Social Gerontology Today

An Introduction

Elizabeth W. Markson
Boston University

Afterword by
Stephen J. Cutler
University of Vermont

Roxbury Publishing Company
Los Angeles, California

An *Instructor's Manual/Testing Program* (available electronically or bound), *free Student Study Guide*, and dedicated *Website* accompany the text.

Library of Congress Cataloging-in-Publication Data

Markson, Elizabeth Warren.
Social gerontology today: An introduction / Elizabeth W. Markson, Afterword by Stephen J. Cutler
p. cm.
Includes bibliographical references.
ISBN 1-891487-89-2
1. Gerontology. 2. Aging. 3. Aged. I. Title

HQ1061 .M345 2003
305.26—dc21   2002018989

Publisher: Claude Teweles
Managing Editor: Dawn VanDercreek
Production Editors: Carla Max-Ryan and Sacha A. Howells
Production Assistants: Heather Setrakian, Phong Ho, and Christine Byrd
Typography: Synergistic Data Systems, sdsdesign@altrionet.com
Cover Design: Marnie Kenney

Printed on acid-free paper in the United States of America. This book meets the standards for recycling of the Environmental Protection Agency.

ISBN 1-891487-89-2

ROXBURY PUBLISHING COMPANY
P. O. Box 491044
Los Angeles, California 90049-9044
Voice: (310) 473-3312 • Fax: (310) 473-4490
E-mail: roxbury@roxbury.net
Website: www.roxbury.net

Photo Credits

COVER PHOTOS: Getty Images; USDA Online Photography Center; Senior Summer School (Courtesy of Seth and Karen Wirshba, Richard D. Holmes, Theresa Comer, Bella Zinovay, Eva Allen, Jean Friedman, and High Mountain Expeditions); U.S. Census Bureau, Public Information download. **TEXT PHOTOS: 1A** E. Markson; **1B** W. B. Burford (Library of Congress, Prints and Photographs Division, [reproduction number LC-USZC4-4246]); **1C** E. Markson. **2A** Courtesy of Lisa Fredman; **2B** U.S. Census Bureau, Public Information Office download. **3A, 3B, 3C, 3D** E. Markson. **4A** U.S. Census Bureau, Public Information Office download; **4B** Courtesy of Robert N. Wilson. **5A** Courtesy of Donald Mulcare; **5B, 5C, 5D** E. Markson; **5E** *Aging Magazine,* Administration on Aging. **6A** B. Boettger. **7A** E. Markson; **7B** Courtesy of Lynne Gershenson Hodgson; **7C** USDA Online Photography Center. **8A** Courtesy of R. Markson; **8B** *Aging Magazine:* Administration on Aging; **8C** R. Markson. **9A** E. Markson; **9B** Courtesy N. and L. Teweles; **9C** Julie Armatidge (Courtesy of Veronica St. Claire). **10A, 10B, 10C** USDA Online Photography Center. **11A** *Aging Magazine,* Administration on Aging; **11B** USDA Online Photography Center; **11C** White House Photo by Eric Draper; **11D** E. Markson; **11E** PhotoDisc (Volume 25); **12A** E. Markson; **12B** USDA Online Photography Center; **12C** E. Markson; **12D** Courtesy of Meals on Wheels West; **13A, 13B, 13C** E. Markson. ✦

Contents

Part I
Understanding Aging as a Social Process

I: The Emergence of Gerontology

Part II
Individuals and Aging

6: Personality, Adult Development, and Cognition

Part III
Aging in Society

9: Sexuality and Intimacy

10: Work, Retirement, and Leisure

12: Elders in the Health Care System

13: Death, Dying, and Bereavement

Acknowledgments

Many people have made this book possible. The very supportive Roxbury staff—Carla Max-Ryan and Sacha Howells, project managers; Ann West, copy editor; and production assistants Heather Setrakian, Phong Ho, and Christine Byrd. I am especially grateful to Claude Teweles, publisher, for his interest in the book and his patience and encouragement.

Special thanks go to Kathleen Jordan, who provided invaluable assistance, information, and insights throughout the early phases of writing this book. She also provided important feedback from her gerontology students, who critiqued early versions of chapters and made suggestions for revision. Carol A. Taylor offered enthusiastic, good-humored, and extensive comments on specific chapters. Thanks also to Rita Edelston, who assisted with preparation of the manuscript.

Thanks to a number of gerontologists at various colleges and universities who reviewed this project at various stages of its development: Jeffrey A. Burr (University of Massachusetts, Boston); Karen A. Conner (Drake University); Donald E. Gelfand (Wayne State University); Deborah T. Gold (Duke University); Roma Hanks (University of South Alabama); Diana Harris (University of Tennessee-Knoxville); William C. Hays (Wichita State University); Rose Jensen (Lynchburg College); Jennie Jacobs Kronenfeld (Arizona State University); Dale A. Lund (University of Utah); Wiley P. Mangum (University of South Florida); Ellen Page-Robin (Western Michigan University); Karen A. Roberto (Virginia Polytechnic Institute and State University); Jon A. Schlenker (University of Maine at Augusta); Barbara H. Settles (University of Delaware); Jennifer Solomon (Winthrop University); Perry G. Thompson (University of Arkansas at Little Rock); Robbyn R. Wacker (University of Northern Colorado); and Ira M. Wasserman (Eastern Michigan University). Their guidance and suggestions were very useful and are much appreciated.

Finally, thanks to Ralph J. Markson, and Alison Markson Bruce, whose ready ears and moral support are much appreciated. ✦

About the Author

Elizabeth W. Markson is Professor of Socio-Medical Sciences and Community Medicine, Research Professor of Medicine, and Adjunct Professor of Sociology at Boston University, where she is also the Academic Director of its Gerontology Center. She received her B.A. from Bryn Mawr College and her Ph.D. from Yale University, and she is a licensed marriage and family therapist. She has published extensively in the area of social gerontology, including *Intersections of Aging* (edited with Lisa A. Hollis-Sawyer), four editions of *Growing Old in America* (edited with Beth B. Hess), *Aging and Old Age* (written with Beth B. Hess) and numerous articles in reviewed journals. She has also published extensively in introductory sociology, with five editions of *Sociology* with Peter J. Stein and Beth B. Hess. Elizabeth Markson has been active in professional organizations and has served as president of the Northeastern Gerontological Society; chair of the Aging and Life Course Division of the Society for the Study of Social Problems; Executive Committee member, the Association for Gerontology in Higher Education; member of the Awards Committee, the Publications Committee, and the Task Force on Older Women of the Gerontological Society of America. She is currently program director of an NIA-funded pre- and post-doctoral training grant on multidisciplinary research in aging at Boston University. ✦

Preface

I should confess that when I was in college, I did not intend to be a gerontologist. I came from a family in which my great-grandmother was born shortly after the middle of the nineteenth century, around the time of the American Civil War, and lived independently until she died at age 98, and I was raised by a live-in grandmother who was active until her massive heart attack at age 93. Not surprisingly, given this family history, I was intimately familiar with elderly family members. Nonetheless, I gave little thought to aging as a lifelong journey—that is, until my first job, as a researcher for a state legislative commission. As the sole "sociopsychological sciences and social service" researcher among a group of economists, I was appointed as "the expert" on issues likely to affect the elderly during the next few years. As I searched the literature, interviewed older people and their families, and began to look at census and other data sources that shed light on aging and old age, I became hooked on the study of aging.

Thus began my career as a gerontologist—a career honed by doctoral work and a subsequent opportunity to study alternative living arrangements for older people who had been diagnosed—often erroneously—as mentally ill. I found myself increasingly curious about the immense differences in the ways people grow old. I also found myself immersed in their life stories. I have now been teaching and doing research in gerontology for over 25 years and am still excited not only by the huge differences among individuals in what life experiences they bring to the ways they grow old, but the different ways that larger social forces—ethnicity, gender, social class, and the slice of history that they live in—shape their lives.

We are constantly being reminded that we are part of an aging society, but the idea of an aging society is often divorced from the experience of growing older. Everyone reading this paragraph will age in many highly predictable ways. From the most minute biological processes to the ways we think, interact with others, and view the world, we are all changing as we age. How each of us ages throughout life and grows old is also immensely variable, influenced by our particular life experiences and the society in which we live. Social gerontologists draw on research and insights from many disciplines to describe and understand the process of aging, for no one discipline captures the entire aging process. Although most academic gerontologists specialize in one particular area of interest, it is also important to have some basic information from a broad range of fields—biology, economics, health sciences, public policy, psychology, sociology, and social work, to name a few—to have an overview of aging and old age. As you read *Social Gerontology Today: An Introduction*, I hope that you will share my enthusiasm and excitement about aging and old age both as an academic topic and as a personal discovery.

How This Book Is Organized

Text

The text is divided into four parts, each of which develops a major gerontological theme.

Part I, Understanding Aging as a Social Process, defines and provides an overview of the study of social gerontology; it introduces the methods by which it is studied, demographic and social characteristics of the elderly, and social theories about aging.

Part II, Individuals and Aging, focuses on biological theories of aging, personality and cognition, mental health, and illness.

Part III, Aging in Society, focuses on family and social relationships; sexuality and intimacy; work, retirement, and leisure; economic security, public policy, and politics; elders in the health care system; and death, dying, and bereavement.

Afterword: The Elderly of Tomorrow, by Stephen J. Cutler, opens a window into aging and old age in the future.

Films and Videos

Films and videos provide useful ways to learn more about a particular topic, and a list of them is provided at the end of each chapter. Most of these are readily available for rental if your college or university does not have them.

Internet Resources

The Internet has become part of everyday life for many of us, and relevant and reliable sites are listed at the end of each chapter. These sites were up-to-date at the time of writing, but since sites change, not every one may be accessed as shown. Also be aware that while the Internet is a wonderful and quick source of information, it is also a huge source of misinformation—so user beware! Always consider the source of the information given at a specific site and the intent of the user—whether to provide accurate factual or research information or to present a specific ideological or political perspective.

Research Articles

Each chapter suggests a specific article that explores a research topic in greater depth.

Supplemental Readings

Suggested supplemental readings are given at the end of each chapter. An additional source of supplemental readings that parallels many of the topics discussed in this text is the reader, *Intersections of Aging: Readings in Social Gerontology,* edited by Elizabeth W. Markson and Lisa A. Hollis-Sawyer (Roxbury Publishing, 2000).

Ancillary Materials

An ***Instructor's Manual/Testing Program*** (available electronically or bound), *free* ***Student Study Guide,*** and dedicated ***Website*** accompany the text. ✦

Part I
Understanding Aging as a Social Process

The Emergence of Gerontology

Introduction

Which of the following statements do you think is true? Take a moment to answer these items and then calculate your score, using the answers given at the end of this chapter.

1.	T	F	At least one-tenth of the aged are living in long-stay institutions (such as nursing homes, mental hospitals, homes for the aged, etc.).
2.	T	F	In general, old people tend to be pretty much alike.
3.	T	F	The majority of old people have no interest in or capacity for sexual relations.
4.	T	F	Older workers usually cannot work as effectively as those under age 65.
5.	T	F	Lung capacity tends to decline in old age.
6.	T	F	Older workers have fewer accidents than younger workers.

These six items are drawn from a series of short tests called the Facts on Aging Quiz (FAQ), designed to bring out misconceptions about older people as well as interesting facts. Developed by gerontologist Erdman Palmore (1988), the quizzes are short and limited to facts that have been documented by empirical research, and they are open to revision as facts change.

Most of us are likely to have preconceptions and sometimes false beliefs about aging and old age, if we have thought about it at all. Few people spend much time thinking about old age and the ways that our culture as well as others have defined it. Each of us is preoccupied with our current lives and our plans for the future: education, friends, romance, careers, and other markers of adulthood. Yet all cultures convey overt or covert messages—sometimes fears—about what old age is.

A basic focus of this book is how people's lives are patterned as they age, and why and how groups and individuals differ from one another in later life. For example, if someone is female, aged 75, widowed, and a member of a minority group, she is much more likely to be poor than a nonminority married woman of the same age. She will also be more likely to be poor than a man of the same age, whether or not he is married or a member of a minority group. What social structural arrangements bring about these differences?

A second focus is myths our culture perpetuates about aging and later life. Throughout the book, emphasis is placed on common but inaccurate beliefs about aging, the elderly, and the process of growing old. Such myths not only pattern our own expectations about aging but also have social and personal consequences for the elderly themselves and can shape social policy.

In this chapter, you will learn more about how society constructs old age as a distinct period of life and the importance of social class, race and ethnicity, and gender in defining the life course. You will also learn more about how gerontology developed as a field of study and how research methods influence what people believe is true about aging and old age. Opportunities for careers, new ideas, new products, and programs in this vital and expanding field are included in the final section.

The Social Construction of Old Age

Definitions Beyond Biology

When we pick up a daily newspaper or magazine, we are likely to see headlines calling attention to the growing older population in the United States. In 2000, more than 34 million people aged 65 or older in the United States represented 13 percent of the population. By 2030, there will be about 70 million older Americans, more than twice their number in 2000. For the first time in history, people aged 65 and over outnumber teenagers, and most middle-aged Americans have more living parents than children! The tremendous growth of the elderly population is not unique to the United States, however. People who are age 65 and older in European and Asian industrialized nations now account for at least 15 to 20 percent of their nations' population. By 2025, the age 60 and older world population is expected to approach 1.2 billion people. In most nations, the older population is growing faster than the population as a whole.

That the elderly are now the most rapidly increasing age group has stimulated intense public debate worldwide about how social and economic resources should be allocated now and in the future. Reflecting the changing age distribution of the American population, Congressional debates about the future of Social Security, Medicare benefits, Medicare use and abuse, educational investments, cost containment of health care expenses, and income transfers for the young and old continue to abound. Because older people are a potentially strong voting bloc, what legislation they are likely to support is important for Congressional and governmental decisions about how tax dollars are spent. Often ignored by marketers, older persons are also being discovered for their economic potency as consumers. What implications do these changes have for your life as the population ages? What will your old age be like? What kind of life can you expect, and will you think or feel different?

When exactly is an individual elderly or old? What is old age? The answer depends on a number of factors. To an American 4-year-old, a 12-year-old sibling is "old"; to a 13-year-old, one's parents may not simply be old, but may possibly have double-dated with George Washington or Abraham Lincoln; to a centenarian, an 80-year-old person may be "young." Each of us has a notion, based on our own age at a particular point in time, about the meaning of the words *old* or *young*.

Aging, however, is a lifelong process—a biological sequence of events that begin at birth and end at death. Every society uses age categories to divide this ongoing process into stages or segments of life. These life stages are socially constructed rather than inevitable.

The *social construction perspective* is based on two assumptions: (1) beliefs that we take for granted as fundamental truths vary in different cultures, periods of history, and social contexts; and (2) the ways in which we understand the world are social artifacts fashioned through people's cooperative efforts, just as are many physical objects like beds, buildings, and computers (Gergen, 1985). According to the particular time, place, culture, historical period, and social organization of any society, treasured beliefs will vary as much as styles of furniture, architecture, music, and clothing.

Age, too, is a social construction. At any point in the life span, age simultaneously denotes not only a number and a mixture of physical characteristics but also a set of social constructs, defined by the norms specific to a given society at a specific point in history. Think about childhood, for example. When you were growing up, childhood was a distinct period of life with particular activities designed especially for your age group: television programs, movies, school, sports, Scouts, perhaps music, dancing, or karate lessons, and so forth. Special products—ranging from furniture to Legos™, Barbie™ dolls to action figures and computer games—were manufactured for you and others of your age. But the notion of childhood, as we now know it, is a relatively new concept that emerged only within the last two centuries (Aries, 1962). As a source of cheap labor, children were considered adult workers very early in life. In nineteenth-century America, a child, not a wife, was likely to become a family's secondary wage earner (Zelizer, 2000). In 1900, according to the U.S. Department of Commerce, Bureau of the Census, 1 in every 6 children aged 10 to 15 was gainfully employed. This figure actually undercounts the number of children in the labor force at that time because many children younger than 10 years old were employed in sweatshops or on farms (Zelizer, 2000)—a far cry from playing in the Little League or on the soccer team!

For similar reasons, adolescence as a distinct life stage is also a new—and distinctly American—invention. Until the last two decades of the nineteenth century, children were expected to learn a trade or to find paid employment as soon as possible unless they had wealthy parents (Demos & Demos, 2000). Benjamin Franklin, for example, began work as a printer's apprentice at age 12. The point here is that the notion of being a child, an adolescent, middle-aged, or elderly is defined by a particular culture during a specific period of history. In industrialized societies such as the United States, age is associated with a particular number of years since birth as well as with specific behaviors and social roles.

When do we become old anyway? In American society, we usually define *old age* as beginning at age 65. Yet nothing magical happens between when we go to bed on the evening before our sixty-fifth birthday and the next morning when we wake up to be 65. We do not turn old overnight. In fact, becoming old at age 65 is a social creation that originated in the nineteenth century when the German Chancellor Bismarck signed legislation making workers who reached the age of 65 eligible for a pension. The choice of 65 as a pensionable age was both cost-effective and politically astute. Because the average life expectancy at birth in Germany, as in most industrialized nations at that time, was less than 50 years, few pension funds had to be paid out; relatively few workers lived long enough to receive benefits. Politically, establishing a governmentally guaranteed pension at a certain age also quieted the demands of trade unions, which had been pressing for more extensive benefits for workers. In short, a specific period of life, such as childhood, adolescence, or old age, is a concept we invent—a social construction. Societies in which

What social construction of later life is this advertising booth for a popular chain of restaurants attempting to promote?

childhood and infant mortality are high and physical conditions hard may define a child as an adult as early as age 7, and an adult may be called an elder in what we consider midlife, age 35 or 40.

Thus, although age is used systematically to distinguish and categorize people, age itself explains very little. Age by itself is not the cause of anything (Hazelrigg, 1997) and gets its meaning only from how we use it to sort people. Moreover, the significance of age as a number is relatively new, as Bytheway (1995) has pointed out:

> In many past societies, it was only the most privileged who had the mathematical and literary skills to keep an accurate record of their date of birth and age. People were judged on their public appearance and this reflected health, gender, status and age—but only according to broad categorizations. . . . The need to measure age numerically developed in the nineteenth century as the law increasingly focused on the institutional control of individuals according to age. (Bytheway, 1995: 18)

What is important about age then is how a society or culture uses it to sort people into categories. As a classification tool, age is important in three ways. First, like sex, age is an *ascribed status* or characteristic; that is, based on attributes over which we have little or no control. At any moment, we are a specific age, and our age provides a basis for division of labor and the kinds of activities we are expected to perform. For example, 12-year-olds in the United States today are expected to go to school rather than to be apprenticed to learn a trade as Benjamin Franklin was at age 12.

Second, unlike sex, a specific age is always transitional. Everyone is constantly moving from one age to another, beginning life at age zero and ending with a certain number at death (Hazelrigg, 1997). Age provides a kind of road map of our lives: where we have been, where we might be going, and how we should get there at particular points in our lives. Moving from one age to another is typically regulated by societal expectations of age-appropriate behavior. Conformity to these expectations is rewarded; violation is punished. If you are a 19-year-old college student, for example, the behaviors expected from you are likely to be very different from those expected from your 2-year-old relative or your 70-year-old retired grandfather.

Third, although in every society some age groups are more powerful, rich, and respected than others, the unique aspect of age as an ascribed status is that everyone can expect to occupy various positions throughout life on the basis of his or her age. All of us were once powerless infants, and for most of us, our power and influence are likely to change as we move from one age category to another. Thus, although every society orders the flow of people into and out of valued positions on the basis of their age, definitions of when particular positions should be occupied are socially constructed and not biologically determined.

Global Glimpses: Definitions of Age in Ancient Greece

In patriarchal ancient Greece, there were four stages of adult life based on gender roles, power, and sexual functioning. At birth, males and females were both classed as *pais* or child, and old age was broadly known as *geras*, but terminology clearly distinguished gender differences in life stages after puberty. Females were defined primarily in sexual and reproductive terms. A young, sexually mature woman was a *kore* or, if still a virgin, a *parthenos*; the mature wife-woman was a *gyne*; and the elderly woman was a *graia*. In contrast, the mature man was an *akme* or at the prime of life, and the elderly man was a *geron* or *presbys*. Women entered old age with the onset of menopause because their primary social value was their ability to bear children. For men, whose social value was higher, the transition into old age was more social and generational than physical, occurring usually around age 60 when a son married at the age of 30 (most often to a female half his age), and the father relinquished control of the family household (Falkner & de Luce, 1992).

Social Class, Race/Ethnicity, and Gender as Classification Tools

Age is only one tool that we use to classify a particular position or status that affects how we grow old. Our lives are also influenced by a variety of other characteristics, such as social class, race, ethnicity, and gender. In all societies, three resources are valued: power, or the ability to impose one's will on others; prestige, or respect from others; and wealth, whether money, goods, or knowledge.

When categories of people are evaluated differently by others, a *social hierarchy* is formed. For example, when one category of people with certain characteristics, such as wealth, skin color, or gender, is regarded more highly than another, the result is a social hierarchy that affects the opportunities and obstacles faced throughout the life course. Wealth, education, gender, race, and ethnicity are all important in determining our social standing, or where we stand in the pecking order of American society.

Social stratification refers to the ways one group is differentiated from another in the social milieu. Specifically, social stratification describes the process of inequity typically built into social relationships and interactions cross-culturally. Most of us think of the United States as a more or less equal society; after all, we have never had a monarchy or a titled nobility. Nonetheless, social hierarchies exist that simultaneously create differences in the distribution of wealth, power, and opportunities throughout our lives. In capitalist societies such as ours, one aspect of social stratification is *social class*, which denotes and describes the unequal distribution of wealth, power, and prestige among groups in relation to certain inherent and extrinsic characteristics that they possess. A social class describes a category of people sharing similar economic circumstances, prestige, education, and political influence. Because of these similarities, the members of a particular social class are likely to share similar lifestyles.

From the conflict perspective, originally proposed by Karl Marx (1818–1883), the basis for social classes in society is *economic control of the means of production* including human labor, technical knowledge and skills, and capitalistic property—land, equipment, and machinery. History is the outcome of struggles between the few who own the means of production and the many who do not. Wealth is power, and both can be used to command respect and dominate others with less wealth.

The sociologist Max Weber (1864–1920), however, emphasized the need to consider three separate types of groupings even though they cannot always be separated in real life: class, status groups, and parties. *Class*, according to Weber, refers to people at the same economic level who may or may not become aware of their common interests. *Status* is based on the degree of prestige of the people in a specific group who tend also to share a similar lifestyle. The respect given a particular status is not necessarily determined by economic level, for in some societies, the greatest respect is given to people who renounce worldly goods. Buddhist monks are one such example. *Parties* are political groupings that may or may not express class interests. For example, the unskilled laborer who belongs to a political party or organization that supports legislation favoring the rich is not expressing the interests of his economic class. Position in any one of these three categories can be used to gain status in another—wealth to gain power, power to gain wealth or respect.

All but the simplest societies construct a hierarchy of their members, based on ability to control power, prestige, wealth, and other objects of value. Although measures of social class (e.g., wealth, education, and influence), are highly related to one another, each reflects different aspects of an individual's position in the social class structure of a society. It is possible to imagine a society in which everyone is equally valued and equally treated, but once a group's economy involves a division of labor, some tasks are considered more important than others. The result is that the people who do different kinds of work are likely to be unequally rewarded.

Social class is thus a characteristic of a society, not simply a reflection of individual talents and abilities. Because both the most and least valued attributes are likely to be relatively rare, status hierarchies tend to be shaped like a diamond, narrower both at the top and at the bottom. American society is no exception, for although we value egalitarianism, power, prestige, and property are unequally allocated. The rich not only control most of the money; they also control access to it and thus its associated benefits. Figure 1-1 shows the percentage in each social class in American society today.

A simple illustration of the way social class operates in everyday life is portrayed in the 1998 film *Titanic;* the rich passengers who traveled first class, thereby occupying the ship's more elegant staterooms and eating far more sumptuous banquets than second or third class passengers, had first crack at the lifeboats. Although 40 percent of the first class passengers died when the Titanic sank, almost twice that proportion—75 percent—of the third class passengers perished. (If you are interested in knowing who survived, see *www.titanic.com.*) Social class differences exist today as well; consider the inequities in political power, education, wealth, and opportunity between the lives of two men. President George W. Bush is the son of a former U.S. president, born into a rich family, a graduate of Yale University, and the former owner of the Texas Rangers. In contrast is George W. Conrad, a Texas tenant farmer. Although he is the same age as President Bush, he was born into a poor family, has only a grade school education, and his job prospects and opportunities are bleak.

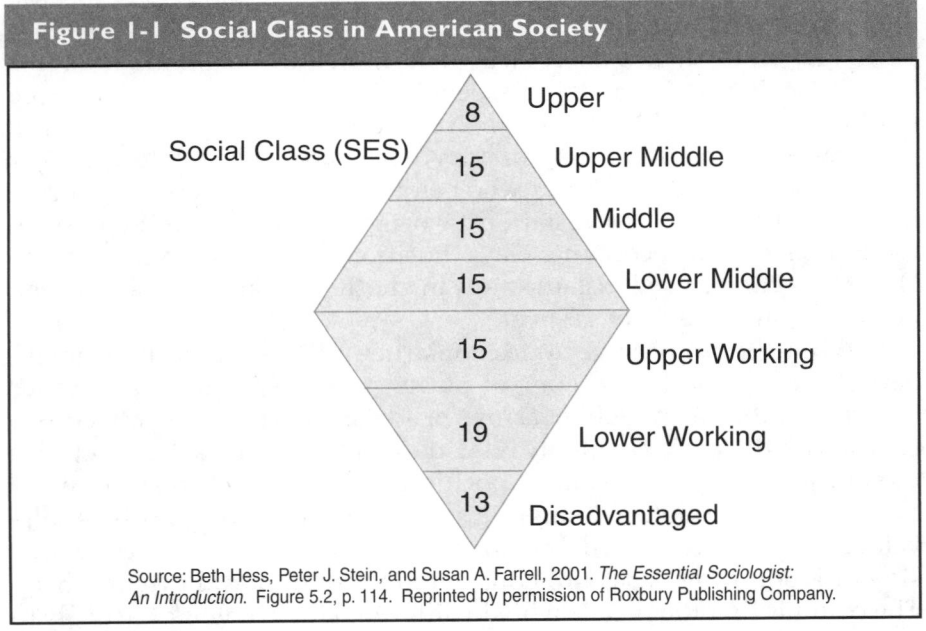

Figure 1-1 Social Class in American Society

Social Class (SES)

8	Upper
15	Upper Middle
15	Middle
15	Lower Middle
15	Upper Working
19	Lower Working
13	Disadvantaged

Source: Beth Hess, Peter J. Stein, and Susan A. Farrell, 2001. *The Essential Sociologist: An Introduction.* Figure 5.2, p. 114. Reprinted by permission of Roxbury Publishing Company.

Like age and social class, race, ethnicity, and gender also are not essential properties of an individual, but are socially constructed to classify and to stratify people according to their perceived worth. Look at the many meanings *race* has had over time. In scientific terms, race is almost impossible to define because human populations are so intermixed that no pure racial types exist today and perhaps never did. As Omi and Winant (1987: 61) observed, race is a mixture of ever-changing meanings and is "defined and contested throughout society in both collective action and personal practice . . . racial categories themselves are formed, transformed, destroyed and reformed." It is the social meaning attached to race that gives it power. For example, throughout much of the history of the United States, drawing a line between "white" and "black" was important in maintaining the dominance of one category of people over another. Although decades of racial mixing had occurred, earlier in the twentieth century many southern states legally defined people as "colored"—and thus subject to unequal treatment—if they had one African American great-great-great grandparent—1/32 African American, 31/32 white.

Similarly, *ethnicity* is a constructed reality, marking one's initial national origin or cultural heritage, such as Irish American, German American, Mexican American, or Japanese American; original language, like Spanish; or religion, such as Jewish American. More fluid than race, we can choose to become "more or less Irish," "more or less Jewish," or "more or less German" throughout our lives. The option to embrace or reject our ethnic identity is, however, not open to everyone in American society. Because visible differences from the majority culture, such as skin color, cannot be changed easily, only white ethnics have this opportunity in the United States (Waters, 1990). Both race and ethnicity not only denote differences but form a hierarchy or stratification system, affecting life opportunities.

Gender is the significance a society attaches to the biological category of male or female. As Hendricks (2000: xiv) has pointed out, "Sex is easy, one X chromosome or two about settles it. Gender is more difficult: it is the *social meaning* that attaches to chromosomes." Gender organizes social structures and shapes how we think of ourselves and how we interact with one another. While gender concerns differences, it also involves hierarchy because it, like age, race, and ethnicity, affects the opportunities and obstacles we face throughout life. Gendered inequality is produced by differential social evaluations of people's worth on the basis of biological sex (Hess, 1990).

Age, race/ethnicity, and gender thus convey public messages that we use to categorize people into hierarchies or stratification systems, in which some have more power, material goods, and influence than others. Ignoring the ways that these hierarchies interlace clouds the patterning of any society, in which differential access to power, prestige, and money affects us throughout our lives. At the individual level, health or sickness, employment or retirement, and social contacts with friends, family, and acquaintances influence our personal views of ourselves as young or old: the notion that "you are only as old or as young as you feel." But being elderly also gets meaning through membership in the hierarchies. Whether a working-class White Anglo-Saxon Protestant (WASP) man; a Latina working-class woman; a white, middle-class, Irish-American man; a middle-class African-American woman; or a recent Vietnamese immigrant woman, in old age each of these people will carry a personal history and the lived experiences of gender, race/ethnicity, and social class. These three constructions will have increased or limited life's opportunities. Like it or not, everyone is likely to have organized her or his self-image around class, ethnicity/ race, and gender. And, although most people seldom think about it at a conscious level, they also share these characteristics with others of similar backgrounds.

The concept of *diversity*, which is produced by social hierarchies, is also important if we are to understand aging and old age. Diversity refers not only to comparisons of similarities and differences across and within groups but also to the social arrangements that construct and shape the different social worlds of groups—whether Irish American, Jewish American, African American, Latino, Native American, Asian, male, female, rich or poor, gay or straight (Calasanti, 1996). The elderly today differ according to their ranking in social hierarchies—a ranking that reflects diversity between different groups. For example, the old age of 65-year-old white middle-class retired corporate executive men is likely to be very different from that of poor rural African-American women of the same age who have worked most of their lives as farm workers. In retirement, their health, wealth, leisure activities, and opportunities take dissimilar courses. The importance of membership in social hierarchies in later life is, however, a relatively new notion, as illustrated in the following section, which examines the ways in which elders have been studied in the past.

Gerontology as a Field of Study

Although human aging and old age are as ancient as humanity, gerontology began to emerge as a scientific field only in the twentieth century. Gerontology (from the Greek word *geras*, meaning old age), usually defined as the scientific study of aging throughout the life course as well as referring to older adults, is a multidisciplinary field that draws from numerous areas, such as anthropology, biology, biochemistry, economics, history, medicine, nursing, psychology, social work, and sociology. *Social gerontology* focuses on what it means to age in society; that is, the personal concerns and social issues associated with growing older and the ways that these topics are influenced by and influence the society in which we live. As Matilda White Riley and her associates have observed, how any of us grows older is molded by the interaction of biological, psychological, and social processes that influence how we change throughout our lives (Riley, Foner, & Waring, 1988).

Social change also plays a role in aging. Not only do people born at different periods of history grow older in different ways, but socio-structural changes in a society (e.g., alterations in the economy, availability of jobs, and governmental requirements for Social Security) influence the ways we are likely to age and grow old (Riley, Foner, & Riley, 1999). Changing norms, governmental practices, and social and economic events outside our personal control but ultimately affecting the courses of our lives are also part of social gerontology. Thus, the lived experiences of growing older and the ways in which social class, gender, race, and ethnicity interplay with broader social change shed light on how we will interpret the meaning of aging.

The Origins of Gerontology

Why bother with the history of gerontology? What can it tell us and what relevance does it have to today's world and our own lives? One reason for this review is to investigate the myths and beliefs about aging that we hold even today. Important also is the gradual scientific unraveling of facts from impressions. Studies of both gerontology and its subfield, social gerontology, are relatively new, but people have probably always attempted to make sense out of growing older and to figure out how long they could live. The Bible (King James Version), for example, mentions a limit for human life:

> And the Lord said, my spirit shall not always strive with man for that he also is flesh; yet his days shall be a hundred and twenty years (Genesis 6:3).

Historically, the search for eternal youth has been a persistent theme; for example, the notion of a "fountain of youth" with magical properties to restore vigor can be traced back to a 700 B.C. Hindu legend (Achenbaum, 1995: 4). Centuries later, the Spanish explorer, Ponce de Leon, unsuccessfully continued this search in his travels through what would later become Florida. Such early—and unsuccessful—attempts to undo or delay death are echoed today in scientific efforts to restore youth and prolong life through embryonic-cell and genetic engineering research which holds the promise of replaceable tissue and body parts.

Despite numerous models of old age proposed throughout the centuries, such frameworks were seldom based on fact. Rather, they reflected broader societal, aesthetic, and religious beliefs (Hendricks & Achenbaum, 1999). The ancient Greeks, for example, valued youth and beauty and regarded the elderly as dried up and ugly, a view that we would describe as overtly *ageist;* that is, stereotyping of and discriminating against people because they are old, just as racism and sexism describe the stereotyping of racial groups and females (Butler, 1969). Early notions of aging pertained to only a few people and usually had little or no relationship to *all* elders and their actual life situations (Hendricks & Achenbaum, 1999). Such models of old age were most often based upon personal reflections about one's own life, often combined with inadequate knowledge of the human body and disease. Moralistic advice on old age as a time to forget the pleasures of the body and devote oneself to spiritual pursuits was also popular—a theme that continues today, along with the myth that people become more religious as they age.

What interpretations of the life course and of male roles are portrayed in this nineteenth-century print?

Critical Thinking: What, Me Ageist?

What personal beliefs do we harbor about old age? How many of the following statements do you agree with? For each statement, count 1 point if you agree, 0 if you disagree; then add up your score. The higher your total, the more likely it is that you have some ageist assumptions. Suggestions on how to combat ageism, corresponding to each statement, are given below.

1. Old age is all in your head (e.g., "you are only as old as you feel").

2. Older people are so cute (e.g., "I think that little old lady is just adorable!").

3. Older people tend to be grumpy or opinionated (e.g., "Old men get so crabby or closed-minded!").

4. I really like older people, but I'd worry about hiring older job applicants if I were an employer because I'm not sure they could keep up with the work and learn new skills.

5. Although many of the older people I know are vigorous and productive, the majority of old people are in bad shape and are boring.

The society we live in is pervaded with negative beliefs about aging. These are as hard to escape as the additives in our food or the pollution in the air. We can, however, fight ageism. Some suggestions include the following:

1. Don't blame old age for tiredness or forgetfulness. Remember that when younger people are tired or forgetful, we blame lack of sleep, inattentiveness, or bad memory!

2. Don't describe older people as cute or grumpy or set in their ways. *Cute* or *adorable* and similar terms infantilize elders. Would you categorize women your age as cute or adorable except as a put-down? Similarly, classifying old people as grumpy or set in their ways robs them of their individuality.

3. Write a letter to the editor of your newspaper when a headline or cartoon about older people is offensive or portrays them as exceptional for their age (e.g., "Grandmother wins marathon"). Is being a grandmother her only claim to fame, or is she a lawyer who took up running in her 60s?

4. Look at birthday cards, films, and television shows. How many of these are ageist? How often are these designed to laugh at rather than laugh with the older person?

5. Think of ways you can combat ageism with knowledge and awareness that everyone, regardless of age, is a unique individual with different strengths, weaknesses, opportunities, and life experiences.

Early Multidisciplinary Approaches

The development of new methods of scientific inquiry in the nineteenth century moved the study of aging from speculation to observation, and gerontology began to emerge as a multidisciplinary scientific field. Surprising as it may sound, science is always a social enterprise; that is, its topics and methods of approach are shaped by the present society and historical period. For example, many of the findings about aging made by nineteenth- and early-twentieth-century scientists were influenced not only by then-current beliefs about old age but also by failure to look at other possible explanations of these results. The way scientists ask questions is also influenced by their own backgrounds and biases—another important reason to specify exactly what is being studied or observed so that future researchers may support or reject the results. A theory can never be absolutely proved; it can merely be disproved. Although some theories are intriguing, they may be difficult or impossible to test and thus are not scientifically sound (Achenbaum & Bengtson, 1994). As you read the following sections of this book, look carefully at the various theories that have been proposed to determine whether they are testable and whether they are substantiated by the results of empirical research. Also, pay attention to the social context in which these theories developed and their generalizability beyond the specific set of people studied.

A notable nineteenth-century study emphasizing the significance of age was conducted by the Belgian mathematician and statistician, L. A. Quetelet, who sought to determine "the age at which faculties reach their maximum or highest energy . . . [and] the time when they commence to decline" (Quetelet, 1842/1969, cited in Haber, 1983: 41). Although Quetelet's study was a landmark in gerontology, his findings echoed old beliefs about the decline of mental abilities in later life. Not surprisingly, because life expectancy at that time was short, he found very few elderly people among those he studied.

Nineteenth-century research based on the elderly poor in medical settings also laid the groundwork to view old age as a pathological condition, requiring medical management—an idea that has influenced thinking even today. For example, Charcot, a physician and author of *Clinical Lectures on the Diseases of Old Age* (1867/1881), based his research entirely on poor women at a Paris medical facility. Dividing the women into two categories (one comprising women over the age of 70; the other, women of every age with chronic diseases), Charcot focused only on disease changes between the two groups. His influential lectures, emphasizing inevitable disease and decline with age, included props, diagrams, photographs, and the exhibition of the passive patients themselves as "the silenced, material resources manipulated by Charcot to ground his theories . . . " (Katz, 1999: 116).

Other French physicians in Paris, also conducting research on aged paupers, repeatedly discovered evidence of general deterioration. From their work, they concluded that the pathologies found in autopsies were not results of illnesses but rather built-in and progressive consequences of growing old. Even when an elderly person might appear to be in perfect health, they reasoned that old age alone meant disability and growing decay of internal organs of the body (Haber, 1983). The stage was set for the medicalization of old age as a pathological physiological process of decline, requiring medical management.

Medicalization describes the use of a medical diagnosis to label individual behavior, such as hyperactivity among children, or a particular social concern, such as old age. Although medicalizing a behavior or social concern can remove it from its previous status as a moral flaw or sin and provide for treatment, this is also a powerful tool for social control. Medical labels not only influence how the condition is handled but also alter other spheres of life, such as job opportunities, family life, legal privileges, social entitlements, social attitudes, and self-definitions.

In the early history of gerontological research, social scientists as well as statisticians and physicians subscribed to negative views of old age. A well-known Englishman, Charles Booth (1894), contended that poverty was an almost inevitable consequence of growing old. In one-third of all poverty cases he studied, he concluded that old age itself was the major cause of poverty because the old were obsolete in an industrialized society. Due to their age, they were destined to be cast aside to depend on charity (Haber, 1983). Research based primarily on the elderly poor also gave birth to the popular belief that the elderly were well-respected in golden, preindustrial times but lost their authority due to industrialization, a topic discussed more fully in Chapter 3.

Why are these historical studies important? They highlight the dangers of ignoring the importance of social hierarchies and diversity in later life. Although Booth, Quetelet, and Charcot were careful researchers, they ignored the fact that all older people are not alike. Rather, they based their conclusions on biased samples—the elderly poor and sick.

Gerontology Challenges the Concept of Age as Decay

Challenges to the view that old age was a period of inescapable poverty, inability to work, and physical decay were advanced by such people as Elie Metchnikoff, who coined the term *gerontology*. The author of *The Nature of Man* (1904) and *The Prolongation of Life* (1908), Metchnikoff proposed that life could be extended and health and ability to work preserved. Others writing in the early twentieth century, such as physician I. L. Nascher (1914), who coined the term *geriatrics* (the specialty of medicine concerned with later life), and psychologist G. Stanley Hall (1922), rejected the belief that old age was a disease and called for research crossing traditional disciplinary lines, marking the establishment of gerontology as a multidisciplinary endeavor (Achenbaum, 1995). It was not until the late 1930s, however, that Cowdry's book, *Problems of Aging* (1939), presented the first multidisciplinary research results, including both the social and biological aspects of aging and old age (Achenbaum, 1995).

Today, as Robert Kastenbaum has pointed out,

Contemporary gerontology includes all of the following: (1) scientific studies of processes associated with aging, (2) scientific studies of mature and aged adults, (3) studies from the perspectives of the humanities (e.g., history, philosophy, literature), and (4) applications of knowledge for the benefit of mature and aged adults. (Kastenbaum, 1995)

Each discipline brings its unique perspective to the study of aging, contributing knowledge about the ways in which aging affects the lives of everyone.

Research for Whom?

Has gerontological research not only expanded knowledge about old age but also served the interests of the elderly? Does gerontology make the scientific method an end in itself rather than addressing issues relevant to the lives of older people now and in the future? Do research, practice, and policy on aging all work together to benefit the elderly, or do they accept and reaffirm the status quo?

Some gerontologists, such as Carroll Estes (1979; 1991) and Harry Moody (1988; 1993; 1998), argue that issues of later life have been emphasized and treated with great scientific efficiency but with little grasp of either their larger political significance or their effect on older people themselves. According to this view, the very policies and agencies established to benefit older adults—the "aging enterprise"—have been creating problems rather than solving them: "The age segregated policies that fuel the aging enterprise are socially divisive 'solutions' that single out, stigmatize, and isolate the aged from the rest of society" (Estes, 1979: 2–3). Research undertaken with good intentions has thus been used to devalue the elderly, guiding social policies and limiting social change by systematically excluding alternative perspectives about old age. The end result is to categorize old people as dependents: more done to than doers in life.

In sharp distinction is research that aims "to make visible the variety, contingency, and inventiveness in any and all efforts to present life" (Gubrium, 1993: 62) and to identify "possibilities for emancipatory social change, including positive ideals for the last stage of life" (Moody, 1993: xv). Rather than attempting to come up with solutions to "the old age problem," this research approach emphasizes the diversity of later life and focuses on identifying positive social changes to enhance opportunities during the last stage of life.

How our society defines old age and the elderly not only shapes beliefs and social and economic policies but also is relevant to our everyday lives. Consider the following personal concerns that many of you may be experiencing or will experience in the future: "My parents are getting a divorce; will my mother be entitled to his Social Security when she turns 62?" "My 67-year-old aunt has just taken her teenaged grandchildren to live with her; can she really handle a bunch of teenag-

ers?" "Will our family life change when my recently-widowed grandfather moves in?" "My 87-year-old grandmother has had a stroke; does
she need to go in a nursing home? How will she pay for it?" "Will Social
Security be there when my parents retire?" "If my parents retire while I
am still in school, will they have enough money for me to continue my
education?" Although it is probably in the distant future, you may even
be wondering about saving for your own retirement! These are just a
few of the personal concerns about later life that many of us undergo.

There is, however, a close relationship between personal concerns
or *private troubles* such as these and *public issues* (Mills, 1959). To
worry about how one's grandmother should be best cared for, whether
one's mother will be able to support herself in old age, or when to start
saving for retirement are private problems, but when large numbers of
people are facing similar personal troubles, these become public issues
that create policy debates and stimulate social changes designed to
relieve them. Knowing how personal concerns and public issues intertwine to shape aging and old age is key if we are to disentangle myths
from the realities of later life and deal effectively with our own lives
and the society in which we live.

Career Opportunities in Gerontology

Gerontology is not only an emerging and intellectually lively field but also one with numerous career opportunities. People in the field of aging work in a variety of settings including social agencies, community and religious organizations, health care and long-term care facilities, governmental agencies at all levels, assisted living and retirement communities, colleges and universities, professional organizations, and business and industry. As you can see from the information that follows, opportunities in this area are almost boundless, offering chances to work with professionals from other disciplines and to maintain and improve the quality of elders' lives. These multiple options exist in part because older people are not homogeneous; their lives differ according to birth cohort (plus their personal experiences, needs, resources, and abilities) and are influenced by membership in social hierarchies.

Jobs and Careers in Aging

Direct Work with Older People

- Developing community or senior center programs (e.g., health promotion, intergenerational activities)

- Counseling older people and their families about employment, retirement, housing, caregiving

- Mental health counseling and psychotherapy with elders and their families

- Legal and paralegal help with estate planning, investments, and long-term care

- Working as a speech therapist or audiologist

- Furnishing physical therapy, occupational therapy, or recreational therapy

- Advising and placing elders in long-term care and providing services after placement

- Working as a certified nurse's aide in a nursing home

- Giving health care as a geriatric physician, dentist, or nurse

Work on Behalf of Older People

- Conducting research on physical, psychological, or social aspects of aging

- Planning and administering community-based services for the elderly

- Working as an architectural or product designer to meet the needs and interests of older people

- Advising businesses, industries, and labor about older workers and consumers

- Advocating with or on behalf of older people

- Teaching courses in colleges, universities, and continuing education programs

Source: Adapted from J. Hendricks, *Careers in Aging.* Washington, DC: Association for Gerontology in Higher Education (*http://www.aghe.org/ciawhatjobs.htm*).

There are many routes to careers in aging. Some students choose aging as a specialty within traditional disciplines or subject areas, such as anthropology, biology, nursing, physical therapy, political science, psychology, social work, or sociology. Others may select an associate or bachelor's degree program at one of the many schools offering a major in the subject. Still others take noncredit continuing education courses designed both for people in new careers and for those interested in specific aspects of aging. Your personal experiences, talents, and personalities also play a role in career pathways.

As a student, you may want to investigate a new career direction by working as a volunteer in a senior center, a church group, a hospital or nursing home, or another agency or organization serving

People of many backgrounds and ages receive academic or continuing education credits to increase their knowledge of aging.

older people. Faculty members at your college or university are probably conducting research on some aspect of aging, and you can offer to help on their research projects. You might also talk with your local or state representative about legislative proposals that affect the aging and volunteer to help on specific aspects thereof, or become active in advocacy organizations, such as the Gray Panthers or the Older Women's League. Attending local, regional, and national professional conferences, such as a state gerontological society, the Gerontological Society of America, and various professional associations (e.g., occupational therapy, physical therapy, public health, psychology, social work, sociology), will give you an opportunity to learn what others in the field are doing. There are also numerous publications and sources of information about the field of aging; a brief listing of useful sources is given at the end of this chapter. Working in the field of aging not only provides an opportunity to learn more about this universal human process but to influence policies, programs, and future directions of older people's lives.

Summary

By 2000, there were more than 34 million Americans who were 65 years of age or older, and the elderly are the most rapidly increasing group in our population. Aging is a lifelong process, and every society uses age categories to assign roles, divide labor, and set rules for behavior. Old age, like childhood or adolescence, is socially defined, and different societies at different times have varied in their definitions of particular ages as related to stages of life. Like age, social class, race, ethnicity, and gender are also used to classify people into hierarchies where some are more powerful than others.

Early views of old age were primarily based on philosophical inquiries and speculations. During the nineteenth century, the study of aging moved from speculation to observation and gerontology began to emerge as a multidisciplinary scientific field. Biased samples led many researchers, however, to conclude that old age was a period of inevitable decline, a notion which has persisted even today and encouraged the growth of stereotypes. During the twentieth century, this notion was challenged, and gerontology began to expand inquiries into both the social and biological aspects of aging and old age.

The challenge in gerontology is to think critically about the assumptions that we personally take for granted plus those that our society takes for granted and reinforces. How any of us grows old will probably be very different from the ways in which our great-grandparents, grandparents, and even our parents have aged. How any of us ages is a personal experience. It also will be shaped by our gender, race, ethnicity, and social class, and by the knowledge and values of the society in which we live today and will grow old in, in the future.

Gerontology is not only an exciting and important field; it also provides many career opportunities in a variety of settings including social agencies, community and religious organizations, health care and long-term care facilities, state, local, and federal governmental agencies, assisted living and retirement communities, colleges and universities, professional organizations, and business and industry.

Key Points

1. By 2000, there were more than 34 million Americans aged 65 and over, and by 2025 the world's population aged 60 and older is expected to approach 1.2 billion people. In most nations, the older population is growing faster than the population as a whole.

2. The rapid growth of the older population has created a demand for people with knowledge and expertise in aging.

3. Gerontology, the scientific study of old age, is a multidisciplinary field that began to emerge within the past century.

4. Social gerontology is the study of old age and the ways that lived experiences, social class, race, ethnicity, and gender interplay with larger social and economic forces in a society.

5. Aging is a continuum, beginning at birth and ending at death, but its meaning is socially constructed.

6. Nineteenth-century studies of the aging process emphasized old age as disease, but reached this conclusion by studying aged, poor, sick people rather than the general elderly population.

7. The view of old age as inevitable decay was challenged in the twentieth century with the advent of multidisciplinary research on aging.

8. The field of aging offers many different employment opportunities, in part because older people are very different from one another. As we grow old, our experiences, needs, resources, and abilities vary according to such factors as social class status, gender, and race and ethnicity.

Discussion Questions

1. What are the advantages and disadvantages of a multi-disciplinary field such as gerontology? Are there any parallels to other fields, such as Women's Studies or African-American Studies?

2. Do medical beliefs about the physical decline in old age proposed by nineteenth-century physicians influence our thinking about the elderly today? If so, how?

3. Have the nineteenth-century views of aging described in this chapter contributed to age-segregated programs, such as senior citizen centers, retirement villages, and nursing homes that separate older people from younger age groups? Have these views influenced social and political policies?

Films and Videos

Surfing for Life: Portraits of Healthy Aging (video; 55 minutes; available from Terra Nova Films, 9848 S. Winchester Avenue, Chicago IL 60643; *www.terranova.org*).

Award-winning view of aging from the perspective of elder surfers, ranging from age 60 to 93, who challenge stereotypes about old age as a time of incapacity, isolation, and sorrow.

Living Longer . . . Aging Well (video; 30 minutes; available from Films for the Humanities and Sciences, P.O. Box 2053, Princeton, NJ 08543-2053; *www.films.com*).

Features stories of older people who, despite ageism, grow old with courage and dignity.

Whisper: The Women (video; available from Terra Nova Films, 9848 S. Winchester Avenue, Chicago IL 60643; *www.terranova.org*).

Winner of a Retirement Research Foundation National Media Award profiling older American women of various cultures who challenge stereotypes and cliches about older women.

Internet Resources

Be aware that although the Internet is a wonderful and quick information source, it is also a huge source of misinformation. When you use the Internet as a source, always be aware of the purposes and sponsorship of the site you are using. The following sites were up-to-date at the time of writing, but because URLs change and sites may come and go, not every one may be accessed as shown. If you are not able to access the site as given, check for the organization by name on the

Internet. Always remember: Evaluate the source of information carefully. User beware!

http://www.aarp.org

The site for the American Association of Retired Persons (AARP), a national organization for people aged 50 and older, provides information for consumers, students, and researchers and links to numerous aging-related topics.

http://www.aghe.org

The Association for Gerontology in Higher Education (AGHE) website contains information relevant to students, including careers in gerontology, publications available through AGHE, its annual meeting, and student scholarships in aging.

http://www.aoa.gov

This site, maintained by the U.S. Administration on Aging, provides up-to-date information on the elderly and on federal programs as well as links to numerous sites with material regarding aging.

http://www.geron.org

The Gerontological Society of America's web site contains material about this multidisciplinary society on aging, its activities, annual meeting, and publications. This is a good starting point to find out about student membership in a national organization for the aging.

Research Article

Featherstone, M. & Hepworth, M. (1989). Ageing and old age: Reflections on the postmodern life course. In T. K. Bytheway, P. Allatt, & A. Bryman (Eds.), *Being and Becoming Old: Sociological Approaches to Later Life* (pp. 143–157). Newbury Park, CA: Sage.

A discussion of growing older in postindustrial society from a British persepctive.

Supplemental Readings

Bytheway, B. (1995). *Ageism.* Philadelphia: Open University Press.

An entertaining treatment of a serious topic from a British perspective, including case studies and illustrations from advertising.

Haber, C. (1983). *Beyond Sixty-Five: The Dilemma of Old Age in America's Past.* New York: Cambridge University Press.

A readable account by a historian of the ways in which old age and the elderly have been defined in American society and the roots of these definitions.

Hendricks, J. (n.d.).*Careers in Aging: Consider the Possibilities.* Washington, DC: Association for Gerontology in Higher Education; also available online at *www.aghe.org.*

An excellent overview of jobs, careers, and training opportunities in the fields of gerontology and geriatrics.

Perls, T. T. & Silver, M. H. (1999). *Living to 100: Lessons in Living to Your Maximum Potential at Any Age.* New York: Basic Books.

Written by a physician and a neuropsychologist, this readable book on the lives of centenarians shows that the longer you live, the healthier you've been.

Rowe, J. W. & Kahn, R. L. (1998). *Successful Aging.* New York: Pantheon.

Summarizing the results of 10 years of research on aging in easily understood terms, emphasis is on lifestyle choices as key factors in how we age.

Answers to the Facts on Aging Quiz

Items 1, 2, 3, 4, and 6 are false, and you will learn more about the reasons why later in this book. Item 5 is true. If you want to check the facts and see the rest of the quiz, see Erdman B. Palmore (1988), *The Facts on Aging Quiz:* 3–10. New York: Springer. ✦

Chapter 2

Doing Social Gerontology Research

Introduction

Social gerontologists conduct research in many places including laboratories, communities, homes, workplaces, hospitals, nursing homes, trailer parks, and even beauty or barber shops—wherever people can be found. They also utilize a variety of different sources, such as data collected by the Bureau of the Census and other national, state, and local agencies, historical documents, large-scale social surveys, and even magazines, books, and other mass media. This chapter discusses some of the research methods used in gerontology. It also focuses on how research methods influence what people have believed to be true about aging and old age and what approaches we use today to study aging and old age.

As you will recall from Chapter 1, the scientific method begins by making very careful and precise observations of different events, behaviors, or other phenomena. This information is then used to produce explanations for the phenomena or particular things observed. These explanations form a theory: a more general explanation that includes and links together many aspects of whatever is being studied. From these theories, hypotheses, or predictions about future events or behaviors are made. These hypotheses then can be tested through more observation and research.

The Logic of Scientific Inquiry

Key to the logic of science is *objectivity* or suspension of bias. Although it is difficult for people to separate themselves from what they study, a careful explanation of the logic used in reaching conclusions allows other scientists to test whether the same results can be obtained. This review is an important part of the scientific method. Important also is careful *specification* of the elements or constructs to be studied so that other researches may duplicate the study. Science is also a social enterprise, shaped by the society and historical period in which it occurs. For example, as described in Chapter 1, many of the findings about aging made by nineteenth- and early-twentieth-century scientists were influenced not only by then-current beliefs about old age but also by failure to take into account other possible explanations of their results.

Can science ever be totally objective? Whether we like it or not, every researcher has personal opinions about the world. Yet scientists aim to be objective, that is, personally neutral, holding to scientific methods while controlling their own attitudes or beliefs that could influence their results. But nobody can be objectively neutral about anything; even the subject a person chooses for study reflects a personal interest of one kind or another. For example, the physician Thomas Perls, who undertook a major study of centenarians, met his first centenarian—his great-grandmother—when he was an infant (Perls & Silver, 1999). That he had personal experiences with a very old relative certainly influenced his later choice of research topic. Although scientific objectivity is an ideal rather than a reality, scientists try to remain detached from their results. If other researchers repeat the study using the same procedures and get the same results, we can be more confident that the results are accurate—an important reason to state exactly what is being studied or observed so that future researchers may support or reject the results obtained.

Doing Research: How I Became an Epidemiologist Who Does Research on Informal Caregivers

Lisa Fredman is an assistant professor of epidemiology at the Boston University School of Public Health, where she is conducting a large-scale study on caregivers of the elderly.

I became an epidemiologist because it combined my interests in research, writing, and psychology. Choosing my own area of research was more difficult. For years, I wrote grant proposals for other investigators. Finally, a colleague said, "Lisa, stop writing grant proposals for other people, and start writing them for yourself." The problem was that no topic was immediately obvious for a grant proposal. The generally-accepted pathways for new investigators to start their research careers didn't seem to apply to me, either. The first pathway was to study an offshoot of one's mentor's research; but I wasn't working with a mentor on any specific research question. The second pathway was to study something one felt passionately about; from a pragmatic perspective, I doubted that passions would get funded very easily. Then, I remembered that my father, a writer, had told me "the best writers write about what they know." I reasoned that this could apply to researchers, too.

I decided to write a proposal to study the health effects of caregiver stress. I knew about caregiving because my family had taken care of my grandmother as her health declined. I had suspected that my mother's stress-related health problems were associated with being a caregiver. In addition, I was collaborating with geriatricians who saw families of elderly patients in hospital, outpatient, and comprehensive geriatric assessment settings. My study evaluated caregivers to elderly patients discharged from a geriatric inpatient unit and other medical settings; data were collected through face-to-face interviews with the caregiver and care recipient. Thus, I further got to know caregiving through discussions with the geriatricians and talking with the caregivers after their interviews. Through researching what I know, I have gained a greater appreciation of caregivers' experiences which, in turn, has influenced, enriched, and improved my research on the health effects of caregiving.

Building Blocks of Science

Basic Elements of Inquiry

A basic element in scientific inquiry is a *concept,* that is, a construct that describes some part of the element of interest. Old age is itself a concept, as are family, race, social class, social support, and so forth. Another basic element is a *variable,* a concept whose value changes from one case or situation to another. Age is one example of a variable; so are health and income. A variable is simply that; it varies from person to person, or time to time, or group to group. Still another basic element in scientific inquiry is *measurement* or the value of a variable of interest. Some variables are easy to measure, like age or income from Social Security. Others are more difficult to assess, such as mental health or successful aging, both of which have been measured in different ways by different researchers. Almost any variable can be measured in more than one way, and one of the first tasks of the researcher is to judge how to measure it. Researchers use *operational definitions,* a topic discussed more fully later, to define how a variable will be measured.

Research Design and Sampling

To ensure that accurate results will be obtained, researchers must ask questions of the appropriate *sample;* that is, a subset of the population of interest. Suppose, for example, you were interested in finding out whether women who are caring for an elderly parent are more likely to be absent from paid work than women who are not. First, you must decide how you will define your *variables* or factors that differ from one person or set of people to another or that change over time. In this situation, your variables are (1) care of an elderly parent; and (2) work absenteeism. You would then decide which is your *independent variable*—that is, the factor thought to cause changes in your *dependent variable*. A dependent variable is just that; it depends on changes in the independent variable.

Your independent variable for this study is parent care, and you must next decide on its *operational definition;* that is, the definition you will use to measure parent care. You might choose to operationalize parent care by limiting your study to women caring for a live-in parent rather than a parent living nearby or a parent living in another town. You will also operationalize how you will measure employed (full-time or part-time?) and absenteeism on the job (number of full days missed within a particular time frame? Number of half-days? and so forth).

Once having decided on your independent and dependent variables and how you will define them, you must ask who and where these working women are. How would you find the appropriate women to study? It would be far too costly and time-consuming to study all women, so you would need to limit your inquiry to a sample. You might decide, for example, to focus on women at a large business in your community and compare those who are employed full time in clerical jobs and caring for a live-in elderly parent, to a similar set of full-time women clerical workers not taking care of a live-in elderly parent. Your results would permit you to know how care of an elderly parent affects absenteeism among these two sets of employed women. Your findings, however, would not necessarily hold true for other women workers in different occupations, businesses, or geographic locales where working conditions (as well as support services for elder care) might differ. In short, your results would not apply (be generalizable) to a larger population as they would not represent all women workers or even all female clerical workers.

A technique often used to insure that a sample is more representative of the characteristics of interest in the population about which inferences are to be drawn is *random sampling,* that is, all people with a particular characteristic or set of characteristics, such as employed women, college students, people over age 65, or registered Democrats, have an equal chance of being included in the study. Random sampling has many uses—in telemarketing, in large-scale opinion surveys, and in the collection of detailed population characteristics data by the U.S. Bureau of the Census. You or members of your family may have been included in a random sample conducted by one or more organizations or government agencies. The advantage of random sampling is that findings can be generalized to the larger population of interest. Recall the research performed by Charcot and Booth discussed in Chapter 1. Had they conducted their research using random sampling of the general population, their findings about old age would have been generalizable rather than confined to the specific sets of people they studied so carefully.

Types of sampling techniques are summarized in Table 2-1. You will notice that there are several variations on random sampling: simple random sampling, stratified random sampling, random sampling within a cluster, as well as nonrandom sampling techniques. Random sampling, although the gold standard, is not always practical or appropriate. Not only is it costly, but it may not fit the problem you wish to study, especially if you are conducting an exploratory study. Very often, researchers use other types of sampling. For example, Mahoney (2001) was interested in health, social support, and religious practice among elderly Soviet-born Jews in the greater Boston area. She planned to conduct interviews rather than distribute questionnaires because she wanted to have conversations with her sample, to ask them follow-up questions, and to pursue topics about which little was known from previous research. Moreover, she wanted to tape-record her interviews so that she could analyze the details of their lives. With limited funding, selecting a large random sample was neither practical nor easy to do. Starting off with people she knew, she asked them to suggest others. This is an example of snowball sampling, so-called because it grows quickly. Although snowball sampling is intuitively appealing, it rarely produces a sample that is representative of the larger population of interest. Mahoney's results, emphasizing the importance of social support, health, self-identification and pride in being Jewish, provide a window on these people's lives since they came to the United States. They are, however, not representative of all Soviet-born elderly Jews or even those living in Boston, for she interviewed only those people fluent in English who were known to each other and willing to talk about their lives.

Like snowball sampling, convenience sampling, as the name implies, is most often used when researchers study easily accessible settings and people. As discussed in Chapter 1, Charcot (1867/1881), in his study of elderly women in the Paris hospital for the poor, used convenience sampling. It is clear from the conclusions reached by Charcot (i.e., the inevitability of old age as a period of decay) that a major problem with convenience sampling is that the results may be biased and not generalizable to other populations, for they do not represent everyone with the particular characteristics of interest, such as the elderly. If snowball and convenience samples are used for exploratory purposes, however, the results can both stimulate knowledge and point to directions for future research on larger populations.

Table 2-1 Sampling Techniques: A Summary

Technique	Characteristics	Examples	Drawbacks
Simple Random Sampling	Includes an equal chance for every element or person to be sampled.	Tossing a coin; using a table of random numbers to select people from a complete numbered list.	Finding a complete list and numbering everyone can be time consuming and the mathematics complex.
Systematic Sampling	Selects every K^{th} element or person from a list.	Selecting every 10th name from a complete list until desired sample size reached.	Arrangement of elements on the list can bias sample (e.g., if list is alphabetical, names beginning with the most common letter will be oversampled).
Stratified Sampling	Organizes the elements or people into subsets and selects randomly from each.	Dividing a list into distinct subsets, such as college class, and then drawing sample from each subset.	Choice of stratification elements may be limited and may not be related to the variables of interest.
Cluster Sampling	Draws sample randomly from elements or people already arranged in subgroups.	Sampling people living in a specific section of the city or attending a particular church.	Need to list the elements in the specific clusters of interest before sampling; even a cluster can vary internally (e.g., if selecting a section of town, the social characteristics of residents of specific blocks can vary).
Snowball Sampling	Selects people the researcher knows and asks them to suggest others to participate.	Beginning with people you know in your neighborhood, asking them to suggest others.	Does not give every person an equal chance to be included; likely to be biased.
Convenience Sampling	Selects elements or people because they are available.	Walking up to people on the street and interviewing them.	Does not give every person an equal chance to be included; likely to be biased as people on one street differ from another.

Types of Research Studies

Sampling is only one issue that affects what we know. The type of study conducted also defines the depth and breadth of information collected. This section briefly describes some of the more common types of studies used in social gerontology.

Cross-Sectional and Longitudinal Studies

Research usually consists of two types: cross-sectional and longitudinal. Not only do the particular methods affect how we choose to study a particular problem, but they also influence the type of information we acquire and what we conclude. Many studies of aging and old age have used *cross-sectional* studies: that is, studies that look at groups of young and old people at one time point. Like a snapshot, they capture what is going on at the moment. Charcot's (1867/1881) studies of the elderly were cross-sectional, showing what the poor elderly patients were like at that time. Data collected in the 2000 U.S. Census were also cross-sectional, as are poverty statistics for a specific year.

Longitudinal studies trace people over a period of time and provide important information about changes that occur. Cross-sectional research is less expensive and easier to undertake, and for these reasons it makes up the majority of studies performed in the social sciences. Many cross-sectional gerontological studies compare the responses of different age groups at a single time period on specific factors. For example, early cross-sectional studies comparing college students and the elderly on intelligence found that older respondents made lower scores than younger respondents on IQ tests, leading to the conclusion that intellectual ability declines as we grow older. What are other possible reasons for this finding? A major factor that could account for the difference is level of education. On the average, college students have had more education and thus greater exposure to the types of information elicited on the test than people who are now old. Moreover, students are more likely to be familiar with test-taking requirements and be far more used to taking timed tests than nonstudents. Students on the average also have lower levels of "test anxiety" than older people (Whitbourne, 1976).

A major shortcoming of cross-sectional studies in gerontology is that they overestimate the importance of chronological age and do not take account of other possible factors that may explain the differences observed. Longitudinal studies avoid this problem and are a powerful tool to dispel myths about aging. There are three major types of longitudinal studies: (1) trend studies; (2) cohort studies; and (3) panel studies.

Longitudinal Trend Studies

These show changes within some general population over time. Examples would be comparison of census data on the proportion of older people in the United States in 1900, 1910, 1920, and so forth up to 2000. This comparison would show trends in the increase of the elderly population over time. Other examples are comparisons of the proportion of people in poverty from 1962 through 2001; types of music records sold to teenagers from 1960 to the present; or changes in the level of support for a political candidate during an election year. Like cross-sectional studies, they take a snapshot at a particular time but differ in that they compare several snapshots to study the direction of change.

Longitudinal Cohort Studies

Cohort studies focus on people who share characteristics, such as members of the graduating class of 2005 or people born during a specific time period. A *birth* cohort is a group of people who, because of their similar years of birth, experience life events at the same age. Research focusing on specific birth cohorts permits study of the "cohort effect": the impact that living through specific historical events, such as the Great Depression of the 1930s, World War II, or the Vietnam War, has on the lives of individuals born during a specific slice of history. For example, a person born in 1910 was a child during both World War I and the great flu epidemic of 1918 (which killed more people than the war itself), a teenager during the "roaring 20s," a young adult during the Great Depression, and may have served in the military during World War II. He or she would have entered midlife during the period of relative economic prosperity of the late 1940s and 1950s and, because mandatory retirement was not totally repealed until 1986, have had to retire at age 65. In comparison, an individual born in 1930 was touched not only by different historical events but experienced them at a different point in the life course. For example, a series of surveys to study the political attitudes of the cohort of people born from 1910 to 1915 might be conducted initially on one sample of people ages 40 to 45 in 1950; a second survey conducted on another sample of people born from 1910 to 1915 in 1960; still another sample interviewed in 1970, and so forth. The specific sets of people studied in each sample would be different but each group would represent survivors of the original cohort of people born from 1910 to 1915. The results of the surveys on the cohort born from 1910 to 1915 may very well differ from surveys on a cohort of people born from 1920 to 1925. Using cohort analysis not only enables us to track changes in a specific birth cohort but adds understanding about why there is no "the elderly." The broad contours of elder's lives vary depending on when they were born into a specific society, as you can see from Figure 2-1.

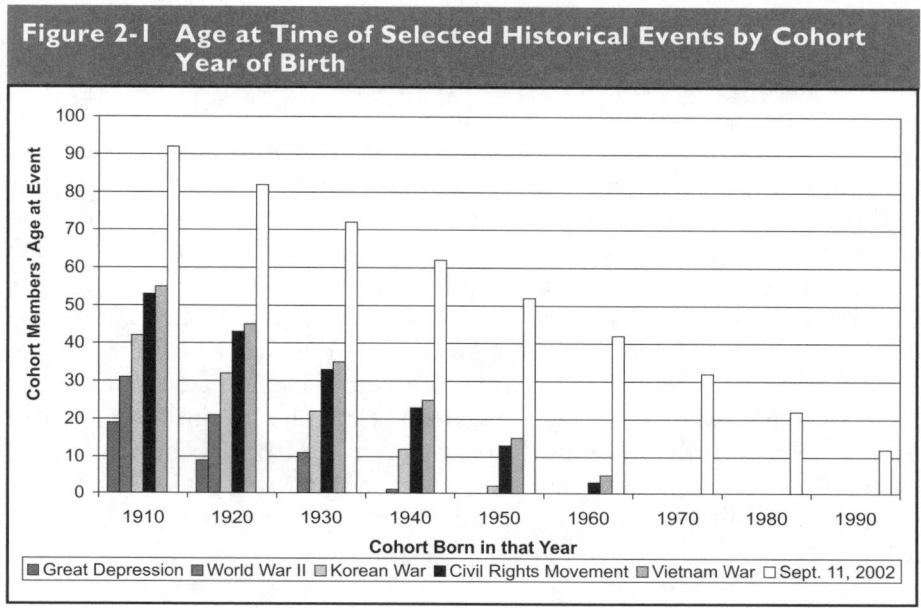

Figure 2-1   Age at Time of Selected Historical Events by Cohort Year of Birth

Panel studies are similar to trend and cohort studies but follow the same group of people over time. For example, the Seattle Longitudinal Study (Schaie, 1996), followed people aged 25 to 81 over two decades to investigate the relationship between aging and intelligence, found that most of the adult life span was characterized by an "absence" of dramatic intellectual declines. A second classic example of longitudinal research is the Framingham Study, begun in 1948 to study factors associated with heart disease. Every two years since 1948, surviving participants in this study have been interviewed and examined medically, providing an invaluable opportunity to study not only heart disease but other diseases, dietary and smoking habits, and physical and psychological functioning. Studies such as that in Framingham have allowed researchers to study the relative influence of different aspects of lifestyles associated with health and illness from midlife into very old age. Unfortunately, longitudinal panel studies are not only expensive and time-consuming but often lose respondents who die, move to a different address, or refuse to continue participation.

Longitudinal studies, whether trend, cohort, or panel, are useful to illuminate how characteristics—size of population, health, attitudes, intelligence, income, relationships, religiosity, political behavior, and so on—change over time. Because all members of a birth cohort are obviously not alike, longitudinal cohort and panel studies also highlight the variation within or between birth cohorts: the importance of the hierarchies of social class, race and ethnicity, and gender on life opportunities and patterns.

Consider the difference in the lifestyles between actor Paul Newman (born in 1925) and his second wife, Joanne Woodward (born in 1930), versus a working-class white couple, Paul Goodman and his wife, Joanne Goodman, who were born in the same years and with the same ethnic backgrounds as Newman and Woodward. Winners of an Academy Award for best actor and actress, Newman and Woodward are philanthropists, social activists, and founders of two charities: the anti-drug Scott Newman Foundation and the Hole in the Wall Gang for children with terminal illness. Newman is also a race car driver and founder of Newman's Own, a line of food products. In contrast, Paul Goodman, who, like Newman, was married twice and fathered six children, was laid off when the plant where he had worked for 35 years closed; he has been unable to find work since. Joanne Goodman went back to work part-time as a supermarket cashier to supplement the Social Security payments both are receiving. Although both couples are of the same age and share common ethnic and racial heritages, their opportunities, life course, and current old age clearly differ.

Large-Scale Social Surveys and Opinion Polls

These are methods of conducting research that involve using questionnaires. Designed to produce information from a representative sample of people, these questionnaires provide the researcher with a standard set of possible responses to gather information from many people in a short time. Such surveys or polls are administered in person, through the mail, over the telephone, and, most recently, over the Internet. If the sample is randomly selected, the results can be generalized to the larger population of interest. The accuracy of the results of a large-scale survey is, however, affected by several factors including the willingness of the respondent to answer truthfully, especially to sensitive questions, and very importantly, the form of the question itself. Common forms of bad questions include those that lead the respondent to a particular answer (e.g., "Don't you agree that the elderly should pay more for Medicare?") and those that are double-barreled, that is, two questions in one (e.g., "Do you agree that taxes should be cut and that private pensions should replace social security?"). Characteristics of the interviewer also can affect the quality of information received; for example, in a study of physical functioning among the elderly, one of the authors found that older men (but not older women) gave different answers to the same questions about their ability to do everyday activities depending on whether they were interviewed by a man or a woman.

Interviewing Older Adults

As in interviewing any group of people, think about how to increase the respondent's comfort as well as your own ease during the research process to make the encounter more pleasant. Some general guidelines are worth keeping in mind:

1. Ensure the respondent's physical comfort as well as your own.

2. Be aware that people become more dissimilar as they grow older. Older respondents are likely to differ from each other even more than Michael Jordan and Michael J. Fox.

3. Explain the general purpose of your study without leading the respondent to agree with a particular statement or point of view.

4. Many interviews require that the respondent give an informed consent in writing that is based on an explanation of the study. Also, explain any informed consent procedures and obtain a written consent if this is required for the research.

5. Unless you are invited to do so, do not address the respondent by her or his first name. For many adults, regardless of age, being addressed as Mary or John rather than Ms., Mr., etc., is a mark of disrespect. If in doubt, ask how the person would like to be addressed.

6. Don't be impatient. Take your time in asking questions and repeat or clarify any question that is unclear, but do not lead the respondent to agree with a particular statement out of politeness.

7. Small vision changes begin for most people in midlife, a topic discussed more fully in Chapter 4. If you are using any printed materials that you will ask the respondent to look at, make sure the print is clear, written in at least 14 point type, and visible under lighting that is good and glare free.

8. Hearing changes also begin to occur in midlife (see Chapter 4), so it is important to speak clearly and distinctly and to minimize background noise as much as possible.

9. Enjoy the opportunity to learn the perspective of your respondent.

Other Research Techniques

In exploratory or pilot research or when more intimate, personal information is required, a large-scale social survey may not be appropriate. A variety of other techniques are available, including *case histories, narratives and life stories, participant observation,* and *comparative studies.* Case histories, providing in-depth information from a few cases, are often used in psychology. The work of Sigmund Freud, the father of psychoanalysis, was based on case histories derived from his practice in the late nineteenth and early twentieth centuries. The narrative or life story denotes "the story we have told ourselves up to that point in time, along with the cultural, social, and personal resources we have available" (Kenyon, Ruth, & Mader, 1999: 44) and yields information about the lived experience or life world of an individual and its specific personal and social context. Jaber Gubrium (1975), for example, undertook a study to learn about the meaning of residents' nursing home situations in the context of their life narratives. He and his assistant conducted in-depth interviews with a total of 58 nursing home residents who were asked to tell their life stories as well as talk about daily living in the facility, the meaning of home and family, self-perception, health, aging, and death. Their life stories "showed that, despite ill health and trying conditions," the respondents were "still able to make meaning, to link together semblances of explanation and understanding and living" (p. 187). The narratives also show that, from the residents' perspective, personal quality of life can be viewed as separate from quality of nursing home care. Had Gubrium used a survey approach, he would have been unable to make the link between people's lived personal history and the ways that these influence how they live their current lives.

Naturalistic observation and participant observation are both ways to find out not what people "say" they do but what they "actually" do. Naturalistic observational studies describe the settings, frequency, and characteristics of certain behaviors. For example, a gerontologist interested in whether more older people shop at a specific store that offers senior discounts on Wednesdays would stand at the doorway for several days to see how many older people came in and out on Wednesdays as opposed to days not offering a senior discount. Researchers making naturalistic observations observe behaviors as they happen, without intervening or interfering in any way.

Naturalistic observations are very time-consuming, as only a few people and situations can be studied within a specific time. As an observer, one is taking the role of "a fly on the wall," but like the fly, no single person can observe everything at once. For that reason, naturalistic observations usually use more than one person as observer. Naturalistic observation has several other limitations: (1) Because people are likely to behave differently when they know they are being watched, observational studies must be restricted to situations where the observer either will not be noticed or will be taken for granted; otherwise they become reactive. If you have ever noticed someone in a store watching you, you probably changed your behavior slightly. You may have put down an object you were handling or moved to a different aisle. That is reactive observation. (2) All of us have selective perception; that is, we are likely to see what we expect to see and miss the unusual—another reason that it is important to have more than one observer for the same behavior.

Some of these barriers can be overcome through *participant observation*, in which the researcher becomes part of the situation under study. For example, Timothy Diamond (1992), a sociologist, was interested in how nursing homes work. To conduct his research, he trained as a nursing assistant and then spent a year working in Chicago area nursing homes. In his study, *Making Gray Gold,* he showed how the facility's priorities—including profits and government regulations—tended to work against the quality of care for residents. Nursing assistants who provided the majority of care were primarily poorly paid minority women who tried to work to increase the dignity and self-regard of the residents but were often at odds with the goals of the nursing home administration. Time that might have been spent with residents was instead devoted to the careful charting required by the nursing home because "if it isn't charted, it didn't happen." Neither a survey nor observation as an outsider would have enabled Diamond to collect such detailed information on daily living in the nursing home—or to discover links to the wider economic, political, and social forces that shape and restrict both the caregivers at the facility and the lives of nursing assistants and residents.

Participant observation such as Diamond's demands not only careful participant observation and careful field notes used to record and reconstruct what has taken place, but also requires that the participant observer be fully accepted in the setting studied. Had he not been a participant as well as an observer in the daily life of a nursing home, Diamond's study would have failed; he simply would not have been able to obtain such detailed information. Participant observation has, however, been criticized as presenting an ethical problem: As a "member" of the group, can one ethically use the information collected for a research study? There is no simple answer. One way researchers have solved this problem is to take what they have collected back to the people observed, asking them to read and discuss the accounts, thus opening a dialogue between the subjects of the research and the researchers (Emerson & Pollner, 1988; 1992).

Growing in popularity are *secondary analyses*—data that have already been gathered and can be reused, often for another purpose. Governmental agencies produce masses of information every day that can be reanalyzed. The census data—collected from American households every ten years as well as yearly or monthly random sample surveys on work, income, housing, voting, family patterns, and other topics—are one major source for secondary analyses. Although far more limited in the information they contain, census data collected annually by cities and towns provide another source for secondary analysis. Other large-scale surveys conducted by organizations (e.g., the Roper Center for Public Opinion Research and the Gallup Polls) and at various universities (e.g., the Health and Retirement Survey, the General Social Survey, and the American Changing Lives Study) also provide useful databases for secondary analysis. A major limitation of secondary analysis of existing data sets is that you are limited to the information that was originally collected, and you may not find the material you need to answer a particular research question more precisely. If, for example, you are interested in knowing whether voting patterns differed among people aged 65 to 69, 70 to 74, 75 to 79, and so forth in the 2000 presidential election, but the data contain information only on voting by people age 65 and over without a more detailed breakdown by their ages, you will be unable to answer your question from the available material.

There are many other sources of material for secondary analyses. Interviews, case histories, anthropological reports, biographies, autobiographies, literature, and crime fiction (Kehl, 1988; Woodward, 1991; Hepworth, 1993; Wyatt-Brown & Rossen, 1993), magazines (Roberts & Zhou, 1997; Featherstone & Hepworth, 1995), historical documents, such as letters, papers, and archives (Haber, 1983; Cole, 1992), newspapers (Gibb & Holroyd, 1996), and even cartoons (Polivka, 1988), birthday cards (Demos & Jache, 1981), television and television commercials (Vernon, Williams, Phillips, & Wilson, 1990; Robinson & Skill, 1995; Riggs, 1996; Roy & Harwood, 1997), and movies (Stoddard, 1983; Walsh, 1989; Fisher, 1992; Markson & Taylor, 2000) have been used as source materials for secondary analysis to study both the experiences of aging and the ways in which older people are portrayed.

Of the various research methods described in this section, *experiments* come the closest to the scientific ideal of control over the variables, a requirement that is seldom met except in laboratory studies. Because behavior is usually influenced by the interpretations people bring to a situation and then modified according to the environment, such control rarely occurs in everyday life. Although the experimental method offers the advantage of control over conditions in which the research occurs, it also has a disadvantage, for participants in such research are generally not representative of the

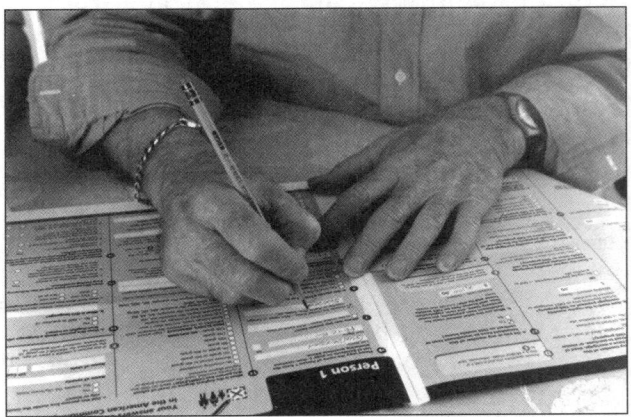

The U.S. Census provides both information about the general population and secondary analyses.

general population; for example, an experiment whose subjects were college freshmen in a psychology class does not represent all 18-year-olds. Thus, it is difficult to generalize the findings to a larger population. Examples of laboratory studies conducted in gerontology are

Aging and Everyday Life: Old Age in Crime Novels

Mike Hepworth, the gerontologist interested in how portrayals in popular novels reflect and shape our attitudes toward old age, selected popular crime novels written by various authors in which older people appeared in a number of roles. In his analysis, he found mixed portrayals of the elderly. They were alternatively depicted as (1) physically and mentally infirm (" . . . the old man's voice droned feebly on. . . . A dribble of saliva came from the corner of the old man's mouth and coursed down his chin" [Bernard, 1990: 5, cited in Hepworth, 1993: 33]); (2) as "the other"; that is, as a different species from younger people; or (3) as examples of "positive aging" (Mrs. Pargeter, an "ample white-haired woman [who] must have been in her sixties, but was carefully and expensively preserved. . . . Though she could not possibly know how many more years she would be allotted, she was determined to enjoy every one of them to the full" [Brett, 1990: 11, cited in Hepworth, 1993: 36]). Hepworth concluded that such depictions not only reproduce and reinforce traditional stereotypes of aging but also provide us with alternative examples of positive aging.

found primarily in psychology in tests of learning, memory, and reasoning. The classic experimental design is shown in Table 2-2.

Table 2-2 Classic Experimental Design

Group	Pre-Test on Dependent Variable	Administer Independent Variable	Post-Test on Dependent Variable
Experimental	Yes	Yes	Yes
Control	Yes	No	Yes

As you can see in Table 2-2, three elements denote classic experimental design: (1) randomly-selected experimental and control groups; (2) independent and dependent variables, where the experimenter is attempting to explain or predict the dependent variable through manipulating the independent variable; and (3) a pre-test and post-test to measure change as a result of manipulating the independent variable. If there are strong differences in the experimental group's pre-test and post-test scores that are not found in the control group, the experimenter can conclude that the independent variable influenced the dependent variable.

Some situations present the opportunity for a *natural experiment;* that is, experiments occurring due to some external event, such as a disaster or famine, that could not be produced in a laboratory. The experience of famine during World War II in the Netherlands provided one such opportunity. When the German army blockaded food supplies to the Netherlands for several months, part of the nation was subjected to severe famine and another portion of the country was not. What, one might wonder, were the long-term effects of severe malnutrition on the infants born to women in the famine versus the nonfamine areas? Because the Dutch famine struck at a precise time and place and in a society able to document its effects, subsequent researchers have been able to compare the incidence of various disorders in adulthood among birth cohorts exposed and not exposed to severe prenatal malnutrition. Several studies indicate that those adults exposed to famine prenatally have a higher incidence of several types of mental disorders believed to occur due to a lack of nutrition while their brains were still developing (Brown, Susser, Lin, Neugebauer, & Gorman, 1995; Hoek, Brown, & Susser, 1998; Neugebauer, Hoek, & Susser, 1999). Although no one would create a famine as an experiment, this natural experiment has implications for health and well-being in any nation or area where severe nutritional deficiency is widespread and aggravated by wars or natural disasters.

Increasingly, gerontologists have become involved in *evaluation research* when new social or economic programs are put into effect. These are essentially natural experiments that can be either large-scale, such as the results of implementing a nationwide or statewide program, or small-scale, such as the results of a program in a specific facility. For example, as of 2000, changes in the Social Security benefit program removed the provision that people between the ages of 65 and 69 would lose a portion of their Social Security payment if they earned over a certain amount per year. A gerontologist might be asked to evaluate the impact of the repeal of this requirement on employment patterns of people aged 65 to 69. Whatever the goal, it should be specified and agreed on, before collecting baseline data and establishing appropriate time intervals for subsequent data collection, to assess whether changes have occurred.

Small-scale evaluation research studies can also be done. Suppose you are asked to evaluate whether people with Alzheimer's disease fare better in a specific unit designed for such patients or in a nonspecialized unit in a nursing home. At the outset of the study, you would need to agree with the program directors about the variables you will use to assess the relative success of the two programs. You might decide to use two relatively simple measures often used in gerontological research: mental status and ability to perform basic everyday activities, such as bathing, dressing, using the toilet, and eating. In the best of all possible worlds, you as the researcher would then work with the facility director to randomly assign new patients with the disease either to the Alzheimer's unit or to the nonspecialized unit and collect baseline data as they entered the two units. Random assignments are not always practical, nor do health and human service providers necessarily agree to such a design. When random assignment is not possible, you would still need to collect the same baseline data on each group of patients. You would follow these two groups over time to determine the amount of improvement, stability, or decline in each setting.

Evaluation research often requires collaboration with the administrators of the program, regardless of its size. The goals of the research are shaped by the goals of the program. Administrators and researchers do not necessarily agree, however, on the ways in which the research should be conducted, and careful negotiation is needed to meet the requirements of both the program and good research.

Basic Statistics: Crunching the Numbers

Once data are collected, researchers examine how the variables are related. The most common statistic is the *percentage* or the number of any given thing in every 100 cases or observations. Percentages allow researchers to compare units of different sizes. For example, although there are far more people age 65 and older in the United States than there are in France, we can compare the percentage of older people in the total population in both nations. In this example, France has a higher percentage of people 65 and older (16 percent) than the United States (13 percent).

Other very common basic statistics are *averages,* also called measures of central tendency—the *mode,* the *mean,* and the *median.* We are all familiar with averages, whether it is the average price of gasoline, the batting average of a particular baseball player, the average salary for new college graduates, or your grade point average. Most commonly used is the arithmetic average—the mean—of a series of numbers. Suppose you want to know the average income of seven older people attending a senior center. Their incomes are as follows: $11,000, $13,000, $14,000, $21,000, $22,000, $25,000, $50,000. The mean income for these seven people is $22,285.71 (or rounded off to the nearest dollar, $22,286). But the mean tells us little about the variability in this group. A more accurate measure of income would be the median, or the midpoint of income: in this case, $21,000 because three incomes are higher and three incomes are lower. When there is an even number of cases, the median is halfway between the two middle cases. Unlike the mean, the median is not affected by an extremely high or low score and gives a better picture of what is average than does the mean.

Another common way to measure the relationship between two or more variables is *correlation:* the relationship in which two or more variables change together. But a correlation does not necessarily mean causality. For example, many people with arthritis notice that their joints ache just before it rains, but this does not mean that their joints affect the weather. A third variable, humidity, is the cause of both the joint aches and the rainstorm. In interpreting the meaning of a correlation, it is important to consider whether the apparent connection between two variables can be explained by one or more additional variables. Otherwise, the apparent connection is a *spurious correlation:* an apparent although false relationship between two or more variables caused by some other variable. To sum up, correlation means only that two or more variables change together. Cause and effect is more complicated and requires three conditions: (1) there is a strong relationship; (2) the independent variable precedes the dependent variable in

---

Controversy and Debate: Is Scientific Research Always Objective?

Is scientific research as objective as we tend to think? Do people inadvertently lie with statistics? Every day we are bombarded by facts and statistics that are presented as scientific results. How can we tell which findings are accurate and which ones represent bias? The best way to disentangle myths from reality, and biased findings from objective ones, is to understand how mistakes in research are made. Here are several ways to understand how findings can be inaccurate:

1. *The people selected for study determine what is learned. If a researcher selects a biased sample, the results will also be biased.* For example, when Charcot (1867/1881) began his research on physical changes in aging, he had a number of potential people to study, but his sample was confined to elderly women in a French hospital for the poor. One cannot learn about the physical changes that occur among all older people by studying only poor or sick individuals. Similarly, when Charles Booth undertook his extensive studies on poverty in nineteenth-century England and Wales, he decided that, because many elders were poor, old age was the primary reason for poverty. By focusing only on the poor, he erroneously reasoned that being elderly rather than other factors, like inadequate income and savings, explained old age poverty.

2. *People interpret their data, often to prove a preexisting belief, and the choice of a method to interpret findings can influence the results.* For example, a very simple measure used in statistics is the arithmetic average (called the mean by statisticians). Quetelet, in his study *A Treatise on Man and the Development of His Faculties* (1969/1842), created a profile for each stage of life using the means derived from large numbers of people. Examining the means, he reached a conclusion that fit in with nineteenth-century thinking about old age: both intellect

and moral sense declined in old age; achievers and nonachievers alike were mere remnants of what they had been in youth and midlife; and old age was a twilight journey to the grave. Although an important step in examining old age, his method of using an arithmetic average to describe an entire period of life is faulty. By using an arithmetic average, Quetelet obscured the immense variability of old age; the few elders who fared poorly detracted from the group.

plications this has for the future. But if age at marriage is charted over a longer period, from 1900 to the present, one can see that age at marriage today is very similar to that in the early twentieth century. Moreover, age at marriage fluctuates over time. The scale used to draw a graph is also important because it can either inflate or deflate a trend. The following graphs present poverty figures for individuals ages 18 to 64 and 65 and over between the years 1979 and 2000. Notice

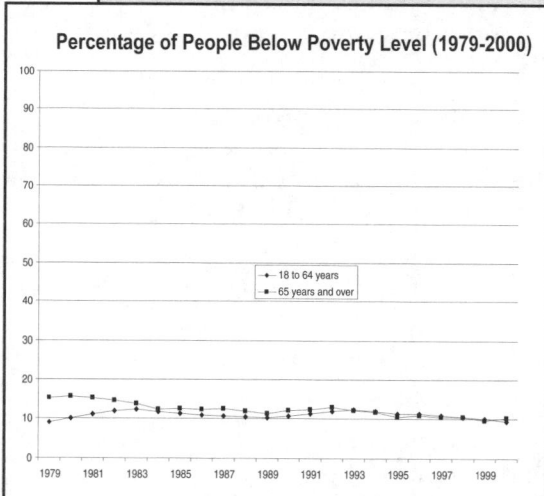

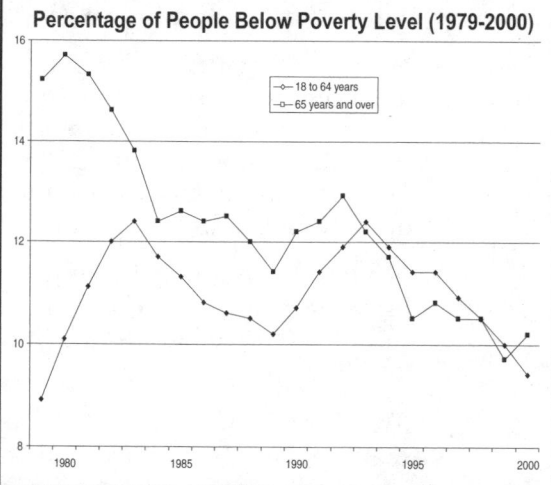

Source: U.S. Bureau of the Census, Historical Poverty Data.

3. *Graphs can sometimes mislead.* In newspapers, news programs, and other media, graphs or charts can misinform us. What we think we see depends in part on the time frame used in a chart. Looking at the age of marriage in the United States over the last few decades, for example, one can see that it is increasing for both men and women and wonder what im-

how the second graph stretches the scale to show a pronounced decrease of the proportion of older people in poverty as compared with the first graph.

Can you find a recent news story in your local paper about the elderly that you think presents biased data or conclusions? What are the sources of bias?

time; and (3) no evidence suggests a third variable is responsible for a spurious correlation between the two.

Putting It All Together: Steps in Gerontological Research

The following checklist puts together many of the concerns gerontologists have in conducting research as well as much of the material in this chapter. Each step raises a question to consider both in reading research reports and in doing your own research.

1. Why is the topic of interest? It is likely to have some personal significance based on experiences or curiosity.

2. What is already known about the topic? Literature searches of what has been done by others are very valuable guides and can both provide guideposts and suggest new approaches.

3. What is the general research question to be answered, and what methods are used? Is it exploratory or descriptive research, what is the group to be studied, and what issues need to be clearly spelled out? If hypotheses are tested, they must be formulated carefully and variables must be clearly operationalized.

4. What is the sample? How is it chosen and why? Are there any limitations imposed on the generalizability because of this sample? If so, what are the limitations and how important are they for the study?

5. Are there any ethical or human subjects concerns? Researchers must be concerned with the rights of human subjects and ensure that any possibility of harm or embarrassment be avoided.

6. How are the data collected or recorded and how is accuracy ensured?

7. How is possible bias on the part of the researcher minimized or controlled?

8. How are the data analyzed? If the study involves specific hypotheses, how convincing are the results to substantiate these? Are there different ways in which these data could be interpreted, and if so, what are they?

9. What does the research contribute to understanding aging and old age? Does it have broader interest to people outside the field of gerontology?

Summary

The scientific method is a key research tool for understanding aging. The scientific method begins by making very careful and precise observations of different events, behaviors, or other phenomena. This information is then used to explain the particular variables observed. These explanations form a theory: a more general explanation that includes and links together many aspects of whatever is being studied. From these theories, hypotheses or predictions about future events or behaviors are made that can be tested through more observation and research.

Basic elements in scientific inquiry include concepts, a construct that describes some part of the element of interest; variables, whose value changes from one case or situation to another; and measurement, or the value of a variable of interest. Some variables are easy to measure, like age or income from Social Security. Others are more difficult to assess, such as mental health or successful aging, both of which have been measured in different ways by different researchers. Almost any variable can be measured in more than one way, and one of the first tasks of the researcher is to judge how to measure it. Researchers use operational definitions to define how a variable will be measured.

Also key in research is objectivity or suspension of bias. Although it is difficult for people to separate themselves from what they study, a careful explanation of how the study was done allows other scientists to test whether they can obtain the same results. Also important is careful specification of the elements or constructs to be studied so that other researches may duplicate the study.

Various methods of sampling have been developed, ranging from simple random sampling to convenience sampling. The choice of a specific sampling method will depend on what is studied. Nonrandom samples are more convenient but the results are not generalizable to a larger population. Research techniques also vary, ranging from large-scale sample surveys to case studies. Cross-sectional studies provide a snapshot of a particular group, or event, or set of characteristics while longitudinal studies, whether trend, cohort, or panel, can show how characteristics change over time. Classic experiments, most often used in a laboratory, include randomly-selected experimental and control groups; independent and dependent variables; and a pre-test and post-test to measure change as a result of manipulating the independent variable. Natural experiments occur due to some external event that could not be produced in a laboratory. Evaluation research is often used to assess programs and can be on either a large or small scale; random assignment to an experimental or control group may not, however, be possible.

Key Points

1. Research methods and sampling procedures influence the types of information collected about later life.

2. A concept describes some part of the element of interest.

3. A variable is a concept whose value changes from one case or situation to another.

4. Operational definitions define how a variable will be measured.

5. Cross-sectional studies give a snapshot of a group or phenomenon at one point in time.

6. Longitudinal studies can show how characteristics change over time.

7. Large-scale social surveys are designed to produce information from a representative sample of people and use standardized questions and response categories.

8. Three elements denote classic experimental design: (1) randomly-selected experimental and control groups; (2) independent and dependent variables; and (3) a pre-test and post-test to measure change as a result of manipulating the independent variable.

9. There are many sources of material for secondary analyses, including census data, historical documents, media, and databases collected in large-scale social surveys.

10. How data are analyzed also influences the results of research.

Discussion Questions

1. What are the advantages of science in learning about aging and old age? Does it have any limitations?

2. Explain the statement: "Science is also a social enterprise." What current examples can you think of to illustrate this point?

3. How can researchers use statistics to favor one interpretation over another?

Films and Videos

Older Voices: Interviewing Older Adults (46 minutes; video; available from Terra Nova Films, 9848 S. Winchester Avenue, Chicago IL 60643; *www.terranova.org*)

A training film for people interested in how structured interviews are conducted with older adults. Includes a 67-page manual.

Internet Resources

http://www.aoa/gov

The site of the U.S. Administration on Aging, it contains information for students and researchers including useful statistical summaries and links to other sites.

http://www.nih.gov/sigs/bioethics/IRB.html

The site of the National Institutes of Health that provides information on ethics in the conduct of research with human subjects.

Research Article

Achenbaum, W. A., & Bengtson, V. L. (1994). Re-engaging the disengagement theory of aging: On the history and assessment of theory development in gerontology. *The Gerontologist, 34*(6), 756–763.

A useful look at theory which can be helpful in understanding how theories are developed and tested.

Supplemental Readings

Gubrium, J. E. (1975). *Living and Dying at Murray Manor.* New York: St. Martin's.

An excellent introduction to participant observation as a research tool and to the different social worlds that exist within a nursing home.

Hepworth, M. (1993). Old age in crime fiction. In J. Johnson & R. Slater (Eds.), *Ageing and Later Life* (pp. 32–37). London: Sage.

An entertaining article summarizing the results of a content analysis of the elderly as depicted in mystery/crime novels. ✦

Chapter 3

Demography, Population, and Housing: The Elderly Today and Tomorrow

Introduction

W*hy are population characteristics important? What difference does it make for a society if there are more elders than children or children than elders?*

Think about the following questions:

- *In what year were you born? How many others were born the same year?*

- *What occupation do you plan to have? What are your chances of promotion? Are they different from those of your parents or grandparents?*

- *What is your racial or ethnic background?*

- *Do you have children or do you plan to? How many?*

- *When do you think you may retire?*

- *Where do you, your parents, and your grandparents live or where have you lived?*

- *How many children did your parents have?*

- *Did your grandparents have more or fewer children than your parents?*

- *How far did your parents go in school? Your grandparents?*

- *In what years were your parents and grandparents born? How many other people were born the same year?*

• *How many people have lived to be as old as your parents? Your grandparents?*

The answers to these questions are all related to characteristics of populations, such as age, marital status, and where people live. The term for the study of the characteristics of population is demography. Demography (from the Greek word demos, *for people) analyzes the size and composition of a population and the flow of people from place to place. Although most of us never think about it, our life chances and those of our grandparents and parents are affected by the demographic characteristics of the society in which we live. Demographic changes affect every social institution (e.g., education, home ownership, and employment) and will continue to shape society not only for the now-old but also for us throughout our lives and beyond.*

Today there are more than 10 times as many Americans 65 and older as there were in 1900. Population changes in the United States and throughout the world have transformed the elderly from a small proportion of people to the fastest growing group. How have population characteristics changed in the past century? Who are the now-old Americans? Where do they live? What are their lifestyles? Who are the old of tomorrow, and how will their lives probably differ from those of their parents?

Today's elderly are pioneering the new frontiers of demographic and social changes. They are growing old in ways that are qualitatively different from their parents and grandparents. Consider a simple example: When your grandparents' grandparents were elderly, they probably got from place to place by train, horseback, streetcar, or horse and buggy, because motor cars did not become common until the 1920s. When your grandparents' parents were old, they probably traveled by car, train, or bus. Your grandparents, however, are likely to travel by car, bus, train, or airplane. Clearly both the ease of travel and the effort of getting from here to there is very different for today's elders than for preceding generations. Older people today are also growing old in ways that are quantitatively different from their parents' or grandparents'; for example, they are more likely to live longer. We also shall grow old differently from our parents; and, if we have children, they will grow old differently than we. This chapter presents key concepts that are used to describe population characteristics and the ways in which everyone's life is patterned by demographic characteristics and changes.

Understanding Population Changes and Aging

Age Structure of the Population

As you will recall from Chapter 1, age is a category we use to distinguish and categorize people in social life. Every society has an age structure of people or age strata; that is, the number of people in each age category, such as age 15 to 19, 20 to 24, 35 to 39, 65 to 69, and so forth. Also, in any society, everyone occupies a status (e.g., child, student, lawyer, or elder) and performs a role, that is, the expected behavior associated with that particular status. The age structure of a nation's population at a specific time is vital in defining how statuses and roles will be allocated according to age and sex.

The relative size of one age group compared with another has important social, economic, and political consequences that affect their opportunities throughout the life course. For example, as the largest generation in the history of the United States (from 1946 to 1965), the baby boom has influenced every aspect of social life. What caused this unprecedented growth in population? The rate of marriage was lowest during the Depression years of the 1930s, increased slowly during World War II, and then shot up just after the war ended in 1945. Although the end of World War II is often cited as a cause, the cessation of hostilities is insufficient to explain an almost 20-year period of closely-spaced childbirths. The major demographic factors causing the baby boom were more people marrying at earlier ages than in the 1930s and having at least two closely-spaced children. Both older and younger women rushed into motherhood during the 1946 to 1964 period (Bouvier & De Vita, 1991)—a movement away from remaining unmarried or having one child or childless families.

Because no other generation had been as large, baby boomers faced scarcities in elementary schools and high schools and colleges. Their sheer numbers swelled schools, increased competition for college admission, and also created a large consumer market for everything from blue jeans to films, magazines, and records. When the boomers finished formal schooling, they left excess numbers of schools, teachers, and colleges in their wake, as they were followed by a smaller cohort of people. By the 1980s, elementary schools built for the baby boomers were no longer needed, and some were converted to housing for the growing elderly population. Colleges bustled to recruit students to fill the slots that had been created for the boomers (McFalls, 1998). Because of their sheer numbers, baby boomers also faced increased competition for jobs and housing in adulthood.

When deaths are subtracted from births, and emi-

As the population has grown older, many schools built for the first wave of baby boomers have been converted into housing for the elderly.

grants from immigrants, the result is a *population pyramid,* a graphic representation of the entire population broken down by sex and age. For example, Figure 3-1 shows the structure of the population of the United States in 2000 and in 2025. The number of males is shown on the left side of the chart and females on the right. Horizontal bars represent age groups in 5-year intervals. The figures on the scale at the bottom give the population in millions in each age group. You can see clearly how sex differences in life expectancy produce more females at the older ages, although at birth there are slightly more males than females. The bulging lines between ages 35 and 54 in 2000 are the baby boomers of the birth cohorts between 1946 and 1964, who will swell the upper age brackets by 2025. Because the boomers were followed by decades of low birth rates, the pyramid turns into a rectangle, characteristic of most modern societies.

Figure 3-1 Population Pyramids for the United States

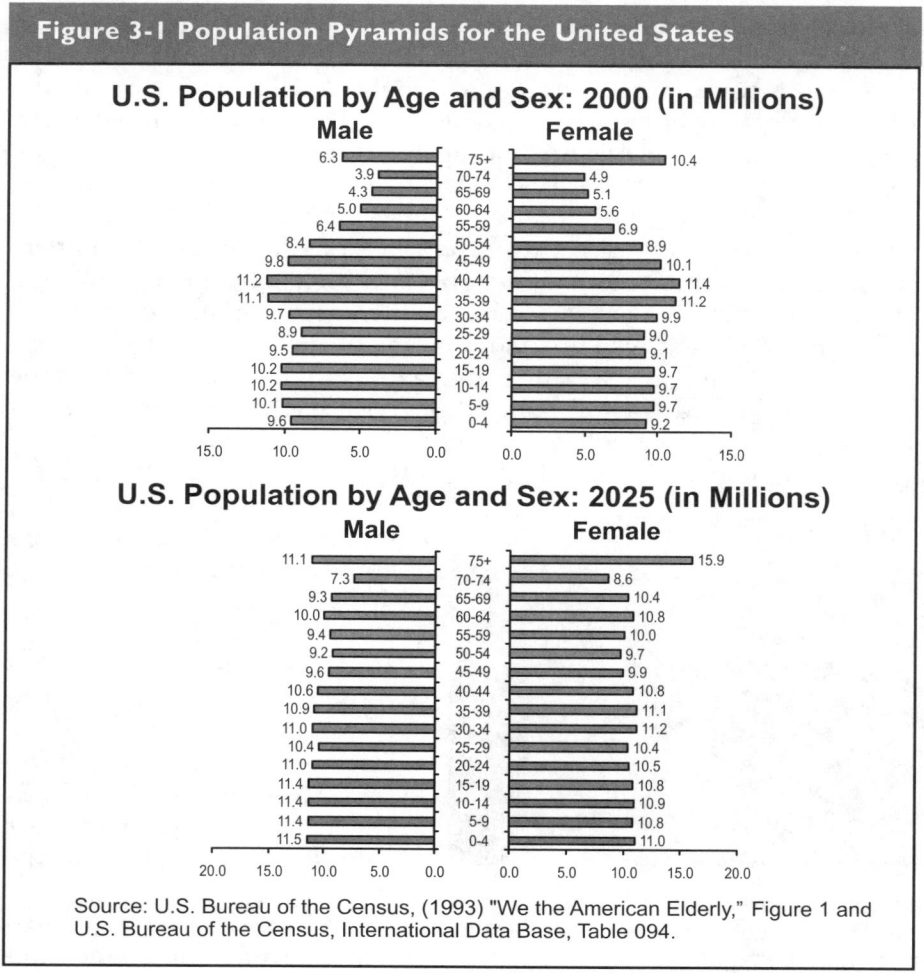

Source: U.S. Bureau of the Census, (1993) "We the American Elderly," Figure 1 and U.S. Bureau of the Census, International Data Base, Table 094.

Spotlight on U.S.: How the Nation Has Grown

The population pyramid derives its name from its original shape when first developed by demographers and is a useful way of summarizing information visually. The shape of a population pyramid gives us two sets of clues: (1) a population's actual past size and (2) its probable future size.

Population size is constantly changing.

The following three pyramids show the United States population by age and sex for three different periods: 1900, 2000, and 2025. As you can see from the figure, in 1900 the population indeed looked like a pyramid, with many children and young adults and fewer and fewer people in the older age groups due to higher mortality as people aged. By 2000, the pyramid had changed its shape. The greater longevity, particularly among women, as well as the aging of immigrants increased the number of older people to almost 13 percent of the population, so the pyramid no longer looked like a triangle. The large bulge created by the baby boom population has moved up to ages 35 to 54. By 2025 the baby boomers will all be age 60 and older.

From the pyramids shown, you can see that the size of a population is never fixed but is constantly changing based on births, deaths, and migration. In the 40-year period between 1960 and 2000, the proportion of Americans aged 65 and older increased from about 9 percent of the population to over 12 percent. As you look at the 2000 pyramid, you can predict with certainty—barring unforeseen disasters—that baby boomers will swell the ranks of the older population when they begin to reach age 65 around 2011.

Population Pyramid Summary for the United States

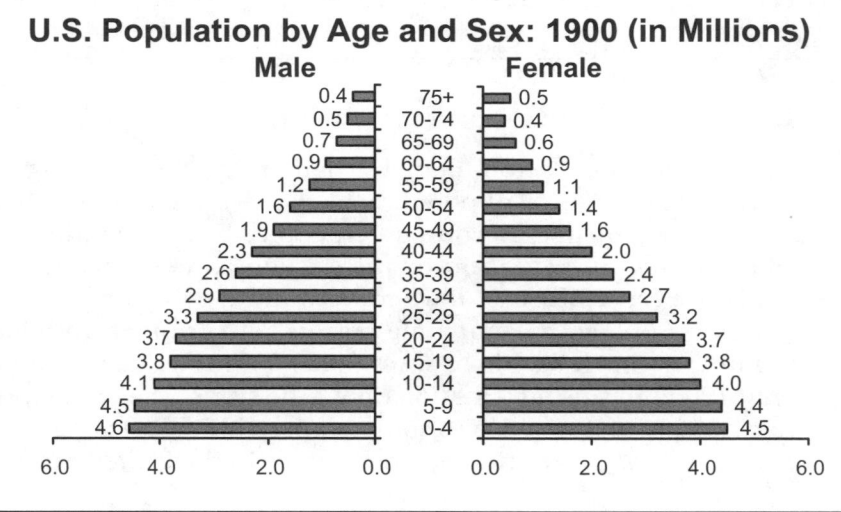

U.S. Population by Age and Sex: 1900 (in Millions)

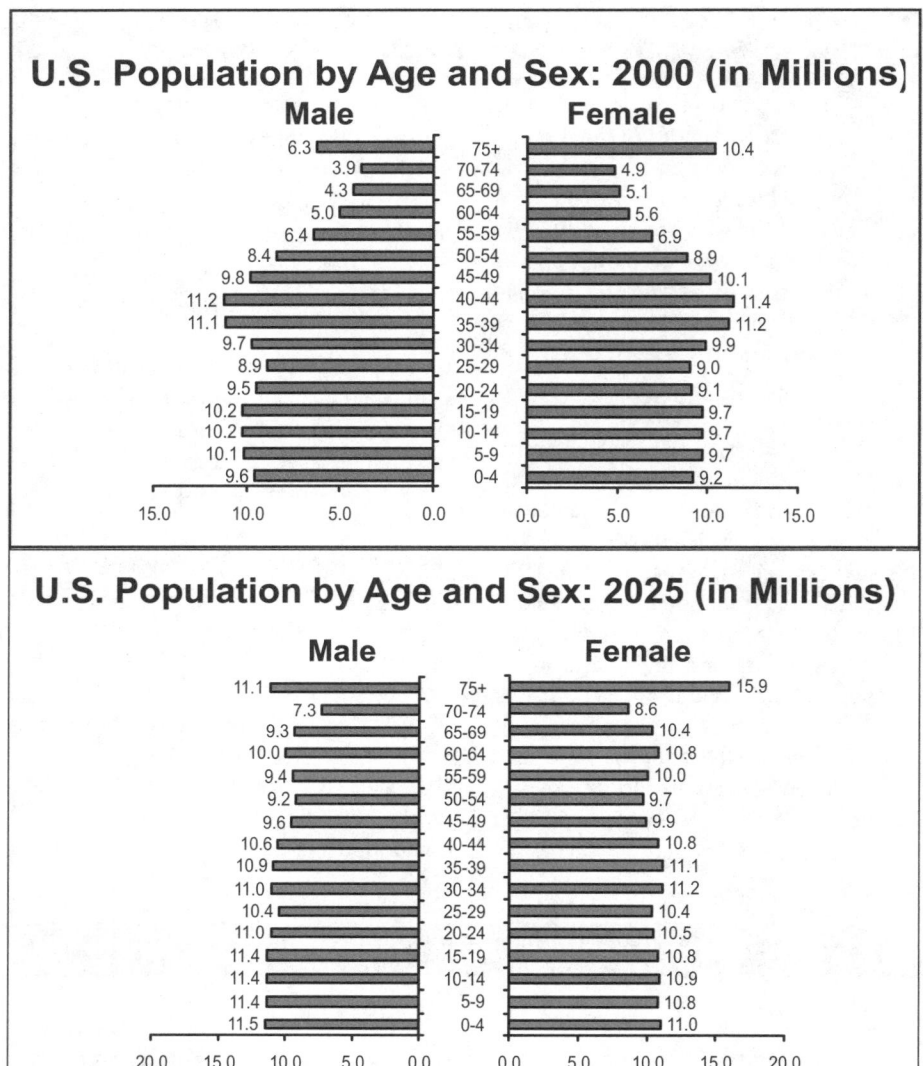

U.S. Population by Age and Sex: 2000 (in Millions)

U.S. Population by Age and Sex: 2025 (in Millions)

Birth Rates, Death Rates, and Migration

To understand population changes, demographers studying the characteristics and patterns of populations use two types of numbers: *absolute numbers,* or actual counts of people, births, deaths, and migration, and *relative numbers* or *rates,* such as percentages and ratios. Rates are especially useful when we want to compare the number of people in one country or time period with another. Although absolute numbers such as "there were 3,000,000 Americans aged 65 and over in 1900" give us information about the size of the population, rates are more useful if we wish to compare populations. If we want to discover whether the proportion of older people in the United States is larger today than in 1900 (or has increased more in Florida or Utah or in the United States or Mexico within the past 10 years), rates are more useful. Rates adjust for the size of the population being studied. Similarly, birth and death rates are more helpful if we want to know the proportion of people born or dying within a specific time. Some common terms used by demographers to study population changes follow.

- *Crude birth rate:* the number of live births in a given year per 1,000 population.

- *Crude death rate:* the number of deaths in a given year per 1,000 total population.

- *Lifespan:* the maximum number of years an organism can live.

- *Life expectancy:* the average number of additional years a person can expect to live if current mortality trends continue for the rest of that person's life, typically calculated at birth.

- *Infant mortality rate:* the number of deaths of infants under one year of age per 1,000 live births during a given year.

- *Migration:* the movement of people into or out of a given geographic area.

- *Immigration:* The movement of people into a given geographic area (in-migration); for example, the number or percentage of a population entering the United States.

- *Emigration:* The movement of people out of a geographic area (out-migration); for example, the number or percentage of people leaving the United States to live in another country.

- *Net migration:* the difference between the in-migration (immigration) and out-migration (emigration) for a geographic area within a specified time period.

- *Population growth:* the sum of natural increase and net migration.

The population of any society is determined by three factors: births, deaths, and net migration. All three influence not only the size of a population but also the life chances and opportunities within that society, a topic that will be discussed more fully. When there is a natural increase (more births than deaths), a population grows. When births are lower than deaths, the population decreases. When immigration is higher than emigration, population increases; when more emigrate than immigrate, population declines. In the United States today, for example, one in every 10 Americans aged 65 or over was born in a foreign country, and over half arrived in the United States before

1970. Other older immigrants began to arrive in the last three decades of the twentieth century to join either family or friends already here or as political refugees.

Deaths are also important in determining the population size. In nations where the infant and childhood mortality rates are high, the population is likely to be smaller than in countries where people can expect to survive infancy and childhood. Those people living in nations with higher infant and childhood mortality rates also have a shorter life expectancy or average number of years they can expect to live.

Social Policy Issue: The Scary Story of the Dependency Ratio

Are we sitting on a population bomb where growing numbers of older Americans will create undue hardship on younger people? Will our sprightly, youthful society be transformed into an America of feeble elders whose support and care drains resources from the young? Some doomsayers, looking at changes in the population, have said "yes." Basic to this argument is the concept of the *old age dependency ratio;* that is, the number of people aged 65 or over per 1,000 people of "working age," defined as between the ages of 18 and 64. In the United States, as in most industrialized nations, the old age dependency ratio is increasing as more people live longer. This demographic fact has raised concern among many people about the nation's capacity to provide pensions, health care, and other needs of older adults.

Often forgotten, however, is that a society's ability to support its dependents hinges not only on the number of people 65 and over (compared with the number of 18- to 65-year-old workers and taxpayers), but also on the *child dependency ratio,* or the number of children under age 18 to be supported per 1,000 persons of working age. Although the elderly dependency ratio is expected to increase as the baby boomers age, the child dependency ratio is expected to decrease. Thus, while the demand for elder services will probably increase, the demand for services for children will decrease.

Also keep in mind that both the child and old age dependency ratios are inexact (i.e., some people are working before age 18 or are not working part or all of the time they are aged 18 to 64, while other people work when aged 65 or older). The dependency ratio can thus be a very misleading figure. More accurate is the actual number of people in the labor force compared with nonworkers at a given time, for they are the people who are most likely to be paying taxes.

Moreover, nobody knows how different future generations of elders will be from the elderly today. The prevalence of chronic disability among the elderly has already begun to decline, and a 70-year-old today more closely resembles a 60-year-old in 1960. The baby boomers, who first popularized healthy lifestyles, may be even healthier in old age. In the United States, smoking and consumption of high fat foods have declined dramatically in the past half century—changes that can potentially reduce both chronic disabilities and the use of health care services in old age. Demographer Charles Longino (1994), observing that Chicken Little lost credibility when he said the sky was falling, suggested that the same destiny may lurk for people who crow about the calamities of population aging or the elderly dependency ratio without challenging the assumptions on which they base their predictions. What do you think? Can you find newspaper or magazine articles that suggest "the sky is falling" as the population ages? What evidence do these sources cite to support their arguments?

Life Expectancy and Life Span

Life expectancy and life span are terms that most of us use but that mean different things. *Life span* is the theoretical maximum number of years that the most robust humans can live. Despite scientific and technological progress, biologic life spans, or the ultimate age that a person can live, have apparently not changed since ancient times. Although experts disagree about the upper limit of the human life span, the greatest age ever authenticated was that of a French woman, Jeanne Calment, who died in 1997 when she was 122 years, 5 months old.

What has changed is *life expectancy,* or the average number of additional years a person can expect to live if current mortality trends were to continue for the rest of that person's life, typically calculated at birth (see Table 3-1). When Christ was born some 2,000 years ago, average life expectancy was only about 22 years. When Benjamin Franklin was born in the eighteenth century, life expectancy at birth was around 35 years. What does a life expectancy of 22 years really mean? Can you assume that an infant born 2000 or so years ago could expect to live only to age 22 or that people born in Franklin's time lived only until they were 35? No, for life expectancy at birth in any given year does not apply to any real group. Its calculation is complex (see Anderson, 1999), but it is most useful to think of as an average. For example, when Benjamin Franklin signed the Declaration of Independence at the age of 70, he had outlived most of his age peers, whose average life expectancy at birth was about 35. This does not mean that most people in Franklin's time suddenly dropped dead at age 35, but if half died in infancy or childhood and the rest lived into their 80s or 90s, you would have an average of about 35. In other words, short life expectancies reflect high infant and childhood death rates.

Many people live shorter or longer lives than average life expectancy predicts. Both biological and social factors influence how long people live, and thus the average life expectancy of a particular population. Life expectancy in the United States was 76.5 years in 1998, the latest year for which such data are available. Life expectancy varies in different societies (e.g., in 2001, Japan had the highest—81 years—and Angola, the lowest—38 years) (Population Research Bureau, 2001). Genetic factors also play a role, as people with similar social characteristics may die of very different causes and at different ages. As people born today move through the life course, mortality conditions may change due to natural disasters, war or civil unrest, new diseases, or life-extending technologies. Social variables—age, sex, social status, political and economic changes, and race/ethnicity—are most closely allied to life expectancy and mortality rates.

The socioeconomic advantages associated with being non-Hispanic, white, and middle class combined with being female increase the likelihood of living to age 90 or beyond.

Sex and Race. At every age, American females of every race can expect to live longer than males. The sex differential in life expectancy reflects both biological and gender influences. Some health issues are unique to women or men because of their biological sex differences, especially in reproduction. Most sex differences in life expectancy today, however, are *gender*-related, that is, resulting from how men and women behave and are treated by others. Throughout their lives, males are at greater risk than females for heart diseases. Female hormones offer protection from heart disease until menopause. After menopause, heart diseases increase rapidly for women but are never as high as for men. Another factor affecting women's life expectancy is the risk of dying in childbirth. At the beginning of the twentieth century, women were far more likely to die in childbirth than they are today. During the past century, both fewer pregnancies and less risk of complications and infections associated with giving birth typically ensured women longer lives.

The two most powerful gender influences on life expectancy today are differences in *lifestyles* and in *health promotion behaviors*. Men are more likely than women to choose risky lifestyles including smoking, driving carelessly, drinking too much, and engaging in dangerous activities and occupations. The death rate among 15- to 24-year-old men, for example, is almost 3 times greater than that for women of the same age. Young men are far more likely to die of homicide, a killer especially of young, poor, African-American men. Men of all ages are also less likely than women to be attuned to behaviors promoting health (e.g., noticing warning signs of illness, seeing a physician, and taking time off from work), at least until they are really ill. Think of the differences between men and women that you know. Are your male or female friends and relatives more likely to drive fast, to drink more, or to go to a doctor?

Despite gender differences in lifestyles and health-related behaviors, the gap in male-female life expectancy grows smaller as we grow older. At age 65, American females can expect to live 3.2 years more than men. Why do sex differences decrease in old age? Again, gender roles are a major factor. As men grow older they are less likely to feel impelled to engage in risk-taking behaviors, perhaps because they no longer feel as much need to show their daring.

At birth, white female infants can expect to live an average of about 5.2 years longer than white male infants, and African-American females about 7.2 years longer than African American male infants.[1] Why is there a racial difference between males and females in life expectancy? The answer lies largely with life chances associated with racial discrimination, limiting opportunities for economic success among minorities. Poverty reduces life expectancy by increasing the likelihood of infant deaths and acute and chronic diseases throughout the life course. African Americans and Latinos of both sexes are more likely than whites to develop chronic diseases, such as diabetes and hypertension (high blood pressure), and African-American males have the highest rate of prostate cancers compared with other race and ethnic groups. High rates of hypertension also exist among Native Americans and Asian Americans, and Native Americans are more likely to develop diabetes, tuberculosis, and pneumonia as well. Deaths from heart disease are 40 percent greater and deaths from stroke 59 percent higher among African Americans than whites. The physical and emotional stress associated with poverty, discrimination, and rapid social change also increases the probability of diseases that relate to earlier death.

As shown in Table 3-1, however, African-American males who make it to age 80 have life expectancies almost equal to white males (7.5 years and 7.1 years, respectively). Among females at age 80, a similar pattern exists; there is only a difference of .4 years (9.1 for whites and 8.7 for African Americans). By age 100, both African American males and females have higher life expectancies than whites of the same age. This decrease is called the *black-white mortality crossover effect*. The reasons for this convergence in life expectancy are unclear, but one hypothesis is that those African Americans who make it to very old are survivors who have been able to overcome the risks associated with disadvantaged minority status.

Table 3-1	Average Expectation of Life in Additional Years for Selected Ages by Sex and Race, 1998			
	White male	**Black male**	**White female**	**Black female**
At birth	74.5	67.6	80.0	74.8
At age 20	55.5	49.5	60.8	56.2
At age 40	36.8	31.9	41.4	37.5
At age 50	27.9	23.9	32.0	28.8
At age 65	16.1	14.3	19.3	17.4
At age 80	7.5	7.1	9.1	8.7
At age 100	2.2	2.7	2.4	2.8

Source: U.S. Department of Health and Human Services, Center for Disease Control. 2001. United States Life Tables, *1998 National Vital Statistics Report 48*, 18, February 7, 2001.

Centenarians. Although the maximum life span has not changed, the proportion of Americans who live to reach 85 or even 100 or more has increased dramatically. According to the 1990 census, there were about 22 centenarians per 100,000 Americans of all ages, and both Social Security Administration and census estimates show that centenarians are among the fastest growing age groups in the United States. However, these data may exaggerate the number of centenarians as they depend on self-reports of age among the now-old (Krach & Velkoff, 1999). Race and ethnicity also play a role: Americans who have lived to be 100 or more are most likely to be non-Latino whites, accounting for 78 percent of those age 100 or over. Making up about 16 percent of those living to be 100 or older, African Americans are the second largest group of centenarians (Krach & Velkoff, 1999).

As with the elderly population as a whole, women centenarians outnumber men. Some centenarians, like Anna Vollmer, live active lives. Widowed and living alone, she has never worn eyeglasses, reads the daily paper and a variety of magazines, rides an exercise bike every day, and takes no prescription drugs. Nor does she fit the stereotype of a sweet grandmother knitting by the fire. When a trespasser brandishing an axe attempted to cut down one of the trees on her property and then ignored her demands that he leave, she loaded her gun and shot out three of his tires! He fled in terror, but she kept his axe. At age 101, this Indiana woman flies annually to Las Vegas, stays at a hotel with a gambling casino where she plays the slot machines, and enjoys an occasional scotch whiskey (Shaw, 1998).

The Demographic Transition

At the end of the twentieth century, there were about three times the number of people that there were in 1900, and within the next

Global Glimpses: Stress, Social Change, and Life Expectancy

When the end of communism opened up a period of economic uncertainty in the former Eastern bloc European nations, life expectancy plummeted, especially for males. Life expectancy in Russia decreased by more than six years after the former Soviet Union broke up and similar patterns have been found in other Eastern European countries. The groups with the highest rates of early death today are relatively young men, dying in their 30s and 40s from heart disease. Their premature deaths have affected life expectancy dramatically as the following table shows.

faced greater economic uncertainty without the social safety nets provided by the communist regimes. Disillusion with the bumpy transition to a market economy led to stress and depression. And stress and depression were forerunners of early death. Men were especially vulnerable, leading some researchers to suggest that the stress they experience is similar to that felt upon the death of a wife: a kind of bereavement reaction. Numerous studies have shown that both European and American men are more likely to die soon after the loss of their wives than are widows, due to a variety of

Nation	Male Life Expectancy	Female Life Expectancy	Difference
Russia	60.6	72.8	12.2
Estonia	63.0	74.5	11.5
Hungary	66.8	74.9	8.1
United States	73.8	79.5	5.7

Why are these men dying in droves? The answers are complex. Smoking, alcoholism, poor diets, and fraying of the health care systems after the end of communism are contributors, but do not provide complete answers. When Russia, Estonia, Hungary, and other European countries overthrew their communist governments, people had greater control of their own lives. Many people had high expectations that their lives would improve, but their hopes were dashed as they

causes including suicide, alcoholism, accidents, and heart disease. Widowers between the ages of 25 and 64 are most at risk because they tend to cope more poorly with the sudden loss of a spouse than their female counterparts. The rocky transition to a capitalist economy has literally touched the hearts of many men.

Source: Richard Stone, "Stress: The Invisible Hand in Eastern Europe's Death Rates." *Science, 288* (5472): 1732–1733, 2000.

decade or so, another billion will be added. In the United States alone, the number of Americans under age 65 tripled during the twentieth century. Although this sounds like a large increase, the number of Americans aged 65 and over was far more dramatic—11 times greater at the end of the century than in 1900. Like other industrialized nations, the United States has undergone a demographic transition, a gradual process that occurs when a society moves from high birth and death rates to low birth and death rates.

The *demographic transition* within a society usually occurs in four stages: (1) increase in birth and death rates; (2) decrease in infant and childhood mortality due to control of infectious diseases and improved living conditions; (3) decline in birth rates associated with greater childhood survival; and (4) decline in both birth and mortality rates, with little difference between the number of births and deaths. In eighteenth- and early-nineteenth-century America, for example, the death rate was extremely high because of poor health and hard living conditions, and people tended to have numerous children because many children would not survive to become adults. By the late nineteenth and early twentieth century, improved living conditions and public health measures decreased the likelihood of infant and childhood deaths from diseases, such as measles, diphtheria, scarlet fever, infant diarrhea, and so forth.

Although improvements in the manufacture of rubber made cheap and effective contraception possible by 1843, those children who survived were still considered an asset to family income among all but the wealthy. However, when legislation was passed that limited child labor and introduced compulsory education for children, working-class children were changed from assets to liabilities. By the 1880s, the diaphragm, developed in the Netherlands, was welcomed as a means for women to control contraception (Tierney, 1999). Parents, realizing that most of their children would survive to adulthood, began to limit the number of births, marking the third stage of the demographic transition. The United States and industrialized nations in Europe and elsewhere are now in the fourth stage of the demographic transition, characterized by little or no natural increase or difference between births and deaths. The stages of the demographic revolution are shown in Figure 3-2.

Most developing nations are still in Stage 2 or the early part of Stage 3. However, if births and deaths continue to decline in developing nations as demographers predict, the overall population age structure of the world will lose its triangular shape and the elderly world population will increase.

Figure 3-2 Demographic Revolution by Stage of Transition

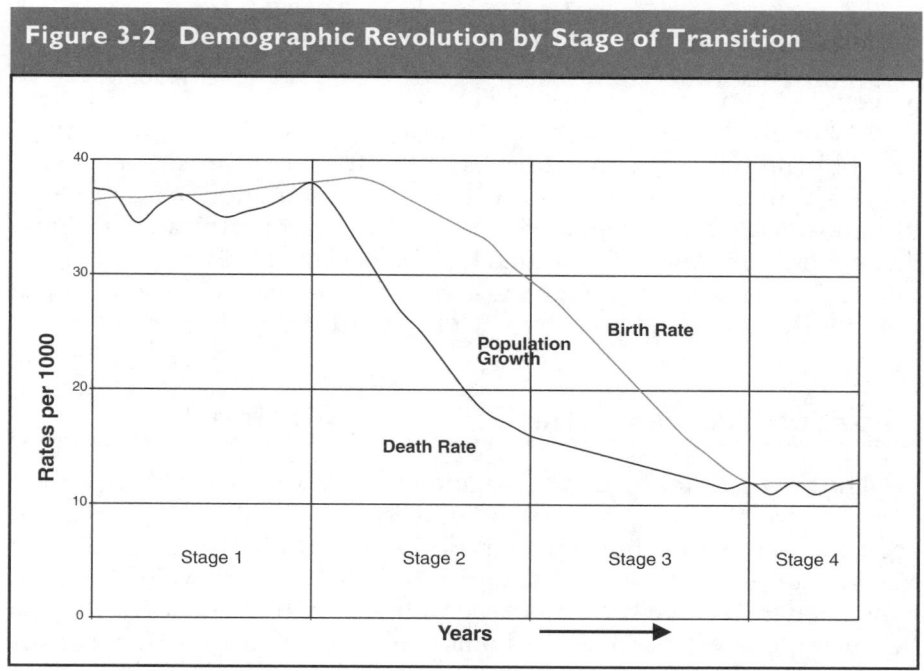

Why When We Are Born Makes a Difference

Important in understanding the ways in which people age are the concepts of *birth cohort* and *life course*. As you will recall from earlier chapters, a birth cohort comprises people born during a specific time, such as 1910 to 1915 or 1980 to 1985. The life course is a sequence of stages that people move through as they mature and go through life. Individuals within a birth cohort appraise and react to events in different ways that are connected to their personal biographies. The concept of birth cohort highlights the point that some of the presumably fixed, built-in life stages proposed by both social scientists and physicians reflect the experiences of a particular cohort rather than a specific stage of life (Riley, Foner, & Johnson, 1972). Just as every person's personal biography and life course are unique, so are every birth cohort's.

Members of a birth cohort—whose size is determined by birth rates and death rates associated with social class, gender, and race/ethnicity, and by in- and out-migration—encounter socially- and historically-based opportunities and obstacles to fulfill social roles as they move through the life course. Although by 1860 the birth rate actually began to drop in the United States (from about 4 births per 1,000 population to around 3 births per 1,000 population by 1910, and slightly less than 2 per 1,000 by 1930), many more people were born during the baby boom years of 1947 to 1967 than during the Great Depression of the 1930s. The large number of baby boom cohorts compared with the smaller numbers of Depression cohorts will clearly influence the number of elderly people in American society by 2020, when the population aged 65 and over is expected to increase from about 13 percent to 20 percent, or 1 in every 5 Americans.

Although declining mortality and the greater life expectancy of now-old and middle-aged cohorts account for the increasing numbers of elderly, their proportion of the American population is also related to trends in births. Except during the baby boom, birth rates declined throughout the twentieth century. Because fewer children were born to fill out the bottom of the population pyramid, the percentage of people in older age groups is now greater (Treas, 1995).

Characteristics of the Older Population

The now-old American population is very diverse, and there are no "the elderly." Not only are all of us living longer, but also the population aged 65 and over is becoming more racially and ethnically diverse. Marital status, living arrangements, and educational levels also vary. How gender, race, and ethnicity combine with birth cohort to shape the life course experiences of the now-old as well as our own lives is discussed in the following pages.

Race, Ethnicity, and Gender

Among people in the United States aged 65 and over in 2000, close to 85 percent were white, about 8 percent were African American, 5 percent were of Latino origin, 2 percent were Asian and Pacific Islander, and less than 1 percent were American Indian, Eskimo, and Aleut. Both Latinos and Asian and Pacific Islanders are very diverse and differ in their cultures and dates of immigration. Several Asian groups, such as many Chinese and Japanese, have been in the United States for generations; others, such as the Vietnamese and Cambodians, are recent arrivals. Latinos include very recent immigrants as well as people whose families have lived in the United States for a century or more, and they represent a range of socioeconomic groups and ethnicities. The major common bond among Latinos is their linguistic origin. In contrast, Asian and Pacific Islanders represent many different linguistic traditions.

In 2000, 12 percent of the foreign-born population in the United States was 65 or older, over half of whom had immigrated when they were much younger. This pattern has been gradually changing; between 1990 and 2000, 1 in every 7 new immigrants was 65 or older. Some of these new immigrants were refugees, but the majority were people who came to be closer to family members already living in the United States. Because of higher birth rates and immigration rates of ethnic and racial minority groups, the elderly population will become even more racially and ethnically diverse in the future. Figure 3-3 shows the anticipated percentage increase in the population aged 65 and over between 2000 and 2050. As you can see, Latinos are expected to increase the most, followed by Asians and Pacific Islanders.

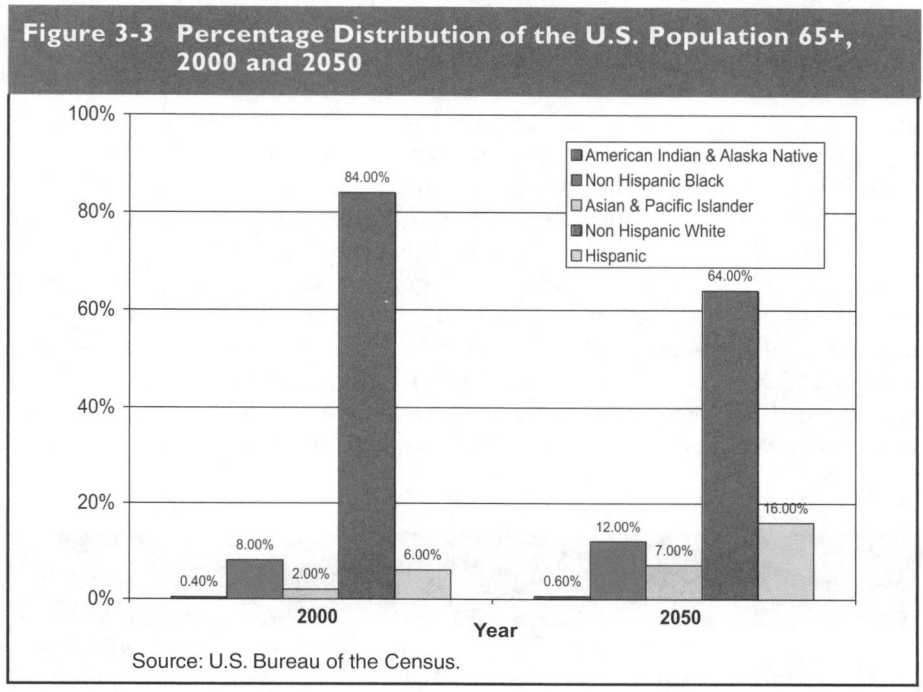

Figure 3-3   Percentage Distribution of the U.S. Population 65+, 2000 and 2050

Source: U.S. Bureau of the Census.

Regardless of race or ethnicity or immigrant status, older women now outnumber older men in the United States as in almost all societies, for women have benefited more from increases in life expectancy during the twentieth century. By 2000, there were 141 older women for every 100 older men; and by age 85 and over, there were 237 women to every 100 men (U.S. Administration on Aging, 2000). This disproportionate sex ratio resulting from greater female life expectancy has definite side effects: widowhood, living arrangements, and late-life poverty (Treas, 1995), all of which are discussed in this chapter.

Marital Status

Why is marital status in later life important? After all, children are grown and the married couples are no longer likely to have more children. But marriage is important in old age for several reasons. Husbands and wives not only have a shared history but also provide daily companionship and affection for one another. Moreover, they often provide help when one partner needs assistance, whether in routine daily chores or in times of illness or incapacity. Older people who are married are also far less likely to be placed in a nursing home or other institution when health fails; research shows that spouses represent at least one third of the caregivers who assisted a noninstitutionalized husband or wife.

Because women live longer than men, it is hardly surprising that most elderly men are married while most elderly women are not (see Table 3-2). Among those 65 and over, men are nearly 2 times as likely to be married and living with a spouse, but women are more than 3 times as likely to be widowed. Given the longer lives of women, it would make sense for women who wish to avoid widowhood to marry men at least 7 years younger than they, but they rarely do. During the 1990s, fewer than 1 in 10 women aged 65 to 74 was married to a man under the age of 65, and 9 in 10 were married to men older than themselves (Hobbs & Damon, 1996). Today, younger birth cohorts of women continue to marry men several years older than themselves, meaning that unless male life expectancy increases dramatically, these women are likely to be widowed in old age. Elderly men and women were about equally unlikely to have never married—less than 5 percent—or to have divorced at some time in their lives and never remarried—about 5 percent.

Table 3-2   Marital Status of the U.S. Population Aged 65 and Over by Gender, 2000

Marital Status	Age 65–74		Age 75–84		Age 85 and over	
	Male	Female	Male	Female	Male	Female
Never married	4.3%	3.7%	3.7%	3.6%	3.9%	3.2%
Married	77.9	54.4	71.7	35.3	55.0	14.1
Widowed	8.3	31.3	19.5	54.7	37.5	79.4
Divorced	7.8	9.3	4.1	5.4	2.8	3.0
Separated	1.7	1.2	0.5	1.0	0.7	0.3
Totals	100%	100%	100%	100%	100%	100%

Source: U.S. Department of Commerce, Census Bureau, *Current Population Survey, March 2000.* Special Populations Branch, Population Division. Internet release date: June 1, 2001.

Although the gender gap in life expectancy explains much of the gender differences in marital status, remarriage rates are also important. Compared with men of the same age, the probability of remarriage is small for women over the age of 45, and even lower at aged 65 or older. In 1993, for example, about 14 in 1,000 widowed men age 65 or over remarried, most often to a woman somewhat younger than themselves, while only about 2 in 1,000 widowed women aged 65 or over remarried (Hobbs & Damon, 1996). Although the reasons why older men prefer younger women have not been systematically studied, it is part of our cultural pattern and even shown in films. For example, in the 1997 film *As Good as It Gets,* 60-year-old Jack Nicholson (winner of the 1997 best actor award) depicted a work-at-home writer. Another 60-year-old performer in the same film was Shirley Knight, who played a minor role as 34-year-old actress Helen Hunt's mother. Romantic involvement, however, focused on the relationship between the characters portrayed by Hunt and Nicholson rather than Knight and Nicholson (Markson & Taylor, 2000).

Education

All of us have probably been told that education is important. How does educational level impact people's lives in old age? One important finding is that research shows that higher levels of education are associated with longer and healthier life expectancy (Land, Guralnik, & Blazer, 1994). Individuals' level of education influences the types of jobs they are likely to have and their level of income. Educational level thus is a useful rough indicator of social class membership that in turn shapes people's life chances. As you can see from Figure 3-4, the now-old are less likely than the general population aged 25 and over to have completed high school or more.

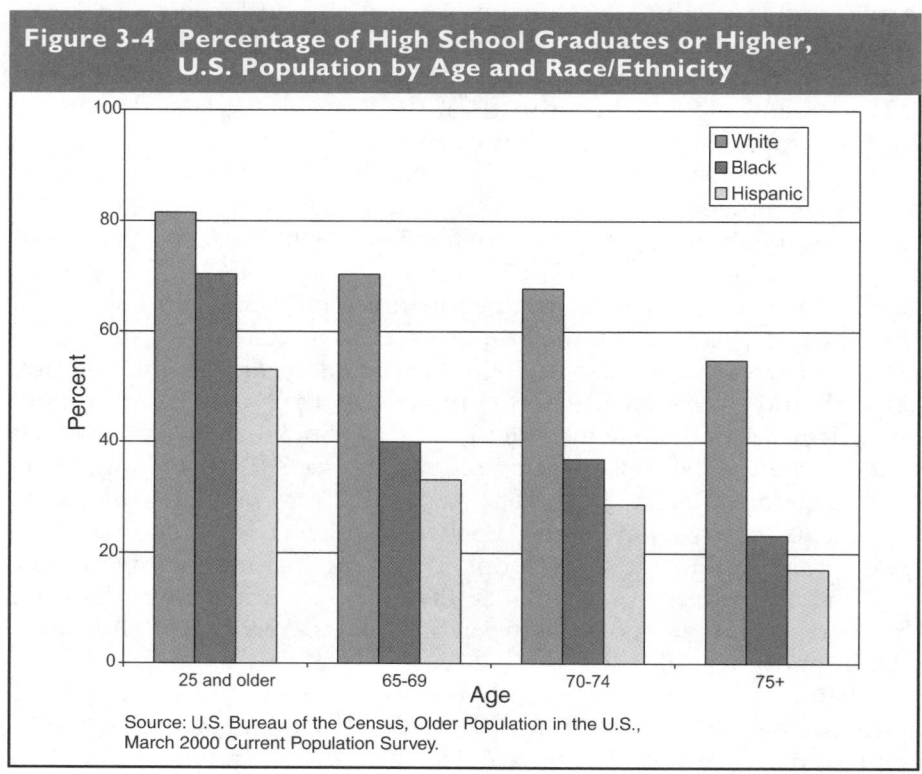

Figure 3-4   Percentage of High School Graduates or Higher, U.S. Population by Age and Race/Ethnicity

Source: U.S. Bureau of the Census, Older Population in the U.S., March 2000 Current Population Survey.

The education of the elderly who are recent immigrants differs markedly from both native and foreign-born who have lived in the United States for many years. For example, these new immigrant elders are less likely to have completed as many years of education. They are also less likely to speak English well. According to the U.S. Census, close to 4 million people aged 65 and over and living in the United States speak a primary language other than English at home, and some do not speak English at all. Inability to speak English fluently can reduce knowledge not only of available goods and services, government entitlements, and other benefits but also of opportunities for participation in the larger society. These now-old are likely to be disadvantaged in the hierarchies of social class and ethnicity/race.

Income and Poverty

It is by now a truism to point out that the income of older people improved markedly during the last four decades of the twentieth century. How poor are the elderly today? The official poverty rate for people 65 and over was 10.2 in 2000. Nonetheless, about 3.4 million elderly people were below the poverty level, and another 2.2 million (almost 7 percent) were classed as "near-poor"; that is, with an income between the poverty level and 125 percent of that level. Poverty, too, is related to gender and race/ethnicity. One out of every 12 elderly whites (8.3 percent) was classified as below the poverty level in 2000, compared with slightly more than 1 in 5 Hispanic (18.8 percent) and African American (22.3 percent) elders (U.S. Bureau of the Census, Internet download, 2000)—a topic discussed more fully in Chapter 10.

Far fewer elders live in poverty today than in 1980, when approximately 16 percent of those in poverty had incomes of less than $3,949 (the poverty threshold for that year). The median yearly income in 2000 for all individuals aged 65 and older was $14,425 (the median denotes a point where half the people are above, half are below). In later life as throughout the life course, men tend to have higher incomes than women. Also in 2000, the median yearly income of men aged 65 and over was $19,168 compared with $10,899 for women. Major sources of income for older people are Social Security (reported by 90 percent of older people), income from assets (reported by 62 percent), public and private pensions (reported by 44 percent), and earnings (reported by 21 percent). Pockets of poverty and near poverty clearly remain. For all older people reporting income in 2000, 8 percent had an income of less than $5,000 and 26 percent indicated that they had an annual income between $5,000 and $9,999 (U.S. Administration on Aging, 2001).

The range of elderly household incomes, however, is wide; in 2000, approximately 1 in every 9 family households with an elderly head (12 percent) had incomes of less than $15,000 per year, and more than 1 in

4 (28 percent) had incomes of $50,000 or more. White households with a head aged 65 or older had higher yearly median incomes ($33,647) than African Americans ($27,952) or Hispanics ($24,330) (U.S.D.H.H.S., 2000). If we look only at median income without considering gender and race/ethnicity, important disparities associated with education, occupation, and life chances are obscured. Income is also discussed in greater detail in Chapter 10.

Living Arrangements

Where the Now-Old Live

The elderly in the United States are not evenly distributed among the 50 states. In 2000, California, Florida, Illinois, Michigan, New Jersey, New York, Pennsylvania, and Texas had very high concentrations of people aged 65 and over (more than 1 million). Although the largest number of elderly reside in California—also the most populous state—Florida has the highest percentage, as many elderly people choose to move there after retirement. Retirement is not the only reason for larger proportions of people 65 and over; for example, some Midwestern states that have a large percentage of farmland also have a high proportion of older people, largely because younger people have migrated to more urban states to find nonagricultural employment. Figure 3-5 summarizes the distribution of the 65-plus population by

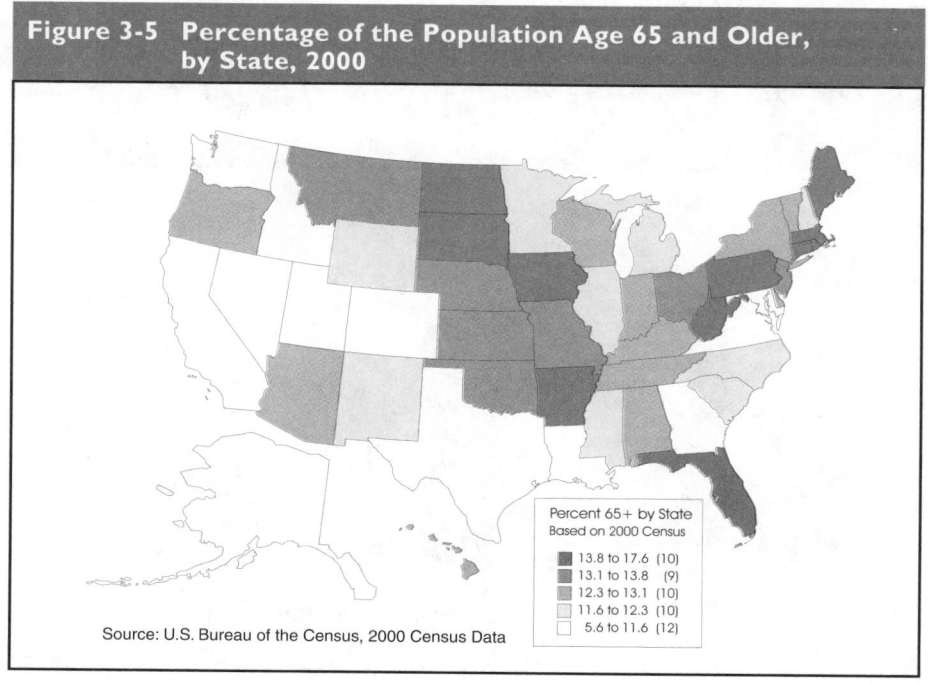

Figure 3-5 Percentage of the Population Age 65 and Older, by State, 2000

Percent 65+ by State
Based on 2000 Census

- 13.8 to 17.6 (10)
- 13.1 to 13.8 (9)
- 12.3 to 13.1 (10)
- 11.6 to 12.3 (10)
- 5.6 to 11.6 (12)

Source: U.S. Bureau of the Census, 2000 Census Data

state. As you look at the figure, think about some other possible reasons that some states have a higher percentage of elders than others.

Housing and Living Arrangements

Living Arrangements. Not only does type of housing vary among the elderly of today, but whether they live with others or alone varies markedly with advancing age and by gender, race, and ethnicity. Among noninstitutionalized people aged 65 to 74, the majority of white, African-American, and Latino men are married and living with their spouse, but white, African-American, and Latina women are much more likely to be widowed. Widowhood increases with age among women, and African-American women over age 75 are far more likely to be widowed than their white or Latina counterparts. The majority of Asian and Pacific Islander, American Indian, Eskimo, and Aleut women aged 75 and older are also widowed (Hobbs & Damon, 1996). Because mortality is greatest among males who have been disadvantaged in the hierarchies of race, ethnicity, and social class, it is not surprising that widowhood is higher in old age among minority women than among their white birth cohort members.

As would be expected given women's greater likelihood of widowhood and lower likelihood of remarriage in later life, the majority of elderly people living alone are women. About 7 in 10 (5.7 million) of these women aged 65 and over are white. Among those 85 years and over, white women are twice as likely to live alone as white men. Among African Americans, women are also more likely to live alone

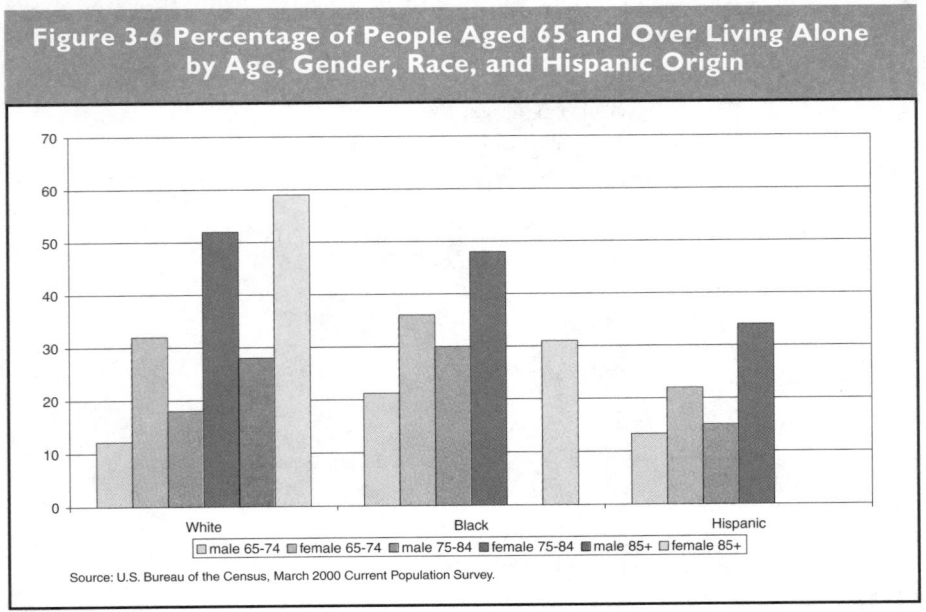

Figure 3-6 Percentage of People Aged 65 and Over Living Alone by Age, Gender, Race, and Hispanic Origin

☐ male 65-74 ☐ female 65-74 ■ male 75-84 ■ female 75-84 ■ male 85+ ☐ female 85+

Source: U.S. Bureau of the Census, March 2000 Current Population Survey.

than men. Figure 3-6 presents U.S. Census data showing the proportion of whites, African Americans, and Latinos living alone by age and sex. As you look at this, you will notice the ways in which gender, race/ethnicity, and age intertwine to affect living arrangements.

Both African-American and white women who have raised more children, who are poor, and who have shorter work histories are most likely to reside with a family member and least likely to live alone (Choi, 1991). African-American widows and divorcees are also more likely to have lower incomes than whites and are more likely to live below the official poverty level. In addition, cultural differences may influence the likelihood of living alone, as elderly women of color who have faced a lifetime of racial discrimination may value family cohesiveness and extended family networks more than whites do (Choi, 1991).

How ethnicity makes a difference: A Latino example. National data often obscure the differences among racial and ethnic groups, combining them into broad categories such as *Asian* or *Latino*. Such categorization often hides the divergence within broad ethnic or racial groups. For example, research on elderly never-married and widowed Latinos living alone shows that living arrangements vary according to national origin, emphasizing the variation in the broad group termed *Latino* or *Hispanic* (Zsembic, 1993). Central and South American men and Puerto-Rican women are most likely to live alone, while Central and South-American women and Cuban men are most likely to live with a family member or members. In part, this reflects the ability of each ethnic group to afford to live alone; older Puerto Ricans have lower family incomes than other Latino groups, are more likely to have been employed in poorly paid blue-collar and service occupations, have less access to a pension plan, and are less likely to own their own homes (Zsembic, 1993). Cubans, although relatively recent migrants, are more likely to have higher educational levels and to have worked in skilled or professional occupations than other Latino groups. Regardless of ethnic origin, men and women who have retirement incomes are more likely to live alone than people relying on savings, Federal programs, or relatives.

Cultural tradition, gender, availability of sons for men and daughters for women, and health, also play roles in living arrangements. That Cuban men prefer to live with family members may reflect the strong ethnic enclave established by Cubans who arrived in the last four decades or so of the twentieth century; these older men may wield more economic power over younger generations and insist on coresidence. Mexican Americans are the most heterogeneous, perhaps due to varying levels of acculturation; more traditional elders and their families prefer coresidence while less traditional elders (or their less traditional children) are less willing to share their households (Zsembic, 1993; 1996). As you think about living arrangements in later life, keep in mind also that, contrary to popular belief, the extended multigenerational family was never the predominant family form in the United States for several reasons. First, because relatively few people survived to reach old age until the twentieth century, the majority of parents had died by the time their last child reached adulthood. Second, the proportion of extended families began to decrease in Western Europe as early as the Middle Ages (Laslett, 1977). The goods once provided in family settings began to decline as other modes of production, such as factories, began to replace them. As a result, the family became less important as an economic unit. Third, today's young-old women, especially white women, are more likely to be in relatively good health and more able to afford to live alone than they were in the past.

Despite popular belief, the majority of the elderly living alone are neither socially isolated nor depressed. Many elders prefer "intimacy at a distance" with their children. Although older people value their family members, they also value their own autonomy even when widowed or divorced and may be reluctant to move in with a child or other relative. Moving in with a child or other relative is likely to require that elders adapt their habits and schedules to that of others—not always a welcome prospect for people who want to do things their way! If you are living in your own apartment or a dormitory, think about how living with your parents requires you to change your habits. Both the improved economic status of the elderly and their wish to live independently as long as possible have contributed to the ever-increasing proportion of older women who deliberately choose to live alone and to defy traditional gender or old-age stereotypes (Treas, 1995).

Within the past 25 years, the number of people living in nontraditional households—without relatives or romantic partners—is also increasing as the population grows older. According to a recent study by AARP, close to 800,000 Americans over age 45 lived with roommates by the early 1990s. Many people, like New Jersey residents Margaret K. White, a 78-year-old retired school teacher, and Bill Potynsky, an 80-year-old retired police captain, who share a house with two others over 65, prefer the company and sense of security provided by the companionship and source of help if needed that such an arrangement provides. They also prefer to share a living unit with people similar in age rather than to live with children or alone. No single person is in charge nor are there any formal rules. Although the residents' habits differ, they count on one another while respecting each other's independence (Newman, 2000).

Housing and Home Ownership. Of the almost 21 million households headed by people aged 65 or over, 79 percent of the household heads own their own home, about 8 in 10 of whom own their homes mortgage-free. An additional 21 percent of elderly householders were renters. Nearly half of all elderly homeowners live in the suburbs and a similar percentage of renters live in central cities. Elderly homeowners are less likely to move than are renters; almost half of all elderly home-owners lived in the same home for more than 25 years compared with renters, half of whom had moved into their home within the past 5 years. Home ownership does decline with age, however, especially in rural areas where the incidence of renting increases from less than 13 percent among those aged 62 to 74 to almost 30 percent among those aged 85 or older (U.S. Dept of Housing and Urban Development, 1999). Of the approximately 21.4 million housing units with one or more elderly householders, 1.4 million are condominiums or cooperative apartments, 82 percent of which are owned rather than rented. According to a 1999 report, the average (median) income of all older home-owner households was $20,280—almost twice that of renters' median income of $10,867 (U.S.D.H.H.S, 1999).

Race and ethnicity interact with income, however. As you can see in Table 3-3, elders living in white non-Hispanic neighborhoods are more likely to own their own homes than African Americans, Asians, or Hispanics. When the overall income level of the neighborhood—an indicator of the probable income level of individuals and families living there—is taken into account, however, much of the difference by race/ethnicity disappears (Bogue, 1999). Home ownership thus reflects socioeconomic status and life chances rather than race or ethnicity alone; in American society, life chances, including opportunities for upward mobility, have been greater for non-Hispanic whites than for African Americans or Hispanics. Note also that there are insufficient data to calculate race or ethnicity for Asians in poverty or near poor neighborhoods or for Hispanics in upper-middle-income neighbor-

Table 3-3	Home Ownership Rates of Elderly Classed by the Most Frequent Income Level and Race/Ethnicity of Neighborhoods			
	Most Common Race/Ethnicity of Neighborhood			
	White Non-Hispanic	**Black**	**Asian**	**Hispanic**
Most Common Income Level of Neighborhood				
Total, all income levels	72%	58%	56%	54%
Poverty level neighborhood	72	58	56	54
Near poor neighborhood	38	45	—*	43
Middle income neighborhood	76	78	77	80
Upper-middle income neighborhood	84	86	85	—*

* not enough cases to compute.
Source: Adapted from Donald J. Bogue. (1999). *Essays in Human Ecology 4: The Ecological Impact of Population Aging.* Chicago: The Social Development Center, Table 4–1.

hoods, emphasizing the relative level of economic success of these two very broad ethnic groups throughout the life course.

In general, however, elders own houses that are older than those owned by younger people. About 50 percent of the homes owned by people aged 65 or older were built before 1960 compared with 33 percent of the homes of younger homeowners. The value of elders' homes is also generally lower than for all homeowners: $89,294 versus $98,815. Owning one's own home—especially an older home that is more likely to need repairs—can be expensive; more than one third of older homeowners spent more than a fourth of their income on housing costs (U.S.D.H.H.S., 1999). According to the U.S. Department of Housing and Urban Development, high housing costs are the most widespread housing problem among older Americans with more than 7.4 million households—30 percent of all elderly households—paying more than they can afford for housing. Some of these elders are homeowners, more or less evenly divided into two groups: (1) people who are still paying off a mortgage; and (2) people who own their own homes free and clear but report problems in meeting the other costs of home ownership (Office of Policy Development and U.S. Department of Housing and Urban Development, 1999).

"Gated communities" are popular with many older adults because they promise privacy and safety. What socioeconomic differences are likely to exist between residents of these two gated housing developments?

Elder renters are even more disadvantaged; the number of very low income, elderly renter households with a severe rent burden is slightly more than 1 million. Renters are 3 times more likely than homeowners to have problems affording their housing. They are also more likely to be women and members of minority groups, to live alone, and to reside in urban areas than homeowners (Office of Policy Development and U.S. Department of Housing and Urban Development, 1999). Many elder renters have had little opportunity to ever own their own homes. Although the Federal government assists about 1.5 million elderly, low-income, renter households with public and assisted housing and rental assistance, there is simply not enough assistance to go around (Office of Policy Development and U.S. Department of Housing and Urban Development, 1999). Table 3-4 summarizes selected characteristics by race and ethnicity in housing units with one or more elderly householders. Contrary to what many people think, the majority of the elderly have not moved within the past year.

Table 3-4	Selected Household Characteristics by Race/Ethnicity of Elderly Householders				
	White	Black	Hispanic	Asian/ Pacific Islander	Native American, Eskimo, Aleut, and Other
	$n =$ 18,942	$n =$ 2,001	$n =$ 870	$n =$ 253	$n =$ 227
Housing Characteristic					
Owner Occupied	82%	68%	67%	54%	56%
Renter Occupied	18	32	33	46	44
Moderate to Severe Problems with Housing Condition	5	15	13	4	11
Moved in Past Year	4	4	5	8	11
Lived in Central Cities	24	57	44	48	44

U.S. Department of Commerce, Bureau of the Census (2000), *American Housing Survey for the United States, 1999 (http://www.census.gov/hhes/www/housing/ahs/ahs99/tab71.html)*.

ECHO housing. This is short for Elder Cottage Housing Opportunity and describes an accessory unit, whether a single family home or a separate apartment, on a single family lot with another primary home. The advantage of ECHO housing is that it provides independence for an older person but closeness to younger family members. Historically, the original ECHO units began in Australia and were mobile or modular rental units moved onto the property. The main home on the lot was occupied by the family and the smaller ECHO unit housed an older family member, usually a mother or mother-in-law. Upon the death of the older relative, the modular or mobile unit was removed to another location and rented to another family.

Sometimes called a "granny flat," the smaller unit may be: (1) an apartment carved out from within the family's home but with a private entrance; (2) above a garage; or (3) a separate building. Building requirements vary, and not all cities or counties permit a second unit on a single family lot. In some communities, the resident of the ECHO unit must be at least 62 years old and be a relative; in others, there is a great deal of variation in the profile of residents. Depending on the regulations of the specific city, county, or town, ECHO housing may be built to encourage the increase of affordable housing units in middle- to upper-priced single family homes.

Age-segregated retirement communities. An age-segregated retirement community is usually like any other neighborhood or community except that it is restricted to people who are 55 years of age or older. Requirements for a minimum age to enter the community are usually established when the original community is founded. Retirement communities appeal to people who do not want to live in areas with people of many different ages and most often emphasize an active lifestyle. Many offer "country-club living" with golf, tennis, swimming pool and Jacuzzi, exercise rooms, a community center, and numerous other clubs and activities. Retirement communities are relatively expensive, and buyers are likely to have additional costs for home maintenance, gardening, landscaping, and membership in the various clubs or facilities provided by the site. More than half of adult retirement community buyers use cash to purchase their home, utilizing a portion of the money they received from the sale of a previous home. An estimated two-thirds of the cash from the sale of the old home goes into the purchase of a new home. The typical buyer in a retirement community is sufficiently well-off to invest part of the proceeds from the previous home to provide a cushion for future income or emergencies (*seniorresource.com* Internet download 3/20/01).

Senior housing developments and retirement hotels. Senior housing developments, sometimes called elder public housing, are government-subsidized housing complexes for low-income elders and are composed of individual apartment units designed for independent living. Income restrictions apply, and some subsidized housing developments have waiting lists. These developments have been providing low-income elders with affordable housing for many years and are usually managed by a local housing authority. Residents may continue to live there as long as they meet the criteria established by the housing authority.

Retirement hotels provide still another option for age-segregated living. Designed for people who wish to lead an independent lifestyle, they provide rooms with a private or shared bath and may be furnished or unfurnished. Maid service is usually provided, as are congregate meals; and some facilities include social activities. Residents pay a monthly fee that covers rent and meals. The retirement hotel, a more low-cost alternative than the retirement community discussed above, is an option for individuals who either are not eligible for subsidized senior apartments or who do not want or need to maintain an apartment, but prefer an age-segregated lifestyle.

Mobile homes and recreational vehicles. There are 1.36 million mobile homes occupied by one or more elders. Because mobile homes provide a low-cost alternative to conventional housing, they tend to attract people who have limited incomes or who do not want to make a major investment in housing. Sometimes called manufactured homes, most mobile homes never move after their trip from the dealer or manufacturer to the consumer's land. Some residents consider the mobile home park their primary or only home; others live there for a few months and elsewhere the remainder of the year. Many "snowbirds" from Northern and Midwestern states spend the winter in mobile home parks in Florida, Arizona, or California.

Although badmouthed by popular culture as "trailer parks," mobile home parks offer an alternative for affordable housing to elders who wish to retire to a warmer climate, a recreational area, or a smaller home. The size of mobile homes ranges from about 900 to 2,500 square feet, and prices run from $10,000 to $100,000, depending on size and options, such as sunken living rooms, Jacuzzi tubs, and fireplaces. Although the ages, educational level, and occupations of mobile homeowners vary, the most frequent occupation is retiree, followed by blue-collar worker, and the majority are high-school graduates (Richardson, 2000; Foremost Insurance Group, 1999).

There are about 50,000 mobile home parks throughout the United States, and the majority are independent operations. Many owners of mobile homes lease the land on which their home sits, often in a mobile home park specifically for people over 55. Regardless of the age of the residents, the conveniences at mobile home parks vary widely, ranging from little more than dirt yards to country-club-like settings with pools, golf courses, and recreation centers. For many people, mobile home parks offer a low-cost alternative to a more expensive

Over the Next Hill: RVing as Home Ownership

Living in motorized, fully equipped, and comfortable vans, full-time RVers view their mobile lifestyle as a way of enjoying retirement. They have been variously described as "gypsies" or "pioneers" as they explore new territories and friendships as they choose. As described by RVers, the qualities that make them seek this lifestyle are: "A spirit of adventure, a love of the outdoors, an outgoing nature, an affinity for meeting people and making friends, a great sense of humor! An independent spirit . . . the freedom first to do what we want with our time. Along with this is the ability to go where we choose, and to

What advantages can living in an RV offer that are not available to less mobile dwellers?

remain or leave as our whim dictates" (Counts & Counts, 1996: 66–67).

Many, like the owners of the RVs pictured, form close friendships and reciprocal exchanges, but differ from residents of towns, villages, or cities as their RV provides freedom to explore relationships based on their ability to hitch up and leave at any time—or simply spend a couple of days "at home" on a beach. Although they value their freedom of movement and leave behind places or people that may be unpleasant, they also quickly establish a sense of community by helping newcomers park and set up, exchanging personal photographs, histories, and interests, and sharing food and information. Many belong to clubs, such as the Escapees, established specifically to foster a sense of "family" among recreational vehicle owners.

Because most RVers are in their 60s, 70s, and sometimes their 80s, many reach a point in their lives where traveling is more difficult due to visual problems and other age-associated infirmities. As one elderly RVer phrased it, "What happens when no one wants you to park your home next to them because your disabling illness is hard to deal with?" (Counts & Counts, 1996: 200). One solution developed by the Escapees club is to set up a nonprofit retirement community, called CARE, for its members who can no longer travel because of disabilities. Participants can lease a site with hookups, shed, and patio and receive a vegetarian lunch. Nursing services and transportation are also available. CARE provides an option for people who do not want to give up freedom, independence, or friends when they can no longer travel from site to site. As the author of an article in the *Escapee Newsletter* (1994: 7) commented:

> Who wants to live in a nursing home when all that is really needed is a little help with bathing, dressing, or getting around? When your home is an RV, how can anyone expect you to give up the freedom of your RV lifestyle. . . . (cited in Counts & Counts, 1996: 199)

Other dedicated RVers reject this alternative and continue to travel indefinitely. One 86-year-old woman who had applied to CARE withdrew her accepted application, saying that she had found a new partner with whom she would continue on the road indefinitely. The lives of full-time RVers challenge stereotypes of aging, such as inactivity and unwillingness to seek new living arrangements, friendships, and even partners. Their lives also indicate the many ways in which older people develop a sense of community even when geographically mobile.

Source: Based on Dorothy Ayers Counts & David R. Counts (1996). *Over the Next Hill: An Ethnography of RVing Seniors in North America.* Peterborough, Ontario: Broadview Press.

retirement community of built (rather than mobile) homes. Those living on leased land can, however, be vulnerable to sudden and unexpected increases in rents on their lots. People who cannot afford the increases or who lose their leases must either move their mobile homes or sell the unit, often to the landlord at a low price (*Consumer Reports,* 1998).

Older Americans tend to be more settled than their children, and residential mobility declines as we grow older. Recreational vehicles (RVs), often confused with mobile homes, offer a more nomadic life-style than mobile homes for retirees. The average price for an RV in 1998 dollars was $47,000. Although there is no exact information on the number of retirees who choose this residential style, estimates range from the hundreds of thousands to more than 2 million Americans, as described in the "Over the Next Hill" box.

Continuing care retirement communities. Still another option that approximately 350,000 older Americans have chosen is to move to age-segregated continuing care retirement communities (CCRCs) where they live independently in their own apartment or town house but where long- and short-term nursing care is available if needed. Offering retirement living, often in a campus-like setting, plus a range of health and other services, about 1,200 CCRCs are currently in operation, often as private nonprofit corporations that are targeted at independent elders. Rather than providing assistance, the goal of CCRCs is to help residents remain healthy and active as long as possible and to maintain normal community living. CCRCs offer housing, meals, and housekeeping as well as various other on-site services, such as a physician or nurse, physical therapy, recreation, and exercise programs. About one-third of CCRCs offer "life care"; that is, lifetime contracts guaranteeing care ranging from independent living to long- and short-term nursing home care. These CCRCs assume the financial risk for long-term care as part of their operating costs. Because the CCRC that provides nursing home care will be financially responsible for its provision, it has a money incentive to promote wellness, disease prevention, and disability reduction. CCRC staff thus may provide immunizations and cancer screening, monitor residents' health, furnish exercise and nutritional counseling, and coordinate both on- and off-site health services.

Living in a CCRC is not cheap. From their savings and income, residents in most CCRCs pay an entry fee to join and a monthly fee thereafter. For example, according to a 1997 GAO (U.S. General Accounting Office) study of 11 sites, entry fees range from about $34,000 for a studio apartment to $439,600 for a two-bedroom home. In addition, yearly fees may range from around $16,500 for an individual to over $51,000 for a couple. Medical expenses are not usually included in these fees. It is perhaps not surprising that CCRCs have attracted primarily well-educated, well-off older people.

Assisted living. Assisted living, a newer concept than the CCRC, provides a combination of housing, meals in a central dining room, personalized supportive services, and health care for people who need help with everyday activities but do not require nursing home care.

Emphasis is placed on a combination of services that permit residents to maintain more dignity and autonomy than a nursing home or other long-term care settings usually provide (Heumann & Boldy, 1993). Packages of services furnished on-site vary from basic assistance, such as meals and weekly housecleaning, to assistance in bathing, dressing, toiletting, and daily housekeeping. Some assisted living facilities also offer units and services specifically designed for those with Alzheimer's Disease or other cognitive impairments. The goal of assisted living is to reduce the likelihood of having to move from facility to facility as needs for help change. A nursing home wing is often maintained on the facility's campus.

An estimated 1.15 million Americans live in assisted living facilities, some of which are independent and others connected to CCRCs or nursing homes. Reflecting their greater life expectancy and probability of widowhood, nearly 80 percent of the residents are women with a median age of 84. About half of the residents lived in their own homes prior to moving to assisted living facilities that most often are located not far from their previous homes (Assisted Living Federation of America, 2001; National Center for Assisted Living, 2001).

An estimated 2 in 5 assisted living residents are cognitively impaired, and about a third are chairbound (Assisted Living Federation of America, 2002). Almost 9 in 10 need or accept help with housework and 8 in 10 need or accept help with their daily medication (National Center for Assisted Living, 2001). The majority of residents need help with one or more basic activities of daily living, as shown in Table 3-5.

Table 3-5 Help with Activities of Daily Living Received by Residents in Assisted Living Facilities			
Activities	**Independent**	**Some Help**	**Dependent**
Bathing	28%	42%	30%
Dressing	43%	33%	24%
Transferring*	64%	19%	17%
Using the toilet	58%	22%	19%
Eating	77%	13%	10%

* *Transferring* is a term used to describe moving from bed to chair, from chair to toilet, and so on.
Source: National Center for Assisted Living (2002). *Assisted Living Resident Profile* (http://www.ncal.org/about/resident.htm). Reprinted by permission.

Like the CCRC, assisted living is not cheap, and Medicare does not pay for assisted living. According to the National Center for Assisted Living (2001), the average monthly fee is $1,873 per month or about $22,476 per year in 2000 dollars. One-third of assisted living facilities charge over $2,000 per month. Additional fees are usually charged for low-level nursing care or extensive attendant care. Individual states sometimes provide funding for assisted living through various programs; however, even in those states that permit use of Medicaid funds for assisted living, these monies can be used only for services. Residents most often pay the cost of room and board themselves. Clearly, not everyone can afford assisted living, and the median annual income of residents is around $25,000 with median assets of $100,000. The average length of stay in assisted living is around 3 years, and residents most often leave to go to a nursing home where they can receive more intensive care.

Board and care homes. Board and care homes are essentially an older version of assisted living facilities and provide rooms, meals, 24-hour supervision, and help with activities of daily living. Meals are provided in a congregate dining room and some social programming may be provided. In some states, board and care homes also serve people who have been discharged from psychiatric hospitals or institutions for the developmentally disabled as well as the elderly. Many board and care homes offer a "homey" atmosphere and are as small as 5 or 6 residents; others may be as large as 100. Residents of board and care homes pay monthly fees that cover room, board, and services. Medicare and Medicaid do not pay for care in board and care homes.

Nursing homes. Although the majority of people aged 65 and over live in the community, the likelihood of being admitted at least once in one's lifetime to a nursing home increases sharply with age. Seven out of 10 residents are women, and approximately one-third are women aged 85 and older, once again reflecting their greater life expectancy and probability of widowhood. Nationally, about 5 percent of the elderly population live in nursing homes—a proportion that has been relatively constant for many decades. However, because of the increase of very old people, both the number of facilities and residents therein are increasing. Demographic characteristics (e.g., marital status, race, gender, socioeconomic status, and prior living arrangements, as well as health and ability for self-care) influence the risk of nursing home placement. Families and physicians use nursing homes for rehabilitation, most often after a stay in an acute hospital; long-term care placement for a person whose needs cannot be met effectively at home; and care of the terminally ill, a topic discussed more fully in Chapter 8.

The Old of Tomorrow

When the oldest cohort of the baby boomers grows old in 2010, they will swell the ranks of people aged 65 and older. For gerontologists, much of the interest in the baby boom generation is based on the fact that it is a numerically large generation between two much smaller generations—the Depression era of the 1930s and the baby bust period, which began in the mid-1960s. It is important, however, to keep in mind that the baby boomers actually represent several different birth cohorts. Some baby boomers became young adults in the flower child era of the 1960s, some during the Vietnam War and still others during the Nixon era. Even the styles of dress, popular music, and social concerns have differed among the broad category of people born during the baby boom years. Not only have boomers experienced different slices of history, based on the period when they were born and became young adults, but their life chances have also varied by the prosperity or decline of the economy plus their socioeconomic status, ethnicity, race, and gender. The first baby boomers became adults who contributed to women's liberation and helped change sexual mores during the social and sexual ferment of the 1960s. How do they differ today from the now-old population?

One major difference between the various baby boom cohorts and the now-old cohorts is marital status. Baby boomers have tended to marry later than their parents and to have higher rates of divorce. Also, a higher percentage of baby boomers remained unmarried than in previous birth cohorts. Nonetheless, slightly more than 6 in 10 baby boomers are currently married and living with their spouse. There are, however, differences by race and gender. White baby boomers are more likely to be married than African Americans, and baby boomer women are more likely to be married or divorced than their male cohort members. Rising housing costs and greater job opportunities for women plus increasing income and wealth discrepancies have also changed the notion that the husband is the single wage earner in married-couple households. Increasingly, dual earner families are the norm among boomers, and mothers with young children are likely to be employed full time. The trend toward dual earner couples has created demands for child care and parental leave not considered in previous generations.

Members of the baby boomer generation also delayed having children. Birth rates began to decrease in the mid-1960s, just as the first wave of baby boomer women began to enter the most likely childbearing years, and their completed families may be smaller than those of their parents. For example, although about 60 percent of women born during the depression years of 1930 to 1935 had three or more children by the time they were between the ages of 35 and 39, the most common pattern for baby boomer women in this age group has been to have two children. Thus, not surprisingly, the number of children born in the late 1960s and 1970s—the baby bust cohort—was smaller than those born during the boomer years. The baby bust cohort was followed by a more recent large baby "boomlet," primarily due to the large numbers of baby boomer families that had children later in life than did their parents. If you are a member of the baby boomlet cohort, you may be distressed to hear that it is likely that the life chances of the baby bust cohorts will be greater than those of the baby boomlet. Because of their smaller numbers, baby bust members face less competition than baby boomlet members for the same advantages, such as education, jobs, and so forth—a difference that will affect them throughout the life course.

Just as there is no "the elderly" or no one way in which we all grow old, each generation is likely to have a different old age from preceding generations. Not only is birth cohort important, but race, ethnicity, social class, and gender will shape the lives of the elders of tomorrow. By 2030, the Latino population aged 65 and over will more than triple, the Asian and Pacific Islander population almost triple, and the Native American and Eskimo population more than double. Members of each of these minority groups will bring varied experiences and histories, preferences, and value systems to old age that will differ according to their life chances and degree of acculturation.

Summary

This chapter focused initially on demography, the study of the characteristics of populations that influence every social institution. The population of any society is determined by three factors: births, deaths, and net migration. The age composition of a society is important in structuring social life, and the United States, like all industrialized nations, has undergone a demographic transition, moving from high birth and death rates to low birth and death rates. Birth cohort is also important, influencing not only the social roles available but specific beliefs and attitudes. Many characteristics assumed to be part of old age are really birth cohort effects. Gender, race, ethnicity, and social class also structure the life course, affecting both lifestyles and opportunities in later life.

In later life, each birth cohort is likely to vary from today's old and will experience different challenges. The demographics show that more people are living longer and remaining energetic at a rate unheard of even a century ago. What effect will better health and longer life expectancy have on the ways in which the boomers experience old age? When large numbers of baby boomers reach age 65 around 2010, will age 65 continue to be considered the "normal" age for retirement? Even today, people are retiring earlier than age 65, for the average age when Americans now retire is 63. Although in other industrialized nations the age at which one becomes eligible for full pension benefits varies, many people both here and in other countries retire even earlier: at age 60. Will the trend toward early retirement continue so that Americans decide to retire even earlier than 62? If so, this will affect the labor force, for baby boomers now account for more than half of all members of the labor force, holding seniority and a large proportion of the more desirable jobs. By 2005, an estimated, 63 percent of the American labor force will be 34 years of age or older with the fastest growing age group of workers between the ages of 45 and 54. As they become truly "older workers," their presence in the labor force is likely to shape future work and retirement policies.

Thinking about your own future, how will the size of your birth cohort influence your personal life chances and opportunities: your job plans, savings opportunities, housing, and even your health care and retirement plans? Thinking far ahead to when you are old, where will you live, and how are these arrangements likely to be influenced by your gender, race and ethnicity, social class, and marital status? Will you live in your hometown, choose a nomadic existence similar to the RVers, or migrate to another part of the United States? Will you live with a spouse, a partner, family members, friends, or people to whom you have no marital or familial ties? Do you think that the number of people in your birth cohort will impact the size of your Social Security or pension if you retire, or the health care coverage you receive when you are 65 or older?

As you think about these questions, also consider the following: Is demography destiny, as some analysts have proposed? The answer would seem to be no. Other factors, such as world events, the economy, and social policies as well as personal characteristics, influence our lives. For example, among the baby boomers, these factors include delayed marriage and higher rates of divorce, and the growing variability of the timing and duration of marriage, childbearing, remarriage, and increased participation of women in the labor force. Changes in health, life expectancy, and shifts in retirement patterns challenge old theories of later life that depend on age alone. Just as your membership in a particular birth cohort and your gender, social class, and race/ethnicity, coupled with the sociohistorical context in which you were born and live, will help form your destiny, these factors also have shaped the lives of those who are now-old.

Endnote

1. Because Federal sources use the terms *Black* and *Hispanic* in statistical data collection, we have used these (rather than *African American*, *Latino*, or *Latina*) when using census tables and other government documents.

Key Points

1. Demography is the study of the characteristics of populations and influences every social institution.

2. Every society uses age to organize social life, and the age structure of a society denotes the number of people within a specific age group.

3. The population of any society is determined by three factors: births, deaths, and net migration.

4. Life span denotes the theoretical maximum number of years an organism can live; life expectancy describes the average number of years an individual born at a specific time is likely to live.

5. The demographic transition describes the process by which a society moves from high birth and death rates to low birth and death rates.

6. Membership in a specific birth cohort affects both the number and types of social roles available as well as beliefs and attitudes.

7. Many characteristics assumed to be part of old age are really birth cohort effects.

8. Life expectancy is influenced by gender, race, ethnicity, and socioeconomic status.

9. Although women live longer than men, both marital status and living arrangements vary markedly by race and ethnicity.

10. Socioeconomic status, ethnicity, gender, and desire to remain independent influence living arrangements in later life.

11. In later life, each birth cohort is likely to vary from today's old and will experience different challenges.

Discussion Questions

1. How have the three components of population change (births, deaths, and migration) contributed to the changing proportion of older Americans?

2. Explain the dramatic shifts in life expectancy since 1900.

3. What might be some of the demographic, social, and economic effects as well as scientific developments that would dramatically increase average life expectancy for men?

4. Select a few social policies or issues that are currently being debated. Discuss how the now-old might be affected by any changes in social policies, such as Medicare, Social Security, and so forth.

5. Are you a member of the baby bust or baby boomlet generations? Or are you a member of the baby boom era, or a child of a baby boomer? Regardless of your birth cohort, what do you envision as your role in planning for the aging of the baby boomers?

Films and Videos

America in the Forties (video; 3 tapes, approx. 3 hours; available from PBS Video, 1320 Braddock Place, Alexandria, VA 22314-1698).

A "nonfiction" musical, providing background on what life was like in the United States for the now-old who were young in the 1940s and who are the parents of the baby boomers.

Centenarians Tell It Like It Is (video; 55 minutes; available from Terra Nova Films, 9848 S. Winchester Avenue, Chicago, IL 60643; *www.terranova.org*).

An entertaining window into the past from centenarians who review politics, premarital sex, and other topics from their perspective as bystanders to history.

My Memories Are Here—Italian Elders (video; 27 minutes; available from Terra Nova Films, 9848 S. Winchester Avenue, Chicago IL 60643; *www.terranova.org*).

Four Italian older people provide views of their past and present lives and the rewards and problems of later life.

Something Left to Do—Elders of Sto-Lo Nation (video; 24 minutes; available from Terra Nova Films, 9848 S. Winchester Avenue, Chicago IL 60643; *www.terranova.org*).

Native American Sto-Lo elders provide insights about how they preserve their culture and link generations.

The Grand Generation (video; 30 minutes; available from Filmmakers Library, 124 East 40th Street, New York, NY 10016; *www.filmakers.com*)

Portrait of six older Americans including a union organizer, a baker, a bayman on the Chesapeake, and three folk artists.

Women of the Georgian Hotel (video; 20 minutes; available from Terra Nova Films, 9848 S. Winchester Avenue, Chicago IL 60643; *www.terranova.org*).

An Emmy Award-winning view of the lives of elderly women that provides information on lifestyles in a Florida retirement hotel.

Internet Resources

www.ameristat.org

Provides instant summaries of U.S. population characteristics including education, income and poverty, race, ethnicity, and marriage and family.

www.aoa.dhhs.gov

A source for current statistical information including "Profile of Older Americans" as well as connections to other sites.

www.census.gov

The source for births, deaths, marriages, and other current information available from the decennial census as well as current population studies on numerous topics relating to aging.

www.demographics.com

The link to *American Demographics*, a readable journal with up-to-date articles on all aspects of population and its effects on social and economic issues.

www.prb.org

The link to the Population Reference Bureau, an organization devoted to information about United States and international population trends and their implications.

Research Article

Riche, M. F. (2000). America's diversity and growth: Signposts for the 21st century. *Population Bulletin, 55* (June): 2.

A good overview of population changes in the United States.

Supplemental Readings

Counts, D.A., & Counts, D. R. (1996). *Over the Next Hill: An Ethnography of RVing Seniors in North America.* Peterborough, Ontario: Broadview Press.

An entertaining account of the various RV lifestyles of recreational vehicle owners, showing that older RVers may go over the next hill for adventure but are far from being over the hill.

Martin, P., & Midgley, E. (1999). Immigration to the United States. *Population Bulletin, 54* (June): 2.

An excellent reference, documenting immigration patterns and their significance in the United States.

McFalls, J. A. (1998). Population: A lively introduction. *Population Bulletin, 53* (September): 3.

A clear and concise introduction to demography that is useful in understanding the role that population change plays in our everyday lives.

Population Reference Bureau. (1999). *World Population: More Than Just Numbers.* Washington, DC: Author.

A useful introduction to population changes throughout the world and their implications for the future. ✦

Chapter 4

Social Perspectives on Aging

Introduction

Mrs. R. is a 72-year-old second generation Japanese-American woman who was born in Los Angeles and lives in Garden Grove, California. She is married and has four children. She was interviewed by a student at the University of Southern California, who asked, "When do you think a person becomes a senior?"

Mrs. R. replied, "You mean what age bracket? . . . Well, my husband is going to laugh at me, because I don't consider myself a senior (she laughs). Because I enjoy life. I like to do a lot of things, and I still, you know . . . when my mother died, and she was 42, I remember her being a very little old lady. But my gosh, I don't consider myself a . . . I don't consider myself a senior. I think it's a state of mind. To me, a senior citizen naturally slows down a little bit and, in that respect, I've slowed down. But I think it's how you feel about life. . . . I like to garden. I am up early in the morning, gardening. I enjoy going to Vegas, I enjoy playing cards, you know, bridge, and going to the movies. . . . Well, I don't know if Matt told you, but my husband had acute leukemia two years ago and look at him now, you know—he's very healthy. And I think somebody's been looking after us all this time. And I tell him, "They don't want you up there yet." So, you know, basically, I think we enjoy going to Vegas. He's gone there more than I have. We've been trying to go once a month. He still enjoys playing golf. I used to play golf, but I gave it up because of my . . . skin.

Mrs. R's view of her own life is but one illustration of how people construct their own aging. Given that age is both a biological fact and a social construct, how can we make sense of Mrs. R's perspective as well as what *we read and observe about aging and old age? How can we link together our findings to make generalizations about a specific observation or set of observations? To understand the nature and consequences of events, scientists use theories, that is, "the construction of explicit explanations in accounting for empirical findings" (Bengtson, Burgess, & Parrott, 1997: S72). A theory is a statement of how and why specific facts are related that allows us to make generalizations about something we want to understand. Suppose you notice that men are more likely to open doors for children and the elderly than for other people. If you place this observation in a theoretical framework, you can understand that this is not random behavior. Rather, it tells you something about the regard in which elders and children are generally held as well as the assumptions being made about their strength and capacity. You will be attempting to explain the why and how of certain behaviors and their relationship to social and cultural norms.*

Similarly, theories in social gerontology encompass more than age as an attribute of individuals; they attempt to explain the how and why of human behavior, and the relationship of age to other social characteristics and to the structure of the society. As Fry (1999: 282) has pointed out: "Theories about age are theories about cultural and social phenomena. . . . How is age used in the regulation of social life? How does age enter into the manipulation and negotiation of daily living?"

Theory thus has several practical uses. First, a theory provides a framework to summarize and link together the many findings of different observations and empirical studies in a meaningful way. Second, theory shows how and why certain events are related in a logical fashion. Third, theories can provide meaning and understanding of the world around us. And fourth, theories are not just abstract ideas but can provide useful directions for practical, real-world interventions. As Havighurst (1961), a leader in the development of social gerontology during the mid-twentieth century, observed more than four decades ago:

> *The science of gerontology has the practical purpose, as we often say, of "adding life to the years" of the latter part of the human life span . . . helping people to enjoy life, and to get satisfaction from life. . . . A theory of successful aging is a statement of the conditions of individual and social life under which the individual person gets a maximum of satisfaction and happiness and society maintains an appropriate balance among satisfactions for the various groups which make it up—old, middle-aged, and young, men and women, etc. (p. 8)*

In investigating old age, gerontologists face four basic questions: (1) What issues or topics should we study? (2) How should we study them—large-scale social surveys, observation, participant observation, published reports (e.g., newspapers, books, and stories), in-depth interviews, historical records, or some other method? (3) Whom do we study; that is, what sample should we select? (4) How do we connect the facts that we have ascertained from our research to form theories about later life? In answering these questions, gerontologists follow one or more theoretical road maps that guide the research. Although it is often assumed that knowledge builds upon knowledge (i.e., scientists work to expand the current theory or set of rules), there is no single theory in gerontology that rules. Gerontologists, like many other scientists, often disagree about what determines the most interesting questions and ways to answer them. This is not necessarily bad, for new theoretical road maps provide new directions for research and social policy.

Aging and old age have been studied from different perspectives including a focus on the individual, a group of people, a specific society, a distinct historical period, comparative studies of societies, and so on. Some researchers seek to find similarities, and others look at change. Despite these differences, distinct theoretical approaches have guided social research on aging in the past and continue to do so today. This chapter discusses important theoretical approaches, the ways in which they have steered research on aging and society over time, and how they have influenced thinking and social planning about the elderly and might do so into our own future old age. As you read this chapter, keep in mind that knowledge is always relative. In gerontology, as well as in other fields of study, each approach and set of new findings has the potential to open up new theoretical directions as road maps to follow.

Was There a 'Golden Age' for the Elderly?

MYTH: IN SOME SOCIETIES, PEOPLE HAVE BEEN
RESPECTED PRECISELY BECAUSE OF THEIR AGE

A common belief is that somewhere, in the past or in some distant society, the elderly were venerated and respected precisely because they were old. Alas, like many of our treasured beliefs, there is little or no evidence to substantiate this. There has probably never been a "golden age" in which elders were automatically respected or loved (Nydegger, 1985). Rather, power and prestige among the elderly have been largely due to their ability to control goods, knowledge, and other resources. In pre-modern Taiwan, for example, the traditional rural family structure was authoritarian, dominated by the oldest male with whom sons lived both before and after marriage. Absolute obedience and complete devotion to parents, and the lower ranking of younger people, was the rule, supporting "a status system that defined authority and fostered control of the young by the old. Within this rigid hierarchy, daughters-in-law were subjugated by mothers-in-law to ensure the stability of the family and security in old age. Such stability and security, however, were achieved at the price of the immeasurable repression of daughters-in-law" (Gallin, 1998: 4). The goal of marriage was continuation of the family, not love or personal satisfaction. Few of us today would welcome such a family structure.

Nor were the elderly automatically venerated in colonial America; the retired, the poor, and widows without husbands or children were often segregated from the rest of society and dependent upon others for support—a topic discussed in greater detail in Chapter 10 (Haber, 1983). Although historians such as Fischer (1977) have argued that a firmly established gerontocracy existed in colonial America, other historians (Demos, 1978; Smith, 1978) have noted that any high status enjoyed by the elderly resulted from their control

How likely do you think a "golden age for the elderly" was for the grandparents of these men?

of resources. Economic power outweighed chronological age (Haber, 1983), and impoverished old men and women, dependent upon the goodwill of their relatives and the community, did not enjoy high status (Haber & Gratton, 1993). By the nineteenth century, according to Cole (1992), "Victorian moralists split the last stage of life into two apparently separate, controllable parts: the 'good' old age of virtue, health, self-reliance, natural death, and salvation; and the bad old age of sin, disease, dependency, premature death, and damnation . . . [setting up] a historical dynamic in which popular perceptions would swing from one pole to the other" (Cole, 1992: 161–162). As you will see in the following section, these two opposing views which have shaped social theories about aging and old age continue to do so today.

Approaches to the Study of Aging

Old Age as Dependence

As discussed in Chapter 1, the nineteenth-century Belgian statistician, Quetelet (1842/1969), called attention to the life course by dividing large numbers of people according to age and accomplishments. He concluded that in old age, both intellect and moral sense decreased. Not only did creative genius disappear, but the older worker could no longer perform adequately when compared with younger workers. Quetelet was not alone in his conclusions. The American physician George Miller Beard (1874; 1881), collecting material from the biographies of famous people through history, computed the mean (arithmetic average) age at which these men and women accomplished their major works. He concluded that "seventy percent of the work of the world is done before forty-five and eighty percent before fifty. . . . It should be noted also [for women] the procreative function ceases between forty and fifty, just the time when physical and mental powers begin to decline, as though nature had foreseen this law and provided that the world should not be peopled by those whose powers had fallen from below their maximum" (Beard, 1874, cited in Cole, 1992: 165).

From a different perspective, social commentators, analyzing various social ills (e.g., the increasing number of poor people, overcrowded labor markets, or growing numbers of unskilled workers in the United States), hypothesized that the elderly declined in status and fell into poverty almost universally; they were cast upon the scrap heap of industrial society. Old age began to be defined by social scientists, reformers, and physicians alike as a social problem, directly linked to poverty and ill health: "At around 50, his [the worker's] abilities began to falter. . . . His strength and flexibility—as well as his salary—all declined with age" (Haber, 1983: 43–44). As one social scientist, Lee Welling Squier (1912), wrote in his study, *Old Age Dependency in the United States:*

> . . . The transition from non-dependence to dependence is an easy stage—property gone, friends passed away or removed, relatives become few, ambition collapsed, only a few years left to live, with death a final and welcome end to it all—such conclusions inevitably sweep the wage-earner from the class of hopeful independent citizens into that of the helpless poor. (pp. 28–29, cited in Haber, 1983: 46)

The connection between dependent old age and living in an institution for the poor seemed clear: "Generations grew up with 'a reverence for God, the hope of heaven, and the fear of the poorhouse' " (Haber & Gratton, 1993: 122). Old age was thus designated not only as physical and mental decline but also as a social problem associated with modernization and industrialization. Much of the research on aging during the first half of the twentieth century accepted the premise that to be elderly was an explicitly or tacitly undesirable state in an individualistic, activist society such as the United States.

Successful Aging Through Individual Adjustment

A key notion in many theoretical approaches to old age has been that of *adjustment* to the status of "old" or "elderly" through specific role behaviors rather than a developmental or life course approach. A *role* is the dynamic aspect of a *status:* individuals hold a status, such as student, and perform a role. For example, in the status of student, the role is to attend class, do homework, write papers, and take exams. Failure to play the role associated with the status of student will probably result in negative consequences, such as failure and loss of student status.

By the 1940s, using the status of "old" or "elderly" as key, social gerontologists used the concept of role to provide a frame for prediction of adjustment or maladjustment in later life. *Adjustment* referred primarily to goodness of fit between the perceived needs of old people and the extent to which they were able to fulfill these needs. Accordingly, while social isolation, declining health, poverty, and retirement were common conditions of old age, these difficulties could be overcome by the individual's efforts. Social researchers, such as Cavan, Burgess, Havighurst, and Goldhamer (1949), emphasized activity and individual life satisfaction as hallmarks of normal (versus pathological) old age.

Examining the relationships among social roles, self-concept, activity, and life satisfaction, advocates of *activity theory* have argued that the individual who ages optimally is one who maintains usual activities as long as possible and finds substitute statuses and roles for relinquished ones. According to activity theory, the elderly are not very different from people in midlife; thus, continued activity in old age preserves self-concept and ensures higher levels of life satisfaction (Cavan, Burgess, Havighurst, & Goldhamer, 1949; Havighurst & Albrecht, 1953).

How to achieve adjustment and avoid maladjustment in old age were also topics for research. For example, one study proposed that reaching the age of 70, retirement, and death of a spouse were equally negative role changes associated with maladjustment. Furthermore, people identifying themselves as elderly or old were expected to be more maladjusted than those who identified themselves as middle-aged. Likewise, fantasizing, absentmindedness, daydreaming about the past, and thoughts of death were regarded as maladjustment indicators (Phillips, 1957). That old age was best handled through "staying young" was the tacit assumption. As Havighurst (1961: 8) summed it up: "Successful aging means the maintenance as far and as long as possible of the activities and attitudes of middle age." Supporters of the activity theory viewed their tasks as "adding life to the years" and giving a series of prescriptions for the individual and society:

> One of the major aims of gerontology is to provide society and individuals with advice on the making of societal and individual choices about such things as retirement policy, social security policy, housing, where and with whom to live, how to relate oneself to one's family, what to do in free time. (Havighurst, 1961: 8)

Although theories focusing on the individual—*micro-level theories*—such as the activity theory are intuitively appealing to Americans who value individualism and personal independence, they are simplistic, ignoring the importance of the social structure in which we grow old. Empirical evidence for the activity theory, for example, has failed to support the importance of continued activity. In a test of the types of social activities and their relationships to life satisfaction in an undiversified retirement community of relatively well-off elders, Lemon, Bengtson, and Peterson (1972) found that only informal activities with friends were significant determinants of life satisfaction; informal activities with relatives or neighbors, participation in voluntary organizations, and solitary leisure and household activities were, however, unrelated. A decade later, Longino and Kart (1982), conducting a second test of activity theory in three different types of retirement communities that were more racially and socioeconomically mixed, again found that only participation in informal activities was associated with life satisfaction. Put differently, the informal social supports provided by friendships are important for life satisfaction in old age, but maintaining a high level of activity itself is not.

Old Age as Continuity

As originally stated by Neugarten (1964), *continuity theory* holds that personality remains stable with aging. Continuity theory is a micro-level and social-psychological theory of adult development. Despite changes in physical functioning, health, and social situations, people tend to respond to various situations in a consistent manner and deal with the world in habitual ways that enable them to adapt to numerous changes without experiencing crisis (Atchley, 1989; 1995a). This approach is based on the assumption that older people assess change from the perspectives of their personality traits, interests, and habits built up over time.

Continuity theory involves four major elements: (1) *internal structure;* (2) *external structure;* (3) *goal setting,* and (4) *maintaining adaptive capacity.* Internal structure describes "the ideas, mental skills, and information stored in the mind . . . that, when combined, form a unique whole that distinguishes one person from another" (Atchley, 1995: 246). The consistency of these elements form individual personality and are important for psychological security. External structures encompass the social roles, activities, relationships, geographic locations, and living environments that differentiate one individual from another; their continuity is important for social security. Goal-setting refers to the assumption that adults set outcomes for how they use life experiences to give their lives direction. Maintaining adaptive capacity describes the ways that people are motivated to use their internal and external structures to maximize life satisfaction (Atchley, 2001). As

Atchley (1995: 229) has summarized: "The heart of continuity theory is the presumption that people are motivated to continue to use the adaptive apparatuses they have constructed throughout adulthood to diagnose situations, chart future courses, and adapt to change."

Continuity theory has intuitive appeal by its emphasis on the point that personality does not magically change with aging; rather, personality remains relatively constant throughout adulthood. It does not take into account, however, the connections between the wider society and the individual. It also leaves unanswered such questions as whether continuity is the most successful way to deal with changes that occur with aging or whether flexibility in gender roles and lifestyles are more beneficial in later life.

Old Age Within a Social System

Nineteen-sixty-one marked the entry of a different perspective with *disengagement theory:* focus on the societal (*macro level*) rather than the individual (*micro level*). Proposed by sociologist Elaine Cumming, a former student of Talcott Parsons, and psychologist William Henry, they argued that aging must be understood *within* the social system in which it occurs. Rather than focusing on individual roles and role adjustment, they emphasized the society as a complex system whose parts work together to maintain equilibrium and thus ensure social survival—a theoretical position associated with a school of thought called *structural functionalism*. Disengagement theory thus centers on the smooth functioning of a society rather than on individual adjustment or attitudes.

As originally stated, disengagement may be summarized by its first two axioms: (1) "Although individuals differ, the expectation of death is universal and decrement of ability is probable. Therefore, a mutual severing of ties will take place between a person and others in that society." (2) "Because interactions create and reaffirm norms, a reduction in the number or variety of interactions leads to an increased freedom from the control of the norms governing everyday behavior. Consequently, once begun, disengagement becomes a circular or self-perpetuating process" (Cumming & Henry, 1961: 211). In other words, because they are elderly, individuals either *choose* to occupy fewer statuses, such as worker or parent of growing children, or are *forced out* of them. As a result, they are less likely to be bound by role behaviors associated with specific statuses.

An additional part of the theory that pays attention to the consequences of disengagement for the individual, however, is often overlooked: "Because the abandonment of life's central roles—work for men, marriage and family for women—results in dramatically reduced social life space, it will result in crisis and loss of morale unless different roles, appropriate to the disengaged state, are available" (Cumming

& Henry, 1961: 215). The importance, not of continuation of activity, but of personally meaningful roles is thus an often overlooked but essential thread running through disengagement theory.

Although they called attention to the obvious—but largely neglected—point that none of us grows old in a vacuum but rather in a social context, Cumming and Henry nonetheless accepted the premise of earlier theorists that old age is inevitably associated with decline. It is precisely this unavoidable decline, they argued, that creates a social imperative for all societies to oust the elderly from key roles. According to this argument, as people age, they become less competent and will weigh down the social system unless they disengage from vital social roles. The social system deals with this by institutionalizing disengagement—"an inevitable mutual withdrawal" between the aged person and society.

Disengagement theory has been heavily criticized for a variety of reasons. Without dwelling on the numerous disputes that disengagement theory has occasioned, its importance is fourfold. First, it called attention to aging not as an individual phenomenon but as a socially patterned event within a social structure where accepted social norms govern withdrawal of the elderly from vital social roles, such as paid employment, in order to maintain continuity and social order. Second, it challenged a major premise of activity theory—that successful old age was a continuation of middle age—by proposing that old age was a distinct life stage characterized by activities different in quantity and quality than those of earlier life. Third, disengagement made perhaps the first explicit recognition of gender differences in aging. Whether, as Cumming (1963) postulated, growing old is easier for men than women remains debatable, but certainly there are gender differences in how old age is experienced. Later work, for example, suggested that flexibility in gender roles—a balance between stereotypically male and female behavior—is associated with both life satisfaction and greater longevity (Monge, 1975; Sinott, 1977). Moreover, there is some evidence that, as we age, we become more androgynous; that is, men become more nurturant and women become more assertive (Gutmann, 1997), a topic discussed more fully in Chapter 7. And lastly, and most important, disengagement theory stimulated theory development during the 1970s and onward—Rose's subculture of aging, Dowd's exchange theory, Cowgill and Holmes' modernization theory examining aging in cross-cultural perspective, and Riley's age stratification are but a few and are discussed in the following sections. Table 4-1 lists the major micro- and macro-level theories discussed in this chapter.

Exclusion of the Elderly From Social Life

Several approaches during the 1960s and 1970s explored social forces associated with the relatively disadvantaged position of the elderly in industrialized society. We briefly examine each of these along with evidence substantiating or refuting the premises. As you read, think about the extent to which each takes account of the diversity and heterogeneity of the elderly. To what extent is membership in the social hierarchies of race, ethnicity, gender, and social class discussed or ignored?

Table 4-1 Micro- and Macro-Level Theories of Aging and Old Age	
Micro-Level Theories	**Macro-Level Theories**
Activity Theory	Disengagement Theory
Continuity Theory	Modernization Theory
Exchange Theory	Subculture of Aging
Selective Optimization with Compensation	Political Economy
Successful Aging	Critical Gerontology

Subculture of Aging. Arnold Rose's (1962) theory of the *subculture of aging* is essentially concerned with how interaction mediates between the attributes of individuals and society: a formulation stemming from a theoretical approach known as symbolic interactionism. Rose, accepting the premise that elders are disengaged from society, focused both on the disadvantages and potential advantages that expulsion from vital social roles can have. Proposing that a pattern of interaction develops when group members have common backgrounds and interests or are excluded from interaction with other groups in the society, or both, Rose argued that elders fit this definition. As a result of both their similarities and social exclusion in later life, the self-concepts and group consciousness of older people change. Many older Americans, he argued, have a diminished self-concept as they age, largely as a result of the emphasis on youth as a desirable attribute in American society. This negative effect may be offset by group identification and consciousness, presenting a potential for unified social action. Older people thus can offset their negative self-concept through becoming a voting bloc, exerting political power within existing political structures or in new ones.

The extent to which the elderly share commonalities, however, is debatable, for both heterogeneity and diversity are the most outstanding hallmarks of later life. Consider, for example, the difference in life experiences between a 65-year-old rural African-American woman who lives below the poverty level in Alabama and a 65-year-old suburban white male who has retired on a handsome pension from his position as a corporate executive. To a young person, they are both old—age 65.

Will membership in the same birth cohort combined with "being old" provide a common self-concept and group identification? Probably not, for their lives and self-concepts have been shaped by their positions in the hierarchies of social class, race, and gender. It is also unlikely that they will take identical political stances, for their ideologies and interests have been formed by their different life courses. Although numerous lobbying groups on behalf of the elderly exist, the elderly have rarely formed a unified political force in American society. As issues regarding Medicare, Social Security, and other programs with a direct impact on the elderly receive increased attention in political elections, however, the potential of "gray power" should not be ignored.

Modernization Theory. As noted earlier in this chapter, social theorists at the turn of the twentieth century cited industrialization and modernization as major culprits lowering the power and influence of the elderly. This perspective was expounded more fully by various theorists (Ogburn & Nimkoff, 1940; Simmons, 1945; Cottrell, 1960) and elaborated as *modernization* theory in the 1970s by Cowgill and Holmes (1972) and Cowgill (1974). Like disengagement theory, this approach is a macro-level formulation, focused more on the social structure of a society than on the individual. Rather than assuming that low regard for the elderly is a hallmark of all societies, as Cumming and Henry proposed, the modernization approach views industrialization as the reason for diminished power and prestige of older people. Briefly, according to modernization theory, as a society moves from a rural, agrarian-based society to an urban, technology-based system, the status of the elderly decreases with respect to leadership roles, power, and influence, and they are more likely to be excluded from community life. In Cowgill's words, modernization describes

> the transformation of a total society from a relatively rural way of life based on animate power, limited technology, relatively undifferentiated institutions, [and] parochial and traditional outlook and values toward a predominantly urban way of life based on inanimate sources of power, highly developed scientific technology, highly differentiated institutions matched by segmented individual roles, and a cosmopolitan outlook which emphasizes efficiency and progress. (Cowgill, 1974: 127)

Like disengagement theory, modernization theory is no longer generally accepted as originally formulated, but it has stimulated research on the status of the elderly in different societies and in different historical periods. As Sokolovsky (1993) aptly points out, there is no simple association between preindustrial and simple societies and a specific view of aging or the status of the elderly. Cultural definitions of old age and the respect accorded to the elderly have varied widely from culture to culture with dramatic implications for how the elderly are treated.

Even within a specific preindustrial society, images of aging are variable and complex, influenced by degree of family support, gender, class position, and health. For example, in one male-dominated Andean society where the prestige of all females is low, older women have unquestioned power over the labor of girls and younger women kin until very old age. In this society, however, female power and prestige are divorced because suffering, rather than age, is the basis on which prestige is assigned to women. Being long-suffering ranges from being overworked as a child or young bride to being abandoned by one's spouse (Mitchell, 1998).

Moreover, the premise that modernization undermined the power and prestige of the elderly is based on another assumption: The current status of the elderly is drastically different from that of previous centuries. Rather than reducing the status of the elderly in the United States, however, recent historical research suggests that modernization resulted in real gains in wealth of the average American so that "by the first decades of the twentieth century, most older persons possessed wealth and assets that were unattainable to all but a few preindustrial elders" (Haber & Gratton, 1994: 175). Moreover, the majority of the old of yesterday and today have never been impoverished or socially isolated, although a persistent minority of elders—widowed women, women without families, African Americans, immigrants, and ethnic minorities—have been mired in poverty over the centuries (Haber & Gratton, 1994).

The notion of the elderly as poverty-stricken discards upon the scrap heap of modern society is deeply rooted in well-intentioned social reform when early-twentieth-century elder advocates inaccurately stressed the neediness of all elders in order to push for retirement pension laws. A heritage of this notion is resentment about elderly entitlements, when the old not living in poverty receive government benefits. This is "cited as evidence of the inordinate greed of an entire generation" (Haber & Gratton, 1993: 184). As you read further in this book, consider the effect that competing definitions of the elderly (i.e., poor, helpless victims versus "greedy geezers") have had on social policies and attitudes toward old age.

Exchange Theory. *Exchange theory*, centering on individual actions within an industrialized society, is an essentially economic, rational-choice model of behavior: In social interaction as well as in economic exchanges, people tend to do that which brings the most benefit at the least cost (Homans, 1974). The more often a particular action of a person is rewarded, the more likely is the individual to repeat it. Building upon this perspective as well as modernization theory, Dowd (1975) placed aging within an exchange framework. Like Rose, Dowd was concerned with the esteem of the elderly in modern society but with a specific focus on their economic and social bargaining power. According to Dowd, "Unlike the aged in more traditional societies, older people in industrialized societies have precious few power resources to exchange in daily social interaction. The net effect is an increased dependence upon others and the concomitant necessity to comply to their wishes" (Dowd, 1975: 592–593). The problems of the aged in contemporary industrial societies are thus problems of decreasing bargaining power. The worker who once exchanged skill for wages loses this bargaining power upon retirement; the widow living with her married children is required to exchange compliance or approval for her housing. The elderly become objects of beneficence rather than able to bargain equally in social exchanges. Simply put, they have few bargaining chips in the chance game of life.

Loss of bargaining power is not inextricably associated with old age because, as Dowd pointed out, the nature and degree of power possessed by the elderly is associated with individual socioeconomic status, ethnicity and race, economic resources, and social policies. Although Dowd accepted the dubious premise that the position of the elderly has grown worse due to modernization, he noted that greater economic autonomy, increased Social Security benefits, and re-employment of older workers after retirement could improve their bargaining ability in the future, as could a coalition of older people to protest their social and economic situation (Dowd, 1975). In the quarter of a century or so since Dowd wrote, to what extent do you believe that the bargaining power of older people has increased or decreased? Why?

Successful Aging Revisited

Much early gerontological theory and research focused not only on the changes that occur in old age but also on the success with which we solve problems throughout later life—a micro approach to aging. During the past decade or so, the concept of *successful aging* has reemerged in gerontology. In the 1960s, when research on successful aging focused on life satisfaction and adaptation to age-related changes, Havighurst suggested that successful aging denoted the ways that an individual maximizes high levels of satisfaction and happiness. Society, too, plays a role, maintaining homeostasis or balance between individual satisfactions and the well-being of elders as a whole (Havighurst, 1961).

This broad view of successful aging, however, is vague. What theoretical perspective points toward maximum levels of satisfaction? Furthermore, how will successful aging, regardless of the theoretical model chosen, be operationalized and measured? When Havighurst first examined determinants of life satisfaction in old age, he focused on two paradigms popular in the 1960s: *activity theory* and *disengage-*

ment theory. Activity theory stresses the continuation of midlife roles and activities as long as possible. Disengagement theory argues that people's roles and relationships differ in quantity and power as they grow old. Which pattern of aging is more "successful"?

Empirical research to disentangle this question indicates that there is no simple answer. Neither activity theory nor disengagement theory adequately accounts for individual differences in patterns of growing old. A team of researchers at the Kansas City Study of Adult Life looked at both men and women to find a personality dimension that would fill the theoretical gap left by activity and disengagement formulations (Reichard, Livson, & Peterson, 1962). They found four very broad personality types: (1) the *integrated,* including activists who maintained old roles, selective activists who dropped some roles but maintained others, and the successfully disengaged or "rocking chair contingent" who contentedly abandoned old social roles; (2) the *armored defended,* encompassing people who denied the aging process as well as those constructed individuals who had less integrated personalities; (3) the *passive-dependent,* including individuals seeking emotional support from others and the apathetic; and (4) the *disorganized.* Surprisingly, only the passive-dependent and disorganized reported medium or low life satisfaction. The "integrated," regardless of their level of activity, and the "armored" who denied their aging, indicated high levels of life satisfaction. The constricted reported high or medium life satisfaction (Reichard, Livson, & Peterson, 1962; Havighurst, 1968). Clearly, life satisfaction as an indicator of successful aging involves "different strokes for different folks," depending on individuals' own values, preferences for lifestyles, and worldviews.

Also emphasizing the importance of basic personality style was a formulation by Cumming who, drawing on the same research studies, suggested a "temperamental variable, basically biological" (1963: 379) as crucial in determining how people age. Proposing two ideal types, the *impinger* or extrovert and the *selector* or introvert, the degree to which an individual more closely resembles one type over the other will affect the way in which she or he grows old. According to this formulation, impingers, characterized by a need for interaction with others and a strong press for dominance, are likely to be active and often appear younger than their age peers. But, if physical disabilities increase, impingers will become progressively less able to control the social situation and will suffer anxiety and panic as a result. Their "problem in old age will be to avoid confusion," noted Cumming (1963: 380). In contrast, selectors, who may have been viewed by others as shy or withdrawn when younger, will seem "age appropriate" when old.

During the 1970s and 1980s, the concept of "successful aging" expanded beyond the notions of life satisfaction and adaptation to old age to encompass three dimensions: (1) survival, (2) physical functioning with a low level of disability, and (3) happiness (Palmore, 1984). Yet

a precise definition of successful aging remains elusive, for it is difficult both to reach a consensus about its dimensions and to develop
valid quantitative and qualitative measures of "success" (Baltes &
Baltes, 1990).

Models of successful aging have been based on theoretically normative psychological outcomes, rooted primarily in middle-class values, most often those of white males. Such standards of success have at
least four limitations: (1) they ignore the importance of individual differences among the elderly; (2) they overlook the importance of social
factors in constructing old age; (3) they neglect the potential for multiple outcomes; and (4) they disregard the fact that there are many different standards of success (Baltes & Carstensen, 1999). Successful
aging remains more a prescription for how to grow old than a theory.

Selective Optimization

Although no one standard has been developed for how to age hap-
pily or well, one more recent micro-level theory emphasizing mastery
of everyday life is *selective optimization with compensation*, a process
of coordinating and balancing the gains and losses associated with
aging to master daily life (Baltes & Baltes, 1990; Baltes & Carstensen,
1999). Developed by two psychologists, Paul and Margret Baltes, this
micro-level model emphasizes processes rather than outcomes. Optimization, defined as the attainment of personally meaningful goals
specific to each person, is fluid. Although age-related shifts in abilities
may occur, people can compensate for losses of capacity or control by
optimizing their strengths, using old strategies and developing new
ones to solve problems. This process is not unique to old age; throughout the life course people select goals and ways to achieve them that
maximize gains over losses. Control over our lives at any age entails a
simultaneous balance between gains and losses in capacity and performance.

A television interview with the late concert pianist Arthur
Rubinstein provides an eloquent example. Rubinstein, then an old
man, described his strategies for successful concert performance in old
age. For example

> . . . (1) In old age he performed fewer pieces, (2) he now practiced
> each piece more frequently, and (3) he introduced more *ritardando*
> [slower segments] in his playing before fast segments, so that the
> playing speed sounded faster than it was in reality. (Baltes, 1993:
> 90)

Rubinstein's techniques show how he used his musical creativity
and knowledge for selective optimization with compensation, shifting
the ratio of gains and losses he experienced in old age.

The concept of selective optimization with compensation applies not only to old age but also to other periods in the life course. Consider how you approach and juggle your own everyday activities in specific contexts of your life. If, for example, you are poor in mathematics but excellent in history, you may decide to register for more courses in history than in math. If you are a good batter but can't shoot a basket, you will probably choose to play baseball rather than basketball. All of us tend to compensate for weaknesses in one area by optimizing our abilities in others in which we do well or excel. There is thus no one simple definition of *successful aging,* or *productive aging,* whether as "active," "disengaged," or whatever. An older person may continue all old activities without any reduction in these, may continue to do some or to modify them, or may choose new (including "disengaged") pursuits. What is important is not the amount or type of activity but the congruency of the choice with the social and personal characteristics of the chooser. Most important is preserving a sense of consistency and continuity so that elders maintain life according to their own standards of well-being and activity. The paradigm of selective optimization with compensation emphasizes the individuality of aging as a process.

Critical Thinking: Disengaged Withdrawal or Selective Optimization With Compensation?

The compensatory mechanisms in the Rubinstein example also apply to many other situations. For example, Abby Jones, now 80, has been a leader in numerous activities in her church for many years (e.g., fund-raising committees, organizing and running the church Bingo and Keno programs). She has also been the church organist and the director of the Teen Outreach program for more than three decades. She now has several age-related health problems, including reduced vision that has made her abandon driving her car. Due to osteoarthritis in her hands and knees, her everyday movements have grown slower and more painful, impeding her ability both to walk long distances and to play the organ. It is also difficult for her to walk eight blocks to the bus stop and to make the two bus transfers required to attend church.

Ms. Jones has resigned from her position as church organist and currently goes to church only for Sunday services. Occasionally, when she has a ride, she attends Bingo. At home, she enjoys listening to music, especially organ concerts, on her CD player and radio and has begun to write poetry. Although she no longer heads the Teen Outreach program, she has taken over the updates for the church teen web page and answers e-mail inquiries sent to the site.

Do you think that Ms. Jones has withdrawn or disengaged from the active life she once knew? Think about what you would do if you were in her situation. It may at first appear that, because she is less active, she has disengaged from her former active roles and has become passive. However, her apparent disengagement can indeed be called an adaptive behavioral strategy: selective optimization with compensation. Ms. Jones has accommodated to her several chronic illnesses by withdrawing from previous roles that are now difficult, relinquishing them to others. Although no longer running the Teen Outreach program or acting as church organist, she has selected and compensated for these role losses by exploring new directions based on her prior knowledge, experience, and skills. Even if she were to withdraw entirely from her formal church roles and stay at home, listening to the music she loves and writing poetry, from her own individual perspective she may view herself as fully engaged in social life on a nonorganizationally-based level. In short, she has selected areas in which she can compensate for losses and optimize these based on her interests and abilities.

Age Stratification

First proposed by Matilda White Riley and her associates (Riley, Johnson, & Foner, 1972), the *age stratification* approach proposes that it is theoretically and practically useful to think of members of a society as stratified by the dimension of age just as social class. According to this view, age becomes a basis of control over resources through age-linked statuses. Inequality among age strata occurs because age is used as a basis for entry or exit from potentially powerful statuses. Calling attention to the importance of *birth cohort*, Riley emphasized the significance of the period in history in which we live and its interaction with our chronological age. For example, members of the large baby boom cohorts born in the decades following World War II faced greater competition for jobs and affordable housing than did cohorts born during the Great Depression years of the 1930s.

The shared history and the opportunities available to one birth cohort thus shape its members' life experiences and aging very differently from those in another birth cohort. An individual's location in a specific birth cohort determines his or her social roles and forms his or her attitudes or actions. The so-called "generation gap" is thus a function of differences between the experiences of different birth cohorts and age norms for appropriate role behavior. All members of a birth cohort age through a particular historical period during which they share common experiences, such as growing up during the Great Depression of the 1930s. Although cohort members encounter the same major events in an era—whether an economic depression, a war, or even the popularity of particular television programs, music, sports, and so forth—the meaning of these happenings varies.

The size of a birth cohort also affects how its members live. Because the baby boom cohorts were so much larger than preceding birth cohorts, you will recall that baby boomers faced much more competition for education and jobs than the smaller size Depression cohorts that preceded them; they also constituted a larger luxury market for goods and services. Businesses (ranging from toys, television shows, movies, and records to designer jeans) were created or expanded just for them. When baby boomers began to buy homes, real estate prices increased and then dropped as members of their cohorts settled down to raise families (McFalls, 1998). An individual's membership in a specific birth cohort influences both the social roles available and attitudes or beliefs.

Everyone's life course is shaped not only by birth cohort but also by social class, gender, race or ethnicity, and personal history. Thus, although members of your birth cohort share a common backdrop of social and historical events that you experience at more or less the same age, each of your *life chances* will differ. The concept of life chances, as defined by Max Weber (1845–1920), a major social theorist, refers to the likelihood of having a particular *lifestyle*. Each individual's lifestyle is shaped by her or his socioeconomic position—the social and economic resources available to that person. Your ability to attain "success," however you may define it, will thus be contoured not only by your individual ability to command economic resources and personal attributes but also by the size of your birth cohort and the life chances or opportunities available to your birth cohort. You will construct your individual biographies in different ways throughout the life course.

Sociohistorical events influence one's present life as well as shape future responses to social and economic stress. As Elder (1974) has shown, living through the Great Depression was not only experienced differently by middle-class and working-class women but also affected their subsequent old age. Although women of both social classes were disadvantaged by their status as females in a male-dominated society and both suffered economic losses during the Depression years, higher-status women were less vulnerable to setbacks. Feelings of mastery and assertiveness in old age characterized those middle-class women who lived through the Great Depression, while feelings of passivity and helplessness were more typical among working-class women. Elder's research emphasized both the importance of birth cohort and the intertwining of gender, social class, and historical events.

Age stratification is especially useful to show that some of the presumably fixed, built-in life stages that have been proposed by social scientists and physicians alike reflect the experiences of a particular cohort (Riley, Foner, & Johnson, 1972). Thus, great caution must be used in making sweeping generalizations about "normal aging" if current or past cohorts of elderly are used as an example. As Riley stated, "Because society changes, members of different cohorts (i.e., born at different times) age in different ways. . . . [Hence,] the lives of those who are growing old today *cannot* be the same as the lives of those who grew old in the past or of those who will grow old in the future" (Riley, 1999: 333).

This is true about even mundane, everyday preferences and behaviors. For example, think about the musical tastes of the now-old, many of whom were teenagers or young adults in the 1940s when the "big band" sounds of Benny Goodman and the crooning of the young Frank Sinatra were popular. They are likely to prefer Sinatra, "big band" sounds and other music of the 1940s and 1950s to rock and roll or hip-hop. When people who grew up in the 1950s grow old, they will probably want to hear music by Fats Domino, Little Richard, and Elvis Presley. Those growing up in the 1960s may prefer the Beatles, Bob Marley, or the Rolling Stones to the music their parents preferred in old age. When those growing up in the 1990s are old, however, they will be more likely to listen to Kurt Cobain and Nirvana or Courtney Love and Hole than to the music loved by their parents or grandparents.

Testing age stratification theory has, however, proved to be difficult. Separating age effects (i.e., the influences of the aging process) from period effects (i.e., the influences associated with each period of time, such as the Great Depression or the war in Vietnam) from the influence of being a member of a specific birth cohort, are notoriously difficult. Are age effects the same for each cohort, or do they vary according to the composition of the cohort and the period? It is likely that both the effects of growing older and the effects of membership in a given cohort will vary through time. For example, the small number of babies born during the Great Depression years meant that they had unusually favorable opportunities in competing for education and jobs. But as younger cohorts born during the first wave of the baby boom entered the labor market, they were able to compete with—and sometimes overtake—the depression cohort for jobs. Similarly, age effects (e.g., biological, social, and psychological aging) can vary widely within a cohort and among cohorts (Glenn, 1976).

Age stratification, however, alerted gerontologists to the ways in which age strata influence and are influenced by the social, political, and economic fabric of a society. Consider current debates about the effect of the large baby boomer cohorts on Medicare and Social Security, for example. As you read further in this book, think about how being a part of a member of a specific birth cohort has defined your own attitudes, beliefs, and opportunities compared with those of your parents, grandparents, and other older relatives.

Theoretical Shifts

Power and Inequality

During the past few decades, a theoretical shift has occurred, setting new directions for examining old age. Social theorists turned their critical lenses inward, examining their previous assumptions about aging. Rather than focusing on how social system needs, modernization, age discrimination, ability to exchange resources, or birth cohorts organize the experience of growing old, theorists challenged the so-called "facts" of aging to criticize the concept of "age-as-leveler"; that is, the notion that once an individual is old, other differences such as race/ethnicity, social class, and gender become irrelevant. As you have seen from the material presented in this chapter, much initial research on aging was built on the premise that old age is almost universally characterized by poor physical health and economic problems. The notion of age-as-leveler ignored the effect that membership in the social hierarchies of social class, gender, and race/ethnicity has upon the many ways in which people grow old. For example, both the activity and disengagement theoretical approaches were based on relatively homogeneous samples of elders living in Kansas City.

Spotlight on U.S.: Lucky 75—Coming Through a Century of Change

Robert N. Wilson is emeritus professor of sociology, University of North Carolina–Chapel Hill, a poet, and a frequent contributor to newspaper columns.

How does birth cohort influence our views of the world around us? The following observations were written by Robert N. Wilson as he approached his 75th birthday in 2000. As you read his comments, think about what theories of aging and old age are relevant to what he says.

Careening toward my 75th birthday, I feel the urge to celebrate a three-quarter century's experience. Of course the millennial moment encourages reflection. Those of us who had the good misfortune to be born into a society of scarcity and repression enjoy a bite, an edge, a spice that seldom visits the children of plenitude. . . .

I should say the first thing that favors us is the sheer fact of being alive during great happenings. . . . Not for us the dull or calm, the serenity of peaceful times. Spawned in the Roaring 20s, fathered by makers of bathtub gin and mothered by dancers of the Charleston, we came alive to the high tide of Modernism and the bleakness of the Great Depression.

Just as the appetite for food is wonderfully sharpened by hunger, the appetite for life may be honed by denial and postponement. In the 1920s and 1930s, we were well-schooled in that habit of "deferred gratification" supposedly underlying middle-class striving. . . . The curtain of Puritan repression that still hung over that America, muffling sensory—especially sexual—experience prepared us for the heady myth of romantic love . . . we thrilled to the favors, however thin, of the closer yet unattainable present one. Thus, for us, in addition to neurotic frustrations and failed dreams, [was] a certain naive joy and poignancy unavailable to the progenitors and heirs of the sexual revolution.

The Great Depression of 1929–1939 meant that many material wants (and some needs) were also subject to deferred fulfillment. Hence for many, good food, secure warmth, clean clothes, and a little spare cash were bounties to inspire lingering gratitude. The trifling pleasures and solid underpinnings of affluence tend to dim the memory of lean times.

But only we who were once deprived can truly savor abundance. As romantic love had its downside of illusory desire, so economic stringency often spawned a sordid longing for do-re-mi, then followed exaggerated striving, and sometimes a mean cash-on-the-barrelhead mentality. On balance, though, perhaps those who knew the ways of priva-tion are best prepared to be thankful for this our life.

The anthropologist Margaret Mead once described people who came of age before World War II as "immigrants in time." She compared our generation to the "immigrants in space" who wrenched themselves from Europe in great waves to come to the United States in the late nineteenth and early twentieth centuries.

Mead argued that the tempo of social and scientific/technological change has been so rapid that today's oldsters confront an alien world as ill-prepared strangers. Although the metaphor may be exaggerated, it is decidedly true that we who grew up before television and jet aircraft transcended geography . . . [and] before the computer/transistor reorganized the flow of communication and resources, may recurrently feel ourselves on a foreign shore.

In parallel, the revolutions in civil rights and gender rights, the unbinding of sexual expression, the belated environmental vigilance, the burgeoning of an incomplete but profound internationalism—all these and more have shaped a social landscape that is in some ways scarcely recognizable by the children of the Great Depression and World War II. [Yet] we are a far more cosmopolitan and sophisticated people than the Americans of pre-1940s vintage. Indeed to call us survivors "lucky" is to understate the case.

Excerpted from Robert N. Wilson, "Lucky 75—Coming Through a Century of Change." *Chapel Hill News*, Sunday, January 16, 2000, A-5. (Used with permission).

Interest in the interplay among race, social class, gender, and ethnicity was in part a response to the age-as-leveler assumption that elders have a uniform experience because of their age. The concept of "double jeopardy," heralding the recognition of the importance of diversity, was initially applied to the odds faced by elderly African Americans as both old and members of an oppressed minority group (Talley, 1956). Double jeopardy has been subsequently expanded to focus attention on lifestyles and problems faced by other elders, such as women, gays, lesbians, and ethnic groups discriminated against by the more powerful.

Emphasis on the importance of diversity and birth cohort also stimulated development of a *life course* approach focusing on individuals and the different patterns of their lives from birth to death, the differential effects of membership in a specific birth cohort, and the importance of the social structure in which they live. Different patterns at the individual level encompass ascribed characteristics (e.g., gender or race/ethnicity) or contextual biographical characteristics (e.g., social class membership when growing up or as a young adult) that have been internalized and that have an enduring significance for one's subsequent life. At the sociostructural level birth cohort and sociohistorical events also shape life opportunities and lifestyle (Dannefer & Uhlenberg, 1999). The life course approach emphasizes the importance of early life experiences, environmental factors, and sociohistorical factors to explain the dramatic heterogeneity and diversity in growing old. Robert N. Wilson, who wrote the excerpt in this chapter, "Lucky 75," gives us one such example: a life filtered through the experiences of growing up in a working class family in upstate New York, serving in the military in World War II, attending a prestigious university on the G. I. Bill, and becoming a college professor at a nationally recognized university. Aging, although a universal process, varies widely among individuals and so do sources of satisfaction in later life. Older people interpret their life experiences in many different ways that relate not only to their individual characteristics but also to their social class, race, and ethnicity.

Studies of older minorities, however, can inadvertently stress the disadvantages their members have faced, such as racial or ethnic discrimination, poverty, and limited life chances, ignoring the positive aspects of ethnicity, race, and minority membership. For example, strong social supports from family, friends, and religion, values in African-American culture emphasizing old age as a natural process, and satisfaction over having survived a lifetime of discrimination and economic disadvantage enhance life satisfaction among very old African Americans (Johnson, 1995). Similarly, for members of minority groups who have faced a lifetime of discrimination and limited opportunities for upward mobility, a racially and/or ethnically homogeneous community can provide a comfortable haven in a hostile world (McAuley,

1998). Nonetheless, as Dressler, Minkler, and Yen (1997) point out, focus on social disadvantage has inadvertently contributed to a deficit thinking mentality that once again portrays disadvantaged elders as victims, ignoring the strengths that disadvantaged groups possess. By emphasizing differences among groups, the meaning and dynamics of aging within groups are ignored.

Focus on the *political economy of aging* has enlarged awareness of the importance of social structure and membership in social hierarchies, such as how the allocation of social resources complements age stratification, which largely ignores power relationships. Implicit— and sometimes explicit—in the political economy approach is concern about whether capitalism as a productive social system can be reconciled with the needs of the elderly. The British sociologist Chris Phillipson (1982), arguing that the priorities of capitalism almost always rank social and individual needs as less important than the search for profits, suggested that the elderly are likely to be caught between the need for better services and the steady decline of facilities and cuts in their standard of living imposed by the most powerful social classes. As summed up by Quadagno and Reid (1999: 355): "The political economy perspective on age highlights how socioeconomic institutions affect individuals over the life course and how they influence their social and economic well-being in old age . . ., [shifting] the focus of gerontological research from the individual's ability to adapt to aging to an examination of broader social processes. . . ." The outcome for any particular person depends both on his or her relative position in the social hierarchies of gender, social class, [and] race/ethnicity and [on] the ways in which governmental policies often reinforce these hierarchies in old age.

A leading American proponent of the political economy approach to aging has been Carroll Estes (Estes, 1979; Minkler & Estes, 1991), who, with her associates, proposed that the course of the aging process is conditioned by each individual's location in the social structure and the economic and social factors that affect that position: "The political economy of aging offers a theoretical and empirical perspective on the socioeconomic determinants of the experience of aging and old age and on the policy interventions that emerge in the context of capitalist society" (Estes, 1991: 19). According to Estes (1991: 25), experts have a disproportionate say in how we define old age and how resources for older people will be allocated:

> Those who control definitions of aging in effect control access to old age benefits such as medical care, as well as the personal and public costs of care and the structure of health care delivery. Currently, public money and professional effort are disproportionately expended on institutional (hospital and nursing home) medical services for the elderly. Both reflect a definition of health

care that is the product of the professional dominance of medicine and a guarantee of a profitable medical care industry.

Social programs designed to benefit the elderly not only have created an "aging establishment" that regulates the distribution of social resources to the elderly but also have often benefited business interests more than the interests of older people. Consider, for example, the drug industry's continued opposition to inclusion of prescription drugs under Medicare. At the same time, many older people have clearly benefited from programs targeted at the elderly; Social Security and Medicare, despite their limitations, are but two examples. A major contribution of political economy has been to call attention to the persistence of social hierarchies and inequities in old age and tie the private problems of individual elders, such as poverty and inequality, to public issues.

Recently, *critical theory*, stressing the need for paradigms of aging to be self-reflective and to consider how models about aging and old age are constructed, interpreted, and applied in real life, has also challenged older theories and assumptions in social gerontology. Of particular interest to critical theory is how models of aging developed by gerontologists have divorced their work on elders' lives from those doing the living with the result that the elderly become the "other," objects rather than subjects of study. In contrast, critical theory seeks to expose patterns of power and domination, show their contradictions, assess potential for change, and criticize the system to bring about change (Moody, 1988). As Moody (1993: xv), a leading spokesperson for the critical approach in aging, has emphasized, "Above all, critical gerontology is concerned with the problem of emancipation from all forms of domination . . . identifying possibilities for emancipatory social change, including positive ideals for later life."

Trends in Applied Research

At the same time, gerontology has moved from theorizing about the basic processes of aging to more *applied models*, focusing on quick-term, program-related studies and large-scale social surveys, often collected for another purpose, at an arbitrary point in time, or repeated at intervals. These data have begun to recast old assumptions about the life course and to challenge beliefs about aging. For example, recent research has shown that family, education, health, work, and leisure patterns occur throughout life at different, and often later ages than were previously believed to occur (O'Rand & Campbell, 1999; Riley, Foner, & Riley, 1999). Moreover, transitions such as completion of education, family formation, divorce, job entry and exit, and retirement have become blurred. The line between worker and retirement has become less defined as many people reenter the labor force in part-time jobs, and education is increasingly not only a pattern both for women and workers learning new skills in midlife but also for people after retirement.

Yet, for these surveys to be valuable, data are needed that span comparable time periods and historical and cultural contexts, and that lend themselves to appropriate in-depth analysis using varied techniques (O'Rand & Campbell, 1999). Moreover, many recent research reports have been atheoretical. As Bengtson, Burgess, and Parrott observed, "in their quest to examine aspects of individual and social aging, researchers have been quick to provide facts but slow to integrate within a larger explanatory framework, connecting findings to established explanations of social phenomena" (1997: S72). Without theoretical frameworks, we are less able to use empirical studies because our ability to integrate specific findings into more general knowledge is limited.

Summary

What can we learn from these road maps or theoretical approaches? The following summarizes key directions within the past half century or so: (1) Attention shifted from a focus on individual adjustment to a broader societal level; (2) assumptions were raised about the effect of modernization on the elderly; (3) researchers concentrated on the political economy of aging (i.e., increased attention to social class and relationship of social class to the modes of production); (4) scientists criticized the so-called "facts" of aging (i.e., the concept of "age as leveler" that ignored the interplay among race, social class, gender, and ethnicity); and, conversely, (5) they used large-scale databases both to test hypotheses and to provide quick answers.

That theoretical research approaches are shifting from what they were in the past is a welcome development. Theoretical models of aging are gradually moving toward more self-conscious examinations, challenging older cultural ideologies and interpretations of aging. It is important, however, not to confuse empirical findings—the "what"—with theories. Empirical findings can challenge old assumptions about who is doing what, but they do not answer the larger question of "why." Theories are needed to address the "why" behind the findings if they are to be truly valuable (Bengtson, Rice, & Johnson, 1999).

How can past theoretical approaches help us to understand aging and the life course, including the coming reality that 1 in 5 people aged 65 or over will be both actors and acted upon in changing lifestyles, social institutions, and social and political policies? As we all live longer, family structures and relationships, living arrangements, housing design, entitlement programs, health care, retirement, and how and where we die are but a few of the areas that will take new shape in the years to come. Our individual lives will remain inextricably connected to social institutions and affected by our membership in the social hierarchies of class, gender, race, and ethnicity. Theoretical models reflect the dynamic interplay among our individual lives, the larger social world in which we all live, and the aging of our parents and ourselves. There is currently no single "grand" theory that satisfactorily explains aging, but various mini theories are useful road maps to navigate disparate research findings (Bengtson, Rice, & Johnson, 1999). For example, which theoretical approaches reviewed in this chapter best explain the fact that elderly African-American women are disproportionately likely to live in poverty? Why? As you read this book, keep in mind the various theories in this chapter. Evaluate which ones best fit the evidence presented as well as what is lacking in the explanatory power of each.

Key Points

1. A theory is a statement of how and why specific facts are related that allows us to summarize findings or observations to make generalizations about something we want to understand.

2. Theories are conceptual road maps that guide research and generate hypotheses for testing.

3. Knowledge is always relative as each new set of findings has the potential to provide new theories or ways of interpreting phenomena.

4. The power and prestige of the elderly are closely related to their ability to control goods, resources, property, or knowledge.

5. Early-twentieth-century theories emphasized old age as a period of dependence.

6. Activity theory stresses continued activity as a way to preserve self-concept and ensure higher levels of life satisfaction.

7. Continuity theory assumes that personality, social relationships, goals, and adaptive mechanisms formed during adulthood remain consistent in old age.

8. Disengagement theory highlights aging within a social system and the social necessity for all societies to oust elders from vital social roles to maintain continuity and stability within the society.

9. The subculture of aging, modernization, and exchange theories emphasize exclusion of the elderly from social life.

10. Age stratification theory points out that age is used as a criterion for entry and exit from different statuses and that birth cohort influences one's opportunities for particular social statuses and role behavior.

11. Newer theoretical approaches include critical theory, the political economy of aging, and the life course approach.

12. There is no "one size fits all" or single "grand" theory that satisfactorily explains aging, but there are mini-theories that provide useful road maps to interpret research and understand the world around us.

Discussion Questions

1. Explain why theories of aging are useful.

2. Look back at the interview with Mrs. R. at the beginning of this chapter. Which of the various theories discussed in this chapter best fits her view of her own age? Why?

3. How has membership in your birth cohort affected the number and types of social roles available for you? Your beliefs and attitudes? Do these options and attitudes differ from those of your parents? If so, what sociohistorical factors do you think are related to these differences?

4. Discuss the following statement: "Those who control definitions of aging in effect control access to old age benefits such as medical care, as well as the personal and public costs of care and the structure of health care delivery."

5. From what you have read in this chapter, to what extent do you agree with the following statement? Models of aging developed by gerontologists have divorced this work on elders' lives from those doing the living with the result that the elderly become the other; objects rather than subjects of study.

6. How might you integrate the Baltes concept of selective optimization with compensation in your own everyday life activities? Give two examples of how you may selectively choose a certain course of action to optimize your progress on something to compensate for an individually or socially perceived limitation. (Hint: Do limitations arising from your personal strengths and weaknesses or your social characteristics, such as birth cohort, gender, social class, or race and

ethnicity, lead you to choose one activity or approach to a problem rather than another?)

7. In 1996, Bob Dole, at age 76, ran for president of the United States and was defeated. To what extent do you think his age was a factor in his defeat? Explain.

Films and Videos

Maggie (video; 30 minutes; available from Terra Nova Films, 9848 S. Winchester Avenue, Chicago, IL 60643; *www.terranova.org*).

An interview with Maggie Kuhn, founder of the Gray Panthers, highlighting issues of power, inequality, aging, and the need for an intergenerational social movement to combat ageism.

Strangers in Good Company (video; 105 minutes; available from First Run Films, 153 Waverly Place, New York, NY 10004; *www.firstrunfeatures.com*).

Semi-documentary of seven very different elderly women stranded in a remote farmhouse and their lives and styles of aging.

Take It With a Smile: Self-Identity and Aging (video; 20 minutes; available from Terra Nova Films, 9848 S. Winchester Avenue, Chicago, IL 60643, *www.terranova.org*).

A useful film to trigger discussion of theoretical approaches to aging that features older adults discussing their self-perceptions and roles as they have grown older.

War Stories Our Mothers Never Told Us (video; 95 minutes; available from First Run Films, 153 Waverly Place, New York, NY 10004; *www.firstrunfeatures.com*).

Seven women of different social classes, races, and cultural backgrounds discuss how World War II affected their lives and loves; This is useful for discussion of period and cohort effects on the lives of the now-old.

Internet Resources

http://www.geronet.med.ucla.edu

This link to the University of California, Los Angeles, leads to various resources. It is useful for examination and discussion of diversity and heterogeneity.

http://www.umich.edu

Follow this link to the University of Michigan and find the Health and Retirement study (i.e., a nationwide, longitudinal data set on retirement and the aging of society), its numerous publications, and other studies.

http://www.rand.org

This site is maintained by the Rand Corporation, an organization engaged in behavioral research on many aspects of aging. Free publications can be ordered online.

Research Article

Bengtson, V. L., Parrott, T. M., & Burgess, E. O. (1996). Progress and pitfalls in gerontological theorizing. *The Gerontologist 36*(6): 768–772.

A useful article summarizing issues in the history of gerontological theory that argues that few shifts in theoretical models have occurred in recent years.

Supplemental Readings

Elder, G. H. (1974). *Children of the Great Depression.* Chicago: University of Chicago Press.

A classic study, showing the interplay of sociohistorical events, gender, and social class and their impact on the depression-years cohorts.

Haber, C. (1983). *Beyond Sixty-Five: The Dilemma of Old Age in America's Past.* New York: Cambridge University Press.

A readable and detailed historical account of how aging has been constructed in the United States.

Haber, C., & Gratton, B. (1993). *Old Age and the Search for Security: An American Social History.* Bloomington: Indiana University Press.

Recommended reading for those interested in the economic status of the elderly in the United States from preindustrial times to the present.

Meigs, M. (1991). *In the Company of Strangers.* Vancouver, B.C., Canada: Talonbooks.

An entertaining account by a painter and writer of the lives of eight very different women who participated in the semi-documentary film, *Strangers in Good Company*, presenting the women's self-images, pasts, and present views of their own old age. ✦

Part II
Individuals and Aging

Chapter 5

Biological Perspectives

Introduction

The desire to be immortal—or at least to remain healthy and active for as long as possible—has been one of humanity's oldest and most treasured dreams. The first Biblical genealogies record legendary life spans of healthy elders, such as Methuselah, who fathered Lemach at 187 years and continued to father children for nearly 800 years more. Sarah gave birth to a child when she was 90. Abraham died still healthy and active at 175, and Sarah at 127. Tales of astoundingly long lives, like the eighteenth-century English farmer, Thomas Parr, who reportedly married for the first time at age 131, fathered one child, and died at age 152 and 9 months due to gluttony and fast living, reflect the belief that in some far distant time or place, remarkably long and healthy life was possible. If only we could learn the secret!

The secret, however, may be unrealistic thinking. Different ways of counting years, lack of documentation, and deliberate falsification of records may have created an illusion of great age (Medvedev, 1974). Moreover, a strong relationship exists between the illiteracy rate of a region and the number of people who claim to be very old. Some areas, such as the Hunza region of Northern Pakistan and the Vilacamba region of Ecuador, either have no written birth records or elders systematically exaggerate their ages to gain status and admiration. Many centenarians in the former Soviet Union are suspected of having assumed others' names and ages to avoid military service (Medvedev, 1974). And in the eighteenth century, Thomas Parr's "longevity" kept a life tenancy lease of a farm cottage going for three generations—father, son, and grandson (Comfort, 1964)! Since accurate birth registration is relatively recent, it is impossible to set maximum life span accurately. Although the number of centenarians is increasing in industrialized nations, the oldest living per-

son whose age has been carefully verified was the French woman, Jeanne Calment, who died at the age of 122 in 1997.

Why do living organisms grow old? Why do living organisms age at different rates? And why do maximum life spans vary within and between species? What are some of the hallmarks of old age? Can aging be reversed? Is there a built-in "biological clock" that affects the maximum amount of time each of us can expect to survive? Are there definite changes in health and levels of activity that are inevitable as we grow old? Does our own self-assessment of our health relate to our actual physical health? Is self-assessed health related to mortality? These are some of the issues discussed in this chapter.

Biological Lifespan and Life Expectancy

Despite scientific and technological progress, biologic life spans for all living organisms have apparently not changed since ancient times. What has changed is *life expectancy,* or the average number of years at birth a person can expect to live. Yet no one has yet found the secret that ensures a long life. As you will recall from Chapter 3, all organisms have a maximum *life span,* or ultimate age that a specific species can apparently live, as Table 5-1 illustrates.

Table 5-1 Maximum Lifespan of Selected Species	
Species	**Maximum Lifespan in Years***
Mouse	3½
Skunk	8
Rabbit	15
Dog	20
American buffalo	26
Domestic cat	30
Chimpanzee	50
Gorilla	55
Human	122
Tortoise	150

* All data except for humans based on zoo data.
Source: Adapted from R. L. Walford (1983). *Maximum Lifespan.* New York: Avon. Table 1.2, p. 11.

The Fountain of Youth: Secrets of Long Life?

MYTH: Certain Substances Can Ensure
a Long Life

Limited research on centenarians indicates that diet, exercise, discipline and hard work, love of family, and social activity contribute to long life (Palmore, 1995; Perls & Silver, 1999). The longevity advice given by centenarians themselves is, however, often contradictory: "One of the two things that men who have lasted for a hundred years always say [is that] either they have drunk whiskey and smoked all their lives or that neither tobacco nor spirits ever made the faintest appeal to them" (Auden & Kronenberger, 1962, cited in Palmore, 1984: 12). Similarly, both a lack of sexual interest and an active sex life are also cited among centenarians. Although diet, nutrition, lifestyle, and genetics play roles in longevity, the fountain of youth still obviously remains undiscovered.

Yet, large sums of money are spent each year by people who hope to reverse the processes of aging. For example, some decades ago, Dr. Paul Niehans in Switzerland developed a therapy using lamb embryo cells. Despite lack of its proven value, this treatment attracted such customers as Winston Churchill, the Duke of Windsor, Pope Pius XII, and former Chancellor Konrad Adenauer of Germany. Another briefly popular therapy for men involved grafts of monkey testicles; an American version of this remedy involved transplanting goat testicles into aging men. No scientific evidence has shown that either "therapy" benefited the recipients, but the practitioners benefited financially!

In the 1950s, Gerovital H2, developed by Dr. Ana Aslan in Romania, became popular. Thousands of people enthusiastically received Gerovital, a procaine and vitamin therapy claiming to reverse the aging process, and traveled to the Geriatric Institute in Bucharest to seek rejuvenation. Although Gerovital does have a mild antidepressant and anti-arthritic effect, controlled studies in the United States and Great Britain fail to show its anti-aging properties.

More recently, ginseng, a Chinese perennial herb, has become popular as a youth-restorer. Used for centuries in China and Korea, ginseng allegedly lowers blood pressure and improves mental activity and organ function. Other popular anti-aging remedies include gingko biloba, DHEA, and melatonin, each of which allegedly improves mental or physical capacities or both. However, claims for these preparations have yet to be validated. For example, DHEA, a hormone made by the adrenal glands on top of the kidney, is sold without a prescription as a remedy to improve energy, strength, immunity, and muscle strength. Yet we have not fully understood its effects. Human growth hormones (HGH) are also claimed to increase muscle, decrease fat, and give energy. Although there is no proof that HGH can prevent or reverse aging, some people spend more than $15,000 a year for shots of this preparation. Melatonin, a hormone that often decreases with age, is another anti-aging and sleep aid that people can buy without a prescription. Although melatonin is apparently an antioxidant (a substance that prevents damage to the body), claims that it can slow or reverse aging are yet unproven (National Institute on Aging, 1996). Other current searches for prolonging life include use of magnetic fields, lowered body temperatures, vitamin E, vitamin A, folate, vegetable "magic bullet" pills, and so forth. Seeking eternal vigor continues now as in ancient times: from Gerovital to ginseng.

Biological Theories of Aging

MYTH: AGING OCCURS AT THE SAME RATE IN ALL ORGAN SYSTEMS

According to biologist Leonard Hayflick (1994: 15), biological aging "represents losses in normal function that occur after sexual maturation and continue up to the time of maximum longevity for members of a species." Aging is not one event but a *process* that occurs at different rates among different groups. Social class membership and economic factors, nutrition, exercise, lifestyle, exposure to industrial hazards and pollution plus genetics all influence the rate at which we age. Strength and muscle coordination peak early in life—around the age of 19 or 20—and then decline; running speed declines gradually after the age of 30; bone loss seems to begin around age 50 (Hayflick, 1994).

Although some slowing down of the body always occurs with age, age is *not* a synonym for decay. Even within the same person, aging of parts of the body may occur at different rates. A college student, for example, may have the kidney function of a 30-year-old, the memory retention of an 18-year-old, and, if a couch potato, the muscles of a 40-year-old, and so on. Even among centenarians, aging is a variable process. Some centenarians are mentally alert and physically active; others are mentally confused and bedridden (Palmore, 1995; Perls & Silver, 1999).

MYTH: SCIENTISTS HAVE DEFINITIVELY PROVEN WHY AGING OCCURS

Why do live organisms age at different rates? And why do maximum life spans vary within and among species? Various biological theories abound but have not yielded precise answers. Moreover, longitudinal research on human aging is difficult to do. Not only does it require an unrealistically long time for study but, to eliminate all complicating factors, it would also require that subjects spend their lives in the controlled setting of a laboratory—an option few of us would choose! Not surprisingly then, most scientifically controlled studies have focused on relatively simple creatures with short life spans, such as fruit flies living in laboratory settings.

Because biological studies of how and why organisms age are relatively new, each theory has had strong advocates plus data both to prove and disprove it. Nor are all theories mutually exclusive; that is, more than one theory may be simultaneously true. We can group theories of biological aging in many ways. One common way of subdividing them is as *program theories* and *damage* or *"wear and tear" theories*. The following are several examples of these theories:

Program Theories. *Program theories* are based on the idea of built-in obsolescence: Nothing works perfectly or lasts forever. Just as mechanical devices will run only for a certain period before they give out, living organisms do the same. According to program theories, a purposeful sequence of events, or *biological clock*, is written in our genetic cellular codes that leads to age changes. Moreover, cells have a limited capacity to divide and function. Even if we eliminated all causes of death from disease, normal physiological declines would result in death at about age 100 or so.

For example, advocates of the *hormonal* or *brain theory of aging* argue that aging is due primarily to programmed changes in hormonal or neural factors. Groups of special cells—glands—make chemicals called hormones and release them into the blood stream; neurons are the basic structural and functional part of the body's nervous system. That neurons and hormones change with age has been recognized for many years.

According to the hormonal theory, the hypothalamus, or portion of the brain that regulates many basic body functions, sends messages to the endocrine glands, which release hormones that in turn release a "death" hormone to stimulate the aging process throughout the body (Denkla, 1975). Whether such a death hormone exists is open to question (Hayflick, 1985). Although a few species (e.g., the Pacific salmon, which undergoes rapid aging due to a massive release of hormones during the period it swims upstream to lay eggs) seem to exhibit a hormone-related death, such specific processes do not appear to exist in most other living organisms.

Other program theories have been proposed including mutation and genetic switching. In mutation, aging is due to changes (i.e., mutations) in the DNA, considered both the chemical basis of heredity and the carrier of genetic information. The mutations occurring in DNA at the cellular level are passed on to so many new cells that an organ of the body declines to the point where its function is reduced.

Genetic switching explanations propose that cellular aging occurs due to the switching off, rather than the mutation, of certain genes. The result of switching is that information needed to produce DNA is not available within the cell, leading to cell death and eventual loss of organ function.

One of the newest program theories explaining biological aging focuses on *telomeres*. Telomeres are repeated as tips on the end of our chromosomes and have a special DNA sequence that maintains the integrity of our chromosomes. The telomeres shorten every time a cell divides. After a certain amount of shortening, cell division no longer occurs and the cell ages and dies.

Telomerase is an enzyme in most cells that repairs and replaces the telomeres, lengthening the lifespan of dividing cells. This fixes the problem and keeps the end of the chromosome from being worn away by repeated cell division. As long as cells have enough telomerase to fill gaps, they keep telomeres that are long enough to allow a cell to divide beyond its usual capacity. Although every cell has the capacity to produce telomerase, it is suppressed in normal cells but activated in cancer cells that have the capacity to divide uncontrollably. When telomerase is introduced artificially into a normal cell, however, it can continue to divide for at least 20 generations longer than normal, remaining "young" (Bodnar et al., 1998). Scientists are currently exploring ways that telomerase may be used to reverse the aging process.

Damage or "Wear and Tear" Theories. *Damage* or *"wear and tear" theories* are based on the idea that cells or organs are unable to repair themselves as they age. For example, the *immune system theory* is based on two scientific findings. First, the ability of the body's immune system to resist disease decreases with age so that the body has less defense against infections and cancer. Second, the immune system becomes less able to detect substances foreign to the body; that is, to discriminate between "part of me" and "enemy alien." That in turn results in chronic autoimmune diseases. The net result of these two processes is an addition in disease and pathology that the body is unable to block. Proponents of the immune theory of aging argue that most diseases of the elderly are due to failure of the body's immune system. Yet this theory remains unproven, for it is not universal: Some animals that age never have well-developed immune systems. Moreover, it is difficult to separate cause from effect: Are the causes of age-related changes due to failure in the immune system or to some other cause (Hayflick, 1994)?

Free radical approaches to aging provide still another explanation of aging due to wear and tear. Free radicals are highly reactive chemicals in the body, triggering processes randomly and irreversibly and altering their proper functioning. Although small amounts of free radicals are created as part of normal body functioning, too many free radicals accumulating in our bodies over time interfere with normal physical processes. Since most free radicals are oxidants that damage tissue, biologists have searched for antioxidants, or substances that can combine with excess free radicals and make them harmless. Antioxidants, such as vitamins E and C, have been fed to experimental laboratory animals and increased their life expectancy but have not altered their maximum lifespan. Similarly, experiments have been done with laboratory animals to test the effects of another antioxidant, melatonin. Current research is investigating the use of antioxidants in human populations, but firm evidence that antioxidants can reverse aging or increase human life expectancy or life span is lacking.

From the above discussion, no single biological theory clearly explains why we age. All theories emphasize the notion that damage or wear occurs in genetic material or cells. All suggest that there is a maximum life span for humans and all other living organisms. Available evidence does not support the impression that modern medicine has lengthened the life span because, as nearly as we know, the life span has remained relatively unchanged for hundreds of thousands of years. Perhaps, as Hayflick (1994), a noted biologist, has pointed out, we are asking the wrong question. Rather than asking "Why do we age?" we should ask "Why do we live as long as we do?" This paradigmatic shift, Hayflick suggests, might reorder the ways in which biologists design experiments and enable them to provide more basic information about aging.

Note on Careers: From Embryology to the Biology of Aging and Beyond

Donald Mulcare is professor of biology and coordinator of the gerontology program at the University of Massachusetts, Dartmouth.

Originally, my interests lay in the undergraduate education of biology majors and students in service courses. My training focused on developmental biology, embryology (especially frog embryology), anatomy, and physiology. Somewhere around 1977, a colleague asked me to take my first step into gerontology. Specifically, I was to write an undergraduate course entitled "Biology of Aging." Although this sounds like a tall order, it was really a small step because the biology of aging is a natural extension of other areas of biology including developmental biology, embryology, anatomy, and physiology. Before teaching this course, I had to do some homework myself, so I acquired a textbook by Rockstein and Sussman and another by Alex Comfort. Still another book, Tanner's *Fetus Into Man* (1979), served as a link between embryology and aging. I used these books plus articles by Leonard Hayflick and David Willoughby to shape my initial approach to the course. In many ways these sources are still with me.

After the third or fourth offering of this course, I was beginning to get the hang of it. After teaching the course more than twenty times, and as I grow older, I am experiencing the Biology of Aging first-hand! Knowledge of the biological changes that may await us helps us to make the most of our lives, and the best time to acquire this knowledge is as soon as possible. The invitation to gerontology has repaid me with useful knowledge.

Across my university, other faculty members also wrote gerontology courses, and a collection of offerings eventually matured into both an undergraduate minor and a certificate program. One of the new courses was "Introduction to Gerontology." This was my first venture in a multidisciplinary gerontology course. My role was to assist the course organizer, Ora De Jesus. I delivered lectures on the biological changes that accompany aging. For the rest of the course, I listened to the other guest speakers and helped with logistics.

Each offering of Introduction to Gerontology since 1987 has featured different presenters and topics. Exposure to the frequently updated content gradually broadened my vision of gerontology as a multidisciplinary field that is constantly changing. It takes some of us a little longer to get the picture! Undergraduate students can learn their course work and leave higher education in about four years, but, strange as it may sound, it can take faculty members twenty or thirty years before they can consider themselves educated in an area!

Circumstances dictated that I become the coordinator for the Introduction to Gerontology course and the gerontology programs. These tasks required still more extensive reading and network building. Ora

De Jesus continued to support the course with lectures and connections to other speakers. Later the students who had received gerontology certificates and minors and who were now elder care providers returned as presenters. They scheduled panel discussions and facilitated field trips to elder housing, nursing homes, and elder day care centers. The same graduates organized a regional Gerontological Society that has served as a bridge between the current undergraduates and elders. The Society has been a reliable source of practicum placements and employment opportunities for students.

The Association for Gerontology in Higher Education (AGHE) offered encouragement and networking events that filled in many of the aspects of gerontology missing from my previous experience. It has proposed guidelines for program development, especially the framework in which UMass Dartmouth placed its existing certificate program courses. AGHE was among the first to promote the union of gerontology and distance education. The AGHE initiative and additional training at UMass Dartmouth allowed me to share the Introduction to Gerontology and Biology of Aging courses (through the two-way video classroom) with remote communities and a partner campus.

Looking back, gerontology has built on my interests in frog embryology and surrounded me with colleagues and students from all disciplines and age groups. Sometimes we meet in person or through distance education. It has been an exciting adventure that is continuing!

Physiological Changes and Health

Individual Differences and Changes in Organ Systems

MYTH: Diseases Are a Part of Normal Aging

Although no two people—even identical twins—necessarily age at the same rate, there are, as discussed in the previous section, gradual declines in the efficiency of the human body. Some years ago, Leaf (1973) noted that the average 75-year-old maintains 92 percent of the brain weight he or she had at age 30, 84 percent of the metabolic rate, 70 percent of the kidney function, and 43 percent of the breathing capacity. Although subsequent research may have challenged these figures, they illustrate two points: (1) not all organs age at the same rate in any given individual; and (2) our bodies slow down as we age.

As we age, various changes occur. Such changes are gradual; after age 30 functional losses in several organs occur at a rate of about 1 percent per year (Hayflick, 1994). Based on findings from the Baltimore Longitudinal Study of Aging, such changes include decreasing kidney function; diminished capacity of some types of white blood cells to fight infectious diseases and cancer; decreasing lung function; and decreasing lower arm and back muscle strength. Nevertheless, because people vary, age alone is a poor predictor of performance; some 85-year-olds may perform as well as a 55-year-old. Maximum heart rate—also called the pulse rate—also changes with normal aging, but when disease-free, the heart of an older person still pumps effectively.

Many conditions people view as "normal aging" are, however, caused by disease. For example, slow losses in physical functioning, such as those due to arthritis (a joint disease afflicting many older people) are actually from a disease, as is hypertension (high blood pressure). Nor is Alzheimer's disease—a condition characterized by slow, progressive, and irreversible memory loss—a part of normal aging. Although short-term memory declines with age, the notion that we become senile as we grow old is simply wrong—a topic that we will discuss more fully in Chapters 6 and 7. Similarly, sudden illnesses (e.g., strokes and heart attacks) are diseases, not normal aging.

Within the past several decades, the effects of chronological age have been examined more carefully. What we have generally assumed to be *normal aging* turns out to be associated with environmental factors, lifestyle, and diseases related to aging. Thus, many physical changes in later life are not directly caused by aging itself but rather by processes which may change with age but are not intrinsic parts of aging. Increasingly, researchers are becoming aware of the distinction between normal aging and *usual aging* (Rowe & Kahn, 1999). As we grow older, however, we are more at risk for chronic diseases, a topic discussed later in this chapter.

Sensory Changes

Inability to see or hear clearly, to taste foods, to smell odors, and to detect pain, warmth, and cold interfere with our daily lives. At any age, such sensory losses may limit our activities in some ways, reduce our enjoyment of everyday life, and contribute to depression, withdrawal, and suspicion. This section reviews what we know—and do not know—about sensory changes in later life. As you will see, changes in any of the five senses vary from person to person and may be due to many factors.

Vision. Various sensory changes—in vision, hearing, taste, smell, and touch—occur as we grow older. Probably the most common is *presbyopia* (from the Greek *presbys* for "older" and *opia* for "vision"), or the gradual inability of the lens of the eye to focus on nearby objects. Presbyopia results from the gradual loss of elasticity in the eye's lens and loss of power in the muscles that help the lens change shape to focus. Although no one understands the reasons why presbyopia occurs, loss generally begins in early childhood but generally is first noticed at midlife when people become aware that it is more difficult to read or see close objects without reading glasses or bifocals (Roberts, 1995). Other relatively harmless visual changes develop with age as well. For example, our eyes may become more sensitive to glare, be less adaptable to changes in lighting, and be less able to discriminate between colors and color gradations.

MYTH: Serious Visual Changes That Make
Seeing Very Difficult Are Normal in Old Age

Eye diseases also increase with age; about two-thirds of all severe visual impairments take place among people 65 and over. Serious visual deficits afflict about 8 percent of men and 5 percent of women aged 65 to 74 and 11 percent of both women and men 75 or over (U.S. Department of Commerce, 2000). The prevalence of legal blindness also climbs beginning at around age 50. For legal blindness, there are no gender differences, but it is almost twice as common in African Americans as in whites.

Many diseases cause low vision and legal blindness in later life, the most common probably being *macular degeneration,* responsible for about 1 in 5 of the cases of legal blindness in the United States. A progressive condition affecting the macula—the part of the eye responsible for perception of fine detail—macular degeneration results in loss of central vision, making it difficult to see anything at close range. If you want to see what macular degeneration is like, make a cardboard set of eyeglasses, cutting out the cardboard around only the edges of the frame but leaving the center part uncut.

Glaucoma, due to an excessive buildup of pressure in the eyeball, and *diabetic retinopathy,* due to poorly controlled diabetes that destroys the blood vessels of the eye's retina (the immediate instrument of vision that receives images from the eye's lens), are also more common as we grow older. *Cataracts,* caused by a change in the protein structure in the lens, produce blurring of vision and sensitivity to glare in bright sunlight. Twenty-five percent of Americans aged 65 or over have cataracts, and removal of cataracts is the most common surgical procedure within this broad age group. Keep in mind, however, that none of these diseases is inevitable for any specific individual. These eye conditions are *not* part of normal aging.

Hearing. Hearing loss is common as we grow older. About 30 percent of men and 18 percent of women aged 65 to 74 have some hearing impairment. Hearing loss has many causes. A buildup of wax in the ears is one common and easily remedied reason. By age 75 or over, 45 percent of men and 31 percent of women have impaired hearing (U.S. Department of Commerce, 2000). An estimated 39 percent of people over the age of 65 have hearing impairments severe enough to benefit from a hearing aid (Tesch-Romer, 1997). Other causes include internal damage to the ear from medications, diseases, genetic factors, and prolonged exposure to loud noises (including loud music from one's stereo or Walkman!). The most common hearing loss associated with aging, however, is *presbycusis* (from the Greek words for "elder" and for "hearing"), first noticed as a loss of ability to hear high-frequency sounds.

Although the age at which presbycusis begins varies, it may start gradually when we are still in our 30s. In midlife, men (aged 30 to 59) are more likely to decline in their ability to hear high notes. Moreover, men lose their hearing at a faster rate in each subsequent decade of life (Hayflick, 1994). Presbycusis also decreases the ability both to hear loud sounds and to hear consonants. Consonants are usually spoken in higher-frequency tones and vowels in low-frequency tones. In a language such as English, where there are only the long and short vowels *a, e, i, o,* and *u,* presbycusis can make understanding what others say very difficult!

How much do hearing aids help? Although hearing aids obviously do improve many types of hearing loss, they are still imperfect devices that do not fully restore normal hearing. Further, wearers of hearing aids find that intrusive background noises, such as traffic, televisions or radio, and so forth, are amplified. This increase in background noise is one reason many people are reluctant to wear hearing aids. According to a recent study, older people with mild to moderate hearing loss who received a hearing aid for the first time reported significant subjective improvement in their ability to hear plus moderate to high satisfaction with the hearing aids. However, their level of social activity, satisfaction with social relationships, and sense of well-being did not increase (Tesch-Romer, 1997). Many people feel that wearing a hearing aid is not only a nuisance but stigmatizes them, marking them as old, deaf, and unattractive.

Aside from its personal meaning to the individual, being fitted for a hearing aid is only a first step. To communicate more effectively, the person with hearing loss may also (1) use lipreading with the hearing aid; (2) ask specific questions to clarify words or phrases; (3) use assertive tactics to control situations in which listening is difficult; and (4) accept and discuss one's hearing loss with others (Montgomery, 1994). Shouting at someone with a hearing loss does not improve hearing and, for those who wear a hearing aid, is likely to create an unpleasant and sometimes incomprehensible noise!

Hearing aids improve many kinds of hearing loss, but do not restore normal hearing. They also increase sensitivity to background noise.

Taste. Does salt lose its savor as we grow older? Evidence suggests that the ability to detect salt, sweet, bitter, and sour—considered the four primary tastes—does decline with aging, although individuals differ widely. Taste is judged by taste buds: little pear-shaped organs on our tongues. Earlier research reported that the number of taste buds declines with age, but more recent and carefully designed studies have not found this decline. Nor is there general agreement about whether our sense of taste declines gradually throughout adulthood or more abruptly in old age (Schiffman, 1995a). What influences changes in taste? Apparently, this is due to degenerative changes within the cells that form our taste buds (Hayflick, 1994). The many causes include medications, nutritional deficiencies, and various diseases. However, evidence shows that we may just prefer stronger, more tart, and less sweet flavors as we grow older (Schiffman, 1995a).

Smell. Most studies have reported a gradual decline in the ability to detect odors as we age. However, these studies often included people who had physical problems or medical conditions, reducing their ability to distinguish odors. As with taste, the sense of smell is affected by many factors. Medications, nutritional states, head injuries, infections such as flu or hepatitis, Alzheimer's disease, and a variety of other diseases, plus smoking and allergies, affect our sense of smell (Schiffman, 1995b). One study of healthy elders (i.e., people who did not have medical conditions negatively affecting their sense of smell) suggested that, on the average, ability to detect and identify odors does decrease with age. However, loss of sense of smell is less than that reported in the studies in which people were not screened for factors negatively affecting sense of smell. Moreover, ability to detect dissimilar smells is not consistently related to specific odors, to gender, or to measures of acuity of smell (Barber, 1996).

Touch. Touch is an important sense throughout the life course as it serves many functions, not only warning us of heat, cold, and injury but also giving comfort and maintaining intimacy. With aging, we are likely to become gradually less sensitive to skin pain than when we were younger, and our sensitivity to touch is also likely to decrease. The density of the skin's blood circulating system is reduced as we grow older, which may be one reason why many older people feel colder when the temperature drops. Diminished sense of touch and awareness of temperature changes may occur in later life also due to other disease-like causes including circulatory problems associated with heart malfunctions and diabetes.

Cosmetic Changes

Of all the biological changes associated with growing old, young people are probably most acutely aware of the cosmetic changes. Hair grays, wrinkles become pronounced, shoulders tend to narrow, and the pelvis widens with increasing age. In American society, these changes are greeted with less than enthusiasm for, although most of us want to live as long as possible, few want to look old. Cosmetic changes associated with aging have been viewed as particularly disastrous for—and by—women, due to the double standard of aging. Over a quarter of a century ago, author Susan Sontag noted: "For most women, aging means a humiliating process of sexual disqualification" (Sontag, 1972: 32)—a statement that still holds true. In contrast, getting older may actually act in men's favor. Masculinity has traditionally been associated with assertiveness, competency, self-control, independence, and power, all qualities that are enhanced with maturity, if not old age. Femininity, however, has been associated with helplessness, passivity, compliance, noncompetitiveness, and warmth, all qualities attributed to "good" children. Moreover, feminine "sexiness" has been associated with youthfulness rather than midlife or old age, an indication that women are valued more for their fecundity than their wisdom (Markson, 1997).

Cosmetic signs of aging may thus trigger concerns about self-worth for women. For example, midlife women may begin to worry about "physical changes of the body," "loss of youthful appearance . . . I fear beginning to look like my mother with a very large stomach," "losing sexual appeal," and so forth (Mansfield & Voda, 1993). Scant wonder that women provide a ready market for health clubs and cosmetics designed to smooth wrinkles away, wash away gray hair, reduce cellulite, and remove unsightly body bulges! Despite the popularity of "older" women such as Candice Bergen, Cher, and Susan Sarandon—all middle-aged—their attractiveness is usually based precisely on the fact that they "do not look their age."

What creates common cosmetic changes in aging? Wrinkles begin below the skin's outer layer (the epidermis) when the dermis (i.e., a layer of tissue filled with glands, nerve endings, and blood vessels) begins to shrink. Males have a thicker dermis than females, which is why women seem to wrinkle more quickly as they grow older (Hayflick, 1994). The main cause of wrinkling, however, is not aging itself but exposure to the sun—that is, our faces wrinkle when our buttocks don't! As they age, sun worshipers are not only likely to accrue more wrinkles but also run more risk of skin cancer and melanoma, a particularly dangerous form of cancer. In addition, environmental toxins, smoking, heredity, and physical disease affect wrinkling.

Graying of the hair occurs due to loss of pigment in the hair follicle. Graying hair is not, however, an indicator of chronological aging. Some people begin to gray while in their teens, others not until their 70s. Hair also thins as we age. Although both males and females experience some hair loss as they grow older, men, even those who are in high school or college, are at particular risk of hereditary "pattern baldness." Baldness and thinning hair supply a set of ready customers for toupees, hair transplants, and preparations designed to reduce hair loss.

Other cosmetic changes associated with aging—"liver" or "age" spots on the skin (associated with an accumulation of melanin, a dark pigment in the skin), slight lengthening of the nose and ears, "dowagers' hump," slight shortening in height, sagging or flabby muscles, and so forth—are familiar negative images of aging. Not all these changes are "normal" aging, however. Rather, they usually result from other processes. For example, sagging or flabby muscles indicate the lack of muscle-building exercise and can be reversed. The so-called dowager's hump may actually be a sign of osteoporosis, a generalized bone disorder characterized by loss of bone mass. Osteoporosis is a serious disease that frequently leads to complications resulting in pain, disability, and immobility and is both costly and disabling, leading to increased risk of hip fracture. Cosmetic changes associated with aging do not appear simultaneously, and some people experience so few that they "do not look their age."

Menopause

One age change that is universal to women is menopause, or the cessation of menses. Unlike the onset of menstruation, there is no single event ushering in menopause. Rather, menopause begins with a gradual decline in ovarian function followed by discontinuation of menstruation. When menopause occurs, the ovaries reduce their output of hormones, and estrogen levels drop. Nevertheless, a woman's body does continue to produce estrogen after menopause although generally in smaller quantities than during her reproductive years. There is no equivalent of menopause among men, for at least some if not all males retain their reproductive capacity throughout their lives, a topic discussed more fully in Chapter 9.

American and European women are a median age of 50 to 51 when their menstrual periods cease. The menopausal median age for women of non-European origin tends to be lower and apparently is associated with poorer nutrition (Weg, 1995). Approximately 38 million women in the United States are now postmenopausal. In the first two decades of the twenty-first century, about 21 million women—members of the current baby boom generation—will enter menopause and have on the average one-third of their lives still to live. Yet, until the Nurses Health Study was undertaken several decades ago, little research focused on the effects of lower estrogen levels on women's health in later life. The Women's Health Initiative, begun in 1992 and currently underway, will also provide useful information on women's health after menopause.

Although menopause affects all women who survive to midlife, and has since the beginning of time, its meaning and symptoms vary from culture to culture, era to era, and person to person. Symptoms reported to be related range from hot flashes, sweating, and dryness of the vagina to mood swings, sleeplessness, and nervousness. Although the most common symptom of menopause remains hot flashes, even this marker varies from culture to culture. For example, Japanese women, who eat diets rich in soy, rarely experience hot flashes (Lock, 1993).

Menopausal and postmenopausal women in Western society are stereotypically prone to depression, anxiety, loss of confidence, and lack of sexual interest. Yet the majority of the evidence suggests the contrary. As psychoanalyst Therese Benedek (1952) argued, menopause is a normal developmental event, offering time for potential psychic expansion. For most women, menopause is *not* a traumatic event. For example, one longitudinal study of midlife women reported that 70 percent felt either relieved or neutral about undergoing menopause (Avis & McKinlay, 1991). In a large-scale study of Canadian women, only 2 percent stated that they felt regret about the cessation of their menstrual periods, and only 11 percent classed menopause as a major life event (Kaufert, 1985). For many women, menopause may indeed provide a welcome relief from fear of pregnancy and childbearing!

What are the implications of menopause for the aging process itself? Traditionally, menopause has been medicalized and regarded by physicians as an estrogen deficiency disease that lends itself to symptom control through estrogen. Yet, this treatment remains controversial (see box). Estrogen therapy is also prescribed as a treatment for *osteoporosis*, a loss of bone mass that weakens the skeleton and often results in broken bones. Recent studies have also examined whether estrogen supplements may delay the onset of Alzheimer's disease, but the results to date are inconclusive (NIA, 1996). *Heart disease,* a topic discussed more fully later in this chapter, may also increase among postmenopausal women who do not take estrogen supplements. Yet, estrogen therapy is not a cure-all and it can have serious side effects.

In sum, an age-old event common to women in midlife remains mysterious. What makes menopause occur? How does it relate to the development of various diseases in later life? Why and how do female versus male hormones prevent or contribute to chronic diseases in old age? As more research is done on the aging process, these questions may have answers. Now there is only enough information to say that the elderly, whether male or female, are more likely than younger people to develop chronic diseases, a topic discussed later in this chapter.

Although vitamin and mineral supplements are useful, no cure for osteoporosis, a chronic disease affecting an estimated 1 in 3 women and 1 in 12 men over the age of 50, has yet been found.

Spotlight on U.S.: Preventing Osteoporosis

According to the National Osteoporosis Foundation, osteoporosis weakens bones and results in an increased loss of bone mass and bone strength. This major public health threat affects approximately 10 million Americans and 18 million more have low bone mass, putting them at risk for this disease (NIH Consensus Conference Panel, 2000). Besides providing structural support, our bones contain most of the stores of the body's calcium. Healthy bone is constantly changing. In childhood and adolescence, bones form at a faster rate than they are reabsorbed. Up to age 40, peak bone mass is maintained through a balance between the formation and the loss of bone. After age 40, however, bone absorption is more rapid than bone formation. Although all of us lose bone mass as we age, this process accelerates in women. Women lose bone mass during the first 10 years or so after menopause at twice the rate of men in the same age group.

Osteoporosis makes people more susceptible to sudden and unexpected bone fractures. For women, wrist fractures are a problem, especially from their late 50s to early 70s; hip and vertebral fractures from their late 70s and 80s; after menopause, all other bone fractures are a problem. Nearly 1 in every 5 people dies within a year after a hip fracture. Greater likelihood of dying is not the only risk associated with a broken hip. Data from the Framingham Study show that hip fracture is the single biggest predictor for subsequent nursing home admission among women (Markson et al., 2000). Moreover, osteoporosis is expensive. The estimated national direct cost for osteoporosis and fractures relating thereto is $10 to $15 billion annually. Most of these estimated costs are for in-patient hospital care and do not include the costs of treatment for people without a history of fractures, nor do they include the indirect costs of lost wages or productivity of either the person or a caregiver (NIH Consensus Conference Panel, 2000). These costs are likely to increase as a greater proportion of the population enters old age (Lindsay, 1995).

What are the symptoms of osteoporosis? Sadly, there is no easy answer because it is commonly asymptomatic and discovered in daily medical practice through X-rays and bone density scans after other diseases that cause bone loss are eliminated. At its later stages, osteoporosis may produce visible changes—loss of height, rounding of the upper back or *dowager's hump*, protruding abdomen, forward thrust of the head—all due to collapsed vertebrae caused by the disease.

What causes osteoporosis is not fully understood, although it is believed to be an estrogen deficiency disease. Yet not all postmenopausal women develop osteoporosis. At high risk are white women with a family history of osteoporosis, of northern European extraction, with small bone frames, and of normal or less than average weight. Women who have suffered from an eating disorder are at increased risk because their bones have not borne enough weight to help prevent bone loss. Smoking, lack of calcium and vitamin D in the diet, some medications, and heavy alcohol or caffeine use also increase risk. Regular exercise, especially resistance and high-impact activity, is important in reducing risk because it increases the mass and strength of bones. (One example: the dominant arm of tennis players is thicker and denser than their nondominant arm by about 15 percent compared with only a 3 percent difference between the right and left arms of most nonathletes!)

The treatment for osteoporosis remains controversial. Calcium and vitamin D supplements are recommended as preventive measures but dosage and effectiveness varies from person to person. Hormone replacement therapy with estrogen is also an established approach to prevent and treat osteoporosis. In 2002, the National Institutes of Health (NIH) stopped a major clinical trial on the use of combined estrogen and progestin due to the risks involved. Estrogen supplements apparently decrease the likelihood of developing osteoporosis, but increase the risk of cancer of the breast and uterus, heart attacks, blood clots, and strokes. More recently, selective estrogen receptor modulators (SERMs) have been developed. The goal of SERMs is to maximize the beneficial effects of estrogen on bones and minimize the risk of cancer. Natural estrogen and progestin, especially found in plants, have also received attention and, although research is promising, no effect on fracture reduction in humans is yet definitive.

Sources: Barzel, U.S., "Osteoporosis," in G. L. Maddox et al. *Encyclopedia of Aging*, New York: Springer, 1995, p. 723; Kane, R. L., Ouslander, J. G., and Abrass, I. B., *Essentials of Clinical Geriatrics*, 3rd edition, New York: McGraw Hill, 1994; Lock, M., *Encounters with Aging*, Berkeley: University of California Press, 1993; National Institute on Aging, "Pills, Patches, and Shots: Can Hormones Prevent Aging?," Bethesda, MD: 1996; NIH Consensus Conference Panel, *Osteoporosis Prevention, Diagnosis, and Therapy*, 2000, March 27–29, 17(1): 1–36; National Institutes of Health, "NHLBI Stops Trial of Estrogen and Progestin Due to Increased Breast Cancer Risk, Lack of Overall Benefit," Bethesda, MD: 2002.

Illness and Recovery

Acute and Chronic Illness

Acute Illness. Since 1900, patterns of illness among all age groups in the United States have changed dramatically: In the past, people were more likely to develop acute illnesses, most often caused by bacteria or viruses, that came on quickly. People with such ailments either died or got better. Today, many acute diseases, (e.g., smallpox, polio, diphtheria, scarlet fever, plague, and measles) have largely been eradicated or checked through immunizations, public health measures, and improved medical treatment. Thus, infectious diseases have become far less common while chronic illnesses (ranging from sinus problems and asthma to heart disease, cancer, arthritis, and diabetes) have escalated. Accidents (especially traffic) and stress-related diseases (e.g., drug dependency, hypertension, and alcoholism) have also increased.

Patterns of both acute and chronic diseases vary by age. Among *acute illnesses*, the common cold occurs most often among children under age 5; injuries are most common among ages 18 to 24, and so forth. Acute conditions also vary by race and gender. Males are more likely to incur injuries and females more likely to have the common cold. Whites are more likely to have injuries but African Americans are more likely to get colds. Despite race or gender, people whose family income is less than $10,000 per year are at greater risk for colds and injuries, influenza, and infective and parasitic diseases (National Center for Health Statistics, 2000).

MYTH: CHRONIC DISEASES OCCUR ONLY IN OLD AGE

Chronic Illness. Chronic diseases develop slowly and can be treated but not cured. Their treatment is symptomatic rather than curable. Their intensity is often unpredictable, and the length of time and the degree of incapacity variable. Acute episodes may be followed by remissions. Moreover, chronic illnesses are often multiple, and the breakdown of one organ may lead to breakdown or impairment of another.

Chronic diseases affect people of all ages, from the very rich to the very poor. Approximately 1 in every 3 Americans has one or more chronic diseases, and one-third of these have some limitation in a major activity (Robert Wood Johnson Foundation, 1996). Contrary to popular belief, only 1 in 4 people living in the community with a chronic illness is elderly. Some chronic diseases are more common among specific age groups. As you can see from Table 5-2, asthma is most often observed among those under the age of 45.

Table 5-2	Percentage of People with Selected Chronic Conditions by Age Group in the U.S.*				
Age	Arthritis	Asthma	Diabetes	Heart Disease	High Blood Pressure
under 45	3%	5%	**	4%	3%
45–64	19%	3%	6%	14%	21%
65–74	39%	4%	12%	26%	31%
75+	44%	3%	13%	39%	27%

* Percentages have been rounded. **Less than 1 percent.
Source: National Center for Health Statistics.

Diseases such as arthritis, hypertension, and heart disease may begin in midlife but progress with age. Arthritis and heart disease are most frequent among the elderly; hypertension (a major risk factor for heart disease and stroke) and diabetes occur most often among both middle-aged and elderly. Among the elderly, nearly 1 in 4 people has one chronic disease, and some have several. As you can see in Figure 5-1, most of the people with more than one chronic condition are middle-aged or older. Over half (51 percent) of Americans aged 45 to 64 have two or more chronic ailments, and over two-thirds (69 percent) of those over age 65 have two or more (Robert Wood Johnson Foundation, 1996).

Less frequently discussed is the growing number of older people who have AIDS or are HIV positive. Transmission of the HIV/AIDS virus among older people takes the same routes—sexual intercourse, drug use, and blood transfusions from infected donors—as among younger people. According to the Centers for Disease Control in Atlanta, the number of new cases of AIDS in people over age 50 is increasing at twice the rate for those younger. Approximately 3 percent of the reported cases of AIDS in the United States are among people 65 and over (Centers for Disease Control and Prevention, 1997). Rates of the disease among people 65 and older are probably underestimated because of the common assumption that sexual activity ends with age. Not only are people living healthier and longer lives, but medications such as Viagra and a more sexually open society mean that more people are dating after widowhood or divorce.

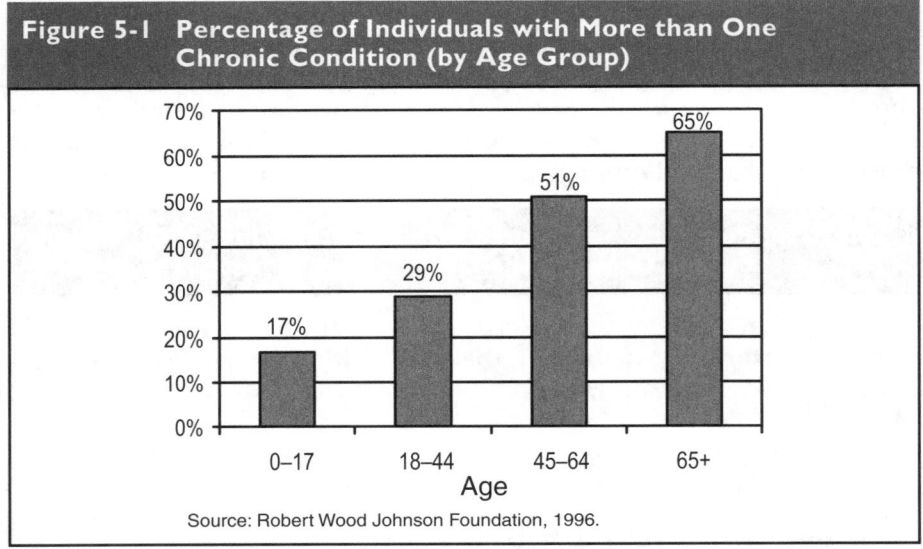

Figure 5-1   Percentage of Individuals with More than One Chronic Condition (by Age Group)

Source: Robert Wood Johnson Foundation, 1996.

Although homosexual contact among those 65 and older accounts for the largest number of reported cases of HIV/AIDS in the U.S., the danger of heterosexual transmission—which accounts for 7 in 10 cases of infection worldwide—may actually increase with age. Postmenopausal women, no longer at risk of pregnancy, are less likely to urge their partners to use protective devices such as condoms. Ads featuring teens and twenty-something people are not targeting this audience. Pregnancy is a fear of the past, and both older men and women are often unaware of the need to practice safe sex. Once an older person is infected, the period between infection with the HIV virus and onset of AIDS may be faster and death earlier because immune systems decline with age. Moreover, diagnosis may be delayed. Few physicians and other health care workers think about the sex lives of older patients, and many other diseases can mimic the symptoms of early AIDS. For example, the mental confusion of AIDS may be mistaken for Alzheimer's Disease (Global Aging Report, 1997).

Whatever the age of the patient, chronic disease costs money. Many chronically ill people "cycle through the hospital, then go to the clinic or doctor's office, return home, go back to the hospital during acute episodes and again back to their homes"—all contributing to higher health costs (Wiener, Fagerhaugh, Strauss, & Suczek, 1997: 26). The indirect costs of chronic disease are also high to patients and their families. Work and daily activity may be limited, special care and equipment needed, drugs, and medical and technical equipment required to maintain the chronically ill person at home. Although difficult to measure, the emotional costs, both to the chronically ill person and her or his family, are also high.

Gender

Chronic diseases vary not only by age but by gender, race, and socioeconomic status. For example, regardless of age, women are more likely to have arthritis; by age 75, the proportion of females reporting that they have arthritis is about 40 percent greater than among males in the same age group (National Center for Health Statistics, 2000). Heart disease is apparently more common in men. However, data from the Framingham Study, which has followed more than 5,000 men and women since 1948, show that the greater resistance to heart disease among women lessens with advancing age. Specifically, after menopause, female risk for heart disease increases two- to threefold. Despite the narrowing gap between males and postmenopausal females with advancing age, women maintain a relative advantage (Kannel & Brand, 1983). This pattern, observed over 20 years ago, continues. In 1999, heart diseases accounted for 19.4 deaths per 1,000 men 65 and over but only 16.7 deaths per 1,000 among their female age peers (but see box).

Spotlight on U.S.: Heart Disease Among Women— The Yentl Syndrome?

Yentl, from a 1983 film of the same name, was a young woman (portrayed by Barbra Streisand) who wanted a formal education but was denied it as she was female. Only by pretending to be male was she able to achieve her goal. In the early 1990s, Bernadine Healy, then Director of the National Institutes of Health, drew from the film's plot to describe the "Yentl syndrome"— the neglect of heart disease among women. Part of the disregard of heart disease among females is not only due to research showing that men are at greater risk for heart attack but to gender-linked differences in symptoms. Because women have not been included in clinical studies of the disease, women and their doctors are often not aware of heart disease risks for women. As Healy noted, when "a woman showed she was just like a man, by having severe coronary disease or myocardial infarction, then she was treated as a man would be" (Healy, 1991: 274).

Yet, although females have a lower prevalence rate of heart disease than men, they have one-third more undetected or "silent" heart attacks than males (age-adjusted rate) according to data from the Framingham study. Why do so many women's heart attacks go undetected? Are females less likely to recognize symptoms, or do they fail to seek timely medical attention for symptoms? To analyze this issue, Iezzoni et al. (1997) examined a large sample of 14,083 patients admitted in 1991 to 100 hospitals. Regardless of the data source or severity measures, women who suffered heart attacks were less likely than men to receive tests to diagnose the extent of heart damage, less likely to undergo bypass surgery, and more apt to die in the hospital.

Differences in age and severity of illness do not explain these differences. Subsequent studies have confirmed that, compared with men, women receive less aggressive treatment during the early management of a heart attack, including early diagnosis in the emergency room, although whether they are more likely to die remains debated (Gan et al., 2000; Herlitz et al., 1999; Keller & Lemberg, 2000). Women are also less likely to receive certain post-heart attack drugs when discharged from the hospital (Dwamena et al., 2000). Clearly there are gender differences in how doctors treat patients.

A major factor explaining the differences in treatment is that women's symptoms differ from men's. Although many women, like men, have chest pain as an initial symptom, they are much more likely to have symptoms of upper abdominal pain, nausea, fatigue, and difficulty in breathing (Mosca et al., 1997). They are also more likely to report pain in the back, neck, and jaw (Herlitz et al., 1999). Because heart attack symptoms can differ by gender, physicians and women themselves may not recognize its initial signs. Until relatively recently, the male model of heart attack was the standard for diagnosis and intervention.

Although sex differences in rates of heart disease are no doubt biologically determined, these studies also emphasize the point that male-female differences in the diagnosis and treatment of heart disease may also be partially socially constructed (McKinlay, 1996). That is, physicians find what they have been trained to find. Women—especially younger women—with symptoms that differ from the male pattern of chest pain are less likely to be diagnosed or to receive treatment as quickly.

Sources: Dwamena et al. 2000. "The use of angiotensin-converting enzyme inhibitors in patients with acute myocardial infarction in community hospitals." Michigan State University Inter-Institutional Collaborative Heart (MICH) Study Group. *Clinical Cardiology* 23(5): 341–346; Gan, S. C., et al. 2000. "Treatment of acute myocardial infarction and 30-day mortality among women and men," *New England Journal of Medicine, 343*(1): 8–15; Healy, B. 1991. "The Yentl syndrome," *New England Journal of Medicine, 325*(4): 274–276; Herlitz, J., Bang, A., Karlson, B. W., & Hartford, M. "Is there a gender difference in aetiology of chest pain and symptoms associated with acute myocardial infarction?" *European Journal of Emergency Medicine,* 6(4): 311–315; Iezonni, L. I., Ash, A. S., Shwartz M., &

Mackiernan, Y. D. 1997. "Differences in procedure use, in-hospital mortality, and illness severity by gender for acute myocardial infarction patients," *Medical Care, 35*(2): 158–171. Keller, K. B., & Lemberg, L. 2000. "Gender differences in acute coronary events," *American Journal of Critical Care, 9*(3): 207–209; McKinlay, J. 1996. "Some contributions from the social system to gender inequalities in heart disease," *Journal of Health and Social Behavior, 37* (March): 1–26; Mosca, L., et al. 1997. *Cardiovascular Disease in Women: A Statement for Health Care Professionals from the American Heart Association.* Washington, DC: American Heart Association.

Race and Ethnicity

With respect to race and ethnicity, potentially serious chronic diseases with the highest prevalence among whites are (in rank order) (1) arthritis, (2) hypertension (high blood pressure), and (3) heart disease. Among African Americans, the prevalence (in rank order) is (1) hypertension, (2) arthritis, and (3) heart disease (Collins, 1997). Racial inequality can influence the type of treatment received. For example, African Americans who suffer a heart attack are significantly less likely to undergo bypass surgery and other invasive procedures than whites with similarly severe heart disease (Kressin & Petersen, 2001). These treatment differences relate to the poorer survival rate among African Americans who are more likely to die than whites within 5 years after a heart attack (Peterson, Shaw, DeLong, et al., 1997). And clot-busting heart medications are used less often among elderly African Americans (9 percent) than whites (17 percent) (Allison et al., 1996).

African Americans live fewer years on the average than whites and live more years with chronic health problems. This racial gap is spread across all areas of health, and socioeconomic conditions, not health risk behaviors, are the primary reasons (Hayward et al., 2000). Minority status thus interacts with socioeconomic status to produce higher rates of all illnesses; members of minority groups are more likely to be living at or below the poverty level. Only 1 in 12 non-Latino/Latina white elders was poor in 2000 compared with nearly 1 in 4 African Americans and 1 in 5 Latinos/Latinas (Dalaker, 2001).

People living in poverty are more vulnerable at any age to chronic conditions such as asthma, arthritis, diabetes, high blood pressure, and heart disease (Collins, 1997). Diabetes, for example, is more prevalent among African Americans than whites. Health data on Latinos/Latinas are more limited, as only recently have separate statistics been gathered for them. Compared with non-Latino/Latina whites, Latinos/Latinas have higher rates of high blood pressure, diabetes, and lung cancer. Keep in mind, however, that Latinos/Latinas are umbrella terms that cover diverse groups, very different from one another in racial and ethnic ancestry, immigrant history, and socioeconomic status.

Medicare

People aged 65 and older are most likely to have health insurance through Medicare, a federal insurance program available nationwide. Medicare has two parts: (1) Part A, hospital insurance; and (2) Part B, medical insurance. Part A helps cover inpatient care in hospitals. Most people do not pay a monthly premium or payment for Part A because they or a spouse paid Medicare taxes while they were working. Part B is optional and helps cover physician services, outpatient, and some other medical services that Part A does not cover. Each person must pay a monthly premium ($50 in 2001), as its cost was not covered by payroll deductions for Medicare taxes. For those people who choose to enroll in Part B, the premium is usually deducted from their monthly Social Security checks or other federal pension. Medicaid is a state-administered program for the poor of all ages. Both eligibility requirements and benefits vary from state to state. Both Medicare and Medicaid are discussed more fully in Chapters 11 and 12.

Limitations in Activities

Chronic diseases do not always get worse, however. Some people with chronic diseases may improve, while others remain the same or deteriorate. Chronic conditions nonetheless remain a major cause of *functional disabilities* that limit ability to perform *activities of daily living* (ADLs). ADLs usually include bathing, dressing, toileting, eating, getting outdoors, moving from bed to chair, and walking. *Instrumental activities of daily living* (IADLs) include preparing meals, shopping, managing money, using the telephone, doing light housework, and doing heavy housework.

The leading causes of functional disabilities among people 65 and over are arthritis and heart disease. Approximately 14 percent of Americans 65 and over have at least one ADL limitation, and 21 percent report difficulties with one or more instrumental activities of daily living (Administration on Aging, 2000). Among the now-old, African Americans are more

Motorized wheelchairs can help people with limited mobility to perform activities of daily living, but they are expensive, and their purchase must be authorized by a physician if Medicare is to pay for it.

likely to be limited in their activities than whites, and this difference increases with age, as may be seen in Table 5-3. Gender as well as race and ethnicity also play a role; more women than men report limitations in their activities.

Yet, defying stereotypes that old age is always synonymous with increasing decline and disability, the *rate* of later life disability has declined sharply. By 1994, there were 1.2 million *fewer* disabled older people than in 1982, and decreases in disability accelerated during the 1989–1994 period (Manton, Corder, & Stallard, 1997) and continue to decrease. The point here is that those patterns of health, disability, and illness throughout the life span are subject to rapid change. Illness and disabilities among members of the baby boom and baby bust generations in old age may thus be very different from those among people 65 and over today.

Table 5-3	Percentage of People Aged 65 and Over with One or More Limitations of Activity Due to Chronic Conditions, 1996					
	Limited but not in major activity		Limited in amount or kind of major activity		Unable to carry out major activity	
Ages	65–74	75+	65–74	75+	65–74	75+
Gender and Race						
Men	13%	23%	8%	9%	11%	9%
Women	12	16	10	16	10	12
Whites	12	19	9	13	9	10
Blacks	12	11	12	20	16	17

Source: National Center for Health Statistics, U.S. Public Health Service, U.S. Department of Health and Human Services. (2000). *Health, United States, 2000*, Table 59.

Self-Perceptions of Health

Given that chronic diseases are more prevalent in later life, how do older people view their health? According to a recent survey by the U.S. Department of Health and Human Services, most people 65 and over rate their health as good to excellent. This finding offers a sharp contradiction to stereotypes of the elderly as dominated by concerns with poor health. There are variations in self-assessed health by gender and race, however. Native American elders, for example, are over twice as likely to report poor health status as are the general public aged 65 and over, reflecting their higher rates of poverty throughout the life course (National Resource Center on Native American Aging at the University of North Dakota, 1998).

Nevertheless, as you can see in Table 5-4, the proportion of people rating their health as good to excellent declines with age despite gender or race, reflecting the greater probability of chronic illnesses as one grows older. You will also note that at all ages shown in the table, non-Hispanic African Americans and Hispanics rate their health as worse than do non-Hispanic whites. Interestingly, although non-Hispanic African American and Hispanic women consistently rate their health worse than do men. There is little gender difference in self-rated health among non-Hispanic whites.

Table 5-4	Percentage of Persons Aged 65 or Older Who Reported Good to Excellent Health, by Age Group, Race, and Hispanic Origin, 1994 to 1996			
	All Persons	**Non-Hispanic White**	**Non-Hispanic Black**	**Hispanic**
65 or Older	72.2	74.0	58.4	64.9
Men				
65 or Older	72.2	73.5	59.3	65.4
65 to 74	74.6	76.3	61.6	68.7
75 to 84	68.3	69.4	56.4	59.7
85 or Older	65.0	67.3	45.0	50.9
Women				
65 or Older	72.4	74.3	57.8	64.6
65 to 74	75.2	77.5	59.3	68.5
75 to 84	69.8	71.7	55.3	59.3
85 or Older	65.1	66.4	56.0	55.1

Note: Data are based on a three-year average from 1994 to 1996. Hispanics may be of any race. Reference population: These data refer to the civilian noninstitutional population Source: Federal Interagency Forum on Aging Related Statistics (2000), Table 17.

Why is self-rated health important? Many studies within the past few decades have shown that self-rated health is an important predictor of mortality and may be more accurate than medical records or self-reports of medical conditions. A review of 27 studies in American and international scientific journals shows consistent findings: Global self-rated health is an important indicator of subsequent death that is independent of other factors (Idler & Benyamini, 1997).

The reasons why this is true are not entirely clear, however. One factor may be self-efficacy, or the degrees of confidence people have in their own abilities to perform specific behaviors in a particular situation or context. A high degree of self-efficacy buffers elders against functional decline even in the face of diminishing physical capacity (Mendes de Leon et al., 1996). As the sociologist W. I. Thomas said long ago, that which we believe to be real is real in its consequences; if we perceive ourselves as relatively healthy and competent, we are likely to perform accordingly.

The Importance of Exercise

Within the past few decades, regular exercise has been demonstrated to be an important insulator against both chronic disease and death. Single exercise sessions boost the body's metabolism; increase blood flow through the arteries, removing fatty deposits from blood vessels; and bolster growth hormone levels. Regular exercise is even more beneficial, reversing all the factors believed to cause aging according to the theories discussed earlier in this chapter. Regular exercise not only increases antioxidants that insulate against disease processes (Alessio & Blasi, 1997) but also functional performance and ability to maintain independent activity (Evans, 1999). Aerobic training can improve heart function even among elders with heart disease (Stahle, Nordlander, & Bergfeldt, 1999). Regular exercise also increases life expectancy. For example, a study of Harvard alumni found a 2- to 7-year increase in life expectancy among men who were physically active (Paffenbarger, Wing, & Hyde, 1978). Age is no barrier to regular exercise, for its benefits can occur with people in their 90s and beyond (Fiatarone et al., 1990). Until further scientific discoveries are made, the fountain of youth may be as simple as becoming and remaining physically active!

What are the benefits of regular exercise for health at any age?

Summary

This chapter has focused on biological changes related to aging processes. Although there are tales of fantastically long lives in far distant times or places, current scientific evidence suggests that the life span, or maximum amount of time an individual can live, is fixed. Dramatic changes have occurred in the past century, however, in life expectancy. Biological aging is a process that begins after sexual maturation and continues throughout life. Although scientists have proposed various theories about why we grow old, no single answer has fully explained the reasons. Death is not necessarily related to aging, as people can die from various causes at any age (i.e., accidents, infectious diseases, and even heart disease and cancer). Death in industrialized societies is associated with aging because the probability of death increases as we grow old. With aging, the efficiency of the body gradually declines; however, not all organs age at the same rate in any given individual. Cosmetic and sensory changes also occur as we grow older. Chronic diseases (e.g., arthritis, diabetes, and heart disease) increase with age and can produce disabilities among many older people. Such diseases are not part of normal aging, and not every older person is equally affected.

Within the past decade or so, the effects of chronological age have been examined more carefully. What we have generally assumed to be "normal aging" turns out to be associated with environment, lifestyle, and diseases that are related to or change with aging. Thus, many physical changes in later life are not directly caused by aging itself but rather by processes which may change with age but are not intrinsic parts of normal aging. Increasingly, researchers are becoming aware of the distinction between *normal aging* and *usual aging.*

Normal aging thus describes those events that are inevitable as we grow older. *Usual aging,* in contrast, is a more statistical definition or average: what many people do or experience as they grow older *but* which are not part of our inevitable fate as we age. For example, many of us think of arthritis as part of "normal" aging. But many people grow old without ever developing this disease. Arthritis thus is "usual" but not "normal" aging. The simple differentiation between usual and normal aging is ushering in a paradigmatic shift in gerontology with implications for every discipline and for the older population now and in years to come. It has spurred the search for "healthy aging." A major factor in healthy aging is regular exercise. One of the major challenges confronting aging researchers in the twenty-first century is to distinguish processes that are inextricably tied to growing old from aging-associated processes and diseases that some, but not all, people experience as they grow old.

Key Points

1. All organisms have a maximum lifespan, or ultimate age that a specific species can apparently reach that has not changed since ancient times. What has changed is life expectancy, or the average number of years at birth a person can expect to live.

2. Aging is not one event but a process that occurs at different rates within and among individuals and is related to socioeconomic factors, nutrition, exercise, lifestyle, exposure to industrial hazards and pollution, plus genetic factors.

3. We can group theories of biological aging in many ways. One common way of subdividing them is as program theories and damage or "wear and tear" theories.

4. Program theories are based on the idea of built-in obsolescence: nothing works perfectly or lasts forever and a "biological clock" of aging is programmed into each of the body's cells.

5. Damage or wear and tear theories are based on the idea that cells or organs are unable to repair themselves as they age.

6. Available evidence does not support the impression that modern medicine has lengthened the life span, for, as nearly as we know, the life span has remained relatively unchanged for hundreds of thousands of years.

7. Although no two people—even identical twins—necessarily age at the same rate, there are gradual declines in the efficiency of the human body, and not all organs age at the same rate in any given individual. Cosmetic and sensory changes also occur as we grow older.

8. Not all these changes are normal aging, however. Rather, they may result from disease processes.

9. One normal age change universal to women is menopause, or the cessation of menses. There is no exact equivalent of menopause among men, for at least some if not all males retain their reproductive capacity throughout their lives.

10. Patterns of both acute and chronic diseases vary by age with some chronic conditions, such as arthritis, hypertension, and heart disease.

11. Chronic diseases vary not only by age but by gender, race, and socioeconomic status.

12. Heart disease is more common in men, but male-female differences in the prevalence of heart disease may be partially socially constructed; women—especially younger women—with symptoms of heart attack are less likely to be diagnosed correctly.

13. Potentially serious chronic diseases with the highest prevalence among whites are (in rank order): (1) arthritis, (2) hypertension (high blood pressure), and (3) heart disease. Among African Americans, the prevalence (in rank order) is (1) hypertension, (2) arthritis, and (3) heart disease.

14. Minority status is also associated with higher rates of all illnesses, as members of minority groups are more likely to be living at or below the poverty level.

15. Compared with non-Latino/Latina whites, Latinos/Latinas have higher rates of high blood pressure, diabetes, and lung cancer.

16. Chronic conditions are a major cause of functional disabilities that limit ability to perform activities of daily living (ADLs) and instrumental activities of daily living (IADLs).

17. Defying stereotypes that old age is always synonymous with increasing decline and disability, the rate of later life disability has recently declined sharply and illness and disabilities among members of the baby boom and baby bust generations in old age may be very different from that of elders today.

18. Most Americans aged 65 or over rate their health as good to excellent, offering a sharp contradiction to stereotypes of the elderly as dominated by concerns with poor health.

19. Regular exercise increases the efficiency of the body and can extend life expectancy.

Discussion Questions

1. Life expectancy at birth in the United States varies by gender. Today, deaths from all three leading causes of death—heart disease, cancer, and stroke—are higher for men than for women. It appears that females have a biological advantage over males from the beginning of life; for example, they are less likely to die in the first month of life. Is the greater life expectancy of females due entirely to biologically based differences between males and female? What social and cultural factors might explain the greater gap between male and female life expectancy today compared with 1900?

2. Explain why health is a social as well as a biological and physical issue.

3. AIDS is an exception to the historical decline in infectious illnesses. What social factors may explain the prevalence of HIV infection among those aged 50 and over?

4. Jane Smith, aged 45, is a recently divorced mother of two children, both of whom are in college. Prior to the birth of her children, she had been employed as an executive in a large corporation. She now plans to resume her career and

hopes to have an active social life, perhaps even remarry. She is, however, concerned that her physical appearance—a middle-aged woman with noticeable wrinkling and graying hair—will be a handicap in both her professional and personal life. She is aware that film stars, such as Cher, Joan Collins, and others have maintained a youthful appearance through plastic surgery. Although such surgery is expensive, she has decided to have a face-lift. Her children think this is ridiculous and a waste of money. What do you think? Justify your answer.

5. Would your view toward maintaining a youthful appearance be different if John Smith, Jane Smith's former husband, who is now growing very bald, decided to have a hair transplant in order to look more youthful? Is there a double standard of aging today?

6. Who benefits most from the emphasis on maintaining a youthful appearance—the recipient, the cosmetic industry, health care professionals, manufacturers of exercise equipment, or others? Explain.

Films and Videos

Age Is No Barrier (video; 25 minutes; available from Filmmakers Library, 124 E. 40th Street, New York, NY 10016; *www.filmakers.com*).

A National Film Board of Canada production, featuring a senior gymnastics team made up of men and women age 55 to 77, who demonstrate the benefits of an active lifestyle.

Death by Design (video; 75 minutes; available from First Run Features, 153 Waverly Place, New York, NY 10004; *www.firstrunfeatures.com*).

A trip through the invisible world of cells, using a variety of metaphors to understand cellular life and death.

I Never Planned on This (video; 46 minutes; available from Filmmakers Library, 124 E. 40th Street, New York, NY 10016; *www.filmakers.com*).

A useful Canadian Broadcasting Corporation video that examines normal healthy aging as part of a biological process beginning at birth; experts include geriatrician John Rowe, M.D.

Old Wives' Tales (video; 40 minutes; available from Filmmakers Library, 124 E. 40th Street, New York, NY 10016; *www.filmakers.com*).

Filmed in Great Britain, this video raises the issue of postmenopausal motherhood via fertility treatments and the question of why older fathers but not older mothers are accepted as normal.

Stealing Time: The New Science of Aging (3 videos; approximately 60 minutes each; available from PBS Video, 1320 Braddock Place, Alexandria, VA 22314-1698; *www.pbs.org*).

"A Quest for Immortality," "Turning Back the Clock" and "Mastering the Mind" present cutting-edge information on aging.

Woman on Fire: Menopause Stories (video; 90 minutes; available from Filmmakers Library, 124 E. 40th Street, New York, NY 10016; *www.filmakers.com*)

Interviews with menopausal women from different cultural backgrounds; animated sequences and recollections of early memories by women explore the transitions of "the change."

Internet Resources

http://www.afar.org

The American Federation for Aging Research provides information on biomedical research, health and life span, and related topics.

http://www.cms.gov

The link for the U.S. Centers for Medicare and Medicaid Services (formerly the Health Care Financing Administration) and the source for information on Medicaid and Medicare statistics, data, laws, regulations, and so forth.

http://www.health.gov

Useful information and links to topics and research on disabilities and managed care; this site is maintained by the U.S. Department of Health and Human Services.

Research Article

Wray, L. A., & Blaum, C. S. (2001). Explaining the role of sex on disability: A population-based study. *The Gerontologist, 41,* 499–510.

This article explores the role of sex on disability and the relative contribution of disease, impairments and demographic and social characteristics on ADLs, mobility and strength.

Supplemental Readings

Charmaz, K. (1991). *Good Days, Bad Days: The Self in Chronic Illness and Time.* New Brunswick, NJ: Rutgers University Press.

Examines how coping with chronic illness reshapes an individual's life and sense of time.

Hayflick, L. (1994). *How and Why We Age*. New York: Ballantine Books.

A very readable introduction to what is known—and not known—about the aging process, including biological changes, life expectancy, and normal versus usual aging.

Strauss, A. L. (1997). Chronic illness. In C. L. Wiener and A. L. Strauss (eds.), *Where Medicine Fails*. New Brunswick, NJ: Transaction Books, pp. 11–24.

An outstanding sociological analysis of the social impact of chronic illness, including coping with the crises associated with some chronic diseases, symptom management, and everyday living.

Waldron, I. (1990). What do we know about causes of sex differences in mortality? A review of the literature. In P. Conrad and R. Kern (eds.), *The Sociology of Health and Illness*. New York: St. Martin's Press, pp. 45–57.

An excellent and still timely review of gender differences in life expectancy. ✦

Chapter 6

Personality, Adult Development, and Cognition

Introduction

> "You are old, Father William," the young man said,
>   "And your hair has become very white;
>   Yet you incessantly stand on your head—
>   Do you think at your age it is right?"
>
> "In my youth," Father William replied to his son,
>   "I feared it might injure the brain;
>   But now that I am perfectly sure I have none,
>   Why, I do it again and again."
>
> —Lewis Carroll, *Alice in Wonderland*

D*o adults, like Father William in the above poem, change their behavioral patterns and ways of thinking as they age? Do memory and intelligence change with age? Or are personalities and thinking patterns fixed early in childhood? Is everyone born with innate predispositions and personality, or is each of us born as a* tabula rasa *(from the Latin, meaning "blank slate") waiting to be filled with experiences and information that ultimately shape what we become? How do memory and intelligence change as we age?*

These are some of the questions explored by social gerontologists from disciplines such as psychoanalysis, psychology and psychiatry, sociology, and anthropology. The approach used by a particular discipline shapes the theories, research, and arguments of that field of study. For example, the concept of "adult development"—one of the topics in this chapter—has been defined in various ways by physicians, psychologists, sociologists, and by elders themselves. Certain approaches become more popular than others, filter into other professional fields, and have specific implications for the ways that the life circumstances, intellectual functioning, and personalities of older people are eventually viewed by the wider society. These approaches also can influence social policies dealing with issues of later life.

This chapter looks at psychosocial development and cognition in midlife and old age. Part of the focus is on adult socialization and the self as well as psychological theories of adult development. The chapter also examines changes in cognitive functioning, including memory and intelligence. As you read, think about the extent to which both theories and results from empirical studies support or challenge common stereotypes of old age. Look at whether the various theoretical perspectives presented are supported or contradicted by empirical studies.

Adult Socialization

Human behavior does not occur automatically but is learned through *socialization*, the process by which we learn to behave in a given society and develop a sense of self. Regardless of the society, basic to the process of socialization are *social norms* or spoken and unspoken rules and guidelines for conduct. Through the process of socialization, we all internalize norms that make social behavior predictable and ensure social order. Although socialization is an integral part of childhood, it is also a lifelong process that ends only when we die.

Norms are enforced by *sanctions*, or the reactions of others that convey approval or disapproval of behaviors. Norms may be either *prescriptive* (guidelines for acceptable behavior) or *proscriptive* (guidelines for unacceptable behavior). Some norms are more important than others and may become laws. For example, "Thou shalt not kill" has much greater weight, reflected in legal sanctions against murder and manslaughter, than norms for correct manners, such as "Don't dunk your doughnut in the coffee." Consider a second example. In adulthood, the most prevalent American cultural norm is to marry prior to bearing children. There is no law, however, requiring people to marry first; indeed, almost one-third of the children born in 1998 were born to unmarried mothers (Statistical Abstract of the U.S., 2000). Nevertheless, although there are no direct formalized sanctions against breaching the normative arrangement of "marriage first, then children," indirect negative sanctions are often evoked against both individuals who decide to have children outside of marriage and their offspring. Withdrawal of economic support by the father or by welfare programs (the recent legal changes regarding length of eligibility for Aid for Families with Dependent Children is one example of the latter), stigmatization of a child or children as illegitimate, and social disapproval by friends, family members, or religious groups are a few examples of informal negative sanctions.

Interestingly, however, unlike this "married with children" example, it is much more difficult to come up with a social gerontological example to point out explicit normative guidelines of life events, and herein lies an important point. The very fact that it is difficult to give an overall illustration of normative conduct in old age serves as an excellent introduction to the topic of adult socialization and its relationship to theories of adult development and successful aging.

Age Norms, Age Status, and Age Grading

As you will recall from earlier chapters, chronological age is one of the social constructs used to set normative standards of behavior, including one's own conduct as well as what one can anticipate or expect from others. Because norms are both required for social order and constructed from individual needs and social concerns, age norms are necessary social results of biological and psycho-social development but often depend on social arrangements. All societies have some system of age-status, or age-grading, within the social order. As a result, rights, expectations, responsibilities, and rewards are stratified (distributed) among people of different groups according to age (Neugarten & Moore, 1968). As people grow older, they leave old roles and take on new ones appropriate for their age. For example, a typical chain of events is that we assume various childhood roles (and the statuses accompanied with those roles) then adult roles. As adults, typical roles include worker, parent, grandparent, and perhaps great-grandparent.

In previous eras in the United States, transitions from one age status to the next were fairly clear-cut. Puberty, for instance, marked the transitional point of adulthood after which all individuals had the same rights and responsibilities. The same holds true with simple societies today. In American society today, however, people move from the dependent status and roles of childhood into another dependent status and set of roles: adolescence. Another transition occurs when individuals move from adolescence to young adulthood at around age 18 to 21. For example, laws require males to register for selective service at age 18, enable young adults to vote at age 18, and allow them to drink alcoholic beverages in most states at age 21. However, the transition into middle age is less clearly marked.

Does middle age occur when one's offspring leave home? If so, then what of adults who have their first child when they are in their late thirties or their early forties as compared with other adults of the same age who begin parenting a decade earlier? Look at a 43-year-old woman whose last child marries and leaves home, another who becomes a grandparent at age 43, and still another who has just given birth to her first child. Comparing these three women, who is "middle-aged" and what are the markers? More cues than chronological age and the occurrence of a specific life event are needed to announce midlife transitions and norms for middle age. Furthermore, what influence does life expectancy have on definitions of middle age?

Table 6-1 Popular Views: When Do People Become Old? (Percentage Distribution of Responses in a 1994 Survey)		
Age at Which the Average Person Becomes Old		
	Average Man	**Average Woman**
Under 40	2%	2%
40–49	5	7
50–59	14	16
60–69	35	31
70–79	24	22
80+	5	6
Other responses*	15	17
Total	100%	100%

*Other responses included "never," "it depends/event" and "not sure."
Source: K. Speas and B. Obenshain (1995). *AARP Images of Aging in America*, Final Report. Copyright © 1995, AARP. Chapel Hill, NC: FGI Integrated Marketing. Reprinted by permission.

Even more difficult to determine are age norms for the elderly. A common belief is that old age begins at age 65—the age at which people currently become eligible for Medicare and full retirement benefits from Social Security. There is, of course, nothing magical about age 65; we don't wake on the morning of our 65th birthday to find that we have suddenly become "elderly" overnight. Age 65 is a socially constructed marker that, as you may recall from Chapter 1, was established by the German Chancellor Bismarck in the late nineteenth century as the point at which German workers became eligible for a pension. As you can see from Table 6-1, the most commonly named age group at which one becomes old is the 60s. There were differences in responses, however; Latinos, for example, tended to perceive women as becoming old at 55 and men at 57. African Americans defined women as old at 59, men at 51. Whites named age 63 as the point when both men and women become old.

Despite the fuzziness of age-grades and norms for behavior in later life, it is inaccurate to conclude that old age represents a state of normlessness. The average age at retirement for all Americans is about 63, yet recent legislative changes to the Social Security act allow people to collect their full entitlement to Social Security at age 65 without penalty for continued employment. Others choose to retire when in their 50s, some continue to work in their 70s or later, and still others start second careers or decide to return to college or university for a degree after their official retirement. To what extent will legislative changes alter current norms for retirement and behavioral expectations?

Not only is age at retirement shifting but life expectancy is increasing. Clearly retirement as a significant marker of "old age" is changing, and few, if any, universal social norms exist about how the remainder of one's life after retirement should be spent. As people age in complex industrialized societies such as ours, age-grades begin to grow rapidly among the elderly as a result of the variety of their life experiences, interests, orientations, and service needs (Atchley, 1995a: 34). The importance of age-grades is neither their rigidity nor their durability. Rather, age-grades need to be sufficiently flexible to reflect heterogeneity and diversity yet to serve as guideposts for the appropriate conduct that makes our social worlds predictable.

Self-Concept and Self-Esteem

The *self-concept* is the picture or image a person has of herself or himself and includes statuses, social roles, body image, personality traits, and self-evaluation or self-esteem. There are some changes in self-concept that occur as we grow older; the 5-year-old does not think of himself as a college student; the 20-year-old college student does not think of herself as a retiree; and so forth. Bodily changes also occur that affect one's self-concept; the 50-year-old basketball player is likely to make fewer baskets than a 20-year old player. But in other areas, such as personality, continuity rather than change is the rule (McCrae, 2001).

The Looking-Glass Self

Does aging affect the image that we have of ourselves? Does it affect the way we feel about ourselves? You may be surprised to learn that at least some aspects of an individual's self-concept appear to be continuous throughout the life course. Self-esteem is rooted in our self-concept—the long-standing beliefs that we have about ourselves. Charles Horton Cooley proposed that people gain a sense of themselves and their self-concepts through the *looking-glass self* (Cooley, 1902/ 1964). Briefly, this idea proposes that we see ourselves as we think others see us and judge ourselves in the way we think others judge us. We do not blindly accept everything we believe others think, however. We tend to accept the reactions of others that reinforce our identity and reject those that do not. As a result we develop feelings about ourselves, such as pride, courage, loathing, and other self-views.

The 'I' and the 'Me'

George Herbert Mead, building on Cooley's idea of how the self develops, hypothesized that the self develops over time through social experience. According to Mead, people learn, primarily through language, to hold the attitudes of others. Mead viewed the self as having two parts. The part that he termed the *I* is spontaneous and initiates social action.

The other part, the *me*, responds to the actions of others. Hence the *self* is formed—the "I" and "me" united—through interaction with others. Each of us internalizes other people's responses to us and thinks about and acts upon these responses. A central part of our self-concept is thus formed by parents, friends and peers, role models, and lovers, as well as by the cultural norms and expectations of the society in which we live. The experiences of people who have been in long-term solitary confinement and those of so-called "feral children" who have no involvement with others have shown how much our notions of ourselves are formed by social interaction. Through continued social experience we develop a sense of self and our relationships with others in the social environment. The self is therefore a dynamic social product, for nobody acts in a vacuum (Mead, 1934/1962).

The Multidimensional Self

Further, everyone's self-concept is multidimensional. It includes self-identity or personality, positive images of the self ("good student," "attractive," "sexy"), negative self-images including personal characteristics and body image ("stupid," "fat," "ugly"), and the social self others see, which one hopes fits one's desired self-concept (George, 2001). The sociologist Erving Goffman (1959), using illustrations drawn from the theater, has termed the social self and its reliance on the setting for a behavioral guide as the *presentation of self.*

Will Your Self-Esteem Change in Old Age?

Part A. In the First Decade of the Twenty-First Century . . .

The following questions tap your self-concept and self-esteem. Think of how you feel about your-self right now. As you answer each question, you may find it helpful to record your answer to each question before going on to the second part.

1. Are you content with yourself?

2. How satisfied are you with your physical appearance?

3. Who are the people that you count on, and who counts on you?

4. What kinds of situations do you find uncomfortable and try to avoid? Why?

5. How do you think others perceive you as a person?

6. Does it match how you think of yourself?

In the second part of the exercise, imagine yourself as old. Now that you have taken some time to think about the questions in Part A of this exercise, combine the following situations and circumstances to the current thoughts that you have about yourself. Assume that you are spending a few hours in your far distant future. As you read, try to carry the image that you currently have of yourself into the vignette, and see how it compares to the futuristic glimpse of you in your late 70s in Part B.

Part B. In the Year 2050: An Afternoon in Your Old Age . . .

You retired from your full-time job 10 years ago, but you continued to work off and on after that to keep up some social contacts and supplement your income. This is no longer possible given your caregiving responsibilities for your partner, but you remain active as a volunteer in the local senior center. This afternoon, you look forward to some time to yourself, doing a few errands, and perhaps taking a long walk to enjoy the spring day. Before going out, you take one final look in the mirror and are aware that your gray hair has thinned, your neck and face seem to have a few more lines, and your figure is not what it was at 20.

As you get on the bus, several younger people dash in front to get on before you, pushing you aside in their hurry to find a seat. When you finally get on, all seats are taken, and you stand until you reach the stop near the mall. At the shopping mall, you enjoy a walk around, window-shopping, but again are pushed aside by a group of teenagers who are checking out the displays. You wonder if they even notice you. Thoughts come back to you from years ago about the elderly couple from whom you rented an apartment when you were in college. Back then you thought they looked so cute, walking arm and arm, as if they still were young and in love. The younger-you thought: "I like old people, they are so adorable, except when they whine and complain." Is this how people see you today—cute but probably a complainer?

You decide to have lunch at your favorite deli in town. At the counter, you are overlooked a few times before the clerk takes your order. You feel mildly annoyed when others who came after you are served first. You begin to wonder if you have become invisible in the eyes of the younger people surrounding you. You finish your meal and decide to have your hair cut. At the hair salon, you listen to the conversations buzzing around you. You make several attempts to start a conversation but are ignored. Despite all the work you have done, and all the experiences that you have had throughout your life, no one seems to take much stock in what you say. It's obvious in their gestures and how their eyes drift away from you in conversation. It might be because other people think you are too old to notice or to be taken seriously. You feel frustrated, for after all you are still the same person that you always have been. You think to yourself: "And now I have something else that I didn't have when I was 20 or 30: more experience and the insight of hindsight and reflection. Isn't that worth something?" You decide that you will walk home.

How did you feel on this afternoon in the future? Did your self-concept change from your answers to the questions at the start of this section? If so, how?

Self-concept has been measured empirically in two basic ways: (1) studies of personality traits or characteristics and (2) concepts and measures derived by particular researchers in specific investigations, often in open-ended interviews. Certain aspects of self-concept, such as the personality traits of introversion or extroversion, remain relatively stable throughout life. More changeable are subjective self-descriptions measured in open-ended questions. Keep in mind, however, that cohort membership, gender, life course experiences, and social and cultural trends have much more effect on self-concept than age alone.

Self-esteem, one aspect of self-concept, is the evaluative and emotive—the self-evaluative—dimension of self-concept. Self-esteem is important for well-being and social behavior; people with low self-esteem are more likely to be depressed, anxious, and conflicted in personal relationships. Results of numerous studies indicate that self-esteem either increases or declines very little in later life, and many aspects, such as achievement, success, good health, and strong interpersonal relationships, are identical for both older and younger populations (George, 2001).

As in everything else, people differ in their levels of self-esteem. If, for example, a person feels "successful" or "satisfied" or "healthy," however defined, self-esteem is likely to be high. Table 6-2 presents cross-sectional data summarizing the satisfaction of both men and women with several aspects of themselves and their lives. As you will notice from the table, both men and women feel as good about themselves today at age 65 and over as younger people do at ages 18 to 34. Nor do feelings about personal physical appearance decline among those 65 or older. It is in midlife rather than old age that both genders regard their physical appearance least positively.

Is the self ageless, as some people have suggested? The answer is yes and no. In one sense, the self is ageless because it is continuous throughout our lives, no matter what our ages or how we physically

Table 6-2	How Satisfied Are People with Themselves as They Age? (Percentage Completely or Somewhat Satisfied)									
	Women					Men				
Satisfaction	Ages 18–34	Ages 35–44	Ages 45–54	Ages 55–64	Ages 65+	Ages 18–34	Ages 35–44	Ages 45–54	Ages 55–64	Ages 65+
Feel good about myself	96%	92%	92%	96%	96%	97%	95%	95%	95%	99%
The way I look for my age	95	90	90	93	92	94	94	95	94	93
My physical appearance	88	86	79	82	93	93	90	86	93	94
My health and fitness	85	81	77	82	82	87	89	80	84	89
My relationship with spouse or significant other	85	87	85	83	63	83	83	84	84	91

Source: AARP, 2001. *Public Attitudes Toward Aging, Beauty, and Cosmetic Surgery: How Americans Really Feel About Physical Appearance.* Copyright © 2001, AARP. Washington, DC: AARP. Reprinted by permission.

change (Kaufman, 1995). Upon seeing their reflections in the mirror, some people in their eighties and nineties say that they are surprised at how old they look; they never thought of themselves as enveloped in such aged bodies. Others state that they don't feel radically different than they did when they were younger. This perception has been termed the mask of aging: "the awareness of an experiential difference between the physical processes of aging, as reflected in outward appearance, and the inner or subjective 'real self' which paradoxically remains young" (Hepworth, 1991: 93). This provides support for continuity theory, which, as you will recall from Chapter 4, is based on the assumption that people are motivated to continue to use the adaptive mechanisms they have developed throughout adulthood to diagnose situations, chart future courses, and adapt to change in later life. But the view that "the self is ageless" can also deny the importance of life experience and physical changes. As modern music composer John Cage commented:

> I now see that the body is part and parcel of the whole being. There isn't a split. . . . When I was younger, I mistreated the body because I thought the mind was what I was really dealing with. But as I get older I see that I'm dealing quite straightforwardly with the body and that I must keep it in good working order as long as I can. (quoted in Berman and Goldman, 1992: 31)

Continuity of the self is thus not agelessness but a dynamic tension between change and constancy. Andrews elaborates on this point:

> Time and time again, old people say they experience the aging process as a continuation of being themselves: their lives are ongoing. But this is not "agelessness." People see value in the years they

have lived; without them they have no history, they have no genuine self. (2000, 316)

Ageism, however, is a potent common force directed at the elderly. It is a prejudice (pre-judgment), most often negative, that stereotypes older people as valueless, poor, frail, burdensome, asexual, and powerless or domineering. On the other end of the ageist spectrum are stereotypes that the elderly are cute, adorable, or automatically wise. Ageism is unique in that the very people who practice it will become its victims if they live long enough.

Despite the tug of ageism on the old, recall that self-esteem does not seem to wane in old age; rather, it can grow stronger. The evidence on self-esteem does not fit Rose's subculture of aging argument (1962): that many older Americans have a diminished self-concept as they age, largely as a result of the emphasis on youth as a desirable attribute in American society. The self-conceptions that older people report having of themselves are thus in sharp contrast to the ways they are often regarded in our society. More important than age or ageism for feelings of low self-esteem, however, is the impact of poverty, racism, and sexism on self-concept and self-esteem.

Foundational Models of Personality and Development

Numerous theories and research on individual personality and development emphasize the importance of childhood and adolescence. Two theorists have been especially influential: Sigmund Freud (1856–1939) and Jean Piaget (1896–1980). Although their theories differ in emphasis and orientation, both offer child-centric models of human psychosocial development. Freud focused on constructing a conceptual base from which personality development could be understood. In contrast, Piaget centered on how cognitive thought processes in the human organism unfold and develop. Crucial to both perspectives is that personality and cognition are formed early in life with little change thereafter.

Both Freud's and Piaget's formulations are examples of *stage theories* of personality development. Stage theories assume that the individual develops in an orderly fashion, somewhat like the steps of a staircase where each step must be successfully mastered before moving on to the next. Otherwise the person will not develop fully.

Although neither theorist was interested in the study of later life, the legacy left by Freud and Piaget has been important both theoretically and practically, drawing attention to early childhood experience in both intellectual and emotional development. Perhaps more important, however, social gerontological theories and perspectives are better understood when seen as part of the life course—aging as a continuum. But theories of adult personality development have been slower to develop, a tacit assumption among researchers being that adult personality is stable and little change occurs after adolescence.

How We Develop: Two Child-Centric Stage Models

Generally regarded as the father of psychoanalytic theory, Austrian physician Sigmund Freud framed human development and survival as a conflict between basic instinctual drives and cultural norms. According to Freud, each of us develops in *five psychosexual stages: (1) oral; (2) anal; (3) phallic; (4) latency; and (5) genital.* Especially crucial in childhood development is the phallic or Oedipal phase between the ages of 3 and 5 when boys experience aggressive, competitive feelings toward their fathers coupled with desires to possess their mothers sexually. Fearing castration by their fathers, male children hide their hostility to them. They finally resolve the Oedipal crisis by identifying with the father to develop a "masculine" identity that rejects "feminine" attributes. Girls experience a similar crisis between the ages of 3 and 5 when they discover that they lack a penis and feel that they are castrated. As a result, females develop a sense of inferiority resolved only through the birth of a child in adulthood.

Whether male or female, each successive stage of development requires specific psychosexual mastery on the part of the individual to reach the next stage successfully. The last, or genital, stage ends at puberty when libidinal energy (sexual drive) is focused on the genitals, rather than on parental figures, and the individual crosses into adult life. By today's standards, Freud's view of females was sexist, overemphasizing biological characteristics and ignoring the role of socialization into gender roles. Freud also viewed females of all ages as distinctly flawed as a result of penis envy: characterized by vanity and a corrupt sense of social justice (Freud, 1961a).

Because of his heavy emphasis on infancy and childhood, Freud had scant interest in older people of either gender and made it clear in the early days of psychoanalysis that, due to the amount of material to be covered and increasing inflexibility of the personality associated with aging, analysis was inappropriate for those age 50 or older. Indeed, for Freud, women as young as 30 were unfit for psychoanalysis because of their psychic rigidity and unchangeability; men at the same age remained youthful and pliable (Freud, 1961b)!

A different but equally child-centered stage theory, focusing on how people intellectually adjust to the world, was proposed by Swiss psychologist Jean Piaget. Through empirical observations of his own children, Piaget, like Freud, emphasized incremental stages occurring during childhood. However, unlike Freud, he focused on *cognitive* rather than emotional development. That is, how do we as human beings go about making sense out of our surroundings and the actions of others? Piaget proposed that everyone's abilities to engage in the world are channeled in very definite and predictable ways. These include adaptation to the environment and organization of thought. *Adaptation* occurs through assimilation (i.e., the ways people make sense of incoming information and integrate this into what they already know) and accommodation (i.e., the process of changing our information to match experience of the real world). *Organization of thought* (i.e., how people put their thoughts together) changes with maturity and has four stages: (1) sensorimotor, occurring in infancy; (2) preoperational, occurring when children develop a capacity for language but are egocentric; (3) concrete operations, or the beginning of logical reasoning in childhood; and (4) formal operations, that is, the development of abstract thought and problem solving.

Rather than conceptualizing the opposition of instinctual forces and social expectations as basic to human development as did Freud, Piaget was concerned with how the processes of physical/biological maturity are tied to one's ability to think creatively and deal with social experiences.

The Discovery of Midlife and Beyond

More recently than Freud and Piaget, theorists have examined personality development as an ongoing process rather than being fixed in childhood. Various theories of adult development, assuming fixed, built-in life stages, have been proposed by psychoanalysts, psychiatrists, and psychologists. Old age is not the most recent portion of the life course to be "discovered" or defined as presenting unique issues of personality development and adaptation. What was once thought to be simply "adulthood" now is divided into early, middle, and late periods (somewhat like history). Most recently, "midlife" or "middle age" has been delineated in both popular and scholarly articles, focusing on such topics as "midlife crisis," "male menopause," "women at midlife," and so forth. Thus, life span developmental psychology focuses on the changes associated with different periods of life and the challenges each stage presents.

The following sections of this chapter review various theories and research evidence about personality development and change in midlife and old age. As you read the following sections, think about the similarities and differences in the theoretical perspectives presented. The majority of these formulations were developed based on the lives of white, middle-class men and most often were cross-sectional rather than longitudinal. How applicable are these theories to women, different racial and ethnic groups, or different social classes? To what extent do they present a static view of old age, untouched by the effect of the birth cohort in which people are born? What social changes affecting the lives of older people have modified these formulations and in what ways?

Introversion in Later Life

Carl Jung, a Swiss psychoanalyst and former student of Freud, was the first psychoanalytic theorist to examine ego and personality development as processes continuing into adulthood rather than becoming relatively fixed during childhood. Like Freud, his theories were based on reflection, personal observations, and clinical experience with small numbers of patients rather than on large-scale studies that included empirical measures of satisfaction, health, or well-being. Jung focused on what he termed the *extroversion of youth* and the increasing *introversion of midlife and old age.* Although he did not deny the importance of sexuality in psychic life, Jung rejected the notion of sexuality as the sole psychic power guiding ego development.

In his 1933 volume, *Modern Man in Search of a Soul,* Jung described a transition from youth to the second period of life, occurring between the ages of 35 and 40, when slow but significant changes in the human psyche begin to happen. During this second period, individual personality traits that disappeared in childhood reemerge and personal convictions and principles grow more fixed. The energies of youthful extroversion with its focus on the social world are replaced naturally by introversion, or the psychological process of drawing inward and becoming more self-preoccupied. In Jung's formulation, a stark division between the preoccupations of youth and the second part of life is both desirable and necessary, for life is qualitatively different as we age. Rather than expanding interests and worldly involvement, the developmental tasks of later life center on a sense of interiority and contraction. In Jung's words,

> . . . we cannot live the afternoon of life according to the programme of life's morning—for what was great in the morning will be little at evening, and what in the morning was true will at evening have become a lie. I have given psychological treatment to too many people of advancing years, and have looked too often into the secret chambers of their souls, not to be moved by this fundamental truth. . . . Aging people should know that their lives are not mounting and unfolding, but that an inexorable inner process forces the contraction of life. For a young person it is almost a sin—and certainly a danger—to be too much occupied with himself; but for the aging person it is a duty and a necessity to give serious attention to himself. After having lavished its light upon the world, the sun withdraws its rays in order to illumine itself. Instead of doing likewise, many old people prefer to be hypochondriacs, niggards, doctrinaires, applauders of the past or eternal

adolescents—all lamentable substitutes for the illumination of the self, but inevitable consequences of the delusion that the second half of life must be governed by the principles of the first. (1933: 125)

Jung's view of midlife and old age, made almost three-quarters of a century ago, emphasize both self-preoccupation and self-discovery as age-appropriate developmental tasks. His reflections were based primarily upon clinical observations of a relatively affluent, white, middle-aged and older clientele. To what extent has social change altered the context in which Jung made his formulations? Would his theory hold true today among different birth cohorts? Different social classes? Men versus women? Diverse racial and ethnic groups? If so, how?

Eight Stages of Life and Generativity

Erik Erikson, expanding upon both Freudian and Jungian formulations of ego development, was concerned with personality development throughout the life course. Erikson's model comprises *eight developmental stages* stretching from birth to death. Each stage poses a crisis in which the individual's ego (or sense of self) is threatened. For the individual to progress from one developmental stage to the next, he or she must successfully deal with the current crisis period. As conflicts emerge through the various stages, healthy (successful) resolution leads to an increased sense of inner unity (1959: 51). The inability to do so retards further development of one's full human potential.

Like Freud, Erikson was more concerned with male development throughout the life course. Also, like Freud's, his formulation may be criticized as sexist by contemporary standards. Erikson's theory of female development was based primarily on observations of the play among 10- to 12-year-old boys and girls. Noting that the boys tended to erect towers, depict busy street scenes, and be concerned with action while girls were more likely to create enclosed peaceful scenes and static figures, he concluded that the essence of female identity development involves inner space—a uterus-based identity centered on anticipation and realization of motherhood. Problems in later life development for females occur when their potential for this fulfillment of inner space is not met. As a result, females were viewed by Erikson as characterized by warmth, tenderness, nurturance, and compassion; males, by activity and creativity.

Table 6-3 summarizes the eight stages of development proposed by Erikson, the life stage conflicts to be resolved, and the successful resolution or skill to be developed if the stage is to be successfully completed. Of particular interest to adult and late life development are the last two stages: Stage 7, *generativity versus stagnation*, involving the desire to become a caring and productive member of society versus feelings of inertia and inactivity, and Stage 8, beginning in midlife and declining in old age as one enters the final stage of life, *integrity versus despair.*

Table 6-3	Erikson's Stages of Development	
Stage	**Life Stage Conflict**	**Strengths/Basic Virtues***
Stage 1	Trust vs. Basic Mistrust	Drive and Hope
Stage 2	Autonomy vs. Shame and Doubt	Self-Control and Willpower
Stage 3	Initiative vs. Guilt	Purpose
Stage 4	Industry vs. Inferiority	Competence
Stage 5	Identity vs. Role Confusion	Devotion and Fidelity
Stage 6	Intimacy vs. Isolation	Affiliation and Love
Stage 7	Generativity vs. Stagnation	Production and Care
Stage 8	Ego Integrity vs. Despair	Renunciation and Wisdom

*After constructing the eight psychosocial stages of human development, Erikson set out to formulate a blueprint of strengths that he saw to be essential to each life stage and to social institutions. Such strengths come into being only if the lasting outcome of a particular stage is favorable.
Source: Adapted from Erikson, Erik H. 1950, 1963. *Childhood and Society* (Second Edition). New York: Norton.

In this last stage of life, people become increasingly aware of their own mortality and either come to terms with the lives they have led as both worthwhile and inevitable or become despondent and anxious. Yet, the stage of integrity versus despair, while intuitively appealing, is very long—especially given current life expectancy. It does not take account of the many changes that can occur from age 60 up to advanced ages of 80 or 100—indeed a long time to reflect upon one's past life achievements or failures!

In his own old age, Erikson modified his views about the last stage of life to include *grand-generativity*—maintaining vital involvement and a sense of autonomy as well as reviewing one's own past years of responsibility for nurturing the next generation and integrating earlier life experiences:

> The task of the elder is not simply to reaffirm life, to reinforce psychosocial strengths by maintaining meaningful involvement with people and activities. The task of the elder also includes coming to accept the inevitability of death's enforced leavetaking. (Erikson, Erikson, & Kivnick, 1994: 63)

To what extent does empirical evidence indicate that generativity peaks in midlife and progressively declines in later life? One study, examining age differences in generativity among three groups—young, middle-aged, and older adults—found that young adults (22–27 years old) showed the lowest levels of generativity. Middle-aged adults (37–42 years old) scored higher than young adults on generativity, but not higher than older adults (aged 67–72). Not only does generativity appear to be more characteristic of midlife and old age than young adulthood, but generativity also does not necessarily decline in old age. Of interest is the fact that generativity was positively associated with life satisfaction, emphasizing the importance of a sense of concern with nurturance and caring for others, including younger generations in both midlife and old age (McAdams, de St. Aubin, & Logan, 1993).

Spirituality and Gerotranscendence

In recent years, *spirituality* has become an increasingly popular topic. Although similarities exist between the many definitions of spirituality and religion, scholars have built upon the work of Jung and Erikson to expand the definition of spirituality more broadly than religious belief. Spirituality thus refers to a personal journey for self-knowledge and personal growth (Wink, 1999; Zinnbauer et al., 1997; Chaffers, 1994). One such definition distinguishing it from religion states that spirituality is a basic source of identity, individuality, and individual creative powers that "awakens us to the essence and greater potential of life as a self-transformative journey" (Chaffers, 1994: 6).

Many years ago, Jung suggested that we are all fated to search for wholeness and the integration of opposing forces in our personalities—an illumination of the self—especially as we age. Although Erikson's model of adult development does not focus on spirituality, his focus on ego integrity, or the acceptance of the inevitability of one's life and kinship with others, implies that healthy personality development in later life involves finding a sense of harmony with the universe. As one woman expressed it: "Spirituality for me has nothing to do with organized religion. It's the way a person lives. . . . That to me is spirituality" (Mattis, 2000: Internet download).

The notion that spirituality is being in touch with the inner self was clearly stated by another woman: "Lately [spirituality] means to me—I sort of developed this understanding that I'm in harmony with nature, and the universe. And, that sort of answers any questions I have when I'm confused about a situation, and not knowing what to do. I think about what's natural in terms of how the universe is run" (Mattis, 2000).

On the basis of work by Erikson, subsequent theorists have proposed a theory of *gerotranscendence,* or a distinctive age-related path toward spirituality in which older adults develop a sense of interconnection between themselves and others and between life and death to make sense of the world (Tornstam, 1999; Fowler, 1981). Yet, the relationship between spirituality and aging remains debatable. Some people may develop a sense of gerotranscendence (Tornstam, 1999), others may rely on religious practices, and still others will not be concerned with a sense of the cosmic at all (see Wink, 1999, for a review). Research on spirituality as a stage in adult personality development is growing, but is still in its infancy.

Life Review in Late Life

Psychiatrist Robert Butler's (1963) theory of the *life review* offers still another view of late life psychosocial development. Butler proposed that the life review process is a naturally occurring universal normative mechanism, prompted by the biological fact of approaching death along with other situations of circumstance, such as retirement and death of significant others. As people become more aware of the inevitability of their own death in the not too distant future, they also take a cumulative look back at their previous life experiences. This personality reorganization is characterized by reminiscence that can be gratifying. Conversely, life review can lead to anxiety, depression, despair, and even suicide, depending on the amount and degree of regret experienced by the individual.

To the degree that an individual takes an inventory of past feelings and behaviors and reexamines old conflicts, Butler's life review and Erikson's final stage of human psychosocial development (ego integrity versus despair) are similar. According to Butler (1963), the life review process is accentuated by retirement because this event provides the opportunity for self-reflection in the absence of the customary "defensive operations" of the world of work. Moreover, although the life review process is a universal and normative mechanism of old age, it can also be experienced by younger people when faced with close or inevitable prospects of impending death. Thus, awareness of impending death is the precipitating factor for undertaking a life review at any age.

Although the concept of life review has become widely accepted, questions about its universality and appropriateness have been raised. How important really is the life review? And is the life review the single most important task of later life? Should everyone who is old be encouraged to spend time performing a life review? To determine whether life review is a naturally occurring and universal process, the Georgia Centenarian Study (initiated in 1988 to investigate how biological, psychological, and social factors contribute to the adaptation to old age among the very old) examined the importance of life review as a process (Merriam, 1995). Assumptions about the process of life review, such as its universality, its relationship to old age, and whether awareness of death was a major factor influencing a person to conduct a life review, were tested among 105 centenarians, 94 people in their eighties, and 90 people in their sixties (Merriam, 1995).

The findings challenged many of the fundamental assumptions of Butler's life review hypothesis. First, close to half of all respondents in each age cohort reported that they have not yet reviewed their lives, suggesting that the life review process is neither universal nor specific to old age. Second, the motivations and rationales of those respondents who conducted a life review varied. Some indicated that they were prompted to review their lives due to major life changes, such as the death of a spouse or other familial changes. Others observed that they were influenced by factors such as important life decisions, by thinking about someone from the past, or by prayer. Still other respondents commented that performing a life review had been a life-long, ongoing process rather than confined to old age.

Furthermore, the centenarians—those respondents statistically most at risk of dying in the near future—were no more likely to engage in a life review than those in younger age cohorts. Indeed, results indicated that death was not even mentioned by any of the respondents as a factor prompting life review. Nor did conducting a life review seem related to satisfaction with past life.

The Seasons of Life Lead to Anxiety and Loss

In contrast to Erikson, who focused on stages of ego development, psychologist Daniel Levinson and his associates (1978) examined developmental changes in terms of life structures or underlying characteristics of a person's life during a particular time period. Levinson's research on adult personality development, which began in the late 1960s, was prompted by two major premises. First, he argued that adult life could not be accounted for by historical, cultural, and social organizational influences alone. Second, he pointed out that knowledge on adult development across disciplinary lines does indeed exist (such as in biology and the social sciences) but is fragmented. Accordingly, rather than focusing on infants or children, Levinson and his associates examined biographical data for a small sample of 40 middle-aged men, born between the years of 1923 and 1934 and representing diverse status characteristics, such as social class, race, ethnicity and religion, education, and marital status. The decision to focus initially on men was guided at least in part by the small sample size.

Using the metaphor of *seasons of life*, he proposed that certain relatively stable and culturally defined segments of the total life cycle evolve that represent distinct parts of a person's life. Like the seasons of weather, each season of life builds upon the previous one to create a greater whole. Levinson identified four seasons or what he termed *eras*, each lasting about 20 years and separated by transitions of about five years each, generally occurring as people perceive changes in themselves or when events such as childbirth or retirement create new roles and relationships.

The seasons of life include the following: (1) Childhood to the end of adolescence (age 0–22); (2) early adulthood (ages 17–45); (3) middle age (40–65); and (4) late adulthood (60 and over). You will note that each season overlaps another at transitional points in the developmental trajectory.

As in Erikson's formulation, middle adulthood (age 40 to 65) is characterized by mentorship and professional peak effectiveness. In late adulthood (age 60 on), anxieties about aging and loss of power and status become predominant. Unlike Erikson, Levinson emphasizes the interaction between the individual and the environment. To develop successfully as an adult, one must adjust both to changing personal circumstances and to the changing social world, creating a satisfactory balance between the two.

Of all the models discussed, this is the most explicit in linking each season or era to specific ages. As you think about this model, consider the extent to which social changes experienced by different birth cohorts can alter the model of eras linked to specific ages. Would you expect differences by social class, race and ethnicity, gender, and other social characteristics?

Androgyny as a Personality Characteristic

Another model of adult personality development involves the concept of androgyny. The word *androgyny* (from the ancient Greek *andro*, meaning "male," and *gyne*, meaning "female") refers to gender-typed personality characteristics and differs from biological characterizations of male or female (Taylor & Hall, 1982). Androgyny thus describes the balance of typically masculine and feminine behaviors in both biological sexes throughout the life course (Richmond-Abbott, 1992).

According to Jung, universal personality archetypes or patterns evolve as we grow older. Throughout our lives, all of us have the potential to experience and express both masculine (the *animus*) and feminine (the *anima*) dimensions within our personality structures. Based on his clinical experience, Jung (1959) proposed that, as people grow older, personality archetypes change. Men develop a sense of their female personality traits and females their masculine personality traits. The concept of androgyny echoes Jung's formulation of *animus* and *anima*.

Psychologists, such as David Gutmann, have been especially interested in the degree to which we incorporate previously suppressed gender traits of the opposite sex into our personalities as we grow older and are freed from the "parental imperative." When children have grown and no longer require emotional and financial security from their parents, men and women are free to explore and adapt gender attributes that were repressed or suppressed while they were involved in active parenting (Gutmann, 1994; 1997).

According to this view, women become more instrumentally- or task-oriented, more aggressive, and more assertive: features most commonly and culturally associated with masculine role behavior. In turn, men become more expressive, self-disclosing, nurturing, and even more passive, behaviors usually associated with feminine gender roles. Older individuals are now able to express more openly behavioral and personality characteristics associated with the opposite gender.

To what extent does empirical evidence support, or refute, the concept of androgyny as people grow old? Some years ago, in a study of collective role and personality images, Neugarten and Gutmann (1968) found that such concepts do change as people age. Drawing samples from two age groups—those aged from 40 to 54 and 55 to 70—respondents included both working-class and middle-class people of European ethnic descent, most of whom were married and Protestant. Respondents were presented with a black and white drawing portraying two men and two women, with one man and woman looking obviously older (in hair color and physique) than the other. This particular drawing was selected to elicit thoughts about familial roles. Results indicated that older respondents, both older men and women, saw the older women in the drawing as the familial authority figure; younger respondents viewed the older man as the familial authority figure.

Androgyny is, however, far more complex than stereotypically masculine and feminine traits because it is multidimensional. For example, Huyck, Zucker, and Angellaccio (2000), studying a middle-class, white, midwestern suburban sample of young adults paired with their same-sex midlife adult parent, found multiple styles of gender identity among both generations. In general, although having a stereotypically feminine appearance and behavior were important attributes among midlife women, they also felt free to adapt so-called masculine characteristics in varied combinations. Similarly, for midlife men a stereotypically masculine identity was anchored in being a good provider or family man; once achieved, however, they felt free to expand into other areas without feeling "unmanned." In short, adults developed varied ways of defining themselves as appropriately and securely masculine or feminine. Surprisingly, birth cohort did not affect gender identity styles. Although young adults tended to rebel against the self-identity of their same-sex parent, once married they were inclined to follow in the footsteps of their same-sex parent, adapting whatever style of gender identity their parent had established earlier (Huyck, Zucker, & Angellaccio, 2000).

A different conclusion about the significance of birth cohort was reached in Turner and Silva's (2000) study of a larger all-female sample, comprising 87 percent white and 20 percent African-American women who ranged in age from 20 to 94 with an average age of 43, most of whom were unrelated to one another. (Because of the small number in the sample, Asians and Pacific Islanders were excluded from analysis.) Members of older birth cohorts were found to be more consistent in their gender identity as feminine than members of younger birth cohorts. Younger cohorts of women incorporated more masculine characteristics in their self-concepts, suggesting a shift toward more androgynous self-definitions among the young.

Why do the findings in these studies reach different conclusions? The first study focused on white, middle-class suburban parent-child pairs, the second on mostly unrelated women from a broad array of ages and social classes, and of different racial and ethnic backgrounds. The cohort differences observed between the two studies thus is likely to have resulted from variations in sampling and research design—a significant point to keep in mind when reading any research studies and determining the extent to which they agree or disagree with one another.

Socialization also plays a role. The younger cohorts of women studied by Turner and Silva had been socialized since the feminist movement of the 1960s and were more likely to have been influenced by its ideologies than older women. Familial differences in socialization patterns may also play a role; however, no data are available to permit this comparison between the two studies. Because of the broad spectrum of gender identity styles found in studies such as those by Huyck, Turner, and their associates, Huyck and colleagues (2000: 98) have suggested that the term *androgyny* should be dropped. More useful than androgyny, they suggest, is to think of "gender expansion" among both men and women throughout the life course. That is, androgyny appears to be influenced by many factors, not simply age or stage in life.

Global Glimpses: Androgyny in Other Societies

To what extent is androgyny in later life found in other cultures? In Druz culture, for example, a unisex status emerges in later life as women become more "masculine"—intrusive and domineering—when their reclaimed aggression is no longer a threat to their young (Gutmann, 1997). A different pattern, however, exists in Central Sudan, a patriarchal society where lineage is traced through the father's family and wives move to the village of their husbands. Gender segregation is fundamental. Although their lives are patterned by life stages, females traditionally are modest and secluded. Trained in girlhood to domestic tasks, females are circumcised. Their lives are restricted from puberty to marriage while their family members investigate marriage options.

Bridehood—a stage of life from marriage through the childbearing years—is marked by public submissiveness, rigid control of sexuality by a wide network of both male and female kin, and heavy child care responsibilities. *Womanhood* (midlife) begins when a female has no small children and is able to delegate many of her duties to her daughters. At midlife she is able to participate in a wider network of women and shift from the ascribed status of bridehood to achieved statuses within the female world, including leadership and ability to travel outside the home. *Old age* is a stage in which respect from others is due but dependency on the family is higher. As Sudanese society has urbanized, numerous changes to the patterns just described have oc-

curred. For example, brides are no longer chosen by the groom's mother; and men have moved to Arab states to find work, leaving many households headed by women. These social and economic changes have created new alliances among middle-aged women who increasingly enjoy financial, educational, and social interaction opportunities hitherto unheard of in this gendered society. It is not the Sudanese old women but those in womanhood, or midlife, who have increased power in the female world and are more androgynous (Kenyon, 1994). The example of Sudanese society shows how the social organization of a society shapes both the status of middle-aged and elderly women and the extent to which they exhibit the androgynous characteristics described earlier in this section.

Does biology play a role in androgyny? Certainly there are biological differences between males and females. There are also biological changes that come about as we grow old. Both suggest hormonal parallels to androgyny. Research on a sample of premenopausal women during various phases of their menstrual cycles on a series of tasks, for example, has indicated that higher levels of estrogen correlate with higher scores on tasks that favored women, such as verbal tests, and lower levels of estrogen correlate dwith higher scores on tasks that favor men, such as spatial relations (Hampson, 1990). Testosterone levels increase in females and decrease in males as they reach old age. Estrogen levels decrease in females, but increase in males (Gutmann, 1997). The extent to which the hormonal differences or age-associated changes in either sex affect behavior, however, remains an open but intriguing question, especially because U.S. notions of masculinity and femininity are not found in all societies. As you will recall from Chapter 1, "sex is easy, one X chromosome or two about settles it. Gender is more difficult: it is the social meaning that is attached to chromosomes" (Hendricks, 2000: xiv).

Is androgynous behavior seen in other species? The answer again is yes and no. Among some nonhuman primates, such as Japanese monkeys who live in a female-bonded society, behavior is structured by age, family relationships, and power. Males disperse at adolescence. Among female Japanese monkeys, social dominance is based on access to desired resources (a stratification system not so different from ours) and maintained through kinship ties among females (McDonald-Pavelka, 1994). Age stratification also exists, but in an unexpected pattern. Although mothers rank above their daughters, younger sisters have more power than older ones. Relative status in the group is not affected by age; rather, social dominance remains the same as the monkeys grow older (McDonald-Pavelka, 1994).

Before making a leap to humans and proof or disproof for androgyny, however, several important distinctions should be made. Japanese monkey society has no real division of labor. Males are not integrated into the social group. Females do not undergo an observable menopause. Various species of nonhuman primates differ widely as well, and not all are female-bonded. Chimpanzee females, for example, disperse and form strong social bonds with their sons who remain with their mothers from birth to death. Mountain gorilla females become part of the harem of a silver-backed male and may move from one such arrangement to another. The variety of nonhuman primate behavior is a reminder of the diversity both of behavior and the aging experience.

Cognition

Cognition (from the Latin word, *cogitare*, "to think") refers to such mental processes as intelligence, learning, and memory. The ways that we all perceive, recall, reason, make decisions, solve problems, and make sense of the world around us are all cognitive processes (Smith, 1995). Does intelligence decline with aging? Is memory loss inevitable as we grow old? These are questions that psychologists studying cognitive processes among older adults have focused on during the past few decades. Two of the most common modes of studying cognition in later life are the psychometric model and the information processing model.

Intelligence and the Psychometric Model

The *psychometric model of cognition* concentrates on measuring intellectual functioning, usually through a series of standardized IQ tests. The extent to which intelligence is innate or molded by life experiences remains a long-standing nature/nurture controversy. Alfred Binet, who developed the first IQ tests in the early 1900s, defined intelligence as the abilities to judge well, to comprehend well, and to reason well. Most IQ tests measure a set of *primary mental abilities* that denote measures of intellectual competence, represented in all meaningful activities of an individual's daily life and work (Schaie, 1996b). Measures of primary mental abilities include the following: (1) numerical reasoning; (2) word fluency or the ability to use words appropriately to describe objects or events; (3) vocabulary; (4) inductive reasoning or the ability to generalize from the specific to the general; and (5) spatial orientation or the ability to orient one's self in space.

Most information on adult intelligence is based on work with IQ tests that measure two types of cognition: (1) *fluid intelligence,* the ability to devise solutions to new problems, drawing general inferences from specific observations, and (2) *crystallized intelligence,* or the knowledge and abilities that people get through education and experience. Fluid intelligence requires flexibility in thinking and reasoning. On intelligence tests, fluid intelligence is most often measured by performance tests that include spatial relations and abstract reasoning and are generally timed.

For example, if you were given three pictures of apples, one with a bite out of it, a second of a whole apple, and a third of an apple core, you would probably arrange them in sequence with the whole apple first, followed by a half-bitten apple, and lastly the apple core. The ability to define a word or to interpret a proverb, such as "a stitch in time saves nine," are illustrations of crystallized intelligence. Other, more everyday, examples of crystallized intelligence involve social judgement, such as managing conflict with a roommate or deciding how to juggle the demands of course work with a part-time job.

Whether intelligence declines with age has been controversial among psychologists. Early research using IQ tests found that older people scored much lower than younger people. A major shortcoming of these studies, however, was their use of cross-sectional studies, comparing measures across different age groups at one time point. The IQ differences observed in cross-sectional studies probably reflect cohort differences, such as educational opportunities and patterns and technological changes. Elders who were socialized in a different era, with less opportunities for education and often not subjected to frequent IQ and achievement tests in school, are less likely to perform well on standardized timed tests when compared with younger cohorts for whom testing was an annual or biennial school routine. Moreover, much of what is known about intellectual functioning is based primarily on whites; more research is needed on minority groups.

Longitudinal panel studies of intelligence, in contrast, test the same set of people several times over a period of weeks, months, or years. Unlike cross-sectional studies, longitudinal research provides the opportunity to assess changes in intellectual functioning from youth to old age. The results of such studies suggest that intelligence endures well into old age among healthy people (Rowe & Kahn, 1998; Palmore et al., 1985). Age changes in psychometric measures of intelligence have been studied most intensively in the Seattle Longitudinal Study, spanning a 35-year period (1956–1991). Study participants (both men and women born between 1889 and 1952 with an educational level ranging from zero up to and including graduate school) were drawn from numerous occupational groups including retirees (Schaie, 1996a). Although all social classes were represented, the sample was "somewhat sparse at the lowest socioeconomic levels" (Schaie, 1996a: 42). Data were collected on the so-called primary mental abilities: verbal meaning, space, reasoning, number, and ability to recall words. During the last two testings, six multiply marked abilities or factors were also assessed. Brief descriptions of these abilities are shown in Table 6-4.

Table 6-4   The Seattle Study of Adult Intelligence

Research Questions Considered

1. Does intelligence change uniformly through adulthood, or are there different life course ability patterns?
2. At what age is there a reliably detectable decrement in ability, and of what magnitude?
3. What are the patterns of generational (birth cohort) differences and of what magnitude?
4. What accounts for individual differences in age-related changes in intelligence in adulthood?
5. Can intellectual decline with increasing age be reversed by educational intervention?

Primary Mental Abilities Assessed Through Testing

Verbal Meaning
Space
Reasoning
Number Fluency
Word Fluency

Multiply Marked Abilities Assessed Through Testing

Inductive Reasoning: the ability to recognize and understand concepts and their relationships.

Spatial Orientation: the ability to visualize and manipulate spatial configurations on a number of dimensions and to perceive the relationships among objects in space.

Number Skills: the ability to understand relationships among numbers and to solve simple quantitative problems quickly and accurately.

Verbal Ability: the ability to understand concepts and put them into words.

Word Fluency: the ability to recall words easily when talking or writing.

Perceptual Speed: the ability to find and identify figures, make comparisons, and carry out simple tasks requiring visual perception with speed and accuracy.

Verbal Memory: the ability to memorize and recall meaningful language units.

Source: Schaie, K. Warner. (1996a). *Intellectual Development in Adulthood: The Seattle Longitudinal Study.* New York: Cambridge University Press: 51–53; 349–360; Schaie, K. Warner. (1996b). "Intellectual development in adulthood." In J. E. Birren and K. W. Schaie (eds.). *Handbook of the Psychology of Aging*, 4th edition. San Diego, CA: Academic Press: 266–286.

Does intelligence change as we grow older? Results from the Seattle studies indicate that, on the average, intelligence actually increases until the late 30s or early 40s and then stabilizes until people reach their mid-50s or early 60s. Although decreases do come about late in life, these declines occur in areas less important and less often used in the respondents' life experience. Individuals thus select the maintenance of certain abilities more important to them, utilizing these to compensate for losses in other areas considered less vital in their lives. They maximize strengths in specific areas of interest to them, an example of selective optimization with compensation (Baltes & Baltes, 1990), as discussed in Chapter 4.

Decreases in abilities demonstrated on such tests vary immensely from individual to individual, regardless of age. Although almost all respondents showed losses as they grew older on at least one of the abilities tested, virtually nobody showed decline in all. Even among those in their 80s or 90s, people with higher scores at initial testing maintain their advantages even after some losses.

Chronic diseases, such as heart disease, cancer, arthritis, and osteoporosis, as well as visual and hearing deficits can reduce intellectual functioning dramatically. Personality characteristics are also important. People characterized by flexibility in midlife are less likely than those who were rigid to experience intellectual decline as they grow older (Schaie, 1996b). Lower educational attainment is associated with poor performance on psychometric tests in later life (Salthouse, 1991). Stereotypes, too, influence how people perform on

Research on intelligence shows that active mental activity and additional educational training enhance intelligence in later life.

tests; if they are expected to perform poorly, they are likely to do so (Steele, 1997).

Membership in the social hierarchies of class and gender also affect psychometric measures of intelligence. Because gender roles are associated with different patterns of socialization, men and women have different performance levels of certain mental abilities throughout adulthood. On the primary mental abilities, men score better on spatial skills while women score higher on reasoning and verbal skills (Schaie, 1996b). Decreases in scores are also lower among people of higher socioeconomic status and high educational attainment, and those in creative occupations rather than highly routinized work (Schaie, 1996a; 1996b). Other factors as well account for individual age-related differences. Evidence indicates that people in long-term marriages to well-educated and intelligent spouses are less likely to show decreases in intellectual ability as they grow older. Measurement of intelligence is rarely, if ever, culture-free. It is hardly surprising that educational opportunities, job attainment, and satisfying marriages appear to enhance intelligence.

Can people be trained to make higher scores on intelligence tests in later life? Results suggest yes. Two-thirds of the people in the Seattle sample who received additional educational training in areas of inductive reasoning and spatial orientation showed significant improvement, again emphasizing the importance of familiarity with what the tests measure. Such improvement lasts. When the two-thirds who improved their scores were tested seven years later, they continued to maintain their gains while people who did not receive such training did not (Schaie, 1996a).

The psychologist Kretch is credited with saying, "He [sic] who lives by his wits dies with his wits." Certainly, educational training plus exposure to stimulating environments and participation in cultural resources play important roles in maintaining our wits—or at least our ability to do well on psychometric tests—throughout the life course. Moreover, cognitive functioning appears to be improving among older Americans; taken as a group, the elderly, especially those in their 80s, appear to have better cognitive functioning than they did a decade ago, especially among those with less than a high school education (Freedman, Aykan, & Martin, 2001).

Testing does not tell it all. Remember that Winston Churchill became the British Prime Minister at age 65 and led the United Kingdom's efforts against Hitler in World War II; Picasso, considered by many to be the greatest artist of the twentieth century, continued to paint until just before his death at age 91; and Sophocles, one of the greatest playwrights of ancient Greece, wrote plays until well into his 80s. Their performances are often described in terms of wonder, rather than as representative of a much larger but less gifted older population. The assumption that accomplishments in later life are unexpected reinforces the notion that decline is normal in old age.

Information Processing, Learning, and Memory

Although there are many theoretical approaches to studying memory, this section focuses on one: the *information processing model*. This approach to cognition is a general framework often used in studying how people both remember old information and learn new material. Most people anticipate increased inability to learn and remember with advancing age, a concern that increases among those aged 75 and over (Scogin & Prohaska, 1993). However, at any age we all forget information because it seems unimportant or we are preoccupied. Severe memory loss is not part of normal aging but rather indicates a pathological condition (see Chapter 7 for a discussion).

Despite popular belief, current research shows our capacity to remember does not decrease as we grow older. What changes are the ways that people process and retrieve information. For example, the tip-of-the-tongue phenomenon (TOT), a temporary blocking of access to a desired word, gets its name from the often-heard statement, "It's on the tip of my tongue, but I can't recall it just now." The word or words are likely to be familiar but not used very often or recently. The largest category of TOT among both young and old is proper names, such as the name of an acquaintance or a seldom-seen film star. Although the tip-of-the-tongue phenomenon seems to be age-related, it is not confined to old age. By about age 37, the TOT begins to increase and continues as we grow older. Think of the mind as a home computer with numerous programs and files stored on its hard disk. As the disk becomes fuller and fuller, the computer may slow down, taking longer to process a request for a specific file and to retrieve it. Similarly, as people grow older, the speed with which they process and retrieve information slows down.

The memory system is complex but has two major subsystems: episodic memory and generic memory. *Episodic memory* refers to the encoding, storage, and retrieval of personally experienced events. *Generic memory,* in contrast, is a repository of knowledge stored with reference to the context in which it was acquired. It encompasses a vocabulary of words and the concepts they represent along with factual knowledge and oneself. Knowing that the word *dog* is in a list to be memorized is an example of episodic memory. Knowing the meaning of the word *dog* is an illustration of generic memory.

Episodic memory also involves two other components: short-term memory and long-term memory. *Short-term memory* (sometimes called working memory) comprises a limited capacity short-term storage and processing center. The ability to remember an unfamiliar phone number while dialing it is an example of short-term memory. Short-term memory can hold about seven pieces of information for a brief time— enough time to remember the information quickly, such as when dialing a phone number. While information is in short-term memory, it may be recalled directly or converted (encoded) and sent to long-term memory where it can be retrieved later. For example, if your first date was memorable in any way, you are likely to have stored it in long-term memory. We are far less likely to store a phone number for a movie theater that we seldom go to or the shopping list for last week's groceries into long-term memory!

A variety of studies have suggested that only small changes occur with aging in the storage capacity of short-term memory (for a review on memory, see Kausler, 1994). What does slow down with aging are (1) the ways of converting or encoding information into long-term memory, and (2) the speed of retrieving information stored in long-term memory. Older adults take longer to store material into long-term memory; for example, laboratory studies have shown slower learning and recall of words among older compared with younger adults (Salthouse, 1991). But even at relatively young ages, as the tip-of-the-tongue phenomenon indicates, adults can take longer to retrieve information.

How can older—and younger—adults improve their memory functioning? Various memory improvement techniques help to organize information into more manageable pieces for better recall. One is *categorization*, a useful way to remember lists. For example, imagine that you need to buy 15 items at the supermarket. Mentally arranging the items to be purchased into categories (e.g., produce, meat, dairy, and frozen desserts) reduces the number of items to recall. You can then go to the areas where these broad categories are stored and hopefully recall what you wanted to buy.

A second technique is *chunking*, which works on the same principle as categorization and can be used to collapse large pieces of information into smaller ones. For example, long-distance phone numbers and social security numbers are usually arranged into chunks. A ten-digit long-distance phone number and a nine-digit social security number are both divided into three chunks even though the number of digits are different in the two sequences. The phone number is chunked into the area code, prefix, and number (800-555-1212) and the social security number is also divided into three sections (xxx-xx-xxxx). *Imagery techniques,* such as associating one item or a person's name with another item, and physical reminders, such as lists, are two other strategies useful in increasing memory. Table 6-5 summarizes various techniques that psychologists have found useful for people at any age who are interested in increasing their capacity to recall.

Cognitive Changes: Inevitable, Myth, or Mediated by Life Chances?

Are cognitive declines in later life the norm? Results from the longitudinal MacArthur Community Study of Successful Aging (Rowe & Kahn, 1998), focusing on patterns of change in physical and cognitive performance of persons ages 70 to 79, echo findings from the Seattle Longitudinal Study (Schaie, 1996a). Although it is widely believed that cognitive changes come about in old age, level of education rather than chronological age is the most consistent predictor of changes in cognitive functioning: The higher the level of education attained, the more likely is a person to remain cognitively intact. Not surprisingly, educational levels are also closely linked to income, gender, and race; higher educational levels are most frequently found among white females of higher socioeconomic status (Rowe & Kahn, 1998). Such findings emphasize the importance of membership in the social hierarchies of race, gender, and social class, all of which shape everyone's life chances and experiences throughout the life course.

Table 6-5 Memory Cue Techniques	
Technique	**Examples**
Organizing	Reducing the number of things into a smaller number of categories (e.g., shirts, pants, dresses). Chunking pieces of information into smaller bits (e.g., area codes, phone numbers).
Visual Imagery	Associating a mental picture with an object or person (e.g., a spring lawn with Mrs. Green or a telephone with the need to make a phone call).
Physical Reminders	Writing lists of tasks or items to do (e.g., homework assignments). Putting objects (e.g., keys or eyeglasses) in a prominent place. Establishing the same location for particular objects (e.g., always putting the television remote controls on a specific shelf).

Source: Adapted from Scogin & Prohaska. (1993). *Aiding Older Adults with Memory Complaints*. Sarasota, FL: Professional Resource Press.

Also important in predicting cognitive change are physical factors, specifically higher levels of physical activity plus pulmonary peak expiratory flow. Greater pulmonary peak expiratory flow increases the level of oxygen to the brain, increasing its function (Albert et al., 1995). Stress can also decrease ability to recall. For example, among elderly women with high levels of cortisol, commonly known as the "stress hormone" because its production increases during stress, verbal memory decreased. When high levels of cortisol diminished, memory improved in over three-fourths of these women. Interestingly, the same results were not found among men (Seeman et al., 1997).

Processes of 'Successful Aging' Revisited

The idea of successful aging is not new, as you will recall from Chapter 4. Robert Havighurst, one of the most influential figures in social gerontology in the 1950s and 1960s, was concerned with how to age successfully. Andrew Young, civil rights activist and the first African-American mayor of Atlanta, is credited with this advice: "I think you've got to find ways to be productive. And I think almost everybody ought to at least think about how they can contribute to life until 100."

But what is successful aging? The desire to remain independent and not burden others illustrates the importance placed on the work ethic deeply ingrained in our culture. However, both successful aging and productive aging are open to many different individual and cultural interpretations. Is successful aging marked by one's life contributions? And what marks a "contribution" or being "productive"? If we live quiet uneventful lives to age 100, is that unsuccessful or unproductive?

What do older people themselves say is "successful aging"? Their advice varies but shares some similarity to both continuity and activity theory: "Stay healthy, exercise," suggested one older person; "Enjoy leisure, recreation, and hobbies," said another. Still another summed up what to do more succinctly: "Get a life!"

The implicit danger in stressing successful aging using these definitions is that people who develop incapacitating illnesses are stigmatized as aging unsuccessfully when indeed they may be optimizing their capacities given their limitations (Baltes & Baltes, 1990). Even very old people who have lived rather unexceptional lives have a sense of well-being despite their limitations (Johnson & Barer, 1997). They are indeed "getting a life." It is the young-old, not the old-old, who complain most about age-related changes. The very old cope using both behavioral and cognitive skills. For example, very old people may contract their environment to make it more manageable and cognitively redefine what they can do to maintain control: "Feeling in control, the world is controllable" (Johnson & Barer, 1997: viii). Recall that a person who feels successful or healthy, however defined, is likely to have high self-esteem.

The Search for New Directions

As the aging population ventures into new social territories not previously explored, new social perspectives, preoccupations, attitudes, and behavior are developing. Often prenormative guidelines are tested and hammered out in the popular press. For example, recent issues of *Modern Maturity*, a bimonthly magazine published by AARP that targets people aged 50+, have tackled such areas as "Great Sex: What's Age Got to Do With It?" "Exclusive Post-Viagra Survey," "Unleash Your Hidden Genius: The Science of Lifelong Creativity," "Live to 100 and Love Every Minute," and "The Perfect Mother-in-law." Headlines such as these reflect both the search for new social definitions and developmental tasks of later life and influence opinions about what new age-appropriate behaviors, attitudes, and norms should be. Like it or not, the popular media play an influential role both in how aging is viewed and in our socialization and aging patterns.

Elders themselves are forging new norms and perspectives on adult development, capacities, and continuity and change. Some remain disadvantaged and desperately poor throughout their lives. Others, more privileged, move into new roles or continue old ones. For example, Dodo Cheney, a tennis player for more than 70 years, is reputed to be the most successful player in history with more victories (285) in her career than either tennis champions Steffi Graf or Pete Sampras and continues to compete in tournaments. Dr. Billy Taylor, jazz pianist and winner of an Emmy, is jazz artistic advisor to the Kennedy Center and his radio program, "Billy Taylor's Jazz at the Kennedy Center" has won rave reviews. As Dr. Joe Wilder, a former lacrosse all-American at Dartmouth College, author of two books on surgery, professor emeritus of medicine at Mt. Sinai Hospital, and a well-recognized painter, summed it up: "I think the greatest resource in the world are men and women over 60. We're a very special group. And I don't mind telling people I'm 78. Everybody says to me, you pass for 60, why do you tell people you are 78? I'll tell you why—cause I'm 78!" (*www.PBS.org/kcet/ agelessheroes;* download 8/2/00). People such as these challenge theories of adult development as a period of passive reflection or inevitable cognitive decline. They also demonstrate that well-being in later life takes many forms.

Summary

This chapter has focused on adult development, cognition, and change with aging. Much of what is known about either adult development or cognition has been based primarily on white, middle-class males. Relatively little research has been done on the ways in which social class, race and ethnicity, and gender influence developmental patterns or changes. The result is a somewhat narrow view of the diversity of the aging experience.

Although chronological age is one way that roles and expectations for behavior are allocated, relatively few norms for later life have been established in American society. Because much of personality theory has focused on childhood and adolescent personality, only relatively recently have theorists turned their attention to adult development in later life. Jung, a former student of Sigmund Freud, called attention to midlife and old age as a distinct period of reflection, contemplation, and integration of opposing forces in our personalities—an illumination of the self—especially as we age. Erikson, broadening this perspective, focused on development throughout the life course and divided psychosocial development progress into eight stages, each of which must be successfully resolved in order to progress to the next stage. The final developmental stage of life was one of integrity versus despair. With integrity, the elder develops a sense of "my kind and mankind [sic]." The concepts proposed by Jung and Erikson have increased interest in spirituality as a developmental task of later life that can be separate from religious belief or practice. Emphasizing the notion of later life as a period of contemplation, Butler viewed old age as characterized by a life review in which each person must come to terms with personal history. For Levinson, developmental changes are not universal but take place through the underlying characteristics of a person's life during a particular time period. Using the metaphor of "seasons of life," he proposed that certain relatively stable but culturally defined segments of the total life cycle evolve that represent distinct parts of a person's life. Like the seasons of weather, each season of life builds upon the others to create a greater whole. The concept of androgyny, referring to the union of gender traits of the opposite sex in our personalities, has also received attention.

Do memory and intelligence change as we age? Evidence from psychometric tests suggests that there is some intellectual decline with age but that it occurs in areas that are not frequently used. Level of education influences performance on tests because no IQ tests are culture free, and intellectual performance in old age can be improved through training. Changes in memory occur as we grow older but extensive memory loss is not a normal part of aging. What changes with aging is the way in which material is stored and retrieved, as both processes take longer than in young people. Successful and productive aging have received attention from both scholars and the popular press. Both notions are particularly appealing to Americans. What constitutes successful aging is, however, defined by both individuals and the culture. As the population grows older, new definitions for both appropriate behavior and the experience of growing old are evolving.

Key Points

1. Socialization is a lifelong process through which we learn to become capable participants in society through the internalization of norms.

2. Chronological age is one of the constructs through which normative standards of behavior are set along with behaviors that one can anticipate, or come to expect from others.

3. Relatively few norms for conduct exist for older adults in U.S. society at the present time.

4. Individual self-concepts appear to be continuous throughout the life course.

5. Self-esteem is anchored in the long-standing conceptions that we have of ourselves and does not diminish in later life.

6. Theories of personality and cognitive development have focused more on infancy and childhood than on later life.

7. Psychoanalyst Carl Jung proposed that, as we age, we become less involved in the external social world and develop a greater sense of interiority.

8. Psychoanalyst Erik Erikson, focusing on development throughout the life course, proposed that human psychosocial development progresses in eight stages, each of which must be successfully resolved in order to progress to the next stage.

9. Levinson's research on adult development dealt with eras or seasons of life and was closely linked to life events and chronological age.

10. Robert Butler's formulation of the life review as a universal process in later life offers still another way to examine old age.

11. Although belief in the life review as a universal process has become part of conventional wisdom in many gerontological circles, empirical research has questioned its assumptions.

12. The concept of androgyny refers to the incorporation of gender traits of the opposite sex into our personalities, where females become more task-oriented and assertive, and males become more expressive and nurturing.

13. Cognition refers to such mental processes as intelligence, learning, and memory.

14. Two of the most common modes of studying cognition in later life are the psychometric model and the information processing model. The study of cognition can be classified into two broad categories of empirical research, with a focus on information processing and psychometrics (statistical measurement of intelligence through testing).

15. The Seattle Longitudinal Study has extended understanding of changes of intelligence in normal aging, its variability, and the effectiveness of intervention strategies to regain, prolong, or maintain cognitive functioning.

16. Although some memory changes occur with aging, memory loss is not a part of normal aging.

17. Memory at any age can be improved by using mnemonic techniques.

18. As the older population ventures into new social territories not previously and collectively experienced, new social perspectives, preoccupations, attitudes, and behaviors take form, including those in the media.

Discussion Questions

1. Discuss the statement: "Continuity of the self is thus not agelessness but a dynamic tension between change and constancy of the self."

2. What is the relevance (if any) of knowing about theories of childhood development when one is interested in adult development and socialization of the older adult?

3. Do theories of human development change? Substantiate your positions from information presented in Chapters 1 through 6.

4. To what extent are the theories proposed by Jung, Erikson, and Levinson affected by the social class and the birth cohorts they studied? Are they applicable to minority groups?

5. Are androgynous people more socially skilled than people who are gender stereotyped? Explain.

6. What are the advantages and disadvantages of the media and popular press influences on age-appropriate behavior in adult socialization?

7. Does memory decline in normal aging? Explain.

8. Discuss how memory can be enhanced at any age.

9. How do occupation and socioeconomic class position affect the potential rate of cognitive intellectual decline?

10. Are there any shortcomings to the psychometric approach in studying intellectual changes with aging? Explain.

Films and Videos

Aging and Saging (video; 24 minutes; available from Films for the Humanities and Sciences, P.O. Box 2053, Princeton, NJ 08543-2053; *www.films.com*).

Provocative discussion of the changing roles of the elderly in cultural perspective with two spiritual leaders, Rabbi Schachter-Shalomi and Ram Das.

Spiritual Dimension of Life and the Will to Meaning (video; 40 minutes; available from Terra Nova Films, Inc., 9848 South Winchester Avenue, Chicago, IL 60643; *www.terranova.org*).

For those interested in exploring the meaning of human existence with the psychiatrist/philosopher Dr. Viktor Frankl.

Forever Young (video; 58 minutes; available from Terra Nova Films, Inc., 9848 South Winchester Avenue, Chicago, IL 60643; *www.terranova.org*).

Older adults sharing their postretirement lives, sources of satisfaction, and views on life and death.

Living Longer . . . Aging Well (video; 30 minutes; available from Films for the Humanities and Sciences, P.O. Box 2053, Princeton, NJ 08543-2053; *www.films.com*).

How older people maintain dignity and self-esteem in our ageist, youth-oriented society.

Memory (video; 57 minutes; available from Films for the Humanities and Sciences, P.O. Box 2053, Princeton, NJ 08543-2053; *www.films.com*).

How information is stored, how aging affects memory, and steps to improve memory by experts from Harvard Medical School, Howard Hughes Medical Institute, and others.

Internet Resources

http://www.nimh.nih.gov

The U.S. National Institute of Mental Health web site, with information on depression, anxiety, and other mental disorders as well as medications to treat psychiatric problems.

http://www.alzheimers.org

A service of the National Institute on Aging, this site provides current educational and referral information on Alzheimer's disease.

http://www.aoa.gov

The web page for the U.S. Administration on Aging and its numerous fact sheets, including information on mental health and illness.

Research Article

Andrews, M. (2000). The seductiveness of agelessness. *Ageing and Society,* *19*(3): 301–318.

This article details the ways in which the concept of agelessness is used and abused.

Supplemental Readings

Johnson, C. J., & Barer, B. M. (1997). *Life Beyond 85 Years: The Aura of Survivorship*. New York: Springer.

A good look at ordinary people and their ways of dealing with the world in very old age.

Langner, E. J. (1999). *The Power of Mindful Thinking*. Cambridge, MA: Perseus Publishing.

Fresh new ways of thinking about the mind based on recent research.

Maxwell, F. (1968). *The Measure of My Days*. New York: Knopf.

A fascinating account of herself in her 80s by a noted author, actress, and consulting psychologist.

Modern Maturity. (Issued monthly). Washington, DC: AARP.

A window on "successful aging" published by AARP.

Terkel, S. (1995). *Coming of Age: The Story of Our Century by Those Who've Lived It*. New York: St. Martin's Press.

Readable interviews, useful in viewing the roles of social class, race, ethnicity, and gender, in which elders describe their lives, activities, and changes throughout the life course. ✦

Chapter 7

Mental Health and Mental Illness

Introduction

Shortly after Aunt Rose went into Ghent Manor nursing home—she went in after she broke her hip—she got kind of remote and spent every day in her room watching television or reading magazines. She didn't even try to get to know her roommate and ate by herself in the dining room. She avoided everybody! We were really taken aback with the way her personality seemed to have changed. . . . Before she came to Ghent Manor—she was 90—Aunt Rose was a real outgoing person. She'd retired from her job as a school clerk a long time ago and was a widow for 20 years, but she had lots of friends—she always called them "the girls"—and they got together regularly to go out to eat and maybe take in a concert, or a lecture. . . . She had lived in the same house for the past 50 years, drove her own car, and attended that "Institute for retired folks at the State University." But after she broke her hip, she needed 'round-the-clock help—more than we could provide at home—and private nurses and home help for 24 hours cost a fortune! None of us could pay for that, and finally she decided to go into the nursing home. . . . But we were worried about how much she had changed after she got to the nursing home, even though she kept saying everything was OK. So, we decided to talk with her doctor at Ghent. He said she had a "depression." He said that we shouldn't worry as this was normal for old people. All of the residents he saw at the nursing home, he said, were depressed (Personal communication, 2001).

Many people, like the physician in the above account, view old age as a period of decline, believing that depression is normal in old age. Similarly, many think that memory loss, dementia, and Alzheimer's are actually normal for the elderly and that it is only a matter of time until such changes occur. How true are these beliefs? What are "normal" changes in mental health as we grow old? Is depression like Aunt Rose's a normal part of aging? Or is it related to changes in health and life situations?

Although a seemingly simple concept, a precise definition of mental health for any age group is elusive. The sociologist John Clausen, who did extensive research on mental illness, is credited with saying that mental health is a state devoutly to be wished but almost impossible to define. Similarly, normal behavior is very hard to define; we are much more likely to be able to describe abnormal behavior that violates our everyday expectations. Whereas both terms seem straightforward, mental health and normalcy are most often described and defined by what they are not—mental illness.

The explanation for judging mental health and normal behavior through the absence of mental illness lies in the rationale of modern scientific medicine and professional dominance of the medical community. Different interpretations of behavior and its meanings are also important in defining mental health and normal behavior. This chapter explores definitions of mental health and mental illness in later life.

Views of Mental Disorders

Conventionally, good mental health at any age is equated with normalcy, but what is normal? Depending on where, when, and who uses the term and makes judgements, the concept of *normal* behavior has many definitions. It is constructed, perceived, and acted upon in distinct ways by psychologists, psychiatrists and other physicians, social workers, social scientists, police, and the lay public. How normal is delineated thus depends both on the disciplinary perspective of the designator and the sociohistorical period and culture in which she or he lives.

Pathological and Statistical Models

The terms *mental illness* and *mental health* are used in many different ways. Although most sociologists and anthropologists define *health* or *illness* from a social-system viewpoint, other scientists use different, clinically-based models. Two clinical models, the pathological and the statistical, are most often used in definitions of mental illness today. Both of these models are designed to detect abnormalities in ways to direct diagnosis and treatment (Mercer, 1973).

The *pathological model* focuses on symptoms and abnormal functioning within an organism. The healthy state of an organ such as a kidney or heart, for example, is the absence of abnormalities detected through clinical history, physical examination, and tests. Normal, healthy functioning, whether of an organ or of behaviors, is thus a residual category, determined through investigations ruling out pathology. The most commonly used model in medicine today, the pathological model (1) seeks biological explanations within the individual; (2) focuses on the individual; (3) emphasizes what is wrong with an individual rather than what is right; and (4) focuses on biological explanations or causes rather than the culture or group (Mercer, 1973). The pathological model has been particularly useful in the diagnosis and treatment of numerous physical illnesses such as pneumonia, tuberculosis, and AIDS, but it has limitations in the study of mental disorders.

Although nineteenth-century biologists, physicians, and social scientists sought biological differences and genetic explanations among racial, ethnic, religious, and nationality groups to explain mental disorders, this search was largely unsuccessful and fueled by fears of immigration and rising rates of poverty. Today it is recognized that many mental illnesses have multiple causes: biological, social, and environmental. Moreover, explanations of mental illness often require an understanding of the society, the social structure in which people live, and their life course and life chances.

The *statistical model* differs from the medical model in that it defines *normalcy* in terms of the usual or average abilities or behaviors found among the majority of the population. Visualize a bell-shaped curve—the so-called normal distribution in statistics (also used in classes in which the professor "grades on the curve"). Specifically, the statistical model (1) defines as normal the average of the group; (2) focuses on the group being evaluated; (3) bases findings on a specific group or population; and (4) does not include cause-effect in the model. In sum, according to this model, normal or average is just that: the arithmetical average of the population being studied. In a particular class, the range of scores that the majority has on an exam is defined as normal or average. Those with unusually high or low scores deviate from the norm. High scorers will be regarded as excellent students; low scorers as needing remedial work if they are to pass the course.

Believing that mental disorders follow the statistical model has several outcomes. First, it emphasizes the largest groups in a population and defines them as normal. Second, it underemphasizes smaller groups and designates them as abnormal. The statistical model has been used extensively in studies of developmental disabilities. For example, Mercer (1973) found that Mexican-American children were much more likely than their white, non-Latino or African-American peers to be labeled as developmentally disabled by schools and agencies dominated by non-Latino whites. Although the school performance of Mexican-American children differed from the majority of Anglo students, within their own community these children were considered normal and as adults they showed no signs of mental retardation. The point here is that culture makes a difference; if, for example, IQ is being measured, each specific group or culture must be reevaluated to determine what is normal. Otherwise, an inaccurate measurement will result that has profound social consequences on the people being evaluated. And third, it can be used as a tool for discrimination. Using the statistical definition based on IQ test results of middle-class whites has had a major impact on poor members of minority groups in two ways: (1) IQ scores were used to prejudge the ability of people to function; and (2) low scores were used to assign people to programs with the fewest resources (Kutchins & Kirk, 1997). When the book *The Bell Curve* (Herrnstein & Murray, 1995), using statistical definitions of IQ to stamp African Americans as inferior, was published, it kindled the old nineteenth-century fire of controversy about the relationship of race, genetics, and IQ to crime, welfare dependency, and failure—a sad example of how a statistical definition can be misused to justify prejudice.

In studies of mental illness as well, a statistical definition based on one set of people can produce biased results when applied in a different context or culture. In a war, for example, it is normal to kill the enemy; this is part of the usual ways of warfare. A soldier who refuses to kill the enemy in combat is likely to be severely sanctioned. But in peacetime, the same person who kills an opponent is likely to be regarded either as mentally unbalanced or criminal.

Nonetheless, the statistical model is less limited than the pathological model. In the pathological model, some physical pathology must be shown if the illness is to be diagnosed. In the statistical model, this is not the case. One can change the percentage of the population to be described as sick either by redefining as normal the behaviors once considered pathological (for example, homosexuality) or by defining as medical problems behaviors previously considered normal (such as grief after the loss of a loved one).

A well-established tool used by mental health professionals that blends the two approaches is the *Diagnostic and Statistical Manual of Mental Disorders* (2000), a volume published by the American Psychiatric Association (APA) and updated periodically by panels of experts. Each edition provides a classification of mental disorders conceived of as clinically significant behavioral or psychological patterns, and associated with painful symptoms or disabilities in functioning. As the authoritative tool for practitioners in the mental health profession, this provides the official terminology and classification system for the differential diagnosis of mental disorders which is the basis for insurance reimbursements.

For some disorders, the physical or biological causes are known or suspected. These disorders are described as *organic mental disorders* and include a broad range of problems, ranging from acute conditions (e.g., delirium) to chronic illnesses (e.g., Alzheimer's disease). However, a physical or biological cause is unknown for most mental disorders. Some may be due to biophysical factors, others due to social or psychological causes, and still others to the interplay of social, biophysical, and psychological variables.

Social Models

Whereas mental health workers such as psychiatrists and psychologists focus on the classification, causes, and treatment of mental illness, sociologists have focused on (1) social factors associated with its occurrence and (2) the process by which individuals are classified as mentally ill. For the sociologist, the definition of what is normal lies in the organization and workings of the social system and the individual's placement within the system. Position in the social hierarchies of race and class plays a role in diagnosis and treatment. Thus, African Americans are more than 6 times as likely to receive a diagnosis of alcohol or substance abuse as whites, and whites are almost 4 times more likely to be diagnosed as suffering from a personality disorder. Even among African Americans of high socioeconomic status, more than 3 times as many individuals as their white counterparts are tested for alcohol or substance abuse, probably due to the belief that African Americans have higher rates of abuse. In fact, the actual rates of abuse are no higher among African Americans than whites. There is also evidence that African Americans are more likely to receive higher doses of antipsychotic medications than whites (Morehouse Medical Treatment and Effectiveness Center, 1999).

Diagnoses of mental illness also reflect the norms of the times. For example, recall that until 1974, homosexuality was classified as a mental disorder by the APA. As a result of lengthy and heated protests both within the psychiatric profession and by civil rights activists, the designation of homosexuality was dropped as a psychiatric diagnosis (Kutchins & Kirk, 1997). It is interesting to note, however, that although homosexuality was dropped from the list of mental disorders in later editions of the APA manual, new illnesses were then added. These include *developmental mathematics disorder* (APA, 2000: 53–54), characterized by impaired development of arithmetic skills unexplained by mental retardation or poor educational opportunities. "Nicotine dependence" and "caffeine intoxication" have also been added as mental disorders (APA, 2000). That smoking emerged as a mental disorder when there is increased awareness that smoking is harmful to health emphasizes the importance of current social norms in defining precisely what kinds of behaviors will be regarded as abnormal. Hence, the concept of normal is both culturally and historically determined. One of the more ridiculous examples of the ways in which diagnosis has varied according to the sociohistorical context is the condition of drapetomania. In the nineteenth century, psychiatrists diagnosed African-American slaves who ran away as suffering *drapetomania* (from the Latin word for "runaway slave" and *mania*, meaning "crazy"), the major symptom of which was running away. The following is a remedy that was advised: neither too lenient treatment nor overly severe whipping (Kutchins & Kirk, 1997)! Thankfully, no one would accept either such a racist diagnostic category or its recommended type of therapy today.

As discussed earlier, old age itself became medicalized during the nineteenth century: a pathological condition to be treated by physicians. Although the notion of old age as a period of inevitable mental decay remains a popular belief, increasingly the distinction between the concepts of normal and usual aging is recognized by researchers and physicians focusing on aging processes. *Normal* in this sense refers to inevitable biophysical and psychological processes; in contrast, *usual* denotes a statistical definition. For example, in adolescence, many Americans develop acne. This is perhaps usual among people with certain types of biological structure but not an inevitable feature of being a teenager. Similarly, in old age, some conditions are more prevalent than others (e.g., certain types of organic mental disorders), but they are not inevitable parts of growing old.

Throughout our lives, mental health is influenced by numerous factors; physical health, changes in social roles, and socioeconomic position are but a few. Declining physical health associated with one or more chronic illness can impair ability to perform activities of daily living. Changing familial and occupational social roles can challenge or enhance the potential for relationships with others. Poverty can worsen physical illnesses and depression. Birth cohort, too, plays a role; for example, the life experiences of people born in the 1920s, who grew up during the 1930s and had children during World War II or the baby-boom years, are vastly different from those of their children or grandchildren (Riley, 1996). Although they have participated in the more affluent society of the past few decades, they may have very different perspectives on saving, as the story of Martha Leary illustrates.

Mental Disorders in Old Age

Alcoholism and Drug Use

An *alcoholic* is defined as a drinker who has reported one symptom of alcohol withdrawal during the past year or at least one symptom of loss of control plus another symptom of dependence, excluding with-

Spotlight on U.S.: Old Age—Hoarder or Product of the Depression?

Martha Leary, a cheerful and outgoing woman now in her 70s, always has a full refrigerator and freezer. Her six children are all grown and no longer live with her and her husband, a retired middle-management business executive. Her children and grandchildren often tease her, wondering whether she is expecting to feed an army that drops in unannounced. Although she delights in cooking meals for family and friends, she always has far more food on hand than she needs. She is also an avid coupon clipper and takes advantage of any bargain at the supermarket or department stores, despite the fact that she has a comfortable income. She saves paper bags and carefully stores the wrapping from gifts she receives, as well as string, rubber bands, glass jars, and other household items with little value. Her grandchildren wonder why she is so concerned with saving objects that strike them as disposable or objects for the recycling bin. They figure that she has gotten stingy as she's gotten old. They are concerned whether this could be a symptom of Alzheimer's or merely a normal part of growing old. But they are confused because she is also a generous person and enjoys giving gifts to her family members and friends for their birthdays and on holidays.

Is Mrs. Leary's behavior an illustration of stinginess and hoarding in old age and possible mental problems? Recall that she grew up in the Great Depression of the 1930s. Albeit from a middle-class family, her parents were forced to sell the land that her father's family had owned

for many years in order to make ends meet and to feed her and her five siblings. That Mrs. Leary is concerned with having an adequate—indeed ample—food supply and economizing whenever possible by reusing inexpensive objects reflects the experiences of many people in her birth cohort rather than mental illness.

Although hoarding may indeed be a symptom of psychological distress, in this situation Mrs. Leary's behavior is normal given her birth cohort and life experiences. Nor is thriftiness or hoarding a universal behavior as we grow older. Her everyday behavior, including her pleasure in feeding her family and in giving to others, suggests that something else explains her thrift. In fact, her behavior has very little to do with her age as she has always been concerned with how to cut costs. To understand why she saves whenever possible, it is important to understand her actions in the context of her personal experiences as a child and young adult during a period when so many families, like hers, underwent economic hardship due to the Great Depression. Her thrift reflects her socialization and life experiences during the Depression and World War II. Both influenced her values, worldviews, and coping and adaptive strategies and are very different from those of her children and grandchildren, whose age cohorts were born into a richer (and disposable) society. Because the Depression occurred at an early stage in Mrs. Leary's life, it created a "Depression mentality" of economizing and preparedness even in an affluent

> economy. It is dangerous to make as-
> sumptions about anyone's behavior
> as either a normal part of growing
> old or a symptom of mental prob-
> lems without considering the con-
> text in which the behavior occurs.

drawal (Williams et al., 1987). Prevalence rates of alcoholism have traditionally been calculated using deaths from cirrhosis of the liver, a
complication of severe alcohol abuse, as an indicator. Because not all
people who are alcoholic die of cirrhosis of the liver nor are they diagnosed and treated for alcohol abuse, the actual prevalence of alcoholism for Americans of any age is unknown. Nor is it known how many
elders are alcoholic. As shown in Figure 7-1, estimates of the prevalence of both alcohol dependence and abuse show that rates are highest among young white males and females (ages 18 to 29) and decline
with age.

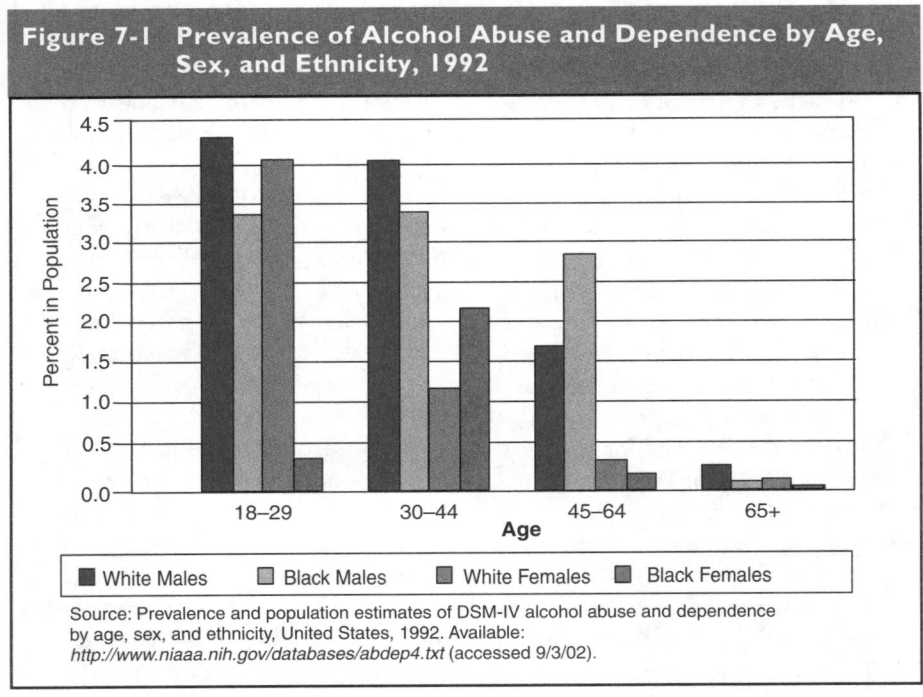

Figure 7-1   Prevalence of Alcohol Abuse and Dependence by Age, Sex, and Ethnicity, 1992

Source: Prevalence and population estimates of DSM-IV alcohol abuse and dependence by age, sex, and ethnicity, United States, 1992. Available: *http://www.niaaa.nih.gov/databases/abdep4.txt* (accessed 9/3/02).

Despite the available evidence that alcohol abuse and dependence
are relatively rare as we grow older, older adults absorb alcohol more
quickly than younger ones. This higher absorption rate can put older
people at greater risk of alcohol-induced disorders. Excessive use of
alcohol at any age can produce anemia, electrolyte imbalances, vitamin B12 deficiency, and unconsciousness. Alcohol abuse can also
cause cognitive decline and dementia. The general consensus is that
light drinking is not harmful to older (or younger) people if they are

reasonably healthy and do not take medications that will interact with alcohol (Gomberg, 1996).

The true prevalence rates of *illegal drug use* at any age are also unknown. Few elderly people are arrested or treated for use of illegal drugs. Whether this is because they do not use street drugs or simply that they have become more adept at concealing their addiction is unclear. There is a small number of elderly heroin users who have managed to live beyond their 60s, and the number is apparently increasing. These are not drug-dependent people who recently started drugs; they are long-term addicts who have survived. Studies of elderly methadone-maintained elders show a number of factors associated with their survival: They had long-lived parents, they avoided violence, and they were careful to use clean needles (Gomberg, 1996). Many elderly hospital inpatients also have been found to have substance abuse disorders, but only about 22 percent received psychotherapy and only 18 percent received any diagnostic mental health services four years after discharge from the hospital. Very few elderly Medicare substance abuse patients get mental health care, perhaps because of health or economic barriers, despite the finding that prompt care predicts lower mortality (Brennan et al., 2001).

More is known about the *misuse* and *overuse* of drugs, such as over-the-counter drugs (aspirin, laxatives, antacids, etc.) and prescription drugs. Older people are likely to use a larger number of different medications, both prescription and nonprescription, which can produce *adverse drug reactions* (ADRs). Although the elderly constitute only about 13 percent of the U.S. population, they consume about 30 percent of all prescription drugs and a disproportionate number of over-the-counter medications.

Physical changes that occur with increasing age can result in alterations in the ability to absorb drugs. Numerous drugs affect cognition: antibiotics, analgesics, steroids, antihistamines, tranquilizers, and drugs for gastrointestinal or cardiovascular disorders, to name a few. Adverse drug reactions and drug interactions may result in unintended side effects, allergies, and toxicity.

The risk of adverse drug reactions depends on the number of medications taken and the ways they can interact rather than on age alone. Other risk factors for adverse drug reactions include greater numbers and more severe illnesses; both are likely to mean that the person takes

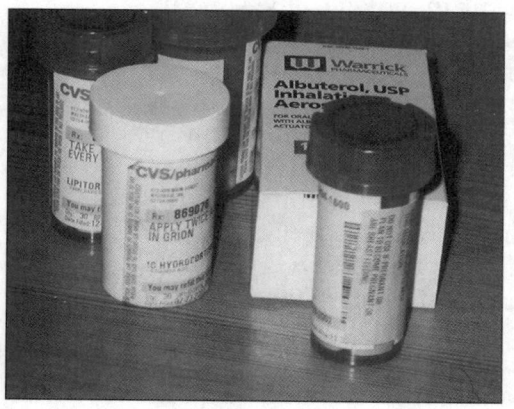

Polypharmacy—the taking of many prescription or over-the-counter drugs—can create drug reactions that are harmful to health.

more medications that can interact and even counteract one another. Adverse drug reactions and drug interactions can produce symptoms of dementia; for example, in some individuals, even an over-the-counter antihistamine can result in confusion, impairing cognitive functioning until the drug is discontinued.

Depression: Prevalence and Incidence

MYTH: The Elderly Have Higher Rates of
Mental Illness Than Other Age Groups

Physicians and epidemiologists make a distinction between prevalence and incidence rates of a disease or condition. *Prevalence* describes the number of cases of a particular illness or disorder during a particular time period. *Incidence* describes the number of new cases during a particular time period. The majority of studies of depression in later life have focused on prevalence, as it is easier to collect data on populations than incidence. Although older people do *not* have higher prevalence rates of mental disorder than younger ones, it is often thought that they do.

As you will recall from the account of Aunt Rose at the beginning of this chapter, it is not unusual to think that depression is to be expected among older people. The physician who felt that depression was normal in old age was using both pathological and statistical definitions. Recognizing the symptoms of depression, he had observed that everyone in the nursing home was depressed and concluded that depression was normal aging rather than a reaction to changes in physical functioning or loss of home, usual activities, and friends, or other role losses common to the residents of the nursing home.

Similarly, it is also frequently believed that some kind of dementia, such as Alzheimer's disease, is bound to occur in old age. One sorority on our campus, whose primary mission is to undertake projects designed to address a social problem, chose the subject of "old age" as its project for a year. When the author was invited to speak to members of the sorority, she was surprised to find that the women almost universally subscribed to the belief that Alzheimer's was the inevitable fate of everyone who grew old! They were very surprised to find out that Alzheimer's disease is neither normal nor usual in old age. In fact, recent data indicate that cognitive functioning among the elderly, especially among those in their 80s, is better today than in the early 1990s (Freedman, Aykan, & Martin, 2001).

Depression is classified by mental health professionals as a functional disorder, that is, with no known organic cause. Although depression is one of the most common diagnoses of functional mental illness for older adults, no agreement exists about how common it is in old age or its causes. Not surprisingly, reported rates among community-based older adults have varied widely: from less than 1 percent to 35 percent depending on the definition used and the population studied (Beekman, Copeland, & Prince, 1999; Mulsant & Ganguli, 1999). Depression affects most aspects of life including physical health, participation in paid employment or social activities, and satisfaction with life.

Symptoms of Depression. Depression is marked by a cluster of symptoms that can occur in numerous combinations depending on the person and the extent of the illness. A person who is depressed will usually describe feeling sad, hopeless, or down in the dumps; lose interest in activities that once provided pleasure; and withdraw. Lack of self-esteem and lack of confidence are also frequent. Other symptoms can include irritability, uncooperativeness, changes in appetite and sleep patterns, lack of energy, and an increase in apathy. Cognitive ability can also be affected, characterized by an inability to concentrate, having fearful thoughts and inappropriate guilt. Mental health professionals make a distinction between major depression and depressive neurosis (dysthymia), although the boundaries are not clear-cut. Symptoms of major depression are listed in Table 7-1. If five of the symptoms are present, the diagnosis of major depression is made. Keep in mind that many elders who are depressed are mistakenly perceived as suffering from *dementia*—an organic brain syndrome discussed later in this chapter—because some of the symptoms are similar.

Depressive symptoms can also be confused with age-related changes, such as problems in sleeping. Not only do many older people complain about waking up frequently during the night, but this subjective complaint is often related to objective findings of increased waking. The effect of this wakefulness is to increase sleepiness during the daytime. Just as many college students may nap during the day after pulling an all-nighter, lack of sleep, not disinterest, is a major reason that many older people catch up on sleep during the day.

Yet, the relationship between sleeplessness and depression in later life is complex. Data suggest that elderly African-American women have significantly higher incidences of insomnia than older white women, or African-American and white men. For both races, the presence of depressed mood increased the likelihood of insomnia. The high prevalence and incidence of other medical conditions, plus depressive symptoms coupled with greater risk of poverty, among elderly African-American women apparently increases sleeplessness (Foley et al., 1999). Lack of energy is also a characteristic of depression yet can be associated with aging-related acute or chronic physical illness as well.

MYTH: Older Women Are More Likely Than
Younger Women to Be Depressed

Table 7-1   DSM-IV-R Symptoms of Major Depression

(*At least five* symptoms present for at least two weeks, as well as *change* from usual functioning.)

- Depressed or sad mood
- Decreased interest in sex
- Loss of interest/pleasure in activities
- Poor appetite or notable weight loss, or increased appetite/ notable weight gain
- Loss of energy or fatigue
- Psychomotor agitation or retardation
- Insomnia or hypersomnia
- Diminished ability to think or concentrate
- Forgetfulness
- Feelings of self-reproach, worthlessness, or inappropriate guilt
- Recurrent thoughts of death, suicidal ideas

Source: Adapted from *Diagnostic and Statistical Manual of Mental Disorders*, 4th ed. Revised. (2000: 356). Washington, DC: American Psychiatric Association.

Depression in Later Life. Contrary to popular belief, the elderly are not the group most likely to be depressed. Persons who are depressed are largely young, female, single, and have low incomes (National Academy on an Aging Society, 2000). Women are twice as likely to suffer from depression, which peaks during the childbearing years. Moreover, recent research suggests that individuals born after World War II—the baby boom generation—are younger than preceding birth cohorts when they first have symptoms of depression. Reasons for any differences between these older and younger birth cohorts are unclear. Various hypotheses have been suggested, such as including sociohistorical events and different life experiences and changes in cultural norms about mental illness that promote greater recognition of the symptoms of depression. Treatment is more acceptable among younger cohorts as well, and new antidepressants have been developed and are widely used. Consider the popularity of Prozac®—a popular antidepressant that has stimulated such books as *Prozac Nation: Young and Depressed in America: A Memoir* (Wurtzel, 1997). There is some evidence that men and women view depression differently, for men are far more likely to regard it as an emotional weakness and women as a health problem (National Academy on an Aging Society, 2000).

Who is likely to be depressed in later life? Research indicates that, although the incidence of *major* depression declines with age, symptoms of *minor* depression increase (Beekman et al., 1995; Blazer, Burchett, Service, & George, 1991.) People of lower socioeconomic status or living in poverty, who are unmarried or unhappily married, have low levels of social and emotional support, and who rate their health as poor, are more likely to have some symptoms of depression (Wilson et al., 1999; Kivela et al., 1999). Although both elderly widowed men and women are more depressed than those still married, death of a spouse has a stronger depressive effect on older men than women; the stronger effect of widowhood on men is apparently due largely to the relatively low levels of depressive symptoms found among men prior to becoming widowers (Lee et al., 2001).

Race and gender differences in the prevalence of depression also exist. Women of color are far more likely to be depressed than white women. Some studies have found that about 1 in 10 white and slightly more than 1 in 4 African-American elderly women were depressed, suggesting that poverty and racial discrimination play important contributing roles (Goldberg, Van Natta, & Comstock, 1985; Comstock & Helsing, 1976). Among younger women (aged 18 to 55), emotional reliance upon others is significantly associated with symptoms of depression (Turner & Turner, 1999). In later life, women with low levels of self-esteem or with little or no confidence in their ability to cope effectively with physical health problems are more susceptible to depression than those who have higher levels of self-esteem or use constructive coping mechanisms. When confronted with life events such as illness or disability, women may rely on a learned response of helplessness and a sense of powerlessness, an ongoing tension between who one is and who one wants to be, and a lack of autonomy—all characteristics fostering depressive symptoms (Wetzel, 1994).

Disability, functional impairment, and poor health increase the probability of becoming depressed in later life for both genders (Mills & Henretta, 2001; Zeiss et al., 1996). Significant correlations between depression and several chronic illnesses including stroke (Steffens et al., 1999), Parkinson's disease (Cummings & Masterman, 1999), and heart disease and cancer (Mulsant & Ganguli, 1999) have been reported. Data from at least one small-scale study indicate that elderly medical inpatients with active major depression are both more likely to die in the hospital than a control group matched by age, functional status, severity and type of medical illness, and extent of disease and, if they survive, to consume more health care resources after release (Koenig et al., 1989).

Functional status is a more powerful predictor of subsequent depression than age, strengthening the suggestion that physical illness and disability may cause older people to report the physical complaints that constitute a major component of depressive symptomatology (Waxman, Carner, & Blum, 1983). Nonetheless, community elders with poor functional status are more likely to score higher on depression on *all* dimensions, not just those associated with physical complaints.

Whether depression predicts later physical disability or physical disability predicts depression remains a chicken-and-egg question, however. For example, increasing disability and declining health have been found to precede the onset of depressive symptoms over a two-year period (Aneshensel, Frerichs, & Huba, 1984). Conversely, chronic illnesses, physical inactivity, and depression have been reported to predict later physical disabilities (Oman, Reed, & Ferrara, 1999). Clearly, depression often occurs along with medical illnesses, such as heart disease, stroke, diabetes, and cancer. Because many older people face such chronic illnesses as well as other problems, health care providers often assume that depression is a normal result, and this attitude is often shared by patients themselves (Lebowitz et al., 1997). These factors conspire to make depression undiagnosed and untreated in later life.

Treatment of Depression. What can be done about depression in the elderly? The treatments are basically the same as those used with younger people. It is important to stress that both major and minor depression are illnesses rather than part of aging. Nor can depression simply be willed away. Many older people were socialized in an era when admitting that they felt depressed or seeking treatment for emotional problems was unacceptable. Trained to be self-reliant, they will deny symptoms of depression, complaining of physical discomfort or problems in sleeping. Currently, many members of the medical community define depression as a chemical illness, much like diabetes. Like diabetes, it is a treatable illness.

Three therapeutic tools are commonly used: antidepressant medications, electroconvulsive therapy (ECT), and psychotherapy. These tools may be used alone or in combination. Drugs, such as selective serotonin reuptake inhibitors (SSRIs like Prozac® or Zoloft®) or tricyclic antidepressants (TCAs) successfully reverse depression for many people. If drugs are not helpful or cannot be used, electroconvulsive therapy (ECT), sometimes called shock therapy, often produces dramatic results for those with major depression. Psychotherapy (talking therapy) offers a nonbiological approach to the treatment of depressive symptoms and is most commonly either cognitively or behaviorally based (Zeiss & Breckenridge, 1997).

Suicide

MYTH: THE HIGHEST SUICIDE RATES ARE AMONG
YOUNG PEOPLE

Depression is a leading cause of suicide in the elderly. Contrary to popular opinion, suicide rates are not the highest among young adults. One reason that people think suicide is most frequent among teenagers and young adults is that it is the third leading cause of death for these ages, largely because relatively few deaths occur among younger age groups due to chronic diseases. Another reason is that the suicide of a young person is far more likely than that of an elder to be noted in the media. However, the rate of suicide (suicides per 1,000 population in an age group) is highest among the elderly, as shown in Table 7-2. Older people also are more likely to use more lethal methods; in 1997, for example, firearms were the most common single means for suicide among both elderly men and women, accounting for about 77 percent of male and 33 percent of female late-life suicides. The elderly also make fewer attempts per completed suicide (National Center for Injury Prevention and Control, 2000).

Table 7-2 Age-Adjusted Suicide Rates per 100,000 Population in 1998 by Age, Sex, Race, and Hispanic Origin

| | **Male** | | | | | **Female** | | | | |
Age	White Non-Hispanic	Black	Hispanic	Asian/ Pacific	Native American	White Non-Hispanic	Black	Hispanic	Asian/ Pacific	Native American
15–24	20.2	15.0	13.4	10.9	41.8	3.6	2.2	2.8	2.7	—
25–44	26.7	15.2	13.0	11.9	33.3	7.2	2.7	2.2	4.0	8.0
45–64	25.1	11.1	11.5	10.2	11.3	7.4	2.2	2.7	4.3	—
65+	37.3	11.6	20.0	21.0	—	5.2	1.2	2.5	7.2	—

— Denotes number too small to be reliable to calculate.
Source: National Center for Health Statistics (2001). *Health, United States 2001*, Table 47.

Throughout the life course, males are more likely to commit suicide than females, with white males more likely to commit suicide than their African American or other racial and ethnic group age-peers. Older men are far more likely to commit suicide than their female counterparts and account for over 80 percent of suicides among the elderly. Suicide rates are highest in old age among white, Asian and Pacific Islander, and Latino men; suicide rates also rise in old age among Asian and Pacific Islander women. African Americans, whether male or female, are most at risk for suicide between the ages of 25 and 34, after which time the rate drops and never reaches its earlier peak.

What social characteristics do those elders who commit suicide share? Suicide is highest among elders who are divorced and widowed, with widowed or divorced men much more likely than their female peers to kill themselves. Major depression among older adults is associated with suicide (Conwell & Brent, 1995). Many older adults who commit suicide have visited their primary care physician close to the time of their suicide: 20 percent on the same day, 40 percent within a week, and 70 percent within one month (Conwell, 1994). Those committing suicide are also more likely than other elderly to have more physical illnesses (National Center for Injury Prevention and Control, 2000).

Most of us believe that people commit suicide due to purely psychological problems. Suicide is, however, also a social act, influenced by the norms and expectations of the society. In his extensive analysis *Suicide* (1897/1966), Emile Durkheim (1858–1917) showed that social forces are at work even in solitary acts of self-destruction. Observing that some categories of people—men, Protestants, the rich, and the unmarried—have higher suicide rates than others, he explained these differences by proposing that suicide is most likely to occur in one of the following situations: (1) when individuals feel at a loss during periods of rapid social change and norms for behavior are unclear (anomic suicide) and (2) when individuals feel socially isolated and unconnected to others (egoistic suicide); or (3) when individuals believe the good of the group will benefit from their deaths (altruistic suicide) (Durkheim, 1897/1966). The common factor in all three types of suicide, according to Durkheim, is *social integration* or the degree to which a person is part of a larger group. In cultures in which the individual is overshadowed or too well integrated by the group, altruistic suicide is most common. Altruistic suicide occurs when individuals are so completely involved in the group that its goals and identity become theirs. Put differently, the norms of the tightly structured society are such that each member of the group is willing to sacrifice life for the sake of beliefs, a cause, or a common good—like the early Christian martyrs, the ritual hara-kiri of the Japanese, or the terrorists who hijacked and crashed commercial airplanes into the World Trade Center and the Pentagon in September 2001. In situations where a person feels no affiliation to others, egoistic suicide is likely. In rapidly changing, confusing times when the norms are unclear, anomic suicide is prevalent; the rash of suicides during the Great Depression of 1929 is one example.

In Durkheim's terms, the majority of late-life suicides are egoistic, due to elders' lack of integration into work, friendship, and family roles, or due to *domestic anomie*, that is, the roleless role of the old who, after the death of significant others, lack clear guidelines for behavior and supportive interaction (Osgood, 1985). Among the now-old, women traditionally have been the kin-keepers and have larger friendship networks than men. Older men, when widowed, chronically ill, or depressed, are less likely than their women counterparts to have extensive social networks upon which to draw. Accordingly, they take action to end their lives. That most personal act—suicide—thus is influenced by social factors including widowhood and social isolation.

Dementia

MYTH: DEMENTIA IS TO BE EXPECTED IN OLD AGE

When an older person forgets the location of the car keys or can't remember a name, it is common to think that this is due to old age or *senility*. When a younger person forgets the same thing, it is described not as senility but absentmindedness. Describing forgetfulness in later life as senility is an ageist bias no longer accepted by gerontologists or mental health professionals. The notion of senility as "normal" in old age is both inaccurate and outdated. Neither researchers in the field of aging nor physicians, psychologists, psychiatrists, or other mental health professionals today expect memory loss to be part of the normal course of growing old. Rather, memory loss is regarded as an indicator of illness.

The terms *dementia* and *organic brain syndrome* (OBS) describe a number of disorders affecting memory, cognition, and mood. Dementia is caused by many different illnesses that affect the brain. These include infections of the central nervous system such as meningitis; central nervous system syphilis; encephalitis and HIV-related disorders; brain injuries; metabolic problems, such as severe anemia, underactive thyroid, and vitamin B12 deficiency; drug reactions; chronic alcoholism; and various neurological diseases, such as Huntington's chorea, Parkinson's disease, Alzheimer's disease, and multiple sclerosis.

Dementia may be irreversible and progress relentlessly, as in Alzheimer's disease, or it may be potentially reversible, as in vitamin B12 deficiency, anemia, and so forth. Although dementia is diagnosed most often in the elderly, it can occur at any age as the above list of causes indicates. Diagnosis and management of dementia are increasingly recognized as important skills in the primary care of the elderly. Once dementia is suspected or diagnosed, potentially reversible or treatable causes should be sought.

A diagnosis of dementia, using criteria established by the American Psychiatric Association, requires impairment in long- and short-term memory. In addition, symptoms of dementia must include at least one of the following: (1) impaired abstract thinking; (2) impaired judgement about interpersonal, family, or job issues; (3) other disturbances of higher brain function, such as language disorder (aphasia), inability to carry out motor activities despite intact comprehension and motor function (apraxia), failure to recognize or identify objects (agnosia); and (4) personality changes ("not himself/herself"). Memory loss and other symptoms must *significantly* interfere with work, usual social activities, or relationships with others. To establish a diagnosis of dementia there must be either (1) evidence from history, physical exam, or lab tests of a specific organic factor related to the cause of symptoms or (2) assumption of an organic factor if symptoms cannot be explained by any nonorganic mental disorder, such as major depression (American Psychiatric Association, 2000).

Alzheimer's Disease

One of the most feared types of dementia is *Alzheimer's disease,* named after the German physician who first identified it in 1906. Other types of dementia include *Pick's disease,* which affects personality and memory, and vascular dementia, which may follow a stroke or a series of small strokes. Alzheimer's disease (AD) is the most commonly diagnosed form of dementia, affecting the parts of the brain controlling thought, memory, and language. Although younger people can also develop Alzheimer's, the risk increases with age. It is important to know, however, that Alzheimer's is *not* part of normal aging.

Among those aged 65 to 74, about 3 percent of men and women have Alzheimer's disease, and by age 85 or older, nearly one-half may have the disorder. Because AD is most common among the old-old and because women have a greater life expectancy than men, women account for about 2 in 3 (68 percent) of people with this disease. Unlike many other chronic conditions, Alzheimer's disease is not associated with income. Education does not insulate against the disease; half the people with AD have less than a high school education and half are high-school graduates or more (National Academy on an Aging Society, 2000).

Alzheimer's is chronic and progressive, reducing cognitive, emotional, and physical functioning. AD begins slowly, and the initial symptom may be mild forgetfulness for recent events, activities, or the names of familiar people or things. As the disease progresses, symptoms become more serious. For example, people can forget how to do simple everyday activities, such as combing their hair, dressing, or eating. They can no longer think clearly, have problems communicating, and may become anxious, aggressive, suspicious, or apt to wander (Yeager, Farnett, & Ruzicka, 1995). With progression of the disease, they are also likely to have limitations in their daily activities, as shown in Table 7-3.

The rate of decline varies from individual to individual with AD, but decline of all abilities is inevitable. About two-thirds of the elderly population with Alzheimer's, compared with a little over one-fourth of the elderly population without the disease, are in poor physical health and are also more likely to have spent time in the hospital and in bed during the past year (National Academy on an Aging Society, 2000). Those people who survive other diseases to reach the advanced stages of Alzheimer's need total care. Because of its lengthy, downhill course that can last up to 15 or more years, victims of Alzheimer's have sometimes been described in the popular media as the "living dead."

Table 7-3   Activity Limitations Among People Age 70 and Older with Alzheimer's Disease

Limitation in Daily Activity	Percentage With Limitation
Managing money	84%
Preparing meals	79
Taking medication	73
Dressing	64
Bathing	61
Eating	58
Walking	53
Getting out of bed	38
Using the toilet	34

Source: Adapted from National Academy on an Aging Society (2000: September). "Alzheimer's Disease and Dementia: A Growing Challenge." *Challenges for the 21st Century: Chronic and Disabling Conditions*, 11:3.

Although research is underway to identify Alzheimer's disease, the diagnosis currently is absolutely confirmed only upon autopsy. An irreversible, progressive brain disorder related to changes in nerve cells, Alzheimer's is characterized by abnormal clumps and tangled bundles of fibers in the brain. Postmortem results can be surprising, indicating the absence of plaques and tangles in an individual who was considered to have had Alzheimer's. The difficulties of a definitive diagnosis lie in the fact that the symptoms of various types of dementia are similar. For example, distinguishing between the symptoms of Pick's disease, a dementia characterized by many of the same symptoms, and Alzheimer's disease can be difficult. Because definite physical evidence is impossible to get from living patients, diagnosis is made through Alzheimer's symptoms, neuropsychological tests of the individual, and interviews with family members.

Scientists now believe that genetic factors are involved. For example, a protein called *apoliproprotein E* (ApoE) may be a factor. Although all of us have ApoE, which helps carry cholesterol in the blood, the gene has several forms, only one of which increases risk for Alzheimer's. Genetic factors alone, however, are not enough to cause the disease; that is, although late onset Alzheimer's may run in some families, not everyone with the gene develops the disease. Other risk factors combine with an individual's genetic makeup to increase his or her chances of developing Alzheimer's. There is also some evidence that the development of Alzheimer's may reflect environmental factors operating over a lifetime. For example, when elders with probable or possible Alzheimer's were compared with healthy control group members, those in the Alzheimer's group were significantly less likely to engage in activities, including intellectual ones, than the control group, even after controlling for age, gender, income, and education. Whether inactivity is a risk factor for the disease, or reflects early effects of the disease, or both remains uncertain (Friedland et al., 2001).

Scientists hope that identification of Alzheimer's risk factor genes plus possible nongenetic factors, such as severe head injury and other environmental elements, can help in the development of treatments to slow or stop the disease (NIA News, 2000b). Experiments with mice provide evidence that a recently identified enzyme, BACE1, begins a process that snips a protein in the brain, producing fragments and making the plaque found in Alzheimer's. Focus on BACE1 suggests that a drug could be developed to inactivate the enzyme and prevent the build-up of the fragments (NIA News, 2001b).

Care for people with Alzheimer's is expensive and costs the United States an estimated $50 billion yearly (Leon, Chang, & Neumann, 1998). The average annual cost of paid home care for a person with Alzheimer's living in the community is $12,572, 62 percent of which is paid for out-of-pocket (National Academy on an Aging Society, 2000). Caregiving takes its emotional toll on family members as well; according to one study (see Table 7-4), 22 percent of the caregivers of a relative with dementia (including Alzheimer's) experienced mental or physical problems (Ory et al., 1999). Dementia (not only Alzheimer's) is a prime reason that elders are admitted to nursing homes; according to one study, almost half of new nursing home admissions were demented (Magaziner, 2000). As the population ages, the number of people with AD is expected to increase. Scientists are searching for ways to prevent or halt the disease. Unless prevention or a cure is dis-

Table 7-4	Effects of Alzheimer's Disease and Dementia on Caregivers' Lives	
Effect	**Percentage of Caregivers Experiencing Effect**	
Took time off from work	57%	
Gave up own leisure activities	55	
Less time for other family members	52	
Went from full- to part-time job or less demanding job	13	

Source: Adapted from Ory et al. (1999). "Prevalence and impact of caregiving: A detailed comparison between dementia and nondementia caregivers," *The Gerontologist*, 39(2): 177–185.

covered, the number of people in the United States with AD is expected to more than triple over the next 50 years (National Academy on an Aging Society, 2000).

Awareness of Alzheimer's Disease. What is it like to know that you have Alzheimer's disease? Morris Friedell, a former college professor, has described his reactions and current life after finding out he was suffering from this organic brain disease. He first became aware that something was amiss when he began to have memory lapses. Younger than the usual Alzheimer's victim, he was initially misdiagnosed as suffering from Pick's disease. His experiences give a firsthand glimpse into the world of an individual diagnosed with early stage Alzheimer's. According to Friedell (2000),

> Atypically, I've always had a little of the dysfunction I [probably] suffer. I couldn't solve the problem of which shoe went on which foot until someone wrote R and L in my shoes. I didn't enjoy playing bridge because the memorizing was onerous. I couldn't follow a basketball game, let alone play it. I was no good at small talk. Hopefully, all this now will help me cope (p. 383). . . . [In an update] I have joined the tiny community of early Alzheimer's victims who communicate by chatting on the Internet. It is a great medium for use because it is relatively slow and provides an instantaneous written record of the conversation. . . . In conclusion, "life goes on," even though it is not the same. (p. 385)

Perhaps because of ageist myths, Alzheimer's disease has been widely publicized in the media as a widespread scourge of old age, and many middle-aged people fearfully forecast that they will develop this form of dementia. Adults who have a family member with Alzheimer's are far more likely than adults whose families do not have a demented elder to have an anticipatory fear of the disease. Because of the genetic evidence linking the ApoE gene to Alzheimer's, adult children who have parents with the disease are particularly alarmed when they notice any memory lapses in themselves. Whether those with an Alzheimer's family member will ever develop the disease is uncertain, for there is currently no test that can detect or predict the likelihood of its onset. But many individuals with an impaired family member are clearly very anxious with even the slightest forgetfulness that they observe in themselves, and their apprehension can spill over into their everyday lives (Hodgson & Cutler, 2000).

Treatment of Alzheimer's Disease. Within the past decade, pharmacological advances have been made that can delay the progression of Alzheimer's in a small but significant portion of people. The Food and Drug Administration (FDA) has thus far approved two drugs for the treatment of Alzheimer's in the United States. These medications are usually prescribed for people like Morris Friedell who are in the early and mid-stage points of the disease. The first drug became available for use in 1993 and is marketed as Cognex®. A second drug, marketed as Aricept®, became available in 1996 and is more frequently prescribed. Both Cognex® and Aricept® inhibit certain chemicals in the brain, and when they work, lucidity is enhanced for a limited period of time, usually 6 to 12 months. Unfortunately, both drugs can have side effects, occasionally producing diarrhea and nausea. Aricept® can also cause an irregular heartbeat, especially among people with heart conditions, and some people taking the drug have had fainting spells. Cognex® affects liver enzymes and requires that patients be tested frequently to monitor liver function. Because frequent monitoring of liver function is required, the number of people taking this drug is limited.

Studying Anticipatory Dementia: A Researcher's View

Lynne Gershenson Hodgson, Ph.D. Professor of Sociology, Quinnipiac University.

I honestly think that researchers choose to study topics that have relevance for their lives; it has certainly been true for me. As a sociologist, with a specialization in gerontology, I've spent most of my career studying two aspects of the family lives of older people: the relationship between grandparents and adult grandchildren, and the concerns of adult children of parents with Alzheimer's disease. My interest in the first topic was an outgrowth of my graduate training in family sociology and gerontology, but it was focused by my personal experience as an adult grandchild and having a close relationship with four grandparents, all of whom lived to see me grow up, get married, and start a family of my own. My interest in the second topic stemmed from an association with a newly developed Alzheimer's facility; the administrator was farsighted enough to see that the facility could combine the best of care for the residents with the more global benefits of providing a site for Alzheimer's research. He urged me to choose a research project focused on the families of people with AD, using his facility to recruit the sample. And so, I did what researchers often do; I turned to colleagues for ideas about what to study.

Research projects are often the result of collaboration with a colleague. My work with the Alzheimer's facility may have moved me to study families of people with Alzheimer's, but it was a colleague, Stephen J. Cutler, with a good research question who directed the precise focus of the project. Himself the child of a parent with Alzheimer's, my colleague wondered if other people with the same family medical history were fearful of developing the disease, and if so, what were the consequences of that fear. And so began a multiyear collaboration—a study, funded by the Alzheimer's Association, on *anticipatory dementia* or the anxieties that arise when middle-aged adults attribute normal, age-associated memory loss to Alzheimer's. In essence, we wanted to find out what happens when a 50-year-old woman can't find her glasses. Does she assume that it's normal to forget where she's put them or does she worry that her forgetfulness is the first sign of Alzheimer's? And is her reaction different depending on whether or not she has a parent with Alzheimer's?

The anticipatory dementia project has gone through many stages, from a small feasibility study that tested whether or not we were tapping into a real phenomenon, to a pilot study that tested the best way to ask questions, to a full-scale telephone survey of 258 men and women. The development of the questionnaire, which entails finding the right questions to ask, took almost a year. So did recruiting the sample—we had to look beyond the original site because, as it turned out, it was very hard to find people who fit the study requirements (in our case, between the ages of 40 and 60, and having a living parent with a probable diagnosis of Alzheimer's disease). We subcontracted with a research firm to do the telephone interviews, and it took a year to collect all the data. And, right now, we're in the middle of analyzing what we have found—presenting our findings at professional meetings and publishing the results in academic journals. The process is a lengthy one from beginning to end, but each step is exciting (and, yes, sometimes frustrating) in and of itself. It's really the lure of science— formulating a question, gathering the applicable data, and arriving at conclusions. You find things you never expected. Take our work, for example. We confirmed our hypothesis that the children of parents with Alzheimer's were more concerned with developing the disease than those in the general population, but anticipatory dementia in the latter group was much more pervasive than we had speculated. It turns out that middle-aged men and women, no matter what their family history of AD, know enough about Alzheimer's to be worried when they lose their glasses.

Research has suggested that use of nonsteroidal anti-inflammatory drugs (NSAIDs) such as Naproxen, which reduces inflammation in the joints and other parts of the body, decreases the risk of Alzheimer's, and the National Institute on Aging is currently sponsoring trials to determine whether such drugs reduce inflammatory processes in the brain associated with AD (NIA News, 2001a). There is also some preliminary evidence suggesting that, when administered to postmenopausal women, estrogen replacement therapy may lower susceptibility to the neurological changes associated with Alzheimer's (NIA News, 2000c). At the level of animal testing, a nasal Alzheimer's vaccine has been tested and found to reduce potentially damaging disease plaques in the brains of mice; this vaccine may be tested with people in the future (NIA News, 2000d).

Critical Thinking: Disentangling Alzheimer's Disease and Depression

Depression and dementia are difficult to disentangle at first glimpse. From the discussion on different types of illness presented in this chapter, what diagnosis would you give to each case (and why)? The professional diagnosis of each case is given at the end of the two cases.

Case Study A: Alonzo Grasset

Alonzo Grasset is a 75-year-old retired tool and die maker brought into the geriatrician's office by his daughter, Maria. She is worried that her father may be senile and may need to be put in a nursing home. Mr. Grasset's wife of 40 years died last year, and he has been living alone ever since. Maria says that he "hasn't been looking after himself, sometimes he doesn't bathe, and he is losing weight." She says that he is forgetful, cannot seem to concentrate, and he is no longer interested in his favorite activities—watching the fights on TV and working in his garden. He has even lost interest in his friends and his children and grandchildren.

Mr. Grasset is an unshaven, thin man whose somewhat dirty and rumpled suit hangs loosely on his body. His speech is very slow and he sits slumped in the chair. Mr. Grasset states adamantly that there is nothing wrong with him except for feeling tired and not being able to sleep.

He has asked for a prescription of sleeping pills to help him get more rest. A physical examination reveals no major physical problems or chronic disease. Administration of a mini-mental status exam used to rule out organic mental illness indicates that, although he asks to have questions repeated and does not seem to concentrate on the task, there are no signs of memory loss. When asked if he has thought about suicide, he says no, but he does miss his wife and that he sometimes wishes he was the one to have died first.

Case Study B: Marlene Marlowe

Marlene Marlowe is a 75-year-old widow, who comes to the geriatrician's office with her daughter, Sonia, who is worried about whether her mother is sick. Mrs. Marlowe is very thin; her hair is uncombed and dirty and her skirt has grease spots. Mrs. Marlowe has been living alone for the past eight years since her husband's death. Mrs. Marlowe receives a pension from the city where she was employed as a clerk for 40 years.

Her daughter says that her mother is "not herself anymore," and that she is becoming more and more forgetful. Last week when Mrs. Marlowe was driving to Sonia's house to celebrate her grandson's birthday, she got lost on her way driving home. Mrs.

Marlowe is not willing to stop driving. She is also not paying her bills, even though there is enough money in her bank account to do so. Although she rarely cooks, she frequently turns on the gas stove for heat because she complains of being cold. She does not always light the oven properly.

Mrs. Marlowe insists that there is nothing wrong with her, but she suspects that her daughter wants to "put me away so she can get ahold of my pension." She says that she doesn't know why Sonia should be concerned with the gas oven because she uses it three times a day to make meals. However, she is unable to recall what she has had for breakfast— "just the usual, you know." Upon a physical exam, Mrs. Marlowe's mouth was very dry, suggesting that she is not drinking enough fluids. There are no other notable physical findings. When she was asked about her ability to perform activities of daily living, she became indignant, stating that she is perfectly competent to do everything she could do in her twenties. On a mini-mental status exam used to rule out dementia, she scored an 18—12 points lower than the perfect score that would be expected as normal.

Source: Adapted from P. P. Barry & E. W. Markson (1998). *Geriatric Module*. Washington, DC: American Medical Student Association.
Although the symptoms in the two cases are similar enough to be confusing at first reading, Mrs. Marlowe's memory loss indicates she is suffering from dementia. Mr. Grasset shows no such memory loss, although he claims to be forgetful.

Geriatrics, Gerontology, and Mental Health

The mental health of the elderly is often assessed using medical and psychosocial information from two emergent fields: geriatric medicine and social gerontology. It is within these two large fields that the pathological, statistical, and social models are incorporated to gain a multidisciplinary understanding of old age. The practice of geriatric medicine in the United States integrates clinical, preventive, and remedial perspectives with social information. Social gerontology thus contributes to treatment and diagnosis as it provides useful knowledge about psychosocial roles and cultural expectations. As primary care providers, geriatricians usually head a team of professionals who undertake a comprehensive multidimensional, interdisciplinary assessment not only of illnesses but also the quality of life of elderly patients (Barry, 1997). Because the physical, psychosocial, and emotional dimensions of illness are inextricably connected, evaluation of an elderly person should include physical, psychosocial, and functional abilities (Barry, 2000). When assessing mental health and mental illness, such information is vital both for the diagnosis and design of the best treatment program for a particular person.

Some behaviors that at first glance appear to be maladaptive can really be healthy adaptations to the person's current situation. The elderly man with severe arthritis, for example, who curtails his activities, such as going to baseball games and boxing matches, and watches sports on television instead may be neither depressed nor withdrawing from social life. Rather, his choice of less vigorous activities can be an adaptive mechanism to his disability. He may be using selective optimization with compensation (Baltes & Baltes, 1990) as discussed in Chapter 4. The development of both geriatrics and gerontology have begun to influence how mental health is perceived, approached, and promoted in later life. Both fields are concerned with the interplay of physical, social, and psychological dimensions of life as well as inter- and intracohort variation.

Physical health is also important for mental health.

Summary

This chapter has focused on mental health and mental illness. Although both normal behavior and mental health sound like relatively simple concepts, they are hard to define. The currently most accepted definitions, of which there are a variety, are published by the American Psychiatric Association in a periodically-revised diagnostic and statistical manual. Although it is commonly assumed that both depression and organic mental illnesses, such as Alzheimer's disease, are a part of normal aging, they are considered mental disorders. Further, alcoholism and adverse drug reactions may result in symptoms of mental illness. Two common diagnoses in later life are depression and dementia. Women are more likely to show symptoms of depression than men throughout the life course, and younger women are more likely to be depressed than older ones. The prevalence of depression is also higher among African American elderly women than among their white age-peers, reflecting their greater vulnerability to poverty and racial discrimination. Many physical illnesses are also associated with depression in later life, although it is unclear whether depression is a forerunner of physical illness or physical illnesses result in feelings of depression.

The terms *dementia* and *organic brain syndrome* (OBS) describe a number of disorders affecting memory, cognition, and mood. Dementia is caused by many different illnesses. Dementia may be irreversible and progress relentlessly, as in Alzheimer's disease, or it may be potentially reversible, as in vitamin B12 deficiency, anemia, and so on. Although dementia is diagnosed most often in the elderly, it can occur at any age. Diagnosis and management of dementia are increasingly recognized as important skills in primary care of the elderly. One of the most feared kinds of dementia is Alzheimer's disease, named after the German physician who first identified it in 1906. Other causes of dementia include Pick's disease, which affects personality and memory, and vascular dementia, which may follow a stroke or a series of small strokes. Alzheimer's disease (AD) is the most commonly diagnosed form of dementia, affecting the parts of the brain controlling thought, memory, and language. Although younger people can also develop Alzheimer's, the risk increases with age. It is important to know, however, that Alzheimer's is *not* part of normal aging. AD begins slowly, and the initial symptoms may be mild forgetfulness of recent events, activities, or the names of familiar people or things. As the disease progresses, symptoms become more serious. With progression of the disease, people are also likely to have limitations in their daily activities. Social gerontology and geriatric medicine, taking account of the individual in a social context, often work in conjunction with each other to improve diagnosis and treatment of mental illnesses in later life.

Key Points

Both normality and mental health are elusive concepts to define absolutely.

1. Various approaches have been used to diagnose illness including mental disorders and normality—the pathological, the statistical, and the social.

2. One of the most common mental health complaints among the elderly is depression, although there is less major depression among the elderly than in other adult populations.

3. The recognition of later-life depression is often confused with the onset of other mental disorders that have an organic origin.

4. Women are more likely than men to be diagnosed as depressed throughout the life course.

5. The prevalence of depression has been found to be higher among African-American elderly women than among their white counterparts, which reflects the former's greater vulnerability to poverty and racial discrimination.

6. In later life, many physical illnesses are associated with depression.

7. Although the true prevalence of alcoholism at any age is unknown, alcohol abuse can create alcohol dementia, characterized by changes in cognitive function; this is considered an organic mental disorder due to changes in the brain.

8. Although the true prevalence of alcoholism and illegal drug use in old age is unknown, some data suggest that both diminish in later life.

9. The use of numerous medications in combination with each other increases in the elderly population, presenting potential risks for adverse drug reactions to occur that can affect cognitive functioning.

10. Some dementias are reversible; others, like Alzheimer's disease, are irreversible at the present time.

11. Geriatric medicine draws on both medical data and psychosocial data in evaluating mental health and illness in elderly patients.

Discussion Questions

1. *Mental health* is an amorphous and sometimes tricky term to define. Explain why.

2. Describe the contributions and shortcomings of how we view "normal" and "normalcy."

3. Explain why alcohol abuse in later life can lead to physical and mental illnesses.

4. Why are adverse drug reactions a risk among the elderly?

5. Describe how Alzheimer's can be interpreted as a disease of the loss of self.

6. What are the symptoms of major depression?

7. Why is depression sometimes mistaken for dementia or Alzheimer's disease?

8. What is meant by "anticipatory fear" of dementia or Alzheimer's?

Films and Videos

Complaints of a Dutiful Daughter (video; 37 minutes; available from Women Make Movies, 462 Broadway, Suite 500, New York, NY 10013).

A documentary of mother-daughter relationships during her mother's gradual descent into Alzheimer's disease by a lesbian filmmaker.

Depression in Older Adults: The Right to Feel Better (video; 30 minutes; available from Terra Nova Films, Inc., 9848 South Winchester Avenue, Chicago, IL 60643; *www.terranova.org*).

Produced by Duke Medical Center, this presents interviews with actual patients and commentary from professionals about later-life depression.

Substance Abuse in the Elderly (video; 30 minutes; available from Terra Nova Films, Inc, 9848 South Winchester Avenue, Chicago, IL 60643; *www.terranova.org*).

Focus on how elders deal with the problems of numerous medications and of diminished ability to absorb alcohol, as well as on prevention programs designed for elders.

Internet Resources

http://www.nia.nih.gov

The site for the National Institute of Aging including "Age Pages" on depression, dementia, and related topics.

http://www.apa.org/psychologists

The site for the American Psychological Association including information on depression and other psychological issues.

http://aging.ufl.edu/apadiv20/apadiv20.htm

The site for Division 20—the aging division—of the American Psychological Association with information on later life issues, syllabi, and so forth.

Research Article

Haynie, D. A., Berg, S., Johansson, B., Gatz, M., & Zarit, S. H. (2001). Symptoms of depression in the oldest old: A longitudinal study. *The Journals of Gerontology Series B: Psychological Sciences and Social Sciences, 56,* P111–P118.

Supplemental Readings

Kleiner, G. (1996). *Where River Turns Into Sky.* New York: Bard/Avon.

A novelistic look at the varieties of aging personalities and experiences.

Mace, N. L., & Rabins, P. V. (1999). *The 36-Hour Day*, 3rd ed. Baltimore, MD: Johns Hopkins University Press.

A well-recognized source of support and factual information about caring for someone with Alzheimer's disease.

Rozelle, R. (2001). *Into That Good Night*. Austin, TX: Texas Review Press.

A poignant memoir of his father's transformation from a quiet, strong role model into dependency due to Alzheimer's disease.

Styron, W. (1991). *Darkness Visible: A Memoir of Madness*. New York: Vintage Books.

An account of the noted author's experience of suicidal depression and his pathway to recovery. ✦

Part III
Aging in Society

Chapter 8

Family Relationships and Social Bonds

Introduction

Merle McEathron, now a centenarian, grew up with her father, stepmother, and two older brothers on a small farm. Her mother died when she was seven; her father withdrew her from school when she reached the eighth grade. Living at home at age 16, Merle's life was a constant round of cooking, washing, cleaning, and taking care of a little stepsister until she met Louis, a dashing young man, who became her husband shortly thereafter. "When my father found out [about the impending marriage]," Merle said, "he wasn't pleased. He had a new red handkerchief in his pocket. He gave it to me, plus $10. 'Now go live with him,' he said, and that was it." After their marriage, Merle had a part-time job in a store, Louis worked as a telegraph operator, and the couple had two sons. The marriage was not happy, however, with the result that Louis suddenly packed up his things and left in the new car the couple had purchased, never to be seen again. At age 20, Merle became a single mother, initially supporting herself and her sons by working in a general store until she was able to buy another general store that she ran successfully for years, enabling her to support her sons' education at business college.

After World War II, she moved to Arizona where she met "a wonderful man, honest and decent." Their marriage of 10 years ended when he died. Lonely after his death, she later met and married a musician who played the organ at her church, but their marriage ended in divorce because he was unfaithful. Her fourth and very happy marriage of nine years to a retired Naval officer ended when he died (Holmstrom, Internet download 8/3/00).

The family history of this centenarian shatters stereotypes of older people's marital and family patterns. To what extent is her family life typical of others in her birth cohort? How is it different? Are there any similarities in Merle McEathron's family life to people you know?

Social relationships such as Merle McEathron's constitute a social convoy; that is, "family and friends who surround the individual and help in the successful negotiation of life's challenges" (Antonucci & Akiyama, 1987: 519). Just as Ms. McEathron's social convoy has varied throughout her life, yours will as well. Each of us has a social convoy whose members are likely to change as we move through the life course. Although the exact composition of our social convoys is fluid, its purpose remains constant—to exchange social supports regardless of age.

Throughout our lives, the social convoys provided by family and friends provide important sources of affection and support. These convoys form our personal social networks, usually marked by feelings of positive regard, commitment, and personal value. The people constituting our social networks are important as sources of both assistance and encouragement, helping us to maintain physical and emotional health. As you will recall from Chapter 3, one in eight Americans is now aged 65 or older, comprising almost 13 percent of the American population. In what ways are their social convoys of family and friendships unique to their birth cohorts? In what ways are they similar to those of younger cohorts? What are the general familial and friendship patterns among the now-old, and how have their social relationships changed as they have grown older? In what ways do these patterns intersect with other social characteristics, such as gender, social class, race, ethnicity, and religion?

On a more personal note, think about your present life and the people who form your circle of intimates, such as family members and friends. How will your family and friendship roles change as you, your family members, and your friends grow older? What will your relationship to these people be 10 years, 20 years, 30 years, and 40 years from now? Now imagine other people whom you have not met, some of whom may not even have been born yet but who will play important roles in your future life. Think also of people who are important to you now but who may not always be part of your life in the future: friends from home, college friends and acquaintances, parents, grandparents, and other relatives. Just as your parents, and perhaps grandparents and other relatives, cared for you when you were growing up, will you be taking care of your grandparents, parents, a spouse or partner, other relatives, or friends at some point in your life? Will others take care of you at some future time? What will your social relationships, including family and friends, be like when you become 65? This chapter explores social convoys provided by family and friends, as well as the role of religion in later life.

Family Ties and Patterns

MYTH: THERE IS ONLY ONE TYPE OF FAMILY
STRUCTURE IN MOST SOCIETIES

Although everyone has an idea of what a family is, or should be, the word *family* describes many patterns with various meanings to different people. Thus, there is no universal definition of *family*, because family forms vary by culture, historical period, and the social structure of a society. This point is especially clear when industrialized and nonindustrialized societies are compared. For example, consider the definitions of *family* used by two very different nonindustrialized societies, the Nayar of India and the Nyakyusa of Tanzania. Among the Nayar, the basic family unit is a kin-based system of women, in which the responsibility of raising children belongs to a woman's family of origin. Households are composed of a woman's children and grandchildren, all of whom live in the home of the woman's brother. This type of family organization is well adapted to the social structure of this particular agriculturally-based society, where the division of labor is determined by gender only. Women perform household and agricultural tasks while men pursue occupations that keep them outside their village and away from home for long periods of time. This female kin-based system prevents social isolation through the social convoy of kin.

In contrast, among the Nyakyusa, who live in the southwest corner of Tanzania, families are organized around villages rather than individual family units. Villages are formed on the basis of age and isolation of adolescent sons from their fathers. When Nyakyusa boys reach the age of 10, they traditionally build their own homes near, but separate from, their families of origin. Boys grow up together in the newly formed age-village and eventually bring their wives to live with them.

Why do the Nyakyusa segregate themselves in this way? The reason reflects their particular social structure. The Nyakyusa are both polygamous (men can have many wives simultaneously) and male-dominated. Competition between fathers and sons for the same wives would likely occur (i.e., kinship tensions could become intolerable, disrupting the society as a whole) if age-based, male-dominated villages were not established.

The Nayar and Nyakyusa family structures illustrate the point that the particular composition and definition of a family reflect the conditions and arrangements associated with the larger social structure of a society. The political and economic social realities of a society are tied directly to how a family is defined. All family patterns, whether industrial or preindustrial, reflect the norms, values, and broader social structural features of that particular society. In the United States, numerous family forms and arrangements exist, and as with all social interaction, they are dynamic rather than static.

Just as the examples of the Nayar and Nayakyusa show that there is no single designation of a family in nonindustrial societies, no single definition applies to the *family* in the United States. Although social scientists have studied the family for many years, the many arrangements and characteristics of U.S. families make it difficult to come up with a single definition. Is the U.S. family an isolated nuclear unit, containing a mother, father, and one or more children as portrayed in reruns of old television shows, such as *Leave It to Beaver* or *Father Knows Best*? Clearly, there are other types of family structures in the United States today that contradict this depiction.

The diversity of family forms in the United States has led some researchers, such as Skolnick and Skolnick (1997), to propose that the general term *family* should no longer be used; rather *families* or *family life* should be substituted. This suggestion is important, for it emphasizes the fact that families are an ongoing, ever-changing process, evolving and altering over time rather than being fixed. *Families* and *family life* describe a composite of many forms and practices in the real world just as other abstract terms (e.g., *the economy*) describe numerous aspects of the financial world (Skolnick & Skolnick, 1997). Newly emerging family structures—same-sex partners, same-sex-parenting couples, stepfamilies, and so on—develop and shift as the wider society undergoes continuous social change. In turn, patterns of family life also affect the broader society in which they occur, creating a dynamic interaction between specific family configurations and the broader social structure.

Although family forms change over time, the family has at least two basic social purposes: (1) meeting private and individualized needs and (2) serving the broader public need of the society. In the public sphere, specific family members (female family members as among the Nayar or dual earner couples in contemporary U.S. society) are socially charged as responsible for the physical care of dependents, such as children, frail elders, and others unable to care for themselves. In the private sphere, family members provide other members with intimacy, nurturance, and emotional connectedness (Cherlin, 1999). Families, however defined, are our first social convoy in life.

How have configurations of family life changed as the population ages? Although the human life span has not changed, life expectancy has dramatically increased with the result that U.S. citizens born today can expect to live at least 30 years longer than those born in 1900. Not only are we living longer as a nation, but many more of us live to grow very old than at any previous time in recorded history. Americans are also more likely to be healthy in old age today than the elderly of yesteryear. People aged 80 and older are now the most rapidly increasing proportion of our population, a trend that is expected to continue during the twenty-first century. Not only will an estimated 1 in 5 Americans be 65 or over by the year 2050, but many of you who are reading this textbook today will also be among those 1 in 5. Given that the proportion of people living to be 60, 70, 80, and even 100 is increasing worldwide, family patterns and relationships face unique challenges in which the aging of the population is likely to change personal and family expectations, attitudes, and behaviors (see Table 8-1).

Table 8-1	Percentage of Population Aged 60 and Over in Selected Industrialized and Nonindustrialized Nations, 1996 and 2050 [Estimated]			
	Percentage Aged 60 and Over*		Percentage Aged 75 and Over*	
Country	1996	2050 Est.	1996	2050 Est.
Industrialized Nations				
Germany	21%	32%	6%	11%
Italy	22	33	7	13
Japan	21	33	6	15
United Kingdom	20	29	7	10
United States	16	25	6	8
Nonindustrialized Nations				
Bangladesh	5%	9%	**	2%
China	10	20	2	5
India	6	12	1	3
Tanzania	5	4	**	1
Uruguay	17	21	5	7

*Percentages rounded.
**Less than 1 percent of the population in that age group.
Source: U.S. Department of Commerce, Economics and Statistics Administration, Bureau of the Census and National Institute on Aging, *Global Aging Into the 21st Century*, December 1996 (wall chart).

The various experiences and ways of being in a family also change with aging. As Matilda White Riley (1983) has pointed out, the longevity revolution requires new views of families. The popular notion of the American family as a private, nuclear system with only casual contacts with other kin no longer fits. Instead, our lives are intertwined with relatives throughout the life course as needs arise. Kinship linkages—whether by blood, marriage, or agreement—that were either inactive or existed only casually are potent potential resources in everyone's social convoy. Its members can be mobilized at any point in the life course when close social relationships are wanted or needed.

Life Chances and the Family

MYTH: All American Families Have
Equal Life Chances

When people become adults, they come from many different types of families and duplicate or change the family structures in which they grew up. Nevertheless, consistent patterns, themes, and trends exist. Especially important in understanding the relationships among individuals, families, and society are the concepts of social stratification, life chances, and social class as discussed in Chapter 1 of this book. These concepts, which we will review briefly, are useful to understand varied familial life circumstances and to clarify patterns among families in later life.

As you will recall from earlier chapters, in capitalist societies such as ours, social stratification describes the unequal distribution of wealth, power, and prestige among groups in relation to certain built-in and acquired characteristics that they possess. Like it or not, everyone's familial and individual positions in a society are stratified (separated and differentiated) into hierarchies by a number of attributes: social class, gender, age, race, and ethnicity. Regardless of one's social class, age, gender, race or ethnicity, or birth cohort, both individual experience in a family and a specific family's position in the larger society are closely connected to the concept of life chances. *Life chances,* as defined by Max Weber (1845–1920), a major social theorist, determine the probability of having a particular lifestyle. *Lifestyle* is shaped by an individual's socioeconomic position, and the degree to which anyone is able to achieve "success," however it is defined, is based on access to social and economic resources (Weber, 1922/1968).

Family life, too, is influenced by life chances. For those families whose resources are few, the probability is greater that the life chances of its members will be limited throughout parts or all of the life course. Limited life chances influence lifestyles and the ways in which any of us will experience old age. For example, the writer Frank McCourt, whose book *Angela's Ashes* became a feature film, was born in the early 1930s in New York City and was one of seven children, only four of whom survived to adulthood. Unable to support themselves in the United States, his parents took the family back to Ireland, hoping for greater social and economic opportunities. Their hopes were dashed because they were not only objects of charity but McCourt and his siblings also had little opportunity for education. Although McCourt and his surviving family members eventually escaped from grinding poverty after their return to the United States, their life chances and subsequent life course, including his mother's poor health and emotional well-being in old age, were branded by their earlier lack of resources. Even though some members of the McCourt family achieved success, their lives were imprinted with the marks of earlier deprivation. Other poor families whom McCourt knew, whether in the United States or Ireland, were even less fortunate throughout their lives, remaining disadvantaged by their position in the social hierarchies of gender, race, and ethnicity as well as social class (McCourt, 1999). Like Frank McCourt and his family, everyone else's past, current, and future lifestyle is tied to life chances.

The Way We Were

MYTH: THE AMERICAN FAMILY HAS BROKEN DOWN

A common belief persists that there was a "Golden Age" of the American family—a time when most Americans lived in extended families, consisting of parents, children, and grandparents from three generations living contentedly in harmony under one roof. This idea also prompts the belief that the American family of today is breaking down. If so, how did Americans move from contented extended families to fragmented nuclear ones, consisting of husband, wife, and minor children or dissolved by divorce? According to some commentators, the strong family ties inherent in the extended family came undone during the nineteenth century when the United States began to shift from a rural economy based on agriculture to an urban, industrialized society. As a result of urbanization and industrialization, family members became physically and emotionally disconnected from one another, preoccupied with self-interests instead of the welfare of the family and society. Often-cited issues by advocates of the family breakdown model are increases in both divorce rates and the proportion of single parent households. That we abandon our elders in nursing homes, or neglect them in lonely isolation, is also a widespread myth, cited as an indication of familial decay. This notion is neither based in nor supported by current sociohistorical research on the family. Rather than the dissolution of the family, new family forms evolved as American society became more economically and socially complex.

Farm, Village, and Urban Family Structures

MYTH: AMERICAN FAMILIES USED TO BE EXTENDED FAMILIES WITH MANY GENERATIONS AND RELATIVES LIVING UNDER ONE ROOF

Despite the myth of the extended family, the most common family form in the United States has been nuclear, consisting of parents and minor children, throughout the nation's history. Thus, the nuclear family is by no means a new invention emerging in the twentieth century. What was the reality of U.S. family life in the past? Historians who have studied the American family point to three significant stages: (1) colonial or agricultural (seventeenth and eighteenth centuries); (2) urban and industrial (nineteenth and early twentieth centuries); and (3) postindustrial (1920s to the present). Each period has been characterized by new social arrangements and preoccupations of life, distinguishing it from the previous era. During the colonial period, most adults spent their lives as parents of children and teenagers with few parents living long enough to see their last child leave home. Although colonial New England particularly emphasized the honor and respect due to elders, those who did live to be old did not automatically hold either wealth or power nor did they form a gerontocracy. Rather, if there was no money or power, there was no respect at any age. Every colonial New England religious meetinghouse seated people by social status indicators that included not only age but also—and very importantly—wealth, public service, and family pedigree. A young rich man was far more likely to be given a front row seat in the meetinghouse, and an old and poor man a back bench (Demos, 1986). Clearly, poor elders were not automatically revered!

Accompanying urbanization and industrialization, very different family structures developed among people living on farms, in villages, and in cities. Among those living on farms, family patterns were affected by social class. Relatively wealthy older farmers encouraged younger family members to remain in the household to work on the farm, with the eldest son inheriting the land and the dominant role in the family. Both poor native-born and foreign-born aging farmers, however, were more likely to work either as hired hands or subsistence farmers and thus unlikely to live in extended families (Haber & Gratton, 1994).

Although there were racial, ethnic, and social class variations, village and urban middle-class families have most often been composed of parents and minor children.

Among people living in villages, family structure most closely resembled the contemporary American nuclear family. During the industrial era, many aging farmers found it more profitable to sell or rent their farmland to others, using the money to establish their own homes and independent lives in villages away from their adult children. Unlike the farm, village life did not promise inheritance or a source of employment, so few adult children remained with their elderly parents. Rather, they migrated to cities to look for jobs and marriage partners (Haber & Gratton, 1994). Table 8-2 summarizes household characteristics for farms, villages, and cities in 1900.

Table 8-2	Household Characteristics for Men and Woman Aged 60+, Living on Farms, in Villages, and in Cities, 1900 (Percentage Distribution)					
	Farm		Village		City	
Relationship to Household Head	Men	Women	Men	Women	Men	Women
Head	81%	13%	74%	32%	77%	30%
Wife	—	44	—	36	—	31
Parent	13	36	6	18	11	25
Children and Other Relatives and Non-kin	6	7	20	14	12	14

Source: Adapted from Public Use Sample of the 1900 U.S. Census, reported in Haber and Gratton, *Old Age and the Search for Security: An American Social History.* Bloomington, IN: Indiana University Press, 1994: 29.

Although urban life has been blamed for the breakup of the family, urbanization and industrialization actually *increased* the probability that elders would live with kin in order to meet the new demands of a changing economy. Complex family structures that included children, grandchildren, siblings, cousins, nonrelatives, and fictive kin (i.e., members not related by blood or marriage but considered family) became more common than the three-generation extended family.

In the city, both extended and complex family structures enabled blue-collar families to improve their economic status by pooling resources. Although extended families became more common among the working classes, the increased economic well-being of middle-class families encouraged establishment of nuclear families in which elders were able to live independently from one another. While the United States continued to industrialize, birth rates fell sharply as the children, once economic assets in an agricultural society, became economic liabilities (Haber & Gratton, 1994).

Race. African-American families differed from both rich and poor whites. Before the Civil War, neither slaves nor freed blacks had opportunities to build wealth or savings for their old age. If slaves, they were dependent on their owners; if free and poor, they were dependent on racist local public welfare systems or charity. After emancipation, African Americans were hired by white landowners as tenant farmers or sharecroppers. Living in extended families whose labor was needed by the white landowners, they had little opportunity to amass savings.

Institutionalized racial discrimination plus historically-based forms of family organization resulted in complex family structures.

The inclusion of fictive kin in the African American household may have historical roots in West Africa, where blood relationships were emphasized at the expense of the marital relationship; such ties are, in any case, believed to have preceded slavery, which in turn reinforced such patterns after the Civil War (Johnson, 1999). Even today, as a legacy of the past and response to continued discrimination, African Americans are more likely to rank their individual needs and desires as less important than the interests of the family unit and its social and economic survival (Slevin & Wingrove, 1998).

Gender. Regardless of race or ethnicity, position in the family—and the structure of a family itself—also varies by gender. During the colonial period, aging wives were a vital component of the farm economy, but widows quickly lost their power as family heads. A scant century ago, elderly farm women were far less likely to be household heads than either village or urban women. In 1900, for example, close to one-third of village and city households were headed by women aged 60 and over, primarily widows who kept their authority as family heads.

Urban family life provided more autonomy for women than did the farm because it was easier for them to find employment or to support themselves by operating boarding houses. The position of older women in the family thus varied, influenced by social class, race and ethnicity, and place of residence. Middle- and upper-class women were expected to be wives, mothers, and (if they lived long enough) grandmothers devoted to hearth and home. Rather than a self-sufficient economic unit, the home was redefined as a refuge for its members: a haven from the heartless industrialized, noisy, urban outside world. Child rearing became the exclusive domain of the mother and was redefined to cover a longer time span. Hence, the home became a child-centered retreat (Hareven, 1982).

Lives of working-class, foreign-born, and African American older women, however, were very different. Their labor, whether in the home or as servants and factory workers, was necessary to maintain the family as an economically viable unit. Impoverished older women faced a difficult future: dependency on charity or the poorhouse.

Family Structure Variations Today

Although various family types established during the colonial and industrial eras survive today, a major change in family structure within the past century has been the size of the nuclear family. In 1900, for example, the average American couple had four children; today, the average couple has one or two. Never before have significant numbers of married couples had more living parents than minor children, a trend brought about both by lower birth rates and unprecedented changes in life expectancy.

U.S. families are also becoming increasingly multigenerational. Ironically, although not often living in the same household, families are coming closer to the myth of the yesteryear extended family. The *beanpole family*, so-called because it is long, tall, and spindly (i.e., characterized by more people in several generations than in one single generation), is becoming common. In the beanpole family, great-grandparents have fewer numbers of children, grandchildren, and great-grandchildren than did people in previous generations but, due to their increased longevity, these elders have unprecedented possibilities to interact with family members of different generations and be parts of each other's social convoy (Bengtson, Rosenthal, & Burton, 1990). By the year 2020, population projections indicate that the typical family will indeed be a beanpole, comprising four or more generations. An estimated 59 percent of the Americans born in 2000 will have both parents alive when they turn 40 in 2040; 27 percent will have both parents still alive at age 50; and at age 70, 7 percent will have one parent still alive (Bengtson, Giarrusso, Silverstein, & Wang, 2000).

Traditional family forms have also been brought by recent immigrants to the United States. Despite their variation in language, country of origin, and life trajectories, these new immigrants from Asian and Latin cultures are likely to share common themes: rigidly defined age- and gender-linked roles and priority of the family unit rather than individual members. Although family patterns differ according to country of origin and level of acculturation, Latinos traditionally have emphasized familism, that is, a "strong identification and attachment of individuals with their families (nuclear and extended), and strong feelings of loyalty, reciprocity and solidarity among members of the same family" (Sabogal et al., 1987: 397–398).

Latino elders are less likely to live alone than elderly non-Latino whites or African Americans and, not surprisingly, given their living arrangements, they have higher levels of family interaction. Latina widows are likely to have the largest household size and number of offspring and to live with others. As discussed in Chapter 3, the social and cultural characteristics of Latinos vary widely, with language being the major common denominator; the degree to which Latino immigrants adapt a specific family structure varies by country of origin, socioeconomic position, gender, and degree of acculturation. Elders' preferences for living arrangements reflect their current social and economic situation; older Latinos who live in their own homes or in public housing prefer to live alone rather than with other family members (Zsembik, 1996).

Asians are even more diverse than Latinos and include Asian and Pacific Islanders, Chinese, Japanese, Korean, Vietnamese, Laotian, Hmong, and Filipino, among others. They have varied languages, cultures, and, very often, incidents of disaster precipitating their emigration. These people bring with them not only different languages but also varying family forms and support networks, expectations, and social and economic needs. Asian families, however, traditionally have emphasized filial piety and respect for the elderly. As Asian families become more acculturated, family forms and definitions are shifting. For example, although expectations for filial piety and close contact with the family remain strong among elderly Vietnamese immigrants, financial responsibility is seen as the duty of the government rather than of adult children (Seelbach & Die, 1988).

Similarly, as socioeconomic conditions for Koreans in the United States have improved and younger generations have become acculturated, modifications in the norm of filial piety, stressing the importance of the marital bond of the children over the parent-child relationship, have taken place and elders' family power has decreased (Kauh, 1999). This modified version of filial piety does not neglect the elderly; rather, married children and their spouses are still expected to provide care and social support to their elderly parents (Kim, Kim, & Hurh, 1991). Financial assistance among Korean Americans flows largely from adult children to aged parents and phone calls and visits between Korean elders and their children are frequent (Kauh, 1997). Preference for family structure among new immigrant families is fashioned and refashioned according to the specific culture, gender, social class, and length of time in the United States as well as by personal taste.

In some African-American families, communal collective activities take precedence over individualism as a value. Institutionalized racial discrimination plus historically-based forms of family organization have resulted in extended and complex family structures for many African Americans. Middle-class African Americans are thus more likely to rank their individual needs and desires as less important than serving the best interests of the family unit and ensuring its economic survival (Slevin & Wingrove, 1998). Many contemporary African-American families include fictive kin, who expand family boundaries and sources of support (Johnson, 1999).

MYTH: Most Older People Prefer to Live with Their Adult Children

Nuclear family structures and independent residential patterns of the elderly imply neither neglect nor the reluctance of younger generations to support their elderly parents. Rather, data suggest that most elders, when economically able to do so, have preferred to live in their own households. The passage of Social Security legislation, enacted in the 1930s, was a landmark, enabling many elders who otherwise would have been dependent on their children or on charity for support to maintain their independence. Whether nuclear or extended, expectations and assumptions of family life based on intergenerational mutual assistance and support characterize most American families today.

Current research suggests that the family as an institution is not dying but is alive and well in its many forms.

Although many current portrayals of older families tend to stress illness and disability rather than the increasing vitality of later-life family relationships, social and structural changes, plus current trends in life expectancy and improved health in old age present new potentials for family life and opportunities for new roles for older people in the twenty-first century. As Hagestad has noted,

> . . . family relationships now have an unprecedented duration. . . . Siblings may share eight decades of life, and for most of those years, they will regard each other as age peers. The majority of parents and children will have about half a century of shared lives. . . . Grandparents and grandchildren will have relationships which last two or more decades. (1987: 266)

The Families of the Now-Old

Marriage

Throughout our lives, marital status and living arrangements in any society are shaped by sociodemographic features: the sex composition of a birth cohort and the proportion of the population constituting that cohort, marital status, health, socioeconomic status, and the availability of supportive family and kin. The elderly are no exception. Most people marry at one point or another in their lives, and only a small number never marry. Others classified as "never married" include both heterosexual and gay and lesbian couples in intimate partnered relationships. Some heterosexual couples choose never to marry, and in most states, lesbian and gay couples are denied the option of legal marriage. Because no count of such couples is made by the census, the actual number of people in stable couple relationships is underestimated.

In the United States, as in many other nations, patterns of marital status in later life vary markedly with advancing age and by gender, race, and ethnicity. Although widowhood rises with age for both men and women, most elderly men are married, but most elderly women are not. As you will recall from Chapter 3, among young-old (65–74) U.S. citizens, the majority of white, African-American, and Latino men are married and living with their spouses, as are over half of the women. Elderly men and women are about equally unlikely to have never married—only about 5 percent—or to have divorced and not remarried—also about 5 percent (Hobbs & Damon, 1996).

Marital Satisfaction

MYTH: Satisfaction with Marriage Goes Down After Retirement

The dynamics of love and marriage throughout the life course—who loves more, who benefits, and who is put at a disadvantage by it—are of interest to social scientists studying relationships, marriage, and family. Cupid does not take aim blindly; we tend to be attracted to people who meet our unspoken personal preferences for a mate (e.g., physical appearance, economic status, race, ethnicity, religion, education). Cupid's arrows are fairly well placed, because couples express a high level of satisfaction at the start of marriage. Marital satisfaction tends to decline in middle age, reflecting challenging or difficult life events (e.g., the complex problems of raising children, earning a living and/or building a successful career, and providing care to elderly parents or other relatives). Marital satisfaction increases in later life for several reasons: (1) many unhappy couples have divorced and (2) couples experience a decrease in the pressure of life events (e.g., freedom from childcare, earning a living, or trying for job promotions).

Compared with middle-aged couples, older husbands and wives are likely to have fewer conflicts and more possibilities for pleasure in several areas of their lives, such as relationships with children, as well as fewer gender differences in sources of pleasure (Levenson, Carstensen, & Gottman, 1993). Both men and women in marriages lasting 45 or more years stress the importance of being married to someone they like as a person, who has a sense of humor, and who is generally in agreement on aims and goals in life, friends, and decisionmaking (Lauer, Lauer, & Kerr, 1990). As couples stay together over time, their shared experiences and accumulated life histories are likely to create strong personal bonds, intimacy, and self-identification as a couple, all enhancing marital satisfaction.

What impact does retirement have on marital satisfaction in later life? The marital relationship generally declines for both husbands and wives when one of the partners begins to move into retirement, but once his or her retirement actually takes place, marital quality is high again, especially if income is adequate (Moen, Kim, & Hofmeister, 2000). More resources, including leisure time, are available to the couple. Retirement is not always a blessing, however. Stressful life changes may occur as couples spend significantly more time with each other, requiring changes in their roles and expectations for their relationship. Again, the past history of the relationship is a factor; postretirement conflicts are fewer when either spouse is attached to the marriage (Szinovacz & Schaffer, 2000).

Being married in later life also apparently insulates against bad health. Married older adults are less likely to develop physical and mental disabilities than the widowed, divorced, separated, or never married. Although illness and disability levels differ among separated, widowed, and divorced elderly, all categories are disadvantaged compared with the married (Waite & Hughes, 1999). Throughout the life course, research on marriage suggests that men are the primary beneficiaries because of the care provided by their wives. It is perhaps not surprising that, regardless of the social class, race, and ethnicity of the couple, marriage appears more crucial for social interaction, life expectancy, and absence of depressive symptomatology among men than among women in old age (Lee, Willetts, & Seccombe, 1998; Lauer, Lauer, & Kerr, 1990).

Many older lesbian and gay couples, although not afforded the institutional support provided by marriage, also have fulfilling and enduring intimate relationships (Peplau & Spalding, 2000). Same-sex couples are apparently as successful in creating satisfying relationships as are heterosexual couples and are no more or less likely to experience dissatisfaction with their relationship as a couple than their heterosexual counterparts. As with heterosexual couples, satisfaction is derived from a long-term exchange relationship that serves as a basis to continue the relationship in the future.

Widowhood

Although women outlive men in all Western industrialized societies and thus are more likely to be widowed, what we may not readily recognize is that the proportion of widows compared with widowers is higher at all points in the life course and increases as we grow old. Among those widowed between the ages of 20 and 39 in the United States, about 8 in 10 are women (Statistical Abstract of the United States, 2000). A major reason for the greater proportion of widows is gender-linked behavior; men are more likely than women to engage in high-risk behaviors throughout the life course. They are likely to drive faster, farther, and less cautiously than women, to violate more traffic regulations, and to die in automobile accidents. Men are also more likely to be employed in more dangerous occupations, to engage in high-risk behaviors (e.g., smoking, drinking alcohol, and using drugs), and to be at greater risk of homicide and suicide. All these behaviors reflect social and cultural influences on marital status and the probability of widowhood that crosscuts race and ethnicity (Waldron, 1976; 1990).

Widowhood at any age represents a loss: the cessation of cumulative experiences and interwoven lives. These losses are often compounded by lack of economic and social resources, especially for women (Hungerford, 2001), and by failing health. Ascribed characteristics, such as gender, race, and ethnicity, plus achieved characteristics, such as education and social class, also affect how a person will experience widowhood. Educational level is important; in general, the higher the educational attainment of the spouse left behind, the better equipped he or she is to handle the loss of a spouse. Higher social class insulates; people whose life chances have been greater are also more likely to have the problem-solving skills needed during this life transition. Friends and associates can provide age-related peer group companionship and promote shared mutual interests toward the enhancement of well-being (McCandless & Conner, 1997; Lopata, 1994; 1996). Although widows are poorer than widowers, widowers fare worse socially and emotionally as they have fewer sources of social, religious, and emotional support and lower test scores of psychological well-being (Fry, 2001).

Although seldom discussed, the death of a spouse can also provide respite from pressures, such as an abusive or unhappy marriage in which separation or divorce could not be considered because of religious or familial taboos, threat of the loss of economic security, or even fear of the stigma of divorce. Death of a spouse can also provide relief from the role of caregiver to a spouse with chronic debilitating or degenerative diseases. One caregiver, Dolores, caring for a husband with terminal cancer, recounted her experiences in the following way:

> My husband died at 75 of cancer, after a long and debilitating illness. . . . This process was spread over a period of eleven years. . . . Gradually he turned into a bedridden invalid, totally dependent on me for his daily care. The last year was devastating; it became a 24-hour job and I got little sleep because of his extreme restlessness. . . . My lack of sleep made deep inroads on my sense of reality. I have several gaps in my memory of that terrible time, probably because I was carrying on as I have been programmed to do. . . . (Sommers & Shields, 1987: 26–27)

Divorce

Contrary to popular belief about the midlife crisis, in which an aging wife is traded in for a new, younger wife, divorce rates do not peak in late middle age. With each succeeding year of marriage, the likelihood of divorce *decreases* (Cooney, 1995). In addition, the number of married couples celebrating their 50th anniversary is on the rise (Edmonson, 1997).

Unhappy couples typically split early on. Nonetheless, extended life expectancy means that more people today than in the past enter old age as divorced, a trend that is likely to continue well into the twenty-first century. Like widowhood, divorce in old age will probably continue to have a greater economic impact on women (Cooney, 1995). Many older women today who have been primarily wives and mothers have fewer skills to offer the job market. Gender and age discrimination further limit their chances of finding employment.

In addition, older divorced women are much less likely to remarry than their male age peers. Even when individuals remarry, the negative economic results of divorce continue into the preretirement years (Holden & Kuo, 1996). Because of increases in divorce rates, it is likely that the proportion of people who do not remarry after divorce will increase among tomorrow's elderly. Older women in particular, who are less likely to remarry than men, will be especially affected. Remarriage rates for elderly widows have remained fairly stable over the last three decades or so, but remarriages among divorced women have tended to decrease. This trend may be offset by the recent rise in median age at first marriage among both men and women; that is, the risk of a marital dissolution is inversely related to age at first marriage.

Ending a marriage through divorce in old age is unlikely to raise issues of child custody or child support, but divorce of one's adult children is another matter and is likely to affect the relationship between grandparents and minor grandchildren. After the divorce of an adult child, grandparents are more likely to be involved with their grandchildren if (1) they live nearby, (2) their adult child—especially a daughter—has custody, or (3) their grandchildren are living in single-father families. Grandmothers are also more likely than grandfathers to have contact with their grandchildren (Hilton & Macari, 1997; Cooney, 1995).

Social Supports

MYTH: The Majority of Older People Are Socially Isolated

There is no one relationship that is called social support; spouse or partner, children, friends, siblings, and the deity are all potential sources for meeting different emotional, social, and instrumental or task needs throughout the life course. This section explores the ways in which older people participate in the networks that form their social convoy. As originally described by Emile Durkheim, a *social network* is the "support accessible to an individual through social ties to other individuals, groups, and the larger community" (1897/1966: 109). Although the number and composition of people in everyone's social network or convoy vary throughout the life course, the social support they provide remains an important source of well-being and sense of identity in old age.

Neither the size of a social network nor the amount of interaction is as important as having intimate and supportive relationships. Even one person in whom one can confide is important for well-being

(Lowenthal & Haven, 1968). Effective social ties reduce psychological distress, offset the impact of stress, and help maintain physical and psychological well-being in later life (Hays et al., 1998). Despite the stereotype of the lonely older person, total social isolation—the absence of any social contacts, interaction, and support networks—is rare among the elderly. The size of social networks apparently decreases with age, however, as does the frequency of contact with its members; the proportion of kin in the network, however, increases with age (Ajrouch, Antonucci, & Janevic, 2001).

Relatives and Friends as Sources of Social Support

Research has shown that married elders almost always feel most intimate with their spouses. Both genders, however, are likely to include more women from whom they generally receive support in their social network. Among never married, separated, widowed, or divorced older people with children, relationships with same-sex children are more important than those with siblings or friends (Akiyama, Elliott, & Antonucci, 1996). Nonetheless, sibling relationships are important in later life, providing mutual support as well as potential and actual support for aged parents. Such relationships can take many forms; brothers and sisters may have the same parents, be adopted, share one biological parent (half brother or sister), share neither biological parent (stepsister or stepbrother), or share neither legal nor biological links as fictive kin (Bedford & Blieszner, 2000). Although sibling ties frequently wane during young adulthood as brothers and sisters focus on their own family and friendship networks, sibling rivalry, envy, and resentment decline with aging. In midlife, death of one or both parents usually brings siblings closer.

Widowhood, death of another sibling, serious illness of a spouse or another sibling, and retirement can also increase intimacy with a sibling during old age (Gold, 1996). Sibling ties provide *generational solidarity,* typified by feelings of closeness, psychological involvement, and acceptance/approval (Gold, 1989a). Generational solidarity increases even in the absence of frequent contact, and merely being aware that a sibling is still alive is important in maintaining positive feelings (Gold, 1989b). Single men and women, those without children, and widows have particularly close sibling ties, especially if the sibling lives nearby. Siblings are also more likely to be confidants, companions, and to give emotional and task-oriented support when one or more children is geographically distant (Campbell, Connidis, & Davies, 1999). Gender also plays a role with sisters feeling closer to one another and women apparently more emotionally connected to their brothers or sisters than men (Miner & Uhlenberg, 1997; Wellman & Wortley, 1989). Friendships can also have familial and siblinglike qualities. When family members are employed, live in a different locale, or are estranged, friends can assume the role of "backup relatives."

Death of a spouse can renew or strengthen old friendship ties and create new ones. As one widow commented, "I've made a very nice friend from the group of women I met down at the Y. . . . I met a new lady friend. And I've renewed a friendship with another lady that I used to be very friendly with" (Lund et al., 1990: 61). Men and women who have been bereaved tend to have closer relationships with others of the same gender (Lund et al., 1990). In general, gender plays a significant role in the structure of social networks, with women likely to have larger support systems and to give and receive more assistance throughout the life course than men. Women traditionally not only have been the "kin keepers" but also their lifelong tendency to have significant friendships often intensifies in old age.

Compared with whites, African Americans have smaller social networks, more family members in their networks, and more contact with them, but this difference tends to decrease among the very old (Ajrouch, Antonucci, & Janevic, 2001). Among African-American elders, fictive kin (i.e., distant relatives and close friends) also provide important sources of social support and caregiving and substitute for family members lost due to changes in the family or through death (Magai, Cohen, Milburn et al., 2001; Johnson, 1999). Because of racial discrimination, African-American families have tended to organize around the need to share resources to survive and to identify with the family unit rather than individual needs. Both inner-city and more economically diverse African Americans have strong sibling ties to draw on in times of need (Johnson & Barer, 1996). Even though both white and African Americans associate more often if they help one another and if they live together, studies show that African Americans are more likely to have closer contact with their brothers or sisters if younger siblings provide help to an older one and the younger sibling has a higher level of education; whites are more likely to interact with their siblings when they share similar values (Suggs, 1989). Popular myths to the contrary, family members—whether blood relatives, fictive kin, or friends who act like family—remain the core of elders' social convoys regardless of race or ethnicity.

Religion as a Source of Social Support

For many people, religious organizations are important informal social supports associated with well-being (Ellison, 1991; 1994). For others, both God and the congregation become "family." Naomi, a 76-year-old African-American widow, whose one son lives with his wife and family in California, has resisted their pleas to join them because she would lose her "church family" (Streff, 2001). When Naomi's boyfriend, an usher in a different church, died several years ago, she found comfort in her church friends.

> When he died, all my church family come round to his church. It was packed there. I mean, it's so nice, you know, how people can turn out for you. . . . Everybody comes shaking my hand. It was wonderful to know that you are cared about. (Streff, 2001)

Although Naomi sees the secret of her successful survival as keeping in touch with Jesus, she was not deeply involved in either church or church friends until she retired:

> When I was out there, I was having a good time, you know. . . . Yes, you know, you go through life, you work hard, you have fun and drinking and you're clowning around. . . . But now you gotta settle down and it's altogether different. You know more about Jesus, you want to be with Him. . . . I learned about Him years, years ago, but I didn't come in until [I was] 73. . . . [When I was working] I wasn't off on Sundays. Every Sunday you had to work . . . so I didn't have much time to go to church. Before, I had a lotta friends. You usually have a lot of friends out there because you're doing everything. But now I'm into church and I have more friends, but they're a different type of friends. These friends here have more love, more understanding. The others are fly by night. . . . I have a whole church full of friends and I go to different churches, you know, and I make friends when I go there. I pay my tithe at one, at my church, and another church I pay tithes too, and the church across the street I pay tithes to. . . . So God is blessing me. . . . It's a family, you know. I wake up in the morning, I thank Jesus Christ and I thank the Holy Spirit and thank my guardian angel for keeping me through the night, and I ask them to direct my path for the day, to protect me from all evil and harm. Get up and I read my Bible . . . I begin my day and end my day, reading my Bible. I look out at the sky and talk to my Jesus, sittin' right over there in that chair by the window. (Streff, 2001)

Others find their major source of support and strength not in religious participation but in their personal relationship with God, Jesus, or the Lord, which provides strength in coping with difficult situations (Poindexter, Linsk, & Warner, 1999), such as that faced by Mrs. Warren, a 90-year-old Catholic white widow crippled from a broken hip. She is alienated from one of her three daughters, has another daughter who is mentally ill, and feels unloved by her children and grandchildren:

> I guess God came along and made it so that I can't walk. I can't go to my daughter's house and straighten this out. I can't do that. I pray, that's all I can do. . . . Oh, God. God. I'll say "He walks with

me and He talks with me and He tells me that I'm his own." (Black & Rubinstein, 2000: 102)

For others, like Rosa, who at age 80 has outlived all her friends, God is her only friend and guides everyday life:

When I was gettin' my [driver's] license, I passed everything except that parallel parking? I just couldn't parallel park. When I went the last time, I said, "Lord, you are gonna have to help me park this car parallel." And I didn't learn to parallel park until after I made my license. That's true. The Lord parked the car; I didn't. . . . I trust God and I ask Him and He give it to me and I don't have to worry. (Streff, 2001)

Informal Caregiving From Family and Friends

MYTH: Adult Children Don't Expect to Take
Care of Their Older Parents

Expectations for Support and Caregiving. As the population grows older, the significance of the growing numbers of elderly for caregiving in the family is a popular topic in the media as well as in social gerontology. What do older parents expect from their children and what do they think their adult children expect from them? At least three major patterns have been found among older white American parents: (1) independence, with no expectations for support to or from children; (2) one-way exchange of support from adult children to older parents; and (3) mutuality, where support will be exchanged as needed between generations.

Although forms of anticipated mutual exchanges varied, reciprocity in exchange was the most common expectation regardless of the age of the respondents (Sherman, 2000). From an exchange theory perspective, providing support to a family member is a delayed trade for past nurturing, whether from parents or other family members. It can also be seen as a moral duty: "the right thing to do." When aged parents receive care from their adult children and do not give respect in return, intergenerational relationships become strained and children are likely to give less care. The norms of reciprocity have been violated (Pyke, 1999).

Expectations for the type of support from adult children vary by race, ethnicity, religion, and social class. Reflecting the greater likelihood and acceptance of extended family structures among some racial and ethnic groups, older African Americans and Latinos are more likely than non-Latino whites to agree that each generation should provide coresident help when needed (Burr & Mutchler, 1999). Although there are few differences in attitudes about exchanging intergenerational financial help among African-American, Latino, and white elders (Burr & Mutchler, 1999), African-American couples are the most likely to sacrifice their own use of goods and services to assist their older parents financially (Wong, Capoferro, & Soldo, 1999). In times of need, children respond regardless of parental expectations (Eggebeen & Davey, 1998).

Family size also plays a role in parent-child expectations in later life. Although the experience of growing up as an only child has been studied, little attention has been given to elderly parents of an only child and their expectations for the parent-child relationship. Evidence comparing elderly mothers of one child and mothers of four or more children, for example, has suggested that mothers of only children are much more likely to depend on their adult child for emotional support and to exclude other potential sources. For mothers of only children, exaggerating the positive aspects of their child's life serves as an adaptive illusion, providing emotional equilibrium and validating their sense of accomplishment as a parent in old age (Goodman & Rubinstein, 1993). It is interesting to speculate whether the dependency on one's child for emotional gratification observed among these mothers is confined to these women's birth cohort, when larger families were the norm, or whether future cohorts of women who elect to have only one child will resemble these mothers.

Caregiving for Elderly Relatives and Friends. As Lund (1995) has pointed out, although caregiving is used to denote a wide range of activities and situations, it most commonly describes the informal or unpaid care that family members, relatives, or friends provide to someone whose independence is limited due to physical, psychological, or social and economic causes. In the past, when elders needed care, most often it was provided by the women of the family, whether wives, daughters, daughters-in-law, or other female relatives, the traditional caregivers. However, the shorter life expectancies characteristic of a century ago meant that the percentage of the population that survived to old age was comparatively small; among those who did survive to grow old, few were infirm enough to require care from others. As birth and death rates have declined, however, the proportion of elders surviving to very old age has increased and the number of younger family members to care for them has decreased. Nonetheless, when elders become disabled today, family members provide most of the long-term care in the community. Selected characteristics of caregivers are summarized in Table 8-3.

Family members, neighbors, and friends are the major source of care and social support for the elderly.

Table 8-3 Selected Characteristics of American Family Caregivers

Age of Caregiver	Percentage of Caregivers*
18–34	22%
35–49	39%
50–64	26%
65 and over	12%
Marital Status	
Currently married or with partner	66%
Single, never married	13%
Separated, widowed, or divorced	21%
Labor Force Participation	
Employed full-time	52%
Employed part-time	12%
Not in labor force	36%

* Totals may not add to 100% due to rounding.
Source: Pandya and Coleman. (2000). *Caregiving and Long-Term Care.* Copyright © 2000, AARP Public Policy Institute. Washington, DC: AARP. (Internet download.) Reprinted by permission.

In the United States today, women still compose about three-fourths (73 percent) of informal caregivers (National Alliance for Caregiving and AARP, 1997). Although how much care a caregiver provides varies, the typical caregiver is a married woman in her mid-forties who provides an average of 18 hours per week of caregiving, lives near the care recipient, and works full time. About 12 percent of caregivers are 65 or older and are most likely to be wives caring for husbands, reflecting women's greater life expectancy. Whether men or women, caregivers for a spouse tend to be in poorer physical health than their noncaregiver peers, with African-American caregivers in poorer health than whites (Wallsten, 2000).

If no wife is available or able to care for a spouse, families begin to look for other candidates as primary caregivers. A daughter (or a daughter-in-law, if no daughter is available) is usually the first choice, followed by other family members, perhaps neighbors and friends, and finally outside sources (Pavalko & Artis, 1997; Coward & Dwyer, 1990). Because women live longer than men, they are more likely to find themselves without a spouse in old age and needing to rely on other family members for care. Even among elders living alone, relatives provide their main source of help. Over two-thirds of old people living alone say that they can depend on help from relatives—most often their children—within a few days, and most can count on relatives' help for a few weeks (Kasper, 1988), a trend that remains true today.

When no family member is available, friends or neighbors often provide care. Data from the National Survey of Families and Households, for which over 6,000 women provided information about caregiving, indicate that slightly more than 5 percent of the respondents had given care within the past 12 months to a female friend not living with them. Women caring for friends tended to be older than those caring for family members. They were also less likely than women caring for family members to be married or to be employed and to have fewer competing obligations that would interfere with caregiving (Himes & Reidy, 2000). The amount of care provided by friends is likely to vary, ranging from friendly visiting to cooking, washing, shopping, paying bills, and so on. As one friendly neighbor providing intensive help to a demented woman living five doors down stated, "I'm basically running two households" (Nocon & Pearson, 2000: 350).

Motivations for friends and neighbors to provide care are many, including a sense of duty, reciprocity for past help, and a feeling of making a difference in someone's life. Offering informal rather than paid help is also a motivation. As one woman said, "I think it helps the older person if you are a friend and it develops from that, because then it helps their self-esteem—you're not there because you've been sent. . . . It's because you want to be involved with them as a person, rather than you want to be involved with any person . . ." (Nocon & Pearson, 2000: 352).

Caregiving is not usually shared equally among family members. Women are both more likely to provide hands-on care and to perform such "feminine" tasks as bathing, dressing, and toileting, meal preparation, and housework (Cancian & Oliker, 2000). Male caregivers more often provide typically "masculine" services, such as transportation, home repairs, financial management, and financial support. As Thompson (2000) has observed, the definition of caregiving as primarily women's work has negative consequences for both genders. Failure to abandon the feminine yardstick of caregiving undermines and makes men caregivers "deviant odd men" (Thompson, 2000: 341). It also supports the sexist notion of women as born caregivers (Cancian & Oliker, 2000). Both genders lose when women are expected to "take care" and men's ability to care is suppressed.

Affection or level of emotional closeness also plays a role in caregiving. According to the Longitudinal Study of Generations, a study tracking the strength of intergenerational ties for almost 30 years, affectional ties have remained high and relatively stable over the 26-year period. Adult children having more affectionate relationships with their mothers at the outset of the study period provided more support than those whose relationships were initially less close. Nonetheless, even when relationships are more strained, adult children give needed assistance to their mothers, providing further refutation for the "decline of the family" myth (Bengtson, Giarrusso, Silverstein, & Wang, 2000).

Despite affectional ties, that caregiving is stressful both for the giver and the recipient has been well established (Gaugler et al., 2000;

Pearlin & Aneshensel, 1994; Lawton et al., 1992; Zarit, 1989). Daughters providing care are more likely than sons to report higher levels of emotional strain (Mui, 1995), perhaps because they are more likely to provide hands-on care. Most research comparing African-American and white caregivers suggests that caregiver stress differs by race; African-American caregivers are likely to report less stress and more rewards than whites (White, Townsend, & Stephens, 2000; Aranda & Knight, 1997; Picot et al., 1997; Lawton et al., 1992). That caregiving is nonetheless stressful is true not only in the United States but also in other nations, even ones in which filial piety is the norm, such as Japan.

Global Glimpses: Caring for the Elderly in Contemporary Japan

A best-selling Japanese novel, *The Twilight Years* by Sawako Ariyoshi, focuses on the problems of caring for a disabled elderly relative in contemporary Japan. The burden of caring for Mr. Tachibana's aged father falls chiefly upon his daughter-in-law, Akiko, an employed middle-aged woman, who feels increasingly trapped by the dual responsibility of a job and caregiving. When she seeks help from the Department of Social Welfare for the Elderly, the social worker comments:

> He's very old isn't he? . . . He's doing fine for a man his age. He lives in such a pleasant environment . . . he has his son, daughter-in-law, and grandson living with him. . . .

Akiko responds:

> You may be right, of course, but, as I've already mentioned, I work full time. I've been suffering terribly from lack of sleep since he gets up in the middle of the night. He's so senile I can't leave him at home on his own. . . . I'm sure I'll find some peace of mind if he's admitted to an institution. (pp. 157–159)

The social worker comments that she thinks he would be happier living at home despite the fact that Akiko works full time. There is no easy solution to problems of caring for an impaired elderly relative, but someone has to make sacrifices. Although caregiving tears many families apart, Akiko should cope courageously. Eventually, Akiko's father-in-law dies at home from pneumonia.

This controversial novel highlights the point that Japan, like the United States, has found no ideal solution to care for a disabled elderly relative. Costs, criteria for service eligibility, and stress on family members remain unsolved problems in many industrialized nations undergoing rapid demographic change. To remedy the problems of caring for infirm relatives, in 1997 the Japanese government passed the Public Long-Term Care Insurance Act, providing home- and community-based or institutional care. Financed through a mix of premiums and taxes, premiums paid by the elderly are deducted from their old age or retirement pensions with the amount determined on a sliding scale based on income. Public funding from taxes is shared by the federal, prefecture, and municipal governments. The program, which was scheduled to begin in April 2000, has presented several potential problems: (1) shortages of existing services that vary in sophistication; (2) lack of trained care managers; (3) domination by a medical model administered by people who do not understand long-term or community-based care; and (4) creation of a for-profit market for home and institutional care that does not necessarily provide the most cost-efficient services (Stone, 1999).

The success of the Long-Term Insurance Act is yet to be demonstrated. Meanwhile, at least one Japanese babysitting service has capitalized on the growing number of elders by expanding its products to include home visits and care for older people. Customers pay a hefty price: a membership fee of $1,665, an annual fee of $832, and $30 per hour of service (costs given in U.S. dollars). But families who can afford it find it worth the cost (editorial, *Global Aging Report,* 1997). Another service, enabling families who live away from their elderly parents to check on their activity was launched in 2001 by a private company. Family members will be able to check through the Internet how often their parents use a special hot-water pot, fitted with a device that records when water is taken from the pot. If an elderly person who uses the pot every few hours suddenly stops using it, the web site record will show that no activity has occurred. Relatives then can follow up with their elderly relative. The cost for this service is an initial sign-up charge of $87.45 plus a monthly charge of $26.24 (Shimbun, 2000).

Sources: Ariyoshi, Sawako. 1984. *The Twilight Years.* Tokyo: Kodansha; Shimbun, Yomiuri. 2000. "Hot-water pots to help check on elderly," *The Daily Yomuiri On-Line,* December 20, 2000. Stone, Robyn. "Long term care in Japan: A window into the future," *The Public Policy and Aging Report, 10*(2): 1–5, ff 15. "Eye on the Business Page," *Global Aging Report,* 2(2), April/May 1997: 7.

Whether in the United States or elsewhere, the dilemma faced by many family caregivers is precisely how to keep in balance demands and resources: demands of care for a disabled elder, job demands, demands of other family members, demands of employment, and economic and personal resources to meet these demands. The majority of caregivers who are employed outside the home have had to make special arrangements or changes at work to provide needed care (Pavalko & Artis, 1997). Both the amount of time and the stress of caregiving can be enormous.

The economic costs of caregiving are also high. According to one study, estimated losses to U.S. employers are between $11.4 and $29 billion dollars per year due to loss of productivity from caregivers who are also employed full-time (MetLife, 1997). As one caregiver commented, "I needed to take care of Mom. I reduced my hours so much that management have to give my accounts to someone else" (MetLife, 1999: 4). Employed caregivers, trying to juggle both job and caregiving, frequently find their paychecks pared and retirement savings decreased due to lost time from work. Yet the value of the unpaid labor contributed by caregivers is often overlooked. The national economic value of informal caregiving was estimated to be $196 billion in 1997 alone—equivalent to about 18 percent of the total national health care spending ($1.1 trillion) in 1997 dollars (Arno, Levine, & Memmott, 1999).

MYTH: Uncaring Relatives Dump Elderly Relatives in Nursing Homes

One of the biggest myths is that uncaring relatives "dump" the elderly in nursing homes. The opposite is true. The typical nursing home patient is a white woman in her 80s with multiple disabilities who has outlived her husband and who needs intensive care that other family members, if living, can no longer give. Families with an elderly relative in a nursing home remain involved in the care of the person. Although involvement in personal care is less, it still continues, and family members take on a new role as advocate for the patient as well as manager for legal and financial concerns. Placement of an elderly relative does not alleviate the effects of caregiving (Gaugler et al., 2000; Stull et al., 1997).

Whatever their race, ethnicity, or sex, the elderly admitted to a nursing home are less likely to have living children than old people in the community, emphasizing the critical role of familial support in preventing or delaying institutionalization. How can families be less burdened as caregivers? Formal services, providing relief from the daily responsibilities of caregiving, help. Although a limited number of community services (e.g., adult day care, in-home services, and respite care enabling the caregiver to have time off from caregiving) are available, many family members are unaware that such formal services exist. Among those who do know of their existence, caregivers who do not use them give various reasons: no immediate need, not wanting to leave the family member with strangers, feeling that their relative has too many emotional problems, and the services would be too expensive (Caserta, Lund, Wright, & Redburn, 1987). In a climate of economic restraint in which formal services are costly, it is important to keep in mind that the informal care system is not a viable alternative to formal support services. Only when both formal and informal services are in place will elderly people with disabilities be assured of the kinds of care they need and want.

Will the need for informal caregiving increase in the future as more and more of us live to grow very old? Some analysts have suggested that, due to current trends in the delay of chronic illnesses in later life, the informal caregiving required of adult children will occur at later points in their family life course. As a result, competing childcare responsibilities and employment conflicts will be fewer because adult caregivers are likely to have retired themselves. Other social trends, such as continued participation in the labor force into old age, however, may result in less availability of older adult children to care for their elderly parents. For example, a rise in the retirement age would influence labor trends and thus the length of one's employment.

Future public policies to ensure both formal and informal caregiving will need to be sensitive both to changing social trends and to the considerable emotional and physical strains imposed by reliance on informal care.

MYTH: Once a Child Who Has a Severe Mental Illness or Developmental Disability Is an Adult, Parents No Longer Have to Provide Care

Parents and Grandparents as Caregivers. Although research on caregiving has focused primarily on adult children or other relatives and friends caring for elderly family members, growing numbers of parents and grandparents are also caregivers to their children or grandchildren. When state mental hospitals and schools for individuals with a severe mental illness or a developmental disability began to deinstitutionalize in the mid-twentieth century, many people were released to the community, often with inadequate community supports. An increasing number of aging parents faced the responsibility of caring for their adult children with a chronic mental illness or developmental disability.

Coupled with deinstitutionalization has been the trend to community-based care that allows an adult child with a developmental disability or a chronic mental illness to remain living at home with parents or siblings. Care of a mentally disabled adult, like care of an older relative, is stressful. Older mothers of adults with a serious mental illness tend to feel more burdened by caregiving and have poorer relationships with their adult child than mothers of adults who are developmentally disabled. They also are more likely to have to deal with a greater number of behavioral problems than mothers whose child is developmentally disabled and to have fewer social supports, including options for a day program for their adult child (Greenberg, Seltzer, & Greenley, 1993).

A concern also for parents of an adult child who is mentally ill or has a developmental disability is how the child will be cared for if the parents become ill or die. Should plans be made for long-term residential care (Freedman, Krauss, & Seltzer, 1997)? What is the role of siblings in providing care (Krauss, Seltzer, Gordon, & Friedman, 1996)? Is it a state or a family responsibility? In a study of New Zealand families with a developmentally disabled member, less than one-fourth of the families had made formal plans for residential care. The majority of caregivers had not discussed the future (Hand & Reid, 2000). As life expectancy has also increased among those with developmental disabilities, many now live into old age and present issues about who will care for them after their parents or siblings are unable to be caregivers.

MYTH: GRANDPARENTS PLAY ONLY A TOKEN ROLE IN THEIR GRANDCHILDREN'S LIVES

Grandparents are also important as caregivers, providing care ranging from occasional babysitting to being a custodial grandparent. Many grandparents also provide day care for grandchildren so that the grandchildren's parents can work. In the United States, for example, 16 percent of preschool children whose mothers worked were cared for by a grandparent, most often the grandmother (Velkoff & Lawson, 1998). There are also many households headed by grandparents caring for grandchildren under age 18 and the proportion is increasing. Among families with children less than 18 years of age, 6.7 percent were headed by grandparents by 1997 compared with only a little over 3 percent in 1970. Reasons why grandparents assume the child care role include familial discontent, economic strains, the AIDS epidemic, child abuse, and substance abuse. In addition, the expanded longevity of older people in relatively good health makes them more available as caretakers when needed (Roe & Minkler, 1998/1999; Minkler & Roe, 1996; Pearson et al., 1997).

The structure of grandparent-headed families varies. Three in every 4 families with coresident grandparents and grandchildren are headed by a grandparent; the remaining families are maintained by a parent of the children with one or more grandparents living in the home. About half (51 percent) of the grandparent-headed families have both grandparents living in the home; the majority (43 percent) of the remainder are headed by a grandmother only with 6 percent headed by a grandfather alone (Bryson & Casper, 1999).

Family structure plays an important role in understanding both variations in caregiving and the types of problems different families are likely to encounter. Grandparents heading a household tend to be younger, in better health, better educated, and more likely to work outside the home than those living in

Grandparents are important as caregivers of their grandchildren, often acting as surrogate parents. What are some of the advantages and disadvantages of such arrangements?

homes maintained by their children. Grandfathers who maintained households for their grandchildren were more likely to be white, to be actively engaged in the labor force, and less likely to be poor than grandmothers. Sixty-six percent of grandfathers were currently employed full-time in 1996 versus 37 percent of grandmothers. Grandfathers are also more likely than grandmothers to own their own homes (81 versus 69 percent). Reflecting the greater probability of poverty among females, grandmothers are almost twice as likely as grandfathers to be poor; 23 percent of grandmother-headed households were poor versus 12 percent of those headed by grandfathers (Casper & Bryson, 1998).

Both white and African-American grandmothers acting as surrogate parents to grandchildren younger than 18 are more likely to become more depressed than grandfathers. Grandmother surrogate parents also are less likely to participate in church activities but to receive more social supports from friends and relatives than they did before assuming the parenting role. Grandfathers reduce church activities and paid employment less than grandmothers after the arrival of grandchildren in the household; they are also more likely to seek an escape from their new "fatherhood" responsibilities by spending more time visiting bars or taverns (Szinovacz, DeViney, & Atkinson, 1999).

Assuming the parenting role is likely to confront grandparents with a stream of questions and dilemmas (Minkler & Roe, 1996). Are they healthy enough for the job? Can they take care of their own physical and mental health needs? Can they continue to work or will they have to quit their jobs to take care of the children? Will they have to reenter the work force in order to meet the additional expenses associated with raising minor children? Although grandparent-headed households exist among all social classes and ethnic groups, such families are most common among low-income inner-city populations (Minkler & Fuller-Thomson, 2000; Minkler & Roe, 1996; Bryson & Casper, 1999). Greater numbers of African-American children live with a grandparent, followed by Latinos and whites (Bryson & Casper, 1999). Grandchildren in grandparent-headed families are more likely to be poor than other children, to have no health insurance, and to live in families receiving public assistance. Especially vulnerable are grandchildren living in grandmother-headed families in which there is no parent present; in this type of family, 84 percent of grandchildren were in households receiving public assistance in 1996 (Bryson & Casper, 1999).

Governmental financial assistance programs have not evolved to address effectively the needs of low-income grandparents in the parenting role. With the continuation of public assistance reforms that limit the amount of time a family may receive welfare and caps on the amount of assistance received, low-income grandparent families will need to find new avenues to support their grandchildren. Access to health insurance, health care, educational and legal services, and employment policies affecting working grandparents who provide care for their grandchildren remain social policy issues that have not been resolved. Inasmuch as family policy in the United States tends to ignore family diversity, family-relevant policies are needed to address the needs of families in both the child-rearing and elder-care phases of the life course.

Summary

The evidence suggests that the family is not declining in importance. Despite the myth of the extended family, the most common family type in the United States has been primarily nuclear, consisting of parents and minor children, throughout the nation's history. Not all families today are nuclear. Rather than one family pattern, family and friendship ties alike resemble Jacob's coat of many colors: a patchwork of multiple shapes and sizes with only an occasionally frayed edge. Marriage and divorce rates tend to decrease with advanced age, but more people entering old age have a divorced status than several decades ago, and divorced women are more likely to be economically insecure than men. Women are also more likely to be widowed in later life than men; men are more likely to remarry after divorce or widowhood.

Family forms vary according to social class, race, and ethnicity, but family members and friends remain important sources of social support throughout the life course. When elders become disabled, family members provide most of the long-term care in the community, with women giving most of the care. One of the biggest myths is that uncaring relatives "dump" the elderly into nursing homes. Grandparents are also important as caregivers, providing care ranging from occasional babysitting to being a custodial grandparent. Many grandparents also provide day care for grandchildren so that the grandchildren's parents can work.

Greater longevity of family members and increases in divorce and remarriage rates have resulted in reconstituted families. These changes have produced varied, complex, and extensive American kinship structures in which family roles and obligations are sometimes unclear; nonetheless, these new family forms also present new chances for close relationships (Riley, 1983). As Bengtson and colleagues (2000: 9) point out,

> The effects of population aging have resulted in longer years of "linked lives" between family generation members. This means more years of potential solidarity and support, as well as more years for potential conflicts. . . . [L]evels of intergenerational solidarity have remained high across the latter decades of the twentieth century, while conflicts between adult generations [have]

occurred over a relatively minor set of issues. We can anticipate these trends continuing throughout the early decades of the twenty-first century. . . . What may be new . . . is the high level of resources provided by the older generation: they are the donors, not the net recipients of cross-generational support. . . . As to the future, contrary to many pundits and politicians, we do not predict a greater degree of intergenerational conflict in the coming decades—primarily because of the micro-social bonds that link generations together as they grow up and grow older together in the twenty-first century.

Key Points

1. Social convoys, composed of family and friends, provide important sources of affection and support throughout life.

2. The concepts of social stratification, life chances, and social class are especially important in understanding the relationships between individuals, families, and society throughout the life course.

3. Despite the myth of the extended family, the most common family type throughout the United States' history has been nuclear, consisting of parents and minor children.

4. Not all families today are nuclear. Recent immigrants to the United States have brought a variety of family forms with them.

5. Marriage and divorce rates tend to decrease with advanced age; however, more people entering old age are divorced than several decades ago.

6. After divorce, women are more likely to be economically insecure than men.

7. Men are more likely than women to remarry after divorce or widowhood.

8. Throughout the life course, more women than men experience widowhood.

9. Widowhood in later life for both genders can challenge their physical and emotional well-being but women are more likely to suffer economically.

10. Family members are important sources of social support throughout the life course.

11. Sibling ties tend to strengthen in later life.

12. When elders become disabled, family members provide most of the long-term care in the community, with women giving most of the care.

13. Among elderly couples, the caregiver is more than twice as likely to be the wife.

14. Grandparents are important providers of care to their grandchildren.

15. Greater longevity and increases in divorce and remarriage have resulted in complex kinship structures that provide new opportunities for close relationships.

Discussion Questions

1. To what extent was Merle McEathron's family life typical of others in her birth cohort? How was it different?

2. Describe the differences in family structure among farm, village, and urban families. What racial, ethnic, and gender differences characterize each?

3. How is family life changing in the United States as the population ages?

4. Describe the *beanpole family* and its implications for family interaction.

5. Is the American family in trouble? Defend your answer.

6. Support or argue against this statement: "Men are the primary beneficiaries of marriage." Substantiate your position.

7. What are some possible issues people may face by being widowed and divorced in old age? How do these differ by gender?

8. What role does gender play in the structure and extent of social networks in later life?

9. What are fictive kin and how do they provide familial support?

10. Provide evidence against the popular belief that relatives "dump" the elderly into nursing homes.

11. What are some social characteristics (in this chapter) of grandparents providing care for grandchildren? In what ways are these characteristics likely to influence the life chances for the grandchildren?

Films and Videos

Complaints of a Dutiful Daughter (video; 37 minutes; available from Women Make Movies, 462 Broadway, Suite 500, New York, NY 10013).

A documentary of mother-daughter relationships from the caregiver's perspective during her mother's gradual descent into Alzheimer's disease.

Gay and Gray in New York (video; 22 minutes; available from Fanlight Productions, 4196 Washington Street, Suite 2, Boston, MA 02131; *www.fanlight.com*).

Interviews with gay and lesbian elders who describe their lives and social networks. Also includes profiles of organizations providing services and support to elders in the gay and lesbian communities.

Grandparents Raising Grandchildren (video; 23 minutes; available from Fanlight Productions, 4196 Washington Street, Suite 2, Boston, MA 02131; *www.fanlight.com*).

Explores issues and problems in three families who are raising grandchildren and explores community programs available to assist grandparents.

Legacy (video; 90 minutes; available from California NewsReel, 149 Ninth Street, San Francisco, CA 94103; *www.newsreel.org*).

An Academy Award documentary film nominee that portrays three generations of inner-city African-American women as they struggle to free themselves from poverty.

My Mother, My Father (video; 35 minutes; available from Terra Nova Films, Inc., 9848 South Winchester Avenue, Chicago, IL 60643; *www.terranova.org*).

Award-winning film of four families dealing with aging parents, who have made different choices for care. Includes study guide.

My Mother, My Father . . . Seven Years Later (video; 42 minutes; available from Terra Nova Films, Inc., 9848 South Winchester Avenue, Chicago, IL 60643; *www.terranova.org*).

Follows up the families in *My Mother, My Father* seven years after the original film to look at changes in family dynamics and caregivers' reflections on their own aging.

The Christmas Cake (video; 27 minutes; available from First Run/Icarus Films, 32 Court Street, 21st Floor, Brooklyn, NY 11201; *www.frif.com*).

Octogenarian sisters-in-law, often at odds with each other throughout adulthood, talk about family ties, politics, and love as they throw light on the permanence and fragility of family ties.

Internet Resources

http://www.census.gov

This Bureau of the Census web site has information on marital status, household composition, size, diversity, and other important information on American families in later life.

http://www.familysearch.org

For those interested in their own family roots, this web site maintained by the Church of Jesus Christ of Latter-Day Saints, also known as the Mormons, provides access to a large family history and genealogy database.

http://www.familiesusa.org

The web site for Familes U.S.A., a national nonprofit organization that advocates for and publishes information on health care for all ages.

Research Article

Usita, P. A. (2001). Interdependency in immigrant mother-daughter relationships. *Journal of Aging Studies, 15*, 183–189.

A small-scale qualitative study of intergenerational mother-daughter relationships among Japanese immigrants from a life-course perspective.

Supplemental Readings

Akiyama, H., Elliott, K., & Antonucci, T. (1996). Same-sex and cross-sex relationships. *Journals of Gerontology, Series B. Psychological Sciences and Social Sciences* 51B (6): P374–P382.

A thorough empirical analysis of the complexities of gender relationships and degree of closeness among men and women in later life.

Black, H. K., & Rubinstein, R. L. (2000). *Old Souls: Aged Women, Poverty, and the Experience of God.* New York: Aldine deGruyter.

A readable portrait of poor elderly white and African-American women, who describe their lives and the social support gained through their relationship with God that has enabled them to survive their financial and emotional problems.

Pruchno, R. A., & Johnson, K. W. (1996). Research on grandparenting: Current studies and future needs. *Generations, 20*, 1: 65–70.

A useful overview of research on grandparenting and its many styles.

Slevin, K. F., & Wingrove, C. R. (1998). *From Stumbling Blocks to Stepping Stones*. New York: New York University Press.

An engaging, readable analysis of surviving sexism, racism, and the pressures of social class plus the importance of family ties throughout the life course among a group of retired, professional African-American women.

Walters, S. D. (1992). *Living Together, Worlds Apart*. Berkeley: University of California Press.

Popular culture's promotion of stereotypical mother-daughter relationships in films viewed from a feminist perspective. ✦

Chapter 9

Sexuality and Intimacy

Introduction

> Will you still need me,
> Will you still feed me,
> When I'm sixty-four?
>
> —The Beatles, "When I'm Sixty-Four"
> (*Sgt. Pepper's Lonely Hearts Club
> Band,* Capitol Records, 1967)

The above lyrics, from a Beatles song popular in the 1960s and 1970s, reflects the quest for lifelong intimacy and desire. Do people still experience sexual desire and intimacy at 64 or older? Are older people interested in and capable of having sexual relationships, and does the sexual behavior of older men and women differ? How sexual expression and intimacy are affected by age, marital status, mental health, and physical health are the topics with which this chapter is concerned.

Obtaining accurate information about sexual behavior among any age group is difficult for several reasons. Much research on sexuality and intimacy is based on small samples of volunteers or on large, nonrandom and scientifically useless samples, such as the readers of popular magazines. Even such heralded research as the Kinsey Reports (Kinsey, Pomeroy, & Martin, 1948; Kinsey, Pomeroy, Martin, & Gephard, 1953), considered both socially shocking and groundbreaking when published half a century ago, and the later work by Masters and Johnson (1966) and Starr and Weiner (1981) were based on self-selected, biased samples. Furthermore, when people do respond to a survey or an interview about their sexuality, they may not give accurate reports. Although sex and sexual behavior are no longer the taboo topics that they were 50 years ago, even today males tend to exaggerate or elaborate and females to minimize their sexual histories depending on the audience! Moreover, even after the so-

called "sexual revolution" of a few decades ago, puritan streaks about acceptable sexual behavior remain. Despite the popularity of frank discussions of sexual experience on talk shows such as Jerry Springer, Oprah, or Donahue, stereotypes persist about appropriate expressions of sexuality for any age group and vary by birth cohort, social class, religion, and other factors.

Finding factual information about sexuality in later life is even more challenging as there is little valid and reliable empirical research. Absence of normative data or a conceptual framework about the biology, psychology, and sociology of sex combined with attitudinal resistance to sexuality in old age have obscured the topic (Wiley & Bortz, 1996). Not only are many elders hesitant to disclose their sexual drives, desires, and activities but ageist assumptions play a role, discouraging awareness of sex as a lifelong drive. Indeed, many younger people are surprised to find out that older people are both sexually interested and active!

Even people in their 40s and 50s find it difficult to think of their parents as having a sex life. The sexual needs and interests of elders are thus often dismissed or ridiculed by younger people as inappropriate or abnormal. Rubin's observation of four decades ago remains apt today:

> *All of us have been accustomed to associate sex and love exclusively with youth. Sexual activity of any kind on the part of older persons is rarely referred to except in derogatory terms. According to our folklore, what is "virility" at twenty-five becomes "lechery" at sixty-five. (Rubin, 1965: 3)*

Sexual Scripts

Sexuality is not only a basic instinctual drive throughout our lives but is socially constructed by the culture in which we live. How we structure our sexual perceptions and experiences throughout the life course is shaped by cultural norms, learned through socialization, and approved or disapproved by our social networks. Simon and Gagnon (1986) have described sexual behavior as governed by a set of three *sexual scripts*. The first and most general of these scripts, *cultural scenarios*, provide us with information and normative guidelines about appropriate sexual behavior including when, where, and how it is permissible to be sexually aroused and what types of feelings are appropriate in a specific context. For example, a classroom situation is typically nonsexual, but if a group of students from the same class go out to a bar at the end of the day, their behavior is likely to change because different scripts apply to the situation. Cultural scenarios are not only shaped by the particular social context but also by historical period, gender, age, race, religion, ethnicity, and other social variables.

Given this broad context of a cultural scenario, each of us develops a specific *sexual script;* that is, we interpret, modify, and apply the general norms for sexual behavior that we have learned to our own particular circumstances. It is through our individual sexual scripts that we actively shape our behaviors to reflect our desires and the situations in which we interact with others within a cultural scenario. *Intrapsychic scripts,* based on sexual scenarios and scripts as well as individual interests and experiences, allow us to develop images about our actual and ideal sexual selves, sexual fantasies, and expectations. The concept of sexual scripts provides a useful perspective to consider how age, cohort, and gender differences shape sexual experiences throughout the life course including old age.

Any discussion of sexuality among people in any birth cohort must address the importance of early socialization. Among the now-old (and many younger people as well), traditional gender socialization during childhood and adolescence has encouraged males to develop qualities such as toughness, initiative, aggressiveness, power, and dominance and to reject feminine qualities. In contrast, female socialization has encouraged gentleness, cooperation, and passivity. Even among young people today, such norms affect how sexual encounters occur. These patterns are particularly important for the birth cohorts of people who are now-old, as both males and females were likely to be socialized to adopt traditional gender roles. For example, among older couples, males and not their female partners typically determine the frequency and nature of sexual activity (Marsiglio & Greer, 1994) because many older women (and men) consider female sexual advances "unseemly."

Stereotypes About Sexuality

Cultural Beliefs Promoting Stereotypes

Myths and stereotypes about sexuality and the elderly abound in our society. Schlesinger (1996: 120) has summarized these as follows:

> (a) elderly people do not have sexual desires; (b) elderly people are not able to make love, even if they wanted to; (c) elderly people are too fragile and might hurt themselves if they attempt to engage in sexual relationships; (d) elderly people are physically unattractive and therefore sexually undesirable (particularly true for elderly women); and (e) the notion of older people engaging in sex is shameful and perverse.

As Schlesinger also points out, these myths are reinforced when people believe that sex is for procreation only, when we are fearful or embarrassed by thinking of our parents, grandparents, or other older relatives enjoying sex, and by our own ageist beliefs and fears about aging that create a barrier between us (younger people) and them (elders).

'Dirty Old Men (or Women)' Versus the Aged as Asexual

MYTH: Interest in Sex in Later Life Is 'Unnatural'

The sexuality of older men is the target of many myths, jokes, and concern because of the commonly held view in U.S. society that emphasizes loss of sexual potency and interest as a "natural" part of later life. The younger man who has many love affairs may be regarded by his contemporaries as a "stud," but an elderly man who displays an interest in sex is likely to be classified as a "dirty old man" or "old lech." When he has a younger sex partner, he runs the risk of scorn for attempts to regain his lost youth, either unsuccessfully or at a heavy price. The latter idea has been a persistent theme in literature and music; for example, Dr. Faustus sold his soul to the devil in order to woo a young woman. Beliefs that older men are asexual, or should be if they are not, impair their self-image and expression of sexuality, making them feel less "masculine."

MYTH: There Is a Male Menopause That Is Comparable to Female Menopause

In recent years, the men's movement has called attention to the "male menopause," which, according to at least one author, begins in midlife and is universal to all men. The most common sexual symptoms of male menopause allegedly include less interest in sex, increased anxiety about losing sexual potency, increased fantasies about having sex with a new and younger partner, and loss of erection during sexual activity (Diamond, 1998). However, whether these symptoms denote a male menopause common to all men, or rather are signs of fear about growing older among some men is certainly debatable. The word *menopause* technically means "the end of female reproductive capacity in midlife." Reproductive capacity is not lost among men as they grow older except in certain conditions (see box on prostate problems in this chapter).

The social construction of aging as a medical problem that characterizes much of the literature on sexuality among middle-aged and older men has fostered the connection of sexual difficulties to biological causes, neglecting the importance of psychosocial factors to sexual well-being and satisfaction (Schiavi, 1996). That male menopause has gained wide currency, however, emphasizes men's apprehensions both about aging in general and about potential declines in virility and sexual potency in particular.

Although middle-aged men may feel apprehensive about their sexuality and find that their sexuality in old age is often ridiculed or ignored in our society, older women fare even worse. In most Western societies, older women traditionally have been at the receiving end of a double whammy: devalued for both age and gender. Older women are usually the focus of labels denoting declining physical attractiveness, such as "old hag." Sexist views of females of all ages lie in part in the interpretation of Genesis in the patriarchal Judeo-Christian tradition, for Eve, through her temptation of Adam, supposedly brought death to humanity. Not only was the female responsible for original sin but she also exemplified lust, sexual excess, and temptation. The dominant view of women according to the early Christian church under Roman influence was summarized by Tertullian in the third century as ". . . the devil's gateway . . . the first deserter of the divine law. . . ." (Tertullian, "On female dress" [*De cultu feminarum*], quoted in Smith, 1992: 76). Another theologian, the ninth-century monk Odo of Cluny, declared: "To embrace a woman is to embrace a sack of manure" (quoted in Smith, 1992: 76). Female value lay primarily in fertility and motherhood. Once past childbearing age, a woman had ceased to be able to "be fruitful and multiply," and her sexuality was either disregarded or viewed as abnormal and even dangerous (Banner, 1992).

The fiction that sexual activity among older, postmenopausal women was abnormal was repeated at the outset of the twentieth century by sexologist Havelock Ellis, who remarked on *old maid's insanity*, a condition where older unmarried women, career women, and lesbians were especially prone to strong sexual drives and sexual aggressiveness (Ellis, 1905/1942)! Even today in contemporary American society, sexism and ageism form a deadly duo for many older women. Although the seasoning, power, and wealth associated with aging may be aphrodisiac qualities for some males, current ideals of female beauty require youthful, unwrinkled faces and lithe figures of adolescence or early adulthood.

Physical youth thus remains more important for a woman's "sexiness," social identity, social regard, and self-esteem than a man's. The female face and body become material commodities to maintain self-respect and community status. Although older women are not expected to perform sexually as much as their male counterparts, they are pressured to remain young and sexually attractive. As Furman has pointed out, taking care of herself is a female moral imperative and must be managed with care:

> . . . looking old reveals the dirty little secret that one *is* old, . . . unvirtuous, . . . potentially depressed. . . . On the other hand, measures taken to appear younger must be carefully selected lest one give away the carefully crafted but appropriately hidden strategies of age disguise. . . . Look youthful but not too youthful, for you

might give away your desperate need to stay looking young: "Who are you kidding?" (1997: 116)

Although social constraints on the appearance and behavior of older men and women differ, both face challenges to their sexuality as they grow old. Men are likely to become anxious when their sexual potency declines from the level of very young men and they feel their virility is threatened. Women are likely to become apprehensive when they cease to meet ideals of youthful sexiness: forever willowy and unwrinkled. Thus, many sexual scripts are rewritten through social pressures.

Sexual Activities and Responsiveness

Although loss of sexual ability and attractiveness in later life is a common fear among young and middle-aged people, a reasonably healthy man or woman should be able to have sexual relations at any age, bound only by his or her personal value system and sexual scripts. The goal for older people—and for all of us—is to break the myths and misconceptions surrounding sexuality in later life so that the realities of later-life sexuality can be understood. Myths about later-life sexuality are not only erroneous but also damaging to older people. As all of us grow old, we are likely to experience some physiological and chemical changes in our bodies, which are reviewed below. It is important to keep in mind that these are changes, *not* a loss of sexuality. Sexuality is more than an urge to procreate as it comprises the lifelong desire for physical and emotional intimacy and affection.

Male Sexual Functioning

MYTH: Impotence Is a Normal Part
of Growing Older

Age-Related Changes. Do changes affecting sexual performance occur in men as they age? The answer is yes, but these changes are normal and generally do not interfere with sexual expression. As they grow older, many men experience a decrease both in circulating the male hormone, testosterone, and in the amount of testosterone available to affect tissue of the penis. Although the significance of these hormonal changes among men is not clear, it is known that aging is associated with a general loss of muscle tone throughout the body and a decrease in elasticity of the skin. As blood vessels in the penis age, the penis becomes less flexible and blood circulation is reduced.

Associated with these physical changes, male ability to have an erection tends to decline during middle and later life. For example, while a typical 18-year-old male needs only about 3 seconds to achieve a maximum erection, a 45-year-old man is likely to require 18 to 20 seconds and a 75-year-old as long as 5 to 6 minutes (Marsiglio & Greer, 1994). Moreover, young men usually can (1) maintain an erection after ejaculation longer than older men; and (2) get another erection within a shorter period of time. In short, older men take longer to achieve erection, their erections are less swollen, and they take longer to get a second erection. These physiological changes may affect men's views of their sexuality and even self-concept because, throughout history, the erect penis has represented sexual vitality and powerful masculinities. Ignorance of normal age-related changes may create anxiety and fear that in turn can cause impotence.

Impotence. Although male impotence has traditionally been a taboo topic, many men experience partial or total impotence at some point in life. For most males this is traumatic because not only is impotence stigmatized in our society but also men have often taken their erectile potency for granted. Even though the prevalence of impotence increases with age, it may occur at any point in adulthood; for example, according to one study of men aged 18 to 59, almost 1 in 3 men (31 percent) regularly experiences some sexual dysfunction (Laumann, Paik, & Rosen, 1999).

What are some reasons for impotence? Within the penis are two spongy cylinders parallel to the urethra. When a male is sexually aroused, the nervous system communicates to the penis, and blood vessels that supply the penis relax, allowing more blood to fill the two cylinders to produce an erection. Impaired physical health as well as performance anxiety may interfere with this process.

Age itself, however, is *not* a cause of impotence; rather, the greater prevalence of chronic diseases in later life may impair sexual functioning. Physical causes for male impotence include chronic diseases, such as heart disease; diabetes; and atherosclerosis (hardening of the arteries); diminished testosterone; surgery for prostate disorders (see Box) as well as bladder or rectal surgery; and physical trauma to the genital area. Drugs (e.g., antidepressants, antihistamines, and drugs used for high blood pressure or to alleviate pain) may also cause impotence. Substance abuse of alcohol, marijuana, and tobacco have also been cited as causes. With physical problems that may be associated with changes in erectile potency, men often become anxious, which in turn leads to further erectile problems. An estimated 1 in 3 cases of male impotence is related to stress, anxiety, or depression, and in turn impotence may cause anxiety and depression (Lawless, 1998).

Concern about male impotence is at least as old as the Bible, in which Sarah wonders about what her sex life with Abraham will be like when they grow old: "After I am waxed old, shall I have pleasure, my lord being old also?" Not only have (usually ineffective) folk remedies for impotence, ranging from ground rhinoceros horn to Spanish fly, existed for many years, but a number of medical treatments, such as penile implants, injections, and other techniques, have been available to treat impotence. None, however, has received the publicity given to Viagra™ (generic name sildenafil), approved by the Federal Drug Administration in 1998. An oral pill specifically for male impotence, Viagra™ increases the ability to produce an erection by increasing blood flow to the penis. Although there is no accurate information on the number of men using Viagra™, the number of prescriptions written has exploded. As the chief executive of a chain of erectile dysfunction clinics in Florida commented,

> Viagra® being a pill really appealed to men. . . . Their attitude is, "Just give me a pill. I need the quick fix". . . . Of course, if it comes down to taking a pill or sticking a needle in your favorite friend, which would you choose? (Morrow, 1999: 2)

Viagra® has also been advertised as a couple's therapy. Not only does one popular consumer advertisement for the drug depict an older man dancing with a somewhat younger, attractive woman, but some women also take Viagra™ (Morrow, 1999). The efficacy of Viagra™ for women, however, remains to be demonstrated. Moreover, the drug is allegedly popular not only among men who are impotent but also among males who want to "boost" their sexual performance. Viagra™ is not appropriate for all men, however. Mild to moderate side effects include headache, flushing, and indigestion (*Bandolier*, 1998). The drug also may have dangerous side effects for those with diabetes, heart disease, or high blood pressure.

Spotlight on U.S.: Prostate Problems

Within the past decade, a male health condition called benign prostatic hyperplasia, or BPH, has received increased attention. The prostate, a walnut-sized gland located just below the bladder, provides part of the fluid necessary for ejaculation. The prostate also surrounds the urethra, the canal through which urine passes out of the body. Although scientists do not know all of the prostate's functions, one of its main roles is to squeeze fluid into the urethra as sperm move through during orgasm. This fluid helps to carry and nourish sperm to aid in the process of conception and makes the female vaginal canal less acidic.

It is common for the prostate to become enlarged as men age. This condition is called benign prostatic hyperplasia (BPH). The prostate begins to enlarge in most men by age 45 and can continue to grow for the rest of their lives. More than half of men in their 60s and as many as 90 percent in their 70s and 80s have some BPH symptoms.

As the prostate continues to enlarge, it can squeeze the urethra, the tube through which urine flows. This may interfere with the normal flow of urine and thus create a need to urinate often, especially at night, hesitation in passing urine, and a difference in the amount of seminal fluid ejaculated in sexual intercourse. Many men with BPH need treatment at some point. Several new medications have been approved, including Proscar™, which inhibits production of a hormone, and other prescription drugs that relax the smooth muscle of the prostate and bladder neck to improve urine flow and reduce bladder outlet obstruction. When drug treatment is not effective, techniques such as microwaves to heat and destroy excess prostate tissue can be used; these procedures can be performed on an outpatient basis and have not been reported to cause impotence. Surgical treatments, most often a procedure called TURP (transurethral resection of the prostate) may also be used. TURP is often cited in medical literature as the "gold standard" against which all other treatments should be measured (National Kidney & Urologic Diseases Information Clearing House, 2002).

Many men worry about whether surgery for BPH will affect their sexual functioning. Most physicians say that, although complete recovery of sexual function may take up to a year, most men will be able to continue to have erections after surgery and find little or no difference in the sensation of orgasm. They may, however, be unable to father children because they have a *dry climax* (retrograde ejaculation), in which semen enters the wider opening to the bladder rather than being expelled

through the penis, to be passed out later with urine.

Extracts from the Saw Palmetto are used by many men to treat the symptoms of BPH, but the remedy has not been approved by the FDA. Do drug companies have vested interests that may have impeded its approval by the government?

Various over-the-counter herbal preparations, most notably saw palmetto, derived from the dried berries of a small scrubby palm found in the Southeastern United States, have also been widely used to treat BPH. Other herbal remedies include South African star grass, nettle, pumpkin seeds, and pygeum africanum. Albeit widely advertised and used by many men both in the United States and abroad, the Federal Food and Drug Administration has not yet approved saw palmetto and other plant extracts for the treatment of BPH. Although there are new scientific studies showing that some plant-derived treatments can be useful in treating symptoms of BPH, an international committee of experts at the Fifth International Consultation on Benign Prostatic Hyperplasia in 2000 reported that the data from these studies were inconclusive due to variations in inspection, manufacturing amount of the active substance in these preparations, and lack of scientific rigor in many studies of these herbal remedies (Carlson, 2000).

BPH is not cancer, nor does it lead to cancer. However, men may have both BPH and prostate cancer at the same time. For this reason, the National Cancer Institute and the American Cancer Society recommend that all men over the age of 40 have a yearly screening for prostate cancer.

Female Sexual Functioning

Age-Related Changes. With the advances in drugs to treat male sexual dysfunction in the past few years, less attention has been paid to sexual functioning among women of any age, despite the finding that 43 percent of women in one large-scale study of people aged 18 to 59 reported experiencing one or more sexual problems during the past year (Laumann, Paik, & Rosen, 1999). The emphasis on male sexual functioning within the mainstream medical community reinforces the double standard and myths about female sexuality; women are either presumed to be content with their current sex lives, or, conversely, their sexual functioning is not considered worthy of concern.

Like men, physiological changes occur among women as they age. As among men, arousal time for women may be longer because slowing of sexual responsiveness is common to both as they grow old. The lips of the vagina (the labia) usually become less firm in postmenopausal women, and more of the clitoris is exposed. Postmenopausal women also experience a decrease in vaginal lubrication associated with lower estrogen levels, a condition correctable with over-the-counter vaginal lubricants or doses of estrogen (see Chapter 5). For women with an estrogen deficiency, support to the sphincter, the muscle that controls urine flow, and to the urethra, the tube that carries urine from the bladder, can cause stress incontinence (leakage of urine). This state may be relieved by estrogen preparations.

MYTH: WOMEN AREN'T REALLY INTERESTED IN SEX AFTER MENOPAUSE

How does menopause affect sexual desire and response, and do the physiological changes affect ability to have intercourse? As you remember from Chapter 5, a hallmark of female aging is menopause. Traditionally, menopause has been medicalized and regarded as an estrogen deficiency disease. In the 1960s, for example, both medical journals and popular women's magazines described postmenopausal women as asexual creatures: "Not really a man but no longer a functional woman, these individuals live in the world of intersex" (Reuben,

1969, cited in Fausto-Sterling, 1985: 299). This negative view of the postmenopausal woman echoes the old assumption, discussed earlier in this chapter, that a woman either becomes asexual or "abnormally oversexed" once her ability to bear children is past.

The notion of postmenopausal women as either asexual or over-sexed is a myth, reflecting female stereotyping. Research indicates that both the emotional and physical capacities for sexual relations remain intact among older women in later life (Weg, 1995). Although the body produces less estrogen, a hormone affecting sexual desire, the male sex hormone, testosterone, made in small amounts by the adrenal glands, increases. This shift in the ratio of testosterone and estrogen maintains or even increases sexual desire, and orgasmic potential remains at a high level. For many women, postmenopausal sexuality also results in increased sexual pleasure in heterosexual intercourse as they no longer fear unwanted pregnancies (Starr, 2001).

Sexual Behavior

How active are older people sexually? Relatively few studies have focused on either sexual activity or satisfaction in later life, and the ones that have tend to use small samples, focus on one gender only, and consider very broad age groups (Roughan, Kaiser, & Morley, 1993). Table 9-1 summarizes the samples for several major studies of sexual behavior. Notice the small proportion of people who were aged 60 or over in most of these studies.

Table 9-1 Samples in Some Major Studies of Sexuality		
Study	**Total Number in Sample**	**Proportion of Sample Aged 60+**
Kinsey	1,980	8%
Masters and Johnson	100	17
George and Weiler	278	17
Starr and Weiner	800	100
Janus and Janus	890	49
Laumann, Paik, and Rosen	3,159	0
AARP/Modern Maturity	1,384	All "45 or older"

Sources: Kinsey et al., 1948, 1953; Masters & Johnson, 1966; George & Weiler, 1981; Laumann et al., 1999; Starr & Weiner, 1981; AARP, 1999; Janus & Janus, 1992.

Little data have been collected on intimacy and sexuality among different racial/ethnic groups, despite the fact that cultural and religious differences affect the ways in which intimate sexual behavior is defined. Research has also most often been cross-sectional, providing only a snapshot of one set of people at a specific point in time. Such snapshots of sexual behavior do not provide information about changes in sexual desire, activity, or ability as people age. Nor are cross-sectional studies useful in sorting out whether age group differences in sexual interest, activity, or satisfaction are birth cohort effects or age-related consequences. The majority of studies focusing on intimacy and sexuality in later life ignore cohort differences. Because many now-old were socialized in a less permissive era than today's, their attitudes and behavior are likely to reflect the norms with which they grew up rather than the effects of aging.

Love, affection, and pleasure in one another do not diminish as we age.

Moreover, as noted at the beginning of this chapter, samples have not been representative of the general elderly population but most often obtained from volunteers and their self-reports. Reliance on self-reported behavior calls into question the accuracy of the findings, for many people, regardless of age, offer gender-based socially-acceptable responses, exaggerating or minimizing their beliefs and experiences. Research also has focused most often on heterosexual behavior with little systematic study of gay and lesbian activity.

Heterosexual Activity

Despite popular myths that older people are uninterested in sex, the available evidence suggests the contrary. A national survey of married people 60 and older found that 54 percent of men and 51 percent of women indicated that they had been sexually active within the past month (Marsiglio & Donnelly, 1991). A more recent survey, conducted by the National Council on Aging and Roper Starch Worldwide and funded in part by Pfizer, the drug company that makes the impotence drug Viagra™, reported that 71 percent of men and 51 percent of women in their 60s had sexual intercourse once a month or more (Fox, 1998). Whether sexual activity declines with age, however, is unclear and is limited by the methodology used. Studies report contradictory findings. Although some researchers have found that level of sexual activity did not decline with age (Starr & Weiner, 1981; George & Weiler, 1981) others have indicated the opposite (Marsiglio & Donnelly,

1991; Mulligan & Moss, 1991; Thomas, 1991; Matthias, Lubben, Atchison, & Schweitzer, 1997).

Making the relationship between sexual activity and age even more complex to disentangle are other factors such as marital status, birth cohort, mental and physical health, and gender. Opportunities for heterosexual intercourse are limited due to lack of a marital partner for many of the now-old, especially women aged 75 or older (AARP, 1999). According to another study, very old women were 24 times more likely to report that they had been sexually active during the last month if they were married than if they were not. Very old men, however, were only about 1.4 times more likely to report such activity if they were married (Matthias, Lubben, Atchison, & Schweitzer, 1997). Not only do women live longer than men and thus are more likely to be widowed as they become old, but there are also fewer older widowers or divorced or single men available as possible partners.

Sexual scripts differ by birth cohort and gender. Many very old adults were socialized in an era when "nice people"—especially "nice women"—did not talk about or admit interest in sexuality. Moreover, it is still more socially acceptable for older men than older women not only to remarry someone much younger but also to seek partners outside of marriage more easily (Starr, 2001).

Physical and mental health also play major roles in sexual behavior. People with chronic illnesses (e.g., diabetes, heart disease, arthritis, stroke, cancer, and lung diseases) or with prostate problems and those who are lonely, anxious, depressed, or cognitively impaired are less likely to be sexually interested and active (LoPiccolo, 1991; Mooradian, 1991; Matthias, Lubben, Atchison, & Schweitzer, 1997; Johnson, 1999; AARP Research Center, 1999). Worrying about one's health "a great deal," poor functional status, and a smaller social network of friends and relatives are also associated with less sexual activity (Matthias, Lubben, Atchison, & Schweitzer, 1997).

It is a major mistake, however, to assume that cross-sectional data, such as that just presented, give a complete picture of sexuality in later life or will apply to future birth cohorts when they age. The sexual scripts of each birth cohort are formed by cultural norms and individual experiences. American men and women today become sexually active at increasingly young ages. For example, the proportion of U.S. women who have had premarital intercourse by age 19 doubled in the two decades between the 1970s and the early 1990s—from about 30 percent to close to 60 percent (Judkins, Mosher, & Botman, 1991; Kost & Forrest, 1992)—and one study of undergraduates at a midwestern university found that males had an average of more than 11 partners and females an average of almost 6 (Reinisch, Sanders, Hill, & Ziemba-Davis, 1992). How this "sexual revolution" among younger birth cohorts will influence their sexual behavior in later life is a question

Spotlight on U.S.: HIV—Not Only a Young Person's Problem

AIDS is a major cause of death among young adults. Yet an increasing number of older Americans have contracted HIV—the virus responsible for AIDS—and the reasons for infection have changed among people aged 50 and older. Until 1990, infection among those 50 and older occurred primarily through receipt of contaminated blood or blood products; 64 percent of all cases of HIV infection were contracted through this transmission route. After voluntary donor deferral and routine blood screening, however, the number and proportion of cases associated with this risk factor declined, but other modes increased. From 1991 to 1996, the proportional increase of new cases of AIDS was higher among those 50 and over than among people aged 13 to 49. In 1996, 11 percent of reported cases of AIDS were in people aged 50 or older. Forty-eight percent of AIDS victims were aged 50 to 54; 26 percent were 55 to 59 years old; 14 percent were aged 60 to 64; and 12 percent were 65 years of age or older (U.S. Centers for Disease Control and Prevention, 1998).

As among younger people, males accounted for over 8 in 10 cases; but, as among younger people, the rate of increase was much higher among older females than males. Although older men who had same-sex relationships accounted for the highest proportion, the percentage contracting the virus through het-

erosexual contact increased dramatically between 1991 and 1996. Among women aged 50 or older, heterosexual contact was not only the major mode of transmission but also rose dramatically during the 1991–1996 period.

Why are the rates of transmission through sexual activity increasing? There are at least five reasons: (1) older men and women are less likely to use condoms or dams if they engage in sexually risky behavior; (2) postmenopausal women are less likely to use protection than younger women as they no longer feel a need to use birth control measures; (3) HIV frequently has a long incubation period with the result that many middle-aged and young-old may have contracted the virus when younger, especially if they engaged in high-risk sexual and drug-use behaviors; (4) primary care physicians are less likely to discuss symptoms of HIV with older patients or to refer them for HIV testing; and (5) many symptoms of AIDS mimic symptoms of other diseases often occurring in the elderly (e.g., Alzheimer's disease, depression, and cancers) and thus are not diagnosed earlier. Data from the Centers for Disease Control and Prevention show that a higher proportion of older than younger patients die within one month following an AIDS diagnosis, stressing the importance of earlier testing and treatment among people 50 and older.

Table 9-2 Number and Percentage of Persons Reported with AIDS, by Age Group and Selected Characteristics— United States, 1996

| | Age group (yrs) | | | |
| | Over age 50 | | 13–49 | |
Characteristic	No.	(%)	No.	(%)
Sex				
Men	6,237	(83.6)	48,416	(79.4)
Women	1,222	(16.4)*	12,598	(20.6)
Race/Ethnicity				
White, non-Hispanic	2,914	(39.1)	23,315	(38.2)
Black, non-Hispanic	3,200	(42.9)	25,146	(41.2)
Hispanic[†]	1,260	(16.9)*	11,706	(19.2)
Asian/Pacific Islander	62	(0.8)	499	(0.8)
American Indian/Alaskan Native	13	(0.2)	194	(0.3)
HIV exposure category				
Men who have sex with men	2,674	(35.9)	24,642	(40.4)
Injecting-drug use	1,430	(19.2)*	15,597	(25.6)
Men who have sex with men and who are injecting-drug users	166	(2.2)	2,801	(4.6)
Heterosexual contact	1,084	(14.5)	7,737	(12.7)
Receipt of blood or blood products[§]	178	(2.4)	91	(1.1)
No risk reported/Other risk	1,927	(25.8)	9,546	(15.6)
AIDS-defining conditions				
HIV encephalopathy	227	(3.0)*	859	(1.4)
Wasting syndrome	514	(6.9)*	2,691	(4.4)
Other opportunistic illnesses	2,802	(37.6)	22,134	(36.3)
Severe HIV immunosuppression	3,916	(52.5)*	35,330	(57.9)
Region[‡]				
Northeast	2,422	(32.4)	18,409	(30.2)
Midwest	678	(9.1)	6,094	(10.0)
South	2,645	(35.4)	22,831	(37.4)
West	1,437	(19.3)	11,642	(19.1)
U.S. territories	273	(3.7)	1,975	(3.2)
Total[**]	7,459	(100.0)	61,014	(100.0)

* $p < 0.05$ (Chi-square). † Persons of Hispanic origin may be of any race. § Includes persons reported with transfusions and hemophilia/coagulation disorders.
‡ Northeast = Connecticut, Maine, Massachusetts, New Hampshire, New Jersey, New York, Pennsylvania, Rhode Island, and Vermont; Midwest = Illinois, Indiana, Iowa, Kansas, Michigan, Minnesota, Missouri, Nebraska, North Dakota, Ohio, South Dakota, and Wisconsin; South = Alabama, Arkansas, Delaware, District of Columbia, Florida, Georgia, Kentucky, Louisiana, Maryland, Mississippi, North Carolina, Oklahoma, South Carolina, Tennessee, Texas, Virginia, and West Virginia; and West = Alaska, Arizona, California, Colorado, Hawaii, Idaho, Montana, Nevada, New Mexico, Oregon, Utah, Washington, and Wyoming.
** Includes persons for whom race/ethnicity or region are missing.

Source: U.S. Centers for Disease Control and Prevention (1998): Table 1 (*http://www.cdc.gov/mmwr/preview/mmwrhtml/00050856.htm*).

that remains to be answered. The AIDS epidemic has also affected sexual activity among both younger and older adults (see Table 9-2).

Homosexual Activity

Most research on aging and sexuality tacitly assumes that the elderly are either heterosexual or abstinent. Only a very small number of studies have focused on samples of older gays or lesbians, many of which examine myths and stereotypes (Friend, 1987; Quam & Whitford, 1992). Yet, in most societies a certain proportion of people have been attracted to members of the same sex since the beginning of history. Whether homosexual (gay and lesbian) and bisexual relationships are punished, ignored, or encouraged is defined by the society and culture in which they occur and has varied over time. As part of the Judeo-Christian and Puritan heritage, U.S. culture has traditionally been homophobic, condemning behaviors that were not "masculine" or "feminine" as deviant and penalizing same-sex lovers. It was not until 1974 that the American Psychiatric Association removed homosexuality from its classification of mental illnesses! Not surprisingly given this cultural backdrop, the number or percentage of older people who engage in homosexual or bisexual activity is unclear. One old but still cited estimate sug-

Lesbian couple celebrates 20 years of living and working together.

gests that 10 percent of the elderly are homosexual (Kimmel, 1978). The proportion of men or women who have engaged in bisexual relationships at any age is unknown.

The roots of homosexuality are currently being debated, and no precise brain or genetic influence that reliably predicts homosexuality or heterosexuality has been discovered. Whether or not homosexuality is biologically based, self-definition and conduct as a gay man or woman are socially learned. Each society and historical era has its own expectation of heterosexual and homosexual behavior. Not all societies have rigid definitions of sexual identity in which two genders are the norm. In some Native American tribes, for example, a third gender, *berdache*, is recognized and admired. The berdaches, albeit biologically male and choosing same-sex lovers, are respected and believed to possess both masculine and feminine personal and social characteristics, such as wisdom and tenderness, as well as supernatural powers (Williams, 1986). The Hijra cult in India represent a third gender as well; the Hijra are males who elect to undergo castration as teenagers, choose to live as women, and spend their lives in close-knit communities where they share the income they make from begging on the street and blessing babies (Nanda, 1990).

In the United States, gay and lesbian sexuality challenges gender norms and sexual identity. Many gay men and lesbians who are now-old have led double lives, fearing that their sexual preferences would cost them not only their jobs but also their status in the community. In urban areas, homosexual subcultures have often offered protection and support from social condemnation. Despite condemnation from the larger society, gay and lesbian older adults are typically comfortable with their sexuality (Quam & Whitford, 1992). Having faced years of dealing with the stigma of bisexuality or homosexuality, they are more equipped than many elders to withstand the stigma of old age and can draw upon the social supports in gay and lesbian society (Kimmel, 1978; Quam & Whitford, 1992; Dorfman et al., 1995). Although generally not discussed openly, many older women, whose average life expectancy is greater than their male counterparts, may find a same-sex partner an alternative easier to achieve than a heterosexual relationship (Jacobs, 1993).

Masturbation

Even less studied than heterosexual activity in later life is *masturbation*. Traditionally, masturbation has been an illicit activity, vigorously discouraged by parents who warned their children that "self-abuse" might cause mental retardation, weaken the body, and shorten life span. As Butler and Lewis (1993) pointed out in their book, *Love and Sex After Sixty*, a vast array of mechanical devices have been invented over the years that were designed to discourage children, especially boys who were considered more likely than girls to masturbate, from self-stimulation. Among adults, too, masturbation has been emphatically condemned, reflecting the Biblical condemnation of Onan, who "spilled his seed upon the ground" (Genesis, 38:9), and from whom another derogatory term for masturbation, onanism, comes. It is thus not surprising that relatively little is known about masturbation among the now-old, for attitudes toward self-gratification traditionally have been repressive (Starr & Weiner, 1981).

In recent years, as sexual standards have changed, masturbation has become increasingly acceptable for males and females of all ages. Starr (2001: 925) summarized current thinking in gerontology as follows: "Most experts agree that masturbation for the elderly is a healthy activity that can reduce feelings of frustration and loneliness while providing needed physical stimulation and release." Most likely to masturbate in later life are those who are single, widowed, or divorced, although many married elders also report masturbating as a gratifying activity (Starr, 2001).

Love and Intimacy

An important aspect of love is *personal intimacy* or pleasuring, which describes any form of physical arousal, such as touch or kissing, that feels good and may or may not encompass masturbation, intercourse, or orgasm. As a way of expressing affection, intimate contact is available to people of all ages, regardless of their physical condition, sexual scripts, or concerns about impotence. Regardless of the activity, sexual pleasure, love, and intimacy are immensely variable for both males and females throughout the life course. It is, like beauty, subject to different interpretations; one person's intrapsychic script of the "ideal" sex life may be vastly different from another's. Satisfaction with current levels of intimacy, sexual activity, frequency of sexual desire, and fantasies about sex vary by gender as well, reflecting socialization to sexual scripts.

Although being sexually active and having good mental health were the two most important predictors of sexual satisfaction in one study of very old adults living in the community, married women with better functional status were more likely to be satisfied with their sex lives than married men. For men, marital status was unrelated to sexual satisfaction, perhaps reflecting the double standard allowing "older men to purchase sex without the guilt or disapproval that it would create for older women" (Matthias et al., 1997: 13). One small-scale study suggested that midlife and young-old men experience higher levels of desire and fantasies than women (Johannes & Avis, 1997). Another small-scale examination of sexuality in later life indicated that sexual satisfaction for both men and women increased with age and that women were more likely to report sexual satisfaction than men in later life (Steinke, 1988). Whether male or female, however, any individual's satisfaction with sexual activity, love, and intimacy in old age appears to be related to satisfaction earlier in life; those people who were happy with their levels of sexual activity and intimacy when younger are most likely to feel contented with their sex lives in old age.

Many older couples find that their sexual relationship is enhanced by the years of love and affection for one another and their knowledge of their partner's preferences and desires. The immediate urgency of the sex drive, characteristic of young adults, has been tempered by many years of experience and intimacy. Older people also can have greater latitude in their sexual scripts than younger people. No longer needing to prove themselves or to play seductive games, some elders find it easier to relate to their partners and meet their needs. In sum, responsiveness is slower, but desire and ability remain. As one man wrote in "Letters to the Editor" of *Modern Maturity:* "Aging slows. For us seniors, learning creative ways to use sexual energy beyond procreation is perhaps a key source of inspired long life. Plus, it's such fun and wonderful for relationships, too" (Asimus, 2000: 10).

Nor does the need for intimacy and sexual activity cease with physical illness. For example, among one sample of men and women aged 36 to 75 who had survived a stroke, sexuality and intimacy continued not only to be important but also were *more* important to the stroke survivors than to their partners (Chadwick, Saver, Biller, & Carr, 1998).

The Institutional Setting: Barrier to Sex, Love, and Intimacy?

Sexuality, love, and intimacy among residents in nursing homes, assisted living facilities, and other long-term care settings raise numerous debatable issues and questions. Do residents have the right to express physical affection or to have sexual relationships with a spouse? With a same-sex long-term partner? With another opposite-sex or same-sex resident? What limits should be placed on intimacy?

The lives of nursing home and other long-term care residents differ from those of elders living in the community in two respects: greater dependency on others and more external constraints over everyday life. A nursing home is a *total institution* (Goffman, 1961) where residents' everyday activities are regulated, ranging from the times and types of meals served to the physical layout of the building and its furnishings. Behavior, too, is regulated, and elders who violate norms for expected behavior are often referred for a psychiatric consultation, medication, and physical restraints.

In many long-term care facilities, sexuality is discouraged as part of the assumption that the elderly are—or should be—sexless. Personnel working in institutional settings bring their own myths and biases about sexuality and intimacy in old age and are often unaware that sexuality in later life is normal rather than deviant. The physical environment also deters sexual expression, for the majority of nursing homes do not have private rooms. Door locks are generally forbidden, and nursing home personnel have access to all areas for reasons of safety. It is thus not surprising that opportunities for conjugal or partner visits are rarely provided, and personnel become apprehensive when confronted by any expression of sexuality by the residents. Masturbation is discouraged and homosexual relationships forbidden. Elders' relatives, too, often discourage any display of sexuality or physical closeness to or by their family member in a nursing home.

What interventions would be useful in accepting sexuality and physical intimacy among long-term care residents? Various proposals have been made including: (1) creating an atmosphere that encourages discussion of sexual feelings; (2) educating staff, family members, and residents with factual information about sexuality in later life; (3) adding sexual data in resident assessments; (4) sexual counseling; (5) providing privacy and time alone for couples; and (6) accepting masturbation among residents (Schlesinger, 1996: 124–125). To these interventions should be added sensitivity of staff, family, and residents to unwelcome or inappropriate sexual advances or harassment in order to protect but not restrict appropriate expression of sexuality and closeness.

Summary

Much research on sexuality is based on inadequate samples and this is particularly true for the now-old as ageist attitudes have limited investigation of sexuality and intimacy in old age. Laws and customs have restrained the sexual behavior of older people in many ways. Expressions of sexuality and needs for intimacy have been especially constrained for now-old women, who have traditionally enjoyed less freedom than men. Demographic factors also constrict older women more than their male counterparts in at least two ways: (1) fewer potential partners are available for heterosexual single, widowed, or divorced elderly women and (2) many of the few available men seek female partners younger than themselves. If male life expectancy approaches that for females in the future, opportunities for heterosexual sexuality and intimacy may very well change.

As all of us grow older, we are likely to experience physiological and chemical changes in our bodies, but these are not loss of sexual desire, ability, or yearning for intimacy. Sexuality, love, and intimacy remain important throughout the life course. Gerontologists, physicians, nurses, and other health and human service professionals, as well as all of us, can help break down myths and misconceptions about late-life sexuality. As the late Sigmund Freud (1915/1958) pointed out,

> Sexual love is undoubtedly one of the chief things in life, and the union of mental and bodily satisfaction in the enjoyment of love is one of its culminating peaks . . . all the world knows this and conducts its life accordingly; science alone is too delicate to admit it. (pp. 169–170)

As you think about sexuality and intimacy in later life, keep in mind that sexual norms are changing and people of all ages are becoming more frank about sexuality. For example, the cover of the February 2000 issue of *Cosmopolitan,* a magazine targeted at women in their 20s and 30s, spotlighted the articles "For Advanced Lovers Only" and "Bigger and Better Love" on its cover. Increased attention to sexual behavior is not confined to Gen Xers. Several months prior to this issue of *Cosmopolitan, Modern Maturity,* a magazine published by the American Association of Retired Persons for an aged 50–plus readership, featured age 50–plus actress Susan Sarandon on its cover and contents of the issue, such as "Great Sex—What's Age Got to Do With It?" and an "Exclusive Post-Viagra™ Survey" (*Modern Maturity,* September/October 1999).

Not only are the now-middle-aged and elderly expressing interest in sexuality and intimacy, but also the currently available cross-sectional data on sexuality in later life may be very different from that of the younger birth cohorts as they grow old even if there are no dramatic changes in life expectancy. The sexual scripts of each birth cohort are formed by cultural norms, gender socialization, and individual experiences. Your parents' sexual scripts may be very different from those of your grandparents, and your script may be dissimilar to your parents'.

Key Points

1. Knowledge about levels of sexual activity and satisfaction is limited and based on cross-sectional studies that neither give longitudinal information about sexuality throughout the life course nor about birth cohort differences in sexual expression.

2. Whether people are young or old, their sexuality is both a basic instinctual drive and socially shaped by the culture in which we live.

3. The concept of sexual scripts provides a useful way to examine how age, birth cohort, gender, and other social variables pattern sexual attitudes and behavior throughout the life course.

4. Due to culturally defined gender roles, middle-aged and older men may feel apprehensive about their sexuality and, in old age, find that their sexual interests and activity are ignored or deprecated.

5. Older women are at double disadvantage, for not only is old age negatively viewed but women also have been traditionally valued for their youthful beauty and fertility.

6. Certain physiological changes affecting sexual responsiveness occur in both men and women as they grow older, including longer arousal time.

7. A common problem among middle-aged and elderly men is benign prostatic hyperplasia (BPH), which affects the amount of semen ejaculated in sexual intercourse.

8. Postmenopausal women usually experience less vaginal lubrication than young women due to changes in estrogen levels.

9. The elderly engage in a variety of sexual practices, including intercourse with opposite-sex and same-sex partners, masturbation, and pleasuring.

10. Confounding the relationship between sexual interest, activity, and satisfaction is inadequate information on different birth cohorts.

11. Marital status, physical health, emotional well-being, and gender are important variables related to sexual activity, intimacy, and satisfaction.

12. In later life, the majority of people retain their emotional and physical capacities for sexual relations and intimacy.

13. An important but often ignored issue about sexuality in old age is the increasing proportion of men and women who are HIV positive and contracted the virus through heterosexual contact.

14. A second, often neglected issue concerns sexuality and intimacy in long-term care settings, such as nursing homes and assisted living facilities.

15. Sexuality, love, and intimacy are important throughout the life course.

Discussion Questions

1. Bring in advertisements and articles reflecting sexuality and intimacy among older people. Discuss what is and is not included.

2. How have norms regarding premarital and extramarital sex changed over the past 50 years for men? Are the changes the same for women? How would you expect these changes to affect the sexual practices of the now-old?

3. Select members of the class to take opposing sides and conduct a debate on the following issue: "Sexual relationships between consenting residents should be permitted in nursing homes."

4. Should mentally impaired elders in institutional facilities be permitted to have sexual relations with a spouse or partner? Why or why not?

5. Make and write down a set of predictions about sexuality, love, and intimacy in old age for three different birth cohorts: baby boomers, Generation Xers, and your own birth cohort. Explain any differences you predict among the three cohorts.

Films and Videos

A Thousand Tomorrows (video; 30 minutes; available from Fanlight Productions at 1-800-937-4112 or *www.fanlight.com*).

This prize-winning video examines the effects of Alzheimer's disease on intimacy and sexuality through interviews with the spouses of those affected.

As Time Goes By (video; 23 minutes; available from Fanlight Productions at 1-800-937-4112 or *www.fanlight.com*).

This documentary, produced by the Canadian Broadcasting Corporation, delineates men and women discussing love, romance, and growing old, challenging many beliefs about sexuality in later life.

Golden Threads (video; 56 minutes; available from Women Make Movies, Inc., at 1-212-925-0606 x360 or *www.wmm.com*).

A profile of the life of a 93-year-old lesbian activist, founder of a global networking service for midlife and older lesbians, that discusses sexuality, life choices, and aging.

The Personals: Improvisations on Romance in the Golden Years (video; 37 minutes; available from Fanlight Productions at 1-800-937-4112 or *www.fanlight.com*).

Winner of the Academy Award for best short documentary, this video depicts single elders on New York's Lower East Side as they perform a play about their search for love and intimacy through personal advertisements.

Internet Resources

http://www.thebody.com

This site, offered by the U.S. Centers for Disease Control, provides useful information about HIV and AIDS including up-to-date statistics.

http://www.siecus.org

The web site for the Sexuality Information and Education Council of the United States (Siecus), a national nonprofit organization providing educational information on sexuality and advocating the right of individuals to make responsible sexual choices.

http://www.gaylesbianretiring.org

The web site for GLARP, an organization specifically interested in gay and lesbian issues in later life.

Research Article

Laumann, E. O., Paik, A., & Rosen, R. (1999). Sexual dysfunction in the United States: Prevalence and predictors. *Journal of the American Medical Association, 281*, 537–544.

An interesting article on sexual dysfunction that provides much information but does not include the elderly.

Supplemental Readings

Brecher, E. M. (1984). *Love, Sex, and Aging: A Consumer's Union Report.* Boston, MA: Little, Brown.

An old but interesting report of a survey conducted by the Consumer's Union.

Butler, R. N. & Lewis, M. I. (1993). *Love and Sex After 60.* New York: Ballantine.

A useful introduction to sexuality and intimacy in later life that will dispel many preconceptions.

Duberman, M. B. (Ed.). (1997). *A Queer World: The Center for Lesbian and Gay Studies Reader.* New York: New York University Press.

A collection of articles on gender and sexuality, including gay and lesbian aging, from the Center for Lesbian and Gay Studies, City College of New York Graduate School.

Mead, J. (Ed.). (1994). *Many and More: A Celebration of Love in Later Life.* New York: Timken.

An anthology of poems, short stories, and drama about love in later life.

Rubin, L. B. (1990). *Erotic Wars: What Happened to the Sexual Revolution?* New York: Farrar, Straus, & Giroux.

An entertaining portrayal of participation in and response to the sexual revolution.

Schiavi, R. C. (1999). *Aging and Male Sexuality.* New York: Cambridge University Press.

An up-to-date view of psychological and physiological aspects of male sexuality, including that of elderly gays.

Simpson, E. (1994). *Late Love: A Celebration of Marriage After 50.* New York: Houghton Mifflin.

Readable interviews of 50 older couples who married in later life and the importance of physical love and intimacy in their lives. ✦

Chapter 10

Work, Retirement, and Leisure

Introduction

Abraham Goldstein began teaching law in 1930 and also had his own law practice until the 1970s. At age 101, he is a professor of business law at Baruch College in New York City where he conducts individual tutorials with law students. He also prepares an annual summary of important business law decisions to distribute to other faculty (National Public Radio, 2000). At age 100, Fred "Demon" Marsh continues his interest in motorcycles. A former motorcycle racer, he won the Northeast Amateur Championship in the 1920s and gained the name "Demon" because of his love for speed. Single all his life, he still owns Marsh Motorcycle Shop, now managed by his nephew, where he lives in the back of his showroom with Romeo, his German shepherd dog, and rides his moped around the parking lot. (Holmstrom, Internet download 11/27/2000)

Both Abraham Goldstein and Demon Marsh are exceptional members of the labor force. Not only do relatively few people live to 100, but among those who do, very few are working. These two men nonetheless provide a dramatic illustration that not all people who are 65 or older are retired. In 2001, almost 17 percent of American men and 9 percent of women who were 65 or more were involved in some kind of paid employment or were actively looking for work.

Although retirement is a simple word, it has many meanings. It is most often defined by two characteristics: (1) nonparticipation in the paid labor force and (2) receipt of income from Social Security and other retirement plans. Someone who works for pay and does not receive income from Social Security or pensions would not be officially retired. Economists usually classify those individuals who receive the majority of their income from Social Security, pensions, and assets as retired even if they continue to work at paid jobs. People who retire from careers in the military or in law enforcement typically receive a pension after 20 years of service and then take on another job. A notable and famous example of a postretirement military career is that of General Colin Powell, a former Chair of the Joint Chiefs of Staff of the U.S. Department of Defense until his 1993 retirement from the Army, who was named secretary of state in 2001 by President George W. Bush. Many other people continue to work part-time to supplement their Social Security or pension income.

Retirement is not only an event but a period in the life course and a social institution. As a social institution, retirement redistributes work from older to younger workers. Retirement also represents one aspect of a wider movement from a work- to a leisure-oriented society (Phillipson, 1982) and has become a new stage in the life course. What are the social purposes of retirement? What are the major reasons people take early retirement? How do people fare after they retire and how do they spend their time? Does retirement benefit everyone? Will retirement patterns change as the American population lives longer in better health than ever before? This chapter focuses on labor force participation in later life, factors associated with retirement (e.g., health, Social Security, and pensions), attitudes toward retirement, and leisure and postretirement life.

Labor Force Participation

Labor force participation is defined by the federal government as the percentage of a population that is either working or actively looking for work. According to census data, men 65 or over today are much less likely to participate in the labor force than their counterparts a half century or so ago. In 1950, about 46 percent participated in the labor force compared with only 17 percent in 1999. By 2008, according to Bureau of Labor statistics projections, the proportion of men aged 65 and over in the labor force will change very little.

The majority of men and women aged 51 to 61 work for pay, but a surprising number—about 1 in 4—does not (National Academy on an Aging Society, 2000a) and more than 8 in 10 of these men compared with about 4 in 10 women in the labor force are retired. Reflecting gender differences in paid employment, almost 3 in 20 (15 percent) men but over half (56 percent) of the women in this age group have never worked on a steady basis (National Academy on an Aging Society, 2000a).

Throughout the life course, white workers of both genders earn more than their African American or Latino counterparts; college graduates earn the most and those with less than a high school diploma the least (U.S. Bureau of Labor Statistics, 2000). Among 55- to 64-year-olds, women earn only about 68 percent of what men earn. In contrast, there is little gender gap in the wages or salary among workers 20 through 24 years of age. Women's earnings are slightly more than 90 percent of men's earnings. Young women at the start of their careers have not yet hit the glass ceiling that limits pay opportunities for women later in their work lives. The timing of childbearing is also a critical factor affecting women's wages; those women who have children at earlier ages are likely to earn less throughout their lives because their career interruptions occurred during the very period when they would be building a career (Taniguchi, 1999).

Most of the historical decline in the labor force among men aged 55 to 64 and 65 and over occurred during the 1950 to 1980 period, as you can see in Table 10-1. The drop in the male labor force is due both to changes in mandatory rules and financial incentives. *Mandatory retirement* rules, setting age 65 as the retirement age and covering half of American workers, were not fully repealed until 1986. Financial incentives to retire include the following: (1) changes in 1962 that set the earliest age of Social Security eligibility at 62 for men and (2) expansion in private pension coverage in the 1950s and 1960s—topics discussed later in this chapter. In contrast, although the labor force participation of women ages 25 to 54 and 55 to 64 has increased dramatically in the last 50 years or so, little change has occurred among women 65 and older.

Table 10-1 Percentage of Labor Force Participation by Age and Sex, 1950–2008*

	Men			Women		
Year	25–54	55–64	65+	25–54	55–64	65+
1950	96%	87%	46%	37%	27%	10%
1960	97	87	33	43	37	11
1970	96	83	27	50	43	10
1980	94	72	19	64	41	8
1990	93	68	16	74	45	9
1999	92	68	17	77	51	9
2008	91	69	18	80	58	9

*Percentages rounded to nearest whole number.
Source: Purcell, P. J. (2000: 21).

Income Relative to Worker Participation

Employed people in their 50s and 60s and older are more optimistic than retired counterparts about their financial futures. Reflecting their better current financial status plus the belief that they have the ability to continue work, they are twice as likely to believe they will be better off financially in the next two years (National Academy on an Aging Society, 2000b). *Race* affects earnings and savings. Employed white workers aged 60 or over have more than three times the net wealth of employed African Americans (National Academy on an Aging Society, 2000b).

Health

Health also strongly influences labor force participation. Workers 60 and older are almost twice as likely to report very good to excellent health as are their unemployed age counterparts. Not only are they healthier but they are more likely than retirees to be white married men with more education (National Academy on an Aging Society, 2000a). Reflecting their greater likelihood of declining physical strength in later life, older workers, especially those 70 and over, are less likely to be in physically demanding jobs. Workers 70 and over are also far more likely to be self-employed than are those aged 40 to 59, and about 1 in 3 of workers aged 70 or older is in a professional or managerial job.

Lifelong lower incomes among many older African Americans, such as this okra farmer, mean less savings for retirement.

Relatively few are in physically demanding jobs, such as farmer (5 percent), laborer (3 percent), or operative and craftsman (14 percent) (National Academy on an Aging Society, 2000a).

Gradual Exit From the Labor Force for the Aging: Phased Retirement, Bridge Jobs, and Displaced and Discouraged Workers

Many people leave the labor force gradually, moving from long-term or career jobs into phased retirement and bridge or transitional employment before they stop all paid work.

Phased Retirement

Phased retirement describes any arrangement that permits older workers to reduce their work hours and responsibility to ease them into full retirement. Although some discussions of phased retirement also include bridge jobs that often involve a change of work and employer, phased retirement here is used to describe work in which employees reduce their work schedules as they approach retirement. Phased retirement is not widely used, and only around 16 percent of employers offer such programs (Townsend, 2001). However, this approach has advantages for both employees and employers, permitting people who wish to work and earn extra money before full retirement to extend their work lives and allowing employers to retain experienced workers when labor is short. Nonetheless, restrictions on some types of pensions plus the potential costs to employers for health insurance benefits and pension plans, as well as stereotypes that see older workers as less productive than younger workers, have discouraged companies from adopting phased employment plans (Townsend, 2001).

Bridge Jobs

Bridge jobs also span the period between full-time employment and retirement. An estimated one-third to one-half of older Americans will work at a bridge job before ceasing all paid work (Quinn, 1999). Motivations to take a bridge job vary, and include the need for additional income and the desire to explore new types of work. For example, 63-year-old James Gray (a pseudonym) was laid off from his job as a physics teacher in a private high school because his progressive hearing loss made teaching difficult. It was impossible for him to find another teaching job, and he was not yet eligible for full Social Security benefits. In good health except for his hearing ability, he had always enjoyed designing and building things in his spare time and decided to start a small business, constructing tile coffee tables and bases for wood stoves and selling them at a minor profit. Mr. Gray's bridge job not only increased his income but also illustrates the process of selective optimization with compensation (Baltes & Baltes, 1990). Given his hearing loss, he selected a line of work where his deafness was not a barrier, optimized the maintenance of his abilities in design and construction, and used these skills to compensate for a physical deficit. As in Mr. Gray's case, bridge jobs frequently involve a switch from wages or salary to self-employment. Bridge jobs are also most often a slide down the occupational ladder and pay lower wages.

Displaced Workers

Displaced workers, as defined by the Department of Labor, are persons who lost a job at which they had worked for at least three years due to one of the following: (1) closing or move of the plant or company where they were employed; (2) insufficient work; or (3) abolition of the position or shift. Approximately 3.3 million people of all ages were displaced between January 1997 and December 1999. Table 10-2 summarizes their labor force status as of February 2000. As you can see from the table, people aged 55 to 64 were less likely to be employed after displacement than younger workers but more likely to find new employment than those 65 and over, most of whom opted for retirement.

Table 10-2	Displaced Workers by Age, Sex, and Employment Status in February 2000*			
	Employed After Displacement	Unemployed After Displacement	Not in Labor Force	Total
Men				
20–24	78%	12%	10%	100%
25–54	82	13	5	100
55–64	63	15	22	100
65 and over	33	10	57	100
Women				
20–24	66	13	21	100
25–54	75	11	14	100
55–64	54	11	35	100
65 and over	33	8	59	100

*Percentages rounded.
Source: U.S. Bureau of Labor Statistics, Table 8 (*www.bls.gov.news.release/disp.t08.htm*; accessed 12/20/01).

African Americans, Latinos, and women aged 51 to 61 are more likely than white men to be displaced. Although health and type of employment partially explain these racial and ethnic differences, African-American men and Latina women are still more likely to be displaced than their white peers with similar socioeconomic and demographic characteristics (Flippen & Tienda, 2000). A 5-year follow-up of displaced workers indicated that earnings, health insurance coverage, and average household income declined among those who were reemployed and that minorities and women showed the greatest losses. Nonwhites and women were the most economically vulnerable and, when reemployed, had significantly lower earnings than whites.

Nor were lost earnings replaced through other sources, such as pensions (Couch, 1998).

Unfortunately, even those workers who find new jobs do not fare as well as they did prior to being displaced. Only 59 percent of displaced workers who find new jobs have health insurance from their current employer or through their spouse, 21 percentage points less than for all workers. Minorities also have significantly lower rates of health insurance coverage, either through their employers or their spouses, than do whites (Couch, 1998). Displacement also takes its toll on physical and mental health. Regardless of race, ethnicity, or gender, older workers' physical functioning and mental health are worse after involuntary job loss even when their health prior to displacement and sociodemographic characteristics are taken into account (Gallo, Bradley, Siegel, & Kasl, 2000).

Discouraged Workers

Discouraged workers, not counted as part of the labor force, are people who want and are available to work and have looked for a job in the last 12 months or since the end of the last job they held, but they are not currently looking for work because they think that no jobs are available or that none exist for which they qualify. Many displaced workers, especially African Americans and Latinos, become discouraged workers; their periods of joblessness last so long that they eventually withdraw from the labor force (Flippen & Tienda, 2000). Moreover, older workers' job searches are often prolonged. They frequently experience age discrimination in the workplace as well as gender and racial discrimination. Moreover, their skills may be obsolete in a rapidly changing economy. Discouraged older workers, for all practical purposes, are "retired" despite their interest in remaining in the labor force. The jobs are simply not available to them.

Retirement

Although the concept of retirement is relatively new in the United States, today nearly two million people retire each year. As the baby boom generation ages, that number will become even larger. Both men and women are retiring earlier than they did a century or so ago. In 1910, the average retirement age for men who lived long enough and could afford to retire was 74; today it is 63. For women just 20 years ago, the average retirement age was 65 but is now just under age 63. Inasmuch as many people today can expect to spend a quarter of their lives in retirement, an entirely new life stage is evolving, increasingly marked by good health and a desire for new and meaningful experiences, including paid and unpaid work.

Retirement as a Labor Management Strategy

Retirement is more than a personal exit from the labor force. Both retirement and early retirement are products of social and economic structures of a society. From a political economy perspective, retirement is a labor management strategy used by employers both to maximize efficiency and profits and to control the flow of workers in and out of the labor force. Retirement and early retirement plans enable an employer to hire younger and less expensive entry-level workers and to cut the costs of benefits, such as health insurance and pension plans.

Since the 1980s, a range of economic and labor policies to reduce costs including the price of labor have resulted in corporate downsizing and incentives for "early retirement" before the age of 65. Older workers have been increasingly viewed as prime targets for cost cutting through early retirement buyouts and layoffs (Herz, 1995). Early retirement plans or "golden handshakes" encourage workers to leave work by offering various combinations of pension plans and cash payouts based on the employee's age and length of time with the company. Corporate downsizing has a similar effect, saving money for the employer by reducing the number of workers to maximize profits.

Spotlight on U.S.: When General Motors Downsized

When General Motors' (GM) fortunes declined in the 1970s and 1980s, its management announced a series of permanent plant closings that would result in the permanent layoff of tens of thousands of workers. Seniority rules established by the company and the United Auto Workers (UAW) required that younger workers with the shortest period of time on the job would be laid off first, a policy that would result in an older work force. Neither GM nor UAW officials felt this policy would be in their best long-run interests. To encourage older workers to retire and enable younger workers to keep their jobs, both company and union administrators agreed to offer special early retirement plans (ERIPs), offering workers, some as young as age 50, an opportunity to retire early with better benefits than the usual ERIPs. A total of 17 percent of the 1,721 workers opted to retire.

Who chose the ERIPs? Those most likely to take an ERIP were workers entitled to higher pensions and in skilled occupations with 12 or more years of education. They were also more likely to be married, to have worked overtime recently, and not to have been laid off in the recent past. Skilled workers with higher levels of education probably chose to retire because they believed they had better post-retirement job chances enabling them to find new jobs. Further, workers doing overtime opted for retirement perhaps because, through working additional shifts, they had thought ahead to retirement, amassing additional savings.

Two other factors also were important: (1) whether the plant was closing or only downsizing and (2) the degree of worker solidarity within a given plant. Although plant closure increased the pressure on older workers to retire and make room for younger workers, lower worker solidarity within a plant, whether or not it was closing, meant that the average worker eligible for an ERIP was less likely to retire. Pen-

sion assets also played a role. Workers eligible for an ERIP that was lower than the amount they wanted resisted retirement, bumped younger workers, and transferred to another plant. Thus, whether or not a worker decided to take a "golden handshake" was influenced by both pension prospects and worker solidarity.

Source: Based on Hardy and Hazelrigg (1999: 275–303).

Management Practices That Affect Retirement Benefits

MYTH: Employers Provide More Postretirement Benefits Today Than in the Past

Shrinking Postretirement Benefits. Due to rising costs that cut into profits, employers have cut back on postretirement benefits with the result that both the number of early retirees and Medicare-eligible retirees with health insurance from a former employer have consistently declined since the late 1980s (U.S. General Accounting Office, 1997). Losing employer-based health insurance presents two major issues for retirees: (1) they are likely to have to pay more for individual plans on their own that have less comprehensive coverage; and (2) until recently, they faced the possibility that insurance would be denied or restricted because of a preexisting medical condition (U.S. General Accounting Office, 1997). Table 10-3 summarizes the characteristics of

Table 10-3 Characteristics of Retirees More and Less Likely to Have Employer-Based Health Benefits

More Likely to Have Coverage	Less Likely to Have Coverage
Work for large firms	Work for smaller firms
Have higher preretirement earnings	Have lower preretirement earnings
Belong to union	Are nonunion
Work in manufacturing, communications/public utilities	Work in retail sector or service industries
Work in government sector	Work in private nongovernment sector
Are men	Are women
Are white	Are African American or other minority

Source: Adapted from U.S. General Accounting Office (1997: 11).

retirees more and less likely to have employer-based health benefits. As you can see from the table, the people most likely to need health insurance—women, members of minorities, and those with lower earnings—are least likely to have coverage.

Flexible Employment. As corporate downsizing and retirement incentives increased, many companies hired older workers in *flexible employment* as independent contractors, temporary workers, and on-call personnel. Flexible employment costs employers less because workers usually do not receive fringe benefits, such as health insurance and pensions. Flexible workers are also easier to lay off during economic downturns or corporate downsizing. Table 10-4 summarizes the proportion of older workers employed in traditional and flexible work by age and gender. Traditional employment decreases with age while independent contracting and on-call work increases. Flexible work is both positive and negative. On the positive side, it provides bridge jobs and an opportunity to supplement Social Security and pensions. On the negative side, it pays no benefits and is most often concentrated in jobs at the bottom of the labor market, as the growing number of older supermarket baggers and fast-food workers illustrates.

Table 10-4   Older Employed Workers in Flexible Versus Traditional Work Arrangements, February, 2001 (Percentages)

	Male		Female	
Type of Employment	**Ages 55–64**	**Ages 65+**	**Ages 55–64**	**Ages 65+**
Independent contractors	12.2%	20.8%	6.9%	11.3%
On-call workers	1.3	3.2	1.4	2.6
Temp agencies	0.6	0.3	1.3	0.6
Contract firm workers	0.5	0.6	0.2	0.7
Traditional employment	85.3	75.2	90.2	84.8
TOTALS	100.0	100.0	100.0	100.0

Source: U.S. Bureau of Labor Statistics (2001), Table 5.

MYTH: JOB DISCRIMINATION NO LONGER EXISTS

Job Discrimination. Employers' beliefs about the abilities of older workers also influence labor force participation and retirement. For example, because older workers make more money than others, employers often seek young people willing to work longer hours for about half the wages that experienced workers command. Despite evidence to the contrary, many employers fear that older workers will not be as productive as younger ones and that they will have more on-the-job accidents and higher rates of absenteeism. Although age discrimination in employment became illegal in 1967 when the Age Discrimination in Employment Act (ADEA) was passed, many employers are not particularly interested in hiring or retaining older workers. Although laws prohibit employers from telling a job applicant that he or she is too old to be hired, they can say instead that the applicant is "overqualified" for a position because of past extensive job experience.

An older worker seeking promotion can also be evaluated as lacking drive or skills rather than being told that she is "too old." Likewise, older workers are often viewed as less flexible by human resource managers, especially by younger human resource personnel (AARP, 2000). The experience, wisdom, loyalty, and high standards that older workers can bring to a job are disregarded. According to a Harris survey, only 1 in 8 of the 400 companies surveyed felt a need to respond to the aging of the labor force, and only 1 in 3 offered older workers the opportunity to transfer to jobs with less responsibility (Administration on Aging, 1999). Even today, many employers remain concerned about the higher costs and lower productivity of older workers and are more interested in structuring incentives for older workers to retire than in encouraging them to stay in the labor force (Crown & Longino, 1997).

Factors Influencing Workers to Retire

MYTH: People Who Take Early Retirement Are
Usually Well-Off and in Good Health

Income and Health. Some people retire voluntarily, others are subtly eased out. Although a common belief is that people are retiring earlier because they have enough money to live on without working, the average person who retires before age 65 is not well-off (National Academy on an Aging Society, 2000b). Early retirees have a family income nearly half that of people of the same age who are still working and have fewer assets, such as savings, stocks, bonds, and property. Poor health is a major reason for early retirement that results in lower income. Both men and women are more likely to retire if their health is poor enough to limit or prevent work.

Most likely to retire before age 60 are people with chronic health problems; 1 in 4 suffers from heart disease, almost 1 in 5 from hearing impairments, and 1 in 6 from high blood pressure or arthritis or other orthopedic impairments. Especially vulnerable to illnesses resulting in early retirement are African Americans and Latinos in physically demanding jobs (National Academy on an Aging Society, 2000a). Regardless of race or ethnicity, people with chronic illnesses are less likely than their healthy age peers to be satisfied with their retirement (National Academy on an Aging Society, 2000c). Nor do they have hopes that their financial status will improve in the foreseeable future. The proportion of early retirees who think their financial prospects will be even worse within the next two years is twice as high as among workers in the same age group—17 percent versus 8 percent (National Academy on an Aging Society, 2000a).

Not surprisingly, retirement is not always voluntary. The younger a worker is when she or he leaves a job, the more likely it is that the departure is involuntary. Only one-fourth of the people leaving a job between ages 55 and 62 retire voluntarily, compared with over half of those leaving a job at age 62 or older (Uccello, 1998). Reflecting their advantage in the hierarchies of social class, gender, and race/ethnicity, those most likely to retire voluntarily are white married males with 13 years or more of education or with pension coverage from their employer. Yet, both men and women are *less* likely to retire if they have health insurance coverage from their employer. They are also less likely to retire if they have a spouse who is still working (Uccello, 1998).

Global Glimpses: Early Retirement in Europe?

The age when workers must retire was abolished in the United States in 1986, mainly to reduce the costs of the Social Security program, and workers now may be employed until age 70 without losing full Social Security benefits. In Europe, however, the opposite policy has been adopted. To reduce unemployment, the retirement age was effectively lowered to open up jobs for younger workers. Current pension schemes tend to encourage early exit, and the actual retirement age is below the normal eligibility age established by law. Early retirement is used as a socially acceptable way to reduce staff levels.

From the employer's viewpoint, it is less expensive to hire an entry-level younger worker than to keep an older one who receives higher wages. Thus, employees over age 55 or even age 50 are targeted for layoffs and early retirement incentives. These policies have affected age stratification patterns, as unemployed European workers over 50 or 55 had little hope of finding other employment. In 1999, for example,

by age 55, only slightly more than 1 in 3 (37 percent) Italians were employed, about 1 in 2 (47 percent) French, and 3 in 5 people in the British Isles (Commission of the European Communities, 2000).

Displaced workers found that their expected movement through the life course was suddenly re-arranged as normative expectations of appropriate midlife roles no longer applied. Removing older workers from the labor force also changed the terms of social exchange, the unspoken agreement between generations, by increasing competition among age strata for social resources. The large number of unemployed people in their 50s is producing a new social age category: the *prematurely retired.* Are they now the "young-old" or are they still middle-aged?

Early retirement incentives have also proved to be costly, for European nations face an ever-growing number of older people to support. Currently, the Commission of the European Communities is seeking ways to create policies to increase overall employment rates and sustainable pension systems in the future.

Source: Commission of the European Communities. (2000). *The Future Evolu-* *tion of Social Protection from a Long-Term* *Point of View: Safe and Sustainable Pen-* *sions*. Brussels, Belgium: Author.

Gaullier, Xavier. (1988). *La deuxieme* *carriere: Ages, emplois, retraites*. Paris, France: Editions du Seuil.

MYTH: Age Is the Major Reason People Retire Today

Changing Attitudes and Policies. Although retirement is a normative event in American society, movement into retirement has become increasingly flexible and blurred and often a gradual process. For the great majority of men and women in modern industrialized societies, increased life expectancy means that they will outlive work roles. But unlike many other life events, such as confirmations or bar mitzvahs, graduations, or weddings, entry into retirement has no specific or standard rituals. Some people retire without fanfare, others give or are given a party by friends and relatives, and still others are given a farewell party at work, where clocks and watches, marking the passage of time, are frequent gifts. For those who can afford it, travel provides a ritual for transition from the status of worker to retiree.

Income and health clearly influence the decision to retire as well as the opportunity and quality of retirement itself. Not only do government and employer retirement policies shape retirement patterns but social and personal factors, including anticipations of what retirement will be like, are important. Many people will stop working entirely; others will take phased retirement or bridge jobs; still others will enter a new type of work, either through preference or economic necessity; and some, like the two centenarians described in the beginning of this chapter, will continue to work at their lifelong adult occupations, curtailing hours or responsibilities of the job.

Age is only an approximate marker of when retirement will occur, and the decision to retire is gradual. About 3 in 4 workers aged 51 to 61 can name a year or an age at which they expect to retire, 1 in 8 say that they haven't thought about retirement, and another 1 in 7 say they will never retire. Those enrolled in a pension plan, associated with a union, or in poorer health are more likely to think and talk about retirement (Ekerdt, Kosloski, & DeViney, 2000). Conversely, men who anticipate good postretirement benefits, including a pension plan and health insurance from their employer, are more likely to retire early (Fronstin, 1999). Expectations for postretirement financial security plus positive views of retirement as a predictable and planned reward for years of work are important both for retirement decisions and retirement satis-faction (Mutran, Reitzes, & Fernandez, 1997).

Attitudes toward retirement also are influenced by the amount of commitment to the job. People in jobs with little independence, rou-tine tasks, and high physical demands are more likely to retire volun-tarily or due to disability at earlier ages, and those less dedicated to their job are more likely to view retirement positively (Mutran, Reitzes, & Fernandez, 1997). On the other hand, workers whose longest period of employment involves significant personal communication and deal-ing with people are more likely to delay retirement, perhaps because their social skills provide them more opportunities to continue work-ing (Taylor & Shore, 1995). As an article in the *Financial Times* pointed out, good jobs provide several benefits: self-identity, a sense of mastery, creativity, control, interdependence with others and a link between the individual and society, social contacts, and a schedule and pattern for daily life (Furnham, 2001). Good jobs also provide money!

Gender and Family Obligations. Although both retirement poli-cies and retirement preparation programs emphasize retirement and financial planning, personal and family characteristics (e.g., including kinship ties, marital status, and gender role expectations) also influ-ence retirement decisions. Men are more likely to decide to retire when their wives are eligible for Social Security benefits; wives are more likely to be influenced by their husbands' decisions and the couple's overall economic situation. Men are also more likely to retire when their wives are in poor health, suggesting that men are not prepared to be both caregivers and employees. On the other hand, women with a husband in poor health are likely to keep on working, playing dual roles as employee and caregiver.

Wives' retirement decisions suggest that men pressure their wives to retire but women do not do likewise to their husbands. For many wives, preservation of their husbands' status as the head family honcho is important (Szinovacz & DeViney, 2000). Obligations to kin, such as frequency of contact with adult children and financial responsibility for adult children, also affect decisions to retire and vary by marital status, gender, and race (Szinovacz, DeViney, & Davey, 2001). Recent research emphasizes that the models of retirement decision-making and the very definition of retirement itself need to take into account the ways that gender, class, and race/ethnicity intersect to structure paths, decisions, and meanings; no "one size fits all" (Calasanti, 1993, 1996; Szinovacz, DeViney, & Davey, 2001).

Sources of Retirement Pensions: Social Security and Private Pensions

The major source of income for many elders after retirement is Social Security; one leg of the three-legged stool that can comprise retirement income; private pensions and assets form the other two legs. Pensions to retirees under Social Security are *life annuities,* paying out a periodic amount of money that lasts for life in exchange for an up-front premium charge. Social Security in the United States is not financed from general revenues as it is in some other industrialized nations; rather it is a "pay as you go system" in which today's retirees are being supported by payroll taxes levied on current workers just as the contributions made by current retirees were used to fund benefits to earlier cohorts of retired workers.

MYTH: Most Americans Have Always Had Retirement Pensions

The Evolution of Social Security. The United States, however, was a latecomer to national social insurance programs and was the last Western nation to establish a social security plan. During the nineteenth century, Otto von Bismarck, Chancellor of Germany, introduced a social insurance fund for disabled and retired workers; France adopted a similar program in 1905, and England instituted an old-age and unemployment insurance program in 1911. When the Social Security Act was passed in 1935, 34 nations already had established some form of national social insurance (Koff & Park, 1999).

Although national old-age pensions similar to Social Security were proposed as early as 1797, the economic well-being of the elderly in the early history of the United States depended on their social status: no money, no respect. Elders who had no money or relatives able to support them were lumped together with other categories of the poor—orphans, the blind, disabled, mentally ill, and developmentally disabled—to receive "home relief" dollars from their local villages or towns (Haber, 1983).

Almshouses. In the late eighteenth and nineteenth centuries, the rising costs of keeping the poor elderly in their own homes led city officials to establish almshouses. The almshouse, also called the poorhouse, housed not only old people but also orphans, unemployed younger people, alcoholics, the mentally or physically ill, and the homeless. This institution both provided economy of scale and discouraged the lazy from seeking financial assistance. Although the elderly were granted more privileges than other residents, almshouse residency was nasty, and the older people who were admitted generally lived there until they died, surrounded by alcoholics, beggars, unwed mothers, orphans, and the mentally and physically disabled (Haber & Gratton, 1994). By the end of the nineteenth century, when new institutions for orphans, the mentally or physically ill, and other groups formerly housed in the almshouse were established, the elderly made up the majority of poorhouse residents. The horror of ending life in the almshouse was the topic of popular poems and songs, such as the following:

For I'm old and I'm helpless and feeble,
The days of my youth have gone by,
Then over the hill to the poor house,
I wander alone there to die.

(Catlin, 1874, cited in Haber & Gratton, 1994: 128)

The first federal retirement benefit legislation, passed in 1861, established pensions for Union Civil War veterans so that they could avoid the stigma of entering the poorhouse. By 1900, about two-thirds of eligible elderly Union Army Civil War veterans and their dependents were receiving such benefits (Koff & Park, 1999); Confederate veterans received no federal benefits. Retirement programs for certain state and local government employees—primarily teachers, police, and firefighters—also date back to the nineteenth and early twentieth centuries. Pension advocates, arguing that impoverishment was the likely fate for everyone in old age, began to press for an all-inclusive system of age-based pensions. The Civil Service Retirement System was established in 1920 for Federal employees and members of the U.S. Congress (Social Security Administration, Internet download), but until the passage of the Social Security Act in 1935, the vast majority of older workers simply worked until they dropped. The very notion of leaving a job permanently was unknown except to the rich, the very ill, or the few guaranteed a regular retirement income (Elman, 1999; Haber & Gratton, 1994).

During the Great Depression of 1929, banks failed and savings were demolished. Neither local communities and states nor private charities had enough financial resources to cope with widespread unemployment and

As a result of the Great Depression, some families, such as this one from Texas, lived in substandard housing without sanitation or water.

economic destitution. By 1930, about 40 percent of the nation's elderly were economically dependent. Two years later, one-third of the American labor force was out of work. Workers went on strike and numerous social movements developed to protest the nationwide economic destitution. These events prompted fears that riot and anarchy might occur unless some sort of national plan was instituted to relieve the prevailing social and economic turmoil (Koff & Park, 1999).

The Townsend Movement. One of the most popular social movements focusing on the elderly in the 1930s was led by Francis Townsend, a 66-year-old California physician whose savings had been wiped out during the Great Depression. Townsend began to advocate for an old age revolving pension plan, calling for payments of $200 per month to people aged 60 and over who in turn would be required to spend it within the next 30 days. Such a plan, he proposed, would not only relieve the economic plight of the elderly but would bolster the lagging economy. To be financed by a national 2 percent tax on all commercial transactions, his plan generated popular enthusiasm.

The Townsend movement was ideologically attractive, blending the issue of old age poverty with the American values of individualism and consumerism (Katz, 1996). The Townsend movement also gave the elderly a new identity of activism, rights, and empowerment (Katz, 1996). About 7,000 Townsend Clubs with more than 1.5 million members were founded throughout the United States. Not only were members expected to participate in politics and community affairs, but within the clubs, older people gained a sense of personal power when politicians appealed to them on their terms for votes and support (Katz, 1996).

The Social Security Act

In response to growing nationwide social protest about poverty and unemployment, President Franklin D. Roosevelt's administration proposed relatively conservative initial economic provisions that resulted in the Social Security Act passed in 1935. This Act established two national social insurance programs to help the elderly and unemployed: (1) a federal system of old-age benefits for retired workers formerly employed in industry and commerce, and (2) a federal-state system of unemployment insurance. The Act also provided federal grants-in-aid to states for the means-tested programs of Old Age Assistance, Aid to Families with Dependent Children, and Aid to the Blind programs later replaced by other legislation. In 1939, Congress added benefits for dependents of retired workers and surviving dependents of deceased workers.

Why was age 65 chosen as the age of eligibility for Social Security retirement benefits? Although the Committee designing the Social Security Act provisions briefly examined European old-age pension programs, notably the German and British systems, the factors determining the retirement age for Social Security were both economic and political. From a political perspective, it met the needs of those demanding some type of national pension scheme. From an economic perspective, it reduced the likelihood of high costs, for at least two reasons: (1) to award benefits to people younger than age 65 would be expensive; and (2) to award benefits to workers older than 65 would keep workers in the labor force longer, increasing unemployment among younger people (Katz, 1996). According to Wilbur Cohen, a major architect of the Social Security Act,

> . . . at no time . . . did the staff of members of the Committee on Economic Security deem feasible any other age than 65 as the eligible age for the receipt of old age insurance benefits. There is, therefore, very little material available to analyze the economic, social, gerontological, or other reasons for the selection of this particular age. However, 65 was widely accepted at the time, almost without controversy, as the minimum retirement age in public and private pension plans (Cohen, 1957, cited in Katz, 1996: 65).

Few changes were made in the provisions of the Social Security Act until the 1950s, when coverage was extended to additional jobs that had previously been excluded from benefits. The act was also broadened through the addition of *Disability Insurance*, providing benefits for severely disabled workers aged 50 or over, for dependents of disabled workers, and for adult disabled children of deceased or retired workers. In the 1960s, requirements that disabled workers be aged 50 or over were removed. Disability benefits were also provided for widows and widowers aged 50 or older.

Two of the most important changes to the Social Security Act are the *Medicare* (Title XVIII) and *Medicaid* (Title XIX) programs established in 1965. *Medicare* created a health insurance program for the elderly, financed through the Social Security System but set up with its own trust funds and earnings tax to provide coverage. This system reduced the cost of hospital care and outlined a voluntary supplementary medical insurance plan financed through premiums paid by individuals.

Medicaid established grants to states for health care for the poor of all ages as determined by a means test. The total insurance package under Social Security became Old Age and Survivors Disability Health Insurance (OASDHI), with three separate trust funds for Old Age and Survivors Insurance (OASI), Disability Insurance (DI), and Hospital Insurance (HI) (Koff & Park, 1999). Numerous changes have been made to the Social Security Act since its inception, such as those summarized in Table 10-5.

MYTH: GOVERNMENT PROGRAMS, LIKE SUPPLEMENTAL SECURITY INCOME (SSI), KEEP OLDER PEOPLE OUT OF POVERTY

Supplemental Security Income. *Supplemental Security Income* (SSI), created in 1972 and put into effect in 1974, is not an old-age pension scheme but replaces several means-tested welfare programs that were originally part of the Social Security Act. SSI (Title XX of the

Table 10-5 Milestones in the Social Security Act	
Year	**Event**
1935	President Roosevelt signs the Social Security Act.
1937	Payroll tax set at one-cent per dollar for a maximum annual deduction of $30 each for employers and employees.
1950	First Social Security tax increase.
1956	Disability insurance extended to workers ages 50 to 64.
1960	Disability insurance at any age approved.
1962	Retirement at age 62 approved with reduced benefits.
1965	Medicare established.
1969	Social Security included in federal budget to offset military expenditures of Vietnam war.
1974	Supplemental Security Income (SSI) replaces Old Age Assistance, Assistance to the Blind, and Aid to the Permanently and Totally Disabled welfare programs.
1975	Beneficiaries given annual cost-of-living adjustment linked to Consumer Price Index.
1977	Benefit formula revised and Social Security taxes increased to avoid shortfall.
1983	Payroll taxes for self-employed increased; retirement age to be raised; up to 50 percent of high-income recipient benefits taxed.
1993	Up to 85 percent of high-income recipient benefits taxed with additional revenue channeled to Medicare.
2000	Social Security Act amended to permit workers ages 65 to 69 to continue working without reduction of their retirement benefits.

Source: Adapted from Koff, T. H., and Park, R. W. (1999: 168).

Social Security Act) is a nationwide federal assistance program that supplanted the Old Age Assistance (OAA), Assistance to the Blind (AB), and Aid to the Permanently and Totally Disabled (APTD) programs of the original Social Security Act. Despite federal funding, these older programs were state-administered, and without federal guidelines for maximum or minimum standards, states differed widely on eligibility criteria and payment levels. The SSI program, designed to correct inequities by setting a uniform amount of money for people with very low incomes, established uniform eligibility requirements for "assistance as last resort" for impoverished people who were 65 or older or blind or disabled. Blind and disabled children can also receive benefits.

SSI is a welfare means-tested program, meaning that people will not be eligible if their income and assets exceed limits established by the government. Federal eligibility criteria include (1) assets (property, savings, etc.) limited to a total of $2,000 for individuals and $3,000 for couples; (2) uniform definitions of disability and blindness; and (3) uniform standards for citizenship and residency. The monthly federal benefit rate of $545 for individuals and $817 for an eligible couple in 2002 is reduced dollar-for-dollar by the amount of their income, determined on a monthly basis (Social Security Administration, 2001). If, for example, an individual received $300 a month in income, the amount he or she would receive from SSI would be computed as $545 minus $300 = $245 monthly.

Although SSI recipients are categorically eligible for Medicaid, there is a hitch; each state can establish its own eligibility requirements for Medicaid. People on SSI can also receive Social Security if they have enough earned income credits, but their SSI will be reduced to take into account the money they get. SSI payments are also reduced by a windfall, such as sale of a home or land:

> Howard is a 76-year-old man who lives alone in a cabin located some 20 miles from even the smallest town in the county [in Appalachia]. . . . He has always owned the house and adjoining land where he and his wife raised five children. . . . Howard worked only sporadically throughout his life and relied on Supplemental Security Income (SSI) for his limited income until recently. . . . Recipients of SSI are allowed to keep their homes and still receive benefits, which is what happened in Howard's case until he sold a portion of the land to a neighbor and used the money (to) pay off old debts. Someone reported the sale to the Social Security Administration and Howard's SSI checks were stopped. The Social Security Administration considered the money from the land sale to be income, which made Howard ineligible for SSI. Hence, Howard gets no monthly income and has lost the medical insurance, Medicaid, which accompanies SSI. (McInnis-Dittrich, 2000: 241–242)

Because Americans have traditionally been concerned that means-tested welfare programs, such as SSI and Aid to Families with Dependent Children, will be abused by people who are ripping off the system by receiving benefits when they should be working or when they have lied about other sources of income, SSI has not abolished poverty. The level of benefits leaves many SSI recipients below the poverty level. Nearly 50 percent of the families receiving SSI currently live below the poverty level.

Although states may supplement the basic SSI payment at various levels, only 27 states provide supplements and in only 2 states does the combination rise above the poverty level (Social Security Administration, Office of the Commissioner, 2000). Not only is it difficult and time-consuming to meet the eligibility requirements, but also individuals and couples receiving the full basic monthly SSI benefit set by the federal government but no state supplement get a payment *below* the poverty level. Over half the SSI recipients have no other source of income. An individual 65 or older and eligible for the full amount of SSI would receive only $6,540 per year—almost $2,000 below the poverty level in 2000. An elderly couple would receive $9,804 per year, again below the poverty level.

Private Pensions

As the baby boomers approach retirement, income security has become a hot topic. As more and more people live longer, will they outlive their resources? Will Social Security be adequate to meet the needs of the large number of retiring baby boomers when there are fewer workers making contributions in this pay-as-you-go system? To increase postretirement income beyond Social Security benefits, some employers have developed company-based pension plans. Various types of individual pension plans also exist, as described in the following sections.

Employer-Sponsored Retirement Plans. Employers can offer two basic types of retirement plans: defined-benefit or defined-contribution. A *defined-benefit* plan is just that: a plan that defines what benefits employees will receive. Like Social Security, defined-benefit pension plans are life annuities. In a typical defined-benefit plan, employers promise to pay a certain annual pension benefit at retirement that usually depends on years of service and average salary over the last few years of employment. Typically, the employer makes contributions to a pension fund; employees usually do not make contributions. If an employer's defined-benefit plan does not have enough money to pay out all its promised benefits, the Pension Benefit Guaranty Corporation, a federal agency created by the Employee Retirement Income Security Act of 1974, will pay the benefits up to a maximum set by law (Pension Benefit Guaranty Corporation, Internet access 10/11/00).

In the usual *defined-contribution plan,* employers promise to make specified annual contributions, usually based on the worker's salary. Retirement benefits depend on the amount contributed and the investment return on the account and are guaranteed for life (Gale, Papke, & VanDerhei, 1999). Each employer can set the pension benefit; for example, 2 percent of the arithmetic average of the best consecutive three years of earnings multiplied by the number of years worked. Employees may or may not be required to contribute to the plan, depending on its design. The employer usually picks the funds into which employer and employee (if any) contributions will be made. Participants in defined-benefit plans still pay Social Security.

A *defined-contribution* plan is really a savings account to which an annual contribution is made for each employee. Employees contribute a portion of their pre-tax salary to a qualified retirement plan, and employers typically match some portion of the employee contribution. Investment earnings accumulate tax-free until withdrawn (Spring stead & Wilson, 2000). The benefit that the employee eventually receives is based on the "vested" portion of the accumulated value of his or her contributions plus any investment earnings.

Private Pensions in a Conservative Era. Defined-benefit pensions provide an incentive for retirement, for workers receive the greatest return on such pensions by retiring as soon as eligible (Fullerton, 1999). Reflecting growing political conservatism, the diminished power of labor unions, and corporate downsizing, employer-sponsored private pensions have undergone changes. Major shifts occurred between 1975 and 1994 in the types of pensions provided by employers. In 1975, 39 percent of the workforce had primary coverage through defined-benefit plans, but by 1995, only 23 percent were covered. Over the same period, primary coverage from employer defined-contribution plans increased almost fourfold: from 6 percent to slightly more than 22 percent (Gale, Papke, & VanDerhei, 1999). As the number of defined-benefit plans (life annuities) declined, defined-contribution plans, such as 401(k) plans (i.e., where the amount of the future benefit varies depending on the amount of earnings on investments), increased. The result of these changes is to shift the financial risk from the employer to the individual worker who is responsible for directing the investments. The worker, not the employer, runs the risk of the ups and downs of the stock market.

Types of Defined-Contribution Plans and Individual Retirement Accounts

Defined-contribution plans include *401(k)* plans for the private sector, *403(b)* plans for the non-profit sector, and *457* plans for state and local governments. These plans offer workers the following: (1) a systematic way to save for retirement; (2) tax deferral on the amount contributed, resulting in reduction of income taxes; and (3) tax deferral on any gains on the value of investments in the plan. If a person retires or changes jobs before age 59 ½ and chooses to withdraw money from a 401(k) rather than roll it over into another retirement plan, the money is subject to a 20 percent federal withholding tax plus a 10 percent early distribution tax although there are certain situations that permit access to all or part of the funds in a 401(k) account, such as buying a home. Participants in 401(k) plans still pay Social Security taxes on their full pay. Their contributions do not result in reduction of Social Security benefits but are additional savings for retirement.

Keogh Plans are designed for self-employed people to set up retirement plans for themselves and their employees with the same tax advantages as the plans described above. Unlike the defined-benefit plan, the money-purchase defined-contribution Keogh plan requires that the individual make the same contribution each year. Still another tax-deferred plan, the *Simplified Employee Pension Plan* (SEP-IRA), is offered by sole proprietors of small businesses and corporations that do not have any other plan. The employer makes contributions to accounts that are controlled by employees. Such plans have a maximum contribution limit both for employers and employees (AARP, 1999).

Individual Retirement Accounts (IRAs) are the most common individual retirement plan. People can contribute up to $2,000 of pre-tax earned income to an IRA per year if an individual or spouse is not covered by a pension plan at work and $4,000 if married and only one spouse is working. They may also make taxable or partially taxable contributions. Investment earnings for all contributions accumulate tax-free until they are withdrawn. A penalty is imposed if funds are withdrawn before age 59½, and income tax must be paid on tax-deductible IRAs when the money is withdrawn. Contributors are required to begin withdrawing money from their IRAs when they reach 70½.

A more recent individual retirement plan is the *Roth IRA*, permitting workers to contribute up to $2,000 of their earned income to an account. Although these contributions are not tax deductible, withdrawals on both the principal and interest are tax-free. Again, penalties apply for early withdrawals but, unlike regular IRAs prohibiting contributions after age 70½, there are no time limits for making contributions.

Although defined-contribution plans allow workers more choice (e.g., including when to retire), than defined-benefit plans, such plans can be risky. Because at least 70 percent of defined-contribution plan participants are not offered a life annuity as a pay-out option upon retirement, those who live very long lives may very well outlive what they have saved in a defined-benefit pension plan if they are not thrifty or if their investments have lost money. Even if they are very penny-wise, they will have a lower standard of living (Brown, 2000). If individual account proposals to reform Social Security, discussed in the following chapter, are implemented, such approaches should take into account how a life annuity can be guaranteed to retirees and their dependents, even in the face of unpredictable economic fluctuations. Otherwise, rising poverty rates among the elderly and reliance on relatives or on welfare programs are likely to occur (Brown, 2000). Neither alternative is attractive nor cost-effective in the long run.

MYTH: ALMOST EVERYONE TODAY CONTRIBUTES TO A PRIVATE PENSION FUND

Private Plan Participation. Given the numerous non–Social Security private pension plans available, how many workers are covered by this confusing array? By 1997, the most recent year for which data are currently available, a total of 79 percent of all full-time employees in medium and large private establishments participated in defined-benefit and defined-contribution plans (Bureau of Labor Statistics, 2001). Not all companies offer either type as a supplement to Social Security, however. Workers in companies without pension plans other than Social Security can choose to save as individuals through IRAs, Roths, or similar plans.

People participating in either defined-contribution or individual retirement plans are disproportionately white, male, and full-time workers and earn more than those who do not contribute. Older workers are also more likely than younger ones to contribute to either type of retirement plan. Women, reflecting their generally lower income, are less likely to make such a contribution, with women part-time workers less likely to contribute to a retirement plan than men part-time workers. When income is controlled, however, participation rates are about equal; for example, among men and women earning $55,000 a year or more, 88 percent of men and 87 percent of women participate in a defined-contribution plan, such as a 401(k) or IRA. African Americans are less likely to have any kind of retirement account than whites; only 53 percent of African-American workers, compared with 68 percent of whites had such a plan. Most likely to participate in IRAs and 401(k)s were "all other races," primarily Asians in professional and technical occupations (Springstead & Wilson, 2000).

What may be concluded from these findings? Obviously, the more money one earns, the more likely one is to contribute to a pension plan, and pension benefits will be higher after retirement. Poorer, less educated people have less chance to learn about such plans or to know how to implement them. If present patterns of contributions to private pensions continue, little change in the income level of those most at risk of late-life poverty—women, African Americans, Latinos, and male white, low-income workers—can be expected. Saving for one's future old age is difficult if not impossible when the money is needed for survival in the present.

Leisure and Retirement Activities

MYTH: PEOPLE FALL APART WHEN THEY RETIRE AS THEY ARE DEPRIVED OF THEIR MAJOR SOURCE OF STATUS AND IDENTITY

The myth that work is central to identity is built on the notion of a stable career that is central to a person's identity. This assertion echoes the Puritan ethic of the value of work as an end in itself and is based on activity theory, assuming that loss of the work role brings about critical changes in life that may result in poor health (see Chapter 3). The belief that retirement is a cessation of meaningful activity was constructed from studies of middle-class white men whose lives were centered on their company, where they worked for ever-greater financial rewards until retirement. Such patterns are not reflected in the experiences of working-class men, people of color, and women (Calasanti, 1996), or even all white middle-class men. Recent research has shown that for most people, retirement is not only a predictable life event but a continuation of many past relationships and activities.

Then what is life like after retirement? Is it freedom from schedules? A time to play golf? Renew old hobbies or develop new ones? To travel? A continuation or expansion of household chores? An opportunity to give to others? The answer is, it depends. Traveling remains an important retirement activity for those who can afford it. Programs such as Golden Passports give older people reduced admissions to national parks; airlines offer discounts to older people; and many businesses offer special prices to senior citizens. Leisure activities, such as sports, television watching, radio and music listening, reading, and spending time with friends and relatives, often expand. But retirement patterns differ not only from person to person but also by social class, gender, and race and ethnicity. Just as there is no single job pattern that characterizes paid work, there is no single retirement model.

Models that view retirement as a period of leisure (often raising the question "How do you keep busy now that you're retired?") do not take into account the ways that social class, gender, and race/ethnicity shape retirement activities. For African Americans, Latinos, and other disadvantaged ethnic minorities whose work histories were fragmented due to racial/ethnic discrimination and the types of jobs available to them, there is no sharp line between work and retirement. Alternating periods as paid worker, displaced worker, and unemployed job seeker blur the differentiation between worker and retiree. Nor is the notion of retirement as freedom from a 35- or 40-hour work week and job pressures true for most older working-class women; they have worked all their lives although not always for pay (Calasanti, 1993; 1996). Their transition from paid to unpaid work is not clear-cut, for they have been working two jobs during most of their adult lives—one paid work, the other unpaid domestic labor.

Although both working-class women and men describe retirement as "freedom," men see themselves as freed from the kinds of activities associated with paid work, such as punching a time clock or being supervised (Calasanti, 1993). Women view themselves as free to arrange their household (and caregiving) tasks in a more relaxed fashion. As one woman commented,

> When I worked I had to do a lot of work at night, household, laundry, ironing, everything, and now I don't even have a certain day to do my laundry. I do it when I want to and I just don't feel like I'm on a tight schedule. (Calasanti, 1993: 144)

A similar theme runs through the experience of working-class African-American women. Retirement is both freedom from constraint and the opportunity to relax as well as to give back to the community and work for others:

> I've been a diet aid helper at two nutrition sites for more than six years. . . . I come to the [senior] center once a week. I belong to the Urban League. I'm financial secretary of the homeowner's association and president of the local chapter of the AARP. I feel I'm going to these meetings and organizations to help other people and more or less to just simply be there. (Allen & Chin-Sang, 1990)

Voluntary Organizations and Volunteering

MYTH: OLDER PEOPLE ARE NOT INTERESTED IN VOLUNTEERING

Americans are a nation of joiners, observed the Frenchman Alexis de Tocqueville when he visited the United States almost two centuries ago (de Tocqueville, 1838–1840). Is membership in voluntary formal organizations more typical of younger people and does this behavior decline in later life? At first glance, the answer would seem to be "yes," but when health and sociodemographic factors are taken into account, membership in voluntary organizations is lowest among younger people, rises in middle age, and remains high until very old age. At least in terms of number of memberships, older age groups are the most involved in voluntary organizations (Cutler & Hendricks, 2001).

Participation as a volunteer is an important part of the economy; according to one estimate, older volunteers contributed over $77.2 billion worth of services in one year alone (Independent Sector, 1998, cited in Cutler & Hendricks, 2001). According to one recent survey of retirees, over half the men and women had either volunteered or done community service in the past year, most often in fund-raising, helping the elderly, or working with children and teenagers (Peter D. Hart Research Associates, Inc., 1999). Such service to the community and "giving back" is unpaid work that clearly departs from the notion of retirement as unstructured leisure to be filled with hobbies or golf games.

For many older people, retirement is a continuation of lifelong activity to improve social conditions. As W. H. "Ping" Ferry, age 85, a Dartmouth College graduate who has had several careers—consultant to labor unions, public relations company executive, and director of philanthropic foundations—summed up,

> I still have a very large correspondence with dozens of people. We [he and his wife] are still in the philanthropy business and trying to get rid of the dough as fast as we can. . . . We're interested in people who can't get help anywhere else: prisoners and poor people. . . . Damned if I know why I work so hard, but I can't quit. I think I'm constantly trying to pay back. I owe somebody something. How will I ever pay back for all this good fortune that's been my lot in life? (Terkel, 1996: 41)

Both government and nonprofit organizations offer many opportunities for community service. The National Senior Service Corps, for example, has several programs, *Foster Grandparent, RSVP,* and *Senior Companion* for people over 55. *VISTA* (Volunteers in Service to America) has a special congressional mandate to include both young people and those 65 and over. The *Peace Corps* also includes older people who make up about 4 percent of its volunteers. A host of organizations exist in the nonprofit sector; for example, *AARP* has chapters at the local level and matches people with jobs through a national Volunteer Talent Bank; the *Services Corps of Retired Executives* (SCORE) enables retired executives to use their expertise to consult with companies in the United States and other nations, and *Civic Ventures,* a California-based nonprofit organization, provides volunteers opportunities to work with schools and youth agencies; and some organizations, like the *Gray Panthers,* an intergenerational advocacy organization, are geared to activists of all ages, working together for social and economic justice on such issues as universal health care, jobs with a living wage and the right to organize, preservation of Social Security, affordable housing, access to quality education, economic justice, and challenging ageism, sexism, and racism.

Education

MYTH: Older People Are Not Interested in Learning New Things. After All, Remember, "You Can't Teach an Old Dog New Tricks."

In addition to volunteering, older people are increasingly becoming sprightly students. The proportion of people age 65 and over participating in educational activities has almost doubled since 1990 (Gardyn, 2000). Contrary to popular belief, learning ability does not decline among healthy older people; at any age, motivation is the key to learning. People such as Nora Welsh (pseudonym), 72 and a black belt in Karate, find that taking continuing education courses helps their work as volunteers. Welsh has taken numerous continuing education courses in gerontology at Boston University since 1994, where she received the certificate of continuing education in the study of aging in 1998. Others, like Sally Schwartz (pseudonym), widow and grandmother of two, decided to return to college or university for a bachelor's or advanced degree. Schwartz completed her doctorate in counseling psychology at the age of 69 and started a thriving private practice in a New England suburb.

In addition to traditional continuing education and academic programs, late-life learning programs have been developed by over 300 colleges or universities. Although the Lifelong Learning Act (Public Law 94–482) was passed in 1976, it was not funded due to disagreements among educational organizations about how appropriations might be spent. Within the past 30 years or so, educational opportunities have expanded, ranging from institutes for learning in retirement based at colleges and universities to *SeniorNet*, a nationwide association of older computer users (Manheimer, 1998). *Elderhostel*, founded in 1975, provides short-term, residential educational programs throughout the United States and abroad for adults aged 55 and over. Most often based at a college or university, courses cover a range of topics from culture to national parks; fees include room, board, class instruction, and activities. The Institute for Retired Professionals at the New School for Social Research in New York established a peer-learning program; led by well-educated retirees, this Institute has been a model for numerous other programs at colleges and universities (Manheimer, 1998). Evergreen College of Boston University developed a different model where people 60 and over participate in specific lecture and physical fitness programs designed for them and can also audit any academic course for a modest registration fee. More recently, the University of North Carolina at Ashville established its community leadership program, designed to give in-depth knowledge about the community. Graduates of the program go on to serve as volunteers in a wide variety of community enrichment projects (Manheimer, 1998). Other state universities and community colleges offer opportunities for lifelong learning; distance learning programs, whether through an educational institution or a television network, also have specific programs that may be taken either for credit or enjoyment.

Numerous other nations have established a program

Lifelong learning is a key to new fields and interests. What opportunities for lifelong learning are available in your community?

known as the *University of the Third Age (U3A)* that had its beginning in 1972 when a French university professor began to conduct a summer school for retirees. Since then, Australia, New Zealand, Poland, and other nations have formed similar Universities of the Third Age. The U3A movement has followed two basic models: the French model, supported by governmental funding and associated with a university, and the British "self-help" model, financed by a private charity plus a small fee of about three dollars per participant and run by its participants, who decide what is to be taught, by whom, how, and at what cost (Williamson, 1995). The United States has, however, been relatively slow to develop programs for older learners on a systematic basis as there is little popular consensus about learning in later life. National funding for lifelong learning is caught in the politics of financing programs. Given relatively limited funding for education, administrators are more likely to devote resources to younger people.

Labor Force Participation and Retirement in the Future

When the oldest baby boomers begin to retire within the next few years, the effects on the economy could be substantial. Occupations with large numbers of older workers include executive, administrative and managerial jobs, airline pilots, and teachers. By 2008, the oldest baby boomers will be near the average retirement age for the population; and by 2018, all but the youngest boomers will be of retirement age. Some analysts predict that there will be a much smaller pool of workers available to fill their jobs, but other analysts have noted that the labor shortage is likely to be offset in the long run by new immigrants even if baby boomers decide to retire at age 63 or so (Dohm, 2000). According to census data, over 7.6 million immigrants, most of whom were then young adults, entered the United States during the 1991–1998 period. Nonetheless, if the baby boomers continue to retire at age 65 or younger, their retirement will create an employment vacuum, with job openings at middle and higher levels, stimulating promotions of younger people in these positions. In that situation younger cohorts in high-demand occupations will have greater incomes if the economy is prosperous (Bogue, 1999). Again, assuming that the economy is relatively prosperous and large numbers of older workers stay in the labor force at age 60, 65, or 70, the age composition of the labor force will shift into an hourglass shape with the huge aging baby boom generation at one end and the baby bust and baby boomlet generations—the boomer's own children—at the other.

An hourglass labor force is likely to raise age-related work issues, in which older workers protest age discrimination and younger workers demand the opportunity to fill the higher-level jobs occupied by their elders. The Age Discrimination in Employment Act (ADEA), passed by Congress in 1967 and amended in 1986 to protect workers aged 40 and over, made age discrimination and mandatory retirement policies illegal. Yet many older workers, even at age 40 or 45, find it harder than younger workers to find new employment today when laid off.

Recent trends also suggest that those baby boomers who do retire are likely to face higher out-of-pocket health care costs as employers reduce the amount of retired workers' health benefits. During the 1984–1995 period, the proportion of employers paying the full cost of family health coverage for retirees aged 65 and over declined sharply. In 1984, employers paid around 40 percent of the full costs of family coverage for retirees aged 65 or older, but by 1995, fewer than 15 percent of employers paid the full costs of such coverage (*Working Age*, 1999: 4).

Social Security and Medicare will also need to take into account the number of workers contributing to these old-age entitlements. Thus, age at retirement, Social Security and pensions, costs of health care packages for retirees, and the ways baby boomers will support themselves after retirement are affected by demographic characteristics as well as by social and political decisions and personal preferences or decisions.

Belief in the value of work, better health, recent changes to Social Security, and the availability of defined contribution pension plans may, however, motivate some baby boomers to stay in the labor force longer (Dohm, 2000). Unlike their parents' generation, about 80 percent of boomers believe they will continue to work during retirement, and only 16 percent expect not to work for pay during retirement. More than 1 in 3 (35 percent) plan to work part-time for the interest or enjoyment work provides, and nearly 1 in 4 (23 percent) expect to work part-time for the money. The majority of boomers do not want to have to depend on their children during retirement (AARP, 1998).

Income and the widening gap between rich and poor in recent years affect how boomers feel; those with incomes less than $30,000 per year are unprepared and pessimistic about retirement, as shown in Table 10-6. Baby boomers' outlook on other aspects of the future also varies according to their income. Fifty-two percent of those with incomes of $70,000 or more plan to work during retirement for fun and self-fulfillment; 35 percent of those with incomes of less than $30,000 say they will have to work for the money it will provide (AARP, 1998).

Differences in pension wealth will affect retirement plans. Pension wealth among baby boomers is unequally distributed. Among full-time workers between the ages of 51 and 61, for example, median pension assets on the current job were 76 percent greater for men than women due to differences in wages, years on the job, and gender-linked patterns of employment. Although employment prospects for women have brightened over the last 30 years or so, many baby boomer women remain more likely than men to hold pink-collar and minor professional jobs that pay less. If their labor force participation, years of work experience, and earnings increase in the future, younger baby boomer women are likely to have larger private pensions and greater economic security when they retire (Johnson, Sambamoorthi, & Crystal, 1999).

Table 10-6 How High- and Low-Income Baby Boomers Assess Their Retirement Prospects		
Assessment of Retirement	**High Income ($70,000+)**	**Low income (<$30,000)**
Very optimistic	36%	18%
Given a lot of thought to retiring	49%	28%
Confident in ability to plan for the future	76%	47%
Can count on IRA, 401(k) or other retirement savings account	82%	46%

Source: Adapted from AARP (1998: *http:research.aarp.org/econ/boomer_seq.html*).

Baby boomers have, however, always had political power. Despite their competition for education, jobs, and housing, they got the vote when they turned age 18, created new markets for consumer goods, and established the second feminist movement. Their protests stopped the Vietnam War. When they reach 65, they are likely to demand changes in social policies that guarantee them a decent standard of living and options for work and retirement.

Summary

Although retirement is a simple word, it has many meanings. It is most often defined by two characteristics: (1) nonparticipation in the paid labor force; and (2) receipt of income from Social Security and other retirement plans. Someone who works for pay and does not receive income from Social Security or pensions would not be officially retired. People who retire from careers in the military or in law enforcement typically receive a pension after 20 years of service and then take on another job. Many will continue to work part-time to supplement their Social Security or pension income. Technically, however, those individuals who receive the majority of their income from Social Security, pensions, and assets are classified as retired even if they continue to work at paid jobs. Not all people who are 65 or older are retired. In 1999, close to 17 percent of men and 9 percent of women in the United States who were 65 or older were in the labor force.

For the great majority of men and women in modern industrialized societies, increased life expectancy means that they will outlive work roles. But unlike many other life events, such as confirmations or bar mitzvahs, graduations, or weddings, entry into retirement has no specific or standard rituals. Some people retire without fanfare, others give or are given a party by friends and relatives, and still others are given a farewell party at work, where clocks and watches, marking the passage of time, are frequent gifts. For those who can afford it, travel provides a ritual for transition from the status of worker to retiree.

The concept of retirement is relatively new in the United States, and retirement for most workers was not attainable until the 1930s. Most people worked until they either became disabled or dropped dead. When the Social Security Act was passed in 1935, all but a few modern nations had long since established some form of national social insurance. Today, nearly two million people retire each year, and as the baby boom generation ages, that number will become even larger. Both men and women are retiring earlier than they did a century or so ago, some voluntarily, others subtly pushed out. When earlier retirement is added to increased life expectancy, many people today will spend a third of their lives in retirement. As a result, an entirely new life stage is evolving, increasingly marked by good health and a desire for new and meaningful experiences, including paid and unpaid work.

From a political economy perspective, retirement is a strategy used by employers to manage workers and maximize efficiency and profits. Retirement is not only a way of controlling the flow of workers in and out of the labor force but also of reducing the costs of labor for the employer. That is, retirement and early retirement plans reduce the amount of money the employer must pay for fringe benefits (e.g., health insurance and pension plans), as well as make it possible to hire younger and less expensive entry-level workers. Both retirement and early retirement are thus products of social and economic structures of a society.

When a corporation's market value depends on continued profits, there is great pressure to reduce labor costs, hence incentives for *early retirement* before the age of 65. For example, early retirement plans or *golden handshakes* encourage workers to leave by offering various combinations of pension plans and cash pay-outs based on the employee's age and length of time with the company. Corporate downsizing has a similar effect, saving money for the employer. Increasingly, many companies are hiring contingent workers as consultants, independent contractors, office temp workers, and on-call personnel, all policies that reduce fringe benefit costs for the employer.

Beliefs about the abilities of older workers also influence retirement. Despite evidence to the contrary, many employers fear that older workers will not be as productive as younger ones, that they will have more on-the-job accidents and higher rates of absenteeism. Older workers are often stereotyped as slow to learn, hard to change, and inclined to coast through their last few years on a job. Not surprisingly, retirement is not always voluntary. The younger a worker is when she or he leaves a job, the more likely it is that the departure is involuntary, whether resulting from job loss or poor health. About 1 in every 100 men, and slightly less than every 200 women 65 and over, was a displaced worker in 2000. Most often due to the closing down or move of the plant or company where they worked, or insufficient work from their prior employer. These are people who, for all practical purposes, are "retired" despite their interest in remaining in the labor force. Social Security, passed in 1935, is a major source of retirement income. Private pension plans, including defined contribution plans and defined benefit plans, are offered by many employers; individuals may also decide to contribute to various individual retirement accounts.

Contrary to popular belief, retirement is not a crisis for the majority of people. Although activities vary according to social class, race and ethnicity, and gender, significant postretirement pursuits for all include "giving back," volunteering, and education.

Key Points

1. Labor force participation is defined by the federal government as the percentage of a population that is either working or looking for work.

2. According to census data, men 65 or over today are much less likely to participate in the labor force than their counterparts in 1950, when about 46 percent participated.

3. The drop in male labor force participation is due to several factors, including changes that reduced the earliest age of eligibility for Social Security to 62 for men, as well as the expansion of private pension coverage in the 1950s and 1960s.

4. The labor force participation of women 65 and older has changed very little. In 1950, about 10 percent of women 65 and over were in the labor force as compared with 9 percent in 1999.

5. Both men and women are more likely to retire if their poor health limits or prevents work or work in physically demanding occupations.

6. Only one-fourth of the people leaving a job between ages 55 and 62 retire voluntarily, compared with over half of those leaving a job at age 62 or older.

7. Voluntary retirement is most common among male workers with 13 years or more of education or with pension coverage from their employer.

8. Both men and women are less likely to retire if they have health insurance coverage from their employer or have a spouse who is still working.

9. Most women workers are not covered by private pension plans.

10. Discouraged workers, not counted as part of the labor force, are people who want and are available to work, have looked for a job in the last 12 months or since the end of the last job they held, but are not currently looking for work because they think there are no jobs available or none for which they are qualified.

11. Social Security is a major source of retirement income and provides a life annuity.

12. A defined-benefit plan specifies the benefits employees will receive upon retirement.

13. A defined-contribution plan is basically a savings account to which the employer and employee make a contribution.

14. Retirement activities are many and range from travel to volunteerism and education.

Discussion Questions

1. Describe the typical displaced worker.

2. Is there a transition from being a displaced worker to a discouraged worker; if so, what are some possible reasons for this?

3. Discuss the advantages and disadvantages of defined-benefit versus defined-contribution pension plans.

4. Imagine that you are the guide for a Vulcan who has been dropped from the starship *Enterprise* to report on retirement in the United States today for his planet's historical and cultural archives. How would you explain the concept of retirement and its advantages and disadvantages in the United States? He is also interested in whether retirement differs for men and women or by race, ethnicity, and social class. Give him as complete and unbiased a report as you can.

5. Is age discrimination likely to affect prospects for older workers in the future? Justify your answer.

6. Will patterns of retirement change in the future? If you think you will retire, do you think your experience is likely to differ from that of your parents or grandparents, and if so, how?

Films and Videos

Forever Young (video; 58 minutes; available from Terra Nova Films, 9848 South Winchester Avenue, Chicago, IL 60643; *www.terranova.org*).

A look at the postretirement life of older adults discussing their lives and activities that range from beekeeping to skydiving.

My Retirement Dreams (video; 60 minutes; available from *www.pbs.org*).

An engaging portrait of retirement by a man who describes himself as "somewhere between a boomer and a geezer" and who began his journey as a tourist in the landscape of old age but ended up an insider.

Old Enough to Know Better (video; 58 minutes; available from First Run/ Icarus Films, 32 Court Street, 21st Floor, Brooklyn, NY; *www.frif.com*).

The story of the Fromm Institute for Lifelong Learning at the University of San Francisco, from the perspective of its faculty and students, all of whom are officially "retired."

Social Insecurity: Work, Family, and Retirement (video; 60 minutes; available from PBS video, 1320 Baddock Place, Alexandria, VA 22314-1698).

A Socratic dialogue approach to issues facing the workplace, families, and the nation as the population ages.

Internet Resources

http://www.aarp.org

Entrance to the American Association of Retired Persons and their numerous services, including policy and research papers on retirement and baby boomer retirement plans.

http://www.ssa.gov

The official site for the U.S. Social Security Administration.

http://www.dol.gov

The site for the U.S. Department of Labor with information and statistics on employment, displaced workers, and numerous other issues related to working and unemployment.

Research Article

Savishinsky, J. (1995). The unbearable lightness of retirement: Ritual and support in a modern life passage. *Research on Aging 17:* 3, 243–259.

An anthropologist looks at retirement rituals, their meanings, and how white, non-Latino/Latina elders view their departure from the work force.

Supplemental Readings

Chinen, A. B. (1990). *In the Ever After: Fairy Tales and the Second Half of Life.* Willmette, IL: Chiron.

A retelling of fairy tales about old age and retirement, interpreted from the life course perspective of psychoanalyst Carl Jung.

Freedman, M., & Roma, T. (1999). *Prime Time: How the Baby-Boomers Will Revolutionize Retirement and Transform America.* Public Affairs, LLC.

A look at older Americans today and in the future as untapped national social assets, and a call for social changes in the ways older people are treated and regarded.

Terkel, S. (1995). *Coming of Age.* New York: St. Martin's Griffin.

Engaging interviews about their work and retirement experiences with elders from various walks of life. ✦

Chapter 11

Economic Security, Public Policy, and Politics

Introduction

"Medicare Premiums and Social Security Will Rise"

"Privatize Social Security: Here's Why"

"Social Security Benefits Face Growth"

"Senators Are Told of Abuses at U.S. Pension Guarantor"

"Our Graying Budget Priorities"

"Older Voters Don't Feel a Connection to Candidates"

These are just a few of the headlines that appeared in newspapers such as the New York Times, Los Angeles Times, and the Christian Science Monitor in the eight weeks preceding the presidential election in 2000. Clearly, issues about later life economic security, including Social Security and private pensions, Medicare costs and benefits, and politicians' appeals to older voters, were important issues that even now are still being played out as you read this chapter. What are the major sources of income for the elderly population in the United States? How much do they depend on Social Security? Private pensions? How do elders spend their money? Are they greedy geezers who are spending their children's inheritance as some conservatives have claimed? Or are they the beneficiaries of a compact between generations? How does the income of older Americans compare with that of elders in other industrialized nations?

Not only is economic security in later life a significant issue, but also, as the above headlines suggest, politics are inextricably intertwined with the economics of later life. Legislative and governmental programs established in the twentieth century have had a major impact on the quality of *life of the elderly. The Social Security Act in the 1930s; the Older Ameri-cans Act, the Age Discrimination in Employment Act, Medicare, and Medicaid, all four of which were passed in the 1960s; and the Family Leave Act in the 1990s are but a few examples of political legislative changes whose passage continues to affect the economic status of elders and their families.*

Elders themselves are not passive recipients of legislative changes because they constitute a potentially strong voting bloc. They thus play a vital role in the adoption and modification of public policies. Various organizations also lobby on behalf of specific groups of older people or the elderly in general. This chapter focuses not only on economic security in later life but also on the politics of aging and the role of the elderly in polit-ical processes.

Income and Expenditures in Later Life

Almost everyone wants to be economically secure: to have enough money to live comfortably and to enjoy life, regardless of differences in the definition of enjoyment. When we are young, retirement is very much in the future. Much more immediate are such goals as paying off student loans, saving enough money to take a vacation or a honey-moon, and buying a house. For those who have children, saving for their education is likely to become a priority initially more important than saving for their own retirement or having enough money should they become disabled or sick. As people grow older, however, their concerns turn more toward their personal economic security and ade-quate income. Like younger people, their concern is having enough money to live comfortably in a safe neighborhood. They also want to be economically secure should disability occur.

Distribution of Income and Assets

How secure economically are the now-elderly, and how does their income vary according to membership in the social hierarchies of race and ethnicity, gender, and social class? Although various measures of income are used by the Census Bureau and other government and nongovernment agencies, one of the most useful is *median income:* the dollar amount denoting the midpoint at which income is ranked according to amount. The median gives a more accurate picture of income than the mean, or arithmetic average, which can be skewed by a few very wealthy (or extremely poor) people. For example, the mean income for American workers of all types in 1995 was $21,900 but the median income was $15,000. Using the mean figure gives an inflated picture of income that is pulled up by the small proportion of very rich.

The distribution of income in any society is complex. *Median household income,* a way of assessing the amount of income received within a given year, is classified by the Census Bureau by characteristics of the household head (i.e., the individual who states that he or she is the head of the household). Not only is the amount of household income affected by membership in the social hierarchies of gender, social class, and race/ethnicity, but it also varies according to the number of earners, geographic location, region, and age of the head of the household. For example, data from the census indicate that the median income of *all* U.S. households, regardless of the age of their head, was $42,148 in 2000. Geographic differences exist, however, with the lowest median household income ($38,410) in the South and the highest ($45,106) in the Northeast. Incomes in the West and Midwest were only slightly below those in the Northeastern states. Nationwide, incomes are highest in the suburbs and lowest outside metropolitan areas (U.S. Bureau of the Census, 2001).

The Influence of Race and Ethnicity. Non-Latino/Latina whites have the highest median household income, followed by Asian and Pacific Islanders—themselves very diverse. Latino and African-American households of all types have the lowest. Type of household and gender of the household head are also important factors. Among all major racial/ethnic groups, married couple families have the highest income. Family households headed by women fare worse, and nonfamily households headed by women are the worst off regardless of race or ethnicity (U.S. Bureau of the Census, 2001). These discrepancies reflect not only the lower earnings and assets of minority groups in the United States but also the persistent gender inequality in salaries and wages. Women tend to spend fewer years in paid employment than men because they are more likely to interrupt such work to take care of children or elderly parents. Similarly, they are more likely to work at part-time rather than full-time jobs. Even when in paid employment, women are less likely to be paid as much as men. For example, in 2000 the median earnings of all full-time, year-round women workers were only $27,355—almost $10,000 less than the median earnings ($37,339) of their male counterparts (U.S. Bureau of the Census, 2001).

The Importance of Age. How does age influence the amount of household income? In 2000, the median household income for all American households headed by people under the age of 65 was $51,418. Among households headed by those aged 65 to 74, median household income was $28,889—a difference of more than $22,000 per year. Median household income continues to decline in old age with those age 75 and over having a median household income of $19,430 (U.S. Bureau of the Census, 2001). Table 11-1 shows the relationship of both age and race/ethnicity to median household income. As you can see from the table, household income peaks between the ages of 45 and

54 for all three race/ethnic categories, dropping thereafter and continuing to fall with age.

Table 11-1   Median 2000 Household Income by Age and Race/Ethnicity of Household Head

Race/Ethnicity	Age of Household Head						
	15–24	25–34	35–44	45–54	55–64	65–74	75+
White non-Hispanic	$29,762	$49,878	$59,784	$63,898	$48,697	$29,572	$19,656
Hispanic	27,850	34,096	38,058	41,107	31,179	20,164	14,512
Black	20,449	31,348	37,547	38,474	28,446	21,017	13,362

Source: U.S. Bureau of the Census, *www.census.gov/hhes/income*.

One reason that income declines with age is retirement. As you recall from the preceding chapter, relatively few people aged 65 and over are in paid employment compared with the adult population as a whole. After retirement, they rely on Social Security, private and government pensions, and other assets for income. Social Security alone accounted for about 38 percent of the income of the elderly; private pensions accounted for another 10 percent and government employee pensions 8 percent. Table 11-2 shows the major sources of income in 1998 from all sources for all U.S. households and for selected age groups.

Table 11-2   Major Sources of Income for All U.S. Households and for Households with Heads 45 and Over by Broad Age Categories, 1998

Sources of Income	Percentage of Income From Source				
	All Households	Head 45–54	Head 55–64	Head 65–74	Head 75+
Wages, salaries, self-employment	84%	94%	80%	30%	10%
Social Security, other pensions	11%	3%	15%	60%	78%
Interest, dividends, rentals, other property	2%	2%	3%	7%	10%
Other sources	3%	1%	2%	3%	2%

Source: U.S. Bureau of Labor Statistics. 1998. *Consumer Expenditure Survey*, Table 3.

As you can see from Table 11-2, the primary sources of income for all American households are salaries, wages, and self-employment when age is not taken into account. You can also see that age is an important variable. Reliance on Social Security and other types of pensions increases sharply with advancing age. By the ages of 65 to 74, only 30 percent of income comes from paid employment, and paid employment accounts for only 10 percent of household income among those household heads 75 or older. Not surprisingly, because they have had more years in which to save, income from interest, dividends, rentals, and other property income increases as well among those 65 and over. The proportion received from other sources of support (e.g., unemployment and workers' compensation, veterans' benefits, public programs such as food stamps, and supplemental security income) only minimally fluctuates with age.

Another way of assessing income and economic security in later life is *net worth:* the value of real estate, stocks, bonds, and other assets minus outstanding debts. Greater net worth permits people to maintain their standard of living when income falls due to retirement, health problems, divorce, widowhood, or other events. Between 1984 and 1999, the median net worth among households headed by people 65 or older increased by about 69 percent. But the disparity in net worth between white and African-American households remains striking. In 1999, median net worth of older white households was estimated at around $181,000–$168,000 more than the estimated net worth ($13,000) of elder African-American households. Clearly, race influences life chances and economic security in old age. Given a lifetime of unequal opportunity, few African Americans have had the opportunity to accumulate stocks, mutual funds, individual retirement accounts, and other assets for their old age. Possibilities for and level of education also interact with race, ethnicity, and gender to influence life chances and net worth in later life. In 1999, household heads who were 65 or older and had at least some college education reported a median net worth more than four times that of heads of household with less than a high school education. To the extent that these factors have reduced individuals' earning capacities, their ability to save is less. Figure 11-1 shows these differences graphically.

Social Security and Income

A somewhat different analysis of how income is distributed among the elderly is provided by data from the Social Security Administration, which periodically surveys income received by married couples living together with husband or wife aged 65 or older (usually the age of the husband, because men are likely to marry women younger than themselves) or an individual 65 or over not living with a spouse. Inasmuch as the Social Security analyses are based on couples and individ-

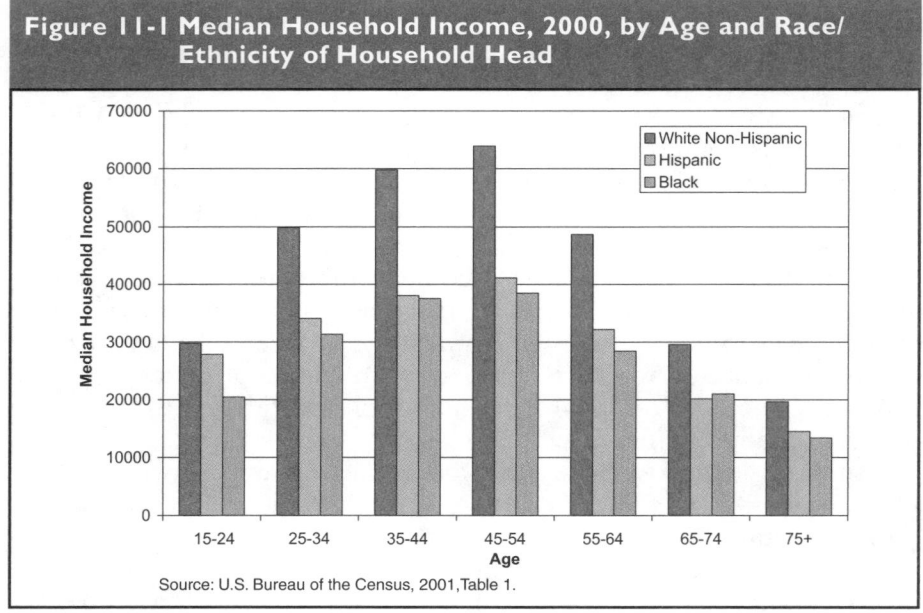

Figure 11-1 Median Household Income, 2000, by Age and Race/ Ethnicity of Household Head

Source: U.S. Bureau of the Census, 2001,Table 1.

uals not living with a spouse (widowed, divorced, separated, and never married), they paint a somewhat bleaker picture of income than household data. The major reason for this is that the income of other members of the household unit (e.g., children, other relatives, or unrelated individuals) is not taken into account. Nor is net worth included in analyses by the Social Security Administration.

Regardless of the measure of income used, income is higher among married couples living with a spouse than any other category of elders.

Social Security is a source of income for about 90 percent of married couples and individuals not with a spouse. Less than half receive retirement benefits other than Social Security, and only about 1 in 5 have earnings. For the majority of beneficiaries of Social Security, it is a major source of income, as Table 11-3 shows. Those 65 and over also differ by birth cohort in their likelihood of receiving income either from earnings or private and other pensions. Inasmuch as participation in the labor force decreases with advancing age, the "young old" are much more likely to receive income from earnings than older cohorts. In 1998, about three times more people (41 percent) ages 65 to 69 received income from earnings than those ages 75 to 79 and a mere 3 percent of those 85 or older in 1998. Private pensions and other pensions are also more common among younger cohorts (Social Security Administration, 2000).

As with measures of household income collected in the census, Social Security data show income is highest for married couples. Married couples had a median income more than two times that of men not living with a spouse and more than two and one-half times that of women not with a spouse. Most married couples on Social Security receive a benefit equivalent to one and one-half times the husband's benefits. For most couples today, this amounts to more than if benefits were calculated on each of their earnings separately. A woman at retirement who earned less than 30 percent of her husband's earnings over the accounting period will receive a Social Security pension based on his higher earnings rather than her own. White couples and individuals had a median income double that of their African American counterparts and more than 90 percent greater than Latinos.

Table 11-3 Percentage of Income From Social Security for Married Couples and Individuals Not with Spouse, 1998

Amount of Income Derived From Social Security	Percentage of Beneficiaries
100 percent of 1998 income	18%
90–99 percent of 1998 income	12%
50–89 percent of 1998 income	33%
Less than 50 percent of 1998 income	37%

Source: Social Security Administration (2000: 9). *Income of the Aged Chartbook 1998.* Washington, D.C.: Social Security Administration, Office of Policy. Office of Research, Evaluation, and Statistics.

Median income declines among both couples and individuals not living with a spouse as they grow older. The dramatic differences by age are due to the larger number of widowed, divorced, separated, and never married women. Most elderly Social Security recipients are women who represent 60 percent of all aged recipients and 72 percent of the beneficiaries age 85 or older (Social Security Administration, 2000). It is both her attachment to the workforce and marital status that determine the type and amount of Social Security retirement benefit a woman receives. A widow is entitled to 100 percent of her husband's benefits. If she is entitled to Social Security based on her own earnings, she will receive either her own worker benefit or the wife or widow benefit, whichever is greater. A divorced and not remarried woman may still claim a wife or widow's benefit if married to the worker for 10 years or more. The majority of divorced or widowed women rely on these benefits upon retirement rather than their own benefits. In 1996, for example, only 35 percent of women received benefits as retired workers, compared with 82 percent of men (*www.ssa.gov/policy/pubs/BGP/bgpWomen.html,* accessed 10/11/00)—a dramatic indicator of the historic differences in the earning patterns of men and women.

Expenditures: Older People as Consumers

As the American population ages, expenditures by older consumers become increasingly important for the economy. People over 50 are a growing and well-off consumer group, with 50 percent of the total discretionary income in the United States (Metlife, 1999). Relatively little attention has been given, however, to the ways that older Americans spend their money, nor have they generally been the target of marketing except for merchandise like pain relievers, laxatives, incontinence wares, and similar items. As one recent analyst of the youth bias in advertising queried, "Why do advertisers insist on directing messages to younger people to such an extreme that they deliberately turn off, blatantly insult, or merely ignore older consumers?" (Lee, 1997). Although those now 45 to 54 years old have the greatest income, households headed by people aged 35 to 44 and those headed by people 75 and older spend similar amounts per person—slightly below the average for all adults (Russell, 1997). The average annual expenditures of all household units and those headed by an individual 65 or older are summarized in Table 11-4.

Table 11-4 Average Annual Expenditures of Household Units, by Percentage Spent on Selected Services, 1998			
Items	**All Consumer Units**	**Head Age 65–74**	**Head Age 75+**
Total average annual expenditures	$35,535	$27,830	$20,987
Percentage spent on selected services			
Food	14%	14%	14%
Housing and utilities	40%	41%	45%
Home furnishings	4%	5%	4%
Clothing	5%	4%	3%
Transportation	19%	18%	14%
Health care/insurance	5%	10%	14%
Personal insurance and Social Security	9%	4%	2%
Other	6%	6%	6%

Source: U.S. Department of Labor. 1998. *Consumer Expenditure Survey 1998.*

Although the average (mean) income for those 65 and over is lower than that for all household units headed by an adult, the proportions spent on various types of goods and services do not differ very much for food, housing and utilities, household furnishings, or "other" expenditures (e.g., entertainment, reading, tobacco, alcoholic beverages). Elders spend more on health care and health insurance per year than do all households and spend less on personal insurance, which includes pensions, Social Security, life, and other insurance. Those 75 and over spend somewhat less on transportation.

How has birth cohort affected older people's spending patterns, tastes, and preferences, and have these changed over time? An analysis of expenditure patterns of older and younger consumers from 1984–1997 showed that spending by older consumers has increased substantially—by 14 percent for those aged 65 through 74 and 18 percent for those aged 75 and over. Although the share of total expenditures by older consumers in different birth cohorts changed very little on such items as clothing, housing and utilities, transportation, and recreation, health care expenditures of all types rose substantially since 1984 for everyone (Paulin, 2000).

Regardless of birth cohort, a larger share of people's health care budget went to health insurance, and expenditures for drugs for those 65 and over increased. Those younger than age 65 in 1997 spent about 9 percent more than people younger than 65 in 1984. More dramatic was the increase in health care expenditures among the elderly with people aged 65 to 74 in 1997 spending around 26 percent more and those 75 or over about 20 percent more than their 1984 age counterparts. Aside from the rising amounts spent on health care, little change in tastes and preferences occurred among those who were 65 and over in 1984 and those 65 and over in 1997 (Paulin, 2000).

As life expectancy and health have improved, older adults are an increasingly heterogeneous group of consumers. Some people in their 60s are working and perhaps still putting their children through college; others are retired. Those in very poor health are seeking help with home and personal maintenance tasks. Some are living near or below the poverty level; still others are traveling or relocating to warmer climes. Those in their 70s and older are also heterogeneous, with some in good health and economically secure and others, especially women and minorities, living in poverty. Clearly, the variations among the now-old affect the amount they spend as well as the ways in which they allocate expenditures.

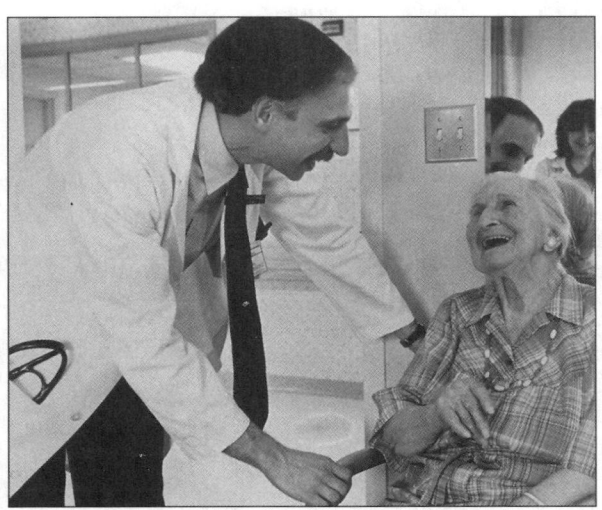

What impact does the increase in health care expenditures, including prescription drugs, have on quality of life?

As the baby boom generation ages, whether their expenditure patterns will differ from the now-old is uncertain. Boomers in general are better educated than today's elders, and they were socialized in a relatively economically prosperous era when they formed a powerful youth market. Economically prosperous boomers may be willing to spend more on luxury items and entertainment than previous birth cohorts. If so, they are likely to become *the* consumer market in the next few decades, wooed by advertisers and merchants.

Poverty and the Distribution of Income in Later Life

The official measure of poverty used by the federal government is based on a family's annual money income before taxes. The official poverty index, based on the U.S. Department of Agriculture's 1961 Economy Food Plan, was developed to reflect different consumption patterns of individuals and families. Although the poverty index is adjusted annually for inflation, two separate indices have existed since its inception: one for the population under age 65, the other for individuals and two-person households aged 65 and over.

The poverty index for elderly individuals living alone or in two-person households is lower than that for those under age 65, apparently based on the supposition that, because elders living in one- or two-person households spent less for food in the 1960s, they need less money than younger individuals! The poverty line in 1999 for one person 65 or older and living alone was $7,990—$677 dollars less than that for a person under age 65. For two people aged 65 or over, the threshold was $10,075—$1,139 less than that for two people aged 64 or younger. For families with three or more individuals, no distinction by age is made (Dalaker & Proctor, 2000).

A 1995 report by the National Academy of Sciences critiqued the current poverty index for not reflecting how noncash benefits (e.g., food stamps, taxes, work-related expenditures, and out-of-pocket medical costs) affect people's economic security. Nor does the poverty index take account of the ways that policy changes in these areas affect income. Moreover, the official poverty measure neither considers how the costs of food, housing, and other basics have changed relative to other items since the early 1960s nor geographic variations in costs (Citro & Michael, 1995). Currently, various experimen-

Women, especially women of color with limited education, are not only more likely to be in low-paying jobs, but to live in poverty in later life.

tal measures of poverty are being developed to address these criticisms (Dalaker & Proctor, 2000).

Whatever the shortcomings of the poverty index, data clearly show that the proportion of people 65 and over living in poverty has sharply declined since 1959 when slightly more than 1 in 3 (35 percent) of the elderly lived in households with money income below the poverty line. By 2000, slightly more than 1 in 10 (10.2 percent) Americans 65 and over lived below the poverty level, compared with a little over 1 in 6 (16.2 percent) children (Dalaker, 2001). This figure, however, obscures those living in near poverty. Although about 3.3 million elders were classified as living below the poverty level in 2000, nearly 5.6 million were "near poor"; that is, with an income between the poverty level and 125 percent of that level. Those living in poverty and near poverty are at high risk of inadequate housing, health care, food, transportation, and other resources.

Spotlight on U.S.: Economic Security for Elderly Women?

Economic security for women in old age is particularly problematic. At least one member of the average American couple who retires today and begins receiving Social Security can expect to live an average of 25 or so more years, and the majority of these will be women. Women at age 65 can expect to live an average of about 3.3 years longer than men and, because they generally marry older men, they are three times more likely to be widowed. An average older female can expect to spend about 15 years as a widow (Schoen & Weinick, 1993). Almost 3 in 4 of all elders with incomes below the poverty level are women (FitzPatrick & Entmacher, 2000). Even more significant is that more than half of elderly widows now living in poverty were not poor before the death of their husbands. Poverty rates are about two times higher among women than among men and three times higher among the unmarried compared with the married. By age 85, almost 1 in 5 of all American women live in poverty. Especially vulnerable are Latina and African-American women who are widowed, divorced, or never married.

Although education decreases the risk of poverty, the interplay of education, race and ethnicity, and marital status make the statistics for older women even bleaker. For example, the probability that a white married woman with less than a high school education will be in poverty between the ages 60 and 85 is estimated to be 37 percent, but 63 percent for her female counterpart who is widowed, separated, divorced, or never married. For African-American women whose education is low, the probability of ever being in poverty between the ages of 60 and 85 is far greater—66 percent for married women but 88 percent if the women are not currently married (Rank & Hirschl, 1999).

Contrary to popular belief, older American women do not fare better than women in other Western industrialized nations; in fact, they have poverty rates 1.5 to 20 times higher (Smeeding, 1999). According to data from the Luxembourg Income Study, a major cross-national study, American elderly women living alone have lower median income than other elders in six other nations including Australia, Canada, France, the Netherlands, Sweden, and the former West Germany. A major reason for their greater rates of poverty is the structure of social insurance programs. During the 1980s, improvements in the economic status of the elderly in other nations resulted from major changes in government-sponsored social insurance pension plans. In Canada, for example, major revisions in social insurance pension schemes included increased benefit levels, increased supplemental means-tested benefits, and a provision to divide pension credits equally between former spouses (Kinsella & Tauber, 1993). In the United States, Social Security benefits depend on the highest 35 years of earnings. Women have far fewer work years than men as they interrupt their work careers to raise children and care for elderly relatives. They are also less likely than men to have private pensions and are more likely to be dependent on Social Security as a major source of income. Social Security provides 49 percent of retirement income for widowed, divorced, and never married women; assets provide 22 per-

cent, earnings 10 percent, and "other sources" 4 percent. Private pensions provide only 15 percent of their income (*http://www.ssa.gov/policy/pubs/BGR/bgpWomen.html*).

Will prospects be brighter for older women in the future? Increasing participation in paid employment by women in the baby boom cohorts translates into more years with earnings toward Social Security. Thus, women born in the early 1940s averaged only about half their husbands' working years, but baby boomer wives born in the 1950s averaged 90 percent of the covered years that their husbands worked. Yet, relatively few wives born in the 1950s earned as much as their husbands, and their occupations, such as clerical workers, teachers, nurses, and other traditionally female and less well-paid occupations, suggest that even baby boomer women will find it more advantageous to rely on their husbands' earnings rather than their own. According to current projections by some analysts, such as Smeeding (1999), the prospects for elderly American women in 2020 are likely to be as gloomy as for now-old women:

> Despite the "good news" of greater labor force participation of women which will increase the number of women with pensions and long earnings careers at higher earnings levels, there is also the "bad news" that divorce, never marrying, and the poor earnings futures of low-skilled women will yield poverty outcomes that mirror those we find today. . . . If we as a society want to reduce poverty among older women, we must

take precautions now to provide even better levels of benefit
adequacy and economic security through the reformed Social Security System. (Smeeding,
1999: 11)

Poverty is also related to race/ethnicity and marital status. One out of every 12 elderly whites (8.3 percent) was classified as below the poverty level in 2000. Latinos and African Americans were far more likely to be poor, with slightly more than 1 in 5 (18.8 percent) Latinos and over 1 in 5 (22.4 percent) African-American elders living in poverty. Regardless of race or ethnicity, married couples are less likely to be poor than widowed, divorced, separated, or never married people (FitzPatrick & Entmacher, 2000).

The Politics of Aging

Social Security: Dissolving the Welfare State?

Issues affecting the economic security of any age group are very much a result of public policies and political forces, as the current controversy about the future of Social Security illustrates. The Social Security Act, sometimes called the "third rail of American politics"— touch it and you die—is no stranger to political controversy, as its roots indicate. Had not the United States been in severe economic crisis in the 1930s as a result of the Great Depression, it is highly unlikely that the Social Security Act would have been passed at that time. Its inception provided not only economic relief for large segments of the population but averted more radical social change. Clearly, subsequent generations of older Americans have benefited from Social Security since its inception. Primarily due to Social Security, poverty rates among the elderly declined from 35 percent in 1959 to slightly more than 10 percent in 2000.

Often ignored in the discussion about privatization of Social Security are its life insurance and disability provisions, for Social Security is more than a retirement fund. In 1999, for example, only 43 percent of the OASDI funds paid out went to retired workers themselves. Forty-one percent of benefits were paid to survivors and dependents of retired workers and sixteen percent to disabled workers (Social Security Administration, 2000). African Americans compose 12 percent of the U.S. population, but they made up 25 percent of the children receiving deceased worker benefits in 1996 and 18 percent of the workers receiving disability benefits (The Century Foundation, 2000).

Is Social Security in crisis or is the *entitlement crisis* a move to shrink the federal government and dissolve the welfare state? Dooms-day demography blames the aging of the population for the current debate about social security. Population aging is but one factor; more important are the political choices made about allocation of resources. During the 1980s, 1990s, and throughout the political campaigns in 2000, Social Security became a political football, tossed in an elaborate political game to the accompaniment of dire predictions from each side. In 1995, for example, *Time* magazine's cover story headlined "The Case for Killing Social Security" cited statistics about the system's imminent bankruptcy as the baby boomers and Gen Xers grow old. Various options for dismantling the social insurance system of Social Security followed: privatize the system, cut benefits, or means-test them. Although by the 2000 presidential campaigns Social Security had a surplus, political controversy about how to "safeguard" or "lockbox" its funds and whether it should be privatized reigned.

How solvent is Social Security today? The facts are relatively straightforward. Using the most commonly accepted demographic and economic assumptions, the trustees of the Old-Age and Survivors Insurance and Disability Insurance Trust Funds predict that funds are sufficient to pay full disability and retirement benefits until 2041. According to its trustees, the combined assets of OASDI—the retirement and disability benefit portions of Social Security—increased from $763.5 billion in December 1998 to $1,213 billion by 2001. From 2002 to 2015, large sums of money are projected to flow into the trust funds and are expected to increase to $3,382 billion by January 2011.

Currently, assets of the Social Security trust funds not needed to pay current benefits are invested in interest-bearing government securities; that is, the trust funds lend money to the U.S. Treasury. These securities can be redeemed at any time to pay benefits or administer the Social Security program by transferring cash from another source, such as income taxes, to the trust funds. Yet both the retirement and disability programs face long-term deficits under current patterns of financing. By 2037, annual income is expected to be only 72 percent of the cost of benefits if no adjustments are made. Of course, the projected deficit may be larger or smaller, depending on economic and demographic patterns.

More murky are the ideological and political disputes about financing. Is Social Security a "compact between generations," in which younger people pledge support to their elders in return for the care they themselves received when younger—a substantial achievement of the welfare state? Or is it a gigantic failed social experiment that not only discourages the free market but individual independence and initiative that could be used to invest in the stock market? As Kingson (2000) summed up the dispute,

> To some budget hawks . . . and especially to some on the right, OASDI's financing problems present an opportunity to tug at the cornerstone of social welfare in the United States by framing the

projected long-term Social Security financing problem as a central part of today's budget problems and as unsolvable without radical reform of the program (i.e., extremely large benefit cuts, privatization, or means-testing). . . . Those favoring the preservation of the existing program tend to frame the financing issue as a problem that can be addressed through prudent planning and some reasonable combination of payroll-taxes and benefit cuts. (pp. 431–432)

Should Social Security Go Private?

A popular proposal to reform Social Security is to supplement or replace traditional publicly financed benefits with a new system of mandatory, private defined-contribution plans. Advocates feel that private plans will offer better returns than the current Social Security plan. To achieve higher returns, however, individuals take greater risks associated with fluctuations in the financial market, as the decline in stocks during the economic recession of 2001 and 2002 indicated. An analysis of the hypothetical pensions American workers would have received during the past century if they had accumulated retirement savings in individual accounts rather than Social Security illustrates this point. If, for example, workers had invested all their contributions in stocks, the average (mean) pension benefit would be a little over half (53 percent) of their peak pre-retirement earnings, but potential benefits could be as low as 20 percent of their peak pre-retirement earnings. The return could also be high—about 110 percent of their peak earnings. The differences are due to variations in stock market returns and interest rates. Even workers who followed identical investment strategies but retired at different times would receive very different pen-

---

Social Policy Issue: Which Strategy?

Various analysts defend and critique privatization of Social Security as shown below. As you read the pros and cons, think about the evidence presented.

Arguments for Privatization	Arguments Against Privatization
All or a percentage of Social Security contributions can be diverted into private accounts without jeopardizing the Social Security system. One trillion dollars could be used from the current Social Security system to purchase back government bonds that are now privately held and placed in individual private accounts where they will pay a higher yield.	If revenues going into the trust funds were diverted into private accounts, there would be fewer resources to pay benefits to future retirees. If 1 trillion dollars for private investment accounts for younger people were taken from Social Security, these funds would be unavailable for retirees in the near future under a pay-as-you-go system.

Arguments for Privatization	Arguments Against Privatization
The Social Security system wastes money that would be saved if individual private accounts were introduced.	The administrative costs for Social Security are less than 1 percent of benefits compared with average administrative costs of 12–14 percent for private insurers.
Small private accounts will get a much better rate of return than the Social Security trust funds and if well-managed, are not risky.	Although private investments could raise the expected rate of return, it increases risk that is not incurred under the present Social Security system.
Private accounts give the average person a better chance to get rich. If, for example, you were born in 1948 and retire at age 66, you will receive only about $17,600 in Social Security per year. But if you had invested in bonds paying 5 percent, you would get $30,132 yearly, and if you had invested in stocks paying an average of 10 percent return, you would get $142,090 annually.	If a system of private accounts were substituted, administrative costs would need to be kept low; and high-risk investments would need to be ruled out unless Americans are willing to let those who mismanage their retirement accounts be hungry and cold.
Most retirees don't really need Social Security, and there is fraud and abuse by people who shouldn't get benefits.	More than 60 percent of the elderly relied on Social Security for at least half of their income in 1998 and 1999, keeping many out of poverty.
Privatization would benefit both men and women.	Privatization would hurt women more than men because they earn less, live longer, and interrupt their working careers to take care of family more often. Current privatization proposals make no provision for these differences and thus poverty among elderly women would increase.
Because, on the average, African Americans have shorter life expectancies and collect retirement benefits for fewer years, privatization would help by allowing them to collect higher benefits for the years that they live.	African Americans have lower average earnings than whites, and they receive a higher annual payoff in comparison with their past tax contributions. They also have fewer assets or private pensions than whites.

The statements above are based on arguments presented by The Century Foundation, a nonprofit politically liberal research organization that focuses on social and political issues, and the Cato Institute, a politically conservative organization whose research focuses on limited government and a free market. Check out their web pages, *www.tcf.org* for the Century Foundation and *www.cato.org* for the Cato Institute. Compare their statements in greater depth. What kinds of assumptions does each make? Whose interests does each organization represent?

sions. Someone retiring in 1969, for example, would have received a pension almost equal to her or his peak pre-retirement earnings, but another individual with the same strategy who retired in 1975 would have received only 42 percent (Burtless, 2000).

A less extreme approach to privatizing Social Security is for a proportion of contributions to be invested in private stock market accounts with the remaining amount placed in Social Security. Proponents of this concept argue that this would not only encourage individual savings but also promise a higher rate of return—and still provide a security net. Some analysts propose that such investments should be deducted from Social Security contributions; others argue that they should be add-ons that encourage additional savings.

Another proposal to reform Social Security is to introduce *means-testing*. Such a program would be a marked departure, ideologically changing the concept of Social Security from a social entitlement program to a public welfare program targeted at the poor: providing benefits only to people living below a certain income or net worth level. If Social Security adapted such a policy, those people who have paid into Social Security but do not meet the means test stand to lose any benefits. Not only might this prove very unpopular among the losers, but means-testing presents several problems. What standards should be used—the official poverty level? The federal eligibility levels for SSI? What would be the cost of administering such a program? How many people who did not meet the means-test criteria would live in near poverty?

Still another proposal is to *increase the age* for full benefits—a policy already adopted in several European nations. Raising the retirement age would reduce the projected deficit. The normal age of eligibility for full benefits will be increased to 66 between 2003 and 2008 and from 66 to 67 between 2021 and 2026, sending a strong political message about the appropriate age for retirement. To what age should it be increased further? Various approaches have been suggested, ranging from gradual but steady raising of the full benefit by two months per year to age 68, increasing the age from 67 to 70 by one month every two years, and rapidly moving the age of retirement to age 73 for full benefits (Rix, 1999). This last proposal would, according to estimates, take care of nearly all the predicted shortfall (American Academy of Actuaries, 1997). How acceptable increases in the retirement age will be, especially if implemented rapidly, certainly remains debatable. Moreover, proposals to increase the age of retirement have been described as "biased against blue-collar folks" (Wildavsky, 1998, cited in Rix, 1999: 13). Blue-collar workers are much more likely than their white-collar age peers to suffer from health problems, and for many blue-collar workers with health problems, staying on the job is likely to be impossible and their savings inadequate for retirement. Proponents of raising the retirement age must also assume that older workers will be in demand to employers—an unlikely proposition at the present when older workers still face long and discouraging searches for jobs if they are displaced (Rix, 1999).

Polls show that perceptions of Social Security were newsworthy topics during the 2000 presidential election year when almost 8 in 10 Americans considered candidates' position on Social Security as an important issue affecting how they would vote. Only about 4 in 10 believed Social Security benefits would be comparable to those today. Paradoxically, while carving out a portion of current Social Security payments for private investments was endorsed by slightly over half of the 2,000 respondents, their support dropped if such an approach were to reduce guaranteed Social Security benefits (Love & Vorek, 2000). The lure of the high returns of the stock market characterizing much of the 1990s and first part of 2000 made private investing an attractive option to Social Security but only if benefits were guaranteed. The subsequent downturn in the stock market and economic recession, however, meant that many private investments declined dramatically in value.

In 2001, President Bush appointed a Commission to Strengthen Social Security. The commission established eight criteria, summarized in the following box, to evaluate various proposals. There are, as yet, no details about how these criteria will be measured, or how much popular support any plans proposed by the Commission will have.

Recommendations of the President's Commission to Strengthen Social Security

1. Encouragement of workers and their families to build personal retirement wealth, giving citizens a legal right to their benefits.

2. Equity of lifetime Social Security taxes and benefits, between and within generations.

3. Adequacy of protection against income loss due to retirement, disability, death of an earner, or unexpected longevity.

4. Encouragement of increased personal and national saving.

5. Rewarding individuals for actively participating in the workforce.

6. Movement of the Social Security system toward a fiscally sustainable course that reduces pressure on the remainder of the federal budget and can withstand economic and demographic changes.

7. Practicality and suitability to successful implementation at reasonable cost.

8. Transparency: Analysis of reform plans should measure all necessary sources of tax revenue, and all benefits provided, including those from the traditional system as well as from personal accounts.

Source: The Interim Report of the President's Commission to Strengthen Social Security (2001:32).

Although the commission's 16 members were handpicked by the president for their support of President Bush's call to add personal investment accounts to the Social Security system, the final report of the commission in December 2001 did not provide a firm blueprint for

the overhaul of the retirement system. Rather, the report proposed three alternative models for reform, each of which involves voluntary personal account options in different amounts. As the commission's co-chair, Daniel Patrick Moynihan, a former democratic senator from New York, was quoted in the press, "This is the first time a national panel appointed by a president has proposed that Americans acquire wealth as part of social insurance" (Stevenson, 2001). Members of the commission indicated, however, that it is up to Congress and the president to make the hard decisions among these approaches, decide on the associated benefit cuts, and come up with the required money.

What implications do the tax cuts of 2001, the slowing of the economy, and the costs of the war on terrorism have on the Social Security budget and proposed reforms of the system?

So what can be concluded from the Social Security controversy? Clearly, it is about money. But even more clearly it is about ideology, guarantee of a minimum income floor to retired and disabled workers and their families, and about the roles of private investment and government. The growing political conservatism that characterized the last two decades of the twentieth century, including the role of social welfare, has provided fuel to fire the debate. Moreover, the Social Security lockbox is not invulnerable. The federal government apparently pried open the "lockbox" to meet the government's deficit in non-Social Security funds in fiscal 2001. In addition to the $38 billion tax rebate given taxpayers in 2001, the September 11 attacks on the World Trade Center and the Pentagon were costly; Congress approved $40 billion in emergency funding, some of which was spent before the end of the 2001 fiscal year. Although national focus on the war on terrorism has eclipsed Social Security as an immediate political issue, the future of Social Security will remain a significant topic in the years to come.

Major Legislation Affecting Elders' Health and Economic Well-Being

The 1960s, unlike the subsequent decades, was a period of legislative activism, including liberalization of Social Security benefits, passage of Medicare, the Older Americans Act, and the Age Discrimination in Employment Act. The United States is now in a period of fiscal constraint for social and human services that began in the 1980s when so-called *generational equity,* described by one of its leading proponents as "nothing more than the present being fair to the future" (Durenberger, 1989), became a popular theme. Also during the 1980s, the aged were targeted as scapegoats for the nation's economic ills and portrayed as greedy, getting rich at the expense of children, and receiving a disproportionate amount of benefits from federal outlays. As one former state Governor, Richard Lamm (a major spokesperson for the lobby group, Americans for Generational Equity [AGE]) stated, "We must recognize that there is a relationship between budgets for the elderly and budgets for the young. . . . Money that is badly needed by poor children in St. Paul is being sent to wealthy retirees in St. Petersburg" (Lamm, 1989: 111). Americans for Generational Equity was funded substantially by private sector organizations (e.g., health care corporations, insurance companies, and banks) with an interest in alternatives to Social Security and Medicare and attempted to alter social policy and benefits for the elderly. Although age has faded from the political forefront, other organizations, ranging from the Concord Coalition to the Third Millennium, have focused on its concerns. The Concord Coalition, founded by two former U.S. senators, has as its aims elimination of the federal deficits and federal entitlement programs contributing to the deficit. In contrast, as an organization, the Third Millennium has blamed the self-indulgence of older Americans for numerous problems, including the federal deficit and neglect of the environment.

Ironically, although the old have been singled out as greedy consumers of resources, no significant U.S. legislation benefiting them has been enacted since 1972. Social Security payments—the major source of income for old women—have been made taxable and cost-of-living increases less generous. Underlying the generational equity position is the premise that our nation faces significant fiscal choices about how to pay for an aging society. Public policy issues thus become framed as intergenerational competition and conflict, as programs for older people are targeted as a major reason for increases in poverty among children. The generational equity debate has become a convenient way to justify shifting social responsibility for vulnerable groups to individuals and the private sector (Quadagno, 1990). Moreover, the premise that the old are selfish, unwilling to pull their own weight, and depleting social resources that justifiably belong to the young, is likely to have unanticipated economic consequences for their children and grandchildren who are likely to be called upon to provide for them if social safety nets are abolished.

Ongoing debates about whether programs for elders should be based on age or need highlight ideological disputes about who should be served and at what cost. Advocates for age-based programs argue that they are less stigmatizing than means-tested programs, set a safety net of protection for elders, minimize eligibility disputes, and promote individual dignity. Advocates for need-based services, such as Neugarten (1982), have argued that age-based programs and policies stigmatize the elderly by painting "the old" as a social problem, thus fueling intergenerational conflicts. Some analysts, like Binstock and Day (1996), have suggested that the trend is to combine age and economic need as policy criteria for old-age programs. Legislation within the past few decades made Social Security payments for higher income recipients taxable and did away with the extra personal exemption for people 65 and older on federal income taxes. Recent proposals for health care reform would separate people by income instead of age. As Parrott, Mills, and Bengtson (2000: 208) have pointed out,

> The untouchable status of old-age policies seems to have evaporated. In addition, there is more talk about individual and family responsibility for elderly persons in conjunction with governmental fiscal responsibility. It is clear that more expectations will fall on families to step in and help their older relatives. The trend in U.S. public policy at the start of the twenty-first century is likely to be toward more state and local—rather than federal—responsibility for aging programs, and less federal money to support state efforts. . . . Families will be asked to do more than they are already doing for the care of their older family members.

Medicare

Medicare (Title XVIII of the Social Security Act) was enacted in 1965 to help older Americans obtain and pay for medical care. Since its beginning, it has been a social insurance program, providing health care benefits to people who have paid into it. That Medicare provides benefits only to the elderly was the result of compromise, as both the medical profession and insurance companies successfully opposed universal health care coverage for all age groups—an opposition that continues today. It is not a means-tested program; all recipients are entitled to the same level of benefits, regardless of their age, health status, or income. Contrary to popular belief, Medicare does not pay for all health care expenses nor cover most long-term care expenses. It was designed to cover acute health problems rather than chronic illness.

Medicare is funded through two trust funds: The Hospital Insurance Trust Fund (HI) and the Supplementary Medical Insurance Trust Fund (SMI). Contributions to the HI are made on a "pay as you go" basis through mandatory contributions from both employees and employers. The SMI is financed by premiums contributed by enrollees and by federal revenues. Today Medicare serves approximately 39 million people, including most Americans aged 65 and over and younger people receiving federal disabilities for at least two years. Since its inception, Medicare has continuously increased the amount of deductibles, copayments, and premiums that individuals must pay out-of-pocket. Since its passage, Medicare spending has grown as a percentage of the federal budget. Increases in the costs of health care and technological change, plus the aging of the population, have driven costs up. In 1988, the Medicare Catastrophic Health Coverage Act was passed. It had as its underlying fiscal premise that new benefits will be met entirely by the elderly themselves through flat increases in the monthly supplemental medical insurance payment plus annual premiums that are surtaxes on elders' income tax liability. This legislation proved so unpopular with the elderly and with organizations lobbying on behalf of the elderly that it was repealed.

More political changes were in the wind, however. By the mid-1990s, expenditure in the HI began to exceed income, leading to the Balanced Budget Act of 1997 and subsequent reductions in coverage. Although Medicare had surpluses in 2000, federal estimates predict that the fund will gradually decline until turning into deficits by 2017 and later.

During the presidential campaigns in 2000, prescription drug coverage—not typically provided by Medicare—became a rallying cry for both Democrats and Republicans who proposed different plans to meet these expenses. Basic to the controversy about prescription coverage remains "who should benefit?" All recipients? Or should such a program be means-tested? And what effect would prescription drug coverage have on the solvency of these plans? Should Medicare itself be means-tested in the future is an implicit question underlying philosophic and political differences. As with OASDI, how to fund Medicare remains the subject of political controversy, dominated by ideological differences—generational equity versus a contract between generations.

Global Glimpses: Social Policy and Financing Health Care in Norway

Compare the current controversies about entitlements, especially about health care, to another nation, Norway. Contrary to popular belief, Norway is not inhabited entirely by tall blond Viking descendants. Not only does the nation include a nomadic Sami (Lapland) population but within the last 40 years, the proportion of people immigrating from other nations to find work has also increased. Although historically a very poor country, the discovery of offshore oil bolstered the Norwegian economy and created a demand for more workers. By 2000, 6 percent of the 4.5 million residents of Norway were classified by *Statistics Norway* (2001) as immigrants, and almost one-third of these were from Asia and Africa. Increasing numbers of immigrants have also sought asylum due to political upheavals in the former Yugoslavia.

Although Norway is a small nation, it, like many other industrialized nations, is confronting how best to deliver health care. Norwegians, like Americans, are strongly individualistic, but they have a long-standing tradition of community-based mutual assistance reflected in social policies (Milgrim, 1977). Unlike the United States, National Insurance provides the primary source of funding for health care, organized on a regional and municipal basis. Responsibility for all health issues lies with the local Board of Health—citizens elected by each municipality—and the local public health officer, usually a general practice physician. All hospital care is provided free of charge to the patient, despite age or length of stay. National Insurance also pays physician fees (Amoako-Addo, 1996a). Residents in long-term care facilities, such as nursing homes, pay an average of around 13 percent of the cost of service, and users of home-based care in the community pay about 5 percent of the operational costs. Payment for both long-term and home-based care is based both on geographic location and on income and property of individual elders using these services (Amoako-Addo, 1996b).

How can Norway afford to pay so much for care of the elderly who constitute 16 percent of the population when the United States apparently cannot? An important factor is

their ideological commitment to a "welfare state"; that is, a society where the provision of social security, health services, universal free education, employment opportunities, elder care, child care, home help services, and housing are considered political rights for every citizen, including immigrants. Such commitment is costly: Norwegians pay one of the highest tax rates in the industrialized world. In return, they receive many services through tax-funded programs that Americans pay for out-of-pocket.

A second and very important factor related to ideology is the different approach to governmental provision of services in the two nations. American social policy, including health care policies, have been based primarily on a "residual social welfare model"; that is, only when the private market and the family cannot meet individual needs should government benefits be provided. In contrast, Norwegians support a "redistributive social welfare model," based on the assumption that everyone, whether rich or poor, should be guaranteed a reasonable standard of living and health care.

A third factor is the relatively high per capita income in Norway—about $1,000 more than the United States per capita income. Related to these three factors are attitudes toward taxation and their relationship to the dominant ideology of the nation. Americans, conscious of the cost of government services and imbued with the residual social welfare model, are often reluctant to support social programs through taxes. In contrast, although, like Americans, Norwegians complain about

taxes, their support of the "redistributive social welfare model" bal-
ances off the perceived personal financial cost of benefits with perceived social benefits. The Norwegian approach is to choose higher
taxes.

How health care, social services, and retirement benefits will be
funded in the future poses a series of American political policy questions. Should eligibility for all such government programs be means-
tested and restricted to the poor? Should the age of eligibility for Social
Security and Medicare be raised? Should Americans support Medicare
through increased tax rates? Should health care to the elderly be
rationed? The ideology guiding future public policies that you support
will influence the health and well-being of elders, our families, and
ourselves in the twenty-first century.

Older Americans Act

Although the Social Security Act met some of the needs for income
security among older Americans, many social service needs remained
unmet. In 1965, the Older Americans Act (OAA), designed to speak for
the elderly and focus attention on problems associated with aging, was
passed by Congress. Its inception was slow and tortuous, bound by
political disagreements about its mission, appropriateness, and location within the federal bureaucracy. Although the first National Conference on Aging, held in 1950 at the request of President Harry Truman, drew over 800 delegates to direct national attention to the needs
of a growing older population, in the ensuing decade at least fifty-three
bills, either to establish an agency on aging within the Department of
Health, Education, and Welfare or to create a separate Commission on
Aging, were introduced in Congress without success. By 1956, President Eisenhower established the Federal Council on Aging, a
subcabinet committee comprising representatives from the various
governmental departments concerned with aging. In 1958, Congress
passed a bill calling for a White House Conference on Aging that was
eventually held in 1961. Shortly thereafter, a Congressional subcom-
mittee recommended that Congress establish an Office on Aging
within the Department of Health, Education, and Welfare (now the
Department of Health and Human Services). Various legislative proposals were made thereafter, but arguments over the placement of the
agency, its funding, and its level of responsibility continued until 1965
when the Older Americans Act was finally signed into law and the
Administration on Aging (AOA) was created as a federal agency,
headed by an Assistant Secretary for Aging within the Department of
Health, Education, and Welfare (Koff & Park, 1999).

The OAA, administered by the Administration on Aging, was intended to create a national network for the planning, coordination, and delivery of services to people 60 and over. At the federal level, the Administration on Aging provides leadership, technical assistance, and support to 57 State Units on Aging, more than 661 Area Agencies of Aging, 222 tribal organizations, and thousands of service providers, caregivers, and volunteers (Administration on Aging, *www.aoa.dhhs.gov/ may97/aoa-oaa.html*). Services provided under the OAA include information and referral, in-home services (e.g., homemaker assistance, home health care), senior center programs, nutrition services, nutrition programs both in-home (meals on wheels) and at senior centers and nutrition sites, and legal assistance advocacy.

How does the downtown location of this Area Agency on Aging influence access for older people?

Eligibility for services under the OAA begins at age 60, yet the majority of Americans at that age are healthy. It is the "old-old," aged 75 or over, who are likely to need services as both health and economic needs increase among this age group. Although the older population has increased, funding for both the Administration on Aging and the OAA has declined, especially since congressional focus shifted from concerns about quality of life for the elderly to cost containment. Given the range of programs encompassed under the Act, a relatively low level of funding has led the Administration on Aging to target services primarily to specific groups at risk: low income, minorities, rural elders, and the frail at risk of long-term care placement. Although the OAA was scheduled for reauthorization in 1991, no such action occurred. Rather, the OAA continued through a Congressional resolution, as Congressional members debated means-testing, budget, and services to be provided. In 2000, the Older Americans Act was reauthorized by Congress. You may want to check its current provisions to see how it meets the needs of the elderly.

Age Discrimination in Employment Act

Age discrimination in employment was not new when the *Age Discrimination in Employment Act* (ADEA) was passed in 1967. Age limits for hiring, negative views of older workers, and beliefs that they were unproductive, impaired, and sickly had existed for over a century. Although protection for older workers was considered in the Civil Rights Act of 1964 that prohibited job discrimination on the basis of sex, race or color, or national origin, age was not included.

When the ADEA was finally enacted, it prohibited age discrimination against those ages 40 to 65, assuming that workers aged 65 or over would be retired. The ADEA also contained other provisions excluding employers from its provisions when (1) age was a "bona fide occupational qualification" for the job or business; (2) fitness for a job was based on "reasonable factors other than age"; (3) the terms of a bona fide seniority system or employee benefit plan must be observed; and (4) an employee is discharged or disciplined for cause. In 1986, Congress amended the ADEA to prohibit mandatory retirement (except for tenured college and university faculty at age 70—a provision later repealed). It was not until 1990 that efforts intensified to pass legislation on behalf of disabled people of any age, culminating in the Americans with Disabilities Act (ADA). Both pieces of legislation prohibit overt discrimination on the basis of age or disability and urge employers to make reasonable accommodations to meet the needs of older or handicapped workers.

How successful has the ADEA been in reducing age discrimination in employment? Corporate downsizing, increased use of part-time and contract employees, automation, and less job security have also put older workers at high risk of losing their jobs to younger workers. Higher pension and health insurance costs are also factors causing older workers to lose jobs but are difficult to prove. For example, in a 1993 U.S. Supreme Court case, *Hazen Paper Company vs. Biggins,* the 62-year-old plaintiff charged that the Hazen Paper Company violated the ADEA by firing him just before he had met the company pension plan's 10-year vesting requirement. The Supreme Court ruled against him, indicating that treating someone differently on factors that may correlate with age, such as pension status, salary level, and length of service, does not necessarily indicate age discrimination. In effect, this decision severed conflicts over pension rights and other age-related factors from age discrimination (Joyce, 1999).

Many employers remain concerned about the higher costs and lower productivity of older workers and are more interested in structuring incentives for older workers to retire than encouraging them to stay in the labor force (Crown & Longino, 1997). Older employees are often offered attractive severance benefits on the condition that they sign an agreement waiving their right to bring a case against their employer alleging age discrimination. Indeed, 1990 amendments to the ADEA permitted early retirement incentives for and spelled out requirements for those taking early retirement to waive allegations of age discrimination.

Family and Medical Leave Act

The FMLA, passed in 1993, mandates public agencies and private sector employers with 50 or more employees to grant eligible employees up to a total of 12 work weeks of unpaid leave during any 12-month period for various documented medical reasons, including birth, adoption, severe personal illness, or care of a family member—spouse, child, or parent—with a serious health condition. Although the FMLA requires that an employee must be restored to her or his original job or an equivalent job with equivalent pay and benefits, it leaves unanswered the question of how the employee will support himself or herself during the leave period—a problematic issue for spouses and adult children providing care to an elderly family member and for employees of any age who may need to take leave due to pregnancy, adoption, or serious health conditions. In contrast, several European nations have developed policies to pay informal caregivers. Britain and the Republic of Ireland adopted a social security model that pays an allowance directly to informal caregivers to replace the income they have lost from their jobs due to their caring responsibilities. Germany instituted a "pay-as-you-go" social insurance model, financed by current workers' and employers' contributions. In those nations, as in ours, ideology and special interests have shaped public policy.

A Tradition of Political Elders

Elders as Politicians

The tradition of elders as political leaders is as old as the Roman Empire, when Plutarch attempted to settle the question of whether old men should withdraw from public life by saying, "Youth ought to obey and old age rule" (Falkner & de Luce, 1992: 26). Various presidents of the United States have been "older": John Adams first became president at age 62, Harry Truman at age 61, George Bush at 65, and Ronald Reagan at 70. The U.S. Constitution sets minimum ages for both members of the House of Representatives (25 years old) and the Senate (age 30). Although the average age of members of Congress today is between 50 and 59, a brief look at the ages of members of the U.S. Congress from 1981 to 1995 clearly shows that age itself is no barrier to holding political office (see Table 11-5). Nor is there any reason to believe that the decisions made by older members of Congress are any worse—or better—than those made by younger members.

Elders as a Political Force

Is there a gray lobby? One popular image of the elderly is that they constitute a major political force, playing special interest politics.

Indeed, amendments to the Social Security Act including Medicare and SSI, the Older Americans Act and establishment of the Adminis- tration on Aging, and passage and revision of the Age Discrimination Act would suggest that there is a substantial voting bloc of elders influ- encing public policy. Yet, there is little reason to believe that senior power is a potent political force advocating for change. Rather, the power of elders and organizations or special interest groups lobbying on behalf of the elderly is more reactive than proactive, that is, more concerned with protecting existing programs and entitlements (Binstock & Day, 1996).

Table 11-5	Percentage of Members of Congress Aged 60–69 and 70+, 1981–1995	
Year	Percentage Aged 60–69	Percentage Aged 70+
1981	13%	4%
1983	14%	4%
1985	16%	5%
1987	14%	6%
1989	18%	6%
1991	21%	6%
1993	21%	5%
1995	20%	6%

Source: U.S. Bureau of the Census. 2000. *Statistical Abstract of the United States 1999*, Table

One reason the elderly have been viewed as a powerful voting bloc is that many people see elders as homogeneous—somewhat like red- woods, which, as one former U.S. president is credited with saying, if you have seen one, you have seen them all. Despite the subculture of aging theory (Rose, 1962) discussed in Chapter 4, there is little evi- dence that the emphasis on youth in American society has created group identification and consciousness among the elderly: a "con- sciousness of kind" that has made elders potent social or political agents. Elders remain both heterogeneous and diverse, influenced by birth cohort, gender, socioeconomic status, race and ethnicity, political preferences, and personal experiences throughout the life course. The impact of these social and personal factors on political behavior persist as more potent forces than chronological age.

Voting Behavior. The 65 plus population is far from apathetic about voting. About two-thirds of the elderly vote, and more than 3 in 5 people 65 and over have voted in presidential elections since 1964 despite decreases in voting among the entire American population of voting age (Hobbs & Damon, 1996). People aged 65 to 74 are more likely to vote than those 75 to 84 or 85 and over. The major reasons elders gave for not voting in the 1996 presidential elections were ill-ness, disability, or an emergency (Casper & Bass, 1998). Table 11-6 presents the percentages voting in the presidential elections of 1972–1996; official reports for the 2000 election are not yet available. Prior to the 1972 presidential elections, national data are available only on 21- to 24-year-olds, as only a few states permitted 18-year-olds to vote. The proportion of people 65 and older voting in presidential elections increased as the proportion of people under 65 decreased. Voting was consistently lowest among those aged 18 through 24.

Table 11-6 Percentage of American Population Reporting Voting in 1972–1996 Presidential Elections by Age of Voters							
	1972	**1976**	**1980**	**1984**	**1988**	**1992**	**1996**
Ages 18–24	50%	42%	40%	41%	36%	43%	32%
Ages 25–44	63	59	59	58	54	58	49
Ages 45–64	71	69	69	70	68	70	64
Ages 65+	63	62	65	68	69	70	67

Source: Casper & Bass (1998): Table 1.

What party or parties do older people favor in presidential elections? Contrary to popular opinion, research suggests that age itself has little impact on political attitudes and behavior. The elderly differ in their voting patterns according to gender, race and ethnicity, and birth cohort. It is birth cohort, not age, that reflects some of the differences in political attitudes between generations (Hudson & Strate, 1985). Although earlier studies of voting behavior, such as Dobson's (1983) analysis, suggested that older people were more conservative than younger people, the apparent political preference for Republican candidates noted in such studies reflects in part birth cohort differences rather than a tendency to become more conservative.

Contrary to popular belief, the young-old are the population most likely to vote in elections.

Prior to the New Deal, new voters tended to identify heavily with the Republican Party and as they grew older remained loyal to their original party. In 1972, those 60 and older were born in 1912 or earlier and would probably have begun to vote before the New Deal of the 1930s, when the two major parties began to realign their political stances. In contrast, voters who were 60 and older in 1996 grew up during the

New Deal years. Moreover, the "generation gap" has narrowed between young and old since the 1970s, reflecting cohort differences between elders in the 1970s and 1990s. According to data from the General Social Survey, the gap between people aged 18 to 24 and those 65+ virtually disappeared on such attitudes as extramarital sex, abortions, and the death penalty from the 1970s to the late 1990s (Smith, 2000).

Gender and race also interact with birth cohort to determine political preferences. In 1996, results from exit poll surveys reported in the *New York Times* suggest that women aged 60 and over were more likely to vote for the Democratic party presidential candidate and their male age peers were more likely to vote for the Republican (Connelly, 1996). Information from the same set of polls for the 1972 to 1996 period shows that older women have shifted their political preferences for presidential candidates from Republican to Democrat, reflecting a cohort difference between these two time periods. In 1972, 70 percent of women 60 and older voted for Nixon, the Republican candidate; 52 percent voted for Reagan in 1980 and 58 percent in 1984. By 1988, slightly more (52 percent) voted for the Democratic candidate, and the trend for older women to vote for a Democratic president continued through the 1996 presidential election. Women of all ages in recent years have been more likely to assume that gender issues, such as equal pay and abortion, are of more concern to Democratic than Republican presidential candidates.

In contrast, older men have been consistently more likely to vote for the Republican presidential candidate with one exception—the 1992 election, when a higher proportion voted for Bill Clinton than George Bush. Consistently, African Americans have been far more likely to vote for the Democratic presidential candidate during the 1972 to 1996 period. Surprisingly, although there are more elderly women than men, proportionately more older men have voted in presidential elections over the years (Hobbs & Damon, 1996). White and African-American men are the most likely to vote and Latinas the least likely. The gender gap in voting, however, has been narrowing over the past few decades (Hobbs & Damon, 1996; Casper & Bass, 1998).

Not only do gender, race, and ethnicity influence the likelihood of voting, but education and higher incomes do as well. People of all ages with more education are more likely to vote, but the elderly, regardless of educational level, are more likely to vote than people between the ages of 25 and 44 (Hobbs & Damon, 1996). Marital status, too, is related to voting; those who are married are more likely to vote than the divorced, separated, widowed, or never married (Casper & Bass, 1998). How a person votes thus results from a constellation of factors including birth cohort, gender, race (and ethnicity), income, religion and religious beliefs, and perception of the candidate's political platform as in line with their own self-interests.

Organizations of and for the Elderly. The belief that age provides a basis for political cohesion and along these lines elders develop a shared consciousness that translates into senior power—a basic tenet of the subculture of aging theory—has yet to be proven. Yet, there are currently over 1,000 separate organized interest groups for older adults, of which at least 100 are national organizations involved in political action on behalf of the elderly (see Binstock & Day, 1996; Hess & Markson, 1980; Koff & Park, 1999; and Internet Resources at the end of the chapter).

The largest and best known of these organizations is the *American Association of Retired Persons* (AARP), which began in the 1940s as an association of retired teachers (National Retired Teachers Association), providing its members with numerous benefits, such as life insurance, travel, prescription services, and other advantages. In 1958, the NRTA founded a spinoff organization for nonteachers that became the AARP, and the NRTA became an organization under the umbrella of the AARP. The AARP's stated mission is to enhance the quality of life of older people, to give leadership in determining older people's roles in society, and to combat ageism. Originally basically conservative, its recent political activity has encompassed advocacy for numerous political changes, including abolition of age-based mandatory retirement and coverage of prescription drugs under Medicare. For a nominal annual fee, people age 50 and older can join and receive a wide array of assistance, ranging from investment services and insurance to travel discounts and genealogical software. Its magazine, *Modern Maturity,* is the most widely circulated membership periodical in the United States.

Less powerful but traditionally less conservative is the *National Council of Senior Citizens* (NCSC), established in 1961 with funds from the labor movement. NCSC, whose purpose is to advocate on behalf of the elderly, was originally launched to help with the passage of Medicare. With primarily a blue-collar membership, among its other activities, NCSC sponsors union-constructed senior housing in 17 states and has advocated for health care and against privatization of Social Security.

The *National Association of Retired Federal Employees* (NARFE), one of the oldest aging-interest groups, was established in 1921 as a membership organization for current and retired federal employees. NARFE's primary purpose is to support legislation and policies designed to benefit federal employees and retirees.

Two grassroots organizations, the *Gray Panthers* and the *Older Women's League*, also advocate on behalf of the elderly. The Gray Panthers, founded by the late Maggie Kuhn, an involuntarily retired YWCA worker, was formed to bring together a coalition of people of all ages to combat ageism and has taken a far more radical stance than the AARP or the majority of other age interest groups, supporting the decriminalization of marijuana, the Equal Rights Amendment, gay rights, and other organizations. The death of Maggie Kuhn, whose physical appearance as a sweet old lady belied her militancy, has left a void in the leadership she provided, but the Panthers continue to survive, committed to goals beyond immediate self-interests.

The Older Women's League (OWL), founded in 1980 by Tish Sommers and Laurie Shields, was the first American grassroots mem-

Table 11-7 Major Interest Groups on Aging and the Elderly, Listed by Date Founded	
Organization and Date Founded	**Type**
American Geriatrics Society (AGS) 1942	Professional society, primarily medical, to encourage and promote study of geriatrics and medical research on aging.
Gerontological Society of America (GSA) 1945	Professional society to promote scientific study of aging and disseminate information on research, education, practice, and career opportunities in aging.
National Council on the Aging (NCOA) 1950	Private, nonprofit organization, providing information, training, technical assistance, advocacy, and leadership on aging.
American Society on Aging (ASA) 1954	Formerly the Western Gerontological Society, founded to improve lives of older people through education, training, and policy analysis.
American Association of Homes and Services for the Aging (AAHSA) 1961	National association of nonprofit organizations for the elderly, promoting quality care.
National Association of State Units on Aging (NASUA) 1964	National association to advance the ability of state aging units to ensure the well-being of elders.
National Caucus and Center on Black Aged (NCBA) 1970	Nonprofit organization focusing on improving the quality of life of older Black Americans.
National Senior Citizens Law Center (NSCLC) 1972	To provide support for legal assistance to elderly poor; funded by the Legal Services Corporation.
Silver Haired Legislatures 1973	To provide opportunity for elders to hold legislative session in their state to sensitize legislators to aging issues.
Association Nacional Por Personas Mayores (ANPM) 1975	To create awareness of needs and status of Hispanic elders and meet these needs through direct services, research, and information.
National Association of Area Agencies on Aging (NAAAA) 1976	To represent area agency interests and provide communication links between area agencies and national organizations and AOA.
National Asian Pacific Center on Aging (NAPCA) 1979	Private organization to improve delivery of health care and social services to elder Asian and Pacific islanders nationwide.

Table 11-7 Major Interest Groups on Aging and the Elderly, Listed by Date Founded (continued)	
Organization and Date Founded	**Type**
National Hispanic Council on Aging 1980	To foster well-being of Hispanic elderly through administration, planning, direct services, research, and education.
Alzheimer's Disease and Related Disorders Association (ADRDA) 1980	To promote research on causes, cures, and treatment for the disease; provide educational programs.

bership organization to focus exclusively on the concerns of midlife and older women. Both activists for displaced homemakers, Sommers and Shields drafted the first displaced homemakers' legislation, initially introduced in California and later in the U.S. Congress. Like the Gray Panthers, membership is open to anyone of any age. Among OWL's numerous advocacy efforts on the national and state level are health care, housing, ending violence against women and the elderly, and improving the image of midlife and older women. Its "Mother's Day Report," issued annually, addresses specific topics for which change is proposed. Numerous other aging interest groups also exist; a partial listing is shown in Table 11-7.

As you can see from the listing of organizations, their purpose differs as does their constituency. Some are special interest groups representing a specific industry, such as nonprofit long-term care facilities; some, like the American Geriatrics Society, are professional organizations; some focus on a specific underserved racial or ethnic group. Still others provide specific services, such as legal advocacy, or promote research and education. Just as in the story of the three blind men who were asked to describe an elephant—where one felt the trunk, another the tail, and a third the ear—each organization concentrates on a specific aspect of aging that is closest to its own interests and purpose. Whether a sustained lobby for the elderly can arise from coalition among these myriad missions remains to be seen.

Summary

The major source of income for many elders is Social Security. Fewer than half of America's retirees receive additional pensions. Only about 1 in 5 has earnings from paid employment. Because participation in the labor force decreases with advancing age, the "young-old" are much more likely to receive income from earnings than older birth cohorts. The majority of married couples on Social Security receive a benefit equivalent to one and a half times the husband's benefits. For most couples today, this amounts to more than if benefits were calculated on each of their earnings separately due to women's lower life-time earnings.

The type and amount of social security benefits a woman receives is determined by both her attachment to the work force and marital status. A widow is entitled to 100 percent of her husband's benefits. A divorced and not remarried woman may still claim a wife or widow's benefit if married to the worker for 10 years or more. The majority of divorced or widowed women rely on these benefits upon retirement rather than their own benefits. Because on the average women live longer than men, most elderly Social Security recipients are women.

The official measure of poverty used by the federal government is based on a family's annual money income before taxes. This index, based on the U.S. Department of Agriculture's 1961 Economy Food Plan, was developed to reflect different consumption patterns of individuals and families. Although the poverty index is adjusted annually for inflation, a little-known fact is that two separate indices have existed since its inception. One is used to assess poverty among the population under age 65; the other is used to assess individuals and two-person households aged 65 and over. Whatever the shortcomings of the poverty index, Census data clearly show that the proportion of people 65 and over living in poverty has sharply declined since 1959. This figure, however, obscures those living in near poverty. Those living in poverty and near poverty are at high risk of inadequate housing, health care, food, transportation, and other resources.

A person's likelihood of living in poverty in old age is influenced by race/ethnicity, marital status, and gender. Economic security for women in old age, especially if they are members of minority groups, is particularly problematic. Regardless of race or ethnicity, poverty rates are about two times higher among women than among men and three times higher among separated, widowed, and divorced women compared with their married age peers. A major reason for their greater rates of poverty is the structure of our social insurance programs. In other industrialized nations, improvements in the economic status of the elderly came from major changes in government-sponsored social insurance pension plans during the 1980s.

Issues affecting the economic security of any age group are very much a result of public policies and political forces, as the current controversy about the future of Social Security illustrates. During the 1980s and 1990s, Social Security became a political football, tossed in an elaborate political game to the accompaniment of dire predictions from each side. How solvent is Social Security today? The facts are relatively straightforward. Using the most commonly accepted demographic and economic assumptions, its trustees predict that reserves are sufficient to pay full disability and retirement benefits until 2041. However, the real issue is not dollars but ideology.

Major legislation affecting elders, such as Medicare, the Older Americans Act, and the Age Discrimination in Employment Act, were enacted in the 1960s. The financing of Medicare is also under discussion: How can it meet the needs of the elderly? The Family and Medical Leave Act, passed in the 1990s, provides up to 12 weeks of leave for personal illness or family care, but does not tackle the issue of how those people taking advantage of its provisions will support themselves or their families while on leave.

Although those aged 65 and older do not form a unified political block, they play important roles in politics, both as officeholders and voters. To the extent that "unified senior power" is exerted, it has so far occurred around only a very small number of issues directly affecting their lives. Likewise, numerous organizations that advocate for the elderly also do not form a unified bloc. Whether a sustained lobby for the elderly will arise from coalition among these groups remains to be seen.

Key Points

1. Reliance on Social Security and other types of pensions increases sharply with advancing age, and paid employment accounts for only 10 percent of household income among those household heads 75 or older.

2. Median household income declines with age and is lowest throughout the life course among African Americans.

3. Household net worth among those aged 65 and older is highest among those with some college or more, reflecting the roles of gender, class, and race/ethnicity on savings throughout life.

4. Two-thirds of those 65 and older receive 50 percent or more of their income from Social Security benefits.

5. Regardless of how income and assets are calculated by various government agencies, married couples are better off economically than individuals living alone or with other individuals in old age.

6. Poverty indices set by the federal government have lower thresholds for individuals and couples aged 65 and older than for younger people.

7. About three-quarters of all elders below the poverty level are female.

8. Especially vulnerable to poverty and near poverty in old age are widowed, divorced, separated, and never married African American women.

9. Political and ideological choices about allocation of resources are a major reason for the "entitlement crisis."

10. Social Security funds are estimated to be adequate to pay OASDI benefits until 2037.

11. Various plans to reform Social Security have been proposed, including privatization, means-testing, and raising the age of eligibility for full benefits.

12. Major legislation affecting elders, such as Medicare, the Older Americans Act, and the Age Discrimination in Employment Act, were enacted in the 1960s.

13. Elders continue to play important roles in politics, both as officeholders and voters, although there is no indication of a unified bloc of senior power.

14. Numerous organizations with different perspectives and ideologies advocate for the elderly but do not form a unified bloc.

Discussion Questions

1. Discuss the risks and benefits of privatizing Social Security. What ideological premises are behind each perspective? Who is likely to benefit the most from privatization? From maintaining the current system?

2. If the age for full benefits from Social Security is raised to 70, what impact do you think this will have on older workers and their economic position? Explain.

3. How would your parents' retirement finances be affected if Social Security were repealed? How do you think your own future retirement income would be affected?

4. Should Social Security be means-tested? Explain the risks and benefits.

5. Discuss the statement: "Should workers who need to take leave from their jobs for documented medical reasons, such as illness or to care for a disabled relative, be paid during their absence?" If so, whose responsibility is it to pay the worker—the government through a federally mandated program or the employer? If the worker is not paid, how should she or he meet expenses?

6. If Medicare will run out of money shortly, what policies would you advocate to ensure a more stable funding base? Would you limit eligibility, and if so, using what standards or criteria?

7. Should age or need be the basis for receipt of services such as those provided by the Older Americans Act and Medicare?

Films and Videos

Social Insecurity: Work, Family, and Retirement (video; 60 minutes; available from PBS video; *www.pbs.org*).

Using dialogue format, this video raises issues of the impact that an aging America will have on society and issues of social responsibility.

To Be Old, Black, and Poor (video; 52 minutes; available from Films for the Humanities and Sciences, P.O. Box 2053, Princeton, NJ 08543-2053).

Documentary of the life of an elderly African American couple and their struggles to survive.

Internet Resources

http://www.aarp.org

Entrance to the American Association of Retired Persons and their numerous services including policy and research papers.

http://www.cato.org

The web site for the Cato Institute, a free enterprise, conservative think-tank that includes policy papers.

http://www.graypanthers.org

The site for the Gray Panthers including information on current activities and membership.

http://www.narfe.org

The official site for information about the National Association of Retired Federal Employees.

http://www.ncoa.org

Site of the National Council on Aging with up-to-date information on legislation, advocacy, programs, and other policy features.

http://www.owl.org

Older Women's League site, including information on "Mother's Day Reports."

http://www.yourcongress.com

A gold mine of information on the inner workings of Congress and congressional representatives.

Research Article

Ekerdt, D. J., & Hackney, J. K. (2002). Workers' ignorance of retirement benefits. *The Gerontologist 42;* 543–551.

Using data from the Health and Retirement Study, this article examines the extent of workers' unfamiliarity with their post-retirement health benefits and future income from pensions and Social Security, and the implications of such ignorance for adequate financial planning.

Supplemental Readings

Abramovitz, M. (1997). *Regulating the Lives of Women: Social Welfare Policy From Colonial Times to the Present.* Cambridge, MA: South End Press.

For the person interested in the ways in which race, class, and gender have intersected to shape social welfare policies in the United States and the influence of ideological factors on women's lives.

Edmunds, G. (2000). *How to Retire Early and Live Well with Less Than a Million Dollars.* Holbrook, MA: Adams Media Corporation.

Written by a former attorney who retired at age 29, this book defines financial needs for retirement and early retirement like his.

Koff, T. H., & Park, R. W. (1999). *Aging Public Policy Bonding the Generations* (2nd edition). Amityville, NY: Baywood.

For the serious student who wants to trace public policies on aging and their development.

Matthews, J. L., & Berman, D. M. (1999). *Social Security, Medicare, and Pensions.* Berkeley, CA: *Nolo.com.*

Written by an attorney and senior citizen center director, a straightforward guide to the complexities not only of Social Security and Medicare, but also SSI, Civil Service pensions, and other topics.

Steckenrider, J. J., & Parrott, T. M. (Eds.). (1998). *New Directions in Old Age Policies.* Albany, NY: SUNY Press.

A useful collection of articles including policy domains, politics and aging policies, and aging policy dilemmas. ✦

Chapter 12

Elders in the Health Care System

Introduction

John Revis, a 70-year-old Korean War veteran, pays a total of $13,003 per year out-of-pocket for the prescriptions he needs to keep him alive after his heart transplant three years ago. He has trouble making ends meet, has not been able to afford to keep his car or pay for gas, and very often has to scrimp on food. Unfortunately, none of his prescriptions are covered by insurance. He is applying to the Veteran's Administration for help in meeting the cost of the drugs he needs. Chris Holden, also 70 years old and a Korean War veteran, recently retired from his job as an executive in a major company. Unlike John, he has been fortunate in enjoying relatively good health. Although his cholesterol is high, he has been able to reduce it through a diet prescribed by his physician and by playing vigorous sets of tennis almost every day. Poor health can be expensive, especially for those least able to afford it!

Many people believe dependency, illness, and frailty inevitably accompany old age. Nevertheless, as the two above illustrations show, poor health is not "normal aging." Increasingly, researchers are becoming aware of the distinction between normal aging and usual aging (Rowe & Kahn, 1998). As they have studied the effects of chronological age more carefully, what they once thought to be inevitable health problems of old age turn out to be associated with environment, lifestyle, and disease— states that may accumulate in their effects as we grow older. For example, although many older people will develop heart disease, many others do not. Changes in many health characteristics in later life are not directly caused by aging itself but by processes that can change with age.

The truth is that as more of us live to be very old, we are more likely to require health care. But poor health is not as prevalent as assumed. About three-fourths of those people aged 65 through 74 years old view their health as good or excellent, and two-thirds of those 75 or over feel similarly. On the other hand, as more people live to be very old, they may face more illnesses or conditions that increase the likelihood of requiring more health care. Those 65 and over are also the only age group in the United States to whom we have provided national health insurance (Medicare) since 1965. At any age, however, how, when, and why we use health care is influenced not only by actual illnesses but by socioeconomic characteristics, race and ethnicity, sex, individual preferences and beliefs, and broader sociostructural factors including the organization of the health care system. This chapter focuses on elders in the health care system and the types of care they receive.

Who Pays for Health Care?

Rising Health Care Costs

A major issue related to the organization and use of health care is how it is financed. Medical care costs now account for about 14 percent of the gross domestic product of the United States (Statistical Abstract of the U.S., 2000). In part, these expenditures reflect the aging of the population because most health care dollars are spent on the treatment of diseases in later life and terminal care. Taken as a group, those 65 and over, who represent about 1 in 8 Americans, account for around 36 percent of our total national health expenditures—more than four times the amount spent on younger people—according to federal estimates. When ill, they enter hospitals twice as often and stay one day longer than the national average (Statistical Abstract of the U.S., 2000). But it is important to keep in mind that these high costs and rates of utilization are confined to a small segment of the elderly, reflecting care for multiple illnesses typically occurring in the last year or so of life (Hogan et al., 2001).

Spending for *Medicare*, the public insurance program providing coverage to nearly all people aged 65 and over, increased from $36.4 billion in 1980 to $244.5 billion by 2000 and, according to federal government estimates, will rise to $329.0 billion by 2005. Nonetheless, the bulk of Medicare spending goes to only a very small proportion of elderly. About 5 percent of Medicare recipients have accounted for 50 percent of the expenditures, and 10 percent of all recipients account for 70 percent of expenditures, again reflecting the occurrence of multiple severe illnesses in the last year or two of life rather than aging itself (Hogan et al., 2001). Clearly, health care use among the elderly has many patterns.

People are eligible for Medicare if they or their spouses worked for at least 10 years in Medicare-covered employment, are 65 years old, and citizens or permanent residents of the United States. Younger people with a disability or chronic kidney disease may also qualify for coverage. As you can see from the following table, Medicare does not cover all medical expenses. Medicare Part A, which covers hospitalization, skilled nursing home care after a 3-day hospital stay, hospice care, and some home health care, is available without premiums to individuals receiving or eligible for retirement benefits from Social Security or the Railroad Retirement Board, who have worked in Medicare-covered employment for the specified period. Part B of Medicare is an optional plan that requires a premium and helps pay for physician services, hospital outpatient care, durable medical equipment, and other services including some home health care. The majority of Medicare's 40 million beneficiaries choose the optional Part B. Approximately 90 percent of Medicare beneficiaries also have some form of third-party payer insurance to help reduce out-of-pocket medical costs.

What Medicare Covers and 2002 Coverage Under Original Medicare Plan

I. PART A (EARNED BENEFIT; NO PREMIUM REQUIRED)

   A. Inpatient Hospital Care (semiprivate room and board, general nursing and other hospital services, and supplies).

      1. Covered for first 60 days less a deductible paid by the patient (a total of $812 in 2002) for each period of acute illness.

      2. Days 61–90 require a copayment by the patient or family of $203 per day.

      3. Beyond 90 days, may draw upon a 60-day lifetime reserve with daily copayment of $406 in 2002.

      4. Beyond 150 days, nothing; patient pays all costs.

   B. Inpatient Psychiatric Care—190-day lifetime maximum.

   C. Skilled Nursing Care Associated with Recovery from Illness.

      1. Covered up to 100 days following a hospitalization.

      2. No copayment for first 20 days.

      3. Daily copayment of up to $101.50 per day for days 21–100.

   D. Home Health Care.

      1. Prescribed by a physician, no deductibles or coinsurance, limits on number of days or required hospitalization.

2.   Copayment of 20% of the Medicare-approved amount for durable medical equipment.

E.   Hospice Care for Terminal Illness.

1.   Patient copayment of up to $5 for outpatient prescription drugs.

2.   Five percent patient-payment of the Medicare-approved amount for inpatient respite care.

II.   PART B (VOLUNTARY WITH A MONTHLY PREMIUM OF $54 IN 2002)

A.   Medical and Other Services.

1.   Patient pays $100 deductible per calendar year.

2.   Patient copayment of 20% of a Medicare-approved amount after the deductible.

3.   Patient copayment of 20% for all outpatient physical, occupational, and speech-language therapy services.

4.   Patient copayment of 50% for outpatient mental health care.

B.   Outpatient Hospital Treatment.

1.   Payment to hospital based on hospital costs.

C.   Clinical Laboratory Services: Generally 100 percent of approved amount.

D.   Blood.

1.   Patient pays for first three pints.

2.   Patient pays 20% of the Medicare-approved amount for additional pints after the deductible unless patient or someone else donates blood to replace what patient has used.

III.   NOT COVERED

A.   Acupuncture.

B.   Outpatient prescription drugs (in most cases).

C.   Routine physical exams.

D.   Dental care and dentures.

E.   Hearing aids and hearing exams.

F.   Routine eye care and most eyeglasses.

G.   Most nursing home care.

H.   Most screening tests or shots (does cover a few).

Source: Adapted from U.S. Department of Health and Human Services, Centers for Medicare and Medicaid Services (2001; 4: 8–11) and U.S. Department of Health and Human Services *HHS News* (2001).

Medicaid, jointly financed by federal and state governments, is the other major governmental source of health care for the elderly. Designed to serve the poor of all ages, Medicaid criteria for eligibility and regulations vary from state to state. About 11 percent of Medicaid recipients are aged 65 or over. Approximately two-thirds of all

Medicaid spending for the elderly is for nursing home care. The demand for health care services is another reason health care costs are increasing. As the baby boomers age, those aged 65 and over will grow from about 13 percent to an estimated 21 percent of the population by 2050. Unless there are major changes in health status, health care costs are likely to increase as the population ages, especially among those aged 75 or over who are at the greatest risk for disabilities.

MYTH: The Increase in the Elderly Population Is the Major Reason for Rising Health Care Expenditures

Factors other than the aging of the population have made health care costs skyrocket. An often cited factor in increasing health costs is the rapid development and use of sophisticated diagnostic and procedural technology. Modern health care is filled with technology—information processing systems, diagnostic devices, and new modes of therapy—that play an increasingly larger role in its delivery. For example, the CT scanner, a diagnostic device that combines X-ray equipment with a computer and a cathode ray tube to produce images of cross-sections of the body, allowed physicians to do things that could not be done before. Technology is also more profitable; fee scales to take a patient's history, conduct a physical exam, or give advice are lower than for using technology.

Medical centers advertise a wide range of services to older people. How useful is such marketing in choosing health care?

Other factors increase costs as well. Increases in the number—and incomes—of health care personnel, high administrative costs, and fraud also play a major role. Health care expenditures for all age groups, not just the elderly, have increased sharply since 1967. Table 12-1 shows the consumer price index in the United States since 1982 to 1984—the index years when the current consumer price index was equal to 100. The costs of medical care for all Americans have increased more rapidly than any other category of personal expenses. The consumer price index for all expenditures rose from 107.6 in 1985 to 166.6 by 1999, and medical care expenditures rose from 113.5 to 250.6. As you can see in Table 12-2, hospital and related services have increased most since 1980.

Population increases plus aging of the population were relatively unimportant factors in the growth of health care spending between

Table 12-1   U.S. Consumer Price Index by Major Categories of Expenditures, 1985–1999 (Index year = 1983–1984)

Year	All Items	Commodities	Energy	Food	Shelter	Clothing	Transportation	Medical Care	Fuel Oil	Electricity	Utility Gas	Utility Phone
1985	107.6	105.4	101.6	105.6	109.8	105	106.4	113.5	94.6	108.9	104.8	111.7
1986	109.6	104.4	88.2	109	115.6	105.9	102.3	122	74.1	110.4	99.7	117.2
1987	113.6	107.7	88.6	113.5	121.3	110.6	105.4	130.1	75.8	110	95.1	116.5
1988	118.6	111.5	89.3	118.2	127.1	115.4	108.7	138.6	75.8	111.5	94.5	116
1989	124	116.7	94.3	125.1	132.8	118.6	114.1	149.3	80.3	114.7	97.1	117.2
1990	130.7	122.8	102.1	132.4	140	124.1	120.5	162.8	98.6	117.4	97.3	117.7
1991	136.2	126.6	102.5	136.3	146.3	128.7	123.8	177	92.4	121.8	98.5	119.7
1992	140.3	129.1	103	137.9	151.2	131.9	126.5	190.1	88	124.2	100.3	120.4
1993	144.5	131.5	104.2	140.9	155.7	133.7	130.4	201.4	87.2	126.7	106.5	121.2
1994	148.2	133.8	104.6	144.3	160.5	133.4	134.3	211	85.6	126.7	108.5	123.1
1995	152.4	136.4	105.2	148.4	165.7	132	139.1	220.5	84.8	129.6	102.9	124
1996	156.9	139.9	110.1	153	171	131.7	143	228.2	97	131.8	107.2	125.9
1997	160.5	141.8	111.5	157	176.3	132.9	144.3	234.6	96.9	132.5	114.6	127.7
1998	163	141.9	102.9	161	182.1	133	141.6	242.1	84.8	127.4	112.4	100.7
1999	166.6	144.4	106.6	164	187.3	131.3	144.4	250.6	86.6	126.5	113	100.1

Source: *Statistical Abstract of the United States* (2000: Table 768).

1985 and 1999. Economy-wide medical-price inflation, and the number of services (including tests) per visit accounted for the major cost increases. Within the past four decades, the earnings of health care workers of all types exceeded the inflation rate, and physicians' earnings grew even faster. The median net income for physicians in the United States in 1997, according to the American Medical Association, was more than $164,000 although incomes varied dramatically by medical specialty. Also contributing to medical care costs were the costs of malpractice insurance, more frequent referrals for tests (especially referrals made by physicians who had invested in health care businesses), high administrative costs, the cost of prescriptions and medical services, hospital and related services, and outright fraud in billing.

Table 12-2 U.S. Consumer Price Index for Medical Care Prices, 1980–1999

Year	Physicians	Dental	Hospital and Related Services	Prescriptions and Medical Supplies
1980	76.5	78.9	69.2	72.5
1990	113.5	114.2	116.1	120.1
1995	208.8	206.8	257.8	235.0
1999	236.0	247.2	299.5	273.4

Source: *Statistical Abstract of the United States* (2000: Table 162).

**Social Policy Issue:
Health Care Across the Border**

The great debate over healthcare policy often centers on a comparison of the United States with its neighbor to the North, Canada. Although attempts to have a "single-payer system" for health care have failed in the United States, where 16 percent of the population remains uninsured, Canada established a national single-payer, provincially administered and publicly financed system in 1971. The Canadian single-payer system, in effect since 1971, is financed through general taxes and administered by the various provinces (provinces are similar to the U.S. states). Canadian doctors, similar to those in the United States, are self-employed, fee-for-service practitioners, but those fees are paid by the national insurance plan according to a schedule worked out between the provincial government and medical association. Hospital budgets are also negotiated. In other words, the Canadians have a private system paid for almost entirely by public money.

How was Canada able to institute a single-payer system? The answer lies in a long history of provincial provision of health care, often through religious agencies acting on behalf of the public at large rather than just their own congregants. In addition, Canadian physicians were less well organized and politically active than their U.S. counterparts. Perhaps most crucial is the structure of the Canadian Parliament that makes its members less vulnerable to lobbying and political fund-raising pressures from pharmaceutical and insurance companies.

Critics of the single-payer system, often described as "socialized medicine," point to high taxes and long waits for elective (not essential or immediately necessary) surgery, and affluent Canadians often travel to private hospitals in the United States. Most recently, a shortage of physicians and a reluctance to raise taxes have added to the hospital waiting lists.

Supporters of a single-payer system point out that the rationing of care in Canada is based on a shortage of doctors and revenue—both of which can be remedied—in contrast to the United States where

care is rationed on the basis of ability to pay, while 44 million are uninsured. In contrast, every Canadian is insured for all essential services, with a wide choice of doctors. Although prescription drugs for people under age 65 are not covered, the price of drugs is lower than in the United States, leading many Americans to cross the border for medications. Because Canada has a lower level of poverty than the United States, and because even its poorest citizens receive quality health care, life expectancy is more than two years longer. Canada outranks the United States on four of the five basic criteria for health established by the World Health Organization.

Are Canadians satisfied? There is widespread concern over the long hospital waits and the shortage of physicians, both of which will require higher taxes, but it is important to note that no mainstream government official or politician has suggested scrapping the system.

Sources: Canadian Intergovernmental Conference Secretariat (2000); Peterson (1994); Graig (1993).

Patterns of Health Care Utilization

Out-Patient Care

As you will recall from Chapter 5, disabilities increase with age, as do visits to physicians and use of other health care services. Because of the greater likelihood of disabilities among those aged 75 or over, the number of outpatient visits to doctors, hospital outpatient clinics, and emergency departments is greater among this age group. Those 75 years of age and over paid for an average of 7.6 outpatient visits compared with an average of 6.4 visits per year among 65- to 74-year-olds in 1998. Although Medicare extended coverage of hospital care and other services to the elderly, visits to physicians are not routinely covered under Part A, the mandatory portion of the program financed by current workers and their employers through a payroll tax. Part B is not financed in the same way and is a voluntary program, so that barriers to health care in old age still exist.

Most elderly, regardless of race, do not visit a dentist regularly despite greater needs. Currently, Medicare does not cover routine dental care. Lack of dental care is a serious problem in later life; by age 75, more than 1 in 3 men and women have lost all their permanent teeth (National Center for Health Statistics, 2001). Many of these do not have properly fitting dentures. Again, finances are a significant reason why older people do not go to dentists.

Inability to negotiate one's way through the health care system, ignorance of entitlements or available services, lack of regular health care providers, and difficulties in transportation (a major reason given by older people that they have not sought health care) also are barriers to using a range of health care services in the community. Some elderly in nonmetropolitan areas, especially counties with six or fewer people per square mile, are likely to have to travel long distances for outpatient care and to have long office waits before being seen. Access barriers such as those just described have added to the "axiom of inequality" of health care.

In 2000 alone, average out-of-pocket charges for medical care amounted to 22 percent of their income among all those aged 65 and over, but 52 percent of their income among low-income elderly women in poor health. Most elderly living below the poverty level are women and members of minority groups, with old women of color the poorest of the poor. Differences among states in Medicaid coverage (the major source of health care coverage for the poor of all ages) and lack of supplemental insurance to the basic Medicare package of Part A further limit the use of the full range of outpatient health services by the poor elderly.

Race, Gender, and Socioeconomic Variations in Out-Patient Care. The health experiences of elderly people today directly affect their use of outpatient and other health care services. Examples include their prior health practices, past and current nutrition, and environmental and industrial exposures to chemicals, all of which affect the likelihood of illness in later life. Socioeconomic deprivation during childhood also influences both health and mortality in adulthood (Wolfson et al., 1999). Although women average longer life expectancies than men, statistics show that they use more outpatient health services and more prescription and over-the-counter drugs than men. Gender differences in health care use among older people at least partially reflect their differences in illnesses; women have more frequent but less fatal health problems than men and are more likely to seek health care throughout their lives.

In the United States, people in the lowest socioeconomic groups and members of racial and ethnic minorities have the highest rates of almost every disease or illness. African Americans are more likely to suffer from high blood pressure (National Academy on an Aging Society, 1999), which puts them at greater risk of heart attacks and strokes.

The racial gap in health spreads throughout a variety of diseases. Socioeconomic conditions, not health risk behaviors, are the primary reason for the racial stratification of health (Hayward et al., 2000). African Americans are less likely to receive lifesaving surgery for early stage lung cancer than whites and are more likely to die (Bach et al., 1999). Similarly, African Americans who have a heart attack are significantly less likely to undergo bypass surgery with the same level of heart disease than whites (Petersen et al., 2002), and less likely to receive clot-busting heart medications (Allison et al., 1996).

Diabetes is two to three times more common in Mexican-American and Puerto Rican adults than in non-Latino/Latina whites, and is especially prevalent among those 50 and over (NIDDK and National Diabetes Information Clearinghouse, Internet download 11/13/00). African Americans, Asians, and Latinos of all ages are less likely to have a specific private physician or dentist, to receive medical care from a specialist, and more likely to have negative experiences with the health care system. Members of minority groups are also less likely to receive important preventive services, such as blood pressure tests, Pap smears, or cholesterol readings compared with white adults (Commonwealth Fund, 1997). It is hardly surprising that almost two-thirds of African Americans and more than 5 in 10 Latinos/Latinas view themselves as receiving lower quality health care than whites (Kaiser Family Foundation, 1999)!

The Rise of Managed Care

Traditionally, payment for health care has been fee-for-service, with the patient, his or her family, or a third-party payer such as Medicare, Medicaid, Blue Cross/Blue Shield, or other insurance paying for the services received. Can we deliver quality care more cheaply and equitably by fee-for-service alternatives to all age groups, including the elderly? Managed care is one such attempt. Managed care plans are designed to control and coordinate use of health care to contain costs, improve quality, or both. Managed care plans have several different models, the most common of which are *Health Maintenance Organizations* (HMOs), *Independent Practice Associations* (IPAs), *Point of Service* (POS), and *Preferred Provider Organizations* (PPOs).

HMOs act as both insurers and providers, providing a full range of medical care. Patients pay a fixed yearly sum in advance with limited copayments for which the individual receiving care is responsible. In return, members of a specific HMO agree to use the physicians and hospitals that are participants of that HMO. Physicians may be either full-time employees of the HMO or paid per-patient. No matter what an HMO spends on a particular patient's care, it assumes the financial risk of providing health care within a fixed budget. HMOs make a profit if their cost of providing services is lower than the agreed-upon payment, but lose if their costs are higher. Unlike the fee-for-service system, HMOs make money when people do not use their services. HMOs emphasize preventive medicine—teaching people to avoid illness.

In contrast to HMOs, *IPAs* contract with individual physicians or groups of physicians to provide services to enrollees at a negotiated rate. Physicians in IPAs maintain their own offices and are also free to contract with other HMOs and see fee-for-service patients. POS plans combine features of both prepaid and fee-for-service arrangements, and patients enrolled in such plans may choose either to use health care providers in the plan or to go outside the plan. Patients generally pay higher copayments when choosing a provider not in the POS. Finally, PPOs are agreements between health care providers and third-party payers to provide care on a negotiated fee schedule. Patients in PPOs may choose any provider, but pay more if they choose non-PPO physicians.

Experimental Medicare managed care programs were launched in the 1980s to learn if shifting from traditional fee-for-service payments for health care to prepaid per capita care would result in lower health care costs. Medicare currently offers several types of contracts to managed care plans, most commonly to HMOs. Medicare sets payments to HMOs at 95 percent of the average cost of a fee-for-service elder in a specific county, adjusted by age, sex, and other characteristics believed to be associated with health risks.

How good is the care older people receive through an HMO? Research suggests that the quality of health care is similar to that given in fee-for-service plans. Medicare enrollees do use less expensive hospital services and intensive services with similar outcomes to fee-for-service elders. Those enrolled in HMOs also tend to use more lower-cost services, such as physician visits and preventive care (Miller & Luft, 1994).

These findings need to be viewed critically, however, as the evidence also suggests that Medicare HMO enrollees are healthier on the average than their fee-for-service counterparts (Brown et al., 1993), at least in part reflecting "creaming" of healthier, low-risk elders by HMOs (U.S. General Accounting Office, 1997). If fewer healthy elders are enrolled in HMOs or similar managed care programs, the quality of care received can deteriorate, for incentives to make a profit can lead to underservice and rationing of expensive procedures to high-cost patients. Some HMOs have been cited for cost-cutting and bad practices, including delays in treatment that resulted in serious illness or death of elders, inadequate care, denial of hospital admission, marketing abuses, denial of coverage for needed services, and nonpayment for out-of-plan services (U.S. General Accounting Office, 1995). Nor have HMOs produced Medicare savings at the targeted rate. Although they were designed to save 5 percent of the Medicare costs for beneficiaries who enrolled, HMOs have actually spent more than fee-for-service health care (U.S. General Accounting Office, 1997).

How satisfied are patients currently enrolled in HMOs with the care they received? Although participation in managed care programs, especially HMOs, has increased rapidly in the past few years, not all Medicare recipients have entered such plans. One reason for the low interest in managed care among the elderly may be that many people find the "alphabet soup" of managed care choices confusing. Moreover, they may prefer greater flexibility in choosing health care options than the usual HMO provides (Wilensky, 1995). Among those who have joined HMOs, the evidence suggests that they make tradeoffs between lower costs and greater satisfaction. That is, HMO participants are less satisfied with either the quality of care they receive or their relationships with their physicians than fee-for-service patients; they are, however, more satisfied with the lower copayments and deductibles they pay and with broader benefits (Brown et al., 1993; Miller & Luft, 1994; Safran, Tarlov, & Rogers, 1994).

Making health care less expensive has been a major goal in Medicare's push for managed care. How successfully has this goal been met? The answer is not very well. According to a 1997 report from the U.S. General Accounting Office, 10 years of research on Medicare's costs under HMOs found that HMO enrollees would have cost Medicare less if they had stayed in fee-for-service plans. Unless problems in rate setting by Medicare are resolved, enrolling more elderly in managed care may increase rather than decrease Medicare spending (U.S. General Accounting Office, 1997).

Methods of Payment, DRGs, and Hospital Use

Methods of Payment and DRGs. Under the original Medicare regulations, hospitals were reimbursed according to "reasonable cost" based on the actual cost figures provided by the hospital for care of particular patients. Because hospital charges and utilization rates increased dramatically after the introduction of Medicare, a *prospective payment system* was introduced in 1985 as an attempt to cap costs. Prospective payment for Medicare patients is based on *diagnosis-related groups* (DRGs) rather than reasonable costs. Under this system, Medicare pays hospitals on a per-case basis with different fixed payments for each of 467 different DRGs. DRGs simplify payment rates: Hospitals are reimbursed in advance based on a diagnosis and anticipated hospital stay. Those hospitals with costs below the DRG rate can keep the difference as profit. Hospitals above the rate will lose the excess expenditure. For example, if the DRG rate for a patient with a hip fracture is set at $800 per day for 10 days, hospitals where hip fracture patients are discharged earlier will profit; hospitals with patients who stay longer will lose money.

The introduction of DRGs was (and remains) controversial. Opponents argue that DRGs encourage early discharge of patients and restrict admission of the very poor or very sick. Proponents of DRGs claim that they have improved efficiency and have eliminated unnecessary services without compromising quality. Evaluating the impact of DRGs on hospital use is difficult because, according to data from the U.S. National Center for Health Statistics, hospital admissions had already declined sharply before their introduction. Nonetheless, their introduction has important implications for health care aspects.

Hospital Use. People 65 and over account for about 2 in 5 discharges from acute care hospitals (Statistical Abstract of the U.S., 2000). During the past few decades, due to changes in both technology and medical practice, use of hospitals has decreased among all age groups. Leading reasons for admission among those 65 and older include heart diseases, cancer, fractures, stroke, and pneumonia. Table 12-3 shows the average length of a hospital stay and leading reasons for hospitalization for men and women aged 45 to 64 and 65 and over. As you can see, major diagnoses and length of stay in the hospital differ slightly among these broad age groups and by sex.

Table 12-3 Hospital Discharges and Length of Stay by Two Most Common First-Listed Diagnoses for Men and Women Age 45 and Over, 1998

Men	Most Common Diagnoses	Average Days of Stay
Age 45–64	1. Heart diseases	4.5
	2. Injuries and poisoning	5.8
Age 65–74	1. Heart diseases	4.8
	2. Cancers	7.5
Age 75+	1. Heart diseases	5.6
	2. Pneumonia	7.1
Women		
Age 45–64	1. Heart diseases	4.8
	2. Injuries and poisoning	5.0
Age 65–74	1. Heart diseases	5.1
	2. Injuries and poisoning	6.7
Age 75+	1. Heart diseases	5.3
	2. Injuries and poisoning	6.3

Source: *Statistical Abstract of the U.S.* (2000: Table 200).

Length (and type) of care varies not only according to the age of the patients but also by location and control of the hospital facilities. Moreover, norms for best practice are set by practitioners in a geographic area rather than by consensus on best practice. A person living in Takoma Park, Maryland, for example, is 10 times more likely to be screened for colon cancer than his or her age peer living in Terre Haute, Indiana, and women in the Northeast, Florida, and Michigan are more likely to receive screening for breast cancer than those living in other parts of the United States (Dartmouth Atlas of Health Care, 1999). What determines the difference in rates relates to the number of hospital beds and surgeons in a given area: more beds lead to more medical admissions, and more surgeons lead to more operations. Rural hospitals, which are more likely to serve a higher percentage of poor and minority elderly, are also more likely than those in urban areas to face the likelihood of closure (Alexander, Aunno, & Succi, 1996). Closures of rural hospitals may further limit access to timely hospitalization.

MYTH: MEDICARE COVERS ALL HOSPITAL EXPENSES

Hospital care is not free under Medicare. Part A of Medicare pays all "reasonable" inpatient hospital care in an acute care or short-stay hospital for the first 60 days less a deductible for each period associated with one acute illness. After 60 days as a hospital inpatient for that specific illness, the patient must pay a copayment. If hospitalization is needed for that illness after 90 days in a benefit period, the patient may draw on a 60-day lifetime "reserve," each day requiring a substantial copayment. A patient who uses up both these forms of coinsurance during a spell of illness nonetheless owes the hospital a substantial amount of money, after which his or her coverage under Medicare coverage would cease for any future illnesses.

Medicare does not offer the elderly protection against extraordinary medical bills. The greatest burden of cost is placed on those who are the sickest. Although less than an estimated one-half of 1 percent face such a level of cost sharing in any given year, the older the patient is the more likely is she or he to be hospitalized, to stay longer, and to spend more out-of-pocket. Patients 80 and older not only stay longer in the hospital but are more often discharged to another facility, such as a nursing home, chronic disease hospital, or rehabilitation institution.

Whoever pays the bill for medical care plays a role in the kind of care received. For example, wealthier patients and those with private health insurance are twice as likely to receive heart transplants, even when there is the likelihood that they will not benefit from them, than those poorer, nonprivately insured patients who would be more likely to benefit from organ transplants (Friedman, Ozminkowski, & Taylor, 1992). That is, the wealthy or famous can jump the queue for a transplant even when the outcome is likely to be poor. For example, the former Yankees' baseball player Mickey Mantle apparently jumped ahead to receive a liver transplant despite a history of alcoholism, only to die of cancer shortly thereafter in 1995.

Long-Term Care

Nursing Homes

MYTH: MOST ELDERS ARE IN NURSING HOMES OR
OTHER LONG-TERM CARE FACILITIES

Who Goes into a Nursing Home and Why? One of the most pervasive myths in American society is that most elders live in nursing homes or other long-term care facilities. The opposite is true: Only about 5 percent of old people are in long-term care facilities at any given point in time. The large increase in numbers (but not percentage) of elderly in nursing homes in recent years is due to (1) more people surviving into very old age and (2) the rapid growth of the nursing home industry that supplanted other long-term care facilities, such as state mental hospital geriatric wards and almshouses.

Long-term care, such as that provided by nursing homes, is designed to deliver health, personal care, and social services to people who have lost or never had some degree of functional capacity. Nursing homes are defined as facilities with three or more beds that routinely provide nursing home care (Gabrel, 2000).

The likelihood of ever entering a nursing home is much greater than 5 percent, however, as residents are often discharged after a few months, often to their own homes or similar living arrangements. The median length of a stay is 51 days for men and 69 days for women (Gabrel, 2000). Due to shorter lengths of stays in acute care hospitals, many elders are admitted to nursing homes or chronic care facilities for rehabilitation or continuing care after an acute illness. The elderly most likely to be discharged after hospitalization to a nursing home were older, lived alone, stayed in the hospital longer, and had poorer functional status than those not admitted (Rudberg, Sager, & Zhang, 1994).

Nursing homes also provide terminal care. About a quarter of the discharges occur due to death (National Center for Health Statistics, 2000). At age 65, the likelihood of spending at least some time in a nursing home during the remainder of one's life is estimated at 52 percent for women but 30 to 33 percent for men.

According to data from the National Nursing Home Survey, the typical nursing home resident is a white, widowed woman, 85-years-old or older, with multiple disabilities. Women comprise about three-fourths of nursing home residents, and almost three-fourths are widowed (Gabrel, 2000). In contrast, only about one-third of the men in nursing homes are widowed at admission; slightly more than one-third are still married, and the remainder are separated or divorced or have never been married. African Americans and Latinos/Latinas are far less likely than whites to enter a nursing home or other long-term care facility. Consequently, their families bear a larger burden for their care when they become severely disabled.

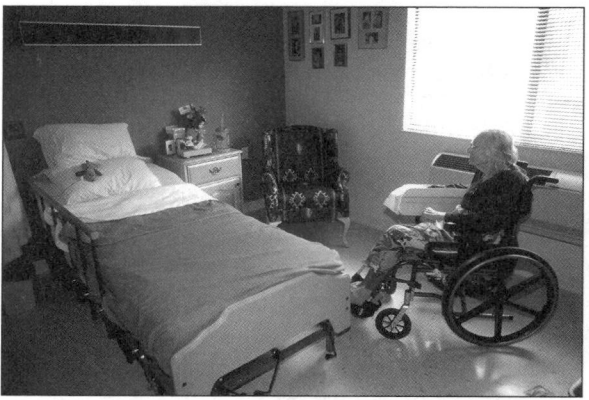

Although the living arrangements of elderly nursing home residents prior to admission vary widely, 46 percent of men and 44 percent of women were admitted from a

What factors contribute to the fact that women will be more likely than men to be admitted and stay longer in a nursing home?

hospital and 31 and 33 percent respectively were admitted from a private household. The majority of nursing home residents need help in performing activities of daily living, as can be seen in Table 12-4.

Table 12-4 Percentage of Nursing Home Residents Aged 65 and Over by Need for Assistance with Activities of Daily Living and Instrumental Activities of Daily Living, 1997		
Received Assistance	**Men**	**Women**
Bathing	94%	99%
Dressing	86	88
Eating	43	46
Moving from bed or chair	23	26
Care of personal possessions	77	77
Managing money	72	72
Securing personal items	75	77
Using telephone	63	62

Source: Gabrel (2000: Table 4). *Monthly Labor Review.* U.S. Department of Labor.

Quality of Life. In future years, many people face the possibility of spending their last months or years in a nursing home or other long-term care facility. How good is the care provided? The answer is, "It depends." Some for-profit facilities are excellent; others are poor. Similarly, some nonprofit or government-owned facilities are outstanding;

others are not. The quality of care is affected by source of payment, social structure of the facility, and sociocultural patterns. Each type of facility has its own peculiar problems: for-profit homes are challenged to maximize profits; public facilities are challenged by the inertia of bureaucracy and uncertainty of appropriations; nonprofit homes are challenged by the availability of funding. Quality of life for patients varies widely. Stories of nursing homes are filled with examples of treating patients as objects, as "senile," agitated, and unreliable—plus incidents of actual physical abuse. Institutional abuse has received much less research attention than domestic abuse, but one study of nurses and nursing home aides found that 36 percent had seen at least one incident of physical abuse by a staff member during the previous year. Ten percent of the nurses reported that they themselves had committed one or more physically abusive acts, and 40 percent admitted to psychological abuse (McDonald, 1996).

Maltreatment of nursing home patients is at least in part a response to highly stressful working conditions. Staff members who are burned out, poorly paid, and who have experienced aggression from residents are at greater risk of being abusive (McDonald, 1996). Although seemingly at the opposite end of the spectrum from abuse is too much care, which can actually turn out to be a type of abuse often overlooked. Specifically, when everything is done for nursing home residents, their activity level and psychological well-being decrease and mortality rates increase (Langer & Avorn, 1985).

The costs of nursing home care, too, are increasingly problematic. The average costs of nursing homes vary widely among states. According to data collected by the AARP, the average cost per day in a nursing home in 1998 was $153, or $56,000 per year (Pandya et al., 2001). Medicare does not cover the cost of nursing home care often, and few elderly or their families can afford to pay for care out-of-pocket for very long. Medicaid, which pays for much of the care, has a "spend-down provision" requiring that the elderly person deplete most of her resources prior to becoming eligible for coverage. In 1998, about $87.8 billion was spent for nursing home care in the United States (Statistical Abstract of the U.S., 2000), and total cost is increasing rapidly as you read this page.

Alternatives to Nursing Homes: Continuing Care Retirement Communities and Assisted Living

Continuing care retirement communities (CCRCs) and *assisted living* are also forms of long-term care for the elderly, but they offer less restrictive settings than a nursing home. As you will recall, approximately 350,000 people reside in CCRCs that provide an age-segregated retirement community with a range of other services, ranging from independent living to nursing home care. Unlike nursing homes, neither Medicare nor Medicaid covers the basic costs of living in a CCRC; expenses for medical care are reimbursed on the same basis as for elders living in their own homes.

How effective are CCRCs in containing health costs? The answer is that we don't know. Studies comparing CCRC residents' health services use with those of non-CCRC residents have not taken into account the atypical characteristics of people choosing a CCRC. Specifically, CCRC residents are better educated, have more money, and are healthier than other people of their age not living in CCRCs. Thus they are likely to use fewer health services than less affluent and more frail elders.

Assisted living, a middle-ground between a nursing home and independent living in the community, provides a range of services to residents up to the point where they need daily nursing or other professional support or assistance on a daily basis. Unlike nursing homes, neither Medicare nor Medicaid covers the cost of assisted living. Assisted living is expensive, with costs ranging from around $31,000 to more than $60,000 per year in 1997 dollars. Although an estimated 15 percent of the elderly could benefit from the services assisted living provides, the cost of such facilities limits their use to the well-off (Heumann & Boldy, 1993).

Although the number of assisted living facilities has grown rapidly in the United States within the past few years, they remain largely unregulated. That the quality of care in assisted living is a primary concern among potential assisted living residents was emphasized in a recent survey of attitudes among a random sample of community-dwelling people aged 50 and over. At least half the respondents voiced worries about having to share a room with another person, receiving low-quality care, being served food they did not like, and having to live with rules and restrictions (AARP Public Policy Institute, 1997). What impact more regulated and affordable assisted living will have on meeting the needs of elders requiring some assistance but not nursing care remains to be seen.

Home and Community Long-Term Care

As health care costs escalate, alternatives to nursing homes have received ever-more attention. Accordingly, a broad array of services has

How likely is it that low-income elders will live in an assisted living facility like this one?

developed to allow older people to remain in their own homes if possible. These include health and home care services, nutrition, adult day care, case management, and other services, some of which are briefly described below.

Health and Home Care. Roughly 1.9 million people over age 65 have chronic physical or mental limitations that require some help at home, and many others have episodes of acute illness making them temporarily dependent on others. The purpose of home health care is to help elders to perform essential activities of daily living that may be difficult because of health problems or functional impairments. It encompasses a range of services to people who need assistance to remain in their own homes: skilled nursing prescribed by a physician; personal care (bathing, dressing, etc.); home help (cooking, shopping, laundry, cleaning); mental health and social services; and legal and financial help. The typical home health care recipient is a white, widowed female over the age of 75 and most likely to be living alone. Heart disease is the most common condition leading to use of home health care; other frequent diseases among home health care users include arthritis, diabetes, and stroke (Statistical Abstract of the U.S., 2000).

Federal law requires all states to provide home health care. Although historically home voluntary and public agencies, such as the visiting nurse service or public health or welfare departments, provided health services, home health care agencies today include both nonprofit and for-profit organizations. About 47 percent of the home health agencies in the United States are for-profit, often local franchises of a health care chain, pharmaceutical company, or other national organization; 44 percent are nonprofit; the remaining are governmental and other agencies (Statistical Abstract of the U.S., 2000). More than 80 percent of these agencies are certified to provide services to Medicare and Medicaid recipients. The Balanced Budget Reconciliation Act passed in the 1990s established prospective payment rates (much like DRGs for hospitals) per-visit, which reduced access to home health care for Medicare recipients (Schlenker, 1996).

Although publicly funded home care usually uses case managers to arrange and monitor services, more recently, Medicaid programs in several states have offered beneficiaries the opportunity to direct their own care. Recipients are responsible for recruiting, hiring, training and supervising the personnel helping them. Although county workers assess the home care needs of applicants based on their level of need and determine the hours of service required, individuals can hire anyone they choose, including family members and spouses. The care recipient certifies the number of hours worked; the state then pays the workers directly. Although numerous variations on this consumer-directed home care pattern exist, research suggests that disabled elders report greater satisfaction and feelings of security when they direct their own long-term care (Tilly, 1999).

Global Glimpses: European Approaches—Paying Caregivers or Elders Directly for Home Care

The United States is not alone in its concern about how to provide less expensive and humane long-term care. Based on the premise that the state has a role to play, several European nations have developed policies to finance long-term care in the community that differ from most current U.S. policies. Britain and the Republic of Ireland have adopted a social security model that pays an allowance directly to informal caregivers to replace the income they have lost from their jobs due to their caring responsibilities. Germany has instituted a "pay-as-you-go" social insurance model, financed by current workers' and employers' contributions. The German social insurance model provides a mix of cash, allowances for services including respite care, and any needed equipment or home adaptations. Benefits are paid directly to dependent elders whose specific benefits vary according to the level of care needed as determined by a medical assessment. France and Italy have adopted a so-called attendance allowance model, which pays a benefit directly to older people for care which they then may use to compensate informal and family caregivers. Entitlement to the allowance depends entirely on the medical and financial situation of the elder.

Each of these different models has strengths and weaknesses, and each makes different assumptions about the role of women as caregivers, the labor market, entitlement to pensions and unemployment in-

surance, and family responsibilities for elder care. A major strength of the social security model in Britain and the Republic of Ireland is its explicit recognition of the rights of caregivers to an income for earnings foregone by caregiving responsibilities. Yet, the payments are very low, with the result that caregivers not only feel underpaid but also have little protection against long-range poverty. Moreover, social security payments are available only to caregivers of working age and thus exclude large numbers of older caregivers, especially women who may be caring for a disabled spouse.

Both the French and Italian models, while recognizing the autonomy of the older person, have the disadvantage of ignoring the needs or circumstances of the caregiver. A basic assumption of this model is that all care needs will be met by the caregiver to whom the payment is transferred, and no additional formal care will be provided. In contrast, the German model, which also provides payments directly to the care recipient, is built on the assumption that formal or informal services, or a combination of both, is possible.

Although the German system of social insurance is the most comprehensive plan when compared with the other nations described above, questions have been raised about the appropriateness of eligibility criteria. Since eligibility is based purely on medical assessment, this scheme is likely to underestimate the social care needs of mentally ill or memory-impaired elders.

Moreover, the program does not recognize the caregiver's right to an independent income. Although the dignity of older people is respected by making direct payments to them, caregivers remain entirely dependent on the older person to reimburse them for the care they provide. Finally, because of the pay-as-you-go nature of Germany's system, future increases in the elderly population may mean that there are not enough workers to pay for needed elder care.

What lessons, if any, can we learn from the experience of these na-tions? Should elders in need of care be paid directly and given options about how they spend this money? Or should informal caregivers be paid directly for providing home care? Should they receive any protection in the form of unemployment insurance and pensions when their caregiving responsibilities end and they need or wish to reenter the job market? How best could eligibility for community-based care be determined?

Source: Based on Glendinning, Schunk, & McLaughlin (1997: 123–140).

A patchwork of funding sources provides coverage for home care in the United States. Medicare Part A covers skilled nursing service ordered by a physician and does not require a deductible or coinsurance; nor does Medicare require prior hospitalization or limit the number of days one may receive services (National Academy on Aging, 1995). Medicare covers home health care only if provided by a Medicare-certified home health agency. Medicaid is the largest source of funding for other home care. Some states provide partial service to persons of any income level, based on functional limitations and family supports, but require participants with higher incomes to share the costs if they are above the poverty level. Other states provide home care only to people of low income. As you will recall from earlier in this chapter, eligibility for Medicaid coverage varies because each state administers its own Medicaid program. Per capita expenditures for home and community-based care also vary widely from state to state; for example, in 1996 California spent $88 per home care visit and Vermont, only $45 (AARP, 1998).

Adult Day Care. Adult day care is designed to allow people to remain in their own homes but get needed services. Usually, a person attends an adult day care center for several hours a day and then returns home. Adult day care comprises four major types of service: (1) day hospitals designed to meet medical needs after an acute illness; (2) social and health centers that provide some nursing and social supports for the chronically ill or disabled; (3) psychosocial centers for the mentally ill or cognitively impaired, including people with Alzheimer's disease or chronic mental illnesses such as schizophrenia; and (4) social centers, such as specialized senior centers (Weiler & Rathbone-

McCuan, 1978). Adult day care gives an individual needed services and social and rehabilitative activities, and gives family members a respite from the day-to-day care of an elderly relative.

Family Caregiving. Families, however, provide the major source of care for infirm elders. Informal caregiving for elders involves activities in two basic areas: (1) providing direct care, such as bathing, dressing, meal preparation, bill paying, and home maintenance; and (2) managing the care provided by others, assessing needs, planning services, arranging for paid or unpaid help, and monitoring the care received. As you will recall from Chapter 8, the majority of family caregivers are women.

Health Care Providers and the Elderly

As a nation, we devote about 80 percent of health care resources to chronic disease, yet available evidence suggests that health care providers stereotype the elderly as much as do people in the general population. Because of stereotypical beliefs, health practitioners may encourage "learned helplessness" among their older patients. Learned helplessness is just that; if we treat someone as helpless, he or she becomes helpless. Learned helplessness is more likely when people are placed in more protected settings (e.g., nursing homes) than they need, if they are given unnecessary home health supports, or if they are left out of decision making about their care. People change their behavior to meet the expectations of those around them, thus losing both ability for self-care and decreasing their quality of life.

How did negative attitudes toward the elderly come to dominate among the health care professions? As you will recall from earlier discussions in this book, old age became medicalized during the past two centuries. Before the nineteenth century, physicians did not prescribe specifically for the elderly, and all adults regardless of age received the same treatment. During the nineteenth and early twentieth centuries, however, old age began to be equated by physicians, welfare workers, and others with mental and physical decay, disease, and poverty. To be old was to be sickly, senile, and in need of supervision.

The notion that old age was a state of decay is reflected today in the lack of education about normal aging and the diverse health needs of people as they grow old. Only recently has geriatrics been recognized as a medical specialty in the United States, and relatively few health professionals take required courses dealing with the biological, social, and psychological aspects of old age. In medical schools, for example, ageism, reinforcement of negative attitudes toward older patients by faculty and medical residents, lack of excitement about treating chronic disease, and lack of positive and rapid "cures" for chronic conditions coupled with competition from other subjects all contribute to lack of enthusiasm for older patients. Physicians report having more problems with elderly patients, provide them with less information and support, and are less egalitarian, less engaged, and less respectful with older patients (Adelman, Greene et al., 1990; Black & Kapoor, 1990). The greater time and effort required to diagnose and treat older patients coupled with knowledge deficits about aging processes also are barriers in communicating effectively with older patients (Beall et al., 1991; Garrity & Lawson, 1989). Even though older patients are slower to provide information, physicians spend less time with older than younger patients (Haug & Ory, 1987). Moreover, physicians rarely discuss personal habits or psychosocial issues with older patients and are less likely to engage them in joint decision-making about care (Adelman, Greene, et al., 1990; 1992). Such attitudes and behavior have a rebound effect on older patients and increase both their passivity and indignation in medical encounters (Greene et al., 1986). The reactions of some older people in a focus group where they were discussing problems in medical encounters are described in Table 12-5. Yet, this situation is gradually changing. Increasing numbers of programs to train health professionals about aging are being established. The ripple effect of greater exposure and knowledge about normal aging versus aging as inevitable decay will hopefully increase not only the quality and context of health care but also elders' abilities to make their health care preferences known.

Health Promotion, Self-Help, and Self-Care

At the same time that the costs of health care have been escalating, emphasis on health promotion and self-care has become more popular. Television shows often feature physicians who discuss medical problems; newspapers include health care columns; and numerous self-care and health promotion books and articles, ranging from low-salt recipes and the benefits of physical exercise to guides on how to live with arthritis, heart disease, and so forth, have been published. Several factors contribute to the current enthusiasm for health promotion and self-care including the following: (1) the consumers' movement in general and demands for improved health care in particular; (2) criticisms of the health care establishment as greedy, expensive, and self-serving; (3) beliefs that individuals should have primary responsibility for their own health care; and (4) very importantly, potential for health promotion to reduce the rising costs of health care in later life.

The passage of the National Consumer Health Information and Health Promotion Act in the 1970s established the federal government's responsibility to inform the public about health promotion through nutrition, exercise, and other preventive health approaches. HMOs and fee-for-service practitioners also stress prevention as a way to preserve health throughout the lifespan. The U.S. Public Health Service report *Healthy People 2000,* emphasized the importance of personal responsibility for health, identifying health promotion and disease prevention as "perhaps our best opportunity to reduce the ever-increasing portion of our resources that we spend to treat preventable illness and functional impairment" (U.S. Department of Health and Human Services, 1991: v).

Table 12-5 Some Older People Speak About Their Health Care Dissatisfaction	
Type of Complaint	**Patient Views**
Insufficient time with a physician	"It's an assembly line—is the doctor reading my chart correctly?"
	"When I go to the vet, my dog gets more individual attention than I do at the clinic!"
	"Some doctors are in such a hurry that it makes me forget why I came."
Insufficient information	"The doctor sits writing things down while I am there; he doesn't tell you what he is writing and you think you may have a horrid disease."
	"Why don't they speak English, not medical terms!"
Insufficient coordination of care	"Why can't I see just one doctor? I have to go to a different doctor for each part of my body, and these doctors don't usually talk with each other."
	"I put together a whole medical record to give to each doctor, but only one read it!"
Long waits to see the physician	"I had an 11:00 a.m. appointment, and I was seen at 3:45! They resented that I dared to complain."
	"I am kept waiting in a small, closed room; the worst time was when I saw the doctor for only 3 minutes."

Source: Personal communication to author, Boston Focus Groups With Elders on Their Medical Care, 10/5/99.

It is ironic, however, that health promotion, self-help, and self-care are seen as newcomers in health care. Self-care accounts for about 85 percent of all health care in the world and makes it possible to save any health care system from being swamped (Butler et al., 1979–1980). In Western industrialized nations, only about one-fourth to one-half of all illnesses result in contact with professional providers of health care, and many of those who do seek formal medical care have already treated their conditions themselves, most often appropriately. And, according to one study, more than 5 out of 6 people (86.3 percent) aged 55 and over treated themselves for at least one medical condition that ranged from minor to serious (Kart & Engler, 1994).

Health promotion, self-care, and self-help are based on the idea that we can increase individual capacity to do what people have always tried to do—take care of themselves—through greater knowledge. Health promotion and self-care are activities related to individual lifestyle. Good health is directly related to such basic and individual self-care activities as adequate nutrition, exercise, regular sleep, stress control, weight control, smoking cessation, and limited alcohol use. Self-care indicates one's deliberate action for one's own well-being and focuses on individuals. Health promotion programs supplement and provide appropriate materials for more informed self-help. Self-help usually refers to a group of people who share common concerns, such as Smokers Anonymous, Alcoholics Anonymous, Widow-to-Widows, Alzheimer's disease support groups, and so forth. Giving a complete listing of health promotion, self-care, or self-help programs for the elderly in the United States is impossible, for activities range from individual exercise to bereavement groups. Top health promotion priorities listed in the recent *Healthy People 2010* that are especially relevant to the older population include nutrition and exercise.

Nutrition. The importance of *nutrition* in health promotion and self-care has attracted particular attention because of its relationship both to disease and to obesity. Diet is associated with 5 of the 10 leading causes of death: coronary heart disease, stroke, some types of cancer and diabetes, and arteriosclerosis. For example, high cholesterol levels in the body put us at risk of heart disease; in turn, high cholesterol has been related to an intake of saturated (animal) fats. Accordingly, nutritionists, physicians, and other health care professions advise diets that include fruits and vegetables, grains, fat-free dairy products, fish, and poultry but limit such high-cholesterol foods as red meat, high-fat dairy products, lard, and so forth. Low-salt diets have also become popular and are believed to reduce hypertension and fluid retention associated with heart disease as well as other conditions. The importance of fiber in the diet has been emphasized as a preventive against bowel cancer, other gastrointestinal disorders, and high cholesterol.

Nutritional status is thus related to chronic disease risk, ability to maintain an independent lifestyle, and rate and length of hospital stays. For example, findings from a study of nuns show that participants with an annual weight loss of 3 percent or more had a 2.7 to 3.9 times greater likelihood of becoming dependent in activities of daily living compared with nuns with no weight change (Tully & Snowdon, 1995). Elderly women who are underweight may also be at greater risk of placement in a nursing home; data from the Framingham study indicate that underweight is a significant predictor of subsequent nursing home admission for elderly females and is related to chronic conditions (Markson et al., 2000).

Obesity, too, is a major health problem for Americans throughout the life course. Fully 54 percent of Americans of all ages are overweight, and 19 percent are classified as obese. Among those 65 and over, 54 percent are also overweight and 16 percent are obese. African Americans are most likely to be overweight and obese and Asian and Pacific Islanders least likely (Statistical Abstract of the U.S., 2000). Obesity has been linked to increased risks of various cancers. Paradoxically, being fat is not an indication of good nutrition, but reflects diets high in cooking fats, fast foods and snacks, spreads, meats, and whole milk dairy products. Lack of exercise also contributes to obesity. *Healthy People 2010* includes control of weight and increased exercise among its 10 top indicators of health.

Although estimates of the extent of malnutrition vary, significant proportions of older Americans are either malnourished or at risk of malnutrition. Several federal programs provide nutritional assistance to Americans, two of which are designed to combat dietary deficiencies among the elderly: the *congregate meals* program and the *home-delivered meals* program. Established by the Older Americans Act, both programs must meet one-third of the daily recommended dietary allowances. Although neither program has an income restriction, funding restrictions limit the numbers of people served. Congregate meals, usually served in senior centers or churches, are often coordinated with other services such as transportation; home-delivered meals (Meals on Wheels) are targeted to the homebound elderly.

According to one survey of congregate and home-delivered meal recipients, over one-fourth were at high risk for malnutri-

Meals on Wheels allows many older people not only to have well-balanced meals delivered to their homes, but to enjoy social contacts with the volunteers who deliver them.

tion (Vailas & Nitzke, 1995). Up to 65 percent of the hospitalized elderly may be protein-energy undernourished at admission or develop serious nutritional deficits while hospitalized (Sullivan, 1995). In addition to specific medical conditions, social factors, psychological factors, sensory impairments, dental problems, and functional impairments contribute to weight loss or malnutrition. Poverty and social isolation can result in inadequate food intakes. Elders living alone or with nonrelatives are more likely to be poor and thus at nutritional risk than older people living in families. Not only do they lack the incentive to prepare a meal which only they will eat, but they often must choose between spending money on food or on prescription medications.

Proportionately more elderly women living alone are at high risk of malnutrition than men, as they are more likely than older men to live at or below the official poverty level. Especially at nutritional risk due to poverty are older African-American women who live alone, about half of whom are poor. Other elders, whether living alone or with a spouse or other relatives, may be at nutritional risk due to lack of knowledge about appropriate foods and food preparation. People who are recently bereaved, depressed, or with caregivers who are employed are also at nutritional risk. Local elder nutrition programs, such as congregate meals or Meals on Wheels, can provide both a source of needed nutrients and social contact. A report evaluating the Elderly Nutrition Program found that, on the average, both congregate and home-delivered meal participants have about 14 more social contacts per month than a matched comparison group of nonparticipants (Ponza & Millen, 1996).

Exercise. Exercise, too, has assumed greater importance as a self-care program for all age groups. Since the 1980s, growing evidence shows that much of the physiological decline associated with old age is due to inactivity. According to the U.S. Public Health Service, over 40 percent of those 65 and over engage in no leisure time physical activity; less than 10 percent engage in any vigorous health activity. Throughout adulthood, women are less likely to exercise than men. Exercise throughout adulthood also varies by race and ethnicity and by level of education. Latina adult females and non-Latina, African-American females are less likely to exercise than are whites, and the likelihood of being sedentary is greatest among women who are poor (see Figure 12-1).

For some time, evidence has indicated that regular physical activity is associated with lower rates of heart disease, high blood pressure, some forms of diabetes, and colon cancer (U.S. Department of Health and Human Services 1991). Exercise also increases bone mineral content, reduces the likelihood of fractures, decreases body fat, and increases lean body mass (Evans, 1999; Frontera & Evans, 1986; Lampman, 1987). It also improves balance and may reduce the likelihood of falls (Rubenstein et al., 2000). Research has shown that even nursing home residents in their 90s can benefit from increased levels

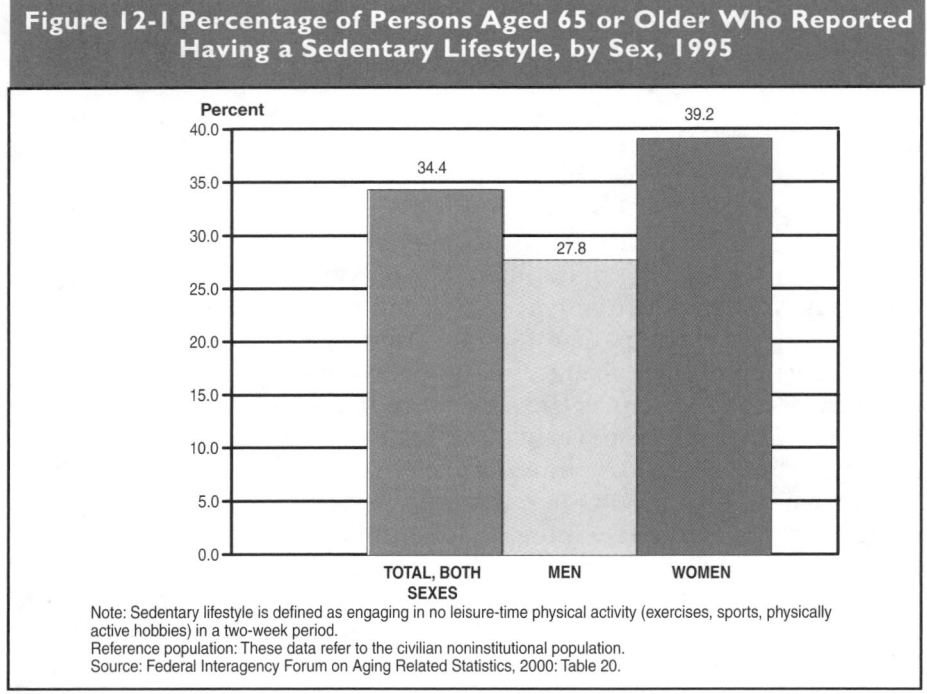

Figure 12-1 Percentage of Persons Aged 65 or Older Who Reported Having a Sedentary Lifestyle, by Sex, 1995

Note: Sedentary lifestyle is defined as engaging in no leisure-time physical activity (exercises, sports, physically active hobbies) in a two-week period.
Reference population: These data refer to the civilian noninstitutional population.
Source: Federal Interagency Forum on Aging Related Statistics, 2000: Table 20.

of exercise (Fiatarone et al., 1994). Moreover, exercise at any age has psychological benefits, reducing anxiety, depression, and boredom.

Issues in Self-Help and Self-Care. The popular appeal of self-care and self-help raises several important social issues: (1) To what extent are these likely to be dominated by commercialism? (2) To what extent do these programs prevent or relieve chronic disease or illness? (3) Do such programs create a false sense of health that result in delays in seeking medical treatment when appropriate? Each of these questions is discussed briefly below.

Commercialism. Although the number of organized health promotion, self-help, or self-care programs for the elderly is unknown, a limited sampling shows that sponsors of such enterprises range from large governmental organizations to small, informal groups. Hospitals, universities, local health departments, municipal councils on aging, churches, private organizations such as the Y, and commercial ventures and franchises all may sponsor health promotion, self-help, or self-care activities. Funds for programs come from numerous sources, ranging from governmental appropriations to participant fees. Although the number of commercial ventures targeted at the elder market is still small, it is not difficult to imagine that organizations, such as weight control and exercise spas, increasingly target their marketing to profit from the increasing numbers of older people. This trend already exists in commercials for high fiber cereals, herbal remedies, vitamins, pain relievers, laxatives, and other self-care products aimed at the health-conscious, often older people. The danger in commercialization of self-help and self-care is that the zeal of entrepreneurs to make a profit can mask the inadequate knowledge base for claims made for the product or program. For example, claims that high fiber cereal reduces the likelihood of cancer could prevent some people from getting regular medical checkups inasmuch as they falsely believe they are no longer at risk.

Prevention and relief. Clearly many health promotion techniques, self-care, and self-help activities are useful. Alcoholics Anonymous and smoking cessation programs are but two illustrations of successful self-help approaches to behavior modification. Disease may be prevented and chronic conditions improved by a wide range of nonmedical techniques, such as regular exercise, adequate nutrition, smoking cessation, and so forth. Knowledge of simple medical procedures, such as taking one's blood pressure, can be used by most people to monitor their health. The outcome of many other programs and activities is hard to evaluate. What is needed is a better understanding of the range of self-interventions that increase health and physical functioning and when they should be used.

Delay. Do self-care and self-help training and practices result in delays in seeking appropriate medical treatment? Again, the evidence is scanty, but common sense would lead us to conclude, "It depends on the practice and on the illness." For example, in a study of adults ranging in age from 55 to 98 (median age 67), about one-third of the respondents recommended self-care *only* for such complaints as "feeling cold much of the time" and "feeling anxious much of the time," and one-fourth advocated self-care only for "loss of appetite" and "frequent indigestion or heartburn." Yet, each of these symptoms may be due to a treatable (even serious) illness requiring medical attention. However, very few people recommended self-care for "rapid heart palpitations" or "chest pain during light exercise" (Kart & Engler, 1994), suggesting that they were aware of some symptoms associated with heart disease.

Much of the initial resistance among health professionals to self-care practices has stemmed from their fear that health care consumers may take important health care functions from them in an uninformed way. Simple self-care practices, such as taking one's blood pressure or checking a stool sample for blood, may be effective indicators of when to seek medical advice. But more knowledge about both the meaning of various symptoms, when to consult a physician or other health practitioner, and the outcomes of different self-care practices is needed if we are to handle symptoms appropriately.

Summary

A major issue related to the organization and use of health care is how it is financed. Medical care costs now account for about 14 percent of the gross domestic product of the United States. Spending for Medicare, the public insurance program providing coverage to nearly all people aged 65 and over, has increased dramatically and is expected to continue to rise. Nonetheless, Medicare spending goes to only a very small proportion of elderly and was designed primarily to cover acute rather than chronic illnesses. Individuals still pay out-of-pocket for a large number of health care expenditures. Medicaid, designed for the poor of all ages, varies from state to state and thus many people do not meet its specific criteria.

Population increases plus aging of the population have been relatively unimportant in explaining the increase in health care spending. Economy-wide medical-price inflation and the number of services (including tests) per visit accounted for the major cost increases. Disabilities associated with aging increase the use of both inpatient and outpatient medical services, and members of economically disadvantaged minorities are more likely to have more illnesses. Barriers to health care still exist, as Medicare does not pay all medical and health-related expenses. Managed care plans are designed to control and coordinate use of health care to contain costs, improve quality, or both, but to date the evidence indicates that they have not resulted in lower costs. Nursing homes, continuing care retirement communities, assisted living, and adult day care provide long-term care. Informal caregiving by relatives and friends remains the major source of long-term care.

Health promotion campaigns emphasize the need to prevent illnesses. Adequate nutrition, exercise, and self-care are increasingly recognized as important in preventing chronic illnesses and in increasing physical functioning. Even people in their 90s or beyond can enhance their functioning with exercise.

Key Points

1. Disabilities increase with age as does use of health care services.

2. In the United States, people in the poorest socioeconomic groups and members of racial and ethnic minorities have the highest rates of almost every disease or illness but are less likely to receive advanced medical procedures.

3. Rapidly rising health costs have stimulated policies, including managed care and HMOs and DRGs, that attempt to re-

duce or contain health care expenditures, but their success is difficult to evaluate as length of hospital stays had already begun to decline before DRGs were introduced.

4. Contrary to popular belief, only 5 percent of the elderly are in a nursing home at any given time.

5. The typical nursing home resident is an 85-year-old white, widowed female with multiple disabilities.

6. Less restrictive alternatives to nursing homes include assisted living and continuing care retirement communities (CCRCs); neither the basic living costs of assisted living nor CCRCs are covered by Medicare or Medicaid.

7. Federal law requires all states to provide some kind of home health care, and payment may be through Medicare, Medicaid, or private funds.

8. The major source of care for impaired elderly remains the family, with women providing about three-quarters of informal home care to older relatives.

9. Although about 80 percent of health care resources are devoted to chronic diseases, health care providers stereotype the elderly as much as the general population does.

10. Two significant health promotion activities are good nutrition and exercise throughout the lifespan.

11. Self-care by the elderly, although valuable, requires information about when certain symptoms indicate illnesses requiring medical attention.

Discussion Questions

1. Using the Internet, you can find many sources of up-to-date information about health care of the elderly. An excellent starting point is the Home Page of the Gerontological Society of America (*http://www.geron.org*). Download one document on health care you find there and provide a brief summary to discuss in class.

2. How inevitable are gender and race differences in illness patterns in later life? Are there ways these can be eradicated?

3. Many Americans think nursing homes would be unnecessary if families would care for their aged relatives. Is this a valid argument? Support your position.

4. If you had a family member with a chronic, debilitating, but not fatal illness, what options for care would you consider?

Would you provide it yourself, use other sources, or both? If additional costs are involved, how would the care be paid for?

5. How feasible are exercise programs for the well elderly? Would you want an intergenerational exercise program for adults regardless of age or one specifically for older people? Why? What steps would you take to establish such a program in your community? How would you interest people in participating?

Films and Videos

Can't Afford to Grow Old (video; 55 minutes; available from Filmmaker's Library; 124 E. 40th Street, New York, NY 10016; *www.filmakers.com*).
Winner of numerous awards and narrated and hosted by Walter Cronkite, it details the issues and options of public versus private sector payment for long-term care.

Don't Take My Sunshine Away (video; 55 minutes; available from Filmmaker's Library, 124 E. 40th Street, New York, NY 10016; *www.filmakers. com*).
A national Film Board of Canada production comparing health care programs for elders in different nations, including home health care in Great Britain and Scandinavia.

Not My Home (video; 45 minutes; available from Fanlight Productions, 4196 Washington Street, Boston, MA 02130; *www.fanlight.com*).
Award-winning look at life in a nursing home including interviews with nurses, aides, residents, and family members.

The Chronically Ill: Pain, Profit, and Managed Care (video; 48 minutes; available from Films for the Humanities and Sciences, P.O. Box 2053, Princeton, NJ 08543-2053; *www.films.com*).
A hard look at how the chronically ill fare today in receiving needed long-term care, comparing treatments by for-profit HMOs with the recommendations of independent experts.

Internet Resources

http://www.ahrq.gov
The link to the Agency for Healthcare Research and Quality within the U.S. Public Health Service, and a source of current information on research on health care and costs for people of all ages.

http://www.cms.hhs.gov
The link for the Centers for Medicare and Medicaid Services (formerly the U.S. Health Care Financing Administration), and the source for information on Medicaid and Medicare statistics, data, laws, regulations, and so forth.

http://www.hhs.gov

A useful link for health information, maintained by the U.S. Department of Health and Human Services.

Research Article

Light, D. W. (2000). The sociological character of health care markets. In G. L. Albrecht, R. Fitzpatrick & S. C. Scrimshaw (Eds.), *The Handbook of Social Studies in Health and Medicine* (pp. 394–408). Thousand Oaks, CA: Sage.

A thorough sociological analysis of the workings of health care markets.

Supplemental Readings

Aneshensel, C. S., Pearlin, L. I., Mullan, J. T., Zarit, S. H., & Whitlatch, C. J. (1995). *Profiles in Caregiving: The Unexpected Career.* San Diego, CA: Academic Press.

Both analyzes and sensitizes the reader to the caregiving experience.

Fox, R. C., & Swazey, J. P. (1992). *Spare Parts: Organ Replacement in American Society.* New York: Oxford University Press.

Broad coverage that raises moral and ethical dilemmas for all age groups.

Markides, K. S., & Miranda, M. R. (Eds.). (1997). *Minorities, Aging, and Health.* Thousand Oaks, CA: Sage.

An excellent reader containing articles on mortality, chronic diseases, diet and nutrition, mental health, and health service and long-term care among African Americans, Asians, Latinos, and Native Americans.

Poplin, C. (1997). The piper's tune. In C. L. Wiener and A. L. Strauss (Eds.), *Where Medicine Fails* (pp. 317–332), New Brunswick, NJ: Transaction Books.

An examination of medical costs, managed care issues, and possible directions for the health care system.

Zola, I. K. (1988). Aging and disability: Toward a unifying agenda. *Educational Gerontology, 14,* 365–387.

Although written some time ago, a relevant and excellent analysis of disabilities, their changing nature, the impact of technology and medicalization on chronic care, and ways of empowering those perceived to need care. ✦

Chapter 13

Death, Dying, and Bereavement

Introduction

At age 78, Morris Schwartz, known to everyone as Morrie, knew he was dying of a degenerative neurological disease, amyotrophic lateral sclerosis (ALS), sometimes called Lou Gehrig's disease. ALS gradually destroys the ability of the nerves to send signals to the muscles. The disease has no cure and is fatal.

Still very much alive, Morrie Schwartz, a professor emeritus of sociology at Brandeis University, used his remaining strength to teach one last lesson: to help people to talk openly about illness, deterioration, and the inevitability of death. To accomplish this goal, he appeared on national television shows, such as Nightline with Ted Koppel three times, spoke on the radio, and wrote. Even when unable to hold a microphone and coughing up phlegm, he dictated his thoughts on life and death into a tape recorder. His reflections were published after his death as the book Morrie: In His Own Words (1997). Some of his words are as follows:

> I don't think you can be totally prepared for diminished capacities. . . . You can think about what might happen . . . but until the time actually arrives, you don't have the experience. . . . (1997: 6).

> Learn how to live, and you'll know how to die; learn how to die, and you'll know how to live. . . . The goals I have set for myself . . . during this illness are not unlike those most of us have aspired to since childhood: to behave with courage, dignity, generosity, humor, love, open heartedness, patience, and self-respect. When you are close to death, it is not easier to achieve these goals than at other stages of your life, just more urgent that you try. (Schwartz, 1997: 125–127)

Morrie Schwartz died peacefully at home on November 4, 1995.

Death is not a topic most of us want to think about. Yet, the grim fact is that the mortality rate in life is 100 percent. Death is a reality for all living organisms. What are the chances of dying at a particular age? What are the leading causes of death today? How are your parents' deaths and your own future death likely to be affected by social factors such as race/ethnicity, social class, and gender? How long are you likely to live? How is mortality viewed in our society and what cultural values do our attitudes to death reflect? How do older people react to the loss of a spouse or significant other? Is there a "right to die"? What kind of end-of-life care do you want for your parents, yourself, and other family members in the future? These are the issues raised in this chapter.

Twentieth-Century Mortality Trends

Today in American society, as in all industrialized nations throughout the world, death is most likely to occur in old age. However, the idea of death as most likely to occur when we are old is relatively new. Surprising as it sounds to us today, childhood and infant mortality rates from acute diseases were so high for many centuries that many young children who died did not even have their names recorded! Because infant and childhood death was so common, the death of one's young child was a predictable event. As a seventeenth-century woman observed, "Before they are old enough to bother you, you will have lost half of them, or perhaps all of them" (Aries, 1962: 38). Nor were the deaths of infants or children always unwelcome, for unlike today, children were not regarded as innocent and impressionable beings to be nurtured or treasured. Until the rubber condom was invented about 150 years ago, children were often regarded as sinful, extra burdens. In poor families with many children, some parents wished openly and loudly for their children to die or to leave home, and smallpox, a major cause of infant and

Tombstones provide information both about family composition and longevity of different birth cohorts. How do the lengths of life of this family compare with current life expectancies for males and females in the United States?

childhood death, was actually known as the "poor man's friend" (Van de Walle & Knodel, 1980). Infanticide, abandonment, and starvation of children were common as late as the nineteenth century. According to one observer commenting on London in the 1860s, "the police seemed to think no more of finding a dead child than they did of finding a dead cat or a dead dog" (Langer, 1972: 97, quoted in Skolnick, 1987).

Spotlight on U.S.: How Do Americans Die?

During the twentieth century in the United States, the top 10 leading causes of death changed dramatically, greatly extending the average length of time people can expect to live. With the exception of pneumonia and flu, the communicable, infectious diseases that accounted for the greatest number of deaths a century ago have been replaced by chronic diseases, suicide, and accidents (including motor vehicle accidents). Further, public health measures, nutrition, improved standards of living, and immunizations drastically reduced the threat of infectious diseases.

Leading Causes of Death, 1900 and 2000, Among the American Population

Rank	1900	2000
1.	Pneumonia and influenza	Heart disease
2.	Tuberculosis	Cancer
3.	Gastroenteritis	Stroke
4.	Heart disease	Lung disease
5.	Cerebrovascular diseases	Accidents
6.	Chronic nephritis	Diabetes
7.	Accidents	Pneumonia and influenza
8.	Cancer	Alzheimer's disease
9.	Senility	Nephritis
10.	Diphtheria	Septicemia

Source: *http://www.cdc.gov/nchs/* (accessed 8/14/02).

Even at the beginning of the twentieth century, average life expectancy at birth in the United States was less than 50 years of age. Today, the average life expectancy is more than 76 years, and, although some individuals survived to become old in 1900, people 65 and over today are far more likely to live into their 70s, 80s, 90s, and even to more than 100.

The Changing Demography of Death

Although death occurs mostly in old age in the United States, infants are particularly vulnerable during their first year of life.

Because of their greater susceptibility during the first year of life, the infant mortality rate (the number of deaths among infants under age 1 per 1,000 births) is often used as a key measure of quality of life. Once children live through their first few years of life, their chances of survival increase substantially.

Heart disease, cancer, and stroke, responsible for more than one-half of all deaths in the United States, occur primarily after age 50. Among those 65 and over, conditions accounting for the principal causes of death are (1) heart disease, accounting for more than 1 in every 3 deaths; (2) cancer, explaining 1 in 5 deaths; and (3) stroke, accounting for about 1 in 10 deaths (Statistical Abstract of the U.S., 2000). Primary cause of death, however, understates the numerous health problems experienced by many elderly toward the end of life, and many older people die of multiple causes. For example, an elderly person who dies of pneumonia may have a compromised immune system due to any number of chronic diseases, such as cancer, heart disease, diabetes, AIDS, and so forth.

The expectation for a longer life is relatively recent. As you will recall from earlier in this book, life expectancy does not describe any one real person. Life expectancy is commonly used because we can see what it stands for: the average amount of time people in a society can expect to live. Surprisingly, the older we are, the longer our probable life expectancy. The longer we live, the healthier we are likely to have been throughout our lives, because people with more severe, life-threatening diseases are likely to die earlier. This was true even centuries ago. In 1900, for example, only about 3 percent of all Americans lived to see their 65th birthday, but those who did could expect, on the average, to live another 11.9 years (Treas, 1995); today, they can expect 17.4 more years. For example, elders who reach age 85 or older can expect to live an average of about six more years. Some will live longer than that and some shorter, but on the average, they will die at age 91.

Although death comes to all of us, any individual's chances of dying are affected not only by age but also by one's membership in the social hierarchies of gender, social class, race, and ethnicity. Political factors also play a role; for example, life expectancy in Russia decreased by more than six years after the former Soviet Union broke up and left public health systems in disorder and many Russians in poverty. Genetic factors also play a role, as people with similar social characteristics may die of very different causes and at different ages. But social variables—age, sex, social status, and race/ethnicity—are most closely allied to life expectancy and mortality rates.

Sex, Race, Ethnicity, and Social Class. At every age, females can expect to live longer than males. The gap in male-female life expectancy declines with aging. Regardless of sex or gender, racial and ethnic minorities are likely to die earlier than whites, primarily because they are more likely to be socioeconomically disadvantaged. In 1900,

African Americans could expect to die about 15 years earlier than whites, and, although this racial gap has narrowed, it has not closed. African Americans are more likely than whites to have heart disease and high blood pressure, and their rate of death from strokes and diabetes is twice as high as whites. At very old ages, however, African Americans have lower mortality rates than whites, a pattern called the "black-white mortality crossover" by demographers. Various reasons have been suggested for this including "survival of the fittest"; that is, those African Americans who live into their 80s have successfully survived the numerous threats to their health imposed by poverty and minority status.

Among other racial and ethnic minorities, life expectancy and mortality vary by race and ethnicity. The two leading causes of death for older Native Americans are the same as for the general population (heart disease and cancer), but, reflecting their greater rates of poverty, they are likely to live an average of about four years less than whites. Differences in life expectancy, however, are greatest among younger age groups and females; by age 76, Native Americans have lower age-specific death rates than whites (John, 1997), again reflecting successful survival despite the numerous threats to their health imposed by poverty and minority status.

Although mortality rates vary widely due to socioeconomic and acculturation differences among the many Latino/Latina groups, which can be of any race, their overall mortality rate is close to the national average for all races and ethnicities. As among non-Latino whites, heart disease ranks first as the leading cause of Latinos' death. For a variety of reasons including lifestyle factors, twice as many Latino elders die of diabetes, chronic liver disease, and cirrhosis (Sotomayor, 1995).

On the average, American-born Asians have a longer life expectancy than their white counterparts (McFalls, 1998), explained in part by their generally high socioeconomic status. Data from the 2000 census show that the average family income for Asians is slightly above that of non-Latino whites, and the poverty rates for most Asian groups are lower than for the nation as a whole. Their educational attainment is also the highest of any racial or ethnic subgroup.

Whether male or female, people in lower socioeconomic groups live shorter lives than their same-sex peers of higher social class. A social class, as you remember, describes people sharing similar economic circumstances, prestige, education, and political influence. The major measures of social class membership, such as income, education, and occupation, show a strong relationship between social class membership and mortality (Marmot, 1996; Winkleby et al., 1992), a relationship that increases at older ages both in the United States and elsewhere (Marmot & Shipley, 1996; Fiscella & Franks, 1997).

Not only are those in more disadvantaged social classes more likely to have work-related accidents and be exposed to greater occupational health hazards but they are also more likely to live in overcrowded, inadequate housing, to have poorer diets, and so forth. Medical care, too, remains a problem, for, despite greater health insurance coverage through Medicare and Medicaid, many poor people are treated within the context of "welfare medicine": long waits in clinics or emergency rooms, lack of a consistent primary care physician, and, for the elderly, inability to pay for expensive prescription medications not covered under basic Medicare policies.

Even today, as Antonovsky (1972: 28) pointed out over a quarter of a century ago, "class influences one's chances of staying alive." In the United States as in many other nations, the lower the social class, the more likely are its members to suffer and perhaps die of infectious diseases more typical a century ago, such as tuberculosis. Chronic, life-threatening diseases such as heart disease, hypertension, and diabetes are also more common among the poor than among the upper and middle classes and take their toll at earlier ages. Paradoxically, it is not in the richest countries that people have the longest lives and the best health but in those nations with the smallest gaps between social classes (Wilkinson, 1996).

Although living in the richest nation in the world, Americans at age 65 are more likely, on the average, to die sooner than their age counterparts in various other nations including Japan and Sweden; Table 13-1 summarizes the life expectancy at birth in various industrialized nations. The reason that the United States ranks lower than these

Table 13-1   Life Expectancy at Birth by Sex, Selected Industrialized Nations, 1995

Nation	Female Life Expectancy at Birth	Male Life Expectancy at Birth
Japan	82.9	76.4
France	82.6	74.2
Switzerland	81.9	75.1
Sweden	81.6	76.2
Canada	81.2	75.2
Australia	80.7	75.0
Italy	80.8	74.4
Norway	80.7	74.9
Netherlands	80.4	74.6
United States	78.9	72.5

Source: Report of the U.S. Surgeon General. (2000). *Healthy People 2010.* (Internet download *www.health.gov/healthypeople/Document/HTML/Volume1/goal.htm*, p. 2; accessed 5/18/00.)

nations is due to the substantial difference in life expectancy among different racial, ethnic, and social class groups. Americans would live longer if all of us enjoyed the longer life expectancies attained by more advantaged, higher-status groups in our society.

Will Women Die Like Men in the Future?

A scant century ago, males and females could, on the average, expect to live about the same length of time. Throughout most of the world, today's women have a clear advantage, in part associated with reductions in mortality associated with pregnancy and childbirth. Although men and women suffer the same types of health problems today, what distinguishes men from women is the frequency of these disorders and the time of death (Verbrugge, 1985). For example, although heart disease is the most common cause of death in the United States for both males and females, it becomes the number one killer of men by ages 45 to 64, but the leading cause of death for women only when they are 65 or older (Statistical Abstract of the U.S., 2000). What explains this discrepancy?

One explanation is biological. Despite popular belief, males appear to be the weaker sex; that is, as organisms, males appear to be more vulnerable to death from conception on. According to the census, the miscarriage rate of male fetuses is greater than of female fetuses, and during the first year of life, male babies are more likely to die than female babies. There is also some evidence that females of nonhuman species live longer than males (Sagan, 1987).

Social and psychological factors also play a role. Males are more likely than females to play violent sports and to engage in high-risk behaviors, such as smoking, drinking alcohol, and driving fast. Between 70,000 and 100,000 Americans die annually from disabling occupational diseases, such as cancers caused by exposure to toxic substances, "miners' asthma," and so forth. Not only are men more likely than women to work in settings where the risk of occupational diseases is high, but such traditionally male jobs as logger, airplane pilot, taxi driver, and construction worker also contribute to the higher male death rate.

Work's pressures plus so-called "Type A behavior," typified by competitiveness, repressed anger, and perfectionism, have been linked by some researchers to coronary heart disease and high blood pressure (Ivancevich & Matteson, 1988; Suls & Sanders, 1988), contributing to greater male physical vulnerability and death at earlier ages. Traditional gender role socialization has encouraged competition more for males than females and greater exposure to job-related psychosocial stress. Psychological stress triggers production of stress hormones that increase irregular heartbeats and the heart's need for oxygen, and narrow the arteries, increasing the likelihood of heart attack (Booth-Kewley & Friedman, 1987). Stress hormones also increase blood glucose in people with diabetes, thereby decreasing effective control of this potentially life-threatening disease (Peyrot, McMurry, & Kruger, 1999).

As gender-linked roles have changed in American society, some people have wondered whether the greater longevity enjoyed by females will change. When women adopt more high-risk behaviors and enter paid employment with job stressors and other risks, will the mortality gap between men and women narrow? Or will a biological advantage persist? Women's unpaid labor as parent and housewife has, however, never been stress-free but rather characterized by long hours, recurring and repetitive tasks, and tedium—qualities similar to factory work (Chavkin, 1984).

Working wives and mothers now carry a double burden—the *second shift* of household tasks in addition to paid employment (Hochschild, 1989). The second shift has consequences; some research has indicated that women's multiple roles result in sustained high levels of stress hormones well after leaving work; men's stress hormones peak during the day and decline when they return home after work (Frankenhaeuser et al., 1989; Theorell, 1991). The long-range effect of the "second shift" on mortality patterns, however, is yet to be determined, for as Fremont and Bird (1999: 128) have pointed out, "Sociologists have examined the effects of gender inequality in the labor force and home on psychological distress, but relatively few have assessed physical health consequences." Perhaps if men were to take fewer risks and better care of their health and both job and household roles were more egalitarian, males might enhance their life expectancy and women maintain their apparent biological advantage! What do you think?

Death in American Society

Almost all of us want to live as long as possible, but few of us want either to grow old or to die. Death, an inevitable biological end is, however, much more than a biological state, as it "throws into relief the most important cultural values by which people live their lives and evaluate their experiences" (Huntington & Metcalf, 1972: 2). Four interwoven values in U.S. society shape Americans' contemporary attitudes toward death. First, as part of the Puritan ethic, work and activity are valued as ends in themselves, and inextricably intertwined with one's sense of personal worth. Since crippling illness and death symbolize the end of productivity, death and feebleness are foes to be beaten whenever possible. Second, ours is a nation where self-determination, individual responsibility, and the belief that anyone can do anything if he or she tries hard enough, are part of our cultural mythology. Third, allied to the high value Americans place on individualism is our belief in technology and its ability to modify or control the environment—and, with the advent of genetic engineering, disease and life itself. Illness and death thus should lend themselves to active control, if not actual defeat. Fourth, as Kalish and Reynolds (1976) pointed out more than three decades ago, if there can be said to be a common religion in the United States, it is health and its high priests are physicians. Once the domain of priests and other religious figures, death is now the dominion of physicians, most often in that modern temple of life and death, the hospital.

Fear of Death and Attitudes Toward Dying

"Men fear death as children fear to go in the dark; and as that natural fear in children is increased with tales, so is the other," wrote the sixteenth-century philosopher Francis Bacon (cited in *Oxford Dictionary of Quotations*, 1980: 26) in a statement that reflects the anxiety with which death is viewed. How do people in later life view death when mortality is more imminent? Although a variety of studies have suggested that death anxiety decreases with advancing age, many such studies have relied on simple death anxiety scales that treat attitudes as single, one-dimensional traits (Neimeyer & Fortner, 1995).

Moreover, as Kalish and Kastenbaum (1995) have pointed out, stereotypes about old age lead us to believe that the elderly are ready to die as their lives have lost most of their value. These stereotypes are usually based on false beliefs including the following assumptions:

> Projection of one's own fears of aging. Younger adults often fear the terra incognita of the later adult years . . . (contributing) to a self-perpetuating cycle in which one avoids intimate relationships with elders and, thus reduces the opportunity for a corrective learning experience. . . .
>
> Salve for the social conscience. If society can convince itself that elderly men and women care little for their own lives and are ready for death, then it is easier to accept age-discriminatory practices in employment, health care, housing, and so forth. There is also less felt need to grieve and mourn. . . . (Kalish & Kastenbaum, 1995: 251)

Just as younger people's feelings and beliefs about death vary according to their social circumstances and life experiences, so do older people's. That the elderly may speak of death or make arrangements for their funeral does not mean that they do not cherish life; rather, they are getting details out of the way so that they may continue the business of living (Kalish & Kastenbaum, 1995).

Dying as a Social Process

Our position in the social class structure influences not only how we live but how we die. The death of a public official or popular culture figure is likely to receive more attention than a drunken derelict, a homeless person, or others considered of low social status. For example, the death of Princess Diana of Britain in a Parisian automobile accident in 1998 was reportedly attended with prolonged, intensive attempts to resuscitate her although she was clearly unlikely to respond. Discrimination (on the basis of gender, race, or ability to pay) about the kind of care given to the dying exists: a survey of organ transplants in 500 hospitals showed that women were nearly half as likely as men and minorities one-fourth as likely as whites to receive heart or liver transplants, and ability to pay also improved the odds of getting a transplant for patients with similar expected years of survival (Ozminskowski, Friedman, & Taylor, 1993).

Older people, too, often receive less treatment than younger people when they are dying, primarily because of ageist assumptions (Blauner, 1968). In one hospital studied by Sudnow (1967: 74),

> Two persons in "similar" physical condition may be differentially designated as dead . . . a young child was brought into the ER with no registering heartbeat, respiration, or pulse—the standard "signs of death" and was . . . revived for a period of eleven hours. On the same evening . . . an elderly person who presented the same physical signs . . . arrived in the ER and was almost immediately pronounced dead, with no attempts at stimulation instituted. . . . During the period when emergency resuscitation equipment was being readied for the child, an intern instituted mouth-to-mouth resuscitation. This same intern was shortly relieved by oxygen machinery. . . . [When the old woman was admitted to the ER], he was the one who pronounced her dead. He reported shortly afterwards that he could never bring himself to put his mouth "to an old lady like that."

The Dying Trajectory. It is important to remember that, while both life and death are biological states, their meanings are social creations. How and when we die and the significance of death itself, as well as how we live, reflect the values of a particular culture within a historical context (Aries, 1974). Dying is thus more than a physiological process or physical act; it is also a social process with a trajectory or path with a specific shape and duration (Strauss, 1997). Duration may vary widely, even among patients with the same illness; for example, a person may be expected to die of a specific cancer within six months but may die sooner or exceed all expectations for survival. Expectations for the duration of a terminal illness are socially defined and vary according to the definers; for example, a physician may define the length of time an individual has to live based on clinical experience and knowledge of the disease, but a family member may base it on intuition and first-hand information about the patient's personal characteristics.

The shape of a terminal illness, too, varies and is socially defined. Some people perceive the terminally ill individual as in a straight, downward, irreversible, and predictable decline; others view the same patient's illness as characterized by peaks and valleys. For example, consider the situation in which an elderly woman goes into a coma after surgery. Nursing personnel may view her death as imminent and advise the family accordingly. Family members, however, may believe that she will regain consciousness and live for some months if not years. The decisions about the kind of care this woman will receive are likely to be influenced by these opposing views about the shape and duration of her condition. Even if the physician and hospital staff agree that she will die without regaining consciousness and urge the family to withdraw active treatment, it is at least possible that she may do otherwise. However defined by the dying individual, physicians, hospital staff, and family members, the duration and shape of the dying trajectory are very likely to influence the care one receives as well as how others interact with the dying person.

Reversing the Dying Trajectory: A Family Member Speaks

When my 70-year-old mother had surgery for an invasive skin cancer, her physician assured both of us that it was routine. Shortly after returning from a successful and uneventful operation in which the cancer was totally removed, however, she took a turn for the worse and went into a coma. I was distressed to hear the floor nurses, interns, and residents describe MY mother as a sweet old lady who really could not be helped any more—whose time had come! They saw an old woman who had gone into a coma; I saw my mother. Their attitude motivated me to do something. Feeling that she needed more care than the floor nurses could provide, I contacted her physician and arranged to hire private registered nurses to be with her around the clock. Because Mother had also become incontinent while in the coma, one private nurse wanted to insert a Foley catheter—an idea that I resisted. After one day, another private nurse informed me that my mother would probably die that night and began to treat mother as if she were already dead, placing her body in tightly wound sheets. Hysterically, I called my husband and told him to come immediately. Although neither my husband nor I knew anything about comas, we saw that Mother was muttering and trying to move.

When I placed an emergency call to her physician to discuss the situation and how she was being treated, he agreed that she should not have a catheter and that we should fire the nurse who expected her to die. Because we did not believe that Mother was dying, we naively decided to stimulate her as much as possible—playing the television, pasting pictures done by her 8-year-old grandchild at eye level next to her bed, and talking to her. With the help of a new and more sympathetic private nurse that her physician recommended, we even dragged her in a comatose state to the bathroom at periodic intervals. This nurse was great—constantly coming up with ways to arouse Mother. After several days of this stimulation (or annoyance!), Mother came out of the coma, was no longer incontinent, and returned home where she lived independently for 23 more years. I think that if I had accepted the judgments of the floor nurse and the private nurse, she would have died in the hospital (anonymous personal communication to author).

Awareness of Dying. How aware the dying person is of impending death is also socially managed. Glaser and Strauss (1965) described awareness of dying among people not in a comatose state as follows: (1) *closed awareness;* (2) *suspected awareness;* (3) *mutual pretense awareness;* and (4) *open awareness.* Closed awareness describes the social situation where the hospital staff and physician know the patient is dying but the patient is unaware of the fact due to inability to recognize the signs of terminal illness. Organization of the hospital to conceal information, reluctance of the staff and the family to discuss dying with the patient, and lack of anyone to help the patient find out the facts maintain a state of closed awareness. Suspected awareness occurs when the patient suspects but is uncertain that the illness is fatal; in this social context, family and staff are also reluctant to disclose information. Mutual pretense awareness is just that; the patient, staff, and family know that the illness is terminal but do not discuss it openly: a kind of "I know that she knows but she doesn't know that I know that she knows" social situation. Open awareness occurs when everyone knows and openly admits that death is approaching.

Physical and Social Death. Regardless of the patient's age or social characteristics, the definition of death is problematic, and various definitions have been proposed, especially with the development of life extension technology. Heart stoppage is no longer the criterion of death because it is possible that heart function can be restored even though the person may never regain consciousness or brain functioning. Kastenbaum (1986) has made a useful distinction between physical death and personal death. *Physical death* is, according to one legal dictionary, "the cessation of life; permanent cessations of all vital functions and signs" (Nolan & Nolan-Haley, 1990: 400). This definition encompasses two states: (1) irreversible arrest of circulation and respiration; or (2) irreversible brain death including the brain stem. Personal death differs from physical death as the individual may remain technically alive but unable to initiate action or to respond to others in a meaningful way. One has lost autonomy and control over even the most basic functions and actions of life.

The term *social death* (Sudnow, 1967: 74) adds still another dimension to the concept of death: "that point at which socially relevant attributes of the patient begin permanently to cease to be operative as conditions for treating him [sic]." Social death does not necessarily coincide with personal death or with physical death but rather describes the situation in which a person is treated as an object. For example, so-called "comatose" patients are treated as essentially dead, and the patients' conditions and future are freely discussed by hospital personnel in their presence. The person is treated as a corpse when he or she is in a coma and does not respond to verbal or visual stimuli. Although some coma survivors have reported details of things said about them while they were in a coma, whether or not the comatose person is able to hear is not considered; nor is the possibility addressed that nonresponsiveness may be due to inability to respond but not to feel or hear, even though personal or physical death has not occurred (Sudnow, 1967). The situation described in the box on the dying trajectory is one example of social death where the woman in a coma was regarded by hospital staff as if she had already ceased to exist.

The Bureaucratization of Death

No longer do most Americans die at home. Over three-fourths of U.S. deaths take place in some kind of health care facility; less than 1 in 5 occur at home; and the remainder occur in other places (Edmonson, 1997). Among those aged 85 and older, slightly less than half die in an acute care hospital because they are most likely to die in a long-term care facility such as a nursing home. Only a very few of the very old (about 6 percent) die at home. The separation of illness and death reduces the average American's exposure to death and dying and to the reminder that we, too, are mortal. It also lessens the social vacuum caused by the disruption in social relationships that ensues when a member of society dies (Blauner, 1968).

Once the province of the family and the community, death has become not only medicalized but bureaucratized; hospitals and nursing homes control and routinize the handling and care of the dying, and funeral homes and cemeteries prepare and arrange cremation or burial of the dead. As defined by the sociologist Max Weber (1946), bureaucratization is characterized by (1) hierarchical authority; (2) structured written communication channels such as records; (3) division of labor implying specialization; (4) expert training for individuals fulfilling specific roles; and (5) impersonality.

As part of the bureaucratization of death, hospitals—and today, nursing homes and other long-term care institutions—are organized to routinize death and make it invisible both to other patients and, whenever possible, to visitors. For example, dying patients may be moved into a private room to avoid troubling other patients and their visitors when death is foreseen, and bodies are generally not removed during visiting hours (Sudnow, 1967). The dying person typically has little control over what is taken out of or put into his or her body; instead, decisions are made by hospital or nursing home personnel, physicians, and family members, with very little input by the dying. He or she has become an object to be processed as effectively and efficiently as possible according to standardized procedures and a set division of labor among physicians, nurses, nurses aides, and orderlies. Written records document the care given and the process of dying.

Medical and nursing personnel also have structured routine procedures to cover, remove, and identify the dead, to inform relatives, and to complete death certificates. In one county hospital described by Sudnow (1967), even the administration of the Catholic last rites is routinized and becomes part of the patient's hospital record; after completing rounds on each ward, the priest rubber-stamps the record of those patients to whom he has given extreme unction to indicate that the rites have been administered. This procedure ensures that the rites are not performed twice on the same person.

Disposal of the deceased follows a hierarchical pattern. After death occurs, death is "pronounced" by a physician according to established procedures. Physicians do not handle dead bodies unless autopsies are to be performed; dealing with corpses, again an established set of procedures, is left to lower-status personnel in the hospital or nursing home hierarchy. The handling of corpses is an unwelcome chore, and, whenever possible, personnel leave a body to be handled by the next shift. Bodies are removed to the facility morgue, usually located on the ground floor in an inaccessible area and with a suitable exit leading to a private loading platform concealed from patients and the public. Funeral home vans to remove the dead from hospitals, nursing homes, or elsewhere are most often unmarked or disguised as ambulances, minimizing the intrusion of death. These structured procedures, record-keeping, clear lines of hierarchy, and division of labor increase the efficiency with which the dying and dead are handled. They also increase the impersonality of the dying experience because the efficiency of hospital and nursing home personnel would suffer if they were deeply affected by each death.

As part of the process of bureaucratization, dying and death have become big business. Hospitals, nursing homes, and the funeral industry employ numerous personnel whose task is to attend the dying and handle the dead—tasks that were once managed by the family and the community without payment. Not only material objects (e.g., medication and space in a hospital or nursing home) but also the whole range of health care services are commodities; that is, they are objects to be purchased, whether through insurance plans or out-of-pocket. Similarly, supervision of the dying and care of the dead are commodities to be bought and sold. Disposition of the body after death is purchased, often at great financial cost, for buying an elaborate funeral in a consumer-oriented culture such as ours is often regarded as a final mark of respect.

Funeral Practices. Funerals, too, have become bureaucratized. No longer do the family and members of the community have primary responsibility for the burial of the dead; the funeral industry has assumed this role. Increasingly, chains dominate the more than $25 billion funeral business in the United States; by 1998, three chains owned 15 percent of the nation's more than 25,000 funeral homes and handled about one in every five funerals (Horn, 1998). In addition, one of these three chains owns a firm that scatters ashes at sea; another has purchased a portion of the largest cemetery in North America. As a web page of the National Academy of Mortuary Sciences states, "Funeral homes that used to be 'mom and pop' operations are selling out by the hundred[s] to large corporations. These corporations, many publicly held, are combining the professionalism of the past with modern business practices. . . ." (*www.drkloss.com*). Two other companies handle two-thirds of all casket and urn sales; one of these also owns the largest prepaid funeral insurance company in the United States (Horn, 1998).

Death is financially costly both for the survivors and people who prepay their own funerals. According to the Funeral and Memorial Societies of America, a national network of memorial societies interested in reducing the financial costs to survivors, the average cost of a funeral in the United States is $4,500, more than three times that in Great Britain ($1,650), and over twice the cost of a funeral in Australia ($2,100) or France ($2,100). Between 1993 and 1998, funeral prices rose three times faster than the cost of living. Although the Federal Trade Commission now requires that funeral homes provide an itemized list of costs to the person responsible for arrangements, under FTC rulings funeral homes can make a "nondeclinable service charge" that is added to other items of service. This charge is for the services of the funeral director and staff and enables the facility to recover its overhead and operational costs. The nondeclinable service charge and other items at one privately owned midwestern funeral home are given in Table 13-2. Although many people believe that embalming is required by law, it is optional except in certain circumstances; however, typical charges for an unembalmed body may include disinfection of the body, refrigeration/sheltering of the body, and dressing and casketing ($425, $75, and $200, respectively, at the midwestern funeral home detailed in Table 13-2).

As you inspect the charges shown in the table, keep in mind that these costs are not at the high end of the scale. Nationwide, prices range according to the geographic locale, ownership, and megamarketing strategies of the facilities; even in the same community, some funeral homes charge more than $10,000 for essentially the same service and casket that costs $1,500 at another. Even at this one funeral home, the cost of caskets ranges widely—from the cheapest, described as "cloth-covered wood," to the most expensive in solid mahogany. Not shown in the table are special items such as clothing that may be purchased for the deceased including under-wear, hosiery, shoes, and suits or dresses specifically designed with a slit in the back for easy prepara-tion of the body. Cremation as an alternative to burial of the body is increasing in popularity; about 21 percent of the dead in the United States are cremated. Although cheaper, cremation can also be expensive; at the same facility shown in Table 13-2, direct cre-mation ranged from $1,495 to $1,810.

This display at a free fair for older people provides incentives for prepayment of funeral expenses. Is prepaying an advantage?

Table 13-2 Basic Costs and Optional Charges at One Midwestern Funeral Home as of January 1999	
Service	**Cost**
Basic nondeclinable service charge	$1,775
Transfer of remains to funeral home (within 20-mile radius)	200
Basic embalming	575
Basic dressing, casketing, cosmetology	325
Use of facilities and staff for visitation/viewing—per hour cost	125
Use of facilities and staff for private viewing	125
Use of funeral coach	175
Transfer car	115
Registration book	40
Acknowledgment cards (25 cards)	5
Casket (from cheapest to most expensive)	350–10,148
Totals	**$3,810–$13,608**

American funeral practices and the funeral industry have been sharply criticized for many years; most notable was the 1963 expose by Jessica Mitford, *The American Way of Death* (published again in 1999 as *The American Way of Death Revisited*). Numerous consumer efforts are being made to inform people about the high cost of dying; these include organizations such as the California-based Natural Death Care Project, the Funeral and Memorial Societies of America, and so on. But mourners seldom shop around and are vulnerable to deceptive sales practices and exorbitant prices. As the baby boomers live to grow old and die, the bureaucratization of the funeral industry is expected to expand as is the financial cost of death.

Is There a 'Right to Die'?

As life extension technology has increased, management of terminal illness and how and when we die have emerged as both medical and ethical issues. During the past few decades, medical technology has made huge strides in caring for critically and terminally ill people of all ages. Accompanying the expansion of lifesaving and extending technology has been concern about the appropriate use of life extending techniques. When should life extension techniques be abandoned? Should life be extended in a society such as ours where chronic, debilitating illness and death are feared and activity valued as an end in itself? Some, like Daniel Callahan (1995), contend that the growth of the elderly population has resulted in too many resources devoted to their care at the expense of the young. According to this argument, the spiraling health care costs in the United States are simply out of control, largely due to the costs of health care for the elderly. Age should thus be used as a criterion for rationing medical treatment, and elders should, out of fairness to the young, accept the fact that they will receive fewer medical resources. Others have criticized this perspective, arguing that it is both ageist and simplistic, ignoring the numerous factors contributing to rising health care costs (see Chapter 12).

The fact remains that dying has become increasingly surrounded by expensive, often futile, technology often misunderstood by patients or their families. Serious problems in end-of-life care have been documented; for example, various studies have found gross deficiencies in pain control; according to one major nationwide study, the final hospitalization for terminally ill people included more than a week in undesirable conditions, including moderate to severe pain despite patient preferences for pain control (Desbiens et al., 1998). Communication between doctor and patient was often poor (Teno et al., 1997a); for example, when describing cardiopulmonary resuscitation (CPR) to patients, physicians often used medical jargon, omitted discussions with the patient about his or her personal goals and values, and failed to give information about either its discomforts or low success rates.

Moreover, physicians write do-not-resuscitate (DNR) orders sooner for patients older than 75, suggesting that doctors use age as a basis for DNR rather than the patients' preferences or the probable outcome of the procedure (Hakim et al., 1996). Despite the success of heroic efforts such as those portrayed on *ER*, only about 15 percent of hospital patients younger than age 70 and almost nobody older than that can expect to live to be discharged when CPR is successful (Nuland, 1994).

Advance Directives

As dying has become more technology-driven and impersonal, death with dignity—a death of one's own—has both romantic and practical appeal. But, as physician Sherwin B. Nuland (1993: 267–268) pointed out in a 1990s best-selling book, death with dignity, although devoutly to be desired, is difficult to achieve: "For most of us, it will prove to be an image of wishfulness . . . usually not attained except by comparatively few. . . . The rest of us must make do with what we are given."

Concern about death with dignity and expanded patient rights to control the types of treatment received coupled with rising health care costs stimulated Congressional passage of the Patient Self-Determination Act in 1990. This act requires that those health care facilities receiving Medicare funds inform patients about their right to prepare *advance directives* or "living wills," stating their preferences for terminal care. An advance directive is a written statement, signed by a mentally competent person, that provides instructions about the kind of care the person does or does not want.

An individual may also select a *health care proxy*, naming another person to make decisions if unable to do so oneself. Advance directives become effective when a person becomes incompetent to make health care decisions during the course of a terminal illness or if the individual is in a permanent coma. *Incompetence* in the context of advance directives means that the person is unable to understand her or his medical condition and the risks and benefits of medical decisions that need to be made.

By 1994, all states and the District of Columbia recognized some type of advance directive, and all states have either general durable power of attorney or specific health care proxy statutes. All, however, provide immunity to physicians and other health care professionals if they do not follow the patient's wishes expressed in a living will and carry no penalty if an advance directive is disregarded. Advance directives also are likely to be ignored in emergency rooms where the patient's record or history is not readily available; they are also often filed in the back of the patient's chart in the hospital or nursing home where they are disregarded. According to one study of more than 4,000 patients, in half the cases where specific instructions were given in the advance directive, care was inconsistent (Teno et al., 1997b).

Although research indicates that the majority of patients—especially the elderly on whom much of the research has been carried out—believe that advance directives are a good idea (Finucane et al., 1988). Few patients, in fact, have prepared documents indicating their preferences for life-sustaining treatment (Markson et al., 1994). An estimated 90 percent of patients do not have advance directives (Pollack, 2000). Nor do all physicians provide adequate details for patients to make informed choices about the range, discomfort, probable success, or cost of available life extension procedures (Covinsky et al., 2000; Hopp, 2000). In addition, physicians may fail to initiate discussions of advance directives because of their busy schedules, fear of upsetting patients, lack of experience with advance directives procedures, and concern about the legal implications (Bedell & Delbanco, 1984).

Most decisions about life-sustaining treatment are made only after people become mentally incapacitated due to illness (Pollack, 2000; Bedell, Pelle, & Majer, 1986; Bedell & Delbanco, 1984), and decisions made by family members or physicians for such patients may not predict patient preferences (Uhlmann, Pearlman, & Cain, 1988; Zweibel & Cassel, 1989). Although the majority of older adults say that they want their family members to make decisions for them if not able to do so themselves, they do not necessarily discuss their wishes or put their preferences in writing (High, 1993). Whites are more likely than African Americans to discuss treatment preferences with relatives before death, to complete a living will, and to have a health care proxy (Hopp & Duffy, 2000), suggesting the need for more research on factors influencing informal communication between older adults and their families on advance directives (Hopp, 2000).

When given various hypothetical cases, older adults are more likely to choose life-sustaining treatments if they would be able to maintain their current quality of life without either being a burden on their families or being permanently mentally confused. As Millie, age 77, summed up her feelings about bypass surgery for heart disease if she were permanently mentally confused: "I don't want to be a burden. And from what I've . . . like with Alzheimer's, I'd hate to burden my family with something like that. They have their own lives, their families to take care of, and I've lived a good life" (Roberto, Weeks, & Matheis-Kraft, 2001: 85).

Little research, however, has been done comparing the choices an individual may make for life-sustaining treatment when relatively healthy versus when actually confronted with the option of life extension or death. Opinions may change when death is imminent. Thus, for example, "Virtually all amyotrophic sclerosis [Lou Gehrig's disease, a progressive and fatal paralytic disorder] patients and others with neuromuscular disease when asked early on, indicate they would rather die than use respiratory support. Virtually all change their minds during periods of acute respiratory failure, particularly when dyspnea can be relieved by noninvasive respiratory supports" (Bach & Barnett, 1994: 138).

Mrs. Candura is a 77-year-old woman with diabetes who was admitted to Central General Hospital for gangrene (death of tissue due to inadequate blood supply) in her right foot. Gangrene can be a complication of diabetes. She has a previous history of gangrene in the same foot and has had two partial amputations of the foot during the past three years. Her physician told her she would die very soon unless her leg were amputated just below the knee. Although she initially agreed to have the surgical amputation, she changed her mind and refused.

Mrs. Candura is clear on some matters but confused on others and sometimes her train of thought wanders. When questioned about why she does not want the amputation, she gives several reasons for her decision. She has been unhappy since her husband's death and she does not want to burden her children or live in a nursing home. She is also discouraged by the failure of the two previous operations and does not believe a third will cure her. She does not fear death but welcomes it.

Her physician made an arrangement for Mrs. Candura to consult a psychiatrist but she refused to speak with him. The psychiatrist believes that she is incompetent to make a rational choice and indicates that her refusal to speak to him shows she is unable to face up to the problem or understand that her refusal to have the surgery constitutes a choice. The psychiatrist also states that her unwillingness to consent to treatment, regardless of the reason, is suicidal and that her mind may be impaired due to the toxic effects of gangrene.

A. If you were Mrs. Candura's physician, what would you do and why?

B. Now assume that Mrs. Candura had never signed an advance directive nor appointed a health care proxy. Mrs. Candura's daughter, Janet, goes to court and asks that her mother be declared incompetent and that Janet be named guardian with power to consent to the surgery. The court grants this request. Do you agree or disagree with the court's decision? Why?

Source: *Lane v. Candura*, 6 Massachusetts Appellate Court 397 (1977).

Hospice

In response to the evidence that many Americans die alone, in pain, and receive medical "heroics," hospice care organizations have developed throughout the United States. The word *hospice* (from the same Latin word as *hospitality* and *hospital*) was first used in 1967 to describe specialized care for the dying at St. Christopher's Hospice in London.

Today *hospice* describes care designed to enable terminally ill people to carry on as an alert, pain-free life as possible and to manage symptoms in their own homes or in homelike settings. Hospice services, available to those who can no longer benefit from curative treatment, are palliative rather than curative and emphasize treating the whole person rather than a disease. Most often provided in one's own home by physicians, nurses, therapists, social workers, and others who furnish medical care and support both to the patient and his or her family and caregivers, hospice care stresses comfort and dignity rather than life extension through technology and thus is usually less costly than conventional care.

Hospices vary with respect to reimbursement patterns, staff interventions, and admissions criteria depending on the percentage of African Americans or Latinos in the hospice service area or served by the hospice. Care for Latinos has been more dependent on Medicaid and free care than for African Americans, whose care has been financed primarily by both Medicaid and Medicare. Problems in serving Latinos and African Americans also differed. The major problems in serving Latinos were identified by hospice personnel as language, reimbursement, and severity of illness; for African Americans the major impediments to care were admission criteria, especially the requirement for an available primary caregiver. Although hospice services are covered by Medicare and most private and Medicaid insurance, their use has been largely among people dying of terminal cancer and more recently AIDS (Statistical Abstract of the U.S., 2000). Regardless of race or ethnicity, relatively few people with heart disease, stroke, and other leading causes of death in later life receive hospice care or are referred to hospices by their physicians.

Euthanasia and Assisted Suicide

The search for "death with dignity" has also called attention to euthanasia (from Greek words meaning "A gentle and easy death"), and whether it is ethical for another to act to end a person's life in order to avoid pain and suffering. The notion of euthanasia in the United States is not new. The first euthanasia bill was drafted in 1906 in Ohio, and the Euthanasia Society of America was founded in 1938. Euthanasia may be passive—withholding or continuing life-sustaining treatments—or active—providing patients with ways to end their own lives.

The right to withhold life-extension treatment (sometimes called passive euthanasia) received national attention in 1976 when the New Jersey Supreme Court allowed Karen Ann Quinlan's parents to disconnect the respirator on which she was placed after going into a coma, apparently induced by drugs and alcohol. In 1990, the U.S. Supreme Court made its first euthanasia decision in the case of Nancy Cruzan, a young woman who had been injured in an auto accident that left her in a permanent coma and had been kept alive for six years through a feeding tube. Although Cruzan had not expressed her wishes to have life supports withdrawn in writing through an advance directive, prior to her accident she had repeatedly verbally expressed a preference not to be kept alive through a feeding tube or other mechanical devices if she were incapable of consciousness. The Supreme Court's decision recognized that competent adults have a constitutionally protected right to refuse medical treatment.

Active euthanasia or "assisted suicide" achieved wide media attention in 1990 when Dr. Jack Kevorkian, a pathologist, assisted in the death of Janet Adkins, a middle-aged woman with Alzheimer's disease. In an influential book, *Medicide* (1991), Kevorkian discussed "the goodness of planned death" as an option not only for the terminally ill but also for others who feel their lives are intolerable. Throughout the 1990s, Kevorkian was the center of both legal action and media coverage as he campaigned for the legalization of assisted suicide. Most notable was his November 1998 appearance on CBS in which a segment of Dr. Kevorkian giving a lethal injection to Thomas Youk, terminally ill with Lou Gehrig's disease, was shown. In 1999, Dr. Kevorkian was convicted of second-degree murder in the death of Thomas Youk. In November 2001, his appeal to reverse this conviction was rejected by the Michigan Court of Appeals and he remains in prison.

Whether there is a moral distinction between withholding life-extending treatment and assisted suicide, euthanasia continues to be debated by clerics, ethicists, and physicians, reflecting the confusion about appropriate norms for dying in the United States and much of the industrialized world. Perhaps echoing the belief that more effective use of available methods of pain relief would erase any need for medical intervention to end life, a recent survey of physicians in Washington State found that hematologists (physicians specializing in blood disorders) and oncologists (cancer specialists), who had more exposure to dying patients than specialists in other fields of medicine, were the strongest opponents of physician-assisted suicide and euthanasia (Cohen, Fihn, & Boyko, 1994). Paradoxically, the same survey reported that psychiatrists, who had the least contact with terminally ill patients, were the strongest spokespersons for physician-assisted suicide.

Those supporting euthanasia claim that patients should be allowed to choose the time and method of their death. As both medical care costs and life extension technology increase, popular support for "death with dignity" is growing. Over a decade ago, a *New York Times–CBS* poll reported that 53 percent of respondents agree that doctors should be permitted to assist a severely ill person to commit suicide (*New York Times*, 1990). Derek Humphry's book, *Final Exit* (1991)—a recipe book for euthanasia—topped the bestseller lists in its first year of publication, and the Hemlock Society, dedicated to the right to choose euthanasia, has members throughout the United States. Over a decade ago, the American Hospital Association recognized that many of the approximately 6,000 hospital deaths per day are in some way planned by patients, their families, or physicians (*New York Times,* 1990). Other estimates suggest that as many as 70 percent of all deaths in hospitals, where most U.S. mortality occurs, are tacit decisions to withdraw care (*Economist,* 1991).

By 1994, Oregon voters had approved an act permitting terminally ill patients to obtain a physician's prescription to end life in a humane and dignified manner; despite legislative attempts to repeal the act, in 1997 Oregon voters refused to repeal it by a 60 percent to 40 percent margin in favor of its retention. On June 26, 1997, the U.S. Supreme Court upheld state statutes that bar assisted suicide. At the same time, however, the Supreme Court noted the concept of *double effect,* acknowledging that death brought about by increased palliative measures is not prohibited as long as the intent is to relieve pain and suffering. The majority opinion stated: "Throughout the Nation, Americans are engaged in an earnest and profound debate about the morality, legality, and practicality of physician-assisted suicide. Our holding permits this debate to continue, as it should in a democratic society" (Vaceo, *Attorney General of New York v. Quill,* 1997; Internet download 12/29/01). As of 2002, only Oregon had a statue allowing physician-assisted suicide and then only for terminally ill patients.

The United States is not alone in its search for norms governing the appropriateness of assisted suicide. Although the British Medical Association has firmly rejected the attempt "by anybody to terminate another person's life" and euthanasia is regarded as attempted murder, in 1990 a brother and sister were conditionally discharged by the court for attempting to kill their terminally ill mother (*Economist,* 1991). In Canada, euthanasia and assisted suicide are generally punishable by up to 14 years in prison, but a highly-publicized case of a woman suing for the right to a physician-assisted suicide created controversy during the 1990s. In France, euthanasia is regarded as homicide but some French doctors apparently "help patients to die." In South Africa, although euthanasia and physician-assisted suicide are regarded as murder, a doctor who administered a lethal injection to his hopelessly ill father received a suspended sentence and had his medical license revoked for two years (*Aging International,* 1994).

The Netherlands is the only European nation where euthanasia is legal, and Dutch physicians have practiced physician-assisted suicide at least since the 1970s. Dutch patients whose lives will be medically terminated must be rational, request death repeatedly with such requests certified by two physicians as reasonable, and must be suffering from unbearable pain without hope of relief although not necessarily terminal illness. "Psychic suffering," "potential disfigurement of personality," and "necessity" have also been noted by Dutch courts as sufficient grounds (Singer & Siegler, 1990).

Even if an individual is convinced that he or she no longer wants to live, should physicians make the decision? For physicians such as Kevorkian, the answer is clearly "yes." But inadvertent potential abuse—the so-called *slippery slope*—is a potential danger if physician-assisted suicide becomes legal. Medical diagnoses are not always accurate, and "miracle" cures, albeit rare, do occur. Not only may people have erroneous beliefs or incomplete information about the nature or prognosis of their illnesses, but many others, who find life intolerable and are with or without chronic, disabling illnesses, suffer from diagnosable and treatable psychological disorders (Mushkin, 1998). Hendin and Klerman (1993) pointed out that the average physician is not trained to evaluate his or her patients for treatable psychological disorders that can make the difference in choosing life versus death. Societal sanction of physician-assisted suicide thus may create pressures on physicians to proceed without adequate training or information about the psychological and social factors associated with the request to terminate life.

The sociologist Robert Merton (1968) noted some years ago that every act has both manifest and latent functions and more than one outcome, often with unforeseen consequences undermining its original goals. What may we learn from the Netherlands about the latent functions of euthanasia to clarify when and how one should die? Although systematic analysis of the incidence, prevalence, and characteristics of those Dutch patients who opt to have their lives ended is not available, in one year alone the number of euthanasia deaths reported to Dutch government officials in the Netherlands had almost tripled: from 590 to more than 1,300. Unofficial estimates prior to legalization range from 3,000 to 16,000 physician-assisted deaths per year or 2 percent to 16 percent of all deaths, typically recorded officially as cardiac arrest (Gomez, 1991). Critics of the Dutch system, such as cardiologist Richard Fenigsen (1989), have argued that euthanasia is differentially applied and not always voluntary; rather, physician-implemented *crypthanasia* (literally, "secret death") takes place, making many infirm and elderly Dutch afraid to seek medical attention when ill. Although this charge has been hotly debated, the point is clear: without formal social control, the potential for murder of those judged to be mentally or physically inferior and a social burden, even in a society with universal health care and well-developed social services such as the Netherlands, is there. According to one source, the majority of the Dutch who have sought euthanasia are in their mid-60s—a period at which major losses of family, work, friendship roles, and diminished power in the larger society are likely to begin for the elderly (Conley, 1992). That their desire to end life is influenced by more than pain and suffering seems likely.

Experience with Oregon's Death With Dignity Act shows that, during three years of legal physician-assisted suicide, a total of 70 patients had their lives terminated. Their characteristics are summarized in Table 13-3.

Table 13-3 Oregon's Death with Dignity Act: Three Years of Experience (1998–2000)	
Characteristics of Patients	**N = 70**
Age range	15–94 years
Median age	70 years
White	97%
Male	51%
Underlying Illness	
Cancer	74%
Other diseases	26%
Type of insurance	
Private	63%
Medicare or Medicaid	37%
None or unknown	1%
Most frequent end-of-life concerns	
Losing autonomy	83%
Poor quality of life	77%
Losing control of bodily functions	66%
Burden on family/friends/caregivers	37%

Source: Adapted from Oregon Health Division (2000: Tables 1 and 3).

Controversy and Debate: Pros and Cons of Assisted Suicide

The following summarizes some of the major arguments people have given for and against assisted suicide. As you look at the table, think about these points and consider which ones you think are most important. Which of the arguments will you support in future legislative and personal decisions and why? To what extent do your ethical and religious beliefs affect your own beliefs about life extension, withdrawal of treatment, or assisted suicide?

Arguments Favoring Doctor-Assisted Suicide	Arguments Opposing Doctor-Assisted Suicide
It is appropriate to have physicians and other health care professionals create a comfortable and peaceful environment in which death occurs.	Physician-assisted suicide is incompatible with the ethics of the profession of medicine, as the intent of medicine is to do good.
Patients have a right to self-determination if they have made a rational competent decision to die.	Patients may be so ill or worried that they may not be able to give a truly informed consent. They may have a treatable depression.

Arguments Favoring Doctor-Assisted Suicide	Arguments Opposing Doctor-Assisted Suicide
Public opinion polls show that almost two-thirds of those polled favor physician-assisted suicide and over half thought they would use it themselves if warranted.	We are debating not how to get compassionate health care to all Americans but how to get suicide to all Americans.
People should not be required to undergo mental and physical decline, to endure emotional and physical pain, and to incur sizable medical expenditures for treatment.	Compassionate and appropriate treatment of the terminally ill is possible. Assisted suicide may create a climate where terminally ill and elderly patients are expected to end their lives.
A very high rate of suicide already exists; an estimated 70 percent of the 1.3 million deaths that occur in American hospitals each year involve some preliminary discussion or consideration, or at the least, an agreement not to take aggressive action to assist the patient's survival.	Right to refuse treatment is not the same as right to die. Assisted suicide avoids the issue of the right to adequate care: As legal scholar George Annas stated, "Why do patients see killing themselves as a better option than putting themselves in the hands of modern American medicine? One reason is that we've done such a horrible job taking care of people."
To prevent abuse, laws could require certain safeguards such as (1) there is intolerable suffering; (2) the patient is mentally competent; (3) a written, witnessed request is provided; (4) the patient consistently and repeatedly over time requests death; and (5) two medical doctors—one who has not participated in the patient's care—agree death is appropriate.	The legality of physician-assisted suicide may interfere with good physician-patient relationships, and the patient may feel implicit pressure to request death. By legalizing physician-assisted suicide, the likelihood increases that suicide will be encouraged for certain people—the developmentally disabled, those with physical disabilities, the very old, the underinsured, and so on.

Bereavement and Grief

Regardless of how or when one dies, the survivors are altered. Not only are they made aware of their own mortality but those closest to the dead person also encounter emptiness in their lives. The following definitions are useful in thinking about the effects of death upon the living. *Bereavement* is the objective situation of having lost someone significant; *grief* is the emotional response to one's loss; and *mourning* denotes the actions and manner of expressing grief, which most often reflects the practices of one's culture.

Bereavement, grief, and mourning are shaped by the historical period in which people live and their culture. As you will recall from the beginning of this chapter, until relatively recently, death was likely to occur at any age and thus was very much a part of everyday life. Indeed, popular art of medieval times often included *steps of the ages,* or rows of people depicting the various ages from birth to death standing on a double staircase. Steps went up one side and down the other, but in the center, ready to meet members of any age group, stood the grim reaper, death (Aries, 1962). In high-mortality societies where death was ever present, the person who died was likely to leave behind a relatively large number of people to whom she or he owed affection, duties, or care. Bereavement was common to people of all ages; children might lose a sibling, a playmate, a parent, or other relatives; adults might experience the death of a child, a partner, a parent, or friend.

One of the results of the shift of mortality to old age characteristic of industrialized societies is not only a smaller circle of people who are bereaved, but also the focus of the loss of a significant other primarily among the elderly, especially older women, who are likely to outlive their spouses. In the United States today, a third of women aged 65 to 74 and more than 6 in 10 of those 75 and older are widowed, compared with less than 1 in 10 men aged 65 to 74 and one in four men 75 and older.

Grief as a response to bereavement is both a symbol of caring for the person who has died and a reaction to the social vacuum created by his or her death. Although a simple word, grief is a complex set of emotions. As described by Erich Lindemann (1944), a psychiatrist who did pioneering work on grieving, acute grief affects all aspects of an individual, inducing physical symptoms, difficulties in concentration, shock, numbness, and depression. Necessary for survivors after the death of a significant other, *grief work* is a process, encompassing "emancipation from the bondage of the deceased, readjustment to the environment in which the deceased is missing, and the formation of new relationships" (Lindemann, 1944: 43).

As urbanization, industrialization, and emphasis on the individual increased in contemporary Western societies, both the likelihood of frequent deaths and the size of the set of people with whom to share grief when bereaved decreased. These social changes have narrowed the circle of bereavement from the community to those most intimately associated with the deceased, such as close family or friends. The death of a significant other thus became potentially more devastating than in preindustrial societies where life expectancy is short and death is a constant visitor (Lofland, 1985). In such societies, when a death occurs, survivors recall the social and emotional gifts they owe the deceased for care and affection; often, too, the survivors think about their lost opportunities to return the benefits of the caring they received from the deceased (Blauner, 1968).

What do people need to ease the loss that they feel when someone whom they know or revere dies? Worden (1982) has proposed that mourning has four tasks: (1) to accept the reality of the loss and that the dead person will not return; (2) to experience the pain of grief rather than suppress or deny it; (3) to adjust to an environment in which the deceased is missing, including loss of roles played by him or her; and (4) to withdraw emotional energy from the deceased and to reinvest it in new relationships. How one actually resolves grief, however, is an individual as well as a cultural matter. Some individuals may work through their feelings and gradually disengage themselves from the deceased. Others may find it more helpful to continue to talk with others about the dead person while moving on with their lives. Grief counseling by a professional may be a poor second best for talking with others who knew the dead person intimately.

How grief is expressed varies widely, not only constructed by historic-cultural patterns but also by the survivors' social characteristics, available social supports, feelings toward the deceased, and individual personalities. Open expression of grief and mourning may be encouraged in some societies or subcultures within a society and discouraged in others. For example, in Black Carib society, public wailing and weeping are expected for women (but not for men), and women who cry quietly or spiritlessly are considered ungrateful (see Box). In contrast, when President John F. Kennedy was assassinated, the dignified and tearless decorum that his wife, Jacqueline, displayed in public was widely admired as was his young son's dignified salute to the funeral cortege.

External demonstrations of grief also vary; during the Victorian era in the nineteenth century, many bereaved people in the United States openly displayed their grief by dressing in black for a year or wearing mourning jewelry that included a lock of the deceased's hair; today, such outward expressions would be considered excessive or peculiar. Religious customs also affect the ways in which grief is shown; for example, in the Jewish religion today, the Shiva, held for the first seven days following a death, is a patterned way for people to come together, reminisce, and acclaim the life and mourn the death of the person. By sharing the grief of the bereaved, such rituals celebrate the life of the dead person and give social support and comfort to the family.

Yet, in American culture the expression of grief is discouraged in public places including funeral establishments. Death is prettified and partially denied, as Wernick has pointed out:

> In flower-bedecked viewing room and chapel, before and even during the service, the embalmed corpse is dressed, cosmetically made up, and displayed as if in good health and only resting. Funerals, as the trade cliche has it, are "for the living." They provide "grief therapy," and some establishments even offer "aftercare" in

addition to the "perpetual care" of remains. . . . Temporarily preserving and beautifying the corpse . . . simulates physical immortality as an iconic sign of enduring personal presence. (Wernick, 1995: 282–283)

Compare this setting with the funereal rites in Black Carib society where open grief and mourning are the norm.

Global Glimpses: Mourning in Black Carib Society

Unlike the United States, in Black Caribbean societies death is neither a private nor family affair nor a business; it is a community concern. Mourning and mourning rites are women's work; every ritual for the dead is organized by a woman who has helped other women in the past. When death occurs, a crowd of people gathers at the home of the deceased or next of kin, and close female relatives of the dead person begin to wail as soon as they hear of the death. Female relatives and volunteers begin preparations almost immediately, washing and dressing the body, preparing refreshments, and giving food to kin and friends of the dead person while a few men construct a coffin. During the night, men gamble or talk; women may sing hymns; and others talk or distribute food and rum—an indispensable part of the wake—until men begin music for dancing. Throughout the night, relatives arrive from other communities and more women begin to wail, expressing their gratitude to the deceased for care and support. Men rarely wail but speak stolidly to the deceased at the open coffin. A church service for the dead person is conducted within 48 hours after death and the mourners walk in a funeral procession to the burial ground, where the female relatives of the deceased display intense emotions at

graveside and are physically supported and helped away from the grave by members of the community.

A novena, following Roman Catholic tradition introduced by missionaries during the colonial era, is held on the first or second Friday after burial to ensure serenity of the deceased's soul and to detach her or him from the world of the living. In addition to the Catholic novena, a few women construct an altar before the novena begins for the ninth-night wake after the novena. The ninth-night wake is sometimes compared to a farewell party by the living for the recently deceased who, according to Carib belief, is resurrected the third day after burial to wander about aimlessly until given a proper goodbye. Prayers, food, rum, and music are part of the ninth-night wake which lasts until morning; many people come and go, dancing, singing, drinking, and talking.

Mourning rituals continue far beyond the ninth-night wake. Close female kin of the deceased must mourn for 6 to 12 months after the death and must follow rules limiting their behavior and clothing. For example, they may attend social events, but only as onlookers. They are to refrain from drinking alcohol and from dancing, refrain from quarreling, and must wear somber colors and not wear jewelry. Six months to a year after the death of a spouse or parent, an obligatory end-of-mourning ceremony is held; the rite includes church prayers and a ritual bath by the mourning woman, at the end of which other women tear the mourning clothes from the mourner's body. To mark the end of mourning, mourners conclude the ceremony by dressing in brightly colored garb and jewelry. The women eat, drink rum, and dance. Other optional mourning ceremonies may be given months and years after a death. A requiem mass may be held. Another commemoration involves giving the spirit of the deceased a "bath"; that is, close relatives and guests dig a pit the size of the grave, throw water into the pit, and address the spirit of the dead. All such rituals include a post-ceremony feast or celebration.

Open and visible expressions of grief are basic to mourning rituals in Black Carib society. The survivors find distraction from their bereavement through supportive interaction with others, emotional outlets, and eventually, enjoyment in living. Through such elaborate commemorations, the loneliness and isolation of the bereaved are lessened, and a sense of belonging to a community of the living is strengthened.

Compare the ways that these mourning practices are similar or different to those with which you are familiar, from the experiences of your family, friends, or neighbors. What are the advantages or disadvantages of these similarities or differences? What are the cultural roots of mourning in your own family? What kinds of expression of grief and bereavement do you think are most useful—open expressions or quiet mourning? Why?

Source: Based on Kerns (1983; 147–166).

Widowhood

How a man or woman responds to the loss of a spouse, for example, will depend on closeness of the marital bond, the extent to which the bereaved person depended on the spouse, and how important the marriage was to the individual's self-definition (Lopata, 1996). In contemporary U.S. society, emphasis on the nuclear family rather than on larger kinship and community-wide networks has boosted the importance of the marital bond. In Lopata's studies of American widows, she found that well-educated, middle-class women were more likely to experience the death of a spouse as disruptive to their self-concept than were working- or lower-class women. Throughout their marriage, middle- and upper-class marital pairs tended to communicate with one another more, sharing issues about household and family roles. They were also more likely to view each other as companions and friends. The death of a husband thus left a greater void and greater probability of feeling lonely, as the wife had lost not only a spouse but her close friend.

Loneliness is not just being alone, for all of us can be alone but not feel lonely. Rather, loneliness describes feelings of relative deprivation—a social and emotional abyss that looms large and colors everyday experience. The widowed are likely to feel lonely for the lost partner for numerous reasons: loss of a companion, a sexual partner, a love object, an escort, someone to argue with, and so forth. Becoming widowed may also lead to idealization of the dead spouse, where he or she achieves near sainthood in the mind of the widowed (Lopata, 1996). Adaptation to widowhood is also affected by the economic resources, supportive social networks, health, and self-concept of the widow or widower (Lopata, 1996). For those people whose economic resources are reduced by the death of a spouse, widowhood is likely to be particularly difficult.

Are men or women more affected by the death of a spouse? Research results are unclear. Regardless of socioeconomic factors, both widows and widowers are more likely to report greater depression, poorer health, and new or heightened illnesses than nonbereaved elders. Widowers are also somewhat more likely to die within a year after bereavement than widows (Gallagher-Thompson, 2001). One explanation for the higher mortality among men is that they are given less latitude to mourn openly for the lost partner. Consequently, they grieve quietly, have fewer social supports, and take less care of their health than women. The higher rates of male suicide in very old age lend some support to this notion. Lund and his associates (Lund, 2000; Lund, Caserta, & Dimond, 1986) have proposed that the differences between men and women in the ways they express grief are often overstated, and that there is considerable variation. The external appearance of "taking it like a man" masks the loneliness, and difficulties in managing activities primarily the responsibility of the deceased spouse are felt equally by both genders. Further research, however, is needed to understand the complex interplay of gender, social class, race, ethnicity, and religion in the grief process.

Summary

Although in the past death occurred at any age, now the elderly are those most likely to die. The eradication of numerous acute illnesses that used to result in death has resulted in dramatic changes in life expectancy and today in the United States, as in all industrialized nations, chronic diseases, such as heart disease and cancer, are the primary cause of death. How long any of us lives is influenced by our social class, ethnicity, race, and gender, all of which affect our life chances and potential for long lives.

Attitudes toward death have varied across time and culture. Americans value life and tend to distance themselves from death, as well as from the process of dying itself. Dying has become increasingly bureaucratized in the United States and placed in the hands of health care professionals rather than the family. Funeral practices, too, have been bureaucratized and the funeral business has become a a money-making industry.

Issues of the right to die, assisted suicide, and euthanasia are receiving attention especially as both medical care costs and life extension technology increase. By 1994, Oregon voters had approved an act permitting terminally ill patients to obtain a physician's prescription to end life in a humane and dignified manner. On June 26, 1997, the U.S. Supreme Court upheld state statutes that bar assisted suicide. At the same time, however, the Supreme Court noted the concept of *double effect*, acknowledging that death brought about by increased palliative measures is not prohibited as long as the intent is to relieve pain and suffering. Americans remain engaged in debates about the morality, legality, and practicality of physician-assisted suicide—a profound ethical and social policy issue.

Status differentials are portrayed even after death; the Maynard family, after whom the town in which they lived was named, not only has the largest tombstones in this cemetery, but the founder of the town is buried in the large mound in the background.

Among the results of the shift of mortality to old age characteristic of industrialized societies is not only a smaller circle of people who are bereaved, but also a focus of the loss of a significant other primarily among the elderly, especially older women who are likely to outlive their spouses. Grief as a response to bereavement is both a symbol of caring for the person who has died and a reaction to the social vacuum created by his or her death. Although a simple word, *grief* is a complex set of emotions. Acute grief affects all aspects of an individual, inducing physical symptoms, difficulties in concentration, shock, numbness, and depression. As urbanization, industrialization, and emphasis on the individual increased in contemporary Western societies, both the likelihood of frequent deaths and the size of the set of people with whom to share grief when bereaved decreased. These social changes have narrowed the circle of bereavement from the community to those most intimately associated with the deceased, such as close family or friends. The death of a significant other thus became potentially more devastating than in preindustrial societies where life expectancy is short and death is a constant visitor. Mourning has been described as comprising four tasks: (1) to accept the reality of the loss and that the dead person will not return; (2) to experience the pain of grief rather than suppress or deny it; (3) to adjust to an environment in which the deceased is missing, including loss of roles played by him or her; and (4) to withdraw emotional energy from the deceased and to reinvest it in new relationships.

How grief is expressed varies widely, not only constructed by historic-cultural patterns but also by the survivors' social characteristics, available social supports, feelings toward the deceased, and individual personalities. Open expression of grief and mourning may be encouraged in some societies or subcultures within a society and discouraged in others. Whether men or women are more affected by the death of a spouse remains unclear, although there is some evidence that while the surface expressions differ by gender, both experience the same feelings of loss.

Key Points

1. In American society today, death is most likely to occur in old age—a dramatic change from the beginning of the twentieth century. Average life expectancy at birth today is more than 76 years, and many people 65 and over survive to very old ages.

2. Causes of death have also changed because public health measures, nutrition, improved standards of living, and immunizations have reduced the incidence of many acute illnesses.

3. Chronic diseases now account for the greatest number of deaths; heart disease, cancer, and stroke are the leading causes of mortality.

4. How long an individual lives is affected not only by genetics but also by sociological variables: age, sex, socioeconomic status, race, and ethnicity, as well as by sociopolitical conditions.

5. Regardless of age, people's feelings and beliefs about death differ due to their social situations and life experiences.

6. The belief that the elderly are more ready to die because their lives are less valuable to them does not reflect reality but ageist assumptions, including projections of our fears about old age, and provides excuses for age discrimination.

7. How we die as well as how we live is affected by our position in the social class structure, and older people often receive less treatment than younger ones.

8. Regardless of the age or social characteristics of the dying person, death is not only a physical state but also encompasses personal death.

9. The process of dying has become bureaucratized; that is, hospitals and nursing homes control and routinize the handling and care of the dying, and funeral homes and cemeteries prepare and arrange cremation or burial of the dead.

10. As family members no longer have responsibility for burial of the dead, funerals, too, are bureaucratized.

11. With the expansion of life extension technology, how to manage terminal illness and dying has emerged as a medical and legal issue.

12. Bereavement denotes the loss of someone significant; grief is the emotional response to loss, and mourning describes the actions and ways of expressing grief.

13. How we grieve and mourn reflects both the culture and the slice of history in which we live and die.

14. In contemporary American society, emphasis on the nuclear family rather than on larger kinship or community-wide networks has changed the experience of widowhood.

Discussion Questions

1. Discuss the statement "It is not the richest nations that have the highest life expectancy but those where there is less difference among social classes."

2. Discuss what is meant by the statement "An individual's awareness of his/her own dying is socially constructed and managed."

3. Describe the dying trajectory.

4. Distinguish between social death and personal death.

5. What are some of the problems and issues that have been experienced with advance directives from the patient's viewpoint? From the physician's?

6. In what ways has death become bureaucratized?

7. Form two debate teams, one to defend assisted suicide, the other to argue against assisted suicide. Present to the class.

8. Read the Social Policy Issue case presented in this chapter. Assume instead that Mrs. Candura's daughter says she does not want her mother to receive the surgery. Her daughter says that for several years before becoming ill, Mrs. Candura cared for her bedridden spouse until his death. Mrs. Candura's experiences as a caregiver prompted her to indicate repeatedly to her daughter that she would not want to live if she were unable to take care of herself. Also assume that before she became ill, Mrs. Candura completed an advance directive stating that she does not want her life "artificially prolonged" if she "cannot care for herself" and there is "no chance of full recovery." The living will also names the daughter as proxy decision maker. How would you treat Mrs. Candura if you were her physician and what are your reasons?

9. How has emphasis on the nuclear family rather than on larger kinship or community-wide networks changed the experience of widowhood?

Films and Videos

Advance Directives and the Elderly: Making Decisions About Treatment Limitations (video; 20 minutes; available from Video Press, University of Maryland School of Medicine, Suite 300, 100 N. Greene Street, Baltimore, MD 21201; *www.videopress.org*).

Nursing home residents discuss artificial feeding, CPR, and use of antibiotics with a physician.

Managing Care, Managing Death: Disguised Euthanasia (video; 29 minutes; available from Films for the Humanities and Sciences, P.O. Box 2053, Princeton, NJ; *www.films.com*).

Winner of the New York Film Festival Award, this film features experts who discuss the use of strong painkillers by doctors to hasten the patient's death and the ethical issues that this "disguised euthanasia" present.

Rose and Zelda (video; 20 minutes; available from Video Press, University of Maryland School of Medicine, Suite 300, 100 N. Greene Street, Baltimore, MD 21201; *www.videopress.org*).

Shot on location at the Levindale Hebrew Geriatric Center and Hospital, 90-year-old Rose and her daughter, Zelda, discuss Rose's preferences for end-of-life care.

Scientific American Frontiers: 21st Century Medicine (5 videos, 60 minutes each; available from *www.pbs.org*).

Explores the many ways computers are changing medicine and life prospects in five episodes.

Surviving Death: Stories of Grief (video; 47 minutes, available from Fanlight Productions, 4196 Washington Street, Boston, MA 02131; *www.fanlight.com*).

Winner of the Wilbur Award for best TV documentary, this video explores responses of people from different backgrounds to the death of people around them. Includes discussion questions.

Tired of Living, Feared of Dying (video; 54 minutes; available from Filmmakers Library, 124 E. 40th Street, New York, NY 10016; *www.filmakers.com*).

Follows seven people who have requested euthanasia in the Netherlands, a nation where physicians can legally grant patients' requests to die.

Internet Resources

http://www.demographics.com/publications

Links to articles in the journal *American Demographics,* a readable source for up-to-date results of population trends including life expectancy and mortality.

http://www.lastacts.org

Established by the Robert Wood Johnson Foundation and contains a wealth of information about care and caring at the end of life, including bibliographic sources for further reading.

http://www.growthhouse.org

A valuable resource for training, research, and educational tools regarding end of life plus links to many other useful sites.

http://www.funeralnet.com

Useful for searches on grief, bereavement, funerals, and cremation plus advertisements from the funeral industry.

http://www.lwc.edu/administrative/library/suic.htm

Maintained by Longwood College, a guide to doctor-assisted suicide including legal decisions.

http://www.nho.org

The site for the National Hospice Organization and a resource for material, including videos, on hospice services.

Research Article

Roscoe, L. A., Malphurs, J. E., Dragovic, L. J., & Cohen, D. (2001). A comparison of characteristics of Kevorkian euthanasia cases and physician-assisted suicides in Oregon. *The Gerontologist, 41*: 439–446.

Compares characteristics of people euthanized by Kevorkian with those receiving physician-assisted suicide in Oregon and notes the importance of gender and marital status.

Suggested Readings

de Beauvoir, S. (1965). *A Very Easy Death.* New York: Warner Books.

A famous French writer examines the day-by-day tragedy of her mother's death and the meanings and mysteries of human life.

Mitford, J. (1999). *American Way of Death Revisited.* New York: Vintage.

An entertaining and highly critical look at the funeral industry in the United States.

Nuland, S. B. (1994). *How We Die: Reflections on Life's Final Chapter.* New York: Knopf.

A thoughtful and illuminating series of portraits and analyses of dying and death by a surgeon and professor of medicine.

Quill, T. E. (1996). *A Midwife Through the Dying Process: Stories of Healing and Hard Choices at the End of Life.* Baltimore, MD: Johns Hopkins University Press.

A fascinating account of the issues surrounding dying and death by the leading-physician plaintiff in the landmark 1997 U.S. Supreme Court case that upheld New York's ban on physician-assisted suicide.

Roth, P. (1991). *Patrimony.* New York: Simon and Schuster.

A sensitive personal account by novelist Philip Roth of his father, including his terminal illness, his advance directive, and eventual death.

Schwartz, M. (with an introduction by P. Solman). (1997). *Morrie: In His Own Words: Life Wisdom From a Remarkable Man.* New York: Walker and Company.

A moving and insightful book of reflections on life and death by a terminally ill man. ✦

Afterword:
The Elderly of Tomorrow

Stephen J. Cutler

Most of you who are just finishing this book (or skipping ahead to the end to find out "who done it") are probably in your late teens or early 20s. Before taking this course, aging may have struck you or your acquaintances as being pretty far removed from your most important everyday concerns. What Professor Markson has demonstrated throughout this volume is that aging ought to be thought of as being of considerable relevance to you. For one thing, lifestyle choices we make as adolescents, teenagers, or young adults may come back to help us or to haunt us in our later years. We know that smoking, little or no exercise, and poor dietary habits have cumulative effects over our lifetimes, resulting in poorer health and higher mortality. Aging is not something that happens to us overnight; how we age is to no small degree the product of decisions we make and how we live over the several decades preceding later life. It's not too early to begin applying the gerontological principles you've learned in this book to your own life.

Perhaps a different slant on aging's relevance comes from the 2000 presidential campaign. To be sure, education was cited by the candidates as a top priority, but much of the campaign seemed to revolve around hot and contentious topics, such as Social Security, Medicare, the cost of prescription drugs, inheritance taxes, and the like. These, of course, are issues that are of particular concern to middle-aged and older voters. Their seeming dominance in the speeches and policy proposals of the candidates was singled out by many pundits as a major reason for the lack of interest, enthusiasm, and involvement of younger persons.

Will this situation change? If you thought that the issues in the 2000 presidential campaign were slanted toward older voters, there is every reason to believe this will continue to be the case. If the demographics of aging are any indication, it's not likely that these sorts of issues will go away or even diminish in importance. Population aging, as Markson makes clear in Chapter 3, is about ready to experience a major growth spurt. Current Census Bureau estimates for the United States project an increase in the number of persons 65 and older from about 35 million in 2000 to over 70 million in 2030 by the time the "baby boomers" will have reached what is (at least now) defined as "old age" (Administration on Aging, 2001).

Now think about the following numbers. In the year 2030, at the point when all of the boomers have reached old age, older persons are projected to be 20 percent of the total population but 26 percent of the voting age population (i.e., 18 years of age and older). Add to this the fact that a higher percentage of the older population votes than any other age group. In 1998, 60 percent of persons age 65+ voted compared with 54 percent of 45- to 64-year-olds, 35 percent of 25- to 44-year-olds, and only 17 percent of persons between the ages of 18 and 24 (U.S. Bureau of the Census, 2000). Making the simplifying assumption that these 1998 age-specific voting rates will hold true for elections in the year 2030, persons 65+ would make up 26 percent of the voting age population but 36 percent of the population that actually voted! Whatever else may be on the political radar screen when many of you are about 50 years old, it's a safe bet that issues of concern to elders will be front and center, ignored by candidates only at great risk to their chances of being elected.

Population aging, as you know from Chapter 3, is not restricted to the United States. We are by no means unique in this regard. International data available through the Census Bureau show a 52 percent increase in the size of the older population of Europe between 2000 and 2030 (see U.S. Bureau of the Census, 2001, for this and subsequent projections). But lest we think of these dramatic changes as confined just to the developed nations, it is clear that the developing nations also are and will be experiencing rapid growth of their older populations. To put a numerical face on it, for the developing nations as a whole, it is expected that the segment of their population that is 65 years of age and older will increase from 5 percent in 2000 to 10 percent in 2030. While this figure may not seem all that impressive (after all, 18 percent of the population of Italy is already 65+), throw in three additional considerations. First, there are almost as many persons 65+ in the developing areas now (250 million) as there are people of all ages in the total population of the United States (275 million). But by the year 2050 (well within the lifetimes of most of you), the projected number of persons 65+ in developing regions of the world (1.2 billion) will *equal the total number of persons of all ages* in the more developed regions. There will be as many old people in developing areas as there are people in the developed regions of the world. The growth of the older populations of developing countries is going to involve unparalleled numbers of persons.

Second, the speed at which this growth is taking place is without historical precedent. It took France 115 years for its older population to increase from 7 percent to 14 percent (1865 to 1980) and Sweden 85 years (1890 to 1975). Contrast this with China, where the percentage of its population 65+ is expected to increase from 7 to 14 percent between 2000 and 2027, a span of only 27 years (Cutler, 2000).

And third, the slower historical pace of population aging in developed nations enabled the creation and expansion of public support (imperfections aside) with relatively unhurried time available for periodic tinkering, fine-tuning, and accommodations. Developing nations, where public support systems are rudimentary or nonexistent, will find themselves having to move very quickly to create appropriate infrastructures in the face of rapidly increasing longevity, changes in family structure, and shifts from rural-agrarian to urban-industrial societies. Recall the concept of "structural lag" and note its applicability to the situation of developing nations, where increasing numbers and changing circumstances of the older population are taking place much more rapidly than societal structures can adapt.

What other implications might population aging have for the future, for what will society look like when you're in your middle and later years? One scenario rests on assumptions about aging and old age that are neither very attractive nor flattering. Over the years, various commentators have not placed aging or the older population in a very positive light (see Cutler, 2000, for sources). Ralph Waldo Emerson spoke of old age as "rest, conservatism, appropriation, inertia, not newness, not the way onward." Sigmund Freud did not believe psychoanalysis was suitable for older patients because ". . . more or less above the fifties, the elasticity of mental processes, on which the treatment depends, is as a rule lacking—older people are no longer educable . . ." (Freud, 1961b). Demographers have expressed the concern that population aging might result in a society that "would not be receptive to change and would have a strong tendency towards nostalgia and conservatism," that "there will be a larger proportion of the population who are less adaptable to social and political change, thus suggesting the possibility of 'social stagnation,' " and that we might "become a society of old people, living in old houses, ruminating over old ideas." Another observer (Wolf, 2001) put it rather succinctly recently when, with a bit of British understatement, he suggested that "middle age countries are likely to be a bit stodgy."

These sorts of concerns about what population aging might mean for social change rest on two implicit assumptions: (1) that people become more rigid in their thinking, beliefs, and values as they grow older; and (2) that aging brings with it a pronounced tendency toward increasingly conservative social and political attitudes. And it's not just ivory tower types who subscribe to these notions about the accompaniments of aging. Survey data from over the past quarter of a century consistently show that the general public has very similar notions of what it means to grow old. For example, the 2000 Myths and Realities of Aging study asked a cross-section of the population about its images of "most people over 65." On the question asking whether most people over age 65 are "very open-minded and adaptable," only 10 percent of persons 18 to 64 thought this was true and only 16 percent of respondents who themselves were 65+ thought that most people over 65 were very open-minded and adaptable (Cutler, N., 2000). To paraphrase the familiar, but ageist, saying: Apparently old dogs and new tricks are widely viewed as fundamentally incompatible.

Is this what society will look like when you're in middle or old age? If living in a "socially stagnant" society is a depressing prospect, take heart. There are at least two lines of evidence suggesting that these concerns about the consequences of population aging are completely unwarranted.

On a macro-level, the fear that population aging will somehow lead to social stagnation, to a society unreceptive to change, is not borne out by recent historical evidence. Take the period 1970 to 2000, for example. After having been enrolled in this course, I don't think you'd allow anyone to claim that the population of the United States was not aging during this period. As Professor Markson points out in Chapter 3, the number of persons 65+ increased by just under 75 percent during this time and there was a three-fold increase in the numbers of the oldest-old (i.e., persons 85+) (Administration on Aging, 2001; U.S. Bureau of the Census, 1996: Table 14). Population aging was well underway. Nor do I think anyone could argue that the decades between 1970 and 2000 demonstrated an era when social change was absent: civil rights, gender roles, family structure, labor force participation of women, and the environment are but a few of the domains in which most people would probably agree that dramatic and profound change has occurred.

There's still a second approach to critically examining the notions that aging is somehow associated with increasing rigidity or with increasingly conservative social and political attitudes. In what has turned out to be a fascinating research project (one which landed us on the front page of the May 15, 2000 edition of the *Christian Science Monitor*), a colleague at the University of Vermont (Nicholas Danigelis) and I have been looking at changes in social and political attitudes in the United States over the 26-year period between 1972 and 1998. We use a series of 22 nationally representative surveys of the adult population that were collected by the National Opinion Research Center at the University of Chicago. These surveys include information from over 38,000 respondents, and we use 61 items to measure attitudes in several social and political domains: attitudes about the legalization of abortion, euthanasia and suicide, support for civil liberties, sexual relations, race relations, the role of government, law and order, family and gender roles, and political identification.

Our basic strategy is to look at changes in social and political attitudes over the 26-year period within cohorts of persons born during the same intervals. Take persons who were born in 1922 or earlier and who in 1972 would be 50 years of age and older. In 1973, persons in that birth cohort would be 51 and older; in 1980, 58 and older; in 1989, 69 and older; in 1998, 78 and older. In this same manner, we can follow cohorts who started out as 18 to 29 in 1972, 30 to 39 in 1972, and 40 to 49 in 1972. By tracing cohort scores on some social or political attitudes over the 26-year period, we can tell whether the attitudes of each cohort have changed, if so whether they became more conservative or perhaps more liberal, whether the direction of change is the same for all of the cohorts, and whether the rate of change is the same or different across the four cohorts.

The results of these analyses show something quite interesting. Let me use the domain of attitudes about race relations as an example (Cutler & Danigelis, 2001). We have nine measures here, looking at attitudes about such topics as interracial marriage, busing students from one school district to another, open housing laws, and voting for a presidential candidate who is a member of a minority group. On seven of the nine measures, attitude change has occurred over time for each of the cohorts, the changes have all been in a liberal direction, and the rate of change has been about the same for each of the cohorts. (For any of you schooled in the language of statistical analysis, this is another way of saying there were no "time by cohort interaction" effects.) On another of the measures (school busing), overall change was also in a liberal direction, but the rate of change was faster for one of the cohorts than for the others. For which cohort was there more rapid change in a liberal direction? The oldest cohort! And on the remaining measure (whether racial inequality is rooted in structural sources rather than being a result of individual ability or initiative), overall change was in a conservative direction, and there were differences in the direction and rate of change among some of the cohorts. Here, the most rapid shift toward conservative attitudes was found in the youngest cohort, while attitude change among the oldest cohort again was in a liberal direction.

Without getting any more bogged down in the specifics of the findings, the results from the area of attitudes about race relations show the following: (1) attitude change was very prevalent and it occurred among all of the cohorts; (2) in the domain of race relations at least, the predominant direction of attitude change was toward more liberal attitudes; and (3) for the most part, the rate at which attitudes changed in a liberal direction was the same for each of the cohorts. So much for the notion that aging is accompanied by greater rigidity! And so much for the notion that change, when it occurs, is inevitably or invariably in a conservative direction!

What seems to be happening here is that as public opinion at large goes, so go the attitudes of the older cohorts. This is what Markson referred to earlier as a *period* effect: Older cohorts may have different starting points, but they tend to be as aware of and are as influenced by the broader currents of change surrounding them as is the case for younger cohorts. At the risk of being excessively repetitive, then, these data provide no support for inevitable connections between aging and rigidity or between aging and the adoption of increasingly conservative attitudes. (To be fair, the overall change in some of the other domains—e.g., law and order—was in a conservative direction, but in most instances all of the cohorts shifted in the same direction and at the same rate. This is further evidence against rigidity and additional support for the existence of a period effect. Interestingly, where rates of change differed among the cohorts in the presence of conservative change, typically it was not the oldest cohort, but the youngest cohort that shifted most quickly in a conservative direction.)

Will population aging make a major dent in social change? Are your middle and later years destined to be spent in a stodgy society? Will population graying impose a poky speed limit on the engines of social, political, and economic change? Not if these findings are valid and applicable, and (not surprisingly) Professor Danigelis and I happen to think that the results are clear, consistent, and entirely convincing.

What then can be said of the future? It's a safe bet that aging will be an impetus for change, not a hindrance to change. It's also a safe bet that change will affect how we age. The nature of the aging experience 50 years from now will likely be very different, just as the aging experience today differs from what it was 50 or 100 years ago. We already have evidence that disability rates among older persons have been declining over the past two decades due to changes in health service delivery and technology and to a greater awareness of healthy lifestyles. As you've seen in earlier chapters, family structure, intergenerational relations, and caregiving are changing as a result of increasing longevity, low birth rates, higher rates of labor force participation among women, and shifts in the basis for health care payment and reimbursement. Technological breakthroughs in medicine and in our understanding of genetics will doubtless lead to new and beneficial diagnostic and treatment procedures, but new technology may also increase longevity in some instances by merely prolonging the dying process. As Professor Markson notes, rapid developments in technology are raising a host of important but perplexing ethical issues. "Smart" houses may have great potential for assisting older persons to remain independent for longer periods of time, but as we marvel at these innovations we cannot forget that satisfying more basic needs, such as adequacy, affordability, and accessibility, will continue to be problematic for significant numbers of older persons, especially women, minorities, and those living alone. Just as modal depictions of elders have shifted from an image of frailty and dependency to one of "greedy geezers," how will our culture depict elders in the future—as an economic drain on society or as a segment of the population capable of making productive and valuable contributions?

Aging has often been described as a growth industry. This is certainly true in terms of the future size of the older population, the number of persons who need to be trained for occupations that serve and care for elders, and in the likely impact that the older population will have on society. What the future portends for older persons and what the older population portends for the future are issues that will only increase in importance. They are also issues that should command your interest, understanding, and involvement. Toward this end, the information, concepts, and tools provided by Professor Markson in *Social Gerontology Today: An Introduction* have gotten you off to a fine start.

* * *

Stephen J. Cutler *is Professor of Sociology and the Bishop Robert F. Joyce Distinguished University Professor of Gerontology at the University of Vermont. He earned his B.A. in sociology from Dartmouth College and his M.A. and Ph.D. from the University of Michigan. Cutler has served as editor of the* Journal of Gerontology: Social Sciences, *as chair of the Sociology of Aging Section of the American Sociological Association, and as president of the Gerontological Society of America. He is the recipient of the 2002 Clark Tibbitt Award from the Association for Gerontology in Higher Education. Stephen J. Cutler's current research focuses on aging and social change, caregiving to frail elders, the social construction and interpretation of normal cognitive changes associated with aging, social participation of older people, and early testing for genetic diseases. Among his extensive scholarly publications are the recent "Emerging Social Trends"* (Handbook of Aging and the Social Sciences, *5th edition, 2001, coauthor) and "Correlates of Personal Concerns About Developing Alzheimer's Disease Among Middle-Aged Persons"* (American Journal of Alzheimer's Disease, *16(6) 2001, coauthor).* ✦

References

AARP. (1997). *Assisted Living: What People Say They Want.* Washington DC: Author.

——. (1998). *Across the States 1998: Profiles of Long-Term Care Systems.* Washington, DC: Author.

——. (1998). Baby Boomers Envision Their Retirement: An AARP Segmentation Analysis. Available: *http://research.aarp.org/econ/boomer_seg.html* (Accessed 10/13/00).

——. (1999, August). AARP/Modern Maturity Sexuality Survey: Summary of Findings. Available: *http://www.aarp.org* (Accessed 12/19/01).

——. (1999). Retirement Savings Options in Financial Planning. Available: *http://www.aarp.org/finance99/retire.html* (Accessed 10/10/00).

——. (2000). *American Business and Older Employees.* Washington, DC: Author.

——. (2000). Various Issues. *Modern Maturity.*

——. (2001). *Public Attitudes toward Aging, Beauty and Cosmetic Surgery: How Americans Really Feel about Physical Appearance.* Washington DC: Author.

Achenbaum, W. A., & Bengtson, V. L. (1994). Re-engaging the disengagement theory of aging: On the history and assessment of theory development in gerontology. *Gerontologist,* 34(6): 756–763.

Achenbaum, W. A. (1995). *Crossing Frontiers: Gerontology Emerges as a Science.* New York: Cambridge University Press.

Adelman, R., Greene, M., Charon, R., & Freidmann, E. (1990). Issues in the physician-geriatric patient relationship. In H. Giles, N. Coupland, & J. Wiemann (Eds.), *Communication, Health and the Elderly* (pp. 126–134). London: Manchester University Press.

——. (1992). The content of physician and elderly patient interaction in the medical primary care encounter. *Communication Research,* 19: 370–380.

Administration on Aging, U.S. Department of Health and Human Services. (1999). Age Discrimination: A Pervasive and Damaging Influence. *U.S. Administration on Aging Fact Sheet* [Online]. Available: *http://www.aoa.dhhs.gov/factsheets/ageism.html* (accessed 7/12/02).

——. (2000). *Profile of Older Americans, 2000.* Available *http://www.aoa.dhhs.gov/STATS* (accessed 12/99).

———. (2002). *A Profile of Older Americans: 2001.* Washington DC: U.S. Department of Health and Human Services. Available *http://www.aoa.gov/ STATS* (accessed 8/21/02).

Ajrouch, K. J., Antonucci, T. C., & Janevic, M. R. (2001). Social networks among blacks and whites: The interaction between race and age. *Journal of Gerontology: Social Sciences,* 56B(2): S112–S118.

Akiyama, H., Elliott, K., & Antonucci, T. (1996). Same-sex and cross-sex relationships. *Journals of Gerontology, Series B. Psychological Sciences and Social Sciences* 51B (6): P374–P382.

Albert, M., Jones, K., Savage, C., et al. (1995). Predictors of Cognitive Change in Older Persons: MacArthur Studies of Successful Aging. *Psychology and Aging,* 10(4): 578–584.

Alessio, H. M., & Blasi, E. (1997). Physical activity as a natural antioxidant booster. *Research Quarterly for Exercise and Health,* 68: 292–302.

Alexander, J., Aunno, T., & Succi, M. (1996). Determinants of profound organizational change: Choice of conversion or closure among rural hospitals. *Journal of Health and Social Behavior,* 37: 238–251.

Allen, K., & Chin-Sang, V. (1990). A lifetime of work: The context and meanings of leisure for aging black women. *Gerontologist,* 30(6): 734–740.

Allison, J. J., Kiefe, C. I., & Centor, R. M. (1996). Racial differences in the medical treatment of elderly Medicare patients with acute myocardial infarction. *Journal of General Internal Medicine,* 11(12): 736–743.

Althausen, A. (1993). Journey of separation: Elderly Russian immigrants and their adult children in the health care setting. *Social Work in Health Care,* 19(1): 61–75.

American Academy of Actuaries. (1997). *Raising the Retirement Age for Social Security.* Washington, DC: Author.

American Association of Homes and Services for the Aged. (2001). Assisted Living. Available: *http://www.aahsa.org* (accessed 3/19/01).

American Psychiatric Association. (2000). *Diagnostic and Statistical Manual of Mental Disorders,* fourth edition text revision. Washington, DC: Author.

Amoako-Addo, Y. (1996a). Values and social policy: The Norwegian experience [Xerox]. Gothenburg, Sweden: University of Gothenburg, Department of Social Work.

Amoako-Addo, Y. (1996b, October). Service delivery for care of the elderly in Norway. Boston, MA: Unpublished seminar paper.

Anderson, R. N. (1999). Method for constructing complete annual U.S. life tables. *Vital Health Statistics,* 2(129): all.

Andrews, M. (2000). The seductiveness of agelessness. *Ageing and Society,* 19(3): 301–318.

Aneshensel, C. S., Frerichs, R. R., & Huba, G. J. (1984). Depression and physical illness: A multiwave, nonrecursive causal model. *Journal of Health and Social Behavior,* 25(4): 350–371.

Aneshensel, C. S., Pearlin, L. I., Mullan, J. T., Zarit, S. H., & Whitlach, C. H. (1995). *Profiles in Caregiving: The Unexpected Career.* San Diego: Academic Press.

Anonymous. (1994). Euthanasia and the law. *Ageing International,* 20: 28.

Anonymous. (nd). Genesis. In *The Holy Bible* (King James Version). Cleveland and New York: World Syndicate Publishing Co.

Antonovsky, A. (1972). Social class, life expectancy and overall mortality. In E. G. Jaco (Ed.), *Patients, Physicians, and Illness* (pp. 5–30). New York: Free Press.

Antonucci, T., & Akiyama, H. (1987). Social networks in adult life and a preliminary examination of the convoy model. *Journal of Gerontology,* 42: 519–527.

Aranda, M. P., & Knight, B. G. (1997). The influence of ethnicity and culture on the caregiver stress and coping process: A socio-cultural review and analysis. *The Gerontologist,* 37: 342–354.

Aries, P. (1962). *Centuries of Childhood.* New York: Random House.

——. (1974). *Western Attitudes Toward Death.* Baltimore, MD: Johns Hopkins Press.

Ariyoshi, S. (1984). *The Twilight Years.* Tokoyo and New York: Kodansha.

Arno, P. S., Levine, C., & Memmott, M. M. (1999). The Economic Value of Informal Caregiving. *Health Affairs,* 18: 182–188.

Asimus, D. (2000, March/April). [Letter]. *Modern Maturity,* p. 10.

Assisted Living Federation of America. (1998). Typical Assisted Living Resident: ALFA's 1998 Overview of the Assisted Living Industry. Available: *http://www.alfa.org/public/articles/details.cfm?id=102* (accessed 3/19/01).

Atchley, R. (1989). A continuity theory of aging. *The Gerontologist,* 29(2): 183–190.

——. (1995a). Age grading and grouping. In G. L. Maddox, R. C. Atchley, J. G. Evans, et al. (Eds.), *The Encyclopedia of Aging* (pp. 33–34). New York: Springer.

——. (1995b). Continuity Theory. In G. L. Maddox, R. C. Atchley, J. G. Evans, et al. (Eds.), *The Encyclopedia of Aging* (pp. 227–230). New York: Springer.

——. (2001). Continuity theory. In G. L. Maddox, R. C. Atchley, J. G. Evans, et al. (Eds.), *The Encyclopedia of Aging* (pp. 246–248). New York: Springer.

Avis, N. E., & McKinlay, S. (1991). A longitudinal analysis of women's attitudes toward the menopause: Results from the Massachusetts Women's Health Study. *Maturitas,* 13: 65–79.

Bach, J., & Barnett, V. (1994). Ethical considerations in the management of individuals with severe neuromuscular disorders. *American Journal of Physical Medicine and Rehabilitation,* 73(2): 134–140.

Bach, P., Cramer, L., Warren, J., & Begg, C. (1999). Racial differences in the treatment of early-stage lung cancer. *New England Journal of Medicine,* 341: 1198–1205.

Baltes, M. M., & Carstensen, L. L. (1999). Social-psychological theories and their applications to aging: From individual to collective. In V. L. Bengtson & K. W. Schaie (Eds.), *Handbook of Theories of Aging* (pp. 209–226). New York: Springer.

Baltes, P. B. (1993). The aging mind: Potential and limits. *Gerontologist,* 33(5): 580–594.

Baltes, P. B., & Baltes, M. M. (1990). *Successful Aging: Perspectives from the Behavioral Sciences*. Cambridge, England: Cambridge University Press.

Bandolier. (1998, July). Erectile dysfunction. In *Bandolier* [Online]. Available: *http://www.jr2.ox.ac.uk/bandolier/band53/b53-2.html* (accessed 6/1/99).

Banner, L. (1992). *In Full Flower: Aging Women, Power, and Sexuality*. New York: Knopf.

Barber, C. E. (1996). El efecto de la edad sobre las medidas de agudeza olfatoria: Un analisis de los datos de estudios correspondientes a diversos paises de Escandinavia, Europa y el Mediterraneo. *Revista de Gerontologia*, 6: 162–173.

Barry, P. P. (1997, February 21). Geriatric education: A team approach. Beverly Lecture at the 23rd Annual Meeting of the Association for Gerontology in Higher Education. Boston, MA.

———. (2000). Assessment of Geriatric Patients. In E. W. Markson & L. Hollis-Sawyer (Eds.), *Intersections of Aging* (pp. 375–380). Los Angeles: Roxbury.

Barry, P. P., & Markson, E. W. (1998). *Geriatric Module*. Washington, DC: American Medical Students Association.

Barzel, U. S. (1995). Osteoporosis. In G. L. Maddox, R. C. Atchley & J. G. Evans et al. (Eds.), *Encyclopedia of Aging* (pp. 722–723). NY: Springer.

Bazargan, M., Bazargan, S., & King, L. (2001). Paranoid ideation among elderly African American persons. *The Gerontologist*, 41(3): 366–373.

Beall, C., Baumhaver, L., Simpson, J., & Pieroni, R. (1991). Teaching Geriatric Medicine: Residents' perceptions of barriers and stereotypes. *Gerontology and Geriatrics Education*, 11(3): 85–95.

Beard, G. M. (1874). *Legal Responsibility in Old Age*. New York: Russells.

———. (1881). *American Nervousness: Its Causes and Consequences*. New York: Putnam.

Bedell, S., & Delbanco, T. L. (1984). Choices about cardiopulmonary resuscitation in the hospital. When do physicians talk with patients? *New England Journal of Medicine*, 310: 1089–1093.

Bedell, S., Pelle, D., Majer, P., et al. (1986). Do-not-resuscitate orders for critically ill patients in the hospital. How are they used and what is their impact? *Journal of the American Medical Association*, 256: 233–237.

Bedford, V. H., & Blieszner, R. (2000). Older adults and their families. In D. H. Demo, K. R. Allen, & M. A. Fine (Eds.), *Handbook of Family Diversity* (pp. 216–231). New York: Oxford University Press.

Beekman, A. T., Copeland, J. R., & Prince, M. J. (1999, April). Review of community prevalence of depression in later life. *British Journal of Psychiatry*, 174: 307–311.

Benedek, T. (1952). *Psychosocial Functions in Women*. New York: Ronald Press.

Bengtson, V. L., Burgess, E. O., & Parrott, T. (1997). Theory, explanation, and a third generation of theoretical development in social gerontology. *Journal of Gerontology: Social Sciences*, 52B(2): S72–S88.

Bengtson, V. L., Rice, C. J., & Johnson, M. L. (1999). Are theories of aging important? Models and explanations in gerontology at the turn of the century. In V. L. Bengtson & K. W. Schaie (Eds.), *Handbook of Theories of Aging* (pp. 3–20). New York: Springer.

Bengtson, V. L., Giarrusso, R., Silverstein, M., & Wang, H. (2000). Families and intergenerational relationships in aging societies. *Hallym International Journal of Aging*, 2(1): 3–10.

Bengtson, V. L., Rosenthal, C. J., & Burton, L. M. (1990). Families and aging: Diversity and heterogeneity. In R. Binstock & L. George (Eds.), *Handbook of Aging and the Social Sciences*, 3rd edition. New York: Academic Press.

Berman, P., & Goldman, C. (1992). *The Ageless Spirit*. New York: Ballantine Books.

Bernard, R. (1990). *At Death's Door*. London: Corgi.

Binstock, R. H., & Day, C. L. (1996). Aging and politics. In R. H. Binstock & L. K. George (Eds.), *Handbook of Aging and the Social Sciences*, 4th edition. San Diego, CA: Academic Press.

Black, H. K., & Rubinstein, R. I. (2000). *Old Souls: Aged Women, Poverty, and the Experience of God*. New York: Aldine de Gruyter.

Black, J., & Kapoor, W. (1990). Health promotion and disease prevention in older people: Our current state of ignorance. *Journal of the American Geriatrics Society*, 38(2): 168–172.

Blauner, R. (1968). Death and social structure. In B. L. Neugarten (Ed.), *Middle Age and Aging* (pp. 531–540). Chicago: University of Chicago.

Blazer, D. G., Burchett, B., Service, C., & George, L. K. (1991). The association of age and depression among the elderly: An epidemiological exploration. *Journal of Gerontology/Medical Sciences*, 46: M210–M215.

Bodnar, A. G., Ouelette, M., Frolkis, M., et al. (1998). Extension of life span by introduction of telomerase into normal human cells. *Science*, 279: 349–352.

Bogue, D. J. (1999). The ecological impact of population aging. *Essays in Human Ecology 4*. Chicago: Social Development Center (1–83).

Booth, C. (1894). *The Aged Poor in England and Wales*. London: Macmillan.

Booth-Kewley, S., & Friedman, H. S. (1987). Psychological predictors of heart disease: A quantitative review. *Psychological Bulletin*, 101: 343–362.

Bouvier, L. F., & De Vita, C. J. (1991). The baby boom—entering midlife. *Population Bulletin*, 46(3): 1–35.

Brecher, E. M. (1984). *Love, Sex, and Aging: A Consumers' Union Report*. Boston, MA: Little, Brown.

Brennan, P. L., Kagay, C. R., Geppert, J. J., & Moos, R. H. (2001). Predictors and outcomes of outpatient mental health care: A 4-year prospective study of elderly medicare patients with substance use disorders. *Medical Care*, 39(1): 39–49.

Brett, S. (1990). *Mrs. Presumed Dead*. London: Pan.

Brown, A. S., Susser, E. S., Lin, S. P., Neugebauer, R., & Gorman, J. M. (1995). Increased risk of affective disorders in males after second trimester prenatal exposure to the Dutch hunger winter of 1944–45. *British Journal of Psychiatry*, 166(5): 601–606.

Brown, J. (2000). *How Should We Insure Longevity Risk in Pensions and Social Security?* [IB #4]. Chestnut Hill, MA: Center for Retirement Research at Boston College.

Brown, R., Clement, D., Jerrold, W., Retching, S., & Bergeron, J. (1993). Do health maintenance organizations work for Medicare? *Health Care Financing Review,* 15: 7–23.

Bryson, K., & Casper, L. M. (1999). Coresident Grandparents and Grandchildren. *Current Population Reports, Special Studies,* vol. P-23-198. Washington DC: U.S. Department of Commerce, Economics and Statistics Administration, Bureau of the Census.

Buckland, P. R. (2001). Genetic association studies of alcoholism—problems with the candidate gene approach. *Alcohol and Alcoholism,* 36(2): 99–103.

Bureau of the Census, and U.S. Department of Commerce. (1995). *Population Profile of the United States, 1995.* Current Population Reports. Washington DC: U.S. Government Printing Office.

——. (2001). *Current Population Survey, March 2000,* Special Populations Branch, Population Division.

Burr, J. A., & Mutchler, J. E. (1999). Race and ethnic variation in norms of filial responsibility among older persons. *Journal of Marriage and the Family,* 61(3): 674–687.

Burtless, G. (2000). Social Security privatization and financial market risk. Working Paper, Center on Social and Economic Dynamics, vol. 10. Washington, DC: Brookings Institution.

Butler, R. N. (1969). Age-ism: Another form of bigotry. *The Gerontologist,* 9: 243–246.

Butler, R. N., & Lewis, M. L. (1993). *Love and Sex After 60.* New York: Ballentine.

Butler, R., Gertman, J., Oberlander, D., & Schindler, L. (1979–1980). Self-care, self-help, and the elderly. *International Journal of Aging and Human Development,* pp. 95–119.

Butler, R. N. (1963). The life review: An interpretation of reminiscence in the aged. *Psychiatry,* 26: 65–76.

Bytheway, B. (1995). *Ageism.* Philadelphia: Open University Press.

Calasanti, T. M. (1993). Bringing in diversity: Toward an inclusive theory of retirement. *Journal of Aging Studies,* 7(2): 133–150.

——. (1996). Incorporating diversity: Meaning, levels of research, and implications for theory. *Gerontologist,* 38(2): 147–156.

Callahan, D. (1995). *Setting Limits: Medical Goals in an Aging Society with a Response to My Critics.* Washington, DC: Georgetown University Press.

Campbell, L. D., Connidis, I. A., & Davies, L. (1999). Sibling ties in later life: A network analysis. *Journal of Family Issues,* 20: 114–148.

Campbell, L. D., & Martin-Matthews, A. (2000). Caring sons: Exploring men's involvement in filial care. *Canadian Journal of Aging,* 19: 57–79.

Canadian Intergovernmental Conference Secretariat. (2000). *First Minister's Meeting Communique on Health.* Canadian Intergovernmental Conference Secretariat. Ottawa: Author.

Cancian, F. (1990). *Love in America.* New York: Cambridge University Press.

Cancian, F., & Oliker, S. (2000). *Caring and Gender.* Thousand Oaks, CA: Pine Forge.

Carlson, R. H. (2000, 6/28). DG Dispatch: BPH: Plant-derived treatments for prostate disease not yet recommended. *DG News* [Online]. Available: *http://www.docguide.com/news/content.nsf/NewsPrint/D6BAA42D B8B07E798525690C* (accessed 12/19/2001).

Caserta, M. S., Lund, D. A., Wright, S. D., & Redburn, D. E. (1987). Caregivers to dementia patients: The utilization of community services. *The Gerontologist,* 27: 209–214.

Casper, L. M., & Bass, L. E. (1998, July). Voting and registration in the election of November 1996. *Current Population Reports, P20-504,* 1–11.

Casper, L. M., & Bryson, K. R. (1998). *Co-Resident Grandparents and Their Grandchildren: Grandparent Maintained Families.* Population Division, vol. Working Paper No. 26. Washington, DC: U.S. Bureau of the Census.

Catlin, G. (1874). Over the hill to the poor house. In M. Scott & B. Wishy (Eds.), *America's Families: A Documentary History* (p. 282). New York: Harper and Row.

Cato Institute. Social Security articles (various). Available: *http://cato.org* (accessed 10/2000).

Cavan, R., Burgess, E., Havighurst, R., & Goldhamer, H. (1949). *Personal Adjustments in Old Age.* Chicago: Science Research Associates.

Centers for Disease Control and Prevention, U.S. Public Health Service, and Department of Health and Human Services. (1997). *HIV AIDS Surveillance Report: U.S. HIV and AIDS cases reported through December 1996.* HIV/AIDS Surveillance Report, 8.

——. (1998, January 23). AIDS among Persons Aged 50 Years, United States, 1991–1996. *Morbidity and Mortality Weekly Report* [Online] (accessed August 23, 1999).

——. (1998). *Health, United States, 1998 with Socioeconomic Status and Health Chartbook.* Available *http://www.cdc.gov/nchs/data/hus/ hus98ncb* (accessed 8/21/02).

Chadwick, L., Saver, J., Biller, J., & Carr, J. (1998). Stroke and quality of life: Intimacy and sexuality poststroke. In W. Sife (Ed.), *After Stroke: Enhancing Quality of Life* (pp. 63–69). New York: Haworth.

Chaffers, J. (1994). *Spiritually—The Missing "i" in Mass Product(i)on: Or Why "Mass Quality" Need Not Be an Oxymoron.* London, England: Conference Proceedings of the Association of Collegiate Schools of Architecture European Conference: The Urban Scene and the History of the Future.

Charcot, J. M. (1881). *Clinical Lectures on the Diseases of Old Age.* New York: William Wood.

Charmaz, K. (1991). *Good Days, Bad Days: The Self in Chronic Illness and Time.* New Brunswick, NJ: Rutgers University Press.

Chatters, L. M., Taylor, R. J., & Jayakody, R. (1994). Fictive kinship relationships in black extended families. *Journal of Comparative Family Studies,* 25: 297–312.

Chavkin, W. (1984). *Double Exposure: Women's Health Hazards on the Job and at Home.* New York: Monthly Review Press.

Chen, L. S., Eaton, W. W., Gallow, J. J., & Nestadt, G. (2000). Understanding the heterogeneity of depression through the triad of symptoms, course, and risk factors: A longitudinal population-based study. *Journal of Affective Disorders,* 59(1): 1–11.

Cherlin, A. (1999). *Public and Private Families.* McGraw Hill.

Chinen, A. B. (1990). *In the Ever After: Fairy Tales and the Second Half of Life.* Willmette, IL: Chiron.

Choi, N. G. (1991). Racial differences in the determinants of living arrangements of widowed and divorced elderly women. *Gerontologist,* 31(4): 496–504.

Cicirelli, V. (1981). *Helping Elderly Parents: The Role of Adult Children.* Boston: Auburn House.

Citro, C. F., & Michael, R. T. (1995). *Measuring Poverty: A New Approach.* Washington, DC: National Academy Press.

Cohen, J., Fihn, S., & Boyko, E. E. A. (1994). Attitudes toward assisted suicide and euthanasia among physicians in Washington State. *New England Journal of Medicine,* 331(2): 89–94.

Cole, T. R. (1992). *The Journey of Life: A Cultural History of Aging in America.* New York: Cambridge University Press.

Collins, J. G. (1997). Prevalence of selected chronic conditions: United States, 1990–1992. In *Vital and Health Statistics, Series 10.* Data from the National Health Survey. DHHS publication no. (PHS) 97-1522. Washington DC: U.S. Department of Health, Education, and Welfare.

Comfort, A. (1964). *The Process of Aging.* New York: Signet.

Commission of the European Communities. (2000). *The Future Evolution of Social Protection from a Long-Term Point of View: Safe and Sustainable Pensions.* Brussels, Belgium: Authors.

Commonwealth Fund. (1997). *Minority Health Care Survey Highlights.* New York: Author.

Comstock, G. W., & Helsing, K. J. (1976). Symptoms of depression in two communities. *Psychological Medicine,* 6(4): 551–563.

Conley, J. J. (1992). Masks of autonomy. *Social Science and Modern Society,* 23(5): 11–15.

Connelly, M. (1996, Sunday, November 10). Portrait of the electorate: The vote under a microscope. *New York Times* [Online]. Available: *http://www.nytimes.com/library/politics/elect-port.html* (accessed 7/12/02).

Consumer Reports. (1998, February). Dream home . . . or nightmare? *Consumer Reports* [Online]. Available: *http://www.consumerreports.org/Special/ConsumerInterest/Reports/9802hom0.htm* (accessed 3/20/01).

Conwell, Y. (1994). Suicide in elderly patients. In L. S. Schneider, C. F. I. Reynolds, B. D. Lebowitz, & A. J. Friedhoff (Eds.), *Diagnosis and Treatment of Depression in Late Life* (pp. 397–418). Washington, DC: American Psychiatric Press.

Conwell, Y., & Brent, D. (1995). Suicide and aging 1: Patterns of psychiatric diagnosis. *International Psychogeriatrics,* 7(2): 149–164.

Cooley, C. H. (1902/1964). *Human Nature and the Social Order.* New York: Schocken Books.

Cooney, T. M. (1995). Divorce. In G. L. Maddox, R. C. Atchley, J. G. Evans, et al. (Eds.), *Encyclopedia of Aging* (pp. 286–287). New York: Springer.

Cosmopolitan Staff. (2000, February). Cover. *Cosmopolitan Magazine.*

Cottrell, F. (1960). The technological and societal bases of aging. In C. Tibbetts (Ed.), *Handbook of Social Gerontology.* Chicago: University of Chicago Press.

Couch, K. A. (1998). Late life job displacement. *The Gerontologist,* 38(1): 7–17.

Counts, D. A., & Counts, D. R. (1996). *Over the Next Hill: An Ethnography of RVing Seniors in North America.* Peterborough, Ontario: Broadview Press.

Covinsky, K. E., Fuller, J. D., Yaffe, K., et al. (2000). Communication and decision-making in seriously ill patients; Findings of the SUPPORT project. The study to understand prognoses and preferences for outcomes and risks of treatments. *Journal of the American Geriatrics Society,* 48(5 supplement): S187–S193.

Coward, R. T., & Dwyer, J. W. (1990). The association of gender, sibling network composition, and patterns of parent care by adult children. *Research on Aging,* 12(2): 158–181.

Cowdry, E. V. (1939). *Problems of Ageing.* Baltimore: Williams and Wilkins.

Cowgill, D. (1974). Aging and modernization: A revision of the theory. In J. Gubrium (Ed.), *Late Life: Communities and Environmental Policy.* Springfield, IL: Charles C. Thomas.

Cowgill, D., & Holmes, L. (1972). *Aging and Modernization.* New York: Appleton-Crofts.

Crown, W. H., Leavitt, T. D., & Rix, S. E. (1996). *Underemployment and the Older Worker: How Big a Problem?* Washington, DC: AARP Public Policy Institute.

Crown, W., & Longino, C. F., Jr. (1997). Labor force trends and aging policy. *Critical Issues in Aging* 1 (Fall): 16–17.

Cumming, E. (1963). Further thoughts on the theory of disengagement. *International Social Science Journal,* 15: 377–393.

Cumming, E., & Henry, W. (1961). *Growing Old: The Process of Disengagement.* New York: Basic Books.

Cummings, J. L., & Masterman, D. L. (1999). Depression in patients with Parkinson's disease. *International Journal of Geriatric Psychiatry,* 14(9): 711–718.

Cutler, N. E. (2000, November 20). Myths and realities of aging 2000. Paper presented at the Annual Meeting of the Gerontological Society of America, Washington, D.C.

Cutler, S. J. (2000). Aging and social change: Toward an interdisciplinary research agenda. In J. M. Clair & R. M. Allman (Eds.), *The Gerontological Prism: Developing Interdisciplinary Bridges* (pp. 9–28). Amityville, NY: Baywood.

Cutler, S. J., & Danigelis, N. L. (2001, July 3). Cohort changes in U.S. racial attitudes: 1972–1998. Paper presented at the 17th World Congress of the International Association of Gerontology, Vancouver, British Columbia.

Cutler, S. J., & Hendricks, J. (2001). Age differences in voluntary association memberships: Fact or artifact? *Journal of Gerontology: Social Sciences,* 55B(2): S98–S107.

Dalaker, J. (2001). *Poverty in the United States, 2000.* Current Population Reports, vol. P 60-214. Washington, DC: U.S. Bureau of the Census.

Dalaker, J., & Proctor, B. D. (2000). *Poverty in the United States.* Current Population Reports: Consumer Income, vol. P60-210. Washington, DC: U.S. Census Bureau.

Dannefer, D., & Uhlenberg, P. (1999). Paths of the life course: A typology. In V. L. Bengston & K. W. Schaie (Eds.), *Handbook of Theories of Aging* (pp. 306–326). New York: Springer.

Dartmouth Atlas of Health Care. (1999). *Dartmouth Atlas of Health Care.* Lebanon, NH: Dartmouth Medical School.

de Tocqueville, A. (translated by Henry Reeves). (1838–40). *Democracy in America.* New York: Craighead and Allen.

Demos, J. (1978). Old age in early New England. In M. Gordon (Ed.), *The American Family in Socio-Historical Perspective* (pp. 220–256). New York: St. Martin's Press.

——. (1986). *Past, Present, and Personal: The Family and the Life Course in American History.* New York: Oxford University Press.

Demos, J., & Demos, V. (2000). Adolescence in historical perspective. In P. S. Fass & M. A. Mason (Eds.), *Childhood in America* (pp. 132–139). New York: New York University Press.

Demos, J., & Jache, A. (1981). When you care enough: An analysis of attitudes toward aging in humorous birthday cards. *Gerontologist,* 21: 209–215.

Denkla, W. D. (1975). A time to die. *Life Sciences,* 16: 31.

Desbiens, N. A., Mueller-Rizner, N., Hamel, M. B., & Conners, A. F. (1998). Preference for comfort care does not affect the pain experience of seriously ill patients. The SUPPORT investigators' study to understand prognoses and preferences for outcomes and risks of treatment. *Journal of Pain and Symptom Management,* 16(5): 281–289.

Diamond, J. (1998). *Male Menopause.* SourceBooks.

Diamond, T. (1993). *Making Gray Gold.* Chicago: University of Chicago Press.

Dobson, D. (1983). The elderly as a political force. In W. Browne & L. K. Olson (Eds.), *Aging and Public Policy.* Westport, CT: Greenwood.

Dohm, A. (2000, July). Gauging the labor force effects of retiring baby boomers. *Monthly Labor Review,* pp. 17–25.

Dorfman, R., Walters, K., Burke, P., Hardin, L., Karanik, T., Raphael, J., & Silverstein, E. (1995). Old, sad and alone: The myth of the aging homosexual. *Journal of Gerontological Social Work,* 24(1/2): 29–44.

Dowd, J. J. (1975). Aging as exchange: A preface to theory. *Journal of Gerontology,* 30(5): 584–594.

Dressler, P., Minkler, M., & Yen, I. (1997). Gender, race, class, and aging: Advances and opportunities. *International Journal of Health Services,* 27(4): 579–600.

Duberman, M. B. (1997). *A Queer World: The Center for Lesbian and Gay Studies Reader.* New York: New York University Press.

Durenberger, D. I. (1989). Education and the contract between the generations. *The Generational Journal,* 11(1): 5–8.

Durkheim, E. (1897/1966). *Suicide.* New York: Free Press.

Dwamena, F. C., El-Tamimi, H., Watson, R. E., et al. (2000). The use of angiotensin-converting enzyme inhibitors in patients with acute myocardial infarction in community hospitals. Michigan State University Inter-Institutional Collaborative Heart (MICH) Study Group. *Clinical Cardiology,* 23: 341–346.

The Economist. (1991). Editorial: Euthanasia: What is the 'good death'? *The Economist,* July 20: pp. 21–23.

Edmonson, B. (1997, April). The facts of death. *American Demographics* [Online]. Available: *http://www.demographics.com/publications/ad/97/9704_ad/ad970427.htm* (accessed 2/3/99).

Eggebeen, D. J., & Davey, A. (1998). Do safety nets work: The role of anticipated help in time of need. *Journal of Marriage and the Family,* 60(4): 939–950.

Ekerdt, D. J., Kosloski, K., & DeViney, S. (2000). The normative anticipation of retirement by older workers. *Research on Aging,* 22(1): 3–22.

Elder, G. H. (1974). *Children of the Great Depression.* Chicago: University of Chicago Press.

Ellis, H. (1905/1942). The sexual impulse in women. In H. Ellis (Ed.), *The Psychology of Sex* (pp. 192–256). New York: Random House.

Ellison, C. G. (1991). Religious involvement and subjective well-being. *Journal of Health and Social Behavior,* 32: 80–99.

——. (1994). Religion, the life stress paradigm, and the study of depression. In J. S. Levin (Ed.), *Religion in Aging and Health: Theoretical Foundations and Methodological Frontiers* (pp. 78–121). Newbury Park, CA: Sage.

Elman, C. (1999). Labor markets and opportunity structures: Modeling the context of retirement in the historical United States. *Research on Aging,* 21(2): 205–239.

Emerson, R. M., & Pollner, M. (1988). On the uses of members' responses to researchers' accounts. *Human Organization,* 47: 189–198.

——. (1992). Difference and dialogue: Members' readings of ethnographic texts. In G. Miller & J. A. Holstein (Eds.), *Perspectives on Social Problems: A Research Annual, vol. 3* (pp. 79–98). Greenwich, CT: JAI Press.

Erikson, E. H. (1950/1963). *Childhood and Society* (2nd Edition). New York: W.W. Norton and Company.

——. (1959). *Psychological Issues, Vol. 1: Identity and the Life Cycle: Selected Papers.* International Universities Press.

Erikson, E. H., Erikson, J. M., & Kivnick, H. Q. (1994). *Vital Involvement in Old Age.* New York: W. W. Norton.

Espenshade, T. J., & Ye, W. (1994). Differential fertility within an ethnic minority: The effect of 'trying harder' among Chinese American Women. *Social Problems,* 41: 97–113.

Estes, C. L. (1979). *The Aging Enterprise.* San Francisco: Jossey Bass.

——. (1991). The new political economy of aging: Introduction and critique. In M. Minkler & C. Estes (Eds.), *Critical Perspectives on Aging* (pp. 3–18). New York: Baywood.

Evans, W. (1999). Exercise training guidelines for the elderly. *Medical Sciences, Sports, and Exercise,* 31: 12–17.

Falkner, T. M., & de Luce, J. (1992). A view from antiquity: Greece, Rome, and elders. In T. R. Cole, D. D. Van Tassel, & R. Kastenbaum (Eds.), *Handbook of the Humanities and Aging* (pp. 3–39). New York: Springer.

Farren, C. K., & Tipton, K. F. (1999). Trait markers for alcoholism: Clinical utility. *Alcohol and Alcoholism,* 34(5): 649–665.

Fausto-Sterling, A. (1985). *Myths of Gender: Biological Theories About Women and Men.* New York: Basic Books.

Featherstone, M., & Hepworth, M. (1995). Images of positive aging: A case study of *Retirement Choice* magazine. In M. Featherstone & A. Wernick (Eds.), *Images of Aging: Cultural Representations of Later Life* (pp. 29–47). London: Routledge.

Federal Interagency Forum on Aging Related Statistics. (2000). *Older Americans 2000: Key Indicators of Well-Being.* Hyattsville, MD: Author.

Fenigsen, R. (1989). Mercy, murder, and morality: Perspectives on euthanasia—A case against Dutch euthanasia. *Hastings Center Reports,* 19(Supplement): 22–30.

Fiatarone, M. A., Marks, E. C., Ryan, N. D., et al. (1990). High intensity strength training in nonagenarians. *Journal of the American Medical Association* 263: 3029–3034.

Fiatarone, M. A., O'Neill, E., & Ryan, N. D. (1994). Exercise training and nutritional supplementation for physical frailty in very elderly people. *New England Journal of Medicine,* 330: 1769–1775.

Finucane, T., Shumway, J. M., Powers, R. L., & Dalessandri, R. M. (1988). Planning with elderly outpatients for contingencies of severe illness: A survey and clinical trial. *Journal of General Internal Medicine,* 3(4): 322–325.

Fiscella, K., & Franks, P. (1997). Poverty or income inequality as predictor of mortality: Longitudinal cohort study. *British Medical Journal,* 314: 1724.

Fischer, D. H. (1977). *Growing Old in America.* New York: Oxford University Press.

Fisher, B. J. (1992). Exploring ageist stereotypes through commercial motion pictures. *Teaching Sociology,* 20(4): 280–284.

FitzPatrick, C. S., & Entmacher, J. (2000). Widows, poverty, and Social Security policy options. *Social Security Brief, vol. 9.* Washington, DC: National Academy of Social Insurance (7 pages).

Flippen, C., & Tienda, M. (2000). Pathways to retirement: Patterns of labor force participation and labor market exit among pre-retirement population by race, Hispanic origin, and sex. *Journals of Gerontology: Psychological Sciences and Social Sciences,* 55B(1): S14–S27.

Foley, D. J., Monjan, A. A., Izmirlian, G., Hays, F. C., & Blazer, D. G. (1999). Incidence and remission of insomnia among elderly adults in a biracial cohort. *Sleep,* 22(Supplement 2): S373–S378.

Foremost Insurance Group. (1999). *Market Facts 1999.* Available: *http://www.foremost.com* (accessed 3/19/01).

Fowler, J. (1981). *Stages of Faith.* New York: Harper and Row.

Fox, M. (1998, September 28). Birds do it, bees do it, even grandma does it. *Yahoo! News* [Online]. Available: *http://dailynews.yahoo.com* (accessed 9/28/98).

Fox, R. C., & Swazey, J. P. (1992). *Spare Parts: Organ Replacement in American Society*. New York: Oxford University Press.

Frank, D. A., et al. (2001). Growth, development, and behavior in early childhood following prenatal cocaine exposure: A systematic review. *Journal of the American Medical Association,* 285(12): 1613–1625.

Frankenhaeuser, M., Lundberg, U., Fredrikson, M., Melin, B., Tuomisto, M., et al. (1989). Stress on and off the job as related to sex and occupational status in white-collar workers. *Journal of Organizational Behavior,* 10: 321–346.

Freedman, M., & Roma, T. (1999). *Prime Time: How the Baby-Boomers Will Revolutionize Retirement and Transform America*. Public Affairs, LLC.

Freedman, R. I., Krauss, M. W., & Seltzer, M. M. (1997). Aging parents' residential plans for adult children with mental retardation. *Mental Retardation,* 35: 114–123.

Freedman, V. A., Aykan, H., & Martin, L. G. (2001). Aggregate changes in severe cognitive impairment among older Americans: 1993 and 1998. *Journals of Gerontology: Psychological Sciences and Social Sciences,* 56B(2): S100–S111.

Fremont, A. M., & Bird, C. E. (1999). Integrating sociological and biological models: An editorial. *Journal of Health and Social Behavior,* 40(2): 126–129.

Freud, S. (1915/1958). *Complete Psychological Works of Sigmund Freud, Vol. 12*. London: Hogarth.

——. (1961a). *Complete Psychological Works of Sigmund Freud. Vol. 12: Types of onset of neurosis* (J. Strachey, Trans.) (Standard Edition). London: Hogarth Press.

——. (1961b). *Some Psychical Consequences of the Anatomical Distinction Between the Sexes* (J. Strachey, Trans.). London: Hogarth Press.

Friedell, M. (2000). Incipient dementia: A victim's perspective. In E. W. Markson & L. Hollis-Sawyer (Eds.), *Intersections of Aging* (pp. 381–385). Los Angeles: Roxbury.

Friedland, R. P., Fritsch, T., Smith, K. A., et al. (2001). Patients with Alzheimer's disease have reduced activities in midlife compared with healthy control-group members. *Proceedings of the National Academy of Science,* 98(6): 3440–3445.

Friedman, B., Ozminkowski, R., & Taylor, Z. (1992). Excess demand and patient selection for heart and liver transplants. *Health Economics Worldwide,* pp. 161–186.

Friend, R. A. (1987). The individual and social psychology of aging: Clinical implications for lesbians and gay men. *Journal of Homosexuality,* 4(1/2): 307–331.

Fronstin, P. (1999). Retirement patterns and employee benefits: Do benefits matter? *The Gerontologist,* 39(1): 37–47.

Frontera, W., & Evans, W. (1986). Exercise performance and endurance training in the elderly. *Topics in Geriatric Rehabilitation,* 2(1): 17–32.

Fry, C. (1999). Anthropological theories of age and aging. In V. L. Bengtson & K. W. Schaie (Eds.), *Handbook of Theories of Aging* (pp. 271–286). New York: Springer.

Fry, P. S. (2001). The unique contribution of key existing factors to the prediction of psychological well-being of older adults following spousal loss. *The Gerontologist,* 41(1): 69–81.

Fullerton, H. N., Jr. (1999). Labor force projections to 2008: Steady growth and changing composition. *Monthly Labor Review,* November, 19–32.

Furman, F. K. (1997). *Facing the Mirror: Older Women and Beauty Shop Culture.* London and New York: Rutledge.

Furnham, A. (2001). Inside Track: Dealing with the shock of retirement. *Financial Times* [Online], January 31. Available: *http://globalarchive. ft.com/globalarchive/articles* (accessed 2/01/01).

Gabrel, C. S. (2000). Characteristics of Elderly Nursing Home Current Residents and Discharges: Data from the *1997 National Nursing Home Survey, advance data, vol. 312.* Washington, DC: National Center for Health Statistics, U.S. Department of Health and Human Services.

Gale, W. G., Papke, L. E., & VanDerhei, J. (1999, September 17). Understanding the shift from defined benefit to defined contribution plans. *ERISA After 25 Years: A Framework for Evaluating Pension Reform.* Washington, DC: National Press Club.

Gallagher-Thompson, D. (1995). Bereavement. In G. L. Maddox, R. C. Atchley, J. G. Evans, et al. (Eds.), *Encyclopedia of Aging,* Second Edition (pp. 105–108). New York: Springer.

———. (2001). Bereavement. In G. L. Maddox, R. C. Atchley, J. G. Evans, et al. (Eds.), *Encyclopedia of Aging,* Third Edition (pp. 117–119). New York: Springer.

Gallego, D. (1980, November). The Mexican American elderly: Familial and friendship support systems . . . fact or fiction? Gerontological Society of America Annual Meetings. San Diego.

Gallin, R. (1998). The intersection of class and age: Mother-in-law/daughter-in-law relations in rural Taiwan. In J. Dickerson-Putnam & J. K. Brown (Eds.), *Women Among Women: Anthropological Perspectives on Female Age Hierarchies* (pp. 1–14). Chicago and Urbana: University of Illinois Press.

Gallo, W. T., Bradley, E. H., Siegel, M., & Kasl, S. V. (2000). Health effects of involuntary job loss among older workers: Findings from the Health and Retirement Survey. *Journals of Gerontology: Psychological and Social Sciences,* 55B(3): S131–S140.

Gan, S. C., et al. (2000). Treatment of acute myocardial infarction and 30-day mortality among women and men. *New England Journal of Medicine,* 343: 8–15.

Gardyn, R. (2000, November). Retirement redefined. *American Demographics,* pp. 52–57.

Garrity, T., & Lawson, E. (1989). Patient-physician communication as a determinant of medication misuse in older minority women. *Journal of Drug Issues,* pp. 245–259.

Gaugler, J. E., Leitsch, S. A., Zarit, S. H., & Pearlin, L. I. (2000). Caregiver involvement following institutionalization: Effects of preplacement stress. *Research on Aging,* 22(4): 337–359.

Gaullier, X. (1988). *La Deuxieme Carriere: Ages, Emplois, Retraites.* Paris: Editions du Soleil.

George, L. K., & Weiler, S. J. (1981). Sexuality in middle and late life. *Archives of General Psychiatry,* 38: 919–923.

George, L. K. (2001). Self-esteem. In G. L. Maddox, R. C. Atchley, J. G. Evans, et al. (Eds.), *Encyclopedia of Aging,* Third Edition (pp. 902–904). New York: Springer.

Gergen, K. (1985). *The Social Construction of the Person.* New York: Springer Verlag.

Gibb, H., & Holroyd, E. (1996). Images of old age in the Hong Kong print media. *Ageing and Society,* 16(2): 151–175.

Glaser, B. G., & Strauss, A. L. (1965). *Awareness of Dying.* Chicago: Aldine.

Glendinning, C., Schunk, M., & McLaughlin, E. (1997). Paying for long-term domiciliary care: A comparative perspective. *Ageing and Society,* 17: 123–140.

Glenn, N. (1976). Cohort analysts' futile quest: Statistical attempts to separate age, period and cohort effects. *American Sociological Review,* 41(5): 900–904.

Global Aging Report Editorial. (1997, April/May). Eye on the business page. *Global Aging Report,* 2(2): 7.

Global Aging Report. (1997). How AIDS claims its older victims: Health and social consequences weigh heavily. *Global Aging Report,* 2.

Goffman, E. (1959). *The Presentation of Self in Everyday Life.* Garden City, NY: Anchor.

———. (1961). *Asylums.* Garden City, New York: Doubleday.

Gold, D. T. (1996). Continuities and discontinuities in sibling relationships across the life span. In Vern L. Bengtson (Ed.), *Adulthood and Aging: Research on Continuities and Discontinuities* (pp. 228–241). New York: Springer.

Gold, D. (1989a). Generational Solidarity: Conceptual antecedents and consequences. *American Behavioral Scientist,* 33(1): 19–32.

———. (1989b). Sibling relationships in old age: A typology. *International Journal of Aging and Human Development,* 28, 37–54.

Goldberg, E. L., Van Natta, P., & Comstock, G. W. (1985). Depressive symptoms, social networks and social support of elderly women. *American Journal of Epidemiology,* 121(3): 448–456.

Gomberg, E. S. L. (1996). Alcohol and Drugs. In James S. Birren (Ed.), *Encyclopedia of Gerontology* (pp. 93–101). New York: Academic Press.

Gomez, C. F. (1991). *Regulating Death.* New York: Free Press.

Goodman, M., & Rubinstein, R. L. (1993). Parenting in later life. *Journal of Aging Studies* 10(4): 295–311.

Graig, L. A. (1993). *Health of Nations.* Washington, DC: Congressional Quarterly, Inc.

Greenberg, J. S., Seltzer, M. M., & Greenley, J. R. (1993). Aging parents of adults with disabilities: The gratifications and frustrations of later-life caregiving. *The Gerontologist,* 33: 542–550.

Greene, M., Adelman, R., Charon, R., & Hoffman, S. (1986). Ageism in the medical encounter. *Language and Communication,* 6: 113–124.

Gubrium, J. E. (1975). *Living and Dying at Murray Manor.* New York: St. Martin's Press.

———. (1993). Voice and context in a new gerontology. In T. R. Cole, A. Achenbaum, P. Jakobi, & R. Kastenbaum (Eds.), *Voices and Visions of Aging* (pp. 46–63). New York: Springer.

Gutmann, D. (1986). Aging and Oedipus. *The Psychoanalytic Review*, 73: 137–148.

Gutmann, D. (1994). *Reclaimed Powers: Toward a New Psychology of Men and Women in Later Life*. New York: Basic Books.

———. (1997). *The Human Elder in Nature, Culture, and Society*. New York: Westview Press: A Division of Harper Collins Publishers.

Haber, C. (1983). *Beyond Sixty-Five: The Dilemma of Old Age in America's Past*. Cambridge: Cambridge University Press.

Haber, C., & Gratton, B. (1994). *Old Age and the Search for Security: An American Social History*. Bloomington, IN: University of Indiana.

Hagestad, G. O. (1987). Able elderly in the family context: Changes, chances, and challenges. *Gerontologist* 27(4): 417–422.

Hakim, R. B., Teno, J. M., Harrell, F. E., Jr., et al. (1996). Factors associated with do-not-resuscitate orders: Patients' preferences, prognoses, and physicians' judgments. SUPPORT Investigators study to understand prognoses and preferences for outcomes and risks of treatment. *Annals of Internal Medicine*, 125(4): 284–293.

Hall, G. S. (1922). *Senescence, the Second Half of Life*. New York: D. Appleton.

Hampson, E. (1990). Variations in sex-related cognitive abilities across the menstrual cycle. *Brain and Cognition*, 14(4): 633–643.

Hand, J., & Reid, P. (2000). Hand-me-down people. In E. W. Markson & L. Hollis-Sawyer (Eds.), *Intersections of Aging* (pp. 345–353). Los Angeles: Roxbury.

Hardy, M. A., & Hazelrigg, L. (1999). A multilevel model of early retirement decisions among autoworkers in plants with different futures. *Research on Aging*, 21(2): 275–303.

Hareven, T. (1982). *Family Time and Industrial Time: The Relationship Between the Family and Work in a New England Industrial Community*. Cambridge, England: Cambridge University Press.

Haug, M., & Ory, M. (1987). Issues in elderly patient-provider interactions. *Research on Aging*, pp. 3–44.

Havighurst, R. J. (1961). Successful aging. *The Gerontologist*, 1(1): 8–13.

———. (1968, Part II). Personality and patterns of aging. *The Gerontologist*, 8(2): 20–23.

Havighurst, R. J., & Albrecht, R. (1953). *Older People*. New York: Longman's Green.

Hayflick, L. (1985). Theories of biological aging. *Experimental Gerontology*, 20, 145–159.

———. (1994). *How and Why We Age*. New York: Ballantine Books.

Haynie, D. A., Berg, S., Johnson, B., et al. (2001). Symptoms of depression in the oldest old: A longitudinal study. *Journals of Gerontology Series B: Psychological Sciences and Social Sciences* 56: P111–P118.

Hays, J. C., Landerman, L. R., George, L. K., et al. (1998). Social correlates of the dimensions of depression in the elderly. *Journal of Gerontology: Psychological Sciences*, 53B: 32–39.

Hayward, M. D., Crimmins, E. M., Miles, T. P., & Yang, Y. (2000, December). The significance of socioeconomic status in explaining the racial gap in chronic health conditions. *American Sociological Review*, 65: 910–930.

Hayward, M. D., Friedman, S., & Chen, H. (1998). Career trajectories and older men's retirement. *Journal of Gerontology: Social Sciences*, 53B(2): S91–S103.

Hazelrigg, L. (1997). On the importance of age. In M. A. Hardy (Ed.), *Studying Aging and Social Change: Conceptual and Methodological Issues* (pp. 93–128). Thousand Oaks, CA: Sage.

Healy, B. (1991). The Yentl syndrome. *New England Journal of Medicine*, 325: 274–276.

Hendin, H., & Klerman, G. (1993). Physician-assisted suicide: The dangers of legalization. *American Journal of Psychiatry*, 150: 143–145.

Hendricks, J. (2000). Foreword. In E.W. Markson & L.A. Hollis-Sawyer (Eds.), *Intersections of Aging* (pp. xiii–xv). Los Angeles: Roxbury.

——. (nd). Careers in Aging. Association for Gerontology in Higher Education [Online]. Available: *http://www.aghe.org/cia* (accessed 3/21/00).

Hendricks, J., & Achenbaum, A. (1999). Historical development of theories of aging. In V. L. Bengtson & W. L. Schaie (Eds.), *Handbook of Theories of Aging* (pp. 21–39). New York: Springer.

Henretta, J. C. (1997). Guest editorial: Changing perspectives on retirement. *Journal of Gerontology: Social Sciences*, 52B(1): S1–S3.

Hepworth, M. (1991). Positive aging and the mask of age. *Journal of Educational Gerontology*, 6(2): 93–101.

——. (1993). Old age in crime fiction. In J. Johnson & R. Slater (Eds.), *Ageing and Later Life* (pp. 32–37). London: Sage.

Herlitz, J., Bang, A., Karlson, B. W., & Hartford, M. Is there a gender difference in aetiology of chest pain and symptoms associated with acute myocardial infarction? *European Journal of Emergency Medicine*, 6: 311–315.

Herrnstein, R. J., & Murray, C. (1995). *The Bell Curve*. New York: Schuster.

Herz, D. E. (1995, April). Work after early retirement: An increasing trend among men. *Monthly Labor Review*, pp. 13–20.

Hess, B. B. (1990). Beyond dichotomy: Drawing distinctions and embracing differences. *Sociological Forum*, 5(1): 75–93.

Hess, B. B., & Markson, E. W. (1980). *Aging and Old Age*. New York: Macmillan.

Heumann, L. F., & Boldy, D. P. (1993). *Aging in Place with Dignity: International Solutions*. Westport, CT: Praeger.

High, D. (1993). Advance directives and the elderly: A study of intervention strategies to increase use. *The Gerontologist*, 33: 342–349.

Hilton, J. M., & Macari, D. P. (1997). Grandparent involvement following divorce: A comparison in single-mother and single-father families. *Journal of Divorce and Remarriage*, 28(1–2): 203–224.

Himes, C. L., & Reidy, E. B. (2000). The role of friends in caregiving. *Research on Aging*, 22: 315–336.

Hobbs, F. B., & Damon, B. L. (1996). *65+ in the United States. Current Population Reports, vol. P23-190*. Washington, DC: U.S. Bureau of the Census.

Hochschild, A. (1989). *The Second Shift*. New York: Viking Penguin.

Hodgson, L. G., & Cutler, S. J. (2000). Anticipatory dementia and well-being. *American Journal of Alzheimer's Disease* 12(2): 62–66.

Hoek, H. W., Brown, A. S., & Susser, E. (1998). The Dutch famine and schizophrenia spectrum disorders. *Social Psychiatry and Psychiatric Epidemiology*, 33(8): 373–379.

Hogan, C., Lunney, J., Gabel, J., et al. (2001). Medicare beneficiaries' costs of care in the last year of life. *Health Affairs 20* (4): 188–95.

Holden, K. C., & Kuo, H.-H. (1996). Complex marital histories and economic well-being: The continuing legacy of divorce and widowhood as the HRS cohort approaches retirement. *The Gerontologist*, 36: 383–390.

Holmstrom, D. (2000). Lives of a Century: Fred Demon Marsh. *Christian Science Monitor* [Online], June 7. Available: *http://www.csmonitor.com/atcsmonitor/specials/centenarians/fred.html* (accessed 11/27/00).

Homans, G. C. (1974). *Social Behavior: Its Elementary Forms*. New York: Harcourt Brace Jovanovich.

Hopp, F. P. (2000). Preferences for surrogate decision makers, informal communication, and advance directives among community-dwelling elders: Results from a national study. *The Gerontologist*, 40(4): 449–457.

Hopp, F. P., & Duffy, S. A. (2000). Racial variations in end-of-life care. *Journal of the American Geriatrics Society*, 48(6): 658–663.

Horn, M. (1998). The deathcare business. *U.S. News* [Online], March 23. Available: *http://www.usnews.com/usnews/search/magazine_search.htm* (accessed 8/19/02).

Hudson, R. B., & Strate, J. (1985). Aging and political systems. In R. Binstock & E. Shanas (Eds.), *Handbook of Aging and the Social Sciences*, Second Edition. New York: Van Nostrand.

Humphry, D. (1991). *Final Exit: The Practicalities of Self-Deliverance and Assisted Suicide*. Eugene, OR: Hemlock Society.

Hungerford, T. L. (2001). The economic consequences of widowhood on elderly women in the United States and Germany. *The Gerontologist*, 41: 103–110.

Huntington, R., & Metcalf, P. (1972). *Celebrations of Death: The Anthropology of Mortuary Rituals*. New York: Cambridge University Press.

Huyck, M. H., Zucker P., & Angellaccio, C. (2000). Gender across generations. In E. W. Markson & L. A. Hollis-Sawyer (Eds.), *Intersections of Aging* (pp. 87–102). Los Angeles: Roxbury.

Idler, E. L., & Benyamini, Y. (1997). Self-rated health and mortality: A review of twenty-seven community studies. *Journal of Health and Social Behavior*, 38: 21–37.

Iezonni, L., Ash, A., Shwartz M., & Mackiernan, Y. (1997). Differences in procedure use, in-hospital mortality, and illness severity by gender for acute myocardial infarction patients. *Medical Care*, 35: 158–171.

Ikels, C. (1991). Delayed reciprocity and the support networks of the childless elderly. In B. B. Hess & E. W. Markson (Eds.), *Growing Old in America* (pp. 441–456). New Brunswick, NJ: Transaction.

Ivancevich, J. M., & Matteson, M. T. (1988). Type A behavior and the healthy individual. *British Journal of Medical Psychology*, 61: 37–56.

Jacobs, R. H. (1993). *Be an Outrageous Older Woman: A R.A.S.P.* Manchester, CT: KIT.

Janus, S. S., & Janus, C. (1992). *The Janus Report on Sexual Behavior.* New York: Wiley.

Johannes, C. B., & Avis, N. B. (1997). Gender differences in sexual activity among mid-aged adults in Massachusetts. *Maturitas,* 26(3): 175–184.

John, R. (1997). Aging and mortality among American Indians. In K. S. Markides & M. R. Miranda (Eds.), *Minorities, Aging and Health* (pp. 79–104). Thousand Oaks, CA: Sage.

Johnson, B. K. (1999). Health status and sexuality in older adults. *Southwest Journal on Aging,* 15(1): 23–28.

Johnson, C. L. (1995). Determinants of adaptation of oldest old black Americans. *Journal of Aging Studies* 9(3): 231–244.

——. (1999). Fictive kin among oldest old African Americans in the San Francisco bay area. *Journal of Gerontology: Social Sciences,* 54B(6): S369–S375.

Johnson, C. L., & Barer, B. M. (1996). *Life Beyond 85 Years: The Aura of Survivorship.* New York: Springer.

Johnson, R. W., Sambamoorthi, U., & Crystal, S. (1999). Gender differences in pension wealth: Estimates using provider data. *The Gerontologist,* 39(3): 320–333.

Joyce, E. (1999, March). Age bias may thwart boomers. *NCOA Networks* [Online]. Available: *http://www.ncoa.org/news/archives/abe_bias.htm* (accessed 12/4/00).

Judkins, D. R., Mosher, W. D., & Botman, S. (1991). National survey of family growth: Design, estimation, and inference. *National Center for Health Statistics,* 2: 1–109.

Jung, C. G. (1933). *Modern Man in Search of a Soul.* London: Kegan Paul, Trench, and Trubner, Ltd.

——. (1959). Concerning the Archetypes, with Special Reference to the Anima Concept. In C. G. Jung (Ed.), *Collected Works, Vol. 9. Part 1.* Princeton, NJ: Princeton University Press.

Kaiser Family Foundation. (1999). *Race, Ethnicity, and Medical Care: A Survey of Public Perceptions and Experiences.* Menlo Park, CA: Henry J. Kaiser Family Foundation.

Kalish, R. A., & Reynolds, D. (1976). *Death and Ethnicity: A Psychocultural Study.* Los Angeles: Ethel Percy Andrus Gerontology Center of the University of Southern California.

Kalish, R. A., & Kastenbaum, R. (1995). Death. In G. L. Maddox, R. Atchley, J. G. Evans, et al. (Eds.), *Encyclopedia of Aging* (pp. 250–252). New York: Springer.

Kane, R. L., Ouslander, J. G., & Abrass, I. T. (1984). *Essentials of Clinical Geriatrics.* New York: McGraw Hill.

Kannel, W. B., & Brand, F. N. (1983). Cardiovascular risk factors in the elderly woman. In E. W. Markson (Ed.), *Older Women.* Lexington MA: Lexington Books.

Kart, C. S., & Engler, C. (1994). Predisposition to self-health care: Who does what for themselves. *Journal of Gerontology: Social Sciences,* 49(6): S301–S308.

Kasper, J. (1988). *Aging Alone: Profiles and Projections.* Baltimore: Commonwealth Fund Commission on Elderly People Living Alone.

Kastenbaum, R. (1995). Gerontology. In G. L. Maddox, R. C. Atchley, J. G. Evans, et al. (Eds.), *Encyclopedia of Aging* (pp. 416–418). New York: Springer.

———. (1986). *Death, Society, and Human Experience,* Third Edition. Columbus, OH: Charles H. Merrill.

Katz, S. (1999). Charcot's older women: Bodies of knowledge at the interface of aging studies and women's studies. In K. Woodward (Ed.), *Figuring Age: Women, Bodies, Generations* (pp. 112–127). Bloomington, IN: Indiana University Press.

———. (1996). *Disciplining Old Age: The Formation of Gerontological Knowledge.* Charlottesville, VA: University of Virginia.

Kaufert, P. A. (1985). Midlife in the midwest: Canadian women in Manitoba. In J. K. Brown & V. Kerns (Eds.), *In Her Prime: A New View of Middle Aged Women.* South Hadley, MA: Bergin and Garvey.

Kaufman, S. (1995). *The Ageless Self: Sources of Meaning in Late Life.* Madison, WI: University of Wisconsin Press.

Kauh, T. (1999). Changing status and roles of older Korean immigrants in the United States. *International Journal of Aging and Human Development,* 49(3): 213–229.

———. (1997). Intergenerational relations: Older Korean-Americans' experiences. *Journal of Cross-Cultural Gerontology,* 12: 245–271.

Kausler, D. H. (1994). *Learning and Memory in Normal Aging.* New York: Academic Press.

Keating, N. C., & Cole, P. (1980). What do I do with him 24 hours a day: Changes in the housewife role after retirement. *The Gerontologist,* 20(1): 84–89.

Kehl, D. G. (1988). The distaff and staff: Stereotypes and archetypes of the older woman in representative modern literature. *International Journal of Aging and Human Development,* 26: 1–13.

Keller, K. B., & Lemberg, L. (2000). Gender differences in acute coronary events. *American Journal of Critical Care,* 9: 207–209.

Kemp, B., Staples, F., & Lopez-Aqueres, W. (1987). Epidemiology of depression and dysphoria in an elderly Hispanic population: Prevalence and correlates. *Journal of the American Geriatrics Society,* 35: 920–926.

Kenyon, G. M., Ruth, J.-E., & Mader, W. (1999). Elements of a narrative gerontology. In V. L. Bengtson & K. W. Schaie (Eds.), *Handbook of Theories of Aging* (pp. 40–58). New York: Springer.

Kenyon, S. M. (1994). Gender and alliance in Central Sudan. In J. Kickerson-Putnam & J. Brown (Eds.), *Women Among Women: Anthropological Perspectives on Female Age* (pp. 15–19). Urbana: University of Illinois Press.

Kerns, V. (1983). *Women and the Ancestors.* Urbana, IL.: University of Illinois Press.

Kevorkian, J. (1991). *Prescription Medicide: The Goodness of Planned Death.* New York: Prometheus.

Kilty, K. M., & Joseph, A. (1999). Institutional racism and sentencing disparities for cocaine possession. *Journal of Poverty,* 3(4): 1–17.

Kim, K. C., Hurh, W. M., & Kim, S. (1993). Generation differences in Korean immigrants' life conditions in the United States. *Sociological Perspectives,* 36(3): 257–270.

Kim, K. C., Kim, S., & Hurh, W. M. (1991). Filial piety and intergenerational relationship in Korean immigrant families. *International Journal of Aging and Human Development,* 33(3): 233–245.

Kimmel, D. C. (1978). Adult development and aging: A gay perspective. *Journal of Social Issues,* 34: 113–130.

Kingson, E. R. (2000). Social Security and aging baby boomers. In E. W. Markson & L. A. Hollis-Sawyer (Eds.), *Intersections of Aging* (pp. 430–441). Los Angeles: Roxbury.

Kinsella, K., & Gist, Y. J. (1995). *Older Workers, Retirement, and Pensions: A Comparative International Chartbook.* Washington, DC: U.S. Department of Commerce.

Kinsella, K., & Tauber, C. M. (1993). *An Aging World II. International Population Reports, Bureau of the Census, vol. P95/92-3.* Washington, DC: U.S. Bureau of the Census.

Kinsey, A. C., Pomeroy, W. B., & Martin, C. E. (1948). *Sexual Behavior in the Human Male.* Philadelphia: W. B. Saunders.

Kinsey, A. C., Pomeroy, W. B., Martin, C. E., & Gephard, P. H. (1953). *Sexual Behavior in the Human Female.* Philadelphia: W. B. Saunders.

Kivela, S. L., Luukinen, H., Sulkava, R., Viramo, P., & Koski, K. (1999). Marital and family relations and depression in married elderly Finns. *Journal of Affective Disorders,* 54(1–2): 177–182.

Kleiner, G. (1996). *Where River Turns Into Sky.* New York: Bard/Avon.

Koenig, H. G., Shelp, F., Goli, V., Cohen, H. J., & Blazer, D. G. (1989). Survival and health care utilization in elderly medical inpatients with major depression. *Journal of the American Geriatrics Society,* 7: 599–606.

Koff, T. H., & Park, R. W. (1999). *Aging Public Policy: Bonding the Generations,* Second Edition. Amityville, NY: Baywood.

Korn, M. L. (2001). Historical roots of schizophrenia. *Psychiatry Clinical Management Modules, Vol. 5.* Medscape (7/2/01).

Kost, K., & Forrest, J. D. (1992). American women's sexual behavior and exposure to risk of sexually transmitted diseases. *Family Planning Perspectives,* 24: 244–254.

Krach, C. A., & Velkoff, V. A. (1999). Centenarians in the United States. *U.S. Bureau of the Census, Current Population Reports, vol. Series P23-199RV.* Washington, DC: U.S. Government Printing Office.

Krauss, M. W., Seltzer, M. M., Gordon, R., & Friedman, D. H. (1996). Binding ties: The roles of adult siblings with mental retardation. *Mental Retardation,* 34: 83–93.

Kressin, N., & Petersen, L. (2001). Racial differences in the use of invasive cardiovascular procedures: Review of the literature and prescription for future research. *Annals of Internal Medicine,* 135(5): 352–356.

Kutchins, H., & Kirk, S. A. (1997). *Making Us Crazy: DSM: The Psychiatric Bible and the Creation of Mental Disorders.* New York: Free Press.

Lamm, R. (1989). Public policy for an aging America. *The Generational Journal,* 11(1): 108–111.

Lampman, R. M. (1987). Evaluating and prescribing exercise for elderly patients. *Geriatrics,* 42(8): 63–76.

Land, K. C., Guralnik, J. M., & Blazer, D. G. (1994). Estimating increment-decrement life tables with multiple covariates from panel data: The case of active life expectancy. *Demography,* 31(2): 297–319.

Lane v. Candura. (1977). 6 Massachusetts Appellate Court 397. Massachusetts.

Langer, E. J., & Avorn, J. (1985). Impact of the psychosocial environment of the elderly on behavioral and health outcomes. In B. Hess & E. Markson (Eds.), *Growing Old in America* (pp. 462–473). New Brunswick, NJ: Transaction Books.

Langer, E. J. (1999). *The Power of Mindful Thinking.* Cambridge, MA: Perseus Publishing.

Laslett, P. (1977). *Family Life and Illicit Love in Earlier Generations.* New York: Cambridge University Press.

Lauer, R. H., Lauer, J. C., & Kerr, S. T. (1990). The long-term marriage: Perceptions of stability and satisfaction. *International Journal of Aging and Human Development,* 31(3): 189–195.

Laumann, E. O., Paik, A., & Rosen, R. (1999). Sexual dysfunction in the United States: Prevalence and predictors. *Journal of the American Medical Association,* 281: 537–544.

Lawless, C. (1998). Oral medications in the management of erectile dysfunction. *Journal of the American Board of Family Practice,* 11(4): 307–314.

Lawton, M. P., Rajagopal, D., Brody, E., & Kleban, M. H. (1992). The dynamics of caregiving for a demented elder among black and white families. *Journal of Gerontology: Social Sciences,* 47: 156–164.

Leaf, A. (1973). Getting old. *Scientific American,* 229: 44–52.

Lebowitz, B. D., Pearson, J. L., Schneider, L. S., et al. (1997). Diagnosis and treatment of depression in late life. Consensus statement update. *Journal of the American Medical Association,* 278(14): 1186–1190.

Lee, G. R., DeMaris, A., Bavin, S., & Sullivan, R. (2001). Gender differences in the depressive effect of widowhood in later life. *Journal of Gerontology/Social Sciences,* 56B(1): S56–S61.

Lee, G. R., Willetts, M. C., & Seccombe, K. (1998). Widowhood and depression: Gender differences. *Research on Aging,* 20: 611–630.

Lee, R. A. (1997). The youth bias in advertising. *American Demographics* [Online], January. Available: *http://www.demographics.com/publications/ad/97_ad9701a47.htm* (accessed 6/20/99).

Lemon, B. W., Bengtson, V., & Peterson, J. A. (1972). An exploration of the activity theory of aging: Activity types and life satisfaction among movers to a retirement community. *Journal of Gerontology,* 27(4): 511–523.

Leon, J., Cheng, C., & Neumann, P. (1998). Alzheimer's disease care: Costs and potential savings. *Health Affairs,* 17(6): 206–216.

Levenson, R. W., Carstensen, L. L., & Gottman, J. M. (1993). Long-term marriage: Age, gender, and satisfaction. *Psychology and Aging,* 8(2): 301–313.

Levinson, D. (1978). *The Seasons of a Man's Life.* New York: Alfred A. Knopf.

——. (1996). *The Seasons of a Woman's Life.* New York: Alfred A. Knopf.

Lindemann, E. (1944). Symptomology and management of acute grief. *American Journal of Psychiatry,* 101: 141–148.

Lindsay, R. (1995). The burden of osteoporosis: Cost. *American Journal of Medicine,* 98: 9S–11S.

Lipman, E. (1996). *Isabel's Bed.* New York: Pocket Books.

Lipschitz, D. A., Ham, R. J., & White, J. V. (1992). An approach to nutrition screening for older Americans. *American Family Physician,* 45(2): 601–608.

Lock, M. (1993). *Encounters with Aging: Mythologies of Menopause in Japan and North America.* Berkeley CA: University of California Press.

Lofland, L. H. (1985). The social shaping of emotion: The case of grief. *Symbolic Interaction,* 8: 171–190.

Longino, C. F., Jr. (1994). Myths of an aging America. *American Demographics, 16* (8): 36–42.

Longino, C. F., Jr., & Kart, C. S. (1982). Explicating activity theory: A formal replication. *Journal of Gerontology,* 37(6): 713–722.

Lopata, H. Z. (1994). *Circles and Settings: Role Changes of American Women.* Albany, NY: State University of New York.

——. (1996). *Current Widowhood: Myths and Realities.* Thousand Oaks, CA: Sage.

LoPiccolo, J. (1991). Counseling and therapy for sexual problems in the elderly. *Clinics in Geriatric Medicine,* 7: 161–179.

Love, J., & Vorek, R. (2000). *Individual Accounts, Social Security, and the 2000 Election.* AARP Research Group. Washington, DC: AARP.

Lowenthal, M. F., & Berkman, P. L. (1967). *Aging and Mental Disorder in San Francisco.* San Francisco: Jossey-Bass.

Lowenthal, M. F., & Haven, C. Interaction and adaptation: Intimacy as a critical variable. *American Sociological Review 33:* 20–30.

Lund, D. A. (1995). Caregiving. In Robert Kastenbaum (Ed.), *Encyclopedia of Adult Development* (pp. 57–63). Phoenix, AZ: Oryx.

——. (2000). *Men Coping with Grief.* Amityville, NY: Baywood.

Lund, D. A., Caserta, M. S., & Dimond, M. F. (1986). Gender differences through two years of bereavement among the elderly. *The Gerontologist,* 26(3): 314–320.

Lund, D. A., Caserta, M. S., Van Pelt, J., & Gass, K. A. (1990). Stability of social support networks after later-life spousal bereavement. *Death Studies,* 14: 53–73.

Mace, N. L., & Rabins., P. V. (1999). *The 36-Hour Day,* Third Edition. Baltimore, MD: Johns Hopkins Press.

Magai, C., Cohen C., Milburn, N., Thorpe, B., McPherson, R., & Peralta, D. (2001). Attachment styles in older European American and African American Adults. *Journal of Gerontology: Social Sciences,* 56(1): S28–S35.

Magaziner, J. (2000). The prevalence of dementia in a statewide sample of new nursing home admissions aged 65 and older: Diagnosis by expert panel. *The Gerontologist,* 40(6): 663–672.

Mahoney, J. P. (2001). Well-Being Among American and Soviet Born Jewish Elders [Doctoral dissertation]. Boston, MA: Boston University.

Manheimer, R. J. (1998). The promise and politics of older adult education. *Research on Aging*, 20(4): 391–414.

Mansfield, P. K., & Voda, A. M. (1993). From Edith Bunker to the 6:00 news: How and what midlife women learn about menopause. *Women and Therapy*, 14: pp. 89–104.

Manton, K. G., Corder, L., & Stallard, E. (1997). Chronic disability trends in elderly United States populations 1982–1994. *Proceedings of the National Academy of Sciences* 94: 2593–2598.

Markides, K. S., & Miranda, M. R. (1997). *Minorities, Aging and Health*. Thousand Oaks, CA: Sage.

Markson, E. W. (1997). Sagacious, sinful, or superfluous?: The social construction of older women. In J. M. Coyne (Ed.), *Handbook on Women and Aging* (pp. 53–72). Westport CT: Greenwood.

Markson, E. W., Kelly-Hayes, M., Wilking, S., D'Agostino, R., & Wolf, P. (2000). The HARP: A gender specific health assessment risk profile for nursing home placement. *Hallym International Journal of Aging*, 2(2): 149–171.

Markson, E. W., & Taylor, C. A. (2000). The mirror has two faces. *Ageing and Society*, 20(2): 137–160.

Markson, L., Fanale, J., Steel, K., Kern, D., & Annas, G. (1994). Implementing advance directives in the primary care setting. *Archives of Internal Medicine*, 154: 2321–2327.

Marmot, M. G. (1996). The social pattern of health and disease. In D. Blane, E. Brunner, & R. Wilkinson (Eds.), *Health and Social Organization* (pp. 42–70). London: Routledge.

Marmot, M. G., & Shipley, M. J. (1996). Do socioeconomic differences in mortality persist after retirement? 25 year followup of civil servants from the first Whitehall study. *British Medical Journal*, 313: 1177–1180.

Marsiglio, W., & Donnelly, D. (1991). Sexual relations in later life: A national study of married persons. *Journal of Gerontology: Social Sciences*, 46: S338–S344.

Marsiglio, W., & Greer, R. (1994). A gender analysis of older men's sexuality: Social, psychological, and biological dimensions. In E. Thompson (Ed.), *Older Men* (pp. 122–140). Thousand Oaks, CA: Sage.

Masters, W. H., & Johnson, V. E. (1966). *Human Sexual Response*. Boston: Little, Brown.

Matthias, R. E., Lubben, J. E., Atchison, K. A., & Schweitzer, S. O. (1997). Sexuality and satisfaction among very old adults: Results from a community-dwelling Medicare population survey. *Gerontologist*, 37(1): 6–14.

Mattis, J. S. (2000). African American women's definitions of spirituality and religiosity. *Journal of Black Psychology*, 26(1): 101–122.

Maxwell, F. S. (1968). *The Measure of My Days*. New York: Knopf.

McAdams, D. P., de St. Aubin, E., & Logan, R. L. (1993). Generativity among young, midlife, and older adults. *Psychology and Aging*, 8(2): 221–230.

McAuley, W. J. (1998) History, race, and attachment to place among elders in the rural all-black towns of Oklahoma. *Journal of Gerontology: Social Sciences* 53B(1): S35–S45.

McCandless, J. N., & Conner, F. P. (1999). Older women and the health care system: A time for change. *Journal of Women and Aging*, 11(2/3): 13–27.

——. (1997). Older women and grief: A new direction for research. *Journal of Women and Aging*, 9(3): 85–91.

McCourt, F. (1999). *Angela's Ashes: A Memoir*. New York: Simon and Schuster.

McCrae, R. M. (2001). Self-concept. In G. L. Maddox, R. C. Atchley, J. G. Evans, et al. (Eds.), *Encyclopedia of Aging*, Third Edition (p. 902). New York: Springer.

McDonald-Pavelka, M. S. (1994). The nonhuman primate perspective: Old age, kinship and social partners in a monkey society. In J. Dickerson-Putnam: J. Brown (Ed.), *Women Among Women: Anthropological Perspectives on Female Age (pp. 89–99). Urbana: University of Illinois Press.*

McDonald, L. (1996). Abuse and neglect of elders. In James E. Birren (Ed.), *Encyclopedia of Gerontology: Age, Aging, and the Aged* (pp. 1–18). New York: Academic Press.

McFalls, J. A., Jr. (1998, September). Population: A lively introduction. *Population Bulletin*, 53(3): 3–47.

McKinlay, J. (1996). Some contributions from the social system to gender inequalities in heart disease. *Journal of Health and Social Behavior*, 37: 1–26.

McInnis-Dittrich, K. (2000). Too little, too late. In E. W. Markson & L. A. Hollis-Sawyer (Eds.), *Intersections of Aging* (pp. 237–246). Los Angeles: Roxbury.

Mead, G. H. (1934/1962). *Mind, Self, and Society*. Chicago: University of Chicago Press.

Mead, J. (1994). *Many and More: A Celebration of Love in Later Life*. New York: Timkin.

Medvedev, Z. A. (1974). Caucasus and Altay longevity: A biological or social problem? *Gerontologist*, pp. 381–387.

Mendes de Leon, C. F., Seeman, T. E., Baker, D., et al. (1996). Self-efficacy, physical decline, and change in functioning in community-living elders: A prospective study. *Journals of Gerontology: Social Sciences*, 51B: S183–S190.

Mercer, J. (1973). *Labeling the Mentally Retarded*. Berkeley, CA: University of California Press.

Merriam, S. B. (1995). Butler's 'life review.' How universal is it? In J. Hendricks (Ed.), *The Meaning of Reminiscence and Life Review* (pp. 7–19). Amityville, NY: Baywood.

Merton, R. K. (1968). *Social Theory and Social Structure* Revised Edition. New York: Free Press.

Metchnikoff, E. (1904). *The Nature of Man*. London: Putnam.

——. (1908). *The Prolongation of Life: Optimistic Studies*. New York: Putnam.

MetLife. (1999). *The Mature Market: Guidelines for Effective Communication*. New York: Metropolitan Life Insurance Co.

MetLife Mature Market Institute. (1999). *The MetLife Juggling Act Study: Balancing Caregiving with Work and the Costs Involved*. New York: MetLife.

Milgrim, S. (1977). *Individual in a social world: Essays and Experiments.* Reading, MA: Addison-Wesley.

Miller, R. H., & Luft, H. S. (1994). Managed care plan performance since 1980: A literature analysis. *Journal of the American Medical Association,* 271(19): 1512–1519.

Mills, C. W. (1959). *The Sociological Imagination.* New York: Oxford University Press.

Mills, T. L., & Henretta, J. C. (2001). Racial, ethnic, and sociodemographic differences in the level of psychosocial distress among older Americans. *Research on Aging,* 23(2): 131–152.

Miner, S., & Uhlenberg, P. (1997). Intergenerational proximity and the social role of sibling neighbors after midlife. *Family Relations,* 46: 145–153.

Minkler, M. & Estes, C. (Eds.). (1991). *Critical Perspectives on Aging.* New York: Baywood.

Minkler, M., & Roe, K. M. (1996). Grandparents as surrogate parents. *Generations,* 20(1): 34–38.

Minkler, M., & Fuller-Thomson, E. (2000). Second time around parenting: Factors predictive of grandparents becoming caregivers for their grandchildren. *International Journal of Aging and Human Development,* 50(3): 185–200.

Mitchell, W. L. (1998). Women's hierarchies of age and suffering in an Andean community. In J. Dickerson-Putnam & J. K. Brown (Eds.), *Women Among Women: Anthropological Perspectives on Female Age Hierarchies* (pp. 52–64). Chicago and Urbana: University of illinois Press.

Mitford, J. (1999). *American Way of Death Revisited.* New York: Vintage.

Moen, P., Kim, J. E., & Hofmeister, H. (2001). Couples' work/retirement transitions, gender, and marital quality. *Social Psychology Quarterly,* 64(1): 55–71.

Monge, R. H. (1975). Structure of the self-concept from adolescence through old age. *Experimental Aging Research,* 1(2): 281–291.

Montgomery, A. A. (1994). WATCH: A practical approach to brief auditory rehabilitation. *The Hearing Journal,* 47: 53–55.

Moody, H. R. (1988). *Abundance of Life: Human Development Policies for an Aging Society.* New York: Columbia University Press.

——. (1993). Overview: What is critical gerontology and why is it important? In T. R. Cole, W. A. Achenbaum, P. L. Jakobi, & R. Kastenbaum (Eds.), *Voices and Visions of Aging: Toward a Critical Gerontology* (pp. xv–xli). New York: Springer.

——. (1998). *Aging: Concepts and Controversies.* Thousand Oaks, CA: Pine Forge Press.

Mooradian, A. D. (1991). Geriatric sexuality and chronic diseases. *Clinics in Geriatric Medicine,* 7: 113–131.

Morehouse Medical Treatment and Effectiveness Center. (1999). *A Synthesis of the Literature: Racial and Ethnic Differences in Access to Medical Care* [Report Prepared for the Henry J. Kaiser Family Foundation]. Henry J. Kaiser Family Foundation.

Morrow, D. J. (1999). Senior Class. *New York Times* [Online], February 17. Available: *http://www.nytimes.com/library/national/science/menshealth/ 17morr.html* (accessed 3/29/99).

Mosca, L., Manson, J., Sutherland, S. E., Langer, R., et al. (1997). Cardio-vascular disease in women: A statement for health care professionals from the American Heart Association. Writing group. *Circulation,* 96(7): 2468–2482.

Mui, A. (1995). Caring for frail elderly parents: A comparison of adult sons and daughters. *The Gerontologist,* 35(1): 86–93.

Muir, F., & Brett, S. (1980). *On Childhood.* London: Heinemann.

Mulligan, T., & Moss, C. R. (1991). Sexuality and aging in male veterans: A cross-sectional study of interest, ability, and activity. *Archives of Sexual Behavior,* 20(1): 17–25.

Mulsant, B. H., & Ganguli, M. (1999). Epidemiology and diagnosis of depression in later life. *Journal of Clinical Psychiatry,* 60(Supplement 10): 9–15.

Mushkin, P. R. (1998). The request to die: Role for a psychodynamic perspective on physician-assisted suicide (The patient physician relationship). *Journal of the American Medical Association,* 279(4): 323–328.

Musick, M. A., Herzog, A. R., & House, J. S. (1999). Volunteering and mortality among older adults: Findings from a national sample. *Journal of Gerontology: Social Sciences,* 54B: S173–S180.

Mutran, E. J., Reitzes, D. C., & Fernandez, M. E. (1997). Factors that influence attitudes toward retirement. *Research on Aging,* 19(3): 251–273.

Nanda, S. (1990). *Neither Man nor Woman: The Hijras of India.* Belmont, CA: Wadsworth.

Nascher, I. L. (1914). *Geriatrics: The Diseases of Old Age and Their Treatment, Including Physiological Old Age, Home and Institutional Care, and Medico-Legal Relations.* Philadelphia: P. Blakiston's Son and Co.

National Academy on Aging. (1995). *Facts on . . . Medicare: Hospital Insurance and Supplementary Medical Insurance.* Washington DC: National Academy on Aging.

National Academy on an Aging Society. (1999, November). Chronic conditions: A challenge for the 21st century. *Challenges for the 21st Century: Chronic and Disabling Conditions,* 1: 1–6. Washington, DC: Author.

——. (2000, September). Alzheimer's Disease and dementia: A growing challenge. *Challenges for the 21st Century: Chronic and Disabling Conditions,* 11: 1–6. Washington, DC: Author.

——. (2000, July). Depression: A treatable disease. *Challenges for the 21st Century: Chronic and Disabling Conditions,* 9: 1–6. Washington, DC: Author.

——. (2000a). *Data Profiles: Young Retirees and Older Workers* [Number 1]. Washington, DC: Author.

——. (2000b). *Data Profiles: Young Retirees and Older Workers* [Number 2]. Washington, DC: Author.

——. (2000c). *Challenges for the 21st Century: Chronic and Disabling Conditions* [Number 10]. Washington, DC: Author.

National Alliance for Caregiving and AARP. (1997). *Family Caregiving in the U.S. Findings from a National Survey.* Washington DC: AARP.

National Center for Assisted Living. (1998). Assisted Living Resident Profile. In *About Assisted Living* [Online]. Available: *http://www.ncal.org/about/resident.htm* (accessed 3/19/01).

———. (2001). *Facts and Trends 2001: The Assisted Living Sourcebook*. Washington, DC: Author.

National Center for Health Statistics, Center for Disease Control and Prevention, U.S. Department of Health and Human Services. (1995). *Highlights of Trends in the Health of Older Americans: United States, 1994*. Hyattsville, MD: National Center for Health Statistics.

———. (1996). *Health, United States 1995*. Hyattsville, MD: National Center for Health Statistics.

———. (2000). *Health, United States*. Hyattsville, MD: National Center for Health Statistics.

———. (2001). *Health, United States 2001*. Hyattsville, MD: National Center for Health Statistics.

National Center for Injury Prevention and Control (n.d.). *Suicide in the United States*. Available: *http://www.cdc.gov/ncipc/factsheets/suifacts. htm* (accessed 3/1/01).

National Institute on Aging. (1996). *Pills, Patches, and Shots: Can Hormones Prevent Aging?* Rockville, MD: National Institute on Aging.

National Institutes of Health National Kidney and Urologic Diseases Information Clearinghouse. (1998; updated 2000). *Prostate Enlargement: Benign Prostatic Hyperplasia* [Publication 98-3012]. Rockville, MD: National Institutes of Health.

National Public Radio. (2000, 8/31). *One Hundred Years of Stories: Abraham Goldstein*. Available: *http://www.npr.org* (accessed 12/11/00).

National Resource Center on Native American Aging at the University of North Dakota. (1998, June). *Comparison of Tribal Elders' Activity Levels and Health Status with the Nation*. Grand Forks, ND: National Resource Center on Native American Aging.

Neimeyer, R. A., & Fortner, B. (1995). Death anxiety in the elderly. In G. L. Maddox, R. C. Atchley, J. G. Evans, et al. (Eds.), *Encyclopedia of Aging* (pp. 252–253.). New York: Springer.

Neugarten, B. L. (1964). *Personality in Middle and Late Life*. New York: Atherton.

———. (1968). The awareness of middle age. In B. L. Neugarten (Ed.), *Middle Age and Aging*. Chicago IL: The University of Chicago Press.

———. (1982). *Age or Need: Public Policies for Older People*. Beverly Hills, CA: Sage.

Neugarten, B. L., & Gutmann, D. L. (1968). Age-sex roles and personality in middle age: A thematic apperception study. In B. L. Neugarten (Ed.), *Middle Age and Aging* (pp. 58–71). Chicago IL: University of Chicago Press.

Neugarten, B. L., & Moore, J. W. (1968). The Changing Age-Status System. In B. L. Neugarten (Ed.), *Middle Age and Aging* (pp. 5–28). Chicago IL: University of Chicago Press.

Neugebauer, R., Hoek, H. W., & Susser, E. (1999). Prenatal exposure to wartime famine and development of antisocial personality disorder in early adulthood. *Journal of the American Medical Association,* 282(5): 455–462.

New York Times. (1990, June 14). Giving death a hand: Rending issue. *New York Times,* p. A-6.

Newman, M. (2000). These roomies share a house, and old age. *New York Times* [Online], March 8. Available: *http://www.nytimes.com/specials/ 030800gen-roommates.html* (accessed 3/8/00).

NIA News. (2000a). Scientists suspect new genetic risk factor for late onset Alzheimer's disease. In *Alzheimer's Disease Research Update* [Online], December 21. Available: *http://www.alzheimers.org/nianews/ nianews36.html* (accessed 3/13/01).

——. (2000b). New study links head injury, severity of injury, with Alzheimer' disease. In *Alzheimer's Disease Research Update* [Online], October 23. Available: *http://www.alzheimers.org/nianews/nianews35.html* (accessed 8/21/02).

——. (2000c). Study suggests ERT stimulates blood flow to key memory centers in the brain. In *Alzheimer's Research Update* [Online], June 27. Available: *http://www.alzheimers.org/nianews/nianews32.html* (accessed 3/13/01)

——. (2000d). Nasal Alzheimer's vaccine successfully tested in mice. In *Alzheimer's Disease Research Update* [Online], September 28. Available: *http://www.alzheimers.org/nianews/nianews34.html* (accessed 3/13/01).

——. (2001a, January 30). Alzheimer's disease anti-inflammatory prevention trial (ADAPT) launched. In *Alzheimer's Disease Research Update* [Online]. Available: *http://www.alzheimers.org/nianews/nianews32. html* (accessed 3/13/01).

——. (2001b). Scientist zero in on enzyme at work in Alzheimer's disease. In *Alzheimer's Disease Research Update* [Online], February 26. Available: *http://www.alzheimers.org/nianews/nianews38.html* (accessed 7/ 17/02).

NIDDK. (2002). *Prostate Enlargement: Benign Prostatic Hyperplasia.* Bethesda, MD: NIH Pub. No. 02-3012.

NIDDK, and National Diabetes Information Clearinghouse. (2000). *Diabetes in Hispanic Americans.* Available: *http://www.niddk.nih/gov/health/ diabetes/pubs/hispan/hispan.htm* (accessed 11/13/00).

NIH Consensus Conference Panel Statement. (2000). *Osteoporosis, Prevention, Diagnosis, and Therapy 2000.* Bethesda, MD: NIH.

Nocon, A., & Pearson, M. (2000). The role of friends and neighbors in providing support for older people. *Ageing and Society,* 20(3): 341–364.

Nolan, J. R., & Nolan-Haley, J. (1990). *Black's Law Dictionary,* Sixth Edition. St. Paul, MN: West.

Nuland, S. B. (1993). *How We Die: Reflections on Life's Final Chapter.* New York: Knopf.

Nydegger, C. (1985). Family ties of the aged in cross-cultural perspective. In B. B. Hess & E. W. Markson (Eds.), *Growing Old in America* (pp. 71–85). New Brunswick, NJ: Transaction.

Office of Policy Development and Research, and U.S. Department of Housing and Urban Development. (1999). *Housing Our Elders: A Report Card on the Housing Conditions and Needs of Older Americans.*

Washington, DC: U.S. Department of Housing and Urban Development.

Ogburn, W. F., & Nimkoff, M. F. (1940). *Sociology.* Boston: Houghton-Mifflin.

Oman, D., Reed, D., & Ferrara, A. (1999). Do elderly women have more physical disability than men do? *American Journal of Epidemiology,* 150(8): 834–842.

Omi, M., & Winant, H. (1987). *Racial Formation in the United States from the 1960s to the 1980s.* New York: Routledge and Kegan Paul.

Oregon Health Division Center for Health Statistics (and Vital Records). (2000). *Oregon's Death with Dignity Act Annual Report 2000.* Available: *http://www.ohd.hr.state.or.us/chs/pas/ar-tbl* (accessed 3/7/01).

O'Neill, G. (2000). The policy clock. *The Public Policy and Aging Report,* 10(4): 9.

O'Rand, A. M., & Campbell, R. T. (1999). On reestablishing the phenomenon and specifying ignorance: Theory development and research design in aging. In V. L. Bengtson & K.W. Schaie (Eds.), *Handbook of Theories of Aging* (pp. 59–78). New York: Springer.

Ory, M., Hoffman, R. R., Yee, J. L., Tennstedt, S., & Schultz, R. (1999). Prevalence and impact of caregiving: A detailed comparison between dementia and nondementia caregivers. *The Gerontologist,* 39(2): 177–185.

Osgood, N. J. (1985). *Suicide in the Elderly: A Practitioner's Guide to Diagnosis and Mental Health Intervention.* Rockville, MD: Aspen.

Ozminkowski, R. J., Friedman, B., & Taylor, Z. (1993). Access to heart and liver transplantation in the 1980s. *Medical Care,* 31(11): 1027–1042.

Paffenbarger, R. S., Wing, A. L., & Hyde, R. T. (1978). Physical activity as an index of heart attack risk in college alumni. *American Journal of Epidemiology,* 108: 161–175.

Palmore, E. B. (1984). *Handbook on the Aged in the United States.* Westport, CT: Greenwood Press.

——. (1988). *The Facts on Aging Quiz.* New York: Springer.

——. (1995). Centenarians. In G. L. Maddox, R. C. Atchley, J. G. Evans, et al. (Eds.), *Encyclopedia of Aging* (pp. 165–166). New York: Springer Publisher Co.

Palmore, E. B., Nowlin, J., Busse, E., Siegler, I., & Maddox, G. (1985). *Normal Aging III.* Durham, NC: Duke University Press.

Paltrow, L. M., Cohen, D. S., Carey, C. A., and Women's Law Project and National Advocates for Pregnant Women. (2000). *Governmental Response to Pregnant Women who use alcohol or other drugs: Year 2000 Overview. An Analysis.* New York: Lindesmith Center Drug Policy Foundation.

Pandya, S. M., & Independent Living/Long-Term Care Team, AARP. (2001, February). *Nursing Homes.* Available: *http://research.aarp.org/health/fs10r_nursing.html* (accessed 3/27/01).

Pandya, S. M., & Coleman, B. (2000, December). Caregiving and long-term care. In AARP Research Center, Public Policy Institute [Online]. Available: *http://research.aarp.org/health/fs82_caregiving.html* (accessed 12/17/01).

Parker, I. The need for positive alternatives to psychiatry's brain-damaging approaches. Available: *http://www.oikos.org/ect.htm* (accessed 6/5/01).

Parrott, T. M., Mills, T. L., & Bengtson, V. L. (2000). The United States: Population demographics, changes in the family, and social policy challenges. In V. L. Bengtson, K.-D. Kim, G. C. Myers & K.-S. Eun (Eds.), *Aging in East and West: Families, States, and the Elderly* (pp. 191–224). New York: Springer.

Paulin, G. D. (2000, May). Expenditure patterns of older Americans, 1984–1997. *Monthly Labor Review*, pp. 3–26.

Pavalko, E. K., & Artis, J. E. (1997). Women's caregiving and paid work: Causal relationships in late midlife. *Journals of Gerontology: Social Sciences*, 52B: 170–179.

Pearlin, L. I., & Aneshensel, C. B. (1994). Caregiving: The unexpected career. *Social Justice Research*, 7: 373–390.

Pearson, J. L., Hunter, A. G., Cook, J. M, et al. (1997). Grandmother involvement in child caregiving in an urban community. *The Gerontologist*, 37: 650–657.

Peek, M. K., Coward, R. T., & Peek, C. W. (2000). Race, aging and care: Can differences in family and household structure account for race variations in informal care? *Research on Aging*, 22(2): 117–142.

Penninx, B. W., Leveille, S., Ferrucci, L., Van Eijk, J. T., & Guralnik, J. M. (1999). Exploring the effect of depression on physical disability: Longitudinal evidence from the established populations for epidemiologic studies of the elderly. *American Journal of Public Health*, 89(9): 1346–1352.

Pension Benefit Guaranty Corporation. *Your Guaranteed Pension* Pamphlet. In U.S. Pension Benefit Guaranty Corporation [Online]. Available: *http://www.pbgc.gov/publications/ygptext.htm* (accessed 10/11/00).

Peplau, L. A., & Spalding, L. R. (2000). The close relationships of lesbians, gay men, and bisexuals. In C. Hendrick & S. S. Hendrick (Eds.), *Close Relationships: A Sourcebook* (pp. 111–124). Thousand Oaks, CA: Sage.

Perls, T. T., & Silver, M. H. (1999). *Living to 100: Lessons in Living to Your Maximum Potential at Any Age.* New York: Basic Books.

Peter D. Hart Research Associates. (1999). *The New Face of Retirement: Older Americans, Civic Engagement, and the Longevity Revolution: A Survey Conducted for Civic Ventures.* San Francisco: Author.

Petersen, L. A., Wright, S. M., Peterson, E. D., et al. (2002). Impact of race on cardiac care and outcome in veterans with acute myocardial infarction. *Medical Care* 40 (1 Supp) I86–96.

Peterson, E. D., Shaw, L. K., Delong, E.R., et al. (1997). Racial variations in the use of coronary revascular procedures. *New England Journal of Medicine 336:* 480–486.

Peterson, M. A. (1994). Institutional change and the health politics of the nineties. In P. V. Rosenau (Ed.), *Health Care Reform in the Nineties* (pp. 149–167). Thousand Oaks, CA: Sage.

Peyrot, M., McMurry, J. F., & Kruger, D. F. (1999). A biopsychosocial model of glycemic control in diabetes: Stress, coping and regimen adherence. *Journal of Health and Social Behavior*, 40(2): 141–158.

Phillips, B. (1957). A role theory approach to adjustment in old age. *American Sociological Review*, 22: 212–217.

Phillipson, C. (1982). *Capitalism and the Construction of Old Age*. London: MacMillan.

——. (1993). The sociology of retirement. In J. Bond, P. Coleman, & S. Peace (Eds.), *Ageing in Society: An Introduction to Social Gerontology*, Second Edition (pp. 180–199). London: Sage.

Picot, S. J., Debanne, S. M., Namazi, K. H., & Wykle, M. L. (1997). Religiosity and perceived rewards of Black and White caregivers. *The Gerontologist*, 37: 89–101.

Poindexter, C. C., Linsk, N. L., & Warner, R. S. (1999). He listens . . . and never gossips: Spiritual coping without church support among older, predominantly African-American caregivers of persons with HIV. *Review of Religious Research*, 40: 230–243.

Polivka, J. S. (1988). Is America aging successfully? A message from media cartoons. *Communication and Cognition*, 21(1): 97–106.

Pollack, S. (2000). A new approach to advance directives. *Critical Care Medicine*, 28(9): 3146–3148.

Ponza, M., Ohls, J. C., & Millen, B. E. (1996). *Serving Elders at Risk: The Older Americans Act Nutrition Programs National Evaluation of the Elderly Nutrition Program*. Newton, MA: Mathematica Policy Research Inc.

Poplin, C. (1997). The piper's tune. In C. L. Wiener & A. L. Strauss (Eds.), *Where Medicine Fails* (pp. 317–332). New Brunswick, NJ: Transaction.

Pruchno, R., & Johnson, K. (1996). Research on grandparenting: Current studies and future needs. *Generations* 20(1): 65–70.

Purcell, P. J. (2000, October). Older workers: Employment and retirement trends. *Monthly Labor Review*, pp. 19–30.

Pyke, K. (1999). The micropolitics of care in relationships between aging parents and adult children: Individualism, collectivism, and power. *Journal of Marriage and the Family*, 61: 661–672.

Quadagno, J. (1990). Generational equity and the politics of the welfare state. *International Journal of Health Services*, 20: 631–649.

Quadagno, J., & Reid, J. (1999). The political economy perspective in aging. In V. L. Bengtson & K. W. Schaie (Eds.), *Handbook of Theories of Aging* (pp. 344–358). New York: Springer.

Quam, J. K., & Whitford, G. S. (1992). Adaptation and age-related expectations of older gay and lesbian adults. *Gerontologist*, 32(1): 367–374.

Quetelet, L. A. J. (1842/1969). *A Treatise on Man and the Development of His Faculties*. Gainesville, FL: Scholars Facsimilies and Reprints.

Quinn, J. (1999). *Retirement Patterns and Bridge Jobs in the 1990s: EBRI Issue Brief No. 206*. Washington, DC: Employment Benefit Research Institute.

Rank, M., & Hirschl, T. (1999). Estimating the properties of Americans ever experiencing poverty during their elder years. *Journal of Gerontology: Social Sciences*, 545(4): 184–193.

Regier, D. A., Farmer, Rae, D. S., et al. (1993a). One-month prevalence of mental disorders in the United States and sociodemographic characteristics: The Epidemiologic Catchment Area study. *Acta Psychiatrica Scandinavica*, 88: 35–47.

Regier, D. A., Narrow, W. E., Rae, D. S., et al. (1993b). The defacto U.S. mental and addictive disorders service system. Epidemiologic Catchment Area prospective 1-year prevalence rates of disorders and services. *Archives of General Psychiatry,* 50: 85–94.

Reichard, S., Livson, F., & Peterson, P. (1962). *Aging and Personality.* New York: Wiley.

Reinisch, J. M., Sanders, S. A., Hill, C. A., & Ziemba-Davis, M. (1992). High risk sexual behavior among heterosexual undergraduates at a midwestern university. *Family Planning Perspectives,* 24: 116–122.

Report of the U.S. Surgeon General. (2000). *Healthy People 2010.* Washington, DC: U.S. Department of Health, Education, and Welfare.

Richardson, R. (2000). Mobile home parks changing from generation ago. *Brainard Dispatch* [Online], Oct. 6. Available: *http://www.brainard dispatch.com* (accessed 3/20/01).

Riche, M. (2000). America's Diversity: Signposts for the 21st Century. *Population Bulletin,* 55: all.

Richmond-Abbott, M. (1992). *Masculine and Feminine: Gender Roles Over the Life Cycle.* New York: McGraw-Hill, Inc.

Riggs, K. E. (1996). The case of the mysterious ritual: Murder dramas and older women viewers. *Critical Studies in Mass Communication,* 13(4): 309–323.

Riley, M. W. (1983). The family in an aging society: A matrix of latent relationships. *Journal of Family Issues,* 4 (3): 439–454.

——. (1996). Age stratification. In James E. Birren (Ed.), *Encyclopedia of Gerontology* (pp. 81–92). New York: Academic Press.

Riley, M. W., Foner, A., & Waring, J. (1988). Sociology of age. In N. J. Smelzer (Ed.), *Handbook of Sociology* (pp. 243–290). Newbury Park, CA: Sage.

Riley, M. W., Foner, A., & Riley, J. W. (1999). The aging and society paradigm. In V. L. Bengtson & K. W. Schaie (Eds.), *Handbook of Theories of Aging* (pp. 327–343). New York: Springer.

Riley, M., Johnson, M., & Foner, A. (1972). *Aging and Society, vol. 3: A Sociology of Age Stratification.* New York: Russell Sage.

Rix, S. A. (1999). *Social Security Reform: Rethinking Retirement-Age policy—A look at Raising Social Security's Retirement Age.* AARP Public Policy Institute, vol. IB 40. Washington, DC: AARP.

Robert Wood Johnson Foundation. (1996). *Chronic Care in America: A 21st Century Challenge.* NY: Robert Wood Johnson Foundation.

Roberto, K. A., Weeks, L. E., & Matheis-Kraft, C. (2001). Health care decisions of older adults: Underlying influences, cognitive status, and perceived outcomes. *Journal of Applied Gerontology,* 20(1): 74–90.

Roberts, J. C. (1995). Eye: Structure and function. In G. L. Maddox et al. (Eds.), *Encyclopedia of Aging* (pp. 357–359). New York: Springer.

Roberts, S. D., & Zhou, N. (1997). The 50 and older characters in the advertisements of *Modern Maturity. Journal of Applied Gerontology,* 16(2): 208–220.

Robinson, J., & Skill, T. (1995). The invisible generation: Portrayals of the elderly on prime-time television. *Communication Reports,* 8(2): 111–119.

Roe, K. M., & Minkler, M. (1998/1999). Grandparents raising grandchildren: Challenges and responses. *Generations*, 22(4): 25–32.

Rose, A. M. (1962). The subculture of the aging: A framework for research in social gerontology. In A. M. Rose & W. A. Peterson (Eds.), *Older People and Their Social World*. Philadelphia: F. A. Davis.

Ross, H., & Milgram, J. (1982). Important variables in adult sibling relationships: A qualitative study. In M. Lamb & B. Sutton-Smith (Eds.), *Sibling Relationships: Their Value and Significance across the Lifespan*. Hillsdale, NJ: Lawrence Erlbaum Associates.

Roughan, P. A., Kaiser, F. E., & Morley, J. E. (1993). Sexuality and the older woman. *Clinics in Geriatric Medicine*, 9: 87–106.

Rowe, J. W., & Kahn, R. L. (1998). *Successful Aging*. New York: Pantheon.

Roy, A., & Harwood, J. (1997). Underrepresented, positively portrayed: Older adults in television commercials. *Journal of Applied Communication Research*, 25(1): 39–56.

Rozelle, R. (2001). *Into That Good Night*. Austin, TX: Texas Review Press.

Rubenstein, L. Z., Josephson, K. R., & Trueblood, P. R. (2000). Effects of a group exercise program on strength, mobility, and falls among fall-prone elderly men. *Journal of Gerontology: Medical Sciences*, 55A: M317–M321.

Rubin, I. (1965). *Sexual Life after Sixty*. New York: Basic Books.

Rubin, L. B. (1990). *Erotic Wars: What Happened to the Sexual Revolution*. New York: Farrar, Straus, and Giroux.

Rudberg, M. A., Sager, M. A., & Zhang, J. (1996). Risk factors for nursing home use after hospitalization for medical illness. *Journals of Gerontology*, 51A(5): M189–M194.

Russell, C. (1997). The ungraying of America. *American Demographics* [Online], July. Available: *http://www.demographics.com/publications/ad/97_ad/9707_ad/ad97073.htm* (accessed 2/18/00).

Russo, N. F. (1995). Women's mental health: Research agenda for the twenty-first century. In C. V. Willie, P. P. Rieker, B. M. Kramer, & B. S. Brown (Eds.), *Mental Health, Racism, and Sexism* (pp. 373–396). Pittsburgh, PA: University of Pittsburgh Press.

Sabogal, F., Marin, G., Otero-Sabogal, R., et al. (1987). Hispanic familism and acculturation: What changes and what doesn't? *Hispanic Journal of Behavioral Sciences*, 9(4): 397–412.

Safran, D. G., Tarlov, A. R., & Rogers, W. H. (1994). Primary care performances in fee-for-service and pre-paid health care systems: Results from the Medical Outcomes Study. *Journal of the American Medical Association* 271 (20): 1579–1586.

Sagan, L. (1987). *The Health of Nations*. New York: Basic Books.

Salisbury, D. L. (1997, Summer). Current and emerging trends in employee benefits. *The Public Policy and Aging Report*, 8(3): 1, ff. 3–5.

Salthouse, T. A. (1991). *Theoretical Perspectives on Cognitive Aging*. Hillsdale, NJ: Erlbaum.

Savishinky, J. (1995). The unbearable lightness of retirement: Ritual and support in a modern life passage. *Research on Aging* 17(3): 243–259.

Schaie, K. W. (1996a). *Adult Intellectual Development: The Seattle Longitudinal Study*. New York: Cambridge University Press.

——. (1996b). Intellectual development in adulthood. In J. E. Birren & K. W. Schaie (Eds.), *Handbook of the Psychology of Aging*, Fourth Edition (pp. 266–286). San Diego, CA: Academic Press.

Scheff, T. J. (1966). *Being Mentally Ill*. Chicago: Aldine.

Schiavi, R. C. (1996). Sexuality and male aging: From performance to satisfaction. *Sexual and Marital Therapy*, 11(1): 9–13.

——. (1999). *Aging and Male Sexuality*. New York: Cambridge University Press.

Schiffman, S. S. (1995a). Smell. In G. L. Maddox, R. C. Atchley, J. G. Evans, et al. (Eds.), *Encyclopedia of Gerontology* (pp. 867–869). New York: Springer.

——. (1995b). Taste. In G. L. Maddox, R. C. Atchley, J. G. Evans, et al. (Eds.), *Encyclopedia of Aging* (pp. 919–922). New York: Springer.

Schlenker, R. E., & AARP. (1996). *Home Health Payment Legislation: Review and Recommendations*. Washington, DC: AARP Public Policy Institute.

Schlesinger, B. (1996). The sexless years or sex rediscovered. *Journal of Gerontological Social Work*, 26(1/2): 117–131.

Schoen, R., & Weinick, R. (1993). The slowing metabolism of marriage: Figures from the 1990 U.S. marital status life tables. *Demography*, 30(4): 737–746.

Schwartz, M., with an introduction by Paul Solman. (1997). *Morrie: In His Own Words*. New York: Bantam Doubleday Dell.

Scogin, F., & Prohaska, M. (1993). *Aiding Older Adults with Memory Complaints*. Sarasota, FL: Professional Resource Press.

Scott, J. P. (1983). Siblings and other kin. In T. H. Brubaker (Ed.), *Family Relationships in Later Life*. Beverly Hills: Sage.

Seelbach, W. C., & Die, A. H. (1988). Family satisfactions and filial norms among elderly Vietnamese immigrants. *Journal of Aging Studies*, 2(3): 267–276.

Seeman, T., McEwen, B., Singer, B., et al. (1997). Increase in urinary cortical excretion and memory declines: MacArthur studies of successful aging. *Journal of Clinical Endocrinology and Metabolism*, 82(8).

Shaw, B. (1998, March 15). Painting the fence green. *Indianapolis Star*, pp. J1–J2.

Sheifer, S. E., Escarce, J. J. & Schulman, K. A. (2000). Race and Sex Differences in the Management of Coronary Artery Disease. *American Heart Journal*, pp. 848–857.

Shenk, D., Zanlotsky, D., & Croom, M. B. (1998). Thriving older African American Women: Aging after Jim Crow. *Journal of Women and Aging*, 10(1): 75–95.

Sherman, S. R. (2000). Intergenerational reciprocity. In E. W. Markson & L. Hollis-Sawyer (Eds.), *Intersections of Aging* (pp. 286–295). Los Angeles: Roxbury.

Shimbun, Y. (2000). Hot-water pots to help check on elderly. *The Daily Yomuiri* [Online], 12/20/00. Available at *http://www.yomuiri.co.jp* (accessed 12/22/00).

Simmons, L. W. (1945). *The Role of the Aged in Primitive Society*. New Haven CT: Yale University Press.

Simon, W., & Gagnon, J. (1986). Sexual scripts: Permanence and change. *Archives of Sexual Behavior,* 15: 97–120.

Simpson, E. (1994). *Late Love: A Celebration of Marriage After 50.* New York: Houghton Mifflin.

Simpura, J., & Tigerstedt, C., in collaboration with Hanhinen, S., Lagerspetz, M., Leifman, H., et al. (1999). Alcohol misuse as a health and social issue in the Baltic Sea region. A summary of findings from the Baltica Study. *Alcohol and Alcoholism,* a34(6): 805–823.

Singer, P. A., & Siegler, M. (1990). Sounding Board: Euthanasia—A Critique. *New England Journal of Medicine,* 322(26): 1881–1883.

Sinott, J. D. (1977). Sex-role inconstancy, biology, and successful aging: A dialectical model. *The Gerontologist,* 17(5): 459–463.

Skolnick, A. S. (1987). *The Intimate Environment: Exploring Marriage and the Family.* Boston: Little, Brown.

Skolnick, A. S., & Skolnick, J. H. (1997). *Family in Transition.* New York: Longman.

Slevin, K. F., & Wingrove, R. C. (1998). *From Stumbling Blocks to Stepping Stones.* New York: New York University Press.

Smeeding, T. M. (1999). Social Security reform: Improving benefit adequacy and economic security for women. *Aging Studies Program Policy Brief, vol. 16.* Syracuse, NY: Syracuse University Center for Policy Research.

Smith, A. D. (1995). Cognitive processes. In George L. Maddox, R. C. Atchley, J. G. Evans, et al. (Eds.), *Encyclopedia of Aging,* Second Edition (pp. 186–188). New York: Springer.

Smith, D. S. (1978). Old age and the 'great transformation': A New England case study. In S. F. Spicker, K. M. Woodward, & D. D. Van Tassel (Eds.), *Aging and the Elderly: Humanistic Perspectives in Gerontology* (pp. 285–302). Atlantic Highlands, NJ: Humanities Press.

Smith, J. (1992). *Misogynies: Reflections on Myth and Malice.* London: Faber and Faber.

Smith, T. W. (2000). Changes in the generation gap, 1972–1998. *GSS Social Change Report, vol. 43.* Chicago: NORC.

Sokolovsky, J. (1993). Images of aging: Cross-cultural perspectives. *Generations,* pp. 51–54.

Sommers, T., & Shields, L. (1987). *Women Take Care.* Gainesville, FL: Triad.

Sontag, S. (1972). The double standard of aging. *Saturday Review,* September, pp. 29–38.

Sotomayor, M. (1995). Hispanic elderly. In G. L. Maddox, R. C. Atchley, J. G. Evans, & et al. (Eds.), *Encyclopedia of Aging* (pp. 458–459). New York: Springer.

Speas, K., & Obenshain, B. (1995). *AARP Images of Aging in America: Final Report.* Chapel Hill, NC: FGI Integrated Marketing.

Springstead, G. R., & Wilson, T. M. (2000). Participation in voluntary individual savings accounts: An analysis of IRAs, 401(k)s, and the TSP. *Social Security Bulletin,* 63(1): 34–39.

Squier, L. W. (1912). *Old Age Dependency in the United States.* New York: Macmillan.

Stahle, A., Nordlander, R., & Bergfeldt, L. (1999). Aerobic group training improves exercise capacity and heart rate variability in elderly patients with a recent coronary event. A randomized controlled study. *European Heart Journal*, 20: 1638–1646.

Starr, B. D. (2001). Sexuality. In E. L. Maddox, R. C. Atchley, J. E. Evans, et al. (Eds.), *Encyclopedia of Aging* (pp. 923–928). New York: Springer.

Starr, B. D., & Weiner, M. B. (1981). *The Starr-Weiner Report on Sex and Sexuality in the Mature Years*. Briarcliff Manor, NY: Stein and Day.

Statistics Norway. (2001). *Statistics Norway 2001*. Oslo, Norway: Norwegian Ministry of Finance.

Steele, C. M. (1997). A threat in the air. How stereotypes shape intellectual identity and performance. *American Psychologist*, 52: 613–629.

Steffens, D. C., Helms, M. J., Krishnan, K. R., & Burke, G. L. (1999). Cerebrovascular disease and depression symptoms in the cardiovascular health study. *Stroke*, 30(10): 2159–2166.

Steinke, E. E. (1988). Older adults' knowledge and attitudes about sexuality and aging. *IMAGE: Journal of Nursing Scholarship*, 20(2): 93–95.

Stevenson, R. W. (2001, December 12). A finale in three-part harmony. *New York Times*, p. 27.

Stoddard, K. M. (1983). *Saints and Shrews: Women and Aging in American Popular Film*. Westport, CT: Greenwood.

Stone, R. (2000). Stress: The Invisible Hand in Eastern Europe's Death Rates. *Science*, 288: 1732–1733.

Stone, R. I. (1999). Long-term care in Japan: A window into the future? *The Public Policy and Aging Report*, 10(3): 1–5, ff. 15.

Strauss, A. L. (1997). Chronic illness. In C. L. Wiener & A. L. Strauss (Eds.), *Where Medicine Fails* (pp. 11–24). New Brunswick, NJ: Transaction Books.

Streff, M. B. (2001). Perceptions of the Present and Future: An Assessment of Relational Experiences, Social Support, and Personal Resources by Women Sixty-Five and Older [Doctoral dissertation]. Boston, MA: Boston University.

Stull, D. E., Cosbey, J., Bowman, K., & McNutt, W. (1997). Institutionalization: A continuation of family care. *Journal of Applied Gerontology*, 16: 379–402.

Sturm, R., & Sherbourne, C. D. (2000). Managed care and unmet need for mental health and substance abuse care in 1998. *Psychiatric Services*, 5(2): 177.

Styron, W. (1991). *Darkness Visible: A Memoir of Madness*. New York: Vintage Books.

Sudnow, D. (1967). *Passing On: The Social Organization of Dying*. Englewood Cliffs, NJ: Prentice-Hall.

Suggs, P. K. (1989). Predictors of association among older siblings. *American Behavioral Scientist*, 33: 70–80.

Sullivan, D. (1995). The role of nutrition in increased morbidity and mortality. *Clinics in Geriatric Medicine*, 11(4): 661–674.

Suls, T., & Sanders, G. S. (1988). Type A behavior as a general risk factor for physical disorder. *Journal of Behavioral Medicine*, 11(3): 201–226.

Surgeon General of the United States. (1999). *Mental Health: A Report of the Surgeon General.* Washington, DC: U.S. Department of Health and Human Services.

Szinovacz, M. E., & DeViney, S. (2000). Marital characteristics and retirement decisions. *Research on Aging,* 22(5): 470–498.

Szinovacz, M. E., DeViney, S., & Atkinson, M. P. (1999). Effects of surrogate parenting on grandparents' well-being. *Journal of Gerontology: Social Sciences,* 54B(6): S376–S388.

Szinovacz, M. E., DeViney, S., & Davey, A. (2001). Influences of family obligations and relationships on retirement: Variations by gender, race, and marital status. *Journals of Gerontology Series B: Social Sciences,* 56B(1): S20–S27.

Szinovacz, M. E., & Schaffer, A. M. (2000). Effects of retirement on marital conflict tactics. *Journal of Family Issues,* 21(3): 367–389.

Talley, T. (1956). The negro aged. *Newsletter, Gerontological Society,* December 6.

Taniguchi, H. (1999). The timing of childbearing and women's wages. *Journal of Marriage and the Family,* 61(4): 1008–1019.

Taylor, M. A., & Shore, L. M. (1995). Predictors of planned retirement age: An application of Beehr's model. *Psychology and Aging 10* (1): A76–83.

Taylor, M. C., & Hall, J. (1982). Psychological androgyny: Theories, methods and conclusions. *Psychological Bulletin,* 92 (2): 347–366.

Teno, J. M., Lynn, J., Wenger, N., et al. (1997a). Advance directives for seriously ill hospitalized patients: Effectiveness with the patient self-determination act and the SUPPORT intervention. SUPPORT investigators. Study to understand prognoses and preferences for outcomes and risks of treatment. *Journal of the American Geriatrics Society,* 45(4): 500–507.

Teno, J. M., Lickes, S., Lynn, J., et al. (1997b). Do advance directives provide instructions that direct care? SUPPORT investigators. Study to understand prognoses and preferences for outcomes and risks of treatment. *Journal of the American Geriatrics Society,* 45(4): 508–512.

Terkel, S. (1995). *Coming of Age.* New York: St. Martin's Griffin.

Tesch-Romer, C. (1997). Psychological effects of hearing aid use in older adults. *Journal of Gerontology: Psychological Sciences,* 52B: P127–P138.

The Century Fund Social Security Network. (2000). *Social Security Privatization: Eleven Myths* [Issue Brief #10]. New York: Century Foundation.

Theorell, T. (1991). On cardiovascular health in women. In M. Frankenhaduser, U. Lundberg, & M. Chesney (Eds.), *Women, Work, and Health* (pp. 187–204). New York: Plenum.

Thomas, L. E. (1991). Correlates of sexual interest among elderly men. *Psychological Reports,* 68: 620–622.

Thompson, E. H. (2000). Gendered caregiving of husbands and sons. In E. W. Markson & L. Hollis-Sawyer (Eds.), *Intersections of Aging* (pp. 333–344). Los Angeles: Roxbury.

Tierney, H. (1999). Contraception. In H. Tierney (Ed.), *Women's Studies Encyclopedia* (pp. 299–304). Westport CT: Greenwood.

Tilly, J. (1999). Consumer-directed long-term care: Participants' experiences in five countries. *Public Policy Institute Issue Brief,* IB 36: 1–22.

Tornstam, L. (1999). Late-life transcendence: A new developmental perspective on aging. In L. E. Thomas & S. A. Eisenhandler (Eds.), *Religion, Belief, and Spirituality in Late Life*. New York: Springer.

Townsend, W. (2001). Phased retirement: From promise to practice. In Cornell Employment and Family Centers Institute (Ed.), *Bronfenbrenner Life Course Center Issue Brief*. Ithaca, NY.

Tran, T. (1994). Bilingualism and subjective well-being in a sample of elderly Hispanics. *Journal of Social Service Research*, 20(1-2): 1–19.

Treas, J. (1995, May). Older Americans in the 1990s and beyond. *Population Bulletin*, 50(2): 2–46.

Tronick, E. Z., & Beeghly, M. (1999). Prenatal cocaine exposure, child development, and the compromising effects of cumulative risk. *Clinical Perinatology*, 26(1): 151–171.

Tsui, M., Huang, H.-Y., & He, Q. (1995, August). The status of elderly women and men in the Chinese urban family. Paper available from *Sociology Express*, email *socio@cerfnet.com*. American Sociological Association.

Tully, C. L., & Snowdon, D. A. (1995). Weight change and physical function in older women: Findings from the nun study. *Journal of the American Geriatrics Society*, pp. 1394–1397.

Turner, B. F., & Silva, P. (2000). Definitions of femininity: Youth to old age. In E. W. Markson & L.A. Hollis-Sawyer (Eds.), *Intersections of Aging* (pp. 103–112). Los Angeles: Roxbury.

Turner, C. B., & Kramer, B. M. (1995). Connections between racism and mental health. In C. V. Willie, P. P. Rieker, B. M. Kramer, & B. S. Brown (Eds.), *Mental Health, Racism, and Sexism* (pp. 3–25). Pittsburgh, PA: University of Pittsburgh Press.

Turner, H. A., & Turner, R. J. (1999). Gender, social status, and emotional reliance. *Journal of Health and Social Behavior*, 40(4): 360–373.

Uccello, C. E. (1998). *Factors Influencing Retirement: Their Implications for Raising Retirement Age*. Washington, DC: AARP.

Uhlmann, R., Pearlman, R. A., & Cain, K. C. (1988). Physicians' and spouses' predictions of elderly patients' resuscitation preferences. *Journal of Gerontology*, 43: M115–M121.

U.S. Bureau of the Census. (1995). *Population Profile of the United States, 1995*. Current Population Reports, vol. Series P23-189. Washington, DC: U.S. Government Printing Office.

——. (1996). *Global Aging into the 21st Century* [Poster]. Washington, DC: U.S. Bureau of the Census.

——. (1996). *Statistical Abstract of the United States 1996* (116th edition). Washington, DC: Government Printing Office.

——. (1999). *American Housing Survey for the United States*. Washington, DC: U.S. Department of Commerce.

——. (2000). *Statistical Abstract of the United States 1999*. Washington, DC: U.S. Government Printing Office.

——. (2000). *Statistical Abstract of the United States 2000: The National Data Book*. Washington DC: U.S. Government Printing Office.

———. (2000). Voting and registration in the election of November 1998. *Current Population Reports* (P20–523RV) [Online]. Available: *http://www.census.gov/prod/2000pubs/p20-523.pdf* (accessed 6/22/01).

———. (2001). *International Database* [Online]. Available: *http://www.census.gov/ftp/pub/ipc/www/idbnew.html* (accessed 6/22/01).

———. (2001). *Money Income in the United States.* Current Population Reports Consumer Income P60-213. Washington, DC: U.S. Department of Commerce.

———. (2001). *Statistical Abstract of the United States 2001: The National Data Book.* Washington DC: U.S. Government Printing Office.

U.S. Bureau of Labor Statistics. (1998). *Consumer Expenditure Survey.* Washington, DC: U.S. Dept. of Labor.

———. (1999). *Employee Benefit Survey, 1997* [Online]. Available: *http://stats.bls.gov/news/release.ebs3.t01.htm* (accessed 10/11/00).

———. (2000). *Highlights of Women's Earnings in 1999.* Report, vol. 943. Washington, DC: U.S. Dept. of Labor.

———. (2000). *Worker Displacement During the Late 1990s.* Economic News Release [Online] USDL 00-223. Available: *http://www.bls.gov.news.release/disp.t08.htm* (accessed 12/20/01).

———. (2001). *Contingent and Alternative Employment Arrangements.* Economic News Release, vol. USDL 01-153. Washington, DC: U.S. Dept. of Labor.

———. (2001). *Labor Force Statistics from the Current Population Survey 2001.* Available: *http://www.bls.gov.news.release/conemp.t05.htm* (accessed 11/10/01).

U.S. Centers for Disease Control and Prevention. (1998). *AIDS Among Persons >50 Years, United States 1991–1996.* Morbidity and Mortality Weekly Report.

U.S. Department of Commerce, Bureau of the Census and National Institute on Aging. (1996). *Global Aging into the 21st Century.* Washington DC: U.S. Department of Commerce.

U.S. Department of Health and Human Services, P. H. S. (1991). *Healthy People 2000: National Health Promotion and Disease Prevention Objectives.* Washington DC: Government Printing Office.

U.S. Department of Health and Human Services. (1995). *Medicare: A Profile.* Washington DC: U.S. Government Printing Office.

———. (2001). Medicare. *HHS News* (3/11/02).

U.S. Department of Health and Human Services, Centers for Medicare and Medical Services (2001). *Medicare and You.* Washington, DC: U.S. Department of Health and Human Services, Centers for Medicare and Medicaid Services.

U.S. Department of Health and Human Services, Centers for Disease Control (2001). *United States Life Table 1998.* National Vital Statistics Report, vol. 18.

U.S. Department of Labor. *Consumer Expenditure Survey 1998* [Online]. Available: *http://BLS/gov/csx/1998/standard/age* (accessed 11/27/01).

U.S. General Accounting Office (GAO). (1995). *Medicare: Increased HMO Oversight Could Improve Quality and Access to Care.* In HEHS-95, vol. 155. Washington DC: General Accounting Office.

———. (1996). *Fraud and Abuse: Providers Excluded from Medicaid Continue to Participate in Federal Health Programs.* Washingtion DC: U.S. General Accounting Office.

———. (1996). *Fraud and Abuse: Medicare Continues to be Vulnerable to Exploitation by Unscrupulous Providers.* Washington DC: General Accounting Office.

———. (1997). *Health Insurance: Erosion in Employer-Based Health Benefits for Early Retirees.* Gaithersburg, MD: Author.

———. (1997). *Medicare HMOs: HCFA Can promptly Eliminate Hundreds of Millions in Excess Payments.* In HEHS-97, vol. 16. Washington DC: General Accounting Office.

———. (1997). *Medicare HMOs: HCFA Could Promptly Reduce Excess Payment by Improving Accuracy of County Payment Rates.* Washington DC: U.S. General Accounting Office.

———. (1997). *Health Care Services: How Continuing Care Retirement Communities Manage Services for the Elderly.* In GAO HEHS-97-36.Washington DC: General Accounting Office.

U.S. National Center for Health Statistics. (2001). *Health, United States 2001.* Washington, DC: Author.

U.S. Social Security Administration. (2000). *Fast Facts and Figures about Social Security.* Baltimore, MD: Office of Policy, Research, Evaluation, and Statistics.

———. (2000). *Historical Development.* Social Security Administration. Available: *http://www.sss/gov/history/brief.html/* (accessed 10/2/00).

———. (2001). *SSI Annual Report: 2001.* The Supplemental Security Income Program. Available: *http://www.ssa.gov/statistics/ssi_annual_stat/2001* (accessed 8/13/02).

U.S. Social Security Administration: Division of Program Studies. (2000). *Income of the Aged Chartbook 1998.* Available: *http://www.ssa.gov/policy.*

U.S. Social Security Administration, Office of the Commissioner. (2000). *The Supplemental Social Insurance Program at the Millenium.* Baltimore, MD: Social Security Administration.

Usita, P. A. (2001). Interdependency in immigrant mother-daughter relationships. *Journal of Aging Studies,* 15: 183–189.

Vailas, L. I., & Nitzke, S. A. (1995). Screening for risk of malnutrition in Wisconsin's elderly. *Wisconsin Medical Journal,* pp. 495–499.

van de walle, E., & Knodel, J. (1980). Europe's fertility transition: New evidence and lessons for today's developing world. *Population Bulletin,* 34(5): all.

Velkoff, V. A., & Lawson, V. A. (1998). *Gender and Aging: Caregiving.* International Brief, vol. IB/98/3. Washington DC: U.S. Department of Commerce, Economics, and Statistics Administration, Bureau of the Census.

Verbrugge, L. M. (1985). Gender and health: An update on hypotheses and evidence. *Journal of Health and Social Behavior,* 26, 156–182.

Vernon, J., Williams, J., Jr, Phillips, T., & Wilson, J. (1990). Media stereotyping: A comparison of the way elderly women and men are portrayed in prime-time television. *Journal of Women and Aging,* 2(4): 55–68.

Waite, L. J., & Hughes, M. E. (1999). At risk on the cusp of old age: Living arrangements and functional status among Black, White, and Hispanic adults. *Journals of Gerontology: Psychological Sciences and Social Sciences*, 54B: 136–144.

Waldron, I. (1976). Why do women live longer than men? *Journal of Human Stress*, 2: 2–13.

——. (1990). What do we know about causes of sex differences in mortality? A review. In P. Conrad & R. Kern (Eds.), *The Sociology of Health and Illness* (pp. 45–57). New York: St. Martin's Press.

Walford, R. L. (1983). *Maximum Life Span*. New York: Avon Books.

Wallsten, S. S. (2000). Effects of caregiving, gender, and race on the health, mutuality, and social supports of older couples. *Journal of Aging and Health*, 12: 90–111.

Walsh, A. (1989). 'Life isn't yet over': Older heroines in American popular cinema of the 1930s and 1970s/80s. *Qualitative Sociology*, 12(1): 72–95.

Walters, S. D. (1992). *Living Together, Worlds Apart*. Berkeley, CA: University of California Press.

Warren, C. A. B. (1991). *Madwives*. New Brunswick, NJ: Rutgers University Press.

Waters, M. (1990). *Ethnic Options: Choosing Identities in America*. Berkeley, CA: University of California Press.

Waxman, H. M., Carner, E. A., & Blum, A. (1983). Depressive symptoms and health services utilization among the community elderly. *Journal of the American Geriatrics Society*, 31(7): 417–420.

Weber, M. (1922/1968). *Economy and Society*. New York: Bedminister Press.

——. (1946). Bureaucracy. In H. Gerth & C. W. Mills (Eds.), *From Max Weber: Essays in Sociology* (pp. 196–244). New York: Oxford University Press.

——. (1978). *Economy and Society*. Berkeley, CA: University of California Press.

Weg, R. B. (1995). Menopause: Biological aspects. In G. L. Maddox, R. C. Atchley, J. G. Evans, et al. (Eds.), *Encyclopedia of Aging* (pp. 622–628). New York: Springer.

Weiler, P., & Rathbone-McCuan, E. (1978). *Adult Day Care: Community Work with the Elderly*. NY: Springer Publishing Co.

Wellman, B., & Wortley, S. (1989). Brothers keepers: Situating kinship relations in broader networks of social support. *Sociological Perspectives*, 32: 273–306.

Wernick, A. (1995). Selling funerals, imaging death. In M. Featherstone & A. Wernick (Eds.), *Images of Ageing* (pp. 280–293). London, England: Routledge.

Wetzel, J. W. (1994). Depression: Women at risk. *Social Work in Health Care* 19 (3–4): 88–108.

Whitbourne, S. K. (1976). Test anxiety in elderly and young adults. *International Journal of Aging and Human Development*, 7: 201–210.

White, T. M., Townsend, A. L., & Stephens, M.-A. P. (2000). Comparisons of African American and white women in the parent care role. *Gerontologist*, 40(6): 718–728.

Wiener, C., Fagerhaugh, S., Strauss, A., & Suczek, B. (1997). What price chronic illness? In C. L. Wiener & A. L. Strauss (Eds.), *Where Medicine Fails* (pp. 25–42). New Brunswick, NJ: Transaction.

Wilensky, G. R. (1995). Incremental health system reform: Where Medicare fits in. *Health Affairs*, 14(1): 173–181.

Wiley, D., & Bortz, W. M., II. (1996). Sexuality and aging—usual and successful. *Journal of Gerontology A: Biological Sciences and Medical Sciences*, 51(3): M142–M146.

Wilkinson, R. G. (1996). *Unhealthy Societies.* London: Routledge.

Williams, G. D., Stinson, F. S., Parker, D. A., et al. (1987). Epidemiologic Bulletin No. 15: Demographic trends, alcohol abuse and alcoholism, 1985–1995. *Alcohol Health and Research World*, 11(3): 80–91.

Williams, W. I. (1986). *The Spirit and the Flesh: Sexual Diversity in American Indian Culture.* Boston: Beacon.

Williamson, A. (1995). *The University of the Third Age (U3A) Movement and Its Rise in New South Wales: In the Great Tradition of Liberal Adult Education?* U.S. Department of Education: EDRS.

Wilson, K. C. M., Chen, R., Taylor, S., McCracken, C. F., & Copeland, J. R. M. (1999, December). Socio-economic deprivation and the prevalence and prediction of depression in older community residents: The MRC-ALPHA study. *British Journal of Psychiatry*, 175: 549–553.

Wilson, R. N. (2000). Lucky 75—coming through a century of change. *The Chapel Hill News*, 1(16): A5.

Wink, P. (1999). Addressing end-of-life issues: Spirituality and inner life. *Generations*, 23(1): 75–80.

Winkleby, M. A., Jatulis, D. E., Frank, E., & Fortmann, S. P. (1992). Socio-economic status and health: How education, income and occupation contribute to risk factors for cardiovascular disesse. *American Journal of Public Health*, 82: 816–820.

Wolf, M. (2001, February 7). Age shall not weary them: Horror stories about the dire consequences of demographic changes in Western societies are exaggerated. *Financial Times* [Online]. Available: *http://news.ft.com/ft/gx.cgi/ftc?pagename=View&c=Article&cid= FT3VP7R0WIC&live=true* (accessed 6/22/01).

Wolfson, M., Kaplan, G., Lynch, J., Ross, & Backlund, E. (1999, October 9). Relation between income inequality and mortality: Empirical demonstration. *British Medical Journal*, 319: 953–957.

Wong, R., Capoferro, C., & Soldo, B. J. (1999). Financial assistance from middle-aged couples to parents and children: Racial ethnic differences. *Journal of Gerontology: Psychological and Social Sciences*, 54B: S145–S153.

Woodward, K., & Schwartz, M. (1986). *Memory and Desire: Aging—Literature—Psychoanalysis.* Bloomington, IN: Indiana University Press.

——. Woodward, K. (1991). *Aging and Its Discontents: Freud and Other Fictions.* Bloomington, IN: University of Indiana.

Worden, J. W. (1982). *Grief Counseling and Grief Therapy: A Handbook for the Mental Health Practitioner.* New York: Springer.

Working Age. (1999, July/August). Statistics in brief. *Working Age*, 15(2): 4.

Wurtzel, E. (1997). *Prozac Nation: Young and Depressed in America: A Memoir.* New York: Riverhead Books.

Wyatt-Brown, A. M., & Rossen, J. (1993). *Aging and Gender in Literature: Studies in Creativity.* Charlottesville, VA: University of Virginia Press.

Yeager, B., Farnett, L., & Ruzicka, S. (1995). Management of the behavioral manifestations of dementia. *Archives of Internal Medicine,* 155(3): 250–260.

Zarit, S. H. (1989). Issues and directions in family intervention research. In E. Light & B. D. Lebowitz (Eds.), *Alzheimer's Disease Treatment and Family Stress: Directions for Research* (pp. 458–486). Washington, DC: U.S. Government Printing Office.

Zeiss, A. M., & Breckenridge, J. S. (1997). Treatment of late life depression: A response to the NIH Consensus Conference. *Behavior Therapy,* 28(1): 3–21.

Zeiss, A. M., Lewisohn, P. M., Rohde, P., & Seeley, J. R. (1996). Relationship of physical disease and functional impairment to depression in old people. *Psychology of Aging,* 11(4): 572–581.

Zelizer, V. A. (2000). The changing social worth of children. In P. S. Fass & M. A. Mason (Eds.), *Childhood in America* (pp. 260–262). New York: New York University Press.

Zinnbauer, B. J., Pargement, K. I., Cole, B., Rye, M. S., et al. (1997). Religion and spirituality: Unfuzzying the fuzzy. *Journal for the Scientific Study of Religion,* 36(4): 549–564.

Zola, I. K. (1988). Aging and disability: Toward a unifying agenda. *Educational Gerontology,* 14: 365–387.

Zsembic, B. A. (1993). Determinants of living alone among older Hispanics. *Research on Aging,* 15(4): 449–464.

——. (1996). Preference for coresidence among older Latinos. *Journal of Aging Studies,* 10(1): 69–81.

Zweibel, N., & Cassel, C. K. (1989). Treatment choices at the end of life: A comparison of decisions by older patients and their physician-selected proxies. *Gerontologist,* 29: 615–621. ✦

Subject Index

Author Index